The Age
of Exuberance

BACKGROUNDS TO EIGHTEENTH-
CENTURY ENGLISH
LITERATURE

Studies in Language and Literature

The Age of Exuberance

BACKGROUNDS TO EIGHTEENTH-CENTURY ENGLISH LITERATURE

Donald Greene

University of Southern California

RANDOM HOUSE   NEW YORK

Library of Congress Catalog Card Number: 67–22327

Manufactured in the United States of America
by H. Wolff Book Mfg. Co., New York
Typography by Jack Ribik

First Printing

❧ Preface

The aim of this book is to provide, for the student of English literature in particular, a guide to the salient historical, ideological, and aesthetic events and circumstances in Britain from the return of Charles II and the restoration of the "old constitution" in 1660 to around the time of the outbreak of the French Revolution in the 1780's. It was a crowded and complicated period of history; it is, moreover, a period which has been subjected to much misunderstanding and misrepresentation, which is only gradually beginning to be cleared away. The task, therefore, of trying to condense into a brief space all that ought to be said about it has been a more than usually frustrating one, and I must apologize for the many omissions and oversimplifications that necessarily result from such condensation. If I dare not say with Samuel Johnson, in the Preface to his great *Dictionary of the English Language*, "In this work, when it shall be found that much is omitted, let it not be forgotten that much likewise is performed," perhaps I may at least repeat H. L. Mencken's aphorism, when reproached for his amateurish but persistent piano playing, "If a thing is worth doing at all, it is worth doing badly"—better crudely executed music than no music. As a teacher I have often felt the need for some short compilation that my students could use in order to help them read the literature of the time with a better understanding of what its authors were talking about and of the assumptions they took for granted their readers would bring to it; and whatever the defects of this book, it is this need that I have had chiefly in mind as I put it together.

The title perhaps calls for explanation. When I was first exposed to the eighteenth century as an undergraduate, or earlier, the current custom of describing it as the "age of reason," or decorum, or restraint, or unemotionality, or "distrust of imagination," or "slavish obedience to rules" never made the slightest sense to me; it still does not. What attracted me to the century then, and what still attracts me, is the magnificent, apparently inexhaustible and indefatigable fund of sheer *energy* that its best art affords—the energy one hears in the firm bass line of a Bach allegro or the apocalyptic choral and orchestral climaxes of a Handel oratorio, that one sees in the fantastic design of a Vanbrugh mansion or the steeple of a Wren church, in the extravagantly imaginative conception of a great Reynolds portrait or a Nollekens bust, in a drawing room decorated by Adam or furnished by Chippendale, that one responds to—unless one's ability to read the plain sense of the words in front of one's nose has been subverted by dogmatic preconceptions about what one is expected to find there—in the *Walpurgisnacht* quality of *Mac Flecknoe, The Dunciad,* and *A Tale of a Tub* (Dryden, Pope, and Swift would have needed to take no lessons in "the literature of the absurd" from its twentieth-century practitioners; why should they, when they had all sat at the feet of its supreme exponent, Rabelais?), in the elaborately baroque diction and sentence structure of Johnson's *Rambler* prose style and the demonic hammer blows with which he demolishes a Lord Chesterfield or Soame Jenyns, in the fervent religious passion that shines out from the poetry of a Christopher Smart or Charles Wesley or William Cowper.

"Poetry," said Keats—we may expand it to "artistic creation" generally—"should surprise by a fine excess, and not by singularity" (by "singularity" Keats means what Johnson meant when he warned the poet not to "number the streaks of the tulip"); and "Its touches of beauty should never be half-way, thereby making the reader breathless, instead of content." The artistic masterpieces of the eighteenth century, as of other centuries, were never guilty of half-heartedness or the failure of nerve that recoils from "fine excess." And if one is looking for *a priori* sociological reasons why this should be so, one can find many in the social and economic history of the "age of expansion."

As to why the nineteenth century should have wanted to think of the eighteenth in the way it did, one can speculate endlessly. One reason was undoubtedly the normal rebellion of any generation against its "image" of its predecessor, in which any stick will do to beat a dog. It is now a cliché that Dryden, Swift, and Johnson had a great many attitudes and values in common, so much so that they have all been lumped together as "Tory humanists" or the like. Yet we find Swift bitterly attacking the Grand Old Man of his youth, his cousin Dryden; and Johnson, in turn, even though as a young writer he had paid Swift the tribute of trying to imitate his satiric idiom, was in the habit of expressing himself with considerably less than enthusiasm about Swift's outlook and achievements. Blake and Wordsworth seized on Johnson as the symbol of what they wanted to revolt from; yet if one can bring oneself actually to examine the evidence, one will find that Blake's views on morality and Wordsworth's on poetry are really not very different from Johnson's. And the great Victorians were to suffer similar injustice in their turn at the hands of the writers of the early twentieth century.

Another reason may be the rise of "Eng. Lit." as a school subject in the middle of the nineteenth century, when the reaction against the eighteenth, or its image, was at its height. The poor academic and journalistic hacks who prepared the first school textbooks of English literary history, needing material to present about the various "periods" they thought it necessary to divide their subject into and desperate for neat generalizations, picked up and passed on such nuggets of vulgar wisdom from the Dick Minims of their day as that the eighteenth century was excessively fond of generalizations. (If the reader thinks I am unduly harsh toward the pioneers of the academic study of English literature, he should spend an hour or two in a large library browsing through the early college textbooks of the subject, which appeared from around the 1840's to the 1870's. They are incredibly awful.) Once enshrined in a widely used textbook, such "knowledge" gets handed on from one textbook writer to the next, attains a prescriptive right to existence, becomes the basis of critical and academic empires, and requires a cataclysm to dislodge it.

Finally, if one wanted to indulge as freely in grandiose generalizations as nineteenth-century critics did, one could venture the suggestion, based on the fact of the sad decline of English music, painting, and architecture in the nineteenth century from the splendor of those arts in the eighteenth—their retreat from the boldly imaginative into the cautiously derivative—that Englishmen of the nineteenth century were in fact a little frightened of the audacity and exuberance of their predecessors, and at the same time (without, of course, being able to acknowledge it to themselves) a little ashamed of their own pusillanimity by comparison, and that they managed both to neutralize the danger and to assuage their own sense of inferiority by creating the preposterous fantasies about the eighteenth century that they did. Psychiatrists could adduce analogous procedures from case histories of father–son relationships. But no doubt a good modern nineteenth-century scholar would have no trouble demonstrating that I am here being as inaccurate and unfair about the nineteenth century as the nineteenth century was about the eighteenth.

Los Angeles   D. G.

❧ Contents

Contents   x

One

The Country and Its People

The Country

It is an old cliché, but one can hardly begin a historical sketch of Britain without affirming it: during most of the past two thousand years, the patterns of British political, economic, and cultural history have to a large extent been determined by the geographical situation of the British Isles in relation to the main routes of communication and trade of the European community and, later, its colonial extensions. During fifteen hundred of those years, from Julius Caesar's time down to Columbus's, the islands were on the fringe of that community, seldom closely involved in its affairs except when, as in the sixth to the tenth century, they found themselves in the path of migrating Teutonic tribes and Viking plunderers, and when, because of dynastic accidents, Norman and Plantagenet rulers led expeditions of military conquest back and forth across the Channel.

There was always some cultural and commercial interchange with the Continent; and missionaries brought the islands, like other outlying parts of Europe, into the orbit of Christendom. Yet the Channel always exercised a powerful isolating influence: Danes, Normans, Continental churchmen might come over determined to impose their ways of living, thinking, and talking on the islanders, but before many generations had passed, manners, ideas, and speech all took on an insular quality, and by the later Middle Ages had been blended

(in the most important quarter of the islands) into a self-sufficient Englishness that sometimes even became (in Church matters, for instance) defiantly anti-Continental. This insularity, or
independence, persists; and it is dangerous at any time for the
student to lump together English literary and intellectual phenomena with those of a Continental movement such as "the Enlightenment" or "Romanticism" without making due allowance
for the stubborn idiosyncrasy of the English.

But in the sixteenth century a fundamental change took
place. With the extension of Europe into the Western Hemi-
sphere, Britain found herself no longer on the fringe but in the
hectic center of international activity. British history during the
four centuries from 1500 to 1900 can perhaps be summed up as
the struggle of the British to come to some kind of terms with
their new position in the world—the struggle between, on the
one hand, the old "isolationism," the desire for self-sufficiency
and the stability that goes with it, and, on the other, the potent
attractions of world power, with its rewards, both material and
psychological, and its dangers, both economic and moral. (In
the twentieth century, the basic terms changed again; and in the
1950's and 1960's it has been the United States which, like Britain in the 1750's and 1760's, has had to face the challenge of
substituting an internationalist for an isolationist posture.)

For Britain, the struggle reached its climax in the middle of
the eighteenth century—specifically, in the Seven Years' War, of
1756–1763 ("The Great War for the Empire," as one of its most
eminent historians, Lawrence Gipson, terms it)—and its outcome, in the political and economic spheres at least, was a deci-
sive victory for expansionism over isolationism. The result was,
for better or worse, the great British territorial and commercial
empire of the nineteenth century; and the theme, explicit or
implicit, of a great deal of the serious British literature of the
time (not unlike that of serious American literature of the mid-
twentieth century) was the probable impact on the spirit of the
individual of this new affluent and *engagé* society. Yet, as perhaps the most acute contemporary observer of these events, Samuel Johnson, noted—in the opening sentence of a magazine first
published, under his editorship, in the month the Seven Years'
War was declared—"The present system of English politics may

properly be said to have taken rise in the reign of Queen Elizabeth." The controlling tendencies of political and cultural life
in eighteenth-century England are merely a continuation of the
tendencies whose power began to be felt in Renaissance England; but the pace becomes much more rapid, and the consequences, for good and bad, become more clearly discernible.

One of the most significant indications of what was happening to Britain in the eighteenth century was the striking increase in its population during the period. After centuries of a
relatively slow and stable rate of increase, it suddenly became a
rapidly expanding society. It began to experience a "boom," a
"population explosion." The population of England (and
Wales) at the end of the seventeenth century is reliably estimated at a little over 5 million—not much more than it had
been a century earlier in the time of Shakespeare (in the densely
populated world of the mid-twentieth century, we are always a
little startled when we recall from what small groups of human
beings the great artistic and intellectual achievements of the
past emerged). At the end of the eighteenth century, however,
when the first government census was taken (1801)—and it is
significant of the changes that were taking place in ways of
thinking that it was not until this late date, and indeed in the
face of strenuous opposition, that the principle of taking a physical count of population was adopted—the figure had nearly
doubled, to almost 10 million. This rapid expansion was to continue throughout the nineteenth century, when the population
of the country quadrupled, and was to level off only at the beginning of the twentieth.

The causes of this phenomenon, as of many others in demog-
raphy, are obscure, and most explanations of it are highly speculative. Since most of the increase seems to have taken place in
the second half of the century, it is natural to connect it with
the "Industrial Revolution," though why the many new factories that sprang up in northern England from 1770 onward
should have found themselves automatically provided with a
supply of operatives is hard to say. The thesis of one of the best
social historians of the period, Dorothy George, is that for all
the emphasis later placed on the miserable living and working
conditions of the early years of industrialization—and they *were*

miserable—they nevertheless represented an improvement over the way the masses had previously lived, and that the concern shown by men like Blake and the seventh Lord Shaftesbury for the workers in the "dark Satanic mills" is testimony of a heightened awareness for the lot of the poor. Earlier in the century this awareness had manifested itself in the organization of many charitable and welfare movements and in improved sanitary and medical facilities, and thus (around 1750) in a striking decrease in the death rate. Even Pope, that bitter satirist of the "degeneracy" of England under the regime of Sir Robert Walpole, conceded, in a complexly ironic epigram "on the large sums of money given in charity in the severe winter of 1740–1741,"

> "Yes, 'tis the time," I cried, "impose the chain,
>   Destin'd and due to wretches self-enslaved";
> But when I saw such charity remain,
>   I half could wish this people should be saved.
>
> Faith lost, and Hope, our Charity begins;
>   And 'tis a wise design in pitying Heav'n,
> If this can cover multitude of sins,
>   To take the *only* way to be forgiv'n.

Hogarth's "Gin Lane" gives a most horrible picture of the effects of the easy availability of cheap gin on the life of the poor in the early part of the century. But the many efforts made by Parliament under Walpole and his successors to enact legislation that would satisfactorily control the sale of liquor—never an easy task, as modern legislators know—are often forgotten. Several unsuccessful or only partially successful acts were passed before the really effective statute of 1751 was arrived at. The consumption of spirits decreased from 8 million gallons in 1743 to around 2 million in 1760. The Act of 1751, Mrs. George says, "was a turning point in the social history of London. . . . The measures to check excessive spirit-drinking had been forced upon the Government in the teeth of vested interests by a general protest in which the middle and trading classes had taken a leading part."[1] It also helped that about this time the price of tea (whose virtues were so stoutly defended by Johnson) dropped enough to make it available to the lower classes. But that there was no deficiency of "social consciousness" in the eighteenth century, a reading of the many essays in the *Tatler* and *Spectator*, the *Rambler* and *Idler* that deal with social abuses—imprisonment for debt, the tyranny of country squires, the hard lot of the prostitute—will readily confirm.

At the beginning of the eighteenth century, then, Britain was still a relatively small, isolated country on the fringe of the European community, which included such larger and seemingly more powerful nations as France (perhaps 16 million people) and Spain (around 10 million). Anomalously, however, she boasted the largest and wealthiest city in Europe—London, whose population, calculated to be 674,000 at the beginning of the century, considerably exceeded that of Paris, its nearest rival, and was many times that of Rome. The influence of London on English life was therefore strikingly great, all the more so since no other English town could come near to challenging its supremacy. The next most populous, the seaport of Bristol and the manufacturing town of Norwich, were each less than 30,000 at the beginning of the century. Toward the end of the century, Birmingham, Liverpool, Manchester, Leeds, and Sheffield were beginning to grow into the great industrial centers they became in the nineteenth century—but only beginning. Most of them did not send members to the House of Commons, nor, in the eighteenth century, was there any great agitation for their representation; this was not to come until 1832.

When by the end of the century the population of London had increased to nearly a million, agrarians like William Cobbett and Romantics like Wordsworth denounced the squalor, materialism, and crime rate of "the Great Wen," and deplored its baneful effects on the primitive virtues still preserved in rural England. (There has never been a time in English history when people have not looked back nostalgically to an earlier "Merrie England.") By this time London, like the similarly denounced New York in the twentieth century, was becoming not merely a national but an international capital; artists and intellectuals from other parts of the world—Voltaire (one of the earliest) and Rousseau, Mozart and Haydn, for instance—were beginning to feel the need either to visit it for at least a time, or actually to emigrate to it, Handel leading the procession that was to culminate in the next century with Karl Marx.

Most of the English population outside London lived in the agricultural south of the country; the great northward shift of the population, to the coal mining region, did not take place until the Industrial Revolution was well under way. The difference between country and town (i.e., London) life was striking, as the ecstasies of many a country wife in the comedies of the time when transported to town testify. Roads were abominable—it was thought a daring innovation when, in 1669, public coaches announced their intention of trying to travel the fifty miles from London to Oxford in one (long) day instead of the two formerly required—and were infested by highwaymen, many of them, like Macheath in *The Beggar's Opera,* glamorous public figures. Communications were difficult, and social amenities in the country limited: Zephalinda, in Pope's charming epistle "To Mrs. Blount on Her Leaving the Town after the Coronation," has to make do with a neighboring squire

Who visits with a gun, presents you birds,

quail and pheasant that he had shot, most unenticing of gifts—

Then gives a smacking buss, and cries—"No words!"
Or with his hounds comes hollowing from the stable,
Makes love with nods, and knees beneath a table.

In the rugged and sparsely populated north, life was more primitive still; it is seldom noticed even in the fiction of the time, though the bleak farmstead of Emily Brontë's *Wuthering Heights* probably represents north English life in the eighteenth century well enough. The north, to be sure, had scenery; but as has often been pointed out, mountains and deserted moorlands seldom provide much aesthetic appeal until the spectator has attained a way of life which makes them no longer hazards and inconveniences. The occasional *avant garde* intellectual, like that cloistered scholar Thomas Gray, might jot down some appreciative comments as he passed through the Lake Country (knowing that he would soon return to the comforts of Cambridge). But a good deal of Romantic propaganda was still going to be required before the delights of local Nature became viable to the average Englishman. Even then, Lady Louisa Stuart, Lady Mary Wortley Montagu's granddaughter, who lived through the "revolution in taste," had her suspicions that much of the ecstasy was affectation: "Can it be that the tastes and pleasures which we now esteem most natural are in fact artificial? What we have merely read, and talked, and rhymed, and sketched ourselves into?"

Politically, the British Isles in the seventeenth century were still fragmented into three nations. The official style of the monarch before 1707 was King (or Queen) of Great Britain, France, and Ireland. Wales had been incorporated in England under the Plantagenets, and given recognition in the title "Prince of Wales" bestowed on the monarch's eldest son. "France" was a relic from the time of Edward III, who had entered a hereditary claim to its throne; it was not, however, dropped from the royal style until 1801. Although King James VI of Scotland succeeded his cousin Elizabeth as King James I of England in 1603, and assumed the title of King of Great Britain, the two nations remained separate throughout the seventeenth century, the Scottish Parliament at Edinburgh legislating for the northern kingdom. By the Act of Union of 1707, negotiated with much difficulty by the English government (with the able assistance of Daniel Defoe), the Parliament at Edinburgh was abolished, and that at Westminster, to which a handful of Scottish peers and commoners were summoned, now legislated for the new nation of Great Britain.

Scotland, a turbulent and, by English standards, impoverished realm of a million or so people, had made trouble for its southern neighbor for many centuries, not excluding the seventeenth. One of the chief bones of contention had been religion, the Scots stubbornly adhering to the stern Presbyterianism introduced by John Knox in the sixteenth century, and refusing any hint of compromise with the episcopacy and liturgy of the Church of England. The great Civil War of the 1640's had been touched off as early as 1637 by Charles I's and Archbishop Laud's attempt to impose a prayer book on the Scots. In July of that year the initial "incident" occurred when, in St. Giles's, Edinburgh, the legendary Jenny Geddes hurled her stool at the officiating clergyman and cried "Will ye say Mass in my lug?"

An indispensable condition of the Union of 1707 had been the recognition of Presbyterianism as the form of the established (state) Church of Scotland, with the anomaly—to later eyes more than to contemporary ones—that the sovereign is head of an episcopal Church south of the Tweed and a nonepiscopal Church north of it. One of the most striking results of the Union was the beginning of that long southward procession of clever and ambitious young Scots whose finest prospect, Johnson grumbled, was the highroad that led them to England—Hume, James Thomson (whose patriotic ditty "Rule, Britannia" pointedly honors *Britain,* not England), Boswell, and many others.

John Bull's other island, Ireland, also furnished many brilliant men to the English intellectual community—Congreve, Swift, Goldsmith, Berkeley, Burke, Sheridan, to mention some. It had a larger population than Scotland (around 2 million), but, if its soil was more fertile, its economy was no more prosperous. Since the time of the Norman kings, the English government had attempted to keep Ireland in strict subjection, such as had never been successfully imposed on Scotland. It retained its own Parliament at Dublin until 1801, when a new Act of Union abolished it and transferred its powers to the Parliament at Westminster which, with Irish representation added to it, now legislated for the whole "United Kingdom," as the realm was then officially designated. But the Irish Parliament in the eighteenth century (in which of course only Protestants could sit) had strictly limited powers, and could pass only legislation approved by the English Privy Council. As a result, as Swift complained in bitter satires like *A Modest Proposal,* the economic needs of Ireland were consistently subordinated to those of England. Unlike Presbyterianism in Scotland, the Roman Catholicism of the vast majority of the (Celtic) population of Ireland received no official recognition and was, at best, ignored, and, at worst, persecuted; the whole population was required to pay tithes to the church of the minority, the (Protestant) Church of Ireland, which was closely affiliated with the Church of England.

As a result of these foolish policies, the history of the relations between England and Ireland for centuries had been one of in-

tervals of ruthless oppression punctuated, whenever England
found itself faced with difficulty elsewhere, by bloody insurrec-
tions—in 1641, at the outset of the Civil War; in 1689, at the
time of the "Glorious Revolution"; and in 1798, during
the French Revolutionary War—in which large numbers of the
Anglo-Irish Protestant "ascendancy" were massacred. Fortunately for the eighteenth century, the years between the two last
mentioned revolts were the longest period of peace that has so
far endured between the two communities. The Celtic Irish, a
half-starved and ignorant peasantry—"Teagues" was one of the
favorite nicknames for them—were, for the English of the seventeenth century, objects of contempt, mixed with some fear; Dryden's pillorying of his enemy Shadwell under the name Mac
Flecknoe is testimony of the attitude. Later the image of the
"stage Irishman," the comic, hot-tempered, rather stupid, but
good-hearted "Paddy" (like Sir Lucius O' Trigger in Sheridan's
The Rivals) began to mitigate that attitude somewhat. But the
sentimentalization of the Celt—the loyal and gallant Scottish
Highlander as well as the warm-hearted Irishman—did not
reach its full maturity until the days of Victoria.

For all that the two fringe regions of Scotland and Ireland
remained remote, primitive, and somewhat ominous places in
the mind of the average Englishman—though Samuel Johnson
paid Scotland the compliment of a serious and thoughtful "socio-
anthropological" study in his *A Journey to the Western Islands of Scotland,* 1775—it should not be forgotten that, as time
went on, their capital cities became far from negligible centers
of culture. Some of the finest city architecture of the eighteenth
century is to be found in Dublin, and it was there that Handel
(in spite of Swift's efforts to sabotage it) conducted the first performance of his *Messiah.* Toward the end of the century, Edinburgh produced an impressive group of philosophers and
writers—a flowering sometimes termed "the Scottish Enlightenment"—and adopted the proud title of "the Athens of the
North." Nevertheless, the intellectual and artistic life of the
British Isles was overwhelmingly dominated (as it still continues to be) by London, and the nearby small but highly influential university communities of Oxford and Cambridge, much as
that of twentieth-century America, in spite of its vast popula-

tion, continues to be dominated by New York and its "suburbs" of Boston, New Haven, Princeton, and Washington.

The Monarchy

Then as now, the official structure of English society was pyramidal, with the monarch at the top. It is well to point out, for the benefit of students brought up to think that the lively propagandist rhetoric of the American Declaration of Independence bears a close relation to historical fact, that England has always been a limited, never an absolute, monarchy. Macaulay summarizes it neatly: the royal power, he points out,

> was limited by three great constitutional principles, so ancient that none can say when they began to exist. . . . First, the King could not legislate without the consent of his Parliament. Secondly, he could impose no taxes without the consent of his Parliament. Thirdly, he was bound to conduct the executive administration according to the laws of the land, and, if he broke those laws, his advisers and his agents were responsible.[2]

Like the American Constitution, which is an offshoot of it, the old English constitution rested on the principle of the division of powers, the executive power being in the hands of the King and his appointed privy councillors (as with the President and his Cabinet), and the legislative power residing in Parliament, consisting of the King and the two representative Houses, the Lords and the Commons. For a law to be placed on the statute books, it must receive the assent of all three constituents (as, in the United States, of the President, the Senate, and the House of Representatives).

The great change in the British constitution by which, in effect, the executive and the legislative powers were transferred to the leadership of the majority party in the House of Commons, making the public actions of both the monarch and Parliament usually no more than a formal ratification of what is decided beforehand in the Cabinet room, was not fully brought about until the mid-nineteenth century. Throughout the seventeenth and eighteenth centuries, including the reign of George

The Houses of Stuart and Hanover (1603–1837)*

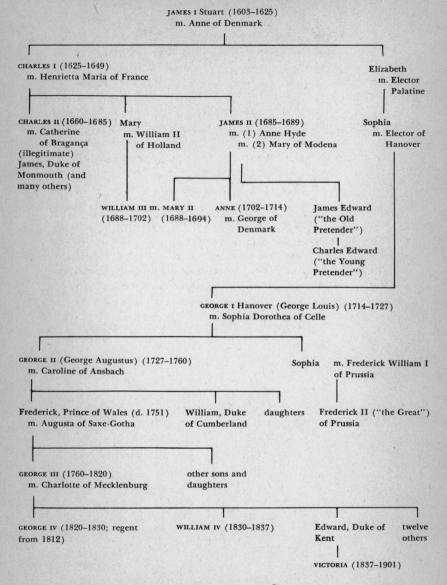

JAMES I Stuart (1603–1625)
m. Anne of Denmark

CHARLES I (1625–1649)
m. Henrietta Maria of France

Elizabeth
m. Elector
Palatine

CHARLES II (1660–1685)
m. Catherine
of Bragança
(illegitimate)
James, Duke of
Monmouth (and
many others)

Mary
m. William II
of Holland

JAMES II (1685–1689)
m. (1) Anne Hyde
m. (2) Mary of Modena

Sophia
m. Elector of
Hanover

WILLIAM III m. MARY II
(1688–1702) (1688–1694)

ANNE (1702–1714)
m. George of
Denmark

James Edward
("the Old
Pretender")

Charles Edward
("the Young
Pretender")

GEORGE I Hanover (George Louis) (1714–1727)
m. Sophia Dorothea of Celle

GEORGE II (George Augustus) (1727–1760)
m. Caroline of Ansbach

Sophia m. Frederick William I
of Prussia

Frederick, Prince of Wales (d. 1751)
m. Augusta of Saxe-Gotha

William, Duke
of Cumberland

daughters

Frederick II ("the Great")
of Prussia

GEORGE III (1760–1820)
m. Charlotte of Mecklenburg

other sons and
daughters

GEORGE IV (1820–1830; regent
from 1812)

WILLIAM IV (1830–1837)

Edward, Duke of
Kent

twelve
others

VICTORIA (1837–1901)

*The student should familiarize himself with this genealogical table. Sovereigns'
names are in small caps; the dates are those of their *de facto* reigns.

III, the King was expected to be the effective chief executive of the country; though, as time went on and Britain became involved in increasingly extensive and expensive international activity, the cooperation of the House of Commons, which held the purse strings of the government, became more and more indispensable. When Johnson said, in 1772, "The crown has not power enough," he was not hankering after absolutism; he was merely complaining about a situation in which the central executive was hampered in giving strong direction to national affairs, as an American President might be when faced with a hostile Congress. Indeed, many seeming puzzles of eighteenth-century British political history become simple enough when translated into modern American governmental terms.

Still, within the traditional limitations of the constitution, there remained much room for maneuver, depending on the personality and ideology of the monarch (as there is in the American system, if one compares the history of, say, President Franklin Roosevelt's administration with President Eisenhower's). It was the genius of the Tudor monarchs that, without overtly infringing those limitations, they were able to create the strong central executive that Britain needed as it emerged from the medieval into the modern world. It was the misfortune of their successors, the Stuarts—at least, of three of them, James I, Charles I, and James II—that they lacked this kind of political tact and failed to heed the danger signals when they trespassed too blatantly beyond the traditional bounds. James I's bizarre treatment of his Parliaments laid the foundations of the scaffold on which his son Charles I was beheaded in 1649. But the fundamental strength and soundness of the old constitution was shown when, eleven years later, after hectic experimentation with various forms of republicanism, culminating in the only real despotism and dictatorship that has ever existed in English history, the English turned with relief to the restoration of the old system, and recalled Charles I's son, Charles II, from exile in France to take his place at the head of it.

The strictures on the political acumen of the other three of the first four Stuarts do not apply to the affable, cynical, and astute Charles II, who, having determined, as he said, "never to set out on his travels again," threaded his way with great skill through the complex and dangerous political mazes of his quarter century on the throne. In particular, his handling of the explosive crisis of the Exclusion Bill, 1678–1682, when it seemed inevitable that the Civil War would break out again in all its fury, was a miracle of political finesse. The British Restoration of 1660 is one of the very few restorations in history that have been successful—for contrast one may turn to the sad spectacles of the monarchist and Napoleonic restorations in nineteenth-century France—and the chief credit for its success must go to Charles himself. Victorian readers, accustomed to their historians' denunciations of Charles's private life, involving a dozen or so mistresses and innumerable illegitimate progeny (he "scattered his Maker's image through the land," as his loyal Poet Laureate, Dryden, wittily put it), must have been puzzled to find the rigidly moral Samuel Johnson praising Charles as the only English monarch for a hundred years who "had much appeared to desire, or much endeavoured to deserve" the affections of his people. But the praise was just.

As the personalities of the British monarchs of the seventeenth and eighteenth centuries (like those of American Presidents) had a good deal of influence in shaping the climate of opinion of their reigns, it will be well to devote some time to reviewing them. The Stuart family were an always interesting, often exasperating, and sometimes charming lot, more capable than any other dynasty that has occupied the English throne of arousing either fervent loyalty or violent antagonism. It has been suggested [3] that the key to an understanding of them is their more-than-average susceptibility to sexual feeling, sometimes overt, sometimes latent. Homosexual tendencies can easily be discovered in the biographies of James I, William III, and Anne; the heterosexual proclivities of Mary, Queen of Scots (James I's mother), Charles II, and James II were notorious; Charles I, after being dominated in his youth by his father's handsome favorite, George Villiers, Duke of Buckingham, was dominated in later life by his French and Roman Catholic wife, Henrietta Maria. Not, of course, that such susceptibility was unique to members of this one dynasty: from, say, William Rufus up to Edward VIII, certainly not excluding Queen Victoria, the sexual feelings of the English royal family have often affected the course of public affairs.

After the death of the popular Charles II in 1685, his near-fanatic brother James II, who, as Duke of York, had narrowly escaped being "excluded" from the throne on account of his religion, was forced into exile after three years of attempting the impossible feat of changing England from a Protestant to a Roman Catholic country. He was succeeded ("usurped," James's "Jacobite" partisans bitterly maintained), after the Glorious Revolution of 1688, by his dourly efficient nephew and son-in-law, William of Orange, Stadholder of Holland, leader of Continental Protestantism against the aggression of Louis XIV of France—like other Stuarts, worshiped by his supporters, execrated by his opponents. Associated with William III as Queen Regnant, though deferring to him in everything, was his wife, James II's elder daughter, the pious Mary II, who died of smallpox in 1694.

William was succeeded in 1702 by Mary's younger sister, "good Queen Anne," staunchly Anglican (but not very intelligently, as Jonathan Swift discovered), always under the domination of some more strong-minded woman—until 1710, of the famous Sarah Churchill, Duchess of Marlborough. Anne, married to the equally dull Prince George of Denmark, had numerous children, all of whom died young. After her death in 1714, the demise (succession) of the crown was controlled by the Act of Settlement, passed by the English Parliament in 1701 and still in force today, which provides that neither the sovereign nor his consort may be a Roman Catholic. Hence the crown went, not to James II's young son ("the Old Pretender"), who was brought up as a Catholic, nor to some fifty other Stuart descendants closer in birth, also debarred because of their Catholicism, but to the nearest Protestant heir, George Louis, Elector of Hanover in Germany, great-grandson of James I, and, as King George I, first of the Hanoverian line of British monarchs.

The Georges have always had a bad press among their subjects. A nineteenth-century wit summed them up:

> George the First was always reckoned
> Vile, but viler George the Second.
> And what mortal ever heard
> Any good of George the Third?
> When from earth the Fourth descended,
> God be praised, the Georges ended.

But the more closely one becomes acquainted with the early Hanoverians, the more one comes to see that they were very far from contemptible or negligible. On the male side, they were the representatives of the ancient German dynasty of Guelph, which in the Middle Ages had furnished emperors for the Holy Roman Empire, and, along with their opponents the Ghibellines, had given their name to a side in the great Italian Wars of Investiture. In the seventeenth century they had astutely promoted their Dukedom of Brunswick to an Electorate—that is, secured for the head of the family the much-sought privilege of being one of the nine great German princes officially charged with the selection of the Holy Roman Emperor; the title of Elector (*Kurfürst*) frequently proved the forerunner to that of King. They were popular rulers in their own dominions and were respected on the Continent as shrewd diplomats and courageous and efficient military leaders.

George's claim to the British throne came from the marriage of his father to Princess Sophia of the Rhine, sister of the daring Cavalier general Prince Rupert.[4] They were the children of James I's daughter, the beautiful and charming Elizabeth, the "Winter Queen" of Bohemia, whose husband's claim to that kingdom (as against that of the Catholic Habsburgs) had precipitated the Thirty Years' War, and who was therefore regarded by suspicious English Puritans as the one really staunch Protestant in the Stuart line. The Electress Sophia inherited her mother's brains and forceful personality, and, though an old lady, looked forward eagerly to becoming Queen Sophia I of Great Britain when her dull cousin Anne should die (she missed the crown by only a few weeks). Sophia was one of three generations of remarkably brilliant and intellectual women connected with the Hanoverian family; her granddaughter-in-law Caroline was the last of the group.

No court which maintained Leibniz as its librarian and historian and Handel as its director of music, as the Hanoverian court did at the beginning of the eighteenth century, deserved the sneers which the English bestowed on it. The fact is that a great deal of English hostility toward the Hanoverians stemmed from sheer provincial ignorance of the wider world of the Continent, even from philistinism (one thinks of Addison's, Swift's, and Johnson's sneers against the Italian opera introduced by Handel, chiefly because it was "un-English" and they knew nothing about it). Apart from George III, the British royal family from George I down to Edward VII has always had a cosmopolitan rather than a nationalist outlook,[5] and it annoyed the English greatly that the first two Georges did not seem to appreciate the great honor that had been bestowed upon them, but were always chafing to get back to their more congenial Continental dominions.

Sophia's son, George Louis, was fifty-four when he acceded to the British throne, and had earned a respected name for himself on the Continent as a diplomat and a general. It vexed his English subjects that he never took the trouble to learn their language. But he had no great need to; well versed in French, German, and Latin, and assisted by able and experienced Hanoverians, he was better able than his English ministers to handle the foreign relations of the country, and did so competently. The story is told of George's conducting in French a lively technical discussion of international affairs with an ambassador from the Continent, and from time to time tossing a perfunctory translation of the gist of it to his English Secretary of State, the Duke of Newcastle, who stood by fidgeting in uncomprehending embarrassment.

Unprepossessing in appearance and stolid in manner, except when alone with a handful of intimate friends, George made little attempt to ingratiate himself with his new subjects. Such social life as there was at court revolved around the Prince and Princess of Wales. The King's marriage to his cousin Sophia Dorothea had ended long before in an ugly scandal and divorce, and he contented himself with his homely mistress, Melusina von der Schulenburg, whom he created Duchess of Kendal,[6] and who exercised considerable political patronage. Like his son's, his interest in literature and painting was minimal; but (again like his son and many of his descendants) he passionately loved music, and stoutly supported his great protégé Handel against politically inspired attacks.

George Augustus (George II) was an impetuous, quick-tempered little man, who quarreled fiercely with his father—a habit of all Hanoverian heirs. But he was a courageous soldier (he was the last British monarch to lead his troops into battle, at Dettingen in 1743, a feat celebrated by Handel with a glorious *Te Deum*). In spite of his apparent indifference to intellectual activity, two great institutions of learning in his dominions were chartered by him and named after him, the Georg-August University of Göttingen in his Electorate of Hanover, and King's College, afterward Columbia University, in his Province of New York (his father had founded the Regius Professorships of Modern History at Oxford and Cambridge). Most important of all, he had the good sense to let himself be governed by his wife, Caroline of Ansbach.

Perhaps the most robust and brilliant intellectual who has ever occupied the British throne, Caroline's hobbies were philosophy and theology. She corresponded with Leibniz and discoursed with Joseph Butler, the most subtle English theologian of the century, whom she appointed her "clerk of the closet" (chaplain-in-chief) and whose promotion to a bishopric she arranged before she died. Her independence of thinking gave rise to rumors of her heterodoxy, even atheism, which her omission on her deathbed to receive the last Communion from the Archbishop of Canterbury did nothing to dispel. She was a plump, blonde, vivacious, outspoken woman, quite beautiful in her youth. Lord Hervey, whose memoir of her and George and their court is a literary classic, was obviously deeply in love with her; so was George Augustus, though he felt he owed it to his position as King to keep a series of mistresses, who, however, stood no chance against Caroline in his affections. Caroline was glad enough to have these ladies take George off her hands from time to time, for his company could be devastatingly boring (her daughters approved these tactics). But any of them foolish enough to embark on a trial of strength with Caroline regretted it, like Pope's friend, Lady Suffolk, to whom Caroline at last felt compelled to remark pleasantly that "it was in my power, if I had pleased, any hour of the day, to let her drop through my fingers—thus." Lady Suffolk soon left court.

Caroline loved power, and, working amiably and efficiently with her father-in-law's and husband's great Prime Minister, Walpole, exercised it competently for a decade. When she died in 1737 (of gangrene resulting from an untreated rupture of the womb, which she concealed lest it should diminish her attraction for her husband, and hence her power over him), George was heartbroken. Hervey recounts the wonderful scene when Caroline begged George, who was lying across the foot of her bed, blubbering uncontrollably, to marry again after she died. "Non—non," he sobbed; "j'aurai des maîtresses!" "Mon Dieu," Caroline murmured, "cela n'empêche pas." [7] (The anecdote shocked virtuous Victorians like Thackeray beyond measure.)

George, however, kept his promise and did not marry again, but immediately sent over to Hanover for his current mistress Amalie von Wallmoden (an action which shocked the virtuous Samuel Johnson) and settled down to another quarter century of uninspired but competent government, generally with the assistance of the Walpolian Whig "connection." The image he projected was anything but glamorous and when he died in 1760 at the age of seventy-seven, Johnson was not the only one of his subjects who felt, as he wrote to a friend, "We were so weary of our old King, that we are much pleased with his successor; of whom we are so much inclined to hope great things, that most of us begin already to believe them."

They were to be disappointed. "The young man is hitherto blameless," Johnson continued, "but it would be unreasonable to expect much from the immaturity of juvenile years, and the ignorance of princely education. He has been long in the hands of the Scots. . . ." The new King was George II's grandson, the twenty-two year old George III, son of the shallow-minded Frederick, Prince of Wales, who had died in 1751. Frederick had been the object of his parents' hearty detestation; at one time George II seems to have speculated on the possibility of separating his dominions, leaving Frederick to rule Hanover and putting his younger brother, the competent William, Duke of Cumberland, on the British throne. Young George III inherited Frederick's feud with both George II and his Walpolian Whig ministers and espoused the "patriotic"—i.e., anti-Walpolian—political line of the opposition, to which Frederick adhered.

Educated by Frederick's counselor, the Scottish Earl of Bute (whom political malice accused of being the lover of George's mother, Augusta, Princess of Wales), young George "gloried in the name of Britain" (not England), as he said in his accession speech; and, as if to point out the difference between himself and his two predecessors, he never set foot out of the country in his long life. His reign, ending in 1820, was exceeded in length only by that of his granddaughter Victoria. Faithful to his ugly wife, Charlotte of Mecklenburg-Strelitz, and father of fifteen children by her—one historian, J. H. Plumb, suggests that the strain and trauma of his connubial duties were a contributory cause of his periodic fits of insanity[8]—he settled down to provide his subjects with an example of bourgeois virtue, and as the simple, good-hearted "Farmer George" he was wildly popular with them.

The American myth that George was a ferocious tyrant has long been exploded by responsible historiography. He was an intensely conscientious and well-meaning individual, determined to fulfill his constitutional duties faithfully and for the good of his country, and to keep its government from being monopolized by coteries of grasping and self-seeking politicians. But he was highly neurotic, and, as Johnson said, immature and ignorant; and mere good intentions were inadequate weapons with which to counter the techniques of intrigue and propaganda used by such skilled practical politicians as John Wilkes and Edmund Burke, and, on the other side of the Atlantic, Sam Adams and Thomas Jefferson. He did much, however, to create —for better or worse—the twentieth-century British image of bourgeois and domesticated virtuous royalty. Unlike some of his successors in this tradition, for example, George V and George VI, but rather like such other historically unsatisfactory monarchs as Charles I and George IV, he was a dedicated and conscientious patron of the arts.

The Church

The elaborate organization of the Church of England was a heritage from the medieval Church, which showed a genius for administration that was in turn a legacy from the Roman Empire. It was Theodore of Tarsus, seventh Archbishop of Canterbury (668–690), born and educated in the Eastern Empire not long after the reign of that great administrator Justinian, who

was largely responsible for imposing on the English Church the
form of organization it retained in the eighteenth century (and
still retains). The country was divided into some 10,000 parishes, each under a rector or vicar, which were grouped into
twenty-six dioceses, each under a bishop. Four large but thinly
populated northern dioceses constituted the Province of York,
the remainder the Province of Canterbury, each with its archbishop; the Archbishop of Canterbury, as senior, held the title
of Primate of All England.

The parish was the unit not only of ecclesiastical organization, but also of local municipal administration: the church-
wardens and other officers of the parish were responsible for the
levying and collection of local property taxes, including tithes
for the maintenance of the church and the support of the parish
priest, and their expenditure for local roads, the relief of the
poor of the parish, and the like. The right of appointment
("presentation") of the parish priest was usually in the hands of
the largest local landowner (formerly the lord of the manor),
though it had sometimes been ceded to an Oxford or Cambridge
college, or to the Lord Chancellor, acting for the crown. The
nominee had, of course, to be approved of and formally "insti-
tuted" by the bishop of the diocese, but this was seldom refused;
the right of presentation ("advowson") was looked on as private
freehold property, and was jealously guarded. So was the right
of the parish priest (the "incumbent"), once presented, to the
fixed revenues allotted to him out of parish funds—hence such
an appointment was called a "benefice" or "living." Once insti-
tuted, it was next to impossible to remove an incumbent against
his will (it still is).

The bishops were (and are) appointed by the crown, on the
advice of the Prime Minister. All bishops of the Church of England were spiritual peers, sat in the House of Lords, and took an
active part in legislating, and sometimes political maneuvering.

Such an establishment was of course postulated on the assumptions that (1) England was exclusively a Christian country;
(2) there is only one Christian church, the Church of England
being a regional division of that universal (catholic) church; (3)
there is no sharp division between Church and State, the function of government generally being to foster the welfare of the

people of the country, spiritually and morally as well as materially. Indeed, in the Middle Ages, the civil affairs of the realm were often ruled by churchmen (as the best qualified administrators); bishops frequently held the office of Lord Chancellor, and the like. The last such appointment was made in the reign of Queen Anne, when John Robinson, Bishop of Bristol, became Lord Privy Seal.

These postulates had been accepted without question throughout Western Europe in the Middle Ages and beyond. But in eighteenth-century Britain the principle of the unity of Church and State was beginning to break down. The machinery of the fully established Church continued to operate (as it still does); the vast majority of the people of England formally adhered to the national Church; and it is clear that the assumptions underlying the establishment still appealed to "High Churchmen" like Swift and Johnson—and John Wesley. But the principle itself had been dealt a mortal blow by John Locke's *Letters on Toleration,* and by the Toleration Act, 1689, which for the first time recognized the legal existence in England of churches other than the national one. Both Locke's work and the legislation were the product of humanitarian and rationalist repugnance at the barbarity of the wars of religion, civil and international, that had vexed Europe for the past century and a half, wars stemming from the principle of *cujus natio, ejus religio*—all the citizenry of a state should be of the same religion. Locke's simple but powerful argument was that the use of force by the state to make men "true Christians" is itself a gross violation of Christian morality, an argument to which even conservatives like Swift and Johnson readily assented.[9] The Toleration Act did not extend its operations very far; it merely permitted Protestant Dissenters (not Roman Catholics) to hold their own services and attend them instead of those of the Church of England. But even to take legal cognizance of the existence of competing religions was looked on by many as a shocking innovation; and in the reign of Anne, the "high-flying" Tories, feeling that toleration had gone much too far, attempted to limit it again by the Occasional Conformity and Schism Acts. These, however, remained a dead letter. It was not until well into the nineteenth century, and only after much violent controversy, that Roman Catholics, Jews, and finally atheists were admitted to full civil equality. Even yet, the sovereign and the sovereign's consort are required by law to be Protestants.

In spite of the gradual decay of the *cujus regio* principle, religious loyalties and animosities were still responsible for many events in the political history of the late seventeenth and eighteenth centuries in England (and in the nineteenth, and even, in its relations with Ireland, in the twentieth). These often stemmed from bitter memories of persecution and aggression on one side or the other. Queen "Bloody" Mary I's burnings at the stake were only a little more than a century old at the time of the Restoration, and were vividly impressed on people's minds by John Foxe's *The Book of Martyrs,* sometimes kept in parish churches along with the Bible. Pope Pius V's excommunication of Queen Elizabeth, the descent of the Spanish Armada, above all the Catholic-inspired Gunpowder Plot of 1605, when Guy Fawkes was found ready to blow up the King and Parliament, were not quickly forgotten (an annual service of thanksgiving concerning the latter was incorporated in the Anglican Prayer Book) and still aroused fierce resentment and very real fear of the Roman Church.

Even more recent and vivid were the memories of the Puritan ascendancy of the 1640's and 1650's; not productive of so much bloodshed as the earlier Catholic activities—though the Archbishop of Canterbury, Laud, did lose his head—yet causing much misery to Anglican clergy evicted from their livings, and irritation to ordinary people through the closing of the theaters, insistence on the "Puritan Sabbath," and the like. About such "blue laws," the average Englishman probably thought much as Macaulay did: "The Puritan hated bearbaiting, not because it gave pain to the bear, but because it gave pleasure to the spectators." [10] And, naturally, Catholics and Puritans also remembered and resented what had been done to them when Anglicans were in power. These memories and resentments were potent political forces in Britain, from the time of the Clarendon Code of the 1660's down to the Gordon Riots of 1780 and beyond; especially so in bringing about the Revolution of 1689 and the settlement of the crown on the Protestant House of Hanover.

It is to the great credit of the leaders of the Church of England in the late seventeenth and eighteenth centuries that on the whole they steadily strove to diminish partisan animosity to other branches of Christianity and irrational exaltation of the status of the Anglican church. Such partisanship was to be found in the lower orders of the clergy—the rural parish priests who shared the isolationist prejudices of their patrons, the squires—and in a small but vociferous group of doctrinaire High Churchmen like Francis Atterbury, Bishop of Rochester, and Henry Sacheverell. But Atterbury was an appointment of the short-lived Tory ministry of the end of Queen Anne's reign, and few eighteenth-century bishops felt as he did.

Anne, curiously, was the only Anglican monarch (and temporal Head of the Church of England) for over a century, between 1649 and 1760. Charles II's conversion to Roman Catholicism was kept secret during his lifetime, but announced after his death. James II was a militant Roman Catholic. William III was a Calvinist, of the Dutch Reformed Church (his wife, Mary II, was Anglican, of course, but was guided by her husband in everything). The first two Georges were Lutherans. It was natural enough then that an ecumenical spirit should have prevailed among the crown-appointed hierarchy, although it was far from prevalent among the ordinary priesthood; indeed, the constant dissension between the two Houses of Convocation, the annual assembly of the Church—the Upper House consisting of the bishops and the Lower House representing the rest of the clergy—was such that from 1716 onward, the government refused to let it deliberate: another grievance, of course, for the more intransigent Anglicans.

The great Whig and latitudinarian bishops of the period have received harsh treatment at the hands of historians, who, for the most part, have followed the anti-Protestant line of the publicists of the Oxford Movement in the nineteenth century.[11] They have been accused of indifference and Erastianism and sloth for not taking a more militantly Anglican stand, for tolerating the encroachments of Dissent, and so on. In the ecumenical climate of the mid-twentieth century, however, it is difficult to condemn Burnet, Tillotson, and the rest for being too friendly to Presbyterians and Baptists.

The great scheme of "comprehension" sponsored in the 1690's by John Tillotson, William III's Archbishop of Canterbury, an attempt to broaden doctrine and ritual so that the Presbyterians and Congregationalists who had been ejected from the Church in 1662 might again join it, was easily sabotaged by Atterbury and the Lower House of Convocation; but the only objection that can now be made to it is that it was 250 years before its time. Not until the 1940's were serious schemes of reunion between Anglicans and other Protestants again devised, and, with the formation of the Church of South India, actually put into practice.

William Wake, Archbishop of Canterbury from 1716 to 1737, a fine scholar, was likewise concerned to establish liaison between his Church and French Huguenots, German Lutherans, and the Eastern Orthodox Church. Men like Edmund Gibson, Bishop of London, the astute administrator who was Walpole's right-hand man in ecclesiastical affairs; Joseph Butler, Bishop of Durham, a great theologian; George Berkeley, Bishop of Cloyne in Ireland, a great philosopher; such lesser but by no means contemptible figures as William Warburton, editor of Shakespeare and Pope and indefatigable controversialist, Robert Lowth, pioneer student of Hebrew poetry, Richard Hurd, a competent literary critic, Richard Watson, professor in turn of chemistry and divinity at Cambridge and a noted radical in politics, to mention some, make up an episcopate which compares very favorably in learning, piety, and energy with that of other periods. The eighteenth century had notable deans, too—Josiah Tucker, pioneer economist, for one; and Jonathan Swift for another. Queen Anne vetoed a bishopric for Swift; yet a Church willing to accept him even as a dean cannot be said to have been completely lacking in courage.

The lesser Anglican clergy were poorly paid and generally poorly educated by comparison with, say, the ministry of the Presbyterian Church of Scotland. To be sure, Fielding's Parson Trulliber and Parson Thwackum were exaggerations, as was Macaulay's "typical" Restoration country parson—

A young Levite . . . might be had for his board, a small garret . . . and might also save the expense of a gardener, or of a groom. Sometimes the reverend man nailed up the apricots, and sometimes

he curried the coach horses. . . . He was permitted to dine with
the family; but he was expected to content himself with the plainest
fare. He might fill himself with the corned beef and the carrots:
but, as soon as the tarts and the cheesecakes made their appearance,
he quitted his seat. . . . Not one living in fifty enabled the incumbent to bring up a family comfortably. As children multiplied and
grew, the household of the priest became more and more beggarly.
Holes appeared more and more plainly in the thatch of his parson-
age and in his single cassock. Often it was only by toiling on his
glebe, by feeding swine, and by loading dungcarts, that he could
obtain daily bread.[12]

But that such pictures could be drawn at all was the result of
Henry VIII's confiscation of the endowments of the medieval
Church, and the refusal of the economical Elizabeth to put it
back on a proper financial basis. There has been much satire
about the more enterprising individuals among the eighteenth-
century clergy, who managed to get possession of plural bene-
fices (though this, too, was a practice going back to the Middle
Ages) and farm out their duties to young curates at a fraction of
the income they received from them, or who, by judicious use of
family or political influence, got themselves translated from a
poor bishopric to a succession of increasingly well endowed ones.
Nevertheless, the eighteenth century took the problem of the
poverty and ignorance of the clergy seriously, and succeeded in
doing something to remedy it. Queen Anne's Bounty, established
in 1703, sought to supply the more than 5,000 parishes in England whose incomes were less than £50 with additional funds.[13]
Energetic bishops like Gibson and Warburton insisted on careful examinations and adequate standards of educational prepa-
ration for their ordinands. In the latter part of the century,
Johnson grumbled that bishops were now being appointed because of their social connections rather than their learning and
piety, and it is true that a number of the bishops during this
period were drawn from families of the nobility. Deplorable as
this might be in itself, it nevertheless indicated a distinct advance in the status of the Anglican clergy generally; and at the
end of the century Jane Austen—herself a daughter of the par-
sonage—can portray, what would have seemed astonishing to
her master Fielding, such personable and intelligent young men

as the Reverend Henry Tilney and the Reverend Edmund Bertram, and even make them the heroes of her novels; though to be sure there is also such a relic of the old regime as the Reverend Mr. Collins.

Was the condition of the Church of England generally stagnant, indifferent, secular minded, materialistic in the eighteenth century, as the standard histories of the period insist? Not extraordinarily so—no more than most churches at most times—as we are shown by the careful researches of Norman Sykes. There were slackers, certainly, as there will always be; but there were many other men in orders who took very seriously their duties of religious instruction and of setting an example to their flock; there were Parson Trullibers but there were also Doctor Primroses. The Communion was celebrated, children were prepared for confirmation, churches were built, sometimes as part of a governmentally sponsored church-building program—architecturally, some of the loveliest churches ever designed, products of the artistic genius of Wren, Gibbs, and Hawksmoor. The marriage laws were reformed (1753) to eliminate earlier scandals. Religious music flourished, both in the hands of great musicians like Purcell and Handel and in the humbler ones of hymn writers: the work of Watts, Doddridge, the Wesleys, Cowper, and others made the century perhaps the greatest period of hymnody in English history.

Of course any church, being an institution of fallible human beings, must always fall short of its exalted ideal. It is *semper reformanda;* and when reformers come along, it will be bound to have its shortcomings examined and condemned and to be exhorted to a higher standard of performance than in the past. The eighteenth-century Church of England was thus subjected to much criticism at the end of the century and the beginning of the next by two sets of reformers, the Methodists (and Evangelicals) and the men of the Oxford Movement. Given their position and their purposes, they were quite right to do so. But secular historians and their readers are not in that position. If the sincerity, devotion, and genuine religious conviction of the whole body of professing Anglicans of the eighteenth century are judged objectively, the period will not make a bad showing by comparison with many other periods in that Church's history, not excluding the twentieth century. Certainly the Church which nurtured laymen who took the fundamentals of the Christian religion so seriously as Johnson, Richardson, Cowper, Smart, Defoe, Steele, and Addison, to mention some literary figures, and Newton, Boyle, Locke, Handel, and Reynolds to mention some extra-literary ones, was somewhat more than moribund.

And the reform movements which produced such scathing criticism of the eighteenth-century Church were themselves, of course, a product of that Church. John and Charles Wesley were, like their inspiration William Law, Anglican priests utterly devoted to their Church, while determined to improve its effectiveness. They were all High Churchmen, a term which in the eighteenth century did not mean men with a leaning toward Roman Catholic ritual and dogma, but men who, like Johnson, felt that the Church should have an important and honored part in the life of the community. There was nothing particularly strange or novel about the Methodist or Evangelical movement of the eighteenth century: it was one of those periodic movements common to the history of Christianity in which a group of men feeling that the influence of the world has caused the Church to stray too far from its original ideals make an effort to return to those ideals. When the Wesleys, at Lincoln College, Oxford, in 1729, encountered Law's newly published *A Serious Call to a Devout and Holy Life*—young Samuel Johnson, a short distance away at Pembroke College, also read it and later reported that "this was the first occasion of my thinking in earnest of religion"—and decided to gather a small band of students to try to put Law's precepts into practice in their daily lives (and were nicknamed "the Methodists" by their fellows), their motives were not very different from those which in earlier times had actuated St. Benedict and St. Francis and Martin Luther and Ignatius Loyola—perhaps one may venture to say, which in the twentieth century actuated Pope John XXIII. The message of the Gospels must again be taken seriously, not allowed to become lost in a welter of man-made formularies and institutional red tape. Religion must be brought to the individual—to all individuals.

"The world is my parish," declared John Wesley, perhaps the

most authentic genius eighteenth-century England produced,
and in his exuberance, determination, and almost incredible
energy highly typical of his age. It was indeed the rigid medieval
parish organization of the Church of England that defeated
Wesley's efforts to reform the Church from within. Unable to
bring his message to the great masses of uninstructed poor
through that organization, he built up one of his own, an action
which led in time to the separation of the Methodist Church
from the Church of England, though Wesley always refused to
regard himself as anything but a loyal priest of the established
Church. (As this is written, the principle of reunion has been
approved in England by both the Methodist and Anglican
bodies. There has never been any doctrinal difference between
the two groups.)

But the impact of Wesley on those who remained within the
Church of England—the Evangelicals—was great. The seventh
Lord Shaftesbury, William Wilberforce, the Stephens, Macau-
lays, Venns, and other members of the "Clapham Sect"—and
their intellectual descendants of the Bloomsbury Circle in the
twentieth century—were to become a potent force in keeping
the Puritan conscience alive and effectively engaged for the bet-
terment of English life. Even the Oxford Movement of the nineteenth century was to begin as an offshoot of Evangelical fervor,
as the life of Newman testifies.

The Church of England, though by far the most important
Christian body in the British Isles, was of course not the only
one. The older English Nonconformist bodies, the Congregationalists, Presbyterians, and others, after a burst of activity following the ejections of 1662—the "dissenting academies" which
they founded at that time, since only Anglicans could be admitted to Oxford and Cambridge, produced many notable men,
including Defoe, Bishop Joseph Butler, and even an Archbishop
of Canterbury, Thomas Secker—lapsed toward the middle of
the century into comparative inaction, vexed with doctrinal disputes. The small English Roman Catholic body prospered
under the ministrations of the energetic Bishop Richard Chal-
loner and the growing spirit of toleration. In Scotland, the Kirk,
the established (Presbyterian) Church of Scotland maintained
its domination over the moral and, through the great Scottish

universities and the admirable Scottish system of elementary schools, the intellectual life of the country. Here it was the Episcopal Church which was the dissenting and unprivileged body— a fact which explains Johnson's insistence, during his tour of Scotland with Boswell, on attending Episcopal and not Presbyterian services.

At the end of the century, however, it was through the Scottish Episcopalians that bishops were first consecrated for the Protestant Episcopal Church of the young United States. The failure of the rigid organization of the Church of England to supply bishops for the Thirteen Colonies—since, of course, its medieval founders had not contemplated its extension overseas —was perhaps one of the contributing causes of the breaking away of those colonies. The best it could do for the empire was the theory that all colonial Anglican churches came under the jurisdiction of the Bishop of London. The American revolt provided a salutary lesson, however, and before the end of the century bishops of Nova Scotia and Quebec, and, a little later, of Calcutta, were appointed. In Ireland, the anomaly continued of the elaborate organization of the established Church of Ireland, supported by public funds, ministering to the small Protestant minority of the population. Its top-heavy hierarchy—it had four archbishops, while the Church of England, with many times its number of adherents, had only two—furnished lucrative sinecures for relations of English noblemen and political friends of the English government. And yet the Church of Ireland nurtured many distinguished men: Swift, Berkeley, Archbishop King of Dublin, Archbishop Boulter of Armagh, and (a little earlier) Bishop Jeremy Taylor and Archbishop James Ussher. The Roman Catholic clergy who ministered to the great majority of the Irish populace were officially ignored, and their history has not yet been properly written.

The Peerage

The status of the titled nobility of Britain from the sixteenth century onward is sometimes misunderstood, especially by American students. It is quite wrong, for instance, to speak of

their "feudal privileges." The feudal power of the English nobility had been destroyed by the Wars of the Roses and the determination of Henry VII, the first of the Tudor monarchs, to
establish a strong central government for the nation without interference from private armies controlled by dukes and earls.
The English lords are "without vassals," Voltaire noted during
his visit to England in the 1720's—unlike the Continental nobles. A slight exception might be made for Scotland, where great
chiefs like the Duke of Argyll, head of the Campbells, and the
Duke of Atholl, head of the Murrays, could still rule their clans-
men despotically in the fastnesses of the Highlands.

But such horror stories as Dickens relates in *A Tale of Two
Cities* about the privileges of the French aristocracy before the
Revolution had been impossible in England since the Middle
Ages. Another important difference from the Continental system was the fact that the children of British peers are not nobles
but commoners—the children of the higher-ranking peers may
have courtesy titles but in law only the current head of the family is a peer. Whereas on the Continent (as readers of Tolstoy
will recall) the dozen offspring of a count are themselves all
counts and countesses, the younger son of the English Earl of
Blankshire is the Honourable Mr. George Smith, and his sons
are not even "Honourable." From shirt sleeves to shirt sleeves
(or commoner to commoner) in three generations is not the exception but the rule. Hence there has never been a closed aristocratic caste in Britain, and the British system of titles has en-
couraged rather than discouraged social mobility.

Very few English titles go back to the Middle Ages (that is, in
the family of the present holder; when an old title becomes ex-
tinct, it may be conferred, by a "new creation," on another family, to the confusion of the unwary student).* The Tudors
brought into being what was virtually a whole new peerage, to
reward useful political and other services to the central government, and many of the most impressively "ancient" English
noble families go back to some astute "operator" of the time of
Henry VII and Henry VIII. The fortunes of the Seymours,
Dukes of Somerset, the second senior English dukedom,[14] began

---

* The Note on Titles on pages 53–55 explains gradations of rank and
titles.

when Henry VIII's roving eye fell on pretty Jane Seymour, whom he made his third wife. Queen Jane produced Henry's only son. Thus her brother, the first Duke, was able to make himself Protector of the Realm when his young nephew, Edward VI, came to the throne. The Russells, Dukes of Bedford, and Cavendishes, Dukes of Devonshire,[15] descend from shrewd lawyers and land agents of that halcyon time of the real estate manipulators, Henry VIII's dissolution of the monasteries. The Churchills, Dukes of Marlborough, owe their position to the enterprise and generalship of John, the first Duke, and Sarah, his equally shrewd Duchess—and historians have not been lacking to accuse the Great Duke of some very sharp practice as he made his way up the ladder of success. The magnificent first Duke of Chandos, a possible model for Pope's Timon in the *Epistle to Burlington,* acquired his enormous fortune from his lucrative post of Paymaster to the Forces during the long and expensive War of the Spanish Succession, when, as the law then permitted, he pocketed for himself the interest on the vast sums of money held for payment of military expenses. The Grosvenors, Dukes of Westminster, got their start when a seventeenth-century Grosvenor married the daughter of a London scrivener, who brought as her dowry some large parcels of land which later became the most expensive real estate in the City of Westminster. Then, of course, there are the dukedoms which Charles II conferred on his numerous illegitimate children—Richmond, Grafton, St. Albans—the "sons of sons of sons of whores," as Pope elegantly designated their contemporary representatives.

Pope's language, published in a widely read poem, and Johnson's equally well publicized snub to the magnificent Earl of Chesterfield may impel us to ask just what the privileges of eighteenth-century noblemen were, if they were not immune to such insult. There were not many. There was the right to sit in the House of Lords and take part in legislation, a right which, as in the twentieth century, only a minority of the peerage normally took advantage of, generally men who had made politics their career to begin with and whose peerages had been conferred on them because of their success in it. Peers had the right, when charged with a felony, to be tried by their fellow peers rather than before an ordinary jury; and if found guilty of a capital crime, the right to be hanged at Tyburn with a silken rather than a hempen rope, as happened to the Earl Ferrers in 1760, when he was convicted of murdering his steward.

The fact is that the power of the peerage stemmed not from the rank itself, which was only a symbol, but, as with untitled men, from political success and the ability to accumulate money and property. Certainly it helped in Britain if one had been fortunate enough to inherit a viscountcy, just as in America it helps if one inherits the surname of Rockefeller or Kennedy and a share of the family fortune and influence—and acumen. But without these, the surname or the title would be of only limited assistance. There were playboy dukes and earls, descendants of men famous in British history, just as there have been playboy Astors and Vanderbilts. Pope scathingly catalogues some of them at the end of *The Dunciad:*

> The cap and switch be sacred to His Grace;
> With staff and pumps the Marquis lead the race;
> From stage to stage the licens'd Earl may run.

There were dukes whose chief diversion was to be amateur jockeys, and the current Earl of Salisbury, descendant of Elizabeth's and James I's great Prime Ministers, amused himself by driving the Hatfield stagecoach. On the whole, the situation of the inheritor of wealth and social position, whether or not graced by a hereditary title of nobility, was not very different in eighteenth-century Britain from what it is in twentieth-century America.

New peerages, then as now, were freely granted to men successful in politics and business, by governments that wanted their support. In particular, the most popular way for the poor but clever boy to make a name for himself in public life was through the legal profession. The eighteenth-century roster of astute lawyers of humble or mediocre origin whose success was symbolized by the acquisition of peerages is long: Lord Somers (to whom Swift dedicated his *A Tale of a Tub*); the Earl Cowper, the Earl of Macclesfield, the Earl of Hardwicke, the great Earl of Mansfield (who, however, was—unusually—the cadet of a minor Scottish noble family); Wedderburn, Lord Loughborough and Earl of Rosslyn; Lord Thurlow; Pratt, Earl Camden. The most striking instances were John and William Scott, sons of a very small tradesman in Newcastle, who became respectively the Earl of Eldon, the great reactionary Tory Lord Chancellor of the early nineteenth century, and Lord Stowell, eminent in maritime and international law. A later perennial Tory Lord Chancellor, John Singleton Copley, Lord Lyndhurst, was the son of the American painter, whose social credentials were minimal.

The military profession also provided a ready means of entry to the peerage for men sufficiently talented, and successful generals and admirals were so rewarded. ("A peerage or Westminster Abbey!" Nelson is supposed to have cried as he began one of his early naval engagements.) Anson, Hood, Howe, Collingwood, Gambier, Keith, Barham, St. Vincent, Ligonier, Amherst, Clive, Marlborough, Wellington are some names of naval and military peerages that come to the mind. Another group in the House of Lords who did not represent a hereditary caste was the twenty-six bishops and archbishops of the Church of England (the spiritual peers). Few of these—at least, before the middle of the eighteenth century—came from families of wealth and position, but rather had made their way by their scholarship and brains—and often, of course, through good luck in finding an influential patron.

A significant attempt was made in 1718 to block this free entry to the peerage. The Tory regime of the last years of Queen Anne's reign had ingeniously forced an unpopular statute through Parliament by promoting, at one blow, twelve of their supporters to peerages, thus securing a majority for the measure in the House of Lords. After the accession of George I, a large number of Whig peers were created; and in order to perpetuate their advantage, one group of Whig politicians introduced a Peerage Bill which would have placed severe restrictions on the number of new peerages the King could create. If it had passed, it would have drastically changed the whole character of the peerage and the position of the House of Lords. But it was defeated, and the peerage continued to be an open-ended institution. Even so, because of the predominance of Whig administrations in the early part of the century, the peerage tended for a time to become something of a closed corporation, the preserve of the Walpole–Pelham–Newcastle–Rockingham–Fox Whig faction, which was the party of the wealthier dukes, marquesses, and earls, such as Burke's patrons, the Duke of Richmond and the Marquess of Rockingham.

Toward the end of the century, however, this "Venetian Oligarchy," as the Tory Disraeli was later to dub them, was rudely shaken. The total number of peers at the beginning of the eighteenth century had been around 150; it remained at almost the same figure in the middle of the century. By its end, however, the number had almost doubled, to around 275. This was the result of the deliberate policy of the younger William Pitt, Prime Minister from 1783, with the hearty cooperation of George III, to crush the "old Whig" domination of the Upper House, by flooding it with newly ennobled lawyers and businessmen willing to support Pitt. Snobs like Jane Austen's Sir Walter Elliot grumbled about this. But the rising middle class (like Jane Austen's two brothers who rose to distinction in the naval profession) approved, and gave Pitt their firm political support. In short, the British peerage in the eighteenth century, as in the sixteenth and the twentieth, was rather a minor political phenomenon than a significant social one.

The Country Gentlemen;
the Agricultural Revolution

If a peerage was generally testimony that its holder or some not very distant ancestor had been one of "the new men"—a clever operator in business, land, or politics, or a professional man whose talent or luck had enabled him to climb the ladder of success—those who considered themselves the genuine old aristocracy of England, the backbone of the nation, the true hundred-per-cent Englishmen were the "gentry." This "squirearchy," proud of the plain designation of "Esquire," or, at most, "Baronet," the hereditary knighthood introduced by James I, lived on manorial estates which had been in the families for innumerable generations, perhaps even since William the Conqueror's *Doomsday Book*—not the huge estates, scattered over several counties, that the wealthy capitalists who acquired dukedoms and marquessates invested in, but relatively small tracts, where the squire and his lady could still take a personal and paternal, and sometimes dictatorial, interest in their tenants' doings.

Even as late as the twentieth century, heads of such families proudly refused to accept peerages offered to them by a government anxious to secure their political support. When they deigned to play an active part in national politics (though they were usually very active in local politics) it was as "Tories"—a word which in the terminology of the eighteenth century was not very different in meaning from the American "Independent"—refusing with equal pride to commit themselves permanently to the support of one or another of the warring Whig factions at Westminster. When one of them, growing bored with the delights of merely local power, did so commit himself, accepting office or a peerage from one of the government potentates, he was written off contemptuously by his former friends as having now become a "Whig." *"Renegado,* one who deserts to the enemy, a revolter; sometimes we say 'a Gower,'" Johnson wrote in the first draft of his *Dictionary,* referring to a Staffordshire magnate, formerly Tory, who had accepted the office of Lord Privy Seal in a Whig ministry, and whose descendants were to become Marquesses of Staffordshire and Dukes of Sutherland.

One of Macaulay's most amusing and memorable passages in the famous Chapter Three of his *History of England,* "The State of England in 1685," is that in which he describes the squirearchy. He stresses their parochialism, ignorance, and crudeness:

Not one in twenty went to town once in five years, or had ever in his life wandered so far as Paris. Many lords of manors had received an education differing little from that of their menial servants. The heir of an estate often passed his boyhood and youth at the seat of his family with no better tutors than grooms and gamekeepers. . . . His chief serious employment was the care of his property. He examined samples of grain, handled pigs, and, on market days, made bargains over a tankard with drovers and hop merchants. . . . His oaths, coarse jests, and scurrilous terms of abuse, were uttered with the broadest accent of his province. . . . The litter of a farmyard gathered under the windows of his bedchamber, and the

cabbages and gooseberry bushes grew close to his hall door.
. . . Strong beer was the ordinary beverage. . . . The coarse jollity
of the afternoon was often prolonged till the revellers were laid
under the table.

No doubt there is some truth in this, but it is after all an account written by a violent Whig about a group which was consistently anti-Whig, a city-bred intellectual writing about the
country, a genteel Victorian shuddering at the vulgar physical
pleasures of a coarser age. Macaulay rather gives himself away in
a footnote where he refers the accuracy of his description of the
country gentleman "to the judgment of those who have studied
the history and *the lighter literature* of that age." Certainly the
loutish squire was a familiar stereotype for the comic dramatist
and comic novelist from Ben Jonson's Kastril, the Angry Boy,
up through Sir Wilful Witwoud, Sir Tunbelly Clumsy, Squire
Trelooby, and others, to Goldsmith's Tony Lumpkin and beyond. Fielding's unforgettable Squire Western probably contributed more than any other single source to Macaulay's portrait.
Fielding too was a Whig, an urbanite, and the cousin of an
earl; and the name of his great creation was intended to remind
his readers that Cornwall, Devonshire, Somerset, and other
western counties, heavily overrepresented in the House of Commons by comparison with other sections of the country, were the
stronghold of Toryism properly so-called—the politics of the
country gentlemen. The West, along with the North, had been
the chief source of Charles I's support in the Civil War, as
against London and the East, the center of Parliamentary and
Puritan strength. Cambridge, in the East, was always the Whig
and Puritan university; Oxford, toward the West, the Tory and
High Church one.

Of course the position of the country gentry was not so simple
as Macaulay described it, and it became more complicated as the
eighteenth century advanced. It is true that there were squires
as ignorant and brutal as those invented by the dramatists and
novelists. For the existence of one of them we have the testimony
of Samuel Johnson, a staunch Tory, but, being an intellectual,
one who wore his Toryism with a difference. This was Sir Wol-
stan Dixie, fourth Baronet, of Market Bosworth, Leicestershire,
in whose home young Johnson spent a few miserable months

when a master at the local grammar school, and whom he later pilloried as Squire Bluster in *Rambler 142*. His chief sports were tyrannizing over his tenants and quarreling with his neighbors. The story is told of his being received by George II, who, wanting to demonstrate his knowledge of English history, remarked, "Bosworth? Big battle there, wasn't it?" "Yes, your Majesty," the baronet replied, "but I thrashed him."

By contrast one may look at Joseph Wright's fine portrait of the elegant and sensitive Sir Brooke Boothby, sixth Baronet, of Ashbourne, Derbyshire, reclining on a grassy bank with a book of poems in his hand (perhaps his own, for he wrote poetry). Johnson was intimately acquainted with his family also—indeed, he may have been in love with Sir Brooke's aunt, Hill Boothby, who had a formidable reputation for learning and piety, and have wished to make her his second wife. The life of their circle is described in Richard Graves's novel *The Spiritual Quixote*, and in its earnest intellectualism and high seriousness is more reminiscent of the Bloomsbury of the 1920's than of Squire Western's abode (though even there, one remembers, Miss Western, the Squire's sister, was a great "politician," and prided herself on her expertise in national and international affairs).

And the more the political structure of England in the seventeenth and eighteenth centuries is studied, the more complex the political position of the squirearchy is seen to be. If in the time of Addison and Fielding it was possible to characterize their stronghold, the western counties, as the center of Tory reaction and isolationist resistance to Whig enterprise, it was also the West which not long before, in 1685, had been the scene of the disastrous uprising against the Catholic James II under the Protestant and "Whig" leader Monmouth, Dryden's Absalom and Shaftesbury's cat's paw. The role of the country gentry in bringing about the great Civil War has recently begun to be stressed; two of the greatest figures on the rebel side were country squires, Hampden and Cromwell, who, as Marvell said, cultivated

> . . . his private garden, where
> He lived reservèd and austere
> (As if his highest plot
> To plant the bergamot).

The controlling political principles of the squirearchy throughout the two centuries may be summed up as suspicion of almost
any central government at Westminster as the source of foreign
involvements and the wars that went with them, defense expenditure and the taxes that went with it, and general interference with the individual; and a reluctance to see agriculture
displaced in favor of commerce as the staple of the English economy.

Like most other branches of the English economy during the
eighteenth century, agriculture, which supported the gentry,
generally prospered, even though commerce and industry
caught up with it and surpassed it. There were ups and downs;
there was the occasional bad harvest, with consequent distress,
and in the late 1730's and early 1740's, and again in the 1750's,
periods of genuine agricultural depression. Nevertheless, by
comparison with the Continental nations, Englishmen in the
eighteenth century were well fed and proud of the fact. Fielding's ditty achieved almost the status of a national anthem:

> When mighty roast beef was the Englishman's food,
> It ennobled our hearts and enriched our blood;
> Our soldiers were brave, and our courtiers were good.
>   Oh, the Roast Beef of Old England,
>   And Old England's Roast Beef!

Hogarth illustrated the point of view in his "Calais Gate,"
where thin, miserable Frenchmen stare longingly at a great rib
roast borne on an Englishman's shoulders. English farms were
able not only to feed and clothe the native population but to
provide grain and wool for export throughout the century:
Arthur Young, writing in the 1760's, reflects complacently on the
fact that France has at last followed England's example and for
the first time has permitted the export of grain for revenue, with
a resulting stimulus to its production—"That nation [Eng-
land]," he says, "became *great* from their exportation of corn."

And during the century, agriculture, like manufacturing,
profited greatly from the general spirit of enterprise and the application for the first time of scientific thought to the problem of
increasing production. Some of the leading figures in this
"agricultural revolution," as it has been called, were Walpole's

brother-in-law, the second Viscount ("Turnip") Townshend, who, after quarreling with Walpole and retiring from politics, devoted himself to encouraging the cultivation of root crops to provide fodder for cattle and swine during the winter months and so make serious mixed farming possible; Robert Bakewell, who initiated the scientific breeding of good strains of farm animals; Jethro Tull, whose influential *Horse-Hoeing Husbandry* (1733) advocated intensive tillage of the ground (to keep down weeds) and the rotation of crops; Thomas Coke of Holkham, Earl of Leicester, who vastly improved methods of estate management. Although the enclosure of small, uneconomical tracts and unproductive commons so as to form fields of large acreage had begun long before, it went on at an increased rate in the eighteenth century, to the accompaniment of Goldsmith's memorable lament in *The Deserted Village*.

What was happening to English agriculture in the eighteenth century was what happened to North American agriculture in the twentieth—the change from farming as a means of scanty subsistence for single families (in effect, a peasantry) to farming viewed as an industry and run on businesslike lines. The result in both cases was a great increase in total productivity, a great decrease in the number of individuals engaged in production, a consequent great shift of population from the countryside to the towns, and general social dislocation. Small tenant farmers and their families were uprooted from their ancestral acres and forced to take employment in the new factory towns or to emigrate. Absentee landlordism increased, as the owners of landed estates were tempted to leave their management in the hands of trained farm managers (stewards) and to seek the more stimulating atmosphere of London. This, in turn, meant the beginning of the end of the gentry as a separate political force: "Toryism" in the old seventeenth- and eighteenth-century sense was to die out in the early nineteenth, much as the not dissimilar Populism of agricultural America was to die out in the twentieth because of a similar shift in social and economic conditions.

All this, however, was perhaps not such a tragedy as Goldsmith thought, or thought he thought. When he wrote his poem, it had been many years since he himself had actually lived in "sweet Auburn," and he at no time demonstrated any great urge to give up London and the society of Johnson, Reynolds, Burke, and the rest to return to it. (Nor did the new class of urban factory workers. Whatever their grievances, as Marx himself pointed out, their lot was at least a cut above the stultification of the farm laborer's life.) The problems of a largely urbanized nation are many and have not yet been completely solved; but once the process has begun, there seems to be no turning back, and in the twentieth century the United States and the Soviet Union are having to face those problems which England, first among the great nations of the world, began to encounter two centuries ago.

The Business Community;
the Industrial Revolution

A comic stereotype as popular as the boorish country squire in Restoration and early eighteenth-century literature was the money-grubbing businessman, the "cit," the bourgeois—Pinchwife, Alderman Gripe, Pope's Balaam in the *Epistle to Bathurst* —whose headquarters was the "City" of London, the old square mile that is still the financial district of the metropolis. His usual role was to be swindled and cuckolded by some gay young "wit" of the "Town"—Westminster, the West End, the seat of the Court, government, the professions, fashion, the arts. There was something more in this plot than merely crude humor: Wycherley, Pope, and the others did sense a threat to traditional moral and cultural values in what they saw as the increasing domination of English life by material and commercial values. It is the natural and proper outcome of the cit's blind devotion to financial success that his pretty wife, whom he has married as a status symbol, should be bored by his intellectual and emotional emptiness, and yield herself to the penniless but lively young "wit." [16] It was not forgotten that the City had been strongly Puritan and Parliamentarian in the Civil War; and Dryden savagely lampooned the London businessmen who had supported Shaftesbury and Monmouth in the struggle over the Exclusion Bill, those who "Adored their fathers' God, and property," and, like Shimei,

Did wisely from expensive sins refrain,
And never broke the Sabbath, but for gain.

But there were literary defenders as well as attackers of the new capitalism, and they were effective ones—Addison, Steele, Defoe; men who held the Whig view that the future happiness of England lay not in preserving the traditional economic and social theories and habits of the squirearchy, but in taking full advantage of her great new commercial, industrial, and financial potentialities. Their hero was not Addison's stupid and ridiculous Tory Fox-Hunter (in the *Freeholder*) or Sir Roger de Coverley (an even more effective piece of propaganda than the Fox-Hunter, since it is purportedly a sympathetic portrait, yet it never leaves us in doubt that we may justifiably patronize Sir Roger's essential stupidity), but his and Steele's Sir Andrew Freeport—the name indicates that he believes in abolishing restrictions on trade—

> a merchant of great eminence in the city of London. A person of indefatigable industry, strong reason, and great experience. His notions of trade are noble and generous. . . . [He] will tell you that it is a stupid and barbarous way to extend dominion by arms; for true power is to be got by arts [i.e., technology] and industry. . . . I have heard him prove, that diligence makes more lasting acquisitions than valour. . . . A general trader of good sense is pleasanter company than a general scholar; . . . having a natural unaffected eloquence, the perspicuity of his discourse gives the same pleasure that wit would in another man (*Spectator* No. 2).

Defoe and many others (for instance, Benjamin Franklin in America) wrote innumerable tracts to prove to the general public the truth and importance of Sir Andrew's maxims that "Sloth has ruined more nations than the sword" and that "A penny saved is a penny got." Samuel Johnson might grumble that "Trade could not be managed by those who manage it if it had much difficulty," but Addison reinforced the *Spectator*'s teaching by declaring that

> There is no place in the town which I so much love to frequent as the Royal [stock] Exchange. . . . [It] gratifies my vanity, as I am an Englishman, to see so rich an assembly of countrymen and foreigners, consulting together upon the private business of mankind,

and making this metropolis a kind of emporium for the whole earth. . . . There are not more useful members in a commonwealth than merchants (*Spectator* No. 69).

Pope's and Dryden's denunciations were in vain; the views of Addison and Defoe triumphed. In a canceled line in Pope's tale of Balaam, the successful City merchant, there occurred the simile "rich as P——." This was Thomas Pitt, Governor of Madras, who, by interloping on the preserves of the East India Company, raised himself by sheer nerve and determination from poverty and obscurity to immense wealth. His grandson and great-grandson, the two William Pitts, became in turn the Prime Ministers of the century who most influenced the course of British history, and both owed their success to their alliance with the business community and their ability to inspire the imaginations of the British public with the glories to be obtained by pursuing the course of commercial expansion and international power.

The City of London became more and more powerful as a political force, and in the 1760's Alderman John Wilkes, Alderman Beckford (father of the writer William Beckford), and a host of others took a very active part in the political struggles of the time. On one occasion, at least, Beckford, in the name of the City, insulted George III to his face and was rewarded for his action by the installation of a large plaque in his honor in the Guildhall, the city hall of London. Bristol, too, was thriving, with the expansion of trade with the Americas—especially with the West Indies, where sugar cane plantations (worked by slave labor) were a source of much wealth to English owners. Seeking to impose its will on its Member of Parliament, Burke, it was snubbed by him in a classic speech on the duty of a representative to the welfare of the nation as a whole rather than to the special interests of his constituents. It may be argued, however, that the force of the business interest in Britain has been somewhat mitigated, from the eighteenth century onward, by the compulsion felt by English businessmen, when they have acquired enough money, to buy rural seats and endeavor to remove the stigma of trade by adopting the habits and views of the squirearchy.

The story of how the British flag followed British trade—the story of the creation of the British Empire—will be told in the next chapter. Meanwhile at home the spirit of enterprise flowered in the "industrial revolution"—the relatively sudden series of advances in industrial technology that, along with the accession of new markets and sources of raw material which resulted from the expansion of the overseas empire, was to make Britain the industrial and commercial colossus she became in the nineteenth century.

The spirit of the "projector"—the modern equivalent might be "operator" or even "wheeler-dealer"—had of course been flourishing from the Renaissance onward; even earlier, for the term is a metaphor from the work of the medieval alchemist who seeks some ingenious process to "get rich quick" by turning base metals into gold. It was satirized by Ben Jonson (in *The Alchemist*) and Swift (in Part Three of *Gulliver's Travels*) among others. But even such a conservative as Samuel Johnson was not immune to its charm: early in life he had dealings with Lewis Paul of Birmingham, who had a (sound) design for cotton-spinning machinery, and his exhortation, when his friend Thrale's brewery was being auctioned, perfectly expresses that spirit—"We are not here to sell a parcel of boilers and vats, but the potentiality of growing rich beyond the dreams of avarice."

The industrial revolution included such incidents as James Watt's invention of a practical steam engine as early as the 1760's; cotton- and wool-spinning and weaving machinery by Crompton, Arkwright, and others; improvements in methods of coal mining and iron smelting, and the establishment of new industrial communities in the North near coal beds, the source of power; improved methods of road building, the construction of canals and iron bridges, the establishment of a ceramics industry in Staffordshire by the Wedgwoods. A still greater expansion was to come in the next century, but even in the eighteenth there were such astonishing statistics as an increase in the output of pig iron from 17,000 tons in 1740 to four times that amount in 1788 and eight times it in 1796; in the value of manufactured cotton exported from £14,000 in 1739 to £303,000 in 1779; in the consumption of raw cotton from one million pounds at the beginning of the century to 22 million in 1787.[17] Britain had, of course, been engaged in industry and com-

merce before the introduction of steam power. Even in the Middle Ages, she had taken pride in her woolen manufacture—
Chaucer's Wife of Bath had "passed hem of Ypres and of
Gaunt" in her weaving, and the Lord Chancellor still presides
over the House of Lords from the Woolsack, which symbolized
its importance. Companies for trading in distant parts of the
world were chartered in Elizabeth's day—the East India and the
Muscovy Companies—and in Charles II's—the Hudson's Bay
Company. When Louis XIV revoked the Edict of Nantes in
1685, withdrawing toleration from French Protestants, many
Huguenots came to England and set up a thriving silk-weaving
industry in Spitalfields.

Up to the mid-eighteenth century, however, such enterprises
had existed along with agriculture in a well balanced and self-
contained economy. Now, with Britain's technological superiority over the rest of the world, it seemed reasonable to many (such
as Adam Smith and his disciple, the younger Pitt) for her to
put all her economic eggs in the one basket of unrestrained
commercial and industrial expansion, buying raw materials
from the outside, manufacturing them cheaply, and selling the
finished product back to the rest of the world at a profit sufficient to enable her to buy food for her population. In the early
stages of this transformation Samuel Johnson had warned, with
remarkable foresight, of its inherent dangers. "Commerce," he
wrote in 1756,

> however we may please ourselves with the contrary opinion, is one
> of the daughters of fortune, inconstant and deceitful as her mother;
> she chooses her residence where she is least expected, and shifts her
> abode, when her continuance is in appearance most firmly settled.
> . . . It is apparent that every trading nation flourishes . . . by the
> courtesy of others. We cannot compel any people to buy from us,
> or to sell to us. A thousand accidents may prejudice them in favour
> of our rivals; the workmen of another nation may labour for less
> price, or some accidental improvement, or natural advantage, may
> procure a just preference to their commodities. . . . Manufactures,
> indeed, and profitable manufactures, are sometimes raised from
> imported materials, but then we are subjected a second time to the
> caprice of our neighbours. The natives of Lombardy might easily
> resolve to retain their silk at home, and employ workmen of their

own to weave it. And this will certainly be done when they grow wise and industrious, when they have sagacity to discern their true interest, and vigour to pursue it.[18]

Something of this nature did, in fact, happen in the early twentieth century, to the consequent distress of the British economy. But in the excitement of the "potentiality of growing rich beyond the dreams of avarice" which gripped the *entrepreneurs* of the eighteenth century, no one was in a mood to pay much attention to Johnson's gloomy long-term predictions.

The Rest

An attempt has been made above to identify the principal interests in British society of the eighteenth century—the "old money" of the peerage, which was generally Whig; the "new money" of the business community, which was "Pittite"; the agricultural interest of the country gentlemen, who constituted the Tories or Independents. What of the remainder, the vast majority of the population? Here a distinction made by Johnson in his *Dictionary* should be noted: under the word "poor," after listing several of its ordinary meanings, he adds *"The poor* (collectively): Those who are in the lowest rank of the community; those who cannot subsist but by the charity of others; but it is sometimes used with laxity for any not rich." It is the distinction of a shrewd and compassionate observer, who had a good deal of bitter personal knowledge about the importance of that distinction—his father, Michael Johnson, had begun life as one of the poor, since he owed his apprenticeship in his trade of bookseller to the generosity of a charitable organization in Lichfield. Johnson expands on the subject in reviewing the complacent arguments of the well-to-do Soame Jenyns that the poor should be content with their lot:

"Poverty" [writes Johnson] is very gently paraphrased by "want of riches." In that sense almost every man may in his own opinion be poor. But there is another poverty, which is "want of competence," of all that can soften the miseries of life, of all that can diversify attention, or delight imagination. There is yet another poverty, which is "want of necessaries," a species of poverty which no care of the public, no charity of particulars [i.e., individuals], can preserve many from feeling openly, and many secretly.

In affluent eighteenth-century England (as in the affluent twentieth-century United States) there were many of the poor: one statistician placed the number of "paupers . . . vagrants, gipsies, rogues and vagabonds," with incomes of less than £10 per family, in England in 1801 at considerably more than one-eighth of the total population. The same writer's figures give an average family income for the whole population of around £115.[19]

There was no thought, in Johnson's day or for long afterward, of allowing the poor in his sense to share in the government of the nation; it was enough of a task to help them ameliorate their condition and to keep them from starving. (Probably few did: there had been, since Elizabeth's time, an elaborate, if far from wholly satisfactory, system of "poor laws" to relieve them.) Between the poor, however, and those at the other end of the scale, the peerage, the gentry, and the magnates of business, lay the vast majority of the nation—"persons in lesser civil offices, lesser clergymen, lesser freeholders, [tenant] farmers, persons of the law, liberal arts and sciences, artisans, labourers employed in manufactures and building, labouring people in husbandry," to quote some of the categories in the statistical analysis mentioned above.

Writers sometimes speak of the rise of the middle class in the eighteenth century, as though no such class had hitherto existed. But evidently it did (though, to be sure, as time went on it exerted more and more influence in public affairs, the proliferation of newspapers, magazines, and books throughout the century making it more knowledgeable and confident in these matters). Throughout the century there were certainly a great many of what Goldsmith called

the middle order . . . that order of men which subsists between the very rich and the very rabble; those men who are possessed of too large fortunes to submit to the neighboring man of power, and yet are too poor to set up for tyranny themselves. . . . This order is known to be the true preserver of freedom, and may be called *the people* (*The Vicar of Wakefield*, Chap. 19).

It is interesting to find Goldsmith, like his friend Johnson a staunch Tory, thus praising the virtues of the middle order, to which he and Johnson belonged, and, in the passage that follows this, acclaiming the monarch (then George III) as the defender of the rights of that order against the attempted encroachments of the men of power (i.e., the aristocratic Whigs of the Walpole–Newcastle–Rockingham–Fox–Burke tradition). "The time is now come," Johnson begins a number of the *Literary Magazine* at the beginning of the Seven Years' War, "in which *every* Englishman expects to be informed of the national affairs, and in which he has a right to have that expectation gratified"—not merely the men of power.

Indeed, by far the greatest number of the English writers of the eighteenth century belonged to that order which proclaimed its rights in such resounding terms. On the whole, the impression one gets from their writings is of a society more closely resembling that of the United States from the eighteenth century to the present time, in which the bulk of the population, in spite of the diversity of their interests and education and economic status, tend to think of themselves as a fairly homogeneous middle order or "the people." It is at least arguable that the literature of the century gives a picture of a society in which class snobbery was less full grown than it became in nineteenth-century Britain, when the newly affluent business families began to find it necessary to send their children to the many recently founded private schools to acquire the proper "U" accent, still the mark of the middle class, as distinguished from the working class. It is perhaps worth noting that Johnson and Goldsmith, however "zealous for subordination" they may have been, use the terms "rank" and "order" instead of the later "class," which has come to imply a hereditary permanency absent in the other more neutral terms.

In his novel *Peregrine Pickle,* Smollett tells a story—an old one, no doubt—of how, as a joke, his hero picks up a common prostitute, and, after giving her a few *weeks'* training in fashionable jargon and drawing room manners, is able to palm her off as a fine society lady. It is significant that, unlike poor Liza Doolittle in Shaw's version of the story a century and a half later, the girl does not have to endure the *months* of agonizing drill needed to change her vowel patterns from non-U to U ones. That is to say, at least one very formidable barrier to rising in the world was absent.

Indeed, social mobility generally seems to have been easier than it was to become in the next two centuries. Able boys from poor backgrounds frequently rose to the highest rank in the legal, ecclesiastical, and military professions, to distinction in the arts and in business. Johnson himself seemed to move with perfect ease on all social levels, talking with the King or dining with the Duke and Duchess of Argyll with as little embarrassment as with an old schoolfellow, one Jackson, who "had tried to be a cutler at Birmingham, but had not succeeded; and now lived poorly at home and had some scheme of dressing leather in a better manner than common." It is Boswell, who was present and gives the account—Boswell, who so often adumbrates the attitudes of the nineteenth century—who was ill at ease in the encounter with this "low man, dull and untaught," as he calls him, wearing a "coarse great coat, greasy leather breeches, and a yellow uncurled wig," and who marvels at Johnson's "genuine humanity and real kindness" in listening politely to Jackson's "low" conversation.

What did it feel like to be an average citizen of Britain living in the eighteenth century? There has been a good deal of fantasy spun by later writers about "the spirit of the age." Early Romantic writers, rebelling as a younger generation always does against its immediate predecessors, and rejoicing in the freedom of their loose-flowing locks and newly invented trousers, took the wigs, brocades, and tight knee breeches of their grandfathers as symbols of restraint and decorum, and condemned the century as rule-bound, formal, artificial, in contrast to the "naturalness" of their own time. (They forgot that nature decks out the male bird in similarly flamboyant attire for very natural purposes, purposes which history shows the Restoration and eighteenth century, from Charles II on, to have been no more hampered in pursuing than the Romantics were.) After time had diminished the spirit of rebellion, the later nineteenth century no longer condemned the eighteenth century's "artificiality," but rather cherished it, as quaint and amusing, a time of

sedan chairs and masquerade balls and bewigged cavaliers and
harmless flirtations.

> When dames wore hoops and powdered hair
> And very strict was etiquette,
> When men were brave and ladies fair
> They danced the minuet

were the words someone of Austin Dobson's generation wrote to
be sung to the melody of Mozart's minuet in *Don Giovanni*—a
piece which, in the opera, takes place in an atmosphere seething
with lust, hatred, and violence, with intrigue, murder, and rape.

It was certainly not a placid, secure time for the ordinary citizen. The century began in the midst of a fierce European, indeed "world" war, against the might of Louis XIV; its midpoint
was marked by the opening of a still greater one, in which, as
Macaulay put it, "black men fought on the coast of Coroman-
del, and red men scalped each other by the Great Lakes of
North America"; it ended in the midst of the greatest of all, that
against Napoleon. On the basis of the number of casualties
suffered, the American Revolutionary War was merely one of
Britain's minor engagements in the century. At home there were
the Jacobite rebellions and invasions of 1715, 1718, and 1745,
the last a very serious threat indeed, with Scotland lost to the
enemy and the rebel army advancing into England as far as the
Midlands; and for decades, the problem of Jacobite subversive
activity played much the same role in British politics as the
Communist threat did in the United States of the 1940's and
1950's. There was frequent rioting and mob violence—over elections, over religious differences, over shortages of food and high
prices: the Porteous riots of 1736, the Wilkes riots in the 1760's,
and, most violent of all, the Gordon "No Popery" riots of 1780,
in which London was in a state of anarchy for a week. Civil
order was maintained with the greatest difficulty by the decrepit
"watch," figures of fun since the time of Shakespeare's Dog-
berry; it was not until the Home Secretaryship of Sir Robert
Peel in the 1820's that Britain acquired an effective police force.
Dorothy George begins the last chapter of her *London Life in
the Eighteenth Century* with a summing up: "The dominating
impression of life in eighteenth-century London, from the

standpoint of the individual, is one of uncertainty and insecurity."

At the same time, it is wrong to react too vigorously to the view of eighteenth-century Britain as a quaint and decorous age of restraint and reason, and to picture it, as some recent historians have, as containing little but crude and callous barbarity. In the opening year of the century, Dryden could look back in disillusionment over the religious and civil strife, the fanaticism and the cynicism that had characterized its predecessor the seventeenth century, and welcome the new era as holding out at least the possibility of something better:

> All, all of a piece throughout:
> Thy chase had a beast in view;
> Thy wars brought nothing about;
> Thy lovers were all untrue.
> 'Tis well an old age is out,
> And time to begin a new.

The promise did not go unfulfilled. The constant threat of civil war and radical political and social upheaval that had plagued England throughout most of Dryden's lifetime at last came to an end when the heirs of the two old warring factions of Cavaliers and Roundheads reached a *modus vivendi* in the wonderfully successful compromise of 1689. It is from this year of the settlement of the Glorious Revolution that "the eighteenth century" perhaps ought to be dated; it is here that one most clearly sees a division in the outlook of those who grew up before and those who grew up after it. In the writings of Dryden and Swift, whose minds were formed in the earlier period, one often detects a nervousness, an underlying insecurity, as if they were never sure when the structure of their society might dissolve beneath their feet, a feeling which is absent in the work of the post-Revolutionary Pope and Johnson, however heartily they may from time to time abuse the contemporary scene.

Savage as the English criminal law was in the eighteenth century, it was less savage than that in France, where the barbarous judicial execution of Robert-François Damien in 1757 raised a horrified protest from the whole of the European intellectual community. It was, after all, the century in which men stopped killing witches, and in which it was judicially decided (by Lord Mansfield in 1772) that slavery could not exist on English soil— nearly a century before a war decided the same thing in the United States.

The increase in the public dissemination of knowledge, in the production and distribution of newspapers, magazines, and books, was phenomenal, and men like Addison and Steele, Johnson and Goldsmith were among the leaders of the movement for enlightened journalism. It was the century when serious writers ceased having to rely on the whims of wealthy patrons in order to be able to pursue their vocation, thanks to such sturdy defenders of the dignity of the creative writer as Pope and Johnson. It was a century with a most distinguished record of sincere and effective charitable and humanitarian activity; and however short it may have fallen of the highest ideal, we of the twentieth century, with its ghastly record of large-scale bloodshed and torture, are hardly in a position to take a supercilious attitude toward the eighteenth in the matter of callousness toward our fellow human beings.

NOTE ON TITLES

A note on British titles of rank, which many students find puzzling, may be helpful. The five ranks of the peerage are, in ascending order, baron, viscount, earl, marquess (the French spelling "marquis" is now seldom used), and duke. Peers of the peerages of England, Great Britain (creations since 1707), and the United Kingdom (creations since 1801) automatically become members of the House of Lords. Members of the peerage of Ireland, before the abolition of the Irish parliament in 1801, were entitled to sit in the Irish House of Lords in Dublin, but not in the British House of Lords; they might, however, be elected to the British House of Commons—Viscount Palmerston, the nineteenth-century Prime Minister, an Irish peer, sat in the Commons as member for an English constituency. The Scottish peers, at the beginning of each new Parliament, elect sixteen of their number to represent them in the British House of Lords—the Earl of Bute, George III's Prime Minister, sat in the Lords as a Scottish representative peer—but the remainder are *not* eligible to the House of Commons. Many Scottish and Irish peers, however, also hold subordinate English (or, after 1707, British) peerages, in right of which they sit in the British House of Lords: e.g., the Earl of Shelburne (peerage of Ireland) sat in the House of Lords as Baron Wycombe (peerage of Great Britain). Baronets (hereditary) and knights (non-hereditary) are not peers, but commoners; they are designated "Sir," with given and family name (as "Sir Robert Walpole"). Wives of peers are, in order, baronesses, viscountesses, countesses, marchionesses, and duchesses. Wives of baronets and knights are "Lady" with the family name only: Maria Skerret, who married Sir Robert Walpole, became "Lady Walpole."

Much confusion is caused by "courtesy titles" and the designations "Lord" and "Lady," none of which are *official* styles of any peer. Eldest surviving sons of earls, marquesses, and dukes are given the "courtesy" title of (usually) the second highest peerage held by the father: e.g., the eldest son of the Duke of Chandos was referred to as the Marquess of Carnarvon (but in official documents merely "Henry Brydges, Esquire, commonly styled Marquess of Carnarvon"). Younger sons of marquesses and dukes bear the courtesy designation "Lord" with given and family names: Lord Sidney Beauclerk, father of Johnson's friend Topham Beauclerk, was fifth son of the Duke of St. Albans. "Lord" with the title only, and without "of," is also the normal designation, except on official occasions, of barons (it would be very unusual to hear a baron addressed as "Baron So-and-so"), and is the informal mode of address of viscounts, earls, and marquesses, but not dukes: e.g., the Marquess of Rockingham was frequently referred to as "Lord Rockingham," but the Duke of Grafton never as "Lord Grafton."

Baronesses (normally) and viscountesses, countesses, and marchionesses (informally) are addressed as "Lady," with the husband's title, but never duchesses. All daughters of earls, marquesses, and dukes are "Lady" with given and family names. When married to a man of lower rank, they change their own family name to their husband's, but retain their own given name: e.g., when Lady Mary Pierrepont, daughter of Evelyn Pierrepont, Duke of Kingston, married Mr. Edward Wortley Montagu, she became Lady Mary Wortley Montagu (her husband remained "Mr. Wortley Montagu"). Marrying a man of higher rank, they assume the title his wife would normally carry: e.g., when Lady Diana Spencer, daughter of Charles Spencer, Duke of Marlborough, married Lord Bolingbroke (2nd Viscount Bolingbroke), she became Viscountess Bolingbroke (Lady Bolingbroke). Divorced from him and married to Topham Beauclerk, she became Lady Diana Beauclerk (Topham remained "Mr. Beauclerk"). The wife of the younger son of a marquess or duke, if of lower rank than her husband, becomes "Lady" with *her husband's* given and family names: Topham Beauclerk's mother was Lady Sidney Beauclerk. Children of peers not entitled to a courtesy "Lord" or "Lady" are "the Honourable" Mr., Miss, or Mrs. So-and-so. But "Right Honourable" is the attribution of members of the King's Privy Council (e.g., the Rt. Hon. Joseph Addison, PC, MP) and of barons, viscounts, and earls (marquesses are "Most Honourable" and dukes "Most Noble"). Dukes, duchesses, and archbishops (but not archbishops' wives) are formally addressed as "Your Grace"; other peers and peeresses and bishops (but not bishops' wives) as "Your Lordship" or "Your Ladyship" (or "My Lord" or "My Lady"). In the Church of England, archbishops are "Most Reverend," bishops "Right Reverend," deans "Very Reverend," and archdeacons "Venerable."

Holders of courtesy titles are not peers but commoners, and may, if elected, sit in the House of Commons: e.g., Lord George Gordon, MP, third son of the Duke of Gordon, and Lord (i.e., Baron—by courtesy)

North, MP, eldest son of the Earl of Guilford ("MP," like "Congressman," indicates a member of the *lower* house of the legislature). However, the heir to a peerage might be summoned (by the Crown) to the House of Lords in one of his father's junior peerages: e.g., John Hervey, second son of the Earl of Bristol, became, on the death of his older brother Carr Hervey in 1723, heir to the earldom; he automatically received the courtesy title Lord (i.e., Baron) Hervey, and was elected to the House of Commons; in 1733, he was given a writ of summons to the House of Lords in his father's peerage of Baron Hervey of Ickworth (i.e., his title was no longer a courtesy but a substantive one, and from a commoner he had become a peer, although his usual designation of "Lord Hervey" remained unchanged).

The title "Lord," with the name of a landed estate, used by Scottish judges has nothing to do with any peerage; it is not hereditary, and it does not confer the epithet "Honourable" on the children of its holders (though Lord Auchinleck's eldest son, James Boswell, used it to impress people on the Continent, who presumably knew no better). Nor does "Lord" in the names of various offices of government (Lord High Chancellor, Lord Keeper of the Privy Seal, Lord Commissioner of the Treasury or Admiralty) have any connection with the peerage, and a Mr. Jones appointed to one of them remains Mr. Jones still.

The numbering of the holders of a peerage begins again each time the title is conferred anew. Thus Aubrey de Vere, 20th and last Earl of Oxford (of the De Vere family) died in 1703; in 1711, Robert Harley was created 1st Earl of Oxford (of the second creation); in the nineteenth century the succession to the earldom died out in the Harley family, and in the 1920's Herbert Henry Asquith was again created 1st Earl of Oxford (of the third creation).

NOTES TO CHAPTER ONE

1. *London Life in the Eighteenth Century* (London: Kegan Paul, 1925; rep. London: London School of Economics, 1951), pp. 36, 42.

2. *History of England* (1849), Chap. I.

3. Maurice Ashley, *The Stuarts in Love* (New York: Macmillan, 1964).

4. It is amusing to find Queen Victoria, born in the last year of her grandfather George III's reign, speaking loftily of "the *bourgeoiserie* of the . . . Russian [imperial] family" (James Pope-Hennessy, *Queen Mary* [New York: Knopf, 1960], pp. 141–142). For all the sneering of the English nobility at them as obscure upstarts, the Hanoverians were fully conscious of their thousand-years descent from Alfred the Great and Guelf the First, and its vast superiority to that of the *parvenu* seventeenth-century Romanovs—and to that of most of the British nobility.

5. The point of view was well expressed in Queen Victoria's objection to a proposal to send the Duke of Clarence, heir presumptive to the throne, and his brother, later King George V, on a tour of the British Empire rather than of Europe: "He & Georgie are charming dear good boys, but very *exclusively* English which you [the Prince of Wales, later

King Edward VII] & your brothers are not, & this is a great misfortune. . . . These Colonies offer no opportunities for the cultivation of art or of any historical interest whatever . . . of Italy, Spain, Austria, Hungary, Russia, Turkey & Holland (very interesting) he knows nothing" (Pope-Hennessy, p. 182).

6. Sir Adolphus Ward (*Cambridge Modern History,* [1902–12] VI, 19) vigorously rebuts the story that Madame Kielmansegge, daughter of his father's mistress, the Countess von Platen, was also George's mistress.

7. "No, no, I'll have mistresses!" "Good Lord, that needn't stop you."

8. Recently two medical researchers, Ida Macalpine and Richard Hunter, have apparently cleared up the old mystery. The few rare attacks of irrationality during George's youth and middle years were the result of the hereditary metabolic disease of porphyria; in old age, he suffered from ordinary arteriosclerotic senility, like Swift. See their *George III and the Mad Business* (London: Allen Lane, 1969).

9. Swift's satire, in *Gulliver's Travels,* of the mutual slaughter of Big-Endians and Little-Endians surely implies Locke's principle, and Johnson frequently affirms it vigorously, e.g., in the preface to his translation of Father Lobo's *Voyage to Abyssinia:* how, he asks, can the Jesuit missionaries to Abyssinia, whose habit was to "preach the gospel with swords in their hands, and propagate by desolation and slaughter the true worship of the God of peace . . . profess themselves the followers of Jesus, who left this great characteristic to his disciples, that they should be known by loving one another, by universal and unbounded charity and benevolence?"

10. An American wit improved on this: "The Puritans thought adultery a greater sin than murder, because adultery gives pleasure to two people but murder only to one."

11. For the student of the Church of England in the eighteenth century, a knowledge of the works of the Very Reverend Norman Sykes, Professor of Ecclesiastical History at Cambridge and later Dean of Winchester, is indispensable. His *Church and State in Eighteenth-Century England* (Cambridge: Cambridge University Press, 1934) and his fine biographies of Archbishop Wake and Bishop Gibson provide a needed corrective to earlier distorted accounts.

12. *History of England,* Chap. III.

13. Because of the rapid fluctuations of the value of money in the twentieth century, it is hard to set a definite equivalent, but a reasonable guess might be that a pound in the eighteenth century was equal in purchasing power to between twenty and forty United States dollars in the 1960's.

14. The premier dukedom of the realm, that of Norfolk, antedated the accession of the Tudor dynasty, but only by two years, having been conferred on John Howard in 1483 by Richard III. On its contemporary holders, Pope commented with his usual pungency,

What can ennoble sots, or slaves, or cowards?
Alas! not all the blood of all the Howards.

15. In the 1960's, apparently for the only time in history, the President of the United States and the Prime Minister of Great Britain were re-

lated by marriage, the Prime Minister's wife, Lady Dorothy Macmillan, being aunt to the late Marquess of Hartington, heir to the Dukedom of Devonshire, who had married a sister of President Kennedy. It was thought piquant that the Prime Minister and the President, both grandsons of poor boys who had risen from the Celtic peasantry to great wealth, should be connected through the "ancient" noble house of Cavendish. Yet the Cavendishes had got their start in the reign of Henry VIII by means of the same shrewdness and enterprise that had characterized the careers of Daniel Macmillan and Joseph Kennedy.

16. Students should acquaint themselves with the battle over "wit" that took place around the turn of the century. It was set off by the Reverend Jeremy Collier's blast against contemporary drama, *A Short View of the Immorality and Profaneness of the English Stage* (1698). Since that drama was distinguished for its "wit," wit was thus charged with being the handmaid of immorality (as probably many people still believe, consciously or unconsciously). Collier was supported by the Whig physician and writer of ponderous epics, Sir Richard Blackmore. Congreve replied in defense of wit, but the anti-wit faction carried the day, in drama at least. There were certainly important political implications in the contest, Whiggism and Nonconformity generally championing "morality" as against wit; and when, after the accession of George I, Steele was rewarded for his services as Whig propagandist by being given the patent to operate the Theatre Royal, Drury Lane, he dropped witty Congrevian drama in favor of his own "sentimental comedy," the ancestor of modern soap-opera. If some events in the history of eighteenth-century taste have been termed "pre-Romantic," this episode may be said to illustrate "pre-Victorianism," the spirit that impelled the Reverend Charles Kingsley to exhort, "Be good, sweet maid, and let who will be clever." However, numerous eighteenth-century writers, from Pope, Swift, and Johnson down to Jane Austen, still adhered to the old-fashioned view that being clever might help one to be good. For further discussion, see William Empson, "Wit in the *Essay on Criticism*," *Hudson Review* (Winter 1950) 559–577 (reprinted in his *The Structure of Complex Words* [New York: New Directions, 1951]), and E. N. Hooker, "Pope on Wit: the *Essay on Criticism*," in R. F. Jones *et al.*, *The Seventeenth Century* (Stanford: Stanford University Press, 1951), pp. 604–617.

17. H. Heaton, "Industry and Trade," in A. C. Turberville, ed., *Johnson's England* (Oxford: The Clarendon Press, 1933), I, pp. 231, 239.

18. "Further Thoughts on Agriculture," *Universal Visiter* (March 1756).

19. P. Colquhon, quoted by Dorothy George, *England in Transition* (Penguin Books, 1953), pp. 152–153.

Two

A Historical Summary: 1660–1789

From the Restoration to the "Glorious Revolution": 1660–1688

Chronology: 1658–1689

1658   Cromwell dies. For a short time his son Richard rules as Protector, but serious divisions occur in the Army leadership. General Monk allows the remnant of the Long Parliament to reconvene; it offers the throne to the exiled Charles II.

1660   Charles II returns, and the "old constitution" is restored. Punitive action is taken against the "regicides" and a few other parliamentary leaders, but an Act of Grace pardons all others. Restrictive laws against Puritanism in religion are passed by the new royalist Parliament (the Clarendon Code, after Charles' chief minister, the Earl of Clarendon). As a result, two thousand Puritan ministers leave the Church of England, becoming Dissenters (Nonconformists). The Royal Society (of London for Improving Natural Knowledge) is founded.

1665   An epidemic of bubonic plague devastates London (see Defoe, *A Journal of the Plague Year*).

1666   The Great Fire of London. The heart of the City is reduced to rubble, including the old Gothic St. Paul's Cathedral. Sir Christopher Wren is commissioned to redesign the City, and later builds a new St. Paul's, in Renaissance–baroque style.

1667   War with Holland, in which the Dutch ravage the English seacoast (see the opening of Dryden's *An Essay of Dramatic Poesy*). Clarendon dismissed and exiled; succeeded by the Cabal, a group of five politicians who seek an alliance with Louis XIV of France. In the secret Treaty of Dover (1670),

Charles accepts Louis' financial aid to enable Charles eventually to restore Roman Catholicism in England.

1668   Sir William Temple (afterward Swift's patron) negotiates the Triple Alliance of England, Holland, and Sweden, a Protestant alliance to curb the growing power of Louis XIV.

1672   William of Orange, the young Stadholder of Holland (next heir to the British throne after James, Duke of York, and his daughters), sets himself up as Louis' chief opponent and leader of Protestantism in Europe. He marries (1677) Princess Mary, eldest daughter of James.

1678   The "Popish Plot"—the informer Titus Oates produces forged "proofs" of a plot of the Catholics to overthrow the government, murder Charles, and place James (a Catholic) on the throne. The agitation is fanned by extreme Protestants led by the Earl of Shaftesbury.

1679–   Shaftesbury introduces the Exclusion Bill in Parliament, ex-
81   cluding James from succession to the throne. It is defeated after Charles dissolves Parliament and summons a new one in the more royalist atmosphere of Oxford. Eventually Shaftesbury dies and the agitation simmers down, followed by severe reprisals on his followers.

1685   Charles II dies. James succeeds as King James II. The Duke of Monmouth, Charles' oldest illegitimate son, one of the extreme Protestant faction, invades England (from Holland) and tries to seize power. He is easily defeated and is executed. His followers are ruthlessly punished by Jeffreys, James' Lord Chief Justice, at the "Bloody Assizes."

1685–   James initiates a campaign to increase the authority of the
88   Crown and to revive Roman Catholicism in England, by use of the royal prerogative of "suspension"—blanket pardons for offenders against anti-Catholic Acts of Parliament—and "declarations of indulgence" of nonconformity with the Church of England. In 1688, the Archbishop of Canterbury (William Sancroft) and six other bishops present to James a petition protesting against his policy; they are imprisoned in the Tower of London on a charge of sedition. The courts triumphantly acquit them. A son (later, the Old Pretender) is born to James' second wife, making the Protestant princesses Mary and Anne no longer heirs to the throne. Great public agitation.

1688   William of Orange is invited by a number of English leaders to come to England with a Dutch army and restore the rights threatened by James. He does so, and wins widespread support. James flees to France with his wife and young son (the "Glorious Revolution").

1689   William and Mary are proclaimed King and Queen by Parliament and accept the Bill of Rights, which asserts, in effect, the supremacy of Parliament over the King. An act requiring office holders to swear to their belief in the right of the new sovereigns to the throne results in a number of Anglican clergymen giving up their appointments in the Church (the "non-jurors"); also in the retirement of Dryden as Poet Laureate. The Act of Toleration practically guarantees freedom of worship to Protestants outside the Church of England. William forms the Grand Alliance with Spain and Austria, and begins war against Louis XIV (the War of the League of Augsburg).

The Search for Political Stability

There have been few periods when the literature of the time has been more politically conscious than that of the Restoration and the eighteenth century in Britain; perhaps the only parallel that comes readily to the mind is that of America in the 1930's. Dryden, Marvell, Pope, Swift, Addison, Steele, Johnson, Goldsmith, Burke, to mention only some of the greater figures writing between 1660 and 1785, were intensely aware of the political issues of their time, deeply committed to one side or the other, and intent on making their readers understand their significance. Dryden, Swift, Addison, Steele and Johnson all acted as quasi-official publicists for the administrations of their day. Dryden and Swift, indeed, at times, were almost Ministers of Propaganda for their governments, as, earlier, Milton had been for his. For the modern reader fully to understand their writings, he needs at least as good a knowledge of the salient historical events of the reigns of the later Stuart and earlier Hanoverian monarchs as he does of the administrations of Herbert Hoover and Franklin D. Roosevelt in order to understand Steinbeck and Dos Passos (or, for that matter, of fifth-century Athens to understand Aristophanes).

But the student needs to use great caution when reading the older standard political histories of seventeenth- and eighteenth-

century Britain—those of Macaulay, J. R. Green, Lecky, and
G. M. Trevelyan, among others. The nineteenth-century historians imposed on the facts of the political structure of Britain
during this period their own "Whig interpretation," as it has
been called. This is probably an unfortunate term. It is true that
the interpretation was largely the work of those staunch Whigs,
Burke and Macaulay, who certainly used it in the service of
their party's welfare. But what is objectionable about it is not
that it tends to present Whigs as the heroes and Tories as the
villains of eighteenth-century political history—a history may be
frankly biased yet useful—but that it grossly oversimplifies and
distorts the highly complex terms of political life of the time,
reducing them to a dichotomy between forward-looking Whigs
and backward-looking Tories. (And, by regarding forward-
looking as necessarily good and backward-looking as bad, implicitly postulating the Victorian state of things as the ideal—
"ratifying the present," as the inventor of the term "the Whig
interpretation," Herbert Butterfield, put it.)

In fact, far from there being a simple two-party system such as
developed in mid-nineteenth-century Britain, there were hardly
parties at all in the modern sense. There were fluctuating
groups of politicians allied for shorter or longer periods of time
to promote common interests, or to aid one another to get and
retain power. Sometimes, to be sure, these political groupings
were based on definite public issues—one notable instance, in
the period between 1708 and 1713, was the question of whether
the war with France should be continued or whether peace
should be made.

But usually the British political structure of the eighteenth
century is better understood by thinking of it in terms of modern
American politics. There the application of the labels "Republi-
can" and "Democrat" is very often only the result of historical
accident and guarantees very little about the ideology of their
possessors, where one group of Republicans and one of Demo-
crats may be far closer to each other on most issues than either
is to another wing of the same party, where a Democratic Chief
Executive may rely on the advice of Republicans whom he has
appointed to his Cabinet and find his strongest opposition in a
group of Democratic congressmen. It may be wrong to suggest,

as Sir Lewis Namier (who demonstrated the falsity of the nine-teenth-century historians' picture) and some of his followers have perhaps done, that eighteenth-century British political history should be analyzed solely in terms of the personal interests and loyalties of the individuals involved in it, ignoring questions of ideology completely. Nevertheless, it is certainly true that during a great deal of the period—as in other times and places—personalities and power-seeking played a much greater role in political maneuvering than did disinterested adherence to abstract principle.

T. S. Eliot once commented that the Civil War in Britain has never ended—that is to say, the basic differences of opinion in politics and religion which divided the country into two war-ring camps in the 1640's still persist today. It is at least true that they were not healed by the Restoration. The return of Charles II from exile in France in 1660, and the replacement of the various short-lived experiments in governmental and ecclesiastical organization under the Parliamentary and Cromwellian regimes by the "old constitution in Church and State"—the resumption of the legislative power by the King-in-Parliament and of the executive power by the King-in-Council, the restoration of the episcopal organization of the Church—were hailed with delight by the vast majority of the English. Pepys' diary gives a striking account of the general rejoicing, and Butler's *Hudibras* is the classic expression of the detestation aroused by the tyrannical dogmatism of the extreme Puritans.

But the sources of discontent which had given rise to the Civil War were by no means eliminated, and again produced bitter strife in 1678, in 1685, and finally in 1688. The political history of the years from 1660 to 1688 is better read as an appendage to that from 1603 to 1660 than as a prelude to that from 1689 onward, and the custom in literary histories of making the seventeenth century terminate and the eighteenth century commence in 1660 seems less and less justifiable the more closely one studies both the history and the literature of the reigns of Charles II and James II. The life of the greatest literary figure of the time, Dryden, overlapped that of Milton by forty-three years, and that of Pope by only twelve; it really makes much more sense to study Dryden and Milton together, as inhabitants of almost the same historical milieu, than it does to lump Dryden together with Pope.

The Restoration of 1660 began as a compromise among the two opposing factions; it was arranged by the Parliamentarian General Monk on the understanding that there would be no reprisals against the Puritan and Parliamentarian side and, for a time at least, this agreement was adhered to. By comparison with the termination of some twentieth-century conflicts, it was a remarkably mild settlement: an Act of Grace initiated by the King guaranteed immunity from prosecution for war crimes to everyone except those who had passed sentence of death on Charles I (the "regicides"), and only a handful of these actually suffered. Even the great propagandist of the regime, John Milton, escaped with no more than a short period of house arrest—a far different fate from that of, for example, Goebbels in the twentieth century. To the Puritan ministers of the Church of England, there was promised a conference to see whether differences could be reconciled, and bishoprics in the Church were offered to two of the Puritan leaders, Baxter and Calamy, though they declined the honor.

Unfortunately, this era of good feeling did not survive the election of the first House of Commons under Charles II, in 1661, the so-called Cavalier Parliament, filled with representatives of the old squirearchy burning for vengeance on those who had confiscated their property and killed their relations in battle (the parallel with what happened in the American South two centuries later is obvious). Its members pushed Charles and his ministers much further than Charles, a most tolerant person even though his tolerance may have stemmed from general political and religious indifference, would himself have gone. Unable, because of the Act of Grace, to inflict civil punishment on their old enemies, they concentrated on ecclesiastical matters, and, with the encouragement of Charles' chief minister, the old Earl of Clarendon, a relic of the days of Charles I and the exile in France, passed a series of stringent statutes (the Clarendon Code) against those in the Church with Puritan leanings.

As a result, some two thousand clergy were forced to leave the Church of England and be classed as "Dissenters" or "Noncon-

formists." The Conventicle Act, the Five-Mile Act, the Corporation Act severely restricted the civil rights and freedom of worship of those who did not adhere to the state church. The Test
Act, passed somewhat later (1672), required all officers of the
state, civil and military, to prove their orthodoxy by taking
communion according to the form of the Church of England
(and produce a certificate to the effect that they had done so),
and to sign a declaration repudiating belief in the doctrine of
transubstantiation. This latter provision was directed at Roman
Catholics rather than Protestant Dissenters, who of course had
no objection to signing such a declaration. Protestant Dissenters,
too, were often willing to receive communion in the Anglican
form at stated times in order to hold a municipal office. An
attempt was made in the reign of Anne to suppress this practice
of "occasional conformity," but without much effect. In fact,
these acts did not really hamper the Nonconformists from prac-
ticing their religion or taking active part in public life, but they
were minor irritations that did not conduce to civil harmony.

It is not necessary here to follow in detail the tortuous political intrigues of the first two decades of Charles' reign, in which
the venerable Clarendon was ousted from power and exiled, and
succeeded first by the Cabal—Clifford, Ashley (later the Earl of
Shaftesbury), Buckingham, Arlington, Lauderdale—and then
by Thomas Osborne, Earl of Danby. In foreign policy, Charles
wavered between friendship with Catholic France under the aggressive Louis XIV, and with Protestant Holland under its
young Stadholder, William of Orange. In the former phase, in
return for a subsidy from France, he agreed by the secret Treaty
of Dover to assist France to crush Holland and (eventually) to
proclaim his own conversion to Roman Catholicism, in the hope
that that of the whole country would follow (it was, however,
kept secret until after his death). In the latter phase, he agreed
to the Triple Alliance of England with Protestant Holland and
Sweden to check the power of Louis, and to the marriage of his
elder niece, Mary, eventual heiress presumptive to the throne,
with William. Mary and her sister Anne, daughters of James,
Duke of York, by his first wife, Anne Hyde, Clarendon's daughter, had been, by Charles' order, educated as Protestants, in
spite of their father's intransigent Catholicism and Charles' own
waverings in that direction.

The question of the future religion of the monarch was to provide a focus for the animosities of the two opposing interests that continued to survive in English political life from the time of the Civil War and earlier. Charles' wife, Catherine of Bragança (of the Portuguese royal family), was sterile, and the immediate heir to the throne was his brother James, who made no secret of his fervent devotion to Rome. Fear of James' succession, however, was mitigated for a time by the assumption that he, in turn, would be succeeded by his staunchly Protestant daughters.

But in the late 1670's, the unscrupulous Anthony Ashley Cooper, first Earl of Shaftesbury (Dryden's Achitophel), found himself out of office and determined to use any means to recover political power. He prevailed on the weak-minded Duke of Monmouth (Absalom), Charles' oldest illegitimate son, to allow himself to be set up as a competitor to James, and, to the accompaniment of a country-wide campaign of anti-Catholic propaganda, introduced into Parliament the Exclusion Bill, which would bar James from succeeding to the throne. All the old antagonisms of the Civil War revived; it was at this time that the terms "Whigs" (to designate supporters of the bill) and "Tories" (to designate its opponents) began to be used—though the student would be wrong to think that these words, at this or any other time in the seventeenth and eighteenth centuries, stood for the tightly organized parties that "Liberal" and "Conservative" came to signify in later nineteenth-century Britain.

At the same time, the rascally Titus Oates "discovered" the great "Popish Plot," in which the Catholics were said to have planned to assassinate Charles and other political leaders and place James on the throne. With Shaftesbury feeding the flames, a small reign of terror against Catholics ensued—some thirty-five individuals were executed for treason. It seriously looked as though the Civil War were about to break out all over again. But Charles, displaying a genius for political maneuver he seldom bothered to exercise—and assisted by his Poet Laureate Dryden's great *Absalom and Achitophel* ("Of this poem," wrote Johnson, "the reception was eager, and the sale so large, that my father, an old bookseller, told me he had not known it equalled but by Sacheverell's Trial," thirty years later)—managed in time, by judicious alternations of compliance and firmness, to quiet the disturbance; Shaftesbury was forced to flee into exile, and at Charles' death in 1685, James peacefully ascended the throne.

He occupied it for only three hectic years, during which his incredible ineptness managed to alienate all factions of his subjects, Whig and Tory, Anglican and Nonconformist. A rebellion raised in the West by Monmouth was crushed and its participants punished (in the "Bloody Assizes" conducted by James' sadistic Lord Chief Justice Jeffreys) with a ferocity which appalled even the great numbers of his subjects who sympathized with James as against Monmouth. The climax came late in 1688, when he sent seven bishops of the Church of which he was officially head, including the Archbishop of Canterbury, to the Tower on charges of sedition, and when his second wife unexpectedly gave birth to a son, who automatically displaced the Protestant Mary and Anne from the succession to the throne and who would assuredly be brought up as a Catholic. This was too much to be borne. An invitation was quickly sent to William of Orange to come over with an army and restore the *status quo*. He did so. James' supporters—including his daughter Anne —flocked to William's banner, and James fled to France without offering any opposition. William and Mary were proclaimed King and Queen, and the Glorious—and bloodless—Revolution was accomplished.

It is hard to resist using the jocular cliché that James II was a "bad King" but a "good thing." No one could have succeeded better in demonstrating to the opposing groups of Englishmen how much they had in common which it was to their interest to preserve. Tories and Whigs, Royalists and Parliamentarians alike were threatened with an absolutism foreign to the English tradition; Anglicans and Nonconformists alike were threatened with domination by Rome. The Revolution of 1688, as has often been pointed out (especially by Burke, contrasting it with the violence and dogmatism of the French Revolution), was an intense expression of *conservatism*. The banner of William's invading army bore the motto of the House of Orange, "Je maintiendrai" ("I will maintain"). What was confirmed by the expulsion of James and by the Declaration of Rights drawn up by the Parliamentary Convention which offered the throne to William and Mary (who signed that Declaration) was the ancient English tradition of limited monarchy and government by consent. The legislative power was to remain in the hands of the King-in-Parliament, and was not to be subverted by suspensions of Acts of Parliament by the king alone, such as James had practiced. Parliament was to have the power to determine the succession to the throne, a power confirmed by the act of William and Mary in accepting their crowns from the hands of Parliament, and a little later, by the Act of Settlement, 1701, which passed over several dozen persons with a better hereditary claim (including James II's son, the Old Pretender) to settle the crown on the Protestant Electors of Hanover. (This was nothing new in English history—the Lancastrian dynasty of Henry IV and the Tudor of Henry VII had been placed on the throne, with Parliamentary consent, to the exclusion of closer heirs.)

Judged on the basis of its results in England, the Revolution of 1688 was enormously successful. There were a few dissentients: some Roman Catholics (but not all—Pope Innocent XI by no means approved of the activities of the Jesuits who guided James' counsels, and refused to make the chief of them, Father Petre, a cardinal when James asked him to do so); some Anglicans (the "non-jurors"), including Archbishop Sancroft of Canterbury, who, maintaining that only James had the hereditary, and therefore divine, right to the throne, refused to take the required oaths recognizing William and Mary as the lawful sovereigns, and were deprived of their appointments (Dryden lost his post of Poet Laureate in this way). But to the vast majority, it was the inevitable solution of an intolerable situation. Tories claimed as much credit for it as Whigs; in later years even "High Tories" such as Swift and Johnson expressed their approval of it. It was the last time that there has been a serious attempt to change the basic terms of government in England by internal force (this is not true, of course, of Scotland and Ireland). A general agreement had at last been reached on what those terms were to be, and, although the old animosities of the seventeenth century were not yet completely healed, it was recognized that a broad enough framework of political agreement existed that minor differences within that framework could be tolerated.

This was finally proven when Harley, Earl of Oxford, fell from power on the change of dynasty in 1714. In the previous century, when such a leader was ousted by his enemies, severe reprisals at once overtook him: Strafford was executed, Clarendon was exiled. For two years Oxford was kept imprisoned and threatened with impeachment on a charge of treason. But the impeachment was at last dropped—thanks to Robert Walpole's maneuverings behind the scenes—and Oxford was released. Even more strikingly, when Walpole in turn fell from power in 1742—and few politicians have made more virulent enemies than Walpole did during his long term of office—although a strenuous effort was made to have him impeached, it too quickly failed; Oxford's son was one of many Tories who refused to vote against Walpole. Since that time the right to the existence of a "loyal opposition" has been recognized, and England—along with other countries, such as the United States, which have inherited the English tradition of government—has been spared the turmoil and bloodshed which in other places has accompanied a shift in political power. The principle of political as well as religious toleration was able to subsist because of the establishment by the Revolution of basic terms of government on which the vast majority of the English could agree. The political stability thus attained has seen England safely through two and a half centuries of internal peace, and certainly accounts for a good deal of the release of national energy which characterized the England of the eighteenth century.

From the Revolution to the Peace of Paris: 1688–1763

Chronology: 1690–1763

1690   Military campaigns against James' supporters in Scotland and Ireland. William defeats James at the Battle of the Boyne (July 12, N.S.) and subdues Ireland.

1694   Queen Mary dies of smallpox. Bank of England founded— modern conception of state financing, with a permanent national debt.

1697   War with France ended by the inconclusive Treaty of Ryswick.

1701   War with France (War of the Spanish Succession) again touched off by an attempt of Louis XIV to place his grandson on the vacant throne of Spain. James II dies in exile in France, bequeathing his claim to the British throne to his son, James Edward (their supporters known as "Jacobites," from Latin *Jacobus,* James). The Act of Settlement provides that after the death of Anne (who has no living children) the Crown go to Sophia, Electress of Hanover in Germany, the nearest Protestant heir, and that the sovereign and his consort must be Protestants (the act is still in force).

1702   William III dies from a fall from his horse. Succeeded by Anne (her husband, Prince George of Denmark, a nonentity, dies 1708). John Churchill, Duke of Marlborough, appointed commander of English and allied forces in the war against France; his wife, Sarah, dominates Anne.

1704   Marlborough decisively defeats the French at the Battle of Blenheim. Whigs, with the Earl of Godolphin as Lord Treasurer (prime minister), control the government and vigorously prosecute the war with France.

1707   Act of Union between England and Scotland. Scotland's separate parliament is abolished and Scots send representatives to the Parliament at London. Official name of the nation becomes "Great Britain" (the geographical name of the island, distinguished from "Little Britain"—Brittany in France).

1709   The Whig administration prosecutes Henry Sacheverell, a Tory High Churchman, for a sermon deploring the Revolution. Sacheverell becomes regarded as a martyr, and the Whigs lose popularity. The Duchess of Marlborough quarrels with Anne and is eventually dismissed, replaced by the Tory Lady Masham as the Queen's confidante.

1710   Whigs dismissed from government, replaced by the Tories Robert Harley, Earl of Oxford, and Henry St. John, Viscount Bolingbroke, with Swift as their chief publicist. Negotiations begun to end the war with France, which the Tories feel is being unnecessarily prolonged for the benefit of Marlborough and the Whigs. Stricter measures against Nonconformists urged by High Church Tories.

1713   War with France ended by Tory-negotiated Peace of Utrecht (chief negotiator, the poet Matthew Prior).

1714   Harley and St. John quarrel. Anne dies; a Whig council of regency (secretary, Joseph Addison) takes over power while awaiting arrival of the new king George I, Elector of Hanover (his mother, Electress Sophia, having died a short time before Anne). On George's arrival, all Tories are dismissed, and the first of a series of Whig administrations takes over, lasting until the end of the century. Bolingbroke, accused of treasonable plotting to restore the throne to the Pretender, flees to France, and joins the Pretender. Oxford is impeached and imprisoned, but eventually released.

1715   Invasion of Scotland by forces headed by the Old Pretender ("the '15"). It is quickly crushed, and the leaders executed. James Edward escapes back to France.

1721   The South Sea Bubble—a vast speculative scheme for trading in the Pacific—collapses and causes financial chaos. Several leading members of the Whig government are implicated and discredited; Robert Walpole, leader of an opposition Whig faction, becomes prime minister (for twenty years).

1727   George I dies; succeeded by his son George II (with whom he has quarreled constantly) and the intellectual and skeptical Queen Caroline.

1733   Opposition to Walpole increased by his attempt to impose a heavy Excise Act (he is forced to withdraw it). The opposition consists largely of Whigs alienated by Walpole ("the Patriots"), led by William Pulteney and Lord Carteret, later joined by William Pitt (the elder), representing the formidable commercial interests which feel Walpole is unnecessarily cautious in promoting Britain's development into a worldwide trading nation. Bolingbroke, permitted to return from exile, and Frederick, Prince of Wales, George II's foolish son and heir, support the opposition against Walpole.

1738   Agitation by the opposition for war with Spain, which has vigorously resisted infringement by British merchants of her monopoly of trading in South American and Pacific waters (guaranteed by the Peace of Utrecht). Captain Jenkins exhibits to a Parliamentary investigating committee an ear allegedly cut off by a Spanish coastguard captain.

1739   Walpole reluctantly declares war against Spain, prosecutes it half-heartedly and unsuccessfully.

1741–   Walpole loses support in a general election, and is finally
42   forced to resign; becomes Earl of Orford. Succeeded by a Whig coalition of former allies and opponents of Walpole,

in which Henry Pelham and his brother, the Duke of New-castle, eventually attain leadership. The Spanish war develops into the War of the Austrian Succession, started by Frederick (the Great) of Prussia's aggression against the territories of Maria Theresa of Austria.

1743   George II personally leads an English and Hanoverian army to victory over the French at the Battle of Dettingen.

1745   Invasion of Scotland by Charles Edward, the Young Pre-tender. The Jacobite forces penetrate as far south as central England. But expected English support is not forthcoming, and Charles retreats to Scotland. His forces are eventually routed at the Battle of Culloden by the Duke of Cumberland, George II's younger son. Charles escapes to France. One result of "the '45" is the beginning of an attempt to civilize the Highlands of Scotland and abolish the remains of the feudal clan system.

1748   The shaky Peace of Aix-la-Chapelle with France is concluded.

1750's   and 1760's. Development of new machinery—James Watt's steam engine, wool- and cotton-spinning and weaving ma-chinery—which is to revolutionize industry in Britain: the beginning of the Industrial Revolution.

1751   Frederick, Prince of Wales, dies; succeeded as heir to the throne by his twelve-year-old son George. His tutor, the Earl of Bute, one of Frederick's political associates (a Scot), brings up George in the "Patriot" and oppositionist tradition of Frederick.

1751–   Continued clashes between neighboring French and British
56   settlements in North America and India, where the French also pursue an expansionist policy. French troops move southward in the Ohio valley, cutting off the British colonies of the Atlantic seaboard from expansion to the west; they seize Fort Duquesne (now Pittsburgh); an expedition to retake it, led by General Braddock, is disastrously defeated.

1756   War between France, on one side, and Britain and Prussia on the other, is declared (the Seven Years' War). William Pitt, a dissident Whig leader, reconciles his differences with the official Whig leadership under Newcastle, and becomes virtual prime minister, conducting the war with great vigor and success. Wolfe later defeats the French in Canada and Clive in India.

1760   George II dies (aged 77); succeeded by his grandson George III (aged 22). The older Whig factions led by Newcastle and

Pitt are in disfavor; Bute becomes Prime Minister, and pursues a policy of bringing the war to a close.

1763   Peace of Paris; Canada and India are ceded to Britain.

The Rise of Greater Britain

William III's twelve-year reign was largely occupied in consolidating the Revolution—Jacobite uprisings in Scotland were crushed, and Ireland, where James himself proceeded with a French army, needed over two years of hard fighting to subdue; mediating among squabbling factions of his English political advisers; and conducting a Continental war against France (the War of the League of Augsburg, concluded by the shaky Treaty of Ryswick, 1697). Two domestic events were of particular significance. The chartering of the Bank of England, conceived by the brilliant financier (and dilettante poet and patron of the arts, possibly a model for Pope's Bufo) Charles Montagu, later Earl of Halifax, provided for the first time a modern scheme of national financing. This included the indispensable national debt, which enabled Britain to engage in long-term military operations and acted as the nucleus for a system of commercial banking on which more ambitious commercial and industrial enterprises could be based. The failure of Parliament to renew or replace the act requiring printed materials to be inspected and licensed before publication put an end to the centuries-old principle of prepublication censorship, and the beginning of an era of freedom of the press; though once published, books and periodicals were subject to the laws of libel and sedition, as of course they still are. (Strangely, censorship, after being removed from the press, was imposed, in 1737, on the London stage, Walpole having lost his patience with the scathing lampoons on him that were being presented. Until 1968, a play to be performed publicly in London had to be approved in advance by the Lord Chamberlain's office.)

William's cold efficiency and his preference for Holland and his Dutch advisers made him few friends in England, and his early death, when his horse tripped over a mole hill, was not much lamented in his adopted country. Indeed, Holland became in the Tories' eyes the symbol of all they did not wish

England to be: it was accused of crass commercialism and materialism, of being a country where wealth was the highest value
and the rich were at liberty to exploit the poor as they pleased.
Yet even Johnson and Swift, who printed as much anti-Dutch
propaganda as anyone—one of Swift's most notable contributions was the conclusion of Book Three of *Gulliver's Travels*
where the Dutch are ascribed the pleasant habit of trampling on
the crucifix to please the Japanese with whom they want to
trade—admit, with varying degrees of reluctance, that the replacement of James II with William III was necessary.

James died in France in 1701, shortly before his nephew and
son-in-law, William; and Louis XIV comforted James on his
deathbed, and helped to set Europe in flames again, by recognizing his son James Edward as King James III of England. Most of
the reign of Anne, William's successor, was occupied with the
War of the Spanish Succession, which Louis' action, among
other things, helped to ignite. The main question at issue was
whether the succession to the Spanish throne should or should
not go to Louis' grandson, who was one of the closest in the hereditary succession. The deeper question was whether French
power should be allowed to expand by the addition of the
power of Spain and her far-flung colonies, so as to dominate the
competition that was developing for world trade and empire
among the European powers. The English Whigs were determined that it should not, and John Churchill, Duke of Marlborough, husband of Anne's favorite, Sarah, and a brilliant
general and diplomat, was resolved to implement that determination. By a series of great victories on the Continent—Blenheim,
Ramilies, Oudenarde, Malplaquet—he crushed French military
might, but at enormous expense in bloodshed. The number of
casualties in these battles of Marlborough surpassed anything
Britain had hitherto known; in its scope and ferocity, the War
of the Spanish Succession might be termed the first of the modern world wars. This casualty rate accounts for at least some of
the animosity Swift and other Tories displayed against Marlborough, for instance, in Swift's bitter "epitaph" on him:

> Behold his funeral appears,
> Nor widows' sighs, nor orphans' tears,

> Wont at such times each heart to pierce,
> Attend the progress of his hearse.
> But what of that? his friends may say,
> He had those honours in his day.
> True to his profit and his pride,
> He made them weep before he died.

Toward 1708 the great issue in English domestic politics became that of the continuation of the war. The Whigs and Marlborough, with their publicists Steele and Addison, insisted that to terminate it before France was eliminated as an important military power was short-sighted. If she were allowed to retain any substantial strength, they maintained, her aggression would eventually have to be checked all over again. Moreover, for Britain to withdraw unilaterally would be a betrayal of her Continental allies. The Tories argued, to the contrary, that Britain's aims in the war had been achieved, that France had learned her lesson, and that Marlborough, the Whigs, and the allies wished to continue the war merely for reasons of aggrandizement and personal advantage. The Tories got their way. In 1710, with the help of the Duchess of Marlborough, whose haughty temper finally overcame Anne's devotion to her, the Whig ministers were dismissed, and the famous Tory ministry of Harley, Earl of Oxford, and St. John, Viscount Bolingbroke, with Swift as their chief propagandist, came into power. The Peace of Utrecht, negotiated largely by the poet Matthew Prior, who was in the diplomatic service, was concluded in 1713.

The hectic political activity of the last years of Anne's reign, when Harley and Bolingbroke engaged in an internecine contest for sole power and both were alarmed by the probability that after Anne's death their Whig opponents, with the support of the new King, would take office, is brilliantly reported in Swift's *Journal to Stella* and (in fictional form) in Thackeray's *Henry Esmond*. There is no real evidence for the suggestion of Thackeray and others that the Tory leaders were plotting to give the crown to James III instead of to George I; yet all of them, including some Whig leaders, kept in some kind of touch with the Jacobite headquarters on the Continent—just in case. The presence of the Jacobite threat during the early decades of the eighteenth century—until after its last desperate attempt in the

Scottish rebellion of 1745—was closely analogous in the political history of the time to the Communist threat in the Western countries in the 1940's and 1950's. Jacobite espionage and subversive activity certainly did go on; at the same time, astute Whigs made political capital for themselves by exaggerating it and freely accusing their opponents of "Jacobite tendencies" when it suited their book to do so. Conversely, thoughtful Tories like Samuel Johnson risked the charge of Jacobitism by condemning these tactics by the Whigs. There is no evidence whatever that Johnson was a Jacobite, in the sense of seriously wishing the restoration of the Stuart family to the throne; but he was certainly an "anti-anti-Jacobite," to adapt a modern phrase.

How little real hold Jacobitism had on the English was demonstrated in "the '45" when the army of Prince Charles Edward (the Young Pretender), managing to advance as far south into England as Derby, found the lip service of the English Jacobites to be no more than that. No crowds of English reinforcements flocked to Charles's banner and he was forced to retreat to Scotland, where English military might soon overpowered him at the Battle of Culloden.[1] The last Stuart claimant to the throne, Charles' younger brother Henry, "Duke of York" and Cardinal of the Roman Catholic Church ("King Henry IX" according to the Jacobites), died in 1807, recipient of a pension from his distant cousin George III to help relieve his necessities.

With the constitutional question settled by the Revolution of 1688, and the problem of French aggression solved, for the time being at least, by the Peace of Utrecht, the energies of English politicians were free to be applied to the great central contest in the history of the first half of the eighteenth century. Britain had to choose whether she was to remain a self-contained, isolationist nation, avoiding foreign and imperial entanglements (a "little England," to use the term that was coined when the question was again debated in the middle of the nineteenth century), or whether she was to take advantage of her naval, military, and industrial strength and her position athwart the world's trade routes to expand into a great commercial world power. The contest was fought primarily between groups of Whigs—no Tories held any governmental office of importance after the accession of George I. Although they occupied from one-fifth to one-fourth of the seats in the House of Commons, they seldom took much of a direct hand in the shaping of national policy, generally throwing their weight, however, when they did intervene, on the side of isolationist rather than internationalist tendencies.

A bitter struggle for power at once developed between the internationally minded Lords Stanhope and Sunderland (Marlborough's son-in-law) on the one side, and Robert Walpole and his brother-in-law Lord Townshend on the other. The Townshends and Walpoles were originally Norfolk country gentry, and Walpole never lost touch with the feelings and values of the squirearchy; indeed the Tory country gentlemen in Parliament saved him from defeat on several occasions, and Samuel Johnson, who as a young man had written vitriolic invective against him, in the end came to admire him ("He was the best minister this country ever had; and if *we* would have let him, he would have kept the country in perpetual peace"). The much too enterprising financial schemes of the South Sea Company, with which the Sunderland–Stanhope administration was closely allied, ended in 1721 with the bursting of the South Sea Bubble— an enormous stock-market boom, in which prices of stocks, led by those of the company, were preposterously inflated, and then collapsed overnight, to the ruin of thousands of speculators, while a few officials of the company, acting in collaboration with members of the government, made fortunes. Stanhope and Sunderland both conveniently died at this time, leaving Walpole, who had been out of office and was not known to be connected with the South Sea Company's activities, in possession of the field.

Walpole's pacific foreign policy, supporting the Quadruple Alliance of Britain, France, Austria, and Holland, which was to ensure the continuance of the peace agreed on at Utrecht, his conservative financial policy at home, and his ruthlessness in getting rid of any colleague who showed signs of being a potential rival for his leadership—in succession, he forced such powerful figures as Townshend, William Pulteney, Lord Carteret, Lord Chesterfield, and the Duke of Argyll out of office—maintained him in office for twenty years, the longest term of any

British Prime Minister.[2] The ejected Whig leaders, however, formed a powerful opposition faction, to which were presently added Bolingbroke, permitted to return from exile in France; Frederick, Prince of Wales, always eager to thwart his parents, who approved highly of Walpole; and, most important of all, the Patriots, headed by William Pitt, grandson of the merchant prince Thomas Pitt. Determined that Britain should obtain a share of the lucrative South American and Pacific trade, hitherto a monopoly of Spain, this group clamored patriotically (that is, jingoistically) against that country, retailing such atrocity stories as that of the patriotic Captain Jenkins, master of a merchant vessel, who resisted the encroachments of the Spanish coast guard, who retaliated by cutting off his ear. Walpole weakly allowed himself to be forced into war against Spain (the War of Jenkins' Ear) and then conducted it feebly and unsuccessfully. He was finally forced out of office in 1742 to the accompaniment of denunciations as "the betrayer of British honor" and "the enemy of British commerce."

However, the Patriots, headed by Pulteney, Carteret, and Pitt, were unable to form, or unwilling to risk forming, an administration made up solely of their own supporters, and made a deal which resulted in a coalition with Walpole's supporters ("Patriotism is the last refuge of a scoundrel," Johnson commented.) For another fifteen years, Henry Pelham and his brother the Duke of Newcastle continued to conduct the government of the country in much the same cautious way as Walpole had done. But in the early 1750's, as French and English interests began to conflict more and more in India and in the Ohio Valley, Pitt once again embarked on a crusade for war, this time with far-reaching results. Forcing himself into a coalition with Newcastle, who was to look after the domestic scene while Pitt took charge of military and diplomatic affairs, he brilliantly conducted the Seven Years' War ("The Great War for the Empire") to a resoundingly successful close. Britain emerged from the Peace of Paris in 1763 the gainer by two subcontinents, Canada and India, with unsurpassed naval and military might, a huge war debt—which was shortly to cause trouble when a later Prime Minister, George Grenville, tried to get the American colonists, now freed from the threat of French aggression to the north and west, to pay part of it—and an irrevocable commitment to commercial and imperial expansion. Writers of these decades, Swift, Pope, Johnson, had seen clearly enough the direction in which Britain was heading, and warned of the dangers involved: the cost in bloodshed, in oppression of native populations, in the moral corruption of a policy which placed material gain above all other values, of a "patriotism" which proclaimed, with James Thomson, that Britain had arisen "at Heav'n's command" and been commanded to "rule the waves." But Thomson found more willing listeners than Swift and Johnson, and the course of Britain's destiny for the next two centuries had been determined.

From the Peace of Paris to the Beginning of the French Revolution: 1763–1789

Chronology: 1763–1789

1763   Bute resigns; George Grenville, Prime Minister, initiates policy of economy (and American taxation) to pay for war costs.

1765   Stamp Act passed; violently resisted in America. Grenville dismissed; Rockingham Prime Minister.

1766   Stamp Act repealed; William Pitt, Earl of Chatham, Prime Minister. Incapacitated, he withdraws from activity, and the Duke of Grafton becomes Prime Minister.

1769   Turmoil over John Wilkes's expulsion from the House of Commons.

1770   Lord North Prime Minister.

1773   American resistance to taxation continues (the Boston Tea Party).

1775   Military actions between British troops and Americans. Battles of Lexington, Concord, Bunker Hill.

1776   American Declaration of Independence.

1777   British army under Burgoyne surrenders at Saratoga.

1780   London mobs riot over proposed extension of Roman Catholic civil rights (the Gordon riots—led by Lord George Gordon).

1781   British surrender at Yorktown.

1782   North resigns; Rockingham, later Shelburne, Prime Minister.

1783   Peace of Versailles ends American War, with recognition of American independence.

1783   After brief coalition government of North and Charles James Fox, William Pitt the younger (aged twenty-four) becomes Prime Minister; retains office 1783–1801 and again 1804–1806.

1789   Summoning of the French States-General, and storming of the Bastille: beginning of the French Revolution.

Confusion and Consolidation

The myth perpetuated by the American Declaration of Independence that George III was a tyrant, trying to turn the clock back to the days of royal absolutism, has long been discredited by responsible historical investigation.[3] He was an immature, inexperienced, conscientious young man who had been brought up in the Patriot tradition of his father, Prince Frederick, and he felt it his duty, on ascending the throne, to try to put into practice the high-sounding principles to which the Patriots gave noisy lip service. Others, like Samuel Johnson, who had been taken in for a time by the lofty ideals they professed, were thoroughly disillusioned when, after Walpole's downfall in 1742, the opposition leaders showed themselves as eager for the spoils of office as any Walpolian. But young George, carefully insulated from political reality by his mother, Princess Augusta, and his tutor, Lord Bute, managed to preserve his idealistic innocence, and when he ascended the throne in 1760, he resolved that the government of the country should no longer be a monopoly of the self-seeking politicians of the Walpole–Pelham–Rockingham faction, which had been in power so long, but should be guided for the good of the country as a whole by a king and ministers who should be "above party."[4] The Whigs of the Walpole tradition, guided by their chief propagandist, Edmund Burke (especially in his influential *Thoughts on the Present Discontents*, 1770), maintained that this cry of nonpartisanship was merely an astute device to hoodwink the public while its advocates (whom Burke termed "the King's friends") unconstitutionally seized power and ruled the country from behind the scenes, in the King's Cabinet. This might very well have been an accurate description of the real motives, conscious or unconscious, of such a Patriot as Bolingbroke; but young George certainly thought it possible to have a nonpartisan, unself-seeking executive. He failed, of course; but the bewildering series of ministerial changes that took place in the first ten years of his reign are testimony to the sincerity of his illusion.

The charge of tyranny made against George is given color for later students by the amount of public clamor that took place against various acts of his administrations. In fact, George's simple and virtuous domestic life and his transparent honesty made him perhaps the most popular sovereign England has ever had —the most popular, certainly, between Charles II and George V; and how accurately he could sometimes judge his subjects' political views was made clear in the general election of 1784, when the younger Pitt, whom George had forced on a hostile House of Commons, was overwhelmingly endorsed by the electorate. The fact was that, as the century progressed, the British public, becoming more and more literate and instructed in affairs of state by journalists like Johnson, was beginning to feel the desire to make its voice heard more loudly than hitherto. The outcome of this movement was to be the Reform Act of 1832 and the subsequent legislation which eventually established virtually universal suffrage in national elections. The sporadic outbursts of petitioning and the passing of resolutions by county associations and large public meetings in the early decades of George's reign were testimony to the development of this desire (and, of course, of the ease with which the public voice could be manipulated by shrewd politicians),[5] rather than to a greater desire on the part of George III than of his predecessors to "thwart the people's will."

Much nonsense has been written about the Wilkes affair being "a stalwart defence of democratic principles against encroachment by the Crown," and the like. Wilkes, a likable but thoroughly unscrupulous amateur in politics—he himself, as he said, was no Wilkite, and probably embarked on the enterprise in order to retrieve his personal fortunes—was voted by the House of Commons unfit, because of his unsavory record, to sit in that House. He was nevertheless reelected to it three times by the voters of Middlesex, to the accompaniment of much public uproar, whereupon the House declared his opponent to have received the larger number of *valid* votes (since Wilkes was ineligible) and to be the new member for Middlesex. A subsequent Parliament permitted him, however, to take his seat. In spite of historians, the incident in no way affected the right which the House of Commons still insists on to determine its own membership. In the twentieth century it has continued to invalidate elections of those who have received the largest number of votes in a constituency (for instance, Irish nationalists) and to declare their "defeated" opponents elected.

George III's reign began with the nation engaged in the concluding stages of the Seven Years' War. As usual in British history, the administration which had conducted a war was not the one which concluded the peace. Pitt, wishing to pursue and extend the war, but opposed by the rest of the Cabinet, resigned in 1762. Old Newcastle was likewise maneuvered into resigning— for all the stories told by Horace Walpole and others of his ineptness and love of intrigue, he had given the country faithful service for half a century, and spent a considerable fortune while doing so. George's mentor, Bute, was thus left without competition as First Minister. The Peace of Paris which he concluded was, however, unpopular (as most Peaces have been), and, unable to endure the scathing attacks made on him as a Scot, an outsider, and (allegedly) the lover of the Princess of Wales, George's mother, he too resigned in 1763. He was replaced by Pitt's brother-in-law, the conscientious but rigid George Grenville. He, however, annoyed the King by his pompous manner toward him, and the Americans by putting through the Stamp Act of 1765, a light but irritating tax on legal documents in the colonies, in an effort to meet part of the cost of the war, and George gladly parted with him the same year.

The King was then forced for a short time to put up with Lord Rockingham, now the leader of the old Walpole–Pelham Whig "connexion," which, under the guidance of Rockingham's secretary, Burke, was beginning to insist that it alone was the sole repository of simon-pure Whiggism, and that all other Whigs were really Tories in disguise. (This is a routine tactic of political propagandists, analogous to that of right-wing American political groups in the 1950's labeling President Eisenhower a crypto-Communist, but it nevertheless has taken in a good many later students; Grenville, North, and the Pitts considered themselves at least as good Whigs as the Rockinghamites.) George and Bute would probably have welcomed the accession of some good Tories to the Court (that is, the support of the administration), but true to their stubborn predilection for independence and opposition, few real Tories came. The Rockingham administration repealed the Stamp Act, which had aroused so much fury in America, but at the same time passed a Declaratory Act, maintaining the constitutional right of the British Parliament to impose taxes on the colonists if it chose. Rockingham's support in Parliament, however, was weak; he resigned in 1766, and Pitt, now the Earl of Chatham, became nominal head of the ministry. But his erratic health (mental as well as physical) caused him to abdicate his responsibilities, and after a short and unhappy period under the inexperienced and incompetent Duke of Grafton, the young Lord North emerged as the strongest figure in the ministry, and, to everyone's surprise, retained the Prime Ministership for twelve years, until 1782.

North, a charming and tactful personality, the heir of a family eminent for its intellectual and artistic interests, and a competent and industrious administrator, succeeded in giving Britain a reasonably stable government, and might have gone down in history as one of her most successful Prime Ministers if it had not been for the dispute with the American colonists. But probably no other British politician available at the time would have handled the situation any better. The trouble was that, thanks to Chatham and the Seven Years' War, Britain had suddenly become an imperial power before she was fully prepared to grasp the responsibilities that that position entailed.

Freed from the French military threat on their northern and western boundaries, the Thirteen Colonies, now containing a population of three million and filled with the same eighteenth-century spirit of enterprise that inspired their cousins in Britain, were obviously not going to rest content with their older status of small and negligible dependencies of the British Crown, but were going to insist on a large share of power in determining their own destinies. Nor did the British on the whole much wish to hamper them in doing so—they were occupied with their own problems. Even Johnson, whose *Taxation No Tyranny* (1775) was one of the most anti-American statements of the time (even the North government insisted that it be softened from its original form), is not really reluctant to "whistle them down the wind," as he misquotes *Othello*. What did bother him, of course, and what bothered Grenville, was the inability of the British taxpayer to recover from the Americans at least some of the very large sums of money expended in freeing the American colonists from the French threat and enabling them to expand westward. That, and the appalling amount of cant found in American patriotic publicity of the time, as in patriotic publicity of most times: "Why is it that we hear the loudest yelps for 'liberty' from the drivers of Negroes?" Johnson shrewdly asks, glancing at men like Patrick Henry and Thomas Jefferson.

What strikes the modern student about the events leading up to the Declaration of Independence in 1776 is the lack of any conscious design by the British to oppress the colonists. Things were allowed to drift through sheer inertia and lack of thought or planning. It was characteristic that the Secretary of State for the Colonies in 1775 should have been the most notoriously inept soldier and politician of the century, Lord George Germain, who in 1760 had been declared by court martial unfit to serve in the British army in any capacity. A century later, after Britain had had more experience in the role of an imperial power, ministers and civil servants might have been found who would have been able to handle such a situation sensibly and tactfully, as, in fact, the relations of Britain with Canada, when that country developed to the stage the Thirteen Colonies had reached in 1776, were handled. As it was, the separation took place in a way that left the utmost resentment on both sides, to the detriment of the future course of history.

The breaking away of the Thirteen Colonies did not result at the time in any great damage to British power. On the contrary, by providing some useful lessons in naval and military administration, and a healthful shock to its complacency, it probably strengthened Britain in the great struggle that was to come with Revolutionary France and Napoleon. The failure of British arms to subdue the colonists at last caused North to resign; he had long wanted to do so, but the King, fearful of what might happen if he lost him, persuaded him to continue. By this time, three fairly distinguishable parties of Whigs were emerging: those led by North, those led by the intellectual Earl of Shelburne, Chatham's political heir (though the younger Pitt was soon to supersede him), and those led by Charles James Fox, supported by Burke. The Tory independents, who had given somewhat reluctant support to North, deserted him when it became apparent that his policy in America had failed. When he resigned, Rockingham succeeded for a few months in keeping Shelburne and Fox together in the one ministry; but on his sudden death in 1783, the hostility between the two erupted, and Fox went into opposition, leaving Shelburne to act as Prime Minister and conclude the peace with the new United States. Shelburne, with young Pitt as his Chancellor of the Exchequer, was presently ousted when Fox and North, who had long been deadly enemies, announced that they had formed a coalition to take over the government.

The general disgust at this seeming cynicism enhanced the position of Shelburne and Pitt. This was reinforced by the introduction of Fox's India Bill, which would have placed the supreme control of the great subcontinent irrevocably in the hands of a few of his and North's supporters. In spite of the great majority which Fox and North together commanded in the House of Commons, George boldly dismissed them and appointed Pitt, then aged twenty-four, his Prime Minister. Fox and the rest angrily denounced this action as a flouting of the "popular will." But when a general election was held in 1784, Fox's supporters were disastrously defeated, and it was seen that the King had, in fact, been perfectly expressing the popular will by his appointment of Pitt, who remained in office, with a short break, for another twenty years. Pitt, the disciple of his father and of Adam Smith, succeeded during his first decade in office in building up Britain's economic and military potential to the point where she was able to endure successfully the long struggle with Revolutionary and Napoleonic France and enter the nineteenth century as a more formidable power than she had ever been before.

NOTES TO CHAPTER TWO

1. The youthful charm of "Bonnie Prince Charlie" has often been made the subject of romance. But his opponent and the victor at Culloden, William, Duke of Cumberland, George II's younger son, was exactly the same age—twenty-five.

2. The term "prime minister" is convenient to use here, but strictly speaking it is anachronistic: it did not come into even unofficial use until the nineteenth century, and was not given official recognition until the twentieth. Before the reign of George I, the most powerful minister was usually the Lord Treasurer; Walpole and his successors were usually, but not always, First Lords of the Treasury (i.e., chairmen of the commissions appointed to execute the office of Lord Treasurer).

3. The student will find a good brief statement of the modern view of the political structure of the time in the first chapter of J. Steven Watson, *The Reign of King George III* (Oxford: The Clarendon Press, 1960), in the Oxford History of England series.

4. The story told by Horace Walpole that George and his mother, the Princess of Wales, were directly influenced by Bolingbroke's *The Patriot King* was discredited by Romney Sedgwick in his introduction to *Letters from George III to Lord Bute, 1756–1766* (London: Macmillan, 1939). The "nonpartisanship" advocated by Bolingbroke was an old cliché, part of the standard equipment of opposition orators. Before Burke defended it, the concept of political party was like sin—everyone was opposed to it in theory, though seldom in practice.

5. See Herbert Butterfield, *George III, Lord North, and the People* (London: G. Bell, 1949).

❧ Three

Ideas and Attitudes

1692   First Boyle Lectures in defense of Christianity delivered (by Richard Bentley; later lectures included Samuel Clarke's *Discourse Concerning the Being and Attributes of God,* 1704– 1705).

1695   *The Post Boy,* the first successful daily newspaper, founded.

1696   John Toland, *Christianity Not Mysterious;* an important early Deist statement.

1699   Richard Bentley, *A Dissertation upon the Epistles of Phalaris;* the crushing answer to the proponents of the Ancients.

Third Earl of Shaftesbury, *An Inquiry Concerning Virtue* (collected in *Characteristics,* 1711).

1702   Archbishop William King, *De Origine Mali;* tr. Edmund Law, later Bishop of Carlisle, as *An Essay on the Origin of Evil,* 1731, with a "Preliminary Discourse" by Rev. John Gay, adumbrating Utilitarian views.

Edward Hyde, Earl of Clarendon, *A History of the Rebellion and Civil Wars in England.*

1704   Sir Isaac Newton, *Opticks;* the physics of light.

Jonathan Swift, *A Tale of a Tub* and *The Battle of the Books* (written about 1697).

1705   Bernard Mandeville, *The Grumbling Hive;* expanded as *The Fable of the Bees,* 1714.

George Hickes, *Linguarum Veterum Septentrionalium Thesaurus;* pioneering investigation of old Germanic literature and antiquities.

1710   George Berkeley, later Bishop of Cloyne, *A Treatise concerning the Principles of Human Knowledge.*

1717   Benjamin Hoadly, Bishop of Bangor, *The Nature of the Kingdom or Church of Christ* (a sermon; its alleged Erastianism precipitated the Bangorian Controversy).

1718   Lady Mary Wortley Montagu introduces inoculation for smallpox from Turkey.

1724   Bishop Gilbert Burnet, *A History of My Own Time* (to 1734); the standard Whig view of the reigns of Charles II, James II, and the Revolution.

1725   Francis Hutcheson, *An Inquiry into the Original of our Ideas of Beauty and Virtue;* an important statement of "benevolist" or "moral sense" ethical theory.

1726   Jonathan Swift, *Gulliver's Travels.*

1728   Alexander Pope, *The Dunciad* (later, much expanded and revised versions in 1729, 1742, 1743).

William Law, *A Serious Call to a Devout and Holy Life.*

1731   *The Gentleman's Magazine,* the first magazine, founded.

1733   Pope, *An Essay on Man.*

1736   Bishop Joseph Butler, *The Analogy of Religion, Natural and Revealed, to the Constitution and Course of Nature;* regarded as the definitive answer to Deism.

   Bishop William Warburton, *The Alliance Between Church and State: or the Necessity and Equity of an Established Religion.*

   The obsolete laws against witchcraft repealed.

1739   David Hume, *A Treatise of Human Nature.*

1748   Hume, *Philosophical Essays* (including "Of Miracles").

1749   Lord Bolingbroke, *On the Idea of a Patriot King.*

   David Hartley, *Observations on Man.*

1750   Montesquieu, *The Spirit of the Laws,* tr. Thomas Nugent.

1750's   Benjamin Franklin's experiments with electricity reported in *Philosophical Transactions* of the Royal Society.

1752   Jean Jacques Rousseau, *A Discourse on the Question of Whether the Revival of the Arts and Sciences Has Contributed to Purify Our Morals,* tr. R. Wynne.

1754   Hume, *A History of Great Britain* (later retitled *A History of England*); to 1762.

1757   Soame Jenyns, *A Free Enquiry into the Nature and Origin of Evil.*

1759   Voltaire, *Candid: or, All for the Best* (and several other translations of *Candide*).

   Samuel Johnson, *The Prince of Abissinia* [*Rasselas*].

1763   Thomas Reid, *An Inquiry into the Human Mind on the Principles of Common Sense;* earliest of the Scottish "Common-Sense" school of philosophy, opposed to Hume.

1765   Sir William Blackstone, *Commentaries on the Laws of England* (to 1768); his lectures as Vinerian professor of law at Oxford; for a century or more the standard introductory textbook of English law.

1766   Henry Cavendish discovers the element hydrogen.

1770   Edmund Burke, *Thoughts on the Present Discontents;* beginning of the Whig interpretation of eighteenth-century British political history.

1772   Lord Mansfield, Lord Chief Justice, rules, in the case of Somerset, a Negro slave brought from Jamaica, that slavery can not exist on English soil.

1774   Joseph Priestley isolates oxygen.

1776   Adam Smith, *The Wealth of Nations.*

Edward Gibbon, *The Decline and Fall of the Roman Empire* (to 1788).

Jeremy Bentham, *A Fragment on Government;* a severe attack on Blackstone, adumbrating the Utilitarianism of the next century.

1781   Sir William Herschel, later Astronomer Royal, discovers the planet Uranus.

1787   Society for the Suppression of the Slave Trade founded by William Wilberforce and Thomas Clarkson.

1790   Edmund Burke, *Reflections on the Revolution in France.*

1791   Thomas Paine, *The Rights of Man;* the famous answer to Burke.

1794   Archdeacon William Paley, *A View of the Evidences of Christianity,* propounding the "argument from design"; for decades the standard textbook of Christian apologetics in English schools.

Mary Wollstonecraft, *A Vindication of the Rights of Woman.*

1796   Edward Jenner practices vaccination.

1798   Rev. Thomas Malthus, *An Essay on Population.*

Introductory

The history of ideas is one of the youngest intellectual disciplines—only some three or four decades old, at least under that name—and is very far from being an exact science. Since the ideas current in any period are bewilderingly numerous and diverse, and since statistical methods for determining their incidence are not known and indeed hardly seem possible,[1] it is a fertile field for unsubstantiated guesswork and ingenious speculation. Many of the accepted notions about the intellectual climate of eighteenth-century Britain seem to stem from the early textbooks of English literary history, full of hastily conceived postulates and generalizations, brought out in the mid-nineteenth century. That such textbooks began to be produced and disseminated on a wide scale in the midst of the nineteenth century's hostile reaction to the art and manners of its predecessor was particularly unfortunate for the eighteenth century. Although scholars and critics of the mid-twentieth century pride themselves on having attained to a fresh appreciation of the time, it is disheartening to see how many modern studies still content themselves with uncritically rehearsing terms and phrases that can be traced back through a succession of literary histories to the inspiration of some obscure pioneer textbook writer of the 1850's or 1860's.

To begin with the most popular of these phrases: it must strike any student who reads the important literary documents of eighteenth-century Britain with clear eyes that it was *not* an "age of reason." Quite the contrary: reason, as signifying the power of the human mind, without external aid, to arrive at valuable knowledge, was seldom if ever in such disrepute. "Dim as the borrowed beams of moon and stars," Dryden begins his confession of faith, *Religio Laici,* "is Reason to the soul." "Reason, an *Ignis fatuus* of the mind," sneers the skeptic Rochester. "So very *reasonable,* so unmoved / As never yet to love or to be loved," Pope condemns the cold-hearted Chloe. "Reason is, and ought always to be, the slave of the passions [i.e., emotions]," writes Hume, summing up the whole tendency of the great British school of empiricism which dominated the philosophy of the century.

If the phrase means that, in fact, the average Englishman behaved, or tried to behave, more reasonably than his counterpart in other centuries, the history of the time, from the panic over the Popish Plot in 1678, through the South Sea mania in 1720, to the Gordon Riots in 1780—and much else in between—will give it the lie. As for the evidence of biography, few of the great figures of the time seem to have been models of emotional decorum and restraint: certainly not Swift, Pope, and Johnson; certainly not such politicians as Bolingbroke and the elder Pitt (whose performances in Parliament were masterpieces of melodrama); nor even such notable members of the traditionally stiff-lipped military profession as the volatile Lord Peterborough and the fervent, uninhibited Nelson. Perhaps the only literary figures whose writings come readily to the mind as exemplifying balance and judiciousness are such minor ones as John Evelyn and Lord Chesterfield. And even Evelyn had his infatuation with Mrs. Godolphin, and the deep neurosis that informs Chesterfield's obsession about the manners of his illegitimate son is readily apparent.[2]

Nor are other phrases that have been coined, or entities that have been postulated, to characterize eighteenth-century Britain more satisfying. There is "neoclassicism"—did writers and thinkers of the time really hold the Latin and Greek classics in greater awe or feel a greater obligation to use them as models for their own works and ideas than did Englishmen of earlier or even later centuries? It is true that a knowledge of the classics and a respect for them were among the hallmarks of any Englishman with pretensions to being educated from the Renaissance down to the beginning of the twentieth century. Yet it would be very hard to show that Dryden, Swift, Pope, and Johnson were more under the spell of the classic writers or that their own writings were more indebted to their example than, say, Spenser and Milton before their time, or Shelley and Tennyson after it. Is there really anything that resembles *Absalom and Achitophel* or *The Dunciad* or *Gulliver's Travels* or *The Lives of the Poets* in Latin and Greek literature? (Pope's and Johnson's "imitations" of Horace and Juvenal could no more be mistaken for Horace and Juvenal than Brahms's *Variations on a Theme by Handel* could be mistaken for Handel.) Like all great artists, Dryden and Swift and Pope did not think of themselves as "neo-" anything: they were attempting to do something new, something that had not been done before; and it is Johnson (whose own ways of writing and thinking are utterly unlike anything that had ever been done before or was to be done afterward) who most loudly applauds their originality, their invention, as an indispensable element of their genius.

"Augustanism," insofar as one can detect any meaning at all in this maddeningly opaque term, seems to imply that the writers of the time thought they were in the same towering class as Virgil, Horace, and Ovid were by comparison with lesser Roman writers of other times. The great admiration of Pope, Dryden, and Johnson for Shakespeare, Spenser, and Milton seems to rebut any such proposition. If it is meant to imply a complacent assumption that they lived in an imperial age, fit to give norms of behavior and thought to other times, the scathing indictments of their own age found in *The Secular Masque, The Dunciad* and Pope's later satires generally, and continually in Swift and Johnson, make it sound more like the age of Domitian than that of Augustus.

The term "the Enlightenment" (*die Aufklärung*), which is

often applied to the intellectual climate of the Continent, especially in the middle and late eighteenth century, seems at first glance to have more to commend it: certainly Pope, Swift, Johnson, and the rest were no friends of intellectual obscurantism. But the primary reference of the term is to the deism and atheism of the *philosophes,* Voltaire, Diderot, D'Alembert, and others: the enlightenment is above all the enlightenment of men's minds from the superstitions of institutional Christianity. It would be a radical mistake to think that Dryden, Swift, Johnson, and the vast majority of the eminent writers of eighteenth-century England, who were sincere and convinced Christians, held this fundamental point in common with their French contemporaries.

"Humanism," a term which has recently attained some popularity in eighteenth-century English studies, is open to a similar objection: if used in a narrow sense, it can mean the stridently antireligious posture of a Swinburne ("Glory to Man in the highest; for Man is the measure of things!") or the Renaissance veneration of (pagan) classicism, attitudes which were alien to Dryden, Pope, Swift, and Johnson.[3] And if the term is broadened so as to mean merely a profound concern for the human condition, there are few great writers, from Aeschylus up through Dante, Chaucer, Shakespeare, and Milton to T. S. Eliot and James Joyce to whom it would not be equally applicable.

The Augustinian Ethic

If we abandon the attempt to find a single neat word or phrase with which to delimit the immense intellectual diversity of eighteenth-century British thought, we can nevertheless easily discover certain important constellations of ideas and attitudes that were undeniably widespread and influential among educated men of the time. One of these, at least, is extremely obvious. As a distinguished historian of ideas has commented,

> However one defines the Age of Reason, however revolutionary and anti-authoritarian one estimates its spirit to have been, it should be noted that neither the Roman Catholic nor the Anglican nor the Lutheran communions ceased their ministrations in 1750. More-

over, in England, men like Burke and Johnson and Goldsmith, as much earlier Pope and Addison, continued to believe in the religion and philosophy of their forefathers.[4]

To this list of English writers of the time who professed orthodox Christian belief (and often used Christian teachings as the material of their writings) could be added Dryden, Defoe, Steele, Young, Smart, Richardson, Fielding, Sterne, Cowper, Crabbe, and a host of others—most strikingly, perhaps, the Very Reverend Jonathan Swift, Doctor of Sacred Theology, priest and dean in the Church of Ireland, whose tombstone, by his own direction, terms him *"strenuum pro virili libertatis vindicatorem"*—"one who defended freedom with all his might." The two greatest British scientists of the age, Newton and Boyle, were devout Christians, as were two of its three greatest philosophers, Locke and Bishop Berkeley.

By comparison, the list of important British writers who unequivocally rejected orthodox Christian doctrine is a small one. Hume and Gibbon are the two who most readily come to mind. Prior, Gray, and Horace Walpole evince some skepticism, but keep rather quieter about it. (Gray presumably subscribed the Thirty-Nine Articles of the Church of England in order to pursue his career at Cambridge.) Then there is a nebulous border region inhabited by the Deists, notably Shaftesbury and Bolingbroke, who profess admiration for the Christian ethic while rejecting its theology, and by Blake, who invented his own theological terminology to expound an ethic not very different from that of the Gospel.

But it is evident, as one makes one's way through the writings of the standard authors of Enlightened England, that their view of man and his place in the universe and his destiny is essentially that of such earlier Christian writers as Spenser and Milton, Donne and Herbert, rather than that of Voltaire and Diderot. They are still writing for an audience thoroughly indoctrinated, from childhood onward, with the King James Bible, the Book of Common Prayer, the Articles, Creeds, and Catechism (and *The Whole Duty of Man* and, later, *The Pilgrim's Progress*)—as, of course, the great majority of educated Englishmen and Americans were until at least the late nineteenth century—and they, the writers, are equally well acquainted with them and accept their teachings whole-heartedly. Any attempt to explicate the intellectual history of the time, or to analyze the thinking of most of its influential writers, which does not take this fact into account is bound to be distorted and misleading.

To the contemporary readers of Pope, Swift, Johnson, and Fielding, intimately familiar with the Book of Common Prayer, it would have seemed a superfluous undertaking to try to expound the elements of the "anthropology," psychology, and ethics found in that document; but since twentieth-century students can no longer be assumed to have such familiarity, an attempt must be made to present them here. To distinguish the fundamental point of view of sixteenth- to eighteenth-century Anglicanism (and Protestant Nonconformity) from variant ones found at other times and in other communions, it may conveniently be termed that of "Augustinianism"—that which Augustine of Hippo (following on St. Paul) was the first to expound forcibly. The following account, from a very reputable modern handbook, is a reliable and useful one:

Augustinianism denotes the interpretation of Christian faith, especially with regard to the doctrine of sin and redemption, which has its origin in the teaching of Augustine. . . . In essence, Augustinianism affirms strongly the fact of original sin—that is, the state in which man finds himself because of the Fall of Adam. In Adam . . . the manhood which we all share is thought to have lost its relationship of communion and fellowship with God. The resultant alienation is passed on to all his descendants, whose situation is thus one of deprivation of the grace of God, and, in consequence, one of chaotic disordering of the will. To be alienated from God results in the human tendency toward self-assertion in contradiction to the will and plan of God. Man is therefore helpless to "save" himself, since his will is perverted at the very root.

In Christ, seen as the embodiment of Divine Charity, God acts to give his "fallen" creatures a new beginning. This is accomplished by Christ as the new and perfect Man in whom God establishes the principle of grace. To this we can only respond in faith, by the surrender of our wills to his. . . . Once man has been caught up into this new relationship, his will is freed. No longer possessed by original sin, he is in the state of grace. The drive to evil which yet abides in him is conquered only by God's active love. . . .[5]

The question of predestination—of election and reprobation
—is, of course, also closely bound up in strict Augustinian
teaching with the matter of original sin and grace. Illogical as it
has seemed to thoroughgoing Protestants of the Calvinist tradition, there has been a tendency in the Church of England from
the very beginning to pass over it lightly. This has been done on
the authority of the somewhat vaguely worded Article XVII,
and it is not a question with which English Christian literary
figures of the eighteenth century (with the notable exceptions of
Defoe and Cowper) have greatly concerned themselves.

Augustinianism, in the Anglican communion, centers then on
the affirmation of man's inherent moral weakness, which he is
unable to rectify merely through his own unaided efforts—
which, indeed, he will never be able to eliminate completely, for
he is destined always to be a sinner and to deserve God's just
punishment. That punishment cannot be averted by the performance of stipulated good works; indeed, works performed by
the unrepentant sinner with a view to assuaging God's wrath
have, Article XIII affirms, rather "the nature of sin." [6] It can be
averted only by the full emotional acceptance of the fact
of one's own imperfection and of God's merciful and forgiving
love, freely offered to the sinner. If this change of heart takes
place, good works—and moral virtue—will automatically follow. But so long as he remains stubbornly attached to his pride
in his own individual superiority as a human being, that change
cannot take place; true humility is required. The most memorable exposition of the doctrine is the great parable of the
"pious" Pharisee, who prayed, "God, I thank thee that I am not
as other men are, extortioners, unjust, adulterers," and the
humble publican who "would not lift up so much as his eyes
unto heaven, but smote his breast, saying 'God be merciful to
me, a sinner.'" "I tell you," Jesus continues, "this man went
down to his house justified rather than the other: for everyone
that exalteth himself shall be abased, and he that humbleth
himself shall be exalted."

Only if the exaltation of the self—pride, the original sin in
the Garden—is diminished, can the individual fulfill the Great
Commandment, "Thou shalt love the Lord thy God . . . and
thy neighbor as thyself." For pride, self-centeredness, inhibits

love.[7] And the disguises of pride are multitudinous, concealing it from its victim in subtle and ingenious ways. Nothing would be easier for the publican, by contemplating his own "humility" approvingly and carrying it on self-consciously (like Uriah Heep), than to transform himself into a Pharisee in a minute fraction of a second. There is never any guarantee that outward behavior, however seemingly commendable, is not the product of Pharisaic motivation; only if the inward workings of the heart were known could we tell.

Hence the examination of motives, searching introspection, the need to stifle any hint of self-complacency we find in ourselves are the continual subjects, of exhortation by the Book of Common Prayer, the two books of Homilies, the sermons and other writings of the Anglican divines of the sixteenth and seventeenth centuries—and the staple of a great deal of the imaginative literature of the eighteenth century, from Defoe and Addison, through Fielding, Richardson, and Sterne, to Johnson and Cowper.[8] "Rend your heart, and not your garments," beseeches one of the introductory scriptural sentences read at the beginning of the Order for Morning and Evening Prayer. Others are: "The sacrifices of God are a broken spirit: a broken and a contrite heart, O God, thou wilt not despise"; "If we say that we have no sin, we deceive ourselves, and the truth is not in us"; "I will arise and go to my father, and will say unto him, Father, I have sinned against heaven, and before thee, and am no more worthy to be called thy son."

The services of Morning and Evening Prayer begin with the great General Confession, recited by the priest and the whole congregation: "Almighty and most merciful Father, we have erred and strayed from thy ways like lost sheep. . . . We have left undone those things which we ought to have done, and we have done those things which we ought not to have done, and there is no health in us; But Thou, O Lord, have mercy upon us miserable offenders." The Collects are insistent on our sinfulness and impotence: "Through our sins and wickedness, we are sore let and hindered"; "Almighty and everlasting God, mercifully look upon our infirmities"; "By reason of the frailty of our nature we cannot always stand upright"; "We put not our trust in anything that we do"; "Create and make in us new and contrite hearts, that we, worthily lamenting our sins, and acknowl-

edging our wretchedness, may obtain . . . forgiveness"; "Grant
. . . by continual mortifying our corrupt affections, we may be
[saved]."

The Litany, the General Confession of the Communion Service, the Homilies appointed to be read in Anglican churches—

> The Holy Ghost, in writing the Holy Scripture, is in nothing more
> diligent than to pull down man's vainglory and pride, which of all
> vices is most universally grafted in all mankind, even from the first
> infection of our first father Adam. And therefore we read in many
> places of scripture many notable lessons against this old rooted
> vice, to teach us the most commendable virtue of humility, how to
> know ourselves and to remember what we be of ourselves. . . . Let
> us all confess with mouth and heart, that we be full of imperfections; let us know our own works, of what imperfection they be,
> and then we shall not stand foolishly and arrogantly in our own
> conceits, nor challenge any part of justification by our merits or
> works[9]

—have much to say to the same purpose. It is hard to see how,
except by an act of conscious rejection (such as we have no reason to suppose that Swift or Johnson or most of their contemporaries among English writers ever made), anyone exposed to
such doctrine week after week from earliest childhood, as the
vast majority of the population of England were throughout the
eighteenth century, could with conviction maintain either the
Stoic view that human nature in itself provides a *datum* for
morality, or the Pelagian one that man has some inherent good
in himself and can, simply by industrious effort, lift himself by
his moral bootstraps.

The great English moral writers of the sixteenth and seventeenth centuries set forth the same doctrine uncompromisingly:
Spenser—

> If any strength we have, it is to ill,
> But all the good is God's, both power and eke will;

Donne—

> I am a little world made cunningly
> Of elements, and an angelic sprite;
> But black sin hath betrayed to endless night
> My world's both parts, and, oh, both parts must die.

and

> Reason, your viceroy in me, me should defend,
> But is captived and proves weak or untrue;

other influential divines like Bishop Lancelot Andrewes—

> Both heathen and holy writers do commend to us that saying
> Γνῶθι σεαυτον ["Know thyself"] but in a diverse sense. The heathen
> use it as a means to puff up our nature, that in regard of the ex-
> cellency which God vouchsafed us above other creatures we should
> be proud thereof; but Christian religion laboreth by the knowledge
> of ourselves "to cast down every high thing that exalteth itself
> against the knowledge of God" . . . *Hoc piarum mentum est, ut
> nihil sibi tribuant* ["Augustine"— marginal note], "This is the part
> of godly souls, that they attribute nothing to themselves" [10]—

the Reverend Henry Hammond, chaplain to King Charles I,
uncle and tutor to Swift's mentor, Sir William Temple—

> I, not I alone, abstracted from Christ, nor I principally, and Christ
> only *in subsidiis* . . . which deceitful considerations drew on Pela-
> gius himself . . . but I, absolutely impotent in myself to any su-
> pernatural duty, being then rapt above myself, strengthened by
> Christ's perpetual influence, having all my strength and ability from
> him, am then by that strength able to do all things myself [11]—

the fluent and popular Robert South—

> [Fallen man] is, as it were, a new kind of species; the plague of man
> has even altered his nature, and eaten into his very essential. The
> passions rebel . . . the light within us is become darkness; and the
> understanding, that should be eyes to the blind faculty of the will,
> is blind itself. . . . So great is the change, so deplorable the deg-
> radation of our nature, that whereas before we bore the image of
> God, we now retain only the image of man[12]—

the saintly Bishop Thomas Wilson, educated at Trinity College,
Dublin, a few years before Swift—

> All these pretend to reason; and indeed God has given all men rea-
> son. But lusts and passions will corrupt and blind our reason.
> . . . You see, Christians, what we are by nature, what men are capa-
> ble of, what they *would* be, when God leaves them to themselves,
> and to their natural corruption. . . . No man can change, can
> mend a corrupt nature, by a reason and will that are both corrupt.[13]

This is the tradition in which Swift and Johnson (and their readers) were raised, and which they continue in their writings.

To the average secularly educated Western man of the late nineteenth and early twentieth centuries, the doctrines of original sin and the depravity of man became little more than curiosities, on the whole repulsive, from the dead past. The writings of Swift, Johnson, Pope (at least, the later, more mature Pope, who "stooped to truth, and moralized his song"), Cowper, and others, in which these doctrines are taken for granted, have therefore appeared to such students to be full of pessimism and misanthropy. The presence of these traits has been generally accounted for by biographical considerations—the writers were the victims of various interesting neuroses, and much use has been made of Freudian terminology to explain them.

But in fact such explanations are as much beside the point as they would be when dealing with the writings of Spenser, Milton, Donne, and Herbert. If pessimism means, as one supposes it does, despair for the possibility of human salvation, the word can be applied to the teachings of neither Donne nor Swift. Both of them well know, and allow the careful reader of their works to know, that the means of salvation are within the reach of the individual—the abasement of human pride and the cultivation of the capacity for love; difficult, no doubt, for the average human individual, but not impossible. If misanthropy means a hatred of human beings and a desire to see them suffer, the term is equally impossible of application. What the individual must do, however, is to strip himself of all illusory self-congratulation on his own high moral status. He must look with clear eyes at the cruelty and devastation which history has testified that his sinful pride has inflicted (and continues to inflict) on himself and his fellows, to turn in revulsion from it, examine his own failings which have made those horrors possible, and endeavor to correct them.

The Dunciad, Gulliver's Travels, The Vanity of Human Wishes, Robinson Crusoe, Tom Jones, Tristram Shandy, The Vicar of Wakefield, Night Thoughts, Jubilate Agno, The Task, Songs of Experience offer little support to the individual who has to sustain his ego by cultivating complacency and self-satisfaction in the thought of the superiority of the human race over the rest of creation (or of the individual over his fellows). They do so because their authors, like Augustine and Spenser and Donne before them, believe that it is precisely such complacency that is responsible for man's self-created miseries and that gets in the way of the attainment of genuine human happiness —that happiness which, as Johnson puts it in the conspicuously *un*pessimistic last line of *The Vanity of Human Wishes,* can be "made" (though not "found"), through the cultivation of mental health, hope, patience, and, above all, love.

Empiricism

Equally potent and widespread an influence on English thinking in the eighteenth century was the "new science" of the Royal Society, and the philosophical tradition underlying it— the great British empiricist tradition. First proclaimed by Francis Bacon, developed by Locke, Berkeley, Hume, and John Stuart Mill, this tradition continues to flourish in the work of Bertrand Russell, Gilbert Ryle, A. J. Ayer, and others in the twentieth century. Except for a brief eclipse by Hegelianism in the later nineteenth century, it has dominated British philosophical investigation for three and a half centuries. And never was this more true than in the eighteenth century, when Locke reigned virtually unchallenged, except by his successors, Berkeley and Hume, who felt that he had not gone far enough in an empiricist direction. British philosophy of the time sharply dissociated itself from contemporary Continental philosophy, where the theorizing of Descartes, Spinoza, and Leibniz, organized in "logical" fashion like that of Euclid and Aquinas, still gave testimony to their confidence in the power of the human mind, unassisted by observation, to juggle words so as to add to our stores of knowledge. It is their age, that of seventeenth-century Continental philosophy, which is properly characterized by the title given to a collection of their writings in a popular series, "The Age of Reason."

Empiricism—the word derives from Greek 'ἔμπειρος, "learned by experience"—is the converse of "rationalism": it insists that the prime, perhaps only, source of genuine knowledge is the individual's experience, gained through the senses, of the world outside himself.[14] It disputes the ability of human reason to attain knowledge through its own isolated activity unaided by such experience; in particular it disputes the effectiveness of "logic," of the great syllogistic system of discourse developed by Aristotle and the scholastics, to furnish useful knowledge.[15] As a corollary, it is "nominalist" in its attitude toward language: words have no magic qualities in themselves—the mere fact that a word is in use does not guarantee, as Plato seemed to think, that there must be, somewhere or other, a reality that it stands for—but are merely meaningless marks and noises, which acquire significance only as men arbitrarily associate sense data with them. Four aphorisms of Bacon's *Novum Organum*— the "new instrument" for attaining knowledge, superseding Aristotle's treatises on logic, the "Organon"—sum all this up:

I. Man, being the servant and interpreter of Nature, can do and understand so much and so much only as he has observed in fact or in thought of the course of nature: beyond this he neither knows anything nor can do anything.

IX. The cause and root of nearly all evils in the sciences is this— that while we falsely admire and extol the powers of the human mind we neglect to seek for its true helps.

XII. The logic now in use serves rather to fix and give stability to the errors which have their foundation in commonly received notions than to help the search after truth. So it does more harm than good.

XIV. The syllogism consists of propositions, propositions consist of words, words are symbols of notions. Therefore if the notions themselves (which is the root of the matter) are confused and over-hastily abstracted from the facts, there can be no firmness in the superstructure. . . .

"Experience," then, not "reason," [16] is the key word of the controlling philosophy of the intellectual life of eighteenth-century Britain. Perhaps never in history have the formal teachings of philosophers been more quickly and widely disseminated among their compatriots as those of Bacon in the seventeenth century and those of Locke in the eighteenth.[17] It is easy, of course, to see why the exaltation of experience should have struck a responding chord in the bosoms of the inhabitants of expanding, exuberant, energetic post-Renaissance England. The most notable outcome (or at least concomitant) of the Baconian philosophy was, of course, the institution of the Royal Society of London for Improving Natural Knowledge, chartered in 1662 by Charles II, and still one of the world's great scientific bodies. The spirit of Bacon and the Royal Society has been condemned (generally by nineteenth-century Romantics and ultramontanists) as materialistic, as wanting to place complete reliance for the attainment of human happiness on the satisfaction of man's material wants. No doubt some scientists, then as now, held such a creed (as have many nonscientists, including such churchmen as Dostoevsky's Grand Inquisitor). Yet if one reads the writings of Bacon and his admirers—Bishop Thomas Sprat and the Reverend Joseph Glanvill, for instance—it is hard not to conclude that they were much concerned with the alleviation of man's moral and psychological ills. These they attributed to his sinful pride in his own mental powers and absorption in his own self-constructed conceits, the remedy being the empiricist recommendation of scholarly humility and a willingness to make contact with experience outside oneself. The unhealthy mental and emotional life of the rationalist is scathingly described by Bacon:

> This kind of degenerate learning did chiefly reign amongst the schoolmen; who having sharp and strong wits, and abundance of leisure, and small variety of reading; but their wits being shut up in the cells of a few authors (chiefly Aristotle their dictator) as their persons were shut up in the cells of monasteries and colleges; and knowing little history, either of nature or time; did out of no great quantity of matter, and infinite agitation of wit, spin out unto us those laborious webs of learning which are extant in their books. For the wit and mind of man, if it work upon matter, which is the contemplation of the creatures of God, worketh according to the stuff, and is limited thereby; but if it work upon itself, as the spider worketh his web, then it is endless, and brings forth indeed cobwebs of learning, admirable for the fineness of thread and work, but of no substance or profit.

And, again, elaborating on the image,

> The men of experiment [i.e., "empirics" in the pejorative sense, aimless collectors of desultory facts] are like the ant: they only col-

lect and use; the reasoners resemble spiders, who make cobwebs out of their own substance. But the bee [the empirical scientist as Bacon conceives him] takes a middle course: it gathers its materials from the flowers of the garden and of the field, but transforms and digests them by a power of its own.[18]

Swift was later to take over these images in a famous passage in *The Battle of the Books* (1697; published 1704). True, it is the Moderns whom he charges with the spider's arrogant rationalism and the Ancients to whom he attributes the bee's humble empiricism,[19] as if to point out, what is true and very important, that the age you live in and the labels you affix to yourself are no guarantee of your mental and moral soundness. Nevertheless, it is Bacon's empiricism he is championing here against the spirit of rationalism (in the actual battle, Bacon escapes the general slaughter of the Moderns: Aristotle shoots an arrow at "the valiant Modern," but it misses him):

Erect your schemes [says Aesop, the moderator, to the spider] with as much method and skill as you please; yet if the materials be nothing but dirt, spun out of your own entrails (the guts of modern brains) the edifice will conclude at last in a cobweb. . . . For anything else of genuine that the Moderns may pretend to, I cannot recollect; unless it be a large vein of wrangling and satire, much of a nature and substance with the spider's poison; . . . As for us the Ancients, we are content, with the bee, to pretend to nothing of our own, beyond our wings and our voice, that is to say, our flights and our language. For the rest, whatever we have got, has been by infinite labour and search, and ranging through every corner of nature; the difference is, that, instead of dirt and poison, we have rather chosen to fill our hives with honey and wax, thus furnishing mankind with the two noblest of things, which are sweetness [of the spirit] and light [of the intellect].

That the new science of the seventeenth century and Christianity were entirely congenial, its contemporary English apologists were profoundly convinced. Even the titles of their books proclaimed this—for instance, *The Christian Virtuoso: Shewing that by Being Addicted to Experimental Philosophy, a Man Is Rather Assisted, than Indisposed, to Be a Good Christian* (1690), by the great Robert Boyle, "the Father of Chemistry," formulator of Boyle's Law, and founder of the Boyle Lectures in defense of Christianity. There were two especially popular lines of argument. One, the "argument from design"—that the deeper insight provided into the ingenuity with which Nature works must convince us more thoroughly of the existence of an omniscient God who planned it all—carries less weight than it used to, perhaps because of its glib use in later times by Archdeacon Paley, of "Paley's watch" fame.

But the other argument deserves being considered more seriously than modern students of intellectual history have tended to do. In its simplest terms, it is that the moral and psychological basis of the "new philosophy," as of Augustinian Christianity, is the derogation of the inherent powers of human nature, in particular human reason. By adopting an attitude of humility as to what man can accomplish without external aid—in morality, from God; in science, from God's creation—one can learn both to love and to know. If this proposition is true, there is no need to marvel at Addison, in a fine hymn, hailing the discoveries of the great Newton (himself a fervent Christian),

> The spacious firmament on high,
> And all the blue ethereal sky,
> And spangled heav'ns, a shining frame,
> Their great Original proclaim:

or at the devout Samuel Johnson choosing as the epigraph for his most labored work of morality, *The Rambler,* the great "skeptical" and "anti-authoritarian" motto of the Royal Society, *Nullius addictus in verba magistri jurare*—"Committed to swearing by the words of no master."

That there was any inherent antagonism between science and religion, the problem that so worried the nineteenth century, the Christian thinkers of the eighteenth century seem to have been unaware; and it may well be that this was because their religious thinking was maturer and full of deeper insight than that of, say, Tennyson or Arnold. It might even be argued that it was closer to that of Barth, Bultmann, or Reinhold Niebuhr in the twentieth century who, seeking to purify religion of anthropomorphic and socially conditioned concepts, find the extension of scientific knowledge no cause for concern as tending to undermine genuine religious belief.

The most explicit apologist of the new science was the Right Reverend Thomas Sprat, Bishop of Rochester, Doctor of Divinity and Fellow of the Royal Society—a combination of honorifics commoner then than now. His arguments are worth attending to as indicative of the official position in the seventeenth and eighteenth centuries. His *History of the Royal Society,* a manifesto rather than a history, since the Society was a mere infant in 1667 when he published the work, contains sections headed "Experiments not dangerous to the Christian religion," "Experiments will not destroy the doctrine of the Godhead," "Experiments not injurious to the worship of God," "Experiments not prejudicial to the doctrine of the Gospel," and much else.

Two sections are of particular interest. One is "Experiments useful for the cure of men's minds": "If we shall cast an eye on all the tempests which arise within our breasts," he remarks, in a passage of which Samuel Johnson and a modern psychotherapist would thoroughly approve,

> and consider the causes and remedies of all the violent desires, malicious envies, intemperate joys, and irregular griefs by which the lives of most men become miserable or guilty, we shall find that they are chiefly produced by idleness, and may be most naturally cured by diversion. Whatever art shall be able to busy the minds of men with a constant course of innocent works, or to fill them with as vigorous and pleasant images as those ill impressions by which they are deluded, it will certainly have a surer effect in the composing and purifying of their thoughts than all the rigid precepts of the Stoical, or the empty distinctions of the Peripatetic, moralists.

Or to put it in modern terms, contact with reality is the best psychotherapy. And in "Experiments not prejudicial to [religious] mortification," replying to the charge that the empirical attitude toward life will hinder what "concerns that which is necessary to a holy life, the mortifying of our earthly desires," Sprat explicitly draws the parallel suggested above, between the humility advocated by the empirical scientist and the humility advocated by Augustinian Christianity:

> I will affirm that it is improbable that even the hardest and most rigorous parts of mortification itself should be injured by these

studies more than others; seeing that many duties of which it is composed do bear some resemblance to the qualifications that are requisite in experimental philosophers. The spiritual repentance is a careful survey of our former errors and a resolution of amend-ment. The spiritual humility is an observation of our defects and a lowly sense of our own weakness. And the experimenter for his part must have some qualities that answer to these: he must judge aright of himself; he must misdoubt the best of his own thoughts; he must be sensible of his own ignorance, if ever he will attempt to purge and renew his reason: So that if that be true, which is commonly observed, that men are wont to prove such kinds of Christians as they were before; and conversion does not destroy, but only exalt our tempers; it may well be concluded that the doubtful, the scrupulous, the diligent observer of Nature is nearer to make a modest, a severe, a meek, an humble Christian, than the man of speculative science, who has better thoughts of himself and his own knowledge.[20]

Abraham Cowley, the most renowned poet of the time, rein-forces Sprat's teaching in his famous *Ode to the Royal Society* prefixed to Sprat's book, where he equates rationalism with the original sin of pride—

> Yet still, methinks, we fain would be
> Catching at the forbidden tree;
> We would be like the Deity
> When truth and falsehood, good and evil, we
> Without the senses' aid, within ourselves would see;

and praises Bacon's nominalism—

> From words, which are but pictures of the thought
> (Though we our thoughts from them perversely drew),
> To things, the mind's right object, he it [philosophy] brought.

To trace in detail the involved history of the development of British empiricist philosophy through Locke, Berkeley, Hume, and the rest is beyond the scope of this work. It is enough to notice that, whatever modifications and subtleties were intro-duced, the underlying assumptions remained the same—knowledge is acquired by observation, by sensory experience, of the world outside oneself; the human mind, unaided by such observation, is an impotent instrument, and the ingenious theories it is capable of weaving out of words in a vacuum are ludicrous and may be dangerous. " 'Words are the daughters of earth, and things are the sons of heaven.' Language is only the instrument of science and words are but the signs of ideas," [21] to quote a formulation of nominalism by that skilled student of words, Samuel Johnson.

Locke is not so thoroughgoing an empiricist as his successors, and is still influenced to some extent by the older rationalist view. His *An Essay Concerning Human Understanding* begins with the assertion, which Sprat and others would have found discouraging, that "it is the *understanding* that sets man above the rest of sensible beings, and gives him all the advantage and dominion which he has over them" and he talks of its "nobleness." Yet even he at once begins filing caveats: "the comprehension of our understandings comes exceeding short of the vast extent of things."

It is the great Bishop of Cloyne, however—it is worth while emphasizing Berkeley's position in the Church—who sharply corrects Locke's hankering after rationalism ("Is the human mind really capable of 'abstract ideas,' as Locke thinks? Can one really visualize an abstract 'triangle,' one that is neither equilateral, isosceles, or scalene?") and whose insistence on the supreme importance, epistemological and moral, of the vivid, direct perception of experience has so appealed to poets. "Look!" his Philonous cries to Hylas, who has been persuaded by Lockean arguments based on the metaphysical postulate of "substance" to doubt the evidence of his senses:

> Are not the fields covered with a delightful verdure? Is there not something in the woods and groves, in the rivers and clear springs, that soothes, that delights, that transports the soul? At the prospect of the wide and deep ocean, or some huge mountain whose top is lost in the clouds, or of an old gloomy forest, are not our minds filled with a pleasing horror? Even in rocks and deserts is there not an agreeable wildness? How sincere a pleasure is it to behold the natural beauties of the earth! [22]

Linked with this experientialist or existentialist epistemology is the remarkable pronouncement that Berkeley made in one of his (to be sure, very early) notebooks: "Sensual Pleasure is the Summum Bonum. This the Great Principle of Morality." [23] And of course, Berkeley maintains, he has devised his formulation of empiricism to support Christian belief: *A Treatise Concerning the Principles of Human Knowledge, wherein the chief causes of error and difficulty in the sciences, with the grounds of scepticism, atheism, and irreligion are inquired into* is the full title of his principal work. *Esse est percipi* ("To be is to be perceived") —existence, life, is experience; God is the creating and sustaining principle of life, the "ground of being":

> It is therefore plain that nothing can be more evident to anyone that is capable of the least reflection than the existence of God, or a Spirit who is intimately present to our minds, producing in them all the variety of ideas or sensations which continually affect us, on whom we have an absolute and entire dependence, in short "in whom we live, and move, and have our being."

When our minds erect a barrier of abstractions—words—between ourselves and experience—reality, God—we begin to introduce confusion and error into our intellectual and misery into our emotional lives.

It may be argued then that in the dominant religious teaching and the dominant philosophy of eighteenth-century Britain there are important common and mutually reinforcing elements which together form a kind of unformulated "ethic." A great many of the important writers of the time implicitly subscribed to this ethic; it underlies and makes intelligible their most important writings, from Bunyan's *The Pilgrim's Progress* to Goldsmith's *The Vicar of Wakefield* (and pushing ahead a little, to the novels of Jane Austen), and certainly including, say, Swift's *Gulliver's Travels* and *A Tale of a Tub,* Johnson's *Rasselas* and *The Vanity of Human Wishes,* and Sterne's *Tristram Shandy.* A crude formulation of some of its salient points might run as follows:

1. What is needed first of all is the willingness to abandon an irrationally exalted view of our own absolute importance—both as individuals and as a species—in the total scheme of things, and of our inherent capacity for moral and intellectual achievement without external aid; a willingness to see ourselves *sub specie aeternitatis* and to accept without resentment our built-in limitations. To do otherwise is tantamount to a complaint that

we are not God. The ideal would be the ability to forget completely the demands of that abstraction "the self," and to lose ourselves wholly in what is outside ourselves, in experience, in others. Being men, incurably burdened with the original sin of pride, we shall never succeed in attaining that ideal; yet we can always approach more closely to it.

2. We must perceive that, in view of our own imperfections and insignificance, concern for our *relative* status, pride in our superiority in some detail over some other creature, is pointless ("The Houyhnhnms . . . are no more proud of the good qualities they possess than I should be for not wanting a leg or an arm, which no man in his wits would boast of": the penultimate sentence of *Gulliver's Travels*). A spirit of competitiveness, of striving for "one-upness" among members of a uniformly imperfect creation, all infinitely below the perfection of its Creator, is thus ruled out as absurd to begin with—apart from the pragmatic reason that it is the cause of the self-inflicted human misery of which history recounts such a ghastly toll.

3. Rather than close our eyes and dwell on the internal fantasies created by our egos in their eternal striving for self-importance, we should develop our receptivity to the rich sources of delight and knowledge, moral as well as material, available through sensory experience. Such a heightened awareness is the prerequisite not only for obtaining the accurate information that enables us to make the best we can of our imperfect earthly existence in material terms, but for developing the capacity for genuine love of our fellow men.

4. We must beware of letting ourselves be taken in by words —by abstractions—which can so easily become vehicles of self-centered illusion, and must always be ready to check these noises, meaningless in themselves, against the concrete experience they are supposed to represent.

There is much more to this "constellation" of attitudes than this primitive sketch—though perhaps it would be unwise to try to reduce it to a more precise formulation—and of course it would be nonsensical to claim it as something peculiar to the English writers of the seventeenth and eighteenth centuries. It is possible to find this ethic implicit in Marlowe's *Faustus* and in Spenser, to take examples from the sixteenth century, and in the plays of Edward Albee and the novels of James Baldwin, to mention two very serious moralists of the twentieth century (who, like Swift, are condemned for the squalid and pessimistic view of humanity they present, as though any imaginative writer could equal in horror the historical reality of what human beings have inflicted on one another in the twentieth century, from Ypres and Verdun, through Belsen and Buchenwald, to Hiroshima and beyond). To provide examples from other literatures, one might name Rabelais (Swift's master) and Tolstoy. But it could perhaps be argued that the English climate of opinion of the eighteenth century was peculiarly favorable to such an ethic.

Deism, Stoicism, Laissez Faire

There were of course many deviant and heterodox positions besides this. Again it must be emphasized, however, that throughout the century these are distinctly minority views. Being minority ones, they naturally stirred up controversy, and so gained publicity for themselves, publicity which has inveigled later students into thinking that they were more widespread and influential than they seem to have been: one sometimes gets the impression from reading intellectual histories of the century that most of the English population were Deists or primitivists, and that there was hardly an orthodox Christian in the land. But on the evidence of the literature of the time, this is nonsense.

The heresy that made the greatest stir in the late seventeenth and early eighteenth centuries was Deism—the affirmation of the existence of a God (or, to use popular Deist expressions, a "Supreme Being" or an "Author of Nature"), while rejecting the need for revealed and institutional religion. Perhaps the best exposition of the Deist argument is given in Dryden's *Religio Laici;* indeed, Dryden states it so effectively that he is hard pressed to answer it in his poem, if it can be said that he answers it at all:

> No supernatural worship can be true:
> Because a general law is that alone
> Which must to all and everywhere be known:

A style so large as not this Book [the Bible] can claim, . . .
And what provision could from thence accrue
To Indian souls, and worlds discovered new?

It is understandable that in the seventeenth century, Europeans, becoming more vividly aware of the existence of millions of human beings in the center of Africa and South America, might well ask whether, unaware of the instruction provided by the Bible and the Church, their souls were therefore doomed to eternal damnation.

The Deist answer (first formulated, apparently, by Lord Herbert of Cherbury—George Herbert's brother—in his *De Veritate,* 1624) was that the ability to recognize the existence of God and to ascertain and obey his commandments must be innate in the human frame, whatever its environment; or, as Pope put it in *An Essay on Man,* 1733: "Lo, the poor Indian! whose untutor'd mind/ Sees God in clouds, or hears him in the wind." The inevitable question, "What need, in that case, for Scriptures, creeds, and a Church to expound them?" was carefully avoided by Herbert and Pope; but other bolder spirits ventured to hint at it—John Toland, in *Christianity Not Mysterious* (1696), Matthew Tindal in *Christianity as Old as Creation* (1730), Henry Dodwell in *Christianity Not Founded on Argument* (1742), and others.[24] Most of these writers, minor figures at best, received a rough reception at the hands of the orthodox, and certainly made few converts among the general public. They were the progenitors of later militant "freethinkers" like Tom Paine (whose *The Age of Reason,* 1793, implies that an age so burdened with religious superstition as the eighteenth century is anything but an age of reason—that is to come in the enlightened future) and Robert Ingersoll, objects of awe and curiosity rather than writers of much real influence.

A related controversy went on about miracles. The Anglican church rejected the modern "miracles" of countless Roman Catholic saints, but accepted those recorded in the Bible. Deists like Anthony Collins (*Discourse on Freethinking,* 1713) and Thomas Woolston (*Discourses,* 1729) gleefully accused the Anglicans of inconsistency; the Reverend Conyers Middleton, defending the Anglican position too lukewarmly, as it was thought, found himself suspected of heresy; but the last word was said by David Hume, whose devastating essay "Of Miracles" (1748) went deep into the fundamental epistemological question of why we should ever believe that any one thing is more likely to happen than any other at any time.

The Deist rejection of the need for revelation, or for formal instruction by a church, in order to know the ways and the will of God entailed (for those who retained the belief in the existence of a Supreme Being) the acceptance of "natural theology" —the doctrine that "Nature," or things as they are, can provide that knowledge. Among natural phenomena is human nature, which in its ideal, uncorrupted state, is assumed to be innately good and to possess the divine spark of reason, which is deemed innately capable of guiding man, by its own unaided power, to the true, the beautiful, and the good. This whole way of thinking derives from pagan Greek epistemology, psychology, and ethics, notably from Stoicism. As has often been pointed out (for instance, in A. O. Lovejoy's *The Great Chain of Being*), it implies a dualistic, rather than a monotheistic, theology. Nature, or the matter which constitutes it, becomes a God, equally powerful with the Supreme Being who is outside Nature; perhaps more powerful, since in some versions of natural law theory, it was maintained that God himself could not contravene the dictates of natural law. To the strictly orthodox, of course, all this was the most pernicious heresy, a denial of the First Commandment, "Thou shalt have no other Gods before me": Nature, including man's reason, was corrupted at the time of the Fall, and no moral norm can be taken from it. Nevertheless, because of the wide diffusion of Greek ideas in the Western world —Cicero, read in all schools as the best introduction to Latin prose, was a particularly fertile source of Stoic thought—it tended to infiltrate Christian thinking from Apostolic times onward.

The best known exponent of the Stoic view in the eighteenth century was Anthony Ashley Cooper, third Earl of Shaftesbury (grandson of Dryden's Achitophel, the first Earl, and ancestor of the seventh Earl, the noted humanitarian reformer and devout Evangelical of the nineteenth century). In his *Characteristics of Men, Manners, Opinions, Times* (1711), which brings together various earlier writings, Shaftesbury propounds, in windy, rhapsodical rhetoric, that Nature is a manifestation of a beneficent, if vague, Deity; that the contemplation of Nature is bound to lead to virtue, happiness, and right thinking; that men instinctively desire the good—indeed, that the Good and the Beautiful are essentially the same, so that the appeal of virtue to men is really an aesthetic appeal. It is true that, in practice, we very often find men attracted to evil rather than good; but this is because their primitive instincts have been corrupted by miseducation. It is easy to see how all this anticipates the teaching of the even more influential later primitivist, Rousseau.[25]

The definitive answer to those who maintained that revealed religion, with its alleged absurdities, should be replaced by the pure light of natural religion was given by Joseph Butler, Bishop of Durham, in his famous *The Analogy of Religion, Natural and Revealed, to the Constitution and Course of Nature* (1736), which argues that when the "course of nature" is actually inspected, it is quite as consistent with the operations of the God of revelation, as taught by orthodoxy, as with those of the Deists' Supreme Being—or, rather, as inconsistent with the God the Deists postulate as with the God of the orthodox. With either deity, there are difficulties. While it is true that revelation has not been bestowed on all men, neither has a Deistic God bestowed on all men equal intellectual ability to deduce moral principles from the universe around them. It is a dangerous line of argument: later men, contemplating a "Nature, red in tooth and claw," were to find it hard to believe that it was presided over by a benevolent God at all, whether Anglican or Deist. But at least Butler effectively establishes that there is no advantage in rejecting orthodoxy for a Deism which leaves just as many questions unanswered.

It is largely the Shaftesburians whom Johnson is pillorying in Chapter XXII of *Rasselas* (1759), where the young Prince of Abyssinia is much impressed by the philosopher who argues,

> The way to be happy is to live according to nature, in obedience to that universal and unalterable law with which every heart is originally impressed: which is not written on it by precept, but engraven by destiny, not instilled by education, but infused at our nativity. . . . Other men may amuse themselves with subtle definition, or intricate ratiocination. Let them learn to be wise by easier

means: let them observe the hind of the forest, and the linnet of the grove.

Johnson makes his point: it is a lazy man's philosophy. He also, interestingly, ties it up with its ancestral Stoicism: "He that lives according to nature," the philosopher asserts, "will suffer nothing from the delusions of hope, or importunities of desire: he will receive and reject with equability of temper." He will, that is, "in ignorance sedate,/ Roll darkling down the torrent of his fate"; as well as passivity of mind, the doctrine entails passivity of emotion, the sort of vegetable existence that Johnson could hardly bear to hear described. Finally, it is essentially arrogant and egocentric, another of the ubiquitous manifestations of the sin of pride. At the conclusion of the philosopher's harangue, Johnson makes a devastating observation: "When he had spoken, he looked round him with a placid air, and enjoyed the consciousness of his own beneficence." Shaftesbury does indeed argue that one of the rewards of virtuous behavior is the pleasant awareness of your own superior virtue, such as the Pharisee in the Gospels enjoyed.[26]

A specialized branch of natural theology was that devoted to answering the age-old question Πόθεν τὸ κακόν; what is the source of evil? How, if we postulate a God who is both omnipotent and benevolent (as both Christians and Deists did), can the existence of evil or pain in the world be accounted for? Either, it seems, God is unable to prevent it, in which case he is not omnipotent; or else he is able to but will not, in which case it is difficult to understand how he can be benevolent.[27] The standard treatise of the time on the subject was the *De Origine Mali* of William King, Archbishop of Dublin, (1702), later translated by Bishop Edmund Law as *An Essay on the Origin of Evil* (1731). King's answer is not a new one; it had been made by Milton, among many others. It is an appeal to the theory of "the great chain of being," a concept whose origins Lovejoy traces back to early Greek philosophy.[28] All existence forms a hierarchical continuum, extending from God (infinity) at the top, down through the nine orders of angels, through man, who is somewhere in the middle, through the lower orders of animals, to the lowest forms of existence, and at last to zero. What seems evil to one member of the chain, then, may be for the good of another member, and for the good of the chain as a whole. Pope popularized the argument in *An Essay on Man:*

> God sends not ill; if rightly understood,
> Or partial Ill is universal Good,
> Or Change admits, or Nature lets it fall;
> Short, and but rare, till Man improv'd it all.
> We just as wisely might of Heav'n complain
> That righteous Abel was destroy'd by Cain,
> As that the virtuous son is ill at ease
> When his lewd father gave the dire disease.

("We" perhaps have no right to complain; but one wonders whether the syphilitic boy may not have some, or how much comfort he would derive from this line of argument.)

Soame Jenyns, a minor and dilettantish politician and writer, again attempted a popularization of it in his *Free Enquiry into the Nature and Origin of Evil* (1757), which would long ago have faded into oblivion if it had not caused Johnson to rise in his wrath and deliver a memorable onslaught on the whole way of thinking. The "great chain" concept is nonsense, Johnson says: between its highest finite member and the infinity of God there must continue to be an infinite interval; likewise between nonexistence and the lowest form of existence. The tendency of the whole line of reasoning is to keep the "have-nots" of the world (of whom Johnson had been one) contented with their lot and to leave the "haves" in untroubled enjoyment of their possessions: "Life must be seen before it can be known. This author and Pope perhaps never saw the miseries which they imagine thus easy to be borne." It is essentially dishonest reasoning, with the end justifying the means, and may even be malicious; to Jenyns' facile argument that ignorance is the desirable "opiate" (Jenyns' word) of the poor, of which they should not be improperly deprived by well meaning busybodies who want to educate them, Johnson retorts:

> I am always afraid of determining on the side of envy or cruelty. The privileges of education may sometimes be improperly bestowed, but I shall always fear to withhold them lest I should be yielding to the suggestions of pride, while I persuade myself that I am fol-

lowing the maxims of policy; and, under the appearance of salutary restraints, should be indulging the lust of dominion, and that malevolence which delights in seeing others depressed.

And Johnson sees quite clearly its derivation from Stoic dualistic theology, charging Jenyns with "dogmatical limitations of Omnipotence" and attempting to revive "Chrysippus's [the most seminal of Stoic philosophers] intractableness of matter."

The affinity of the doctrines of the *Characteristics,* the *De Origine Mali,* and *An Essay on Man* to the constellation of political attitudes termed laissez faire seems obvious. With whatever subtleties Pope and the others may have surrounded the affirmation "Whatever is, is right" in order to reconcile it with the orthodox view of the corruption of nature and human reason since the Fall (and with the experience of Johnson and others of the lower economic levels that whatever is is often very wrong indeed), to the average prosperous British entrepreneur of the eighteenth century it must have sounded like a ratification of free enterprise and a warning to meddling governments and moralists to keep their hands off the workings of the divinely established law of supply and demand. British merchants appealed in high-sounding terms to the wisdom of God as manifested in "the present order of things" when defending their "natural right" to infringe the Spanish monopoly of trade in the South Seas; so did Americans (as the Declaration of Independence testifies) when unwilling to be subjected to taxation by London; so even did defenders of the slave trade. Boswell, for instance, reprobates

> The wild and dangerous attempt which has for some time been persisted in to obtain an act of our Legislature, to abolish so very important and necessary a branch of commercial interest. . . . To abolish a *status,* which in all ages GOD has sanctioned, and man has continued, would not only be *robbery* to an innumerable class of our fellow-subjects; but it would be extreme cruelty to the African Savages [whom it] introduces into a much happier state of life.[29]

Locke's argument (in his *Second Treatise of Government*) that all society springs from the individual's need to protect the investment of his own labor in his own property, and his affirmation that the end of government is to preserve the individ-

ual's "life, liberty, and property"—with the stress on the last—
was of course also tremendously influential throughout the century, and beyond. But affluent and expanding societies seem
naturally to be the breeding ground of laissez-faire thinking:
the average person is reasonably prosperous, expects to become
more so, and is reluctant to have the economic terms which have
worked so well for him changed. God's in his heaven, all's right
with the world, and if other people remain poor, it is the result
of their own willful folly and laziness.

Bernard Mandeville's *The Grumbling Hive* (1705), a dog-
gerel poem of some four hundred lines, which, with long prose
appendices and replies to its critics, was later transformed into a
substantial volume entitled *The Fable of the Bees, or Private
Vices, Public Benefits* (1714), is certainly one of the most striking presentations of laissez-faire doctrine ever written, and was
the great *succès de scandale* of the early eighteenth century. It
tells of a hive of bees, "That liv'd in luxury and ease/ And yet
as famed for laws and arms"—England, in short—whose economy prospers because of the pride, greed, and emulation of its
inhabitants. The luxury trades flourish because of the desire to
keep up with the Joneses. Doctors become rich because of the
bees' self-indulgence and lawyers because of their striving to out-
cheat one another, and both do what they can to advance the
numbers and welfare of their own professions. So do the members of other trades, the slothful clergy, the cowardly soldiers,
the corrupt and teeming civil service. Vanity and fashion make
"built-in obsolescence" an essential feature of the economy:

> Their darling folly, fickleness,
> In diet, furniture, and dress,
> That strange ridic'lous vice, was made
> The very wheel that turn'd the trade.

So the gross national product remains at a high level, and everyone prospers: "the very poor/ Liv'd better than the rich before."

Then some moralistic busybody prays to Jove to remedy the
immorality of this affluent society, and Jove grants the prayer
and miraculously makes all the bees virtuous. They begin to
live honestly and sanely. Doctors, lawyers, even clergymen,
find no need for their services, and join the growing ranks

of the unemployed; the luxury trades are ruined; the expenditures of a government purged of grafting and ambitious politicians drop to new lows. But Mandeville knows that this picture of a plain living and high thinking society is not in itself going to fill his readers with too much alarm; some misguided moralists might even applaud it. So he makes the crucial addition: as well as other industries founded on immoral motivation, the military establishment decays:

> Vain cost is shunn'd as much as fraud;
> They have no forces kept abroad;
> Laugh at th'esteem of foreigners,
> And empty glory got by wars.

And, inevitably, the defenseless colony is at once attacked by aggressive neighbors eager to take advantage of its weakness. Mandeville does not quite have the courage to bring his tale to its logical conclusion, and show the foolishly virtuous community wiped out completely; its few courageous remnants, by dint of Spartan self-denial and self-sacrifice, beat off the invaders, saving it from annihilation. But in order to preserve it from future aggression, they have to emigrate from the conveniences of the hive, and "flew into a hollow tree, / Blest with content and honesty." Translating this, the only solution would be for a society to isolate itself from the modern world and retreat into a primitive fastness—if such could be found, and it seems fairly certain that Mandeville does not think it can be.

Mandeville's argument is familiar in modern industrial (and advertising) circles. The spirit of emulation, waste, and conspicuous consumption is desirable, indeed essential, if industry is to be kept in so healthy a condition that, when need arises, it can quickly convert to effective defense production. It is usually said that Mandeville's book was an attack on Shaftesbury: insofar as it mocks Shaftesbury's admiration of the primitive life of nature, it is. But this is only an incidental part of Shaftesbury's teaching. In fact, Mandeville and Shaftesbury are basically in agreement: what both are saying, in effect, is "Trust human nature, and all will be well." Shaftesbury, to be sure, paints a different picture from Mandeville of what a laissez-faire world would look like, but both are satisfied that men do very well when left to the guidance of their own instincts. It takes a miracle by Jove to make Mandeville's bees "virtuous," and Mandeville is confident that no such miracle will take place. His "private vices" are intended not to be seen as vices at all, since they confer "public benefits"; moralists are wrong who label as vices material self-seeking and cutthroat competition with one's neighbors—these are the fundamental social and economic virtues. What both Mandeville and Shaftesbury are attacking, that is to say, is the orthodox Christian ethic, which maintains that human instincts are a very poor guide indeed and need constantly to be corrected by reference to a higher standard of conduct. The Christian answer to Mandeville is, of course, a very simple one: if the ultimate sanction for a vicious society is the need to sustain military power against aggression by other vicious societies, this is a further reason why the Christian ethic should be extended, not restricted, so as to eliminate the nationalistic pride and competitive spirit which makes such military action necessary.

Mandeville's book is slight, though far from insignificant either for his own or for later times. A much more weighty and influential work, of course, was Adam Smith's *The Wealth of Nations* (1776), for nearly a century and a half the Bible of "liberal" or "classical" or "Manchester school" economics. Smith, a Scottish academic of literary interests, would seem to have had no special qualifications for embarking on an economic treatise. His earlier book, *The Theory of Moral Sentiments* (1759), is a curious work, in which some of his data for a study of human motivation are drawn from the actions and speeches of the characters in the popular drama of the time, often not far removed in quality from modern soap opera. But it was a century when "every man was his own economist." The prevailing doctrine in pre-Adamite England (though not in France, where the physiocrats worked out a body of theory to which Smith was considerably indebted) had been for the most part what is called "mercantilism," in which the individual nation is regarded as a self-sufficient economic unit, and government action, in the way of protective tariffs, subsidies, and the like, is called for to keep the national economy healthy and balanced. Smith argues with great effectiveness that "free trade"— the removal of government controls on industry and commerce, both internally and externally—is bound to lead to great prosperity. The natural "law of supply and demand" will see to it that goods will find their proper price levels, and the full potential of the world's natural resources will be developed to the best advantage of its inhabitants. There is no room here to consider the many sharp critiques (notably Marx's) that were later made of the classical economics that derived from Smith, and the bitter controversies that arose over it (and still go on). But it is clear, at least, that, like all economic theories, it has profound moral implications that cannot be ignored.[30]

The hints thrown out by Mandeville and Adam Smith were to become dogma in the even more affluent Britain of the mid-nineteenth century (where it was called "Liberalism"—that is, freedom from government interference) and in mid-twentieth-century America (where, confusingly, it is called "Conservatism"). It is also closely linked with the notion of inevitable progress. Its classic formulation was by Macaulay in 1830:

> History is full of the signs of this natural progress of society. We see in almost every part of the annals of mankind how the industry of individuals . . . creates faster than governments can squander. . . . We see the wealth of nations increasing, and all the arts of life approaching nearer and nearer to perfection, in spite of the grossest corruption and the wildest profusion on the part of rulers. . . . It is not by the intermeddling of . . . the omniscient and omnipotent State, but by the prudence and energy of the people, that England has hitherto been carried forward in civilisation. . . . Our rulers will best promote the improvement of the nation by strictly confining themselves to their own legitimate duties, by leaving capital to find its most lucrative course, commodities their fair price, industry and intelligence their natural reward, idleness and folly their natural punishment. . . .[31]

All this had been answered in advance by Goldsmith, who puts the case for a strong, responsible, and enlightened central government in Chapter XIX of *The Vicar of Wakefield:*

> [The great] who were tyrants themselves before the election of one tyrant are naturally averse to a power raised over them, and whose weight must ever lean heaviest on the subordinate orders. It is the interest of the great, therefore, to diminish kingly power as much as possible; because whatever they take from it is naturally restored to

themselves; . . . What they may then expect may be seen by turning our eyes to Holland, Genoa, or Venice where the laws govern
the poor, and the rich govern the law. I am then for, and would
die for, monarchy . . . every diminution of [the monarch's] power
. . . is an infringement upon the real liberties of the [people].

Swift, Pope, and Johnson are very much on the same side as
Goldsmith, and are equally skeptical that uncontrolled economic enterprise will lead to the Utopia that Macaulay foresaw.
What has been called "the gloom of the Tory satirists"—and it
is an oversimplification of contemporary political terminology
to label Pope and Swift Tories—is no more than a gloom about
what may happen in a community where "leaving capital to
find its most lucrative course" becomes the highest political
(and therefore moral) principle.[32]

NOTES TO CHAPTER THREE

1. Apart from the elementary one of counting the number of books
published on a certain topic and attempting to estimate the number of
their readers. Even this will hardly be feasible for the eighteenth century until a Short Title Catalogue of publications is extended beyond
the present limit of 1700.

2. "Reason" has been supposed to connote a fondness for "logical structure" in the writings of the time. But see my article " 'Logical Structure'
in Eighteenth-Century Poetry," *Philological Quarterly*, XXXI, 2 (July
1952) 315–336.

3. To Johnson in particular, who frequently sneered at the praise given
by historians to the Romans and their empire—"a people, who while
they were poor robbed mankind, and as soon as they became rich, robbed
one another" (review of Blackwell's *Memoirs of the Court of Augustus*)—
and whose scathing comments on the use of classical mythology and
hackneyed classical literary conventions (e.g., by Milton) are one of the
commonplaces of his criticism. Swift can—mildly—recommend the reading of the Greek philosophers, as a limited source of useful instruction;
but his considered opinion of them is given in his sermon on the text
"The wisdom of this world is foolishness with God," a sustained attack
on them from Socrates onward: "this vein of affecting to raise the reputation of those sages so high, is a mode and a vice but of yesterday, assumed chiefly, as I have said, to disparage revealed knowledge, and the
consequences of it among us." Swift and Johnson never forgot that the
Greeks and Romans were, after all, heathens. Dryden did not hesitate
(in *An Essay of Dramatic Poesy*) to express his admiration of the drama
of Shakespeare and his contemporaries, for all its flouting of the conven-

tions of classical drama, nor was Pope reluctant to use the conventions of the classical epic as material for broad humor in *The Dunciad*. Certainly they all admired good classical literature, but they were far from being overawed by it.

4. George Boas, "In Search of the Age of Reason," in Earl R. Wasserman, ed., *Aspects of the Eighteenth Century* (Baltimore: Johns Hopkins, 1965), p. 18. The false dichotomy between religion ("authoritarian") and rationality ("anti-authoritarian"), found in so many attempts to view the century (in England) as the age of reason, is readily apparent in this passage. But there is nothing counterrevolutionary or authoritarian in the teachings of the Gospel when taken seriously, as presumably some, at least, in the Roman Catholic, Anglican, and Lutheran communions took them. One thinks of the toast of that devout Anglican, Samuel Johnson, "Here's to the next insurrection of the Negroes in the West Indies" (Boswell, *Life*, 23 September 1777). In the Roman Catholic church, the eighteenth century saw the pontificates of Benedict XIV, a worthy predecessor of John XXIII, and of Clement XIV, who dissolved the Jesuit Order: it might be argued that the *aggiornamento* of that church in the twentieth century is merely a rejection of the ultramontanism of the nineteenth century and a return to its eighteenth-century tradition. But Boas' essay is virtually an announcement of the abandonment of that search by one of the most senior and eminent historians of ideas.

5. W. Norman Pittenger (Professor of Christian Apologetics in the General Theological Seminary, New York), "Augustinianism," in *A Handbook of Christian Theology* (New York: Meridian Books, 1958), pp. 22–23. Other contributors to the volume include such distinguished theologians as Paul Tillich, Reinhold and H. Richard Niebuhr, and W. A. Visser 't Hooft. "Paulinism" would be an equally valid designation; so perhaps would "Erasmianism"—see J. K. McConica's *English Humanists and Reformation Politics* (New York: Oxford University Press, 1965), Chap. 2. McConica sums up Erasmus' teaching thus: "Above all, Christianity is to be comprehended by the inner spirit of man; it is an affair of commitment (*affectibus*) rather than of syllogisms, of life itself rather than disputation, of inspiration rather than learning, of conversion rather than reason" (p. 27).

6. Modern students are often surprised to find that "morality"—meaning the ritual observance of good conduct without the inner motivation of faith and love—is sometimes a bad word in seventeenth- and eighteenth-century texts. The condemnation, in *The Pilgrim's Progress*, of Mr. Legality, who dwells in the village of Morality, should be pondered. Sir John Hawkins says that he has treated of Johnson's religious life in considerable detail in order "to refute the objections of many infidels, who, desirous of having him thought to be of their party, endeavoured to make it believed, that he was a *mere moralist*" (B. H. Davis, ed., *The Life of Samuel Johnson, LL.D.* [New York: Macmillan, 1961], p. 246; my italics). But Johnson makes his position quite clear in his Sermon XIII: some men "please themselves with a constant regularity of life, and decency of behaviour. . . . Some are punctual in the attendance on public worship, and perhaps in the performance of private devotion. . . . Their religion is sincere; what is reprehensible is that it is partial, that the

heart is not yet purified" (*Works* [1825], IX, pp. 408–410). All thoughtful Christians of the time knew their *Epistle to the Romans,* and no modern student should attempt to expound their religious position without digesting it.

7. This axiom is also central to the post-Freudian psychiatry of Karen Horney and Erich Fromm and (one gathers) to Zen Buddhism and other non-Christian moral systems.

8. What Lionel Trilling has said of the modern novel ("Manners, Morals, and the Modern Novel," in *The Liberal Imagination* [New York: Viking, 1950], p. 222) as "the most effective agent of the moral imagination in our time"—"Its greatness and its practical usefulness [lies] in its unremitting work of involving the reader himself in the moral life, inviting him to put his own motives under examination, suggesting that reality is not as his conventional education has led him to see it"—will not surprise us if we consider its origins in the work of Bunyan and Defoe, Richardson, Fielding, and Sterne. Indeed, if there is any dominant motive in serious contemporary literature, it is surely the same contempt and rejection of the soul-destroying and ego-centered values of society— the socially inculcated concerns for money making, status seeking, image creating, power grabbing, ego gratification as the chief ends of life—that is found in dominant moral tradition in eighteenth-century English literature.

9. *Certain Sermons or Homilies Appointed by the King's Majesty to be Declared and Read by All Parsons, Vicars, and Curates, Every Sunday in Their Churches Where They Have Cure:* The Second Homily, "Of Faith" (probably by Cranmer).

10. *Ninety-Six Sermons* (Oxford: Parker, 1841), V, pp. 301, 308.

11. *Thirty-One Sermons* (Oxford: Parker, 1849), I, pp. 309–310.

12. *Sermons Preached upon Several Occasions* (London, 1737), I, pp. 68, 71.

13. *Works* (Oxford: Parker, 1847), II, p. 226.

14. For the orthodox Christian, of course, another source is revelation.

15. "All men are mortal; Socrates is a man; therefore Socrates is mortal." But, argues Mill, this conclusion, the product of the reasoning process allegedly unique to man, gives us no *new* knowledge: the fact was already known to us when we stated the major premise, *"All* men are mortal." Bertrand Russell amusingly illustrates the two kinds of epistemology: Aristotle, he says, by closing his eyes and cogitating, was able to deduce from the major premise that females are inferior to males, that women have fewer teeth than men. All Aristotle needed to do to verify this, Russell points out, was to ask Mrs. Aristotle to open her mouth for a few moments while he counted. But such a menial operation was beneath the dignity of rational man. This is perhaps unfair to Aristotle, who had a good deal of the empiricist spirit about him. Yet Sir Thomas Browne, in the wake of the Baconian revolution, properly derides Aristotle for asserting that "a man doth cough, but not an ox or cow; whereas the contrary is often observed by husbandman"; also that horses, oxen, and asses have no "eructation or belching" and that "man alone hath gray hairs" (*Vulgar Errors* [1646], Chap. VI).

16. The word "reason" of course has many meanings. Johnson's *Dictionary* (1755) distinguishes eleven, the first of which, "The power by which man deduces one proposition from another, or proceeds from premises to consequences," is the one intended in this sentence and generally in this chapter. But the other ten range through a wide spectrum of popular usage; and "reasonable," in the eighteenth as in other centuries, very often means no more than "appropriate, admirable, approved of by the speaker."

17. The popularizers of Baconianism were legion—Thomas Browne, Joseph Glanvill, Bishop Sprat, among others. One of the great popularizers of Locke was the Reverend Isaac Watts, whose life Johnson insisted be included in his *Lives of the Poets,* and to whom he pays the tribute, "Few books have been perused by me with greater pleasure than his *Improvement of the Mind,* of which the radical principles may indeed be found in Locke's *Conduct of the Understanding;* . . . Whoever has the care of instructing others may be charged with deficience in his duty if this book is not recommended" (*Life of Watts,* 1781).

18. *The Advancement of Learning,* in Sidney Warhaft, ed., *Francis Bacon, A Selection of His Works* (Toronto: Macmillan, 1965), p. 225; *The New Organon, ibid.,* p. 360. Cf. Christopher Hill, *Intellectual Origins of the English Revolution* (New York: Oxford University Press, 1965), p. 93: "It is important to realize that this religious element in early Baconianism was genuine. . . . Bacon professed no such narrow utilitarianism as later went under his name. In this respect he was as little a Baconian as Karl Marx was a Marxist."

19. *"La querelle des Anciens et Modernes"* began with the publication in France in the 1680's of works by Charles Perrault and Fontenelle complimenting the age of Louis XIV on its superiority in art, literature, and science over the relative crudeness of the Greeks and Romans. Boileau, Racine, and others properly rebutted this self-congratulation. Sir William Temple initiated the controversy in England by his *Essay upon the Ancient and Modern Learning* (1690), in which he takes an extravagantly anti-Modern position: everything has deteriorated since classical times; even in such minor genres as the fable and letter writing, the best practitioners were the early Greeks, Aesop and Phalaris. This "rediscovery" of the legendary Phalaris inspired the young Oxford scholar, Charles Boyle (with considerable unacknowledged assistance by senior classical scholars at Oxford), to publish an edition of "his" letters. This edition, in turn, was torn to pieces in a superb *Dissertation* (1699) by the great Richard Bentley of Cambridge, the foremost English classical scholar of all time. Bentley had no trouble in demonstrating that the works attributed to Aesop and Phalaris, far from being ancient, were very late Greek, and that Boyle and his helpers were very ignorant of what they professed to expertise in. Swift intervened in defense of his patron Temple with *The Battle of the Books* (1697; published 1704), satirizing Bentley's pugnacious temperament and his cousin Dryden's conceit as illustrations of Modern arrogance.

Though the implications of the *querelle* are worth examining—among other things, there were strong political overtones, Oxford being Tory and Cambridge Whig—the importance of the incident in the general history of ideas has perhaps been exaggerated by modern scholars. The complacent believer in the superiority of his own time is not unique to the seventeenth century, nor is the uncritical worshiper of the past, like Temple. Perrault's and Temple's essays are very trivial stuff, and even *The Battle of the Books,* charming as it is, is more of a *jeu d'esprit* than a serious treatment of the question; indeed, much of the humor of the piece comes from the devastating burlesque of the epic clichés of the Ancients, whose literary prowess Swift is supposed to be defending.

20. *History of the Royal Society* (1667), pp. 345, 366–367.

21. Preface to *A Dictionary of the English Language,* 1755. Robert South preached a series of sermons on "The fatal influence of words and names falsely applied," in which he says, "The generality of mankind is wholly and absolutely governed by words and names. . . . The multitude, or common rout, like a drove of sheep, or an herd of oxen, may be managed by any noise, or cry, which their drivers shall accustom them to. . . . They suffer themselves to be carried away with these puffs of wind, even contrary to knowledge and experience itself" (*Sermons Preached upon Several Occasions* [London, 1737], II, p. 33).

22. *Three Dialogues Between Hylas and Philonous,* beginning of the second dialogue. The profound seriousness and importance of Berkeley's epistemology has seldom been appreciated. Any reader who has an inclination to dismiss it with a smile should study A. A. Luce's short and readable analysis, *Berkeley's Immaterialism* (Edinburgh: Nelson, 1945).

23. *Philosophical Commentaries,* No. 769, in Berkeley, *Works,* ed. A. A. Luce and T. E. Jessup (Edinburgh: Nelson, 1948), I. If the basis of existentialism is, as we are told, the doctrine that "existence is prior to essence," it is hard to see what distinguishes it from philosophical empiricism. The teachings of Kierkegaard, with his fervent Augustinianism and violent anti-Hegelianism, deserve to be considered in connection with Swift and Johnson as much as with, say, Kafka and Sartre. Born in 1813, he is closer in time to the eighteenth century than to the twentieth.

24. Discussed in detail in Leslie Stephen's *English Thought in the Eighteenth Century* (1881)—a misnomer, since Stephen, a militant agnostic, is concerned chiefly to describe the deviations from orthodoxy.

25. The woolly and incoherent philosophical writings of the one-time political leader, Henry St. John, Lord Bolingbroke, have a somewhat similar Deist tendency. But they were little read by the general public, and were supposed (probably erroneously) to have made an impact by their assimilation by Pope in *An Essay on Man.*

26. The passage in *Rasselas* seems also to be satirizing the teaching of the Reverend Samuel Clarke, perhaps the one true rationalist of eighteenth-century English thought—Pope's "gloomy Clerk," who "took the high priori road,/And reasoned downward till we doubt of God." Clarke's Boyle Lectures (*A Discourse Concerning the Being and Attributes of God,* delivered 1704–1705), in which he proves the existence of God, and many other things, in a strictly logical, or mathematical, series of theorems, are an amazing performance. "The fitness arising from the relations and qualities of causes and effects," one of the phrases of the philosopher in *Rasselas,* is Clarkean terminology, though Clarke inherits it from the general Stoic tradition.

27. It may be noted that the practice of capitalizing pronouns referring to the Deity is nineteenth-century usage, not earlier. Serious theological writing in the twentieth century seems to have abandoned it.

28. A. O. Lovejoy, *The Great Chain of Being* (Cambridge, Mass.: Harvard University Press, 1936). Because of the popularity of Lovejoy's book, students sometimes tend to assume that everyone in the eighteenth century must have believed in the existence of the "great chain." This is not so. Johnson's devastating attack on the concept will be noted; and it is hard, apart from King, Pope, and Soame Jenyns, to find extended discussions of it in eighteenth-century English writing. Thomson and Addison refer to it; perhaps traces of "chain of being" thinking can be detected in Burke; but on the whole the century was certainly not under its spell.

29. *The Life of Samuel Johnson LL.D.*, September 23, 1777.

30. When, late in the century, the younger Pitt, a student of Adam Smith, initiated the policy of government withdrawal from economic intervention that was to become the rule in nineteenth-century Britain, the Secretary of the Treasury of the young United States, Alexander Hamilton, enunciated (in his *Report on Manufactures*) and initiated the opposite policy of close protection of American industry by means of import tariffs imposed by the federal government. To what extent the subsequent economic histories of the two countries is evidence of the ultimate wisdom of either theory is a complex question; but in 1929 Britain formally abandoned free trade, and has shown no signs of wanting to return to it.

31. Review of Robert Southey, *Sir Thomas More; or Colloquies on the Progress and Prospects of Society.*

32. A version of part of this chapter appeared as an article, "Augustinianism and Empiricism," in *Eighteenth-Century Studies*, I (Fall 1967), 33–68.

General Chronology: Some Dates in the History of the Arts and Aesthetics

1660   Theaters reopened in London (under royal patronage), after the Puritan ban in 1641.

1660's   and 1670's. Sir Peter Lely (born and trained in Holland) active; painted luscious portraits of the ladies of Charles II's court.

1666   The Great Fire destroys much of the old City of London, including the old Gothic St. Paul's cathedral. Sir Christopher Wren commissioned to redesign the City (though his plans were not carried out). But his many baroque City churches and his great baroque St. Paul's (built 1675 to 1710) were erected.

1671   Grinling Gibbons, woodcarver, discovered in Holland by John Evelyn, and brought to England; carved woodwork for Wren's St. Paul's and new London churches.

1675   Godfrey Kneller, later Sir Godfrey, Bart., born in Germany and trained in Holland, arrives in England. Leading portraitist of next four decades. Noted for his set of portraits of the Kit-Cat Club, leading Whig politicians and intellectuals, like Addison and Steele.

1680   Caius Gabriel Cibber, statues of Madness at gates of Bethlehem Hospital (Bedlam).

1680's   and 1690's. Henry Purcell active. Organist of Westminster Abbey and the Chapel Royal. His opera *Dido and Aeneas,* 1689.

1699   Castle Howard designed by Sir John Vanbrugh and Nicholas Hawksmoor (completed 1710); Blenheim Palace designed 1705, completed 1724.

1708   William Croft, organist of Westminster Abbey.

1710   George Frederick Handel comes to England; his opera *Rinaldo,* 1711, stirs up controversy. Naturalized a British subject 1726.

1711 Parliamentary act subsidizing building of fifty new metropolitan churches (only a few actually built).

1716 Burlington House rebuilt by the third Earl of Burlington and Colin Campbell in Palladian style. Burlington later becomes patron of William Kent.

1718 Maurice Greene appointed organist of St. Paul's.

1718– Handel director of music to the Duke of Chandos at Canons.
20

1726 James Gibbs, St. Martin's-in-the-Fields.

1728 John Gay, *The Beggar's Opera.*

1732 Vauxhall pleasure gardens under management of Jonathan Tyers.

1733 Thomas Arne, music for Addison's opera *Rosamund.*

1735 William Hogarth, "The Rake's Progress."

1740 Thomas Arne, music for James Thomson's masque, *Alfred* (includes "Rule Britannia").

1740's and later. Lancelot ("Capability") Brown active in landscape gardening; designs the gardens at Blenheim and Kew.

1742 Handel, *Messiah* first performed (in Dublin); Ranelagh gardens opened.

1747 Horace Walpole begins Gothic additions to Strawberry Hill.

1750's to 1770's. Richard Wilson active in landscape painting.

1750's to 1780's. Thomas Gainsborough active in portrait and landscape painting.

1750's to 1790's. Sir Joshua Reynolds active in portrait painting.

1754 Thomas Chippendale, *The Gentleman and Cabinet Maker's Director.*

1753 Hogarth's aesthetic treatise, *The Analysis of Beauty.*

1755 William Boyce, master of the King's band of musicians.

1756 Edmund Burke, *A Philosophical Inquiry into the Origin of Our Ideas of the Sublime and Beautiful.*

1757 Sir William Chambers, *Designs of Chinese Buildings, Furniture, etc.;* beginning of "chinoiserie" in architecture and interior decoration.
      Robert Adam, *The Ruins of the Palace of Diocletian.*

1760's to 1790's. Joseph Nollekens active in statuary.

1762 Johann Christian Bach (eleventh son of Johann Sebastian) settles in England.
      Henry Home, Lord Kames, *Elements of Criticism;* James ("Athenian") Stuart, *The Antiquities of Athens.*

1762– Horace Walpole, *Anecdotes of Painting in England,* based on
71   the collections of George Vertue.

1764   Mozart (aged eight) visits England; performs before royal family.

1768   Royal Academy of Arts founded; Reynolds first president, Gainsborough, Wilson, and most other eminent artists of the time members.

1775   Sir William Chambers, Somerset House.

1776   Sir John Hawkins, *General History of Music;* Charles Burney, *History of Music* (to 1789).

1784   First Handel festival, in Westminster Abbey.

1790   Archibald Alison, *Essay on the Nature and Principles of Taste.*

1791   Franz Josef Haydn's first visit to England; his "London" symphonies performed; awarded Doctor of Music degree by Oxford.

Introductory: The Baroque

As many have complained, the word "baroque" has come to be used as loosely, and is as impossible of strict definition, as, say, "Romantic." Its original signification seems to have been "bizarre, *outré,* barbaric," which, interestingly, is exactly what "Gothic" and its cognate "grotesque" originally meant as descriptions of art. Yet it is meaningful to say that the dominant artistic idiom of Restoration and eighteenth-century Britain is essentially that of the baroque and its child, the rococo. Perhaps as good a definition of baroque as any is the use of exuberant ornamentation on a carefully planned, symmetrical base; rococo is a more delicate version of the same. They are *dramatic* performances, rejoicing in bright colors, exaggeration, startling contrast, overpowering the spectator or auditor with sheer energy and diversity. One thinks of Handel's great choruses, Vanbrugh's Blenheim Palace, Reynolds' more florid portraits, the portrait sculpture of Roubiliac and Nollekens, Chippendale's furniture (especially of the "Chinese" variety), and, to pick some literary examples in various genres, Dryden's *Ode on the Death of Mrs. Anne Killigrew,* Congreve's *The Way of the World,* the fourth book of Pope's *The Dunciad,* Sterne's *Tristram Shandy.*

To the nineteenth century, all this kind of thing was anath-

ema: it connoted frivolity, lack of "high seriousness," artificiality
—as though all art were not, by definition, artificial!—deca-
dence, and general immorality. Ruskin becomes almost hysteri-
cal as he denounces the moral degeneracy of baroque architecture, and the respected historian John Richard Green sums it
up in a sentence of almost incredible self-righteousness: "We
instinctively feel the great, the immeasurable distance that severs
this age [he is writing in 1859], so proud of its truth, its earnest-
ness, its energy, its high and noble aims, from the heartlessness,
the indifference, the frivolity—in one word, the utter world-
liness of the eighteenth century." [1]

Only fairly recently has the image created by the neurotic
blindness of the Victorians to this great period of art started to
disappear. It first began to do so in music: it became harder and
harder to accuse Bach's great B-minor mass, supremely baroque
as it is, of frivolity and "lack of depth," though one still occasionally finds the older person who carries on the Victorian tradition of accusing Bach's music of "arid, mathematical rationality." Most North Americans are still a little suspicious of the
splendor of Wren's St. Paul's Cathedral, gleaming in white and
gold, and feel the "dim, religious light" of Victorian pseudo-
Gothic churches somehow more "moral." Why bright light and
splendor should be thought irreligious is hard to say, considering that light has always been the prime symbol of deity. But
more recent church architecture has gone back to the earlier
conception and is not afraid to let in plenty of light on religious
"mystery."

The use of "baroque" as a strict descriptive term in art criticism is probably of less value than the role it plays in reminding
the modern student that a whole continent of exciting aesthetic
experience may lie outside the boundaries of his limited education. Thus Evelyn Waugh (whose early training was as an artist)
makes the word symbolize the freeing of an Oxford undergraduate of the 1920's, the protagonist of his most intimately autobio-
graphical novel, *Brideshead Revisited,* from the cold, self-centered inhibition of his essentially Victorian upbringing. As an
adolescent, Charles Ryder says,

> . . . though in opinion I had made that easy leap, from the puri-
> tanism of Ruskin to the puritanism of Roger Fry, my sentiments at
> heart were insular and mediaeval.

His release is effected when he becomes acquainted with a great eighteenth-century English country house, Brideshead Castle:

> This was my conversion to the baroque. Here under that high and insolent dome, under those tricky ceilings; here, as I passed through those arches and broken pediments to the pillared shade beyond and sat, hour by hour, before the fountain, probing its shadows, tracing its lingering echoes, rejoicing in all its clustered feats of daring and invention, I felt a whole new system of nerves alive within me, as though the water that spurted and bubbled among its stones was indeed a life-giving spring.[2]

Many young Englishmen and Americans, on whom the dead hand of Ruskin, whether they know it or not, lies heavy even today, probably need to experience a similar "conversion" if they are really to appreciate the glories of English literature of the eighteenth century (and, indeed, the seventeenth as well). The dazzling ornamentation of Pope's poetry, the breath-taking power of Swift's wit, the elaborate grandeur of Johnson's prose —for that matter, the exotic diction and involuted sentences of Milton—have much in common with the coloratura and verve of Bach's and Handel's music, the sheer melodrama of Vanbrugh's and Hawksmoor's architecture (pushed to even further lengths in South German and Hispanic baroque), the extravagant curlicues of Grinling Gibbons's woodcarvings, the exuberance of line and color in a drawing room decorated by Adam or furnished by Chippendale or Sheraton.

Such a conversion is probably one from a state in which the chief response to an object of art is not aesthetic at all, but "social" or self-regarding—one "likes" a Victorian pseudo-Gothic church or a piece of sentimental Victorian poetry because one knows that this is the way churches ought to look and poetry ought to read, and the pleasure one gets from the experience is largely that of feeling pleased with oneself for doing the right thing—to a state in which one begins to react directly and vividly to the materials of art themselves, the sound, the line, the color, the imagery. As Waugh puts it, a new, or at least hitherto unused, system of nerves begins to operate. Eighteenth-century art is never derivative in the sense of seeking to get its effects by appealing to the observer's historical knowledge—as nineteenth-century art so frequently did. A writer in the eleventh edition of the *Encyclopaedia Britannica* contrasts them (rather unexpectedly, for this publication of 1910 often presents the ripest fruit of the Victorian sensibility),

> The 19th century is the period *par excellence* of architectural "revivals." The great Renaissance movement in Italy . . . was something more than a mere revival. It was a new spirit affecting the whole of art and literature and life, not an architectural movement only; and as far as architecture is concerned it was not a mere imitative revival. The great Italian architects of the Renaissance, as well as Wren, Vanbrugh, and Hawksmoor in England, however they drew their inspiration from antique models, were for the most part original architects; they put the ancient materials to new uses of their own. The tendency of the 19th-century revivals, on the other hand, except in France, was distinctly imitative in a sense in which the architecture of the great Renaissance period was not. Correctness of imitation, in the English Gothic revival especially, was an avowed object; and conformity to precedent became, in fact, except with one or two individual architects, almost the admitted test of excellence.[3]

"Correctness of imitation" and "conformity to precedent" as avowed objects on the part of artists! It is exactly the charge Victorian critics were fond of making against eighteenth-century literature, and if it could be substantiated, it would be a damning one. But of course it cannot be; there is nothing in earlier literature remotely like the great writings of Dryden, Pope, Swift, and Johnson, to name the most important figures. Like all great artists their genius is original, and they had no intention of merely duplicating what had been done before. In Victorian architecture, alas, the charge is only too easy to document. In many ways, important aspects of both Romanticism and Victorianism in England seem to represent a failure of nerve after the eighteenth-century's full-blooded acceptance and extension of the Renaissance spirit of invention and exploration. Certainly few critics could now be found to deny that English painting, architecture, and music in the nineteenth century constitute an inglorious decline from the brilliance of those arts in the eighteenth.

As in other matters, what happened in English art in the seventeenth and eighteenth centuries was a cross-fertilization between sturdy, independent, if provincial, native energy and the wider vision and technical expertise of the Continental tradition. This is well put in the opening paragraph of the volume of the Oxford History of Art series dealing with the seventeenth and early eighteenth centuries:

> The Stuart period is one of the richest and most absorbing in the history of the arts in England. The sheer quantity of works of art that were produced between the reigns of James I and George I was far greater than in the age of the Tudors and, though much of it would be deservedly neglected by a historian of European or even of English art, it contained some of the most vigorous and beautiful expressions of the English genius.

But this is only the prelude to full maturity:

> The flowering of that genius in the Hanoverian age grew partly out of a fusion in the earlier period of native and continental influences, and the English reaction to the full baroque style of the Continent is the central problem: a problem affected by growing consciousness of the arts, by rapidly increasing first-hand acquaintance with renaissance and modern art on the Continent and by varied trends in patronage, from the highly developed cosmopolitan tastes of some of the Stuart sovereigns and the aristocracy to the reactionary, or actively hostile, views of less sophisticated patrons.[4]

It need only be added that the first two Hanoverian monarchs were at least as cosmopolitan in taste as their Stuart ancestors—indeed, their cosmopolitanism was held against them by disaffected English oppositionists, who sneered at their patronage of Handel—and that George III did not extend the insularity of his political outlook to artistic matters, but gave his patronage to the Venetian Canaletto as well as to the native Gainsborough, and recognized no national boundaries in his encouragement of music. Continental painters from Lely and Kneller to Angelica Kauffmann and Henry Fuseli (following in the footsteps of Holbein, Rubens, and Van Dyck) came to practice their art in England and often found so receptive a clientele that they settled there.

For young English painters and architects, an extended visit to Italy, the home of their art, became almost a compulsory part of their education. Handel, a Saxon, spent three years maturing his art in Italy before moving to England. The tours of the Continent in 1770 and 1772 by Johnson's friend, the pioneer musicologist Charles Burney, and the volumes he published describing them, *The Present State of Music in France and Italy* and *The Present State of Music in Germany, the Netherlands, and the United Provinces,* are significant of the concern he felt that music in England should be regarded in an international, not merely a local, context, a concern which is also present in his monumental *History of Music,* as well as in its rival, Hawkins' *General History of Music.* The most noted sculptors of the time, Cibber, Rysbrack, Roubiliac, Scheemakers, were immigrants; one, the most popular and best of the latter part of the century, Nollekens, was the son of an immigrant painter. Singers, then as now, wandered over the world, and if some of Handel's most famous *prime donne* were imports, like the notorious rivals Faustina and Cuzzoni, he also found competent native singers, like Susanna Arne (Mrs. Theophilus Cibber), who first sang the great contralto solos in *Messiah;* and British singers in turn began to perform on the Continent, like Michael Kelly, who sang Basilio in the first performance of Mozart's *Nozze di Figaro.*

The question of the influence of the cosmopolitan spirit of the time on literature is, of course, a harder one, because of the necessarily isolating influence of the language in which it is written. Yet Dryden, Pope, and Johnson were properly insistent on the necessity of an acquaintance with serious Continental literatures, and, without in any way sacrificing their own originality, of recognizing that English literature, like the other arts, must be amenable to judgment by international, not merely insular, standards of excellence. Many writers, as well as painters and musicians, made a kind of extended Grand Tour of the Continent in their youth. Gibbon and Hume, Beckford and Horace Walpole and Boswell were genuine cosmopolitans, as much at home on the Continent as in Britain, almost as fluent in French as in English (Gibbon and Beckford both composed important works in French; Hume retired to France to write his masterpiece, *A Treatise of Human Nature*).

At the end of the century, the long ordeal of the French Revolutionary and Napoleonic wars, lasting over two decades—and, perhaps, the nationalistic and introvertive tendencies of Romanticism—again tended to isolate English writing. Not until the voices of T. S. Eliot and Ezra Pound were heard in the twentieth century did something like the eighteenth century's recognition of literature as a supranational art again exist, and it is questionable whether even yet in the twentieth century Eliot's and Pound's exhortations to a more than national outlook on literature have been much heeded in practice by the average writer and reader of English literature.

Music

English music of the late seventeenth and the eighteenth centuries has more continuity with its past than do the other arts of the time. The Continental influence began to be felt in the reign of Charles II, chiefly the influence of Italian monody—the emphasis on the solo with accompaniment—such as Monteverdi's, in displacing the older polyphonic tradition, and also perhaps some French influence, stemming from the operatic work of Lully, Louis XIV's court composer. But, as did not happen in painting and architecture, it encountered and merged with a thriving and vigorous native professional tradition.

Since early Tudor times, various musical organizations in Westminster and London had maintained high standards of performance and repertoire, notably the choir of the Chapel Royal and the royal band of musicians, maintained by the Court[5] and the choir and organists of Westminster Abbey, St. Paul's, and the larger churches of the metropolis. For some decades, musical societies commissioned and performed an ode on Saint Cecilia's Day, November 22, in honor of the patroness of music, which called forth some of the finest achievements of librettists (such as Dryden, Congreve, and Pope), composers (both Purcell and Handel), and performers. The composition of a setting of the Poet Laureate's annual Birthday Ode and New Year's Ode in honor of the sovereign, and its performance at Court on the stated day, at least gave employment and practice to composers, singers, and instrumentalists, even though the poetic texts were notorious for their badness and not much of the music seems to have been inspired (though Handel's setting of Nahum Tate's ode for Queen Anne's birthday in 1713 has been given a modern recording). Coronations, royal funerals and returns from abroad, military victories and peace treaties called for public ceremonies for which fine music was written by the best composers available.

To serve these institutions and occasions there existed a closely knit community of singers, instrumentalists, and composers—all three functions sometimes united in a single individual —perpetuating itself by training youngsters (often their own children) as apprentices and eventually successors. Thus there was a continuity of tradition from Taverner, in Henry VII's reign, through Byrd in Elizabeth's and Lawes in Charles I's, to Purcell in the reigns of the later Stuarts and Handel in those of the early Hanoverians.[6] As well as this great musical center in London, the college chapels at Oxford and Cambridge and the provincial cathedrals also often maintained fine choirs—those of the two Protestant cathedrals in Dublin combined for the first performance of Handel's *Messiah* and no doubt had much to do with forming and sustaining the fine musical tradition of that city which persisted to the time of Shaw and Joyce, and beyond. Occasionally, enlightened and wealthy noblemen—Milton's Earl of Bridgewater, Pope's Earl of Burlington and Duke of Chandos—had their domestic musicians and musical directors, that of Chandos no less than Handel himself. Throughout the century, one of the regular attractions of the immensely popular public pleasure gardens of Ranelagh and Vauxhall was what would now be called "pop concerts," at which the most notable singers, orchestras, and conductors performed—even Handel participated—while the audience strolled, ate, and drank.

The rich musical fare provided during the period of the Restoration and the eighteenth century did not lack appreciative auditors. Much has been written about the musical versatility and taste of the average Elizabethan gentleman. Not much formal study of the question seems to have been made, but certainly amateurs of music abounded in the seventeenth and eighteenth centuries. Pepys' constant delight in music is one of the most striking features of his wonderful *Diary:* few days pass when the hard-working, efficient civil servant cannot find time to practice on his viol, sing part-songs with his friends, criticize some new singer or composition, even compose songs of his own. All of the eminent North family were musical; its head, Lord Guilford, told Evelyn that he had been brought up from childhood to read music at sight, and another member, Roger North, wrote pioneering treatises of musicology and music criticism. Garrett Wesley or Wellesley, Earl of Mornington, distant cousin of John and Charles Wesley and father of the great Duke of Wellington, the Marquess Wellesley, and other distinguished sons, was Doctor and Professor of Music in Trinity College, Dublin, and a respectable composer. Many portraits of families engaged in making music exist, notably that by the elder Nollekens of Frederick, Prince of Wales, as a boy, playing the cello in company with his sisters the Princesses, who are playing the lute and harpsichord and singing (it was these Princesses, George II's daughters, for whom Handel wrote much of his keyboard music by way of supplying them with lesson material). Late in the century, the young ladies of Jane Austen's novels are expected, as a matter of course, to sing and to perform on "the instrument," as she amusingly calls it—the new pianoforte, which was replacing the harpsichord—and, as Mary Bennet's father acidly puts it, "delight" the guests of the family.

With the great Handel commemoration of 1784, the first music festival in history designed to honor a composer, and with the inauguration of the annual Three Choirs festival, those of the cathedrals of Worcester, Gloucester, and Hereford, the taste for oratorio singing, still widespread in the English-speaking world, began to flourish. George III patronized both activities, and even Samuel Johnson, notoriously unsusceptible to music—though he did once admit to being fond of "Let Ambition Fire Thy Mind"—condescended to write the noble dedication to the King of Charles Burney's official account of the Handel commemoration. It was an Englishman, Samuel Wesley, son of Charles, the poet, and nephew of the great John, who discovered and first publicized to the world at large the achievement of the obscure Johann Sebastian Bach.

It was the great age of "catch" clubs and glee societies. More "popular" music that is still current probably comes from the eighteenth century than from any other. The traditional patriotic songs of the English-speaking world are of that period—

"God Save the King" (alias "America"), "Rule Britannia" (music by Thomas Arne), "Heart of Oak" (music by William Boyce), "Men of Harlech," "Scots Wha Hae," "The Minstrel Boy" and other tunes of Moore's *Irish Melodies,* the tune of "The Star-Spangled Banner." So are many of the most familiar (and best) hymn tunes—even "Adeste, Fideles," which most people think of as vaguely medieval, but which is a perfectly typical eighteenth-century song. So are most of the traditional repertoire of country dance tunes, such as "Sir Roger de Coverley," after whom Addison named his hero (the dance and the tune are better known in America as "the Virginia Reel"). There was never a period that had a greater flair for a catchy melody. Many of the best of them are collected in the six volumes of Tom Durfey's popular *Pills to Purge Melancholy,* the last of the many recensions of which he published in 1720—Addison tells us (in *Guardian* 67) that he remembered seeing Charles II leaning familiarly on Durfey's shoulder and humming a song along with him—and were immortalized in Gay's *The Beggar's Opera.*

The period is dominated by two of the greatest names in the history of music, Henry Purcell, who lived during the reigns of Charles II, James II, and William III, and George Frederick Handel, who served the courts of Anne, George I, and George II. The work of each is a large subject for study in itself; few musicologists, not to mention mere amateurs of music, are thoroughly familiar with the extensive *oeuvre* of either (it has been estimated that the total "output" of Handel equals that of Beethoven and Bach combined). Most of it is extant, and each year more and more neglected masterpieces by both are being resuscitated and performed to the delight of listeners.

Purcell was the son of a court musician, a tenor singer of the Chapel Royal, and later successor in the royal "private music" to Milton's friend, Henry Lawes; his uncle was master of the choristers of Westminster Abbey. Henry was enrolled as a chorister of the Chapel Royal, perhaps as early as the age of six, and during the rest of his life he was occupied in some official post or other in the musical organizations of the capital, succeeding his teacher Dr. John Blow as organist of Westminster Abbey at the age of twenty. He was thus responsible for the music at the coronations of James II and William and Mary. His official duties produced birthday odes and songs of welcome for Charles II, James II, Queen Mary II, and the little Duke of Gloucester, Queen Anne's last surviving child. Most impressive, perhaps, of all these compositions is the great funeral anthem for Queen Mary in 1694, "Thou knowest, Lord, the secrets of our hearts." His *Te Deum* and *Jubilate,* composed for the St. Cecilia's Day celebration of 1694, continued to be performed annually at St. Paul's, and later alternately with Handel's *Te Deum* and *Jubilate* for the Peace of Utrecht. But many other examples of his church music—anthems, settings of psalms and canticles and of the Anglican services—survive and deserve being performed.

The work of Purcell's most widely known today is his opera *Dido and Aeneas,* with libretto by Nahum Tate. Fine as it is, it is only a small sampling of his dramatic music; he wrote five other operas, including versions of two plays by Dryden, two by Shakespeare, and one by Beaumont and Fletcher, and incidental music, including well over a hundred songs, for forty-three other plays (the high musical content of Restoration drama is often forgotten by students), dozens of other songs and catches, and a respectable amount of excellent instrumental music.

Critics have always found it hard to agree on a neat assessment of Purcell's achievement, except that it is that of a rare and authentic genius (though certainly not a neglected one—both he and Handel received an immense amount of acclaim from their contemporaries). Perhaps the best is the saying that Purcell is "not for timid souls." Much has been made of the assertion that he was the last genuinely English composer, and lamentations used to be heard that the triumphs of the "foreigner" Handel had given "native" music, as represented by Purcell, its quietus. Great music is not so easily nationalized as this; what the statement probably means is simply that Purcell, raised in the school of Byrd and Lawes, was still in the process of turning from the older polyphonic to the newer monodic tradition. But like all real artists he was glad to learn what he could from other masters of his trade, such as the Italian Corelli and the Frenchman Lully.

Contrariwise, lamentations have been heard that he did not make this transition cleanly enough: Sir Donald Tovey goes so

far as to talk of "the almost tragic blending of genius and failure" in the English church music of the Restoration, and of the
"patchiness" of Purcell's work, maintaining that he "is probably
the only instance in music of a man of really high genius born
out of due time." Such teleological approaches seem beside the
point to those who are willing simply to obtain delight from the
technical brilliance and emotional depth of *Dido and Aeneas,*
the *Te Deum,* and the funeral anthem for Queen Mary, and
the enduring charm of the songs and incidental music to the
plays. Purcell's musical voice *is* idiosyncratic; he has his own
unique and unmistakable idiom. This makes him exasperating
for critics who would like to pigeonhole him neatly, but it no
more prejudices the excellence of his music than a similar
uniqueness prejudices the excellence of the poetry of Purcell's
great admirer, Gerard Manley Hopkins, who wrote of him that
"he has . . . uttered in notes the very make and species of man
as created both in him and in all men generally," and of his
music,

> . . . so some great stormfowl, whenever he has walked his while
> The thunder-purple seabeach plumèd purple-of-thunder,
> If a wuthering of his palmy snow-pinions scatter a colossal smile
> Off him, but meaning motion fans fresh our wits with wonder.

Purcell was great; but Handel, one of the supreme musical
giants of all time, transcends classification. Haydn said of the
oratorio *Joshua* that he "was perfectly certain that only one inspired author ever did, or ever could, pen so sublime a composition." Mozart painstakingly reorchestrated *Messiah, Acis and
Galatea,* and the settings of Dryden's two St. Cecilia's Day odes
for modern orchestra. Beethoven said of him, "He was the greatest composer that ever lived. I would uncover my head and
kneel before his tomb." Bach, then an obscure provincial organist, painfully trudged some twenty-five miles hoping to get a
glimpse of his world-famous contemporary, who was back in his
native town of Halle for a short visit, only to miss him and
trudge back again.

An infant prodigy like Mozart (but, unlike him, without paternal encouragement), Handel early learned the harpsichord,
organ, violin, and oboe; the last instrument was his early love,

and to judge from his use of it in his compositions, always a favorite; but it was on the keyboard instruments that he—unusually for a great composer—became the greatest virtuoso performer of his time. He had a better academic education than most composers of his age—he attended the University of Halle for a time—and a sound musical education in the fine idiom of church music of Schütz and Buxtehude. In his late teens Handel nearly succeeded Buxtehude as organist as Lübeck, but declined the post when he learned that the offer entailed his marrying Buxtehude's elderly daughter (he remained a bachelor all his life). Between the ages of twenty-one and twenty-four he lived in Italy, where he was lionized by the Italian musical community; more than with any other composer, the cross-fertilization of northern and Mediterranean culture bore rich fruit in Handel's music.

Well aware of his capabilities and determined to realize them, Handel accepted from the Elector Georg Ludwig the splendid appointment of musical director to the Hanoverian court, only to absent himself, with or without permission, for the even richer opportunities of London. When Queen Anne died, the Elector, now King George I, and Handel were reunited (it is a pity that the charming story of Handel's regaining George's good graces by composing the lovely *Water Music* has turned out to be a myth). For the next half century he bestrode English music like a colossus; indeed, even longer, for George III, only twenty-one when Handel died, worshiped him even more fervently than his predecessors had done, and helped to institute the cult of Handel which still flourishes enthusiastically among English (and American) amateurs of choral music.

Handel wrote fifty operas, twenty oratorios, a hundred cantatas and "serenatas," fifty concerti for various instruments (including the eighteen wonderful *concerti grossi* and the seventeen organ concerti), some thirty anthems, two (early) Passions, much solo music for harpsichord, violin, flute, and oboe, and incidental music to a few plays. The operas, marvels of composition which seem to explore the whole potential of the human voice, used to be sneered at because of their lack of dramatic action. But the drama of Handel is in his music; few aspects of human tragedy, comedy, fear, pathos, awe, rejoicing are left un-

expressed in the operas, more and more of which are being revived and performed as twentieth-century audiences discover
their glories. Most of the oratorios were kept alive during the
nineteenth century by English amateur choirs, often of work-
men in the industrial districts of the North, who would not be
deterred by the objections of Victorian critics to what they
thought to be Handel's lack of romanticism. But some of these
oratorios still deserve to be better known than they are.

The instrumental music, to judge from mid-twentieth-century
record catalogues, is beginning to be done justice to; so is the
fine ceremonial music for public occasions, the Coronation Anthems and the fine *Te Deums* for the Peace of Utrecht and the
victory of Dettingen (one can imagine the piercing trumpets
and thundering kettledrums resounding among the white-and-
gold baroque glories of Wren's St. Paul's, as the monarch and
his court, resplendent in their ceremonial robes, give thanks on
behalf of the nation), the lovely *Water Music,* the impressive
music for the Royal Fireworks celebrating the Peace of Aix-la-
Chapelle. For the last, since it was an outdoor occasion, Handel
introduced twenty-four oboes, twelve bassoons, nine trumpets,
nine horns, three pairs of kettledrums, and no less than 101 can-
non, of various calibres, equivalent to several regiments of artil-
lery. After that, no one can continue to talk of the eighteenth
century's restraint—Tchaikowsky is hopelessly outclassed.

It is useless to argue that Handel is not the greatest *English*
composer. English monarchs, since his time, have been regularly
crowned and buried to Handel's music ("Zadok the Priest" and
the Dead March in *Saul*); and a sizable number of George II's
many sins should be forgiven him for the occasion on which the
irascible little monarch, irresistibly moved by the sound, rose to
his feet when he first heard the Hallelujah Chorus in *Messiah,*
since when—for no one should remain seated when a king
stands—all subsequent audiences have followed his example.
The Germans, seeking to adopt Handel as they have adopted
Shakespeare, often translate the English words of his oratorios
back into his native German; but Handel in German merely
sounds silly.

Students of literature should be particularly interested in
Handel's settings of English poetry, which often provide a won-

derfully intelligent and sensitive commentary on the poetic text.
The best known are those of Dryden's two great St. Cecilia's Day
odes, which superseded settings by earlier musicians. Handel's
reinforcement of Dryden's attempt, in the earlier ode, to characterize the contrasting "passions" roused by music is brilliant, and
the concluding "last trumpet" passage is breathtaking—a single,
unaccompanied soprano voice sings a steeply ascending broken
chord, presently joined, on a prolonged high note, by a single
trumpet; and, when it seems that the note cannot possibly be
sustained any longer, the entire chorus and orchestra suddenly
come crashing in like a gigantic thunder stroke, as of worlds
breaking asunder, and continue fortissimo with a monumental
and intricate fugue on the words "The dead shall live, the living
die, And music shall untune the sky," as though Handel, with
consummate audacity, were actually trying to reproduce the
music of that untuning.

Handel's settings of the words of the King James Bible, in
Messiah and other oratorios, do justice to its magnificent
poetry. Milton's *L'Allegro* and *Il Penseroso* are perfect material
for Handelian tone painting (at which Handel is at least as
adept as Richard Strauss). The best introduction for the beginner to the exquisiteness of Pope's poetry is Handel's setting of
two couplets from the pastoral "Summer" inserted in the
masque *Semele* (libretto by Congreve):

> Where'er you walk, cool gales shall fan the glade;
> Trees, where you sit, shall crowd into a shade;
> Where'er you tread, the blushing flow'rs shall rise,
> And all things flourish, where'er you turn your eyes.

Few could tamper with Pope's versification without disaster; but
Handel's change of Pope's "where" in the last line to
"where'er," necessitated by the music, does not make it worse.
Finest of all, perhaps, is the setting of Gay's *Acis and Galatea,*
the quintessence of modern pastoral—both Gay and Handel at
their most subtly sophisticated. That Gay and Handel achieved
this magnificently successful collaboration seems to discount the
assertion, encountered so frequently in literary histories, that
The Beggar's Opera expressed Gay's dislike of Italian (Handelian) opera and indeed succeeded in extinguishing it. *The Beg-*

gar's Opera is a masterpiece of drama, and Gay's handling of the
folk tunes he uses in it is masterly, their charming simplicity
adding another level to the already complex texture of irony in
the piece. But it is certainly not a serious contribution to *musical* art.

These two great names, Handel and Purcell, tend to eclipse
the rest; yet besides them the Restoration period and the eighteenth century produced a group of native musicians as respectable, to say the least, as their counterparts in the nineteenth
century. Among them were holders of appointments in the
cathedrals and at the Court, at Oxford and Cambridge, compilers
of useful musicological treatises, composers whose music, on the
comparatively rare occasions it is now heard, gives genuine
pleasure; and, thanks to modern recordings, the occasions are
becoming less rare. Some of them are Jeremiah Clarke (whose extremely popular "Trumpet Voluntary" has often been attributed to Purcell); William Croft and Maurice Greene, editors of
a fine collection of English church music; William Boyce, master
of the royal band and composer of charming orchestral symphonies. The music of these men is sometimes heard without the
authorship being recognized, often in the way of familiar hymn
tunes—"St. Anne's," the noble tune of Isaac Watts's noble
hymn "O God, our help in ages past," is by Croft; so is "Hanover" ("O worship the King all glorious above")—and "traditional" songs, like Boyce's lively setting of Garrick's tribute to
the *annus mirabilis* 1759, "Come, cheer up, my lads, 'tis to glory
we steer,/ To add something new to this wonderful year. . . .
Heart of oak are our ships,/ Jolly tars are our men. . . ."

Best known, and probably best, of these lesser composers is
Thomas Augustine Arne, "Doctor Arne" after Oxford conferred
its Doctor of Music degree on him. (Handel had indignantly
refused the offer of such a degree, it was said, when he learned
that the honor would cost him some £5 in registration fees. But
later in the century the university redeemed itself by bestowing
one on Haydn, *gratis* one hopes.) Arne was a prolific composer
of successful light opera, settings of operas and masques by Addison, Fielding, Congreve, and others, and incidental music to
plays, notably Shakespeare's. His settings of Shakespearean
songs—"Where the Bee Sucks," "When Daisies Pied," "Under

the Greenwood Tree," "Blow, Blow, Thou Winter Wind"—are still almost the standard settings, and are indeed praiseworthy attempts to capture something of the Elizabethan spirit in baroque idiom. The soprano arias in his serious opera *Artaxerxes* were for a long time part of the standard coloratura repertoire and are happily beginning to be heard again.

Architecture, Interior Decorating, Landscape Gardening

Georgian architecture is one of the glories of the English past. Economically speaking, it was, like other things in the eighteenth century, a by-product of an expanding and affluent individualistic society. As has happened in all times and places, when men have grown wealthy they have invested their wealth in more lavish buildings and furnishings; and from the reign of Elizabeth through that of Victoria, England experienced a more or less continuous building boom. "Housing developments" in the cities, especially London, were undertaken on a speculative basis then as now. Sometimes (as now) they were unsuccessful— the investor lost his money, or the result was a set of jerry-built houses that rapidly fell to pieces; when Samuel Johnson wrote in his poem *London, 1738,* that "falling houses thunder on your head," he was not merely using poetic license.

When sound financing and architectural finesse were combined, however, as often happened in the later seventeenth and eighteenth centuries, the result was the noble series of "squares," still one of the finest features of London. These squares were named after the aristocratic families who had (usually) inherited the land and astutely invested their capital in the buildings—Berkeley Square, Grosvenor Square, Manchester Square; the Russells' Bedford Square, Bloomsbury Square, Russell Square, Tavistock Square; the Harley–Cavendish family's Cavendish Square, with nearby Harley, Wimpole, Welbeck, Mortimer, and Portland Streets. The square was simply the Mediterranean "piazza" or "plaza" and was consciously imported by the fourth Earl of Bedford and Inigo Jones, whose Covent Garden, in the mid-seventeenth century, was the prototype of the others. (Because two sides of it were lined by an arcade, on which the front doors of the houses opened, the word "piazza" came to mean in English a porch or veranda.) In other cities the Royal Crescent and the Parades in Bath, and Merrion Square in Dublin are similar examples of artistically planned developments. All those mentioned were designed for occupancy by the wealthy; but even in domestic architecture intended for those of small means, eighteenth-century builders produced charming rows and terraces of well designed houses, unlike the mean and higgledy-piggledy constructions of the nineteenth and twentieth centuries.

There was also much construction of fine public buildings, particularly churches, a fact which must seem odd to those who think the century an age of religious indifference. Wren's great baroque St. Paul's Cathedral, completed in the reign of Anne, is of course the masterpiece; Wren is buried there, under the fine epitaph *Si monumentum requiris, circumspice*—"If you seek his monument, look around you." But Wren also built some fifty churches in the old City of London, which had been devastated by the Great Fire, churches with a dazzling diversity of lovely baroque steeples and splendid interiors—St. Clement Danes, St. Magnus Martyr, St. Stephen's, Walbrook, and the rest. Later, a Tory Parliament under Anne passed an act providing for the construction of another fifty churches in London and its environs, to take care of the expanding population. All of the fifty were by no means built, but among those that were were such lovely creations as James Gibbs' St. Mary-le-Strand, and Nicholas Hawksmoor's St. Mary Woolnoth and St. George's, Bloomsbury. Gibbs' St. Martin's-in-the-Fields was not erected under the Act of 1711, but from funds raised by the parish; its novel design of the façade of a Greek temple surmounted by a baroque spire became the model for innumerable New England churches. Every visitor to London and every student of the eighteenth century should become acquainted with the achievement of these men and of Thomas Archer, Henry Flitcroft, and other fine church architects.

Not too many of the important secular public buildings of London date from the eighteenth century—William Kent's Palladian Horse Guards, Sir William Chambers' Somerset House,

and George Dance's Mansion House (the residence of the Lord
Mayor) are the most important of those that survive. In the environs of London are Wren's fine Greenwich Hospital and additions to Hampton Court Palace. The university cities preserve
fine baroque buildings in Wren's Sheldonian Theatre and
Gibbs' Radcliffe Camera at Oxford, and Wren's library of Trinity College, Cambridge; and the public buildings of Dublin—
Trinity College, the Four Courts, the Parliament House (later
the Bank of Ireland), the latter two by James Gandon—make it
architecturally one of the finest capitals in Europe.

The great architectural achievement of the age, however, was
in "the stately homes of England"—the splendid variety of
country seats of wealthy noblemen and successful merchants and
politicians. As has been pointed out, important differences between the history of France and that of England may be traced
to the fact that the French aristocracy tended to neglect their
country estates and flock to the court of Versailles, whereas in
England (then as now) everyone who could afford to do so
seized any chance to flee into the country and stay there as long
as possible: a seat in the country was the ultimate ambition of
every City businessman. The fashion had begun long before,
but the Prime Minister, Sir Robert Walpole, put his seal on it
by pouring his questionably-got fortune into Houghton Hall,
Norfolk (architect, Colin Campbell), and its magnificent collection of art.[7] Seats ranged in size and elaborateness from Sir John
Vanbrugh and Nicholas Hawksmoor's grandiose Blenheim Palace, given by the nation to the great Duke of Marlborough, in
gratitude for his military victories, Seaton Delaval, and Castle
Howard, down to so unpretentious an establishment as that of
Edmund Burke near Beaconsfield (eyebrows have been lifted
about how an impecunious intellectual like Burke could have
financed even it).

Many other affluent societies have built lavishly, but few with
such artistic effectiveness as eighteenth-century Britain. The origins of its architecture can be traced to the early seventeenth
century, when Inigo Jones, after visiting Italy and studying the
work of the great Renaissance architects there, brought back to
England a determination to make buildings that were not
merely the rather shapeless functional masses of Tudor times

but works of art, a joy to look at. His lovely Banqueting House (the scene of the execution of his patron, Charles I) still shines out amid a mass of uninspired civil service architecture in Whitehall. His great successor, Wren, a many-sided genius in the Renaissance tradition—he was a distinguished scientist as well as architect, President of the Royal Society and Savilian professor of astronomy at Oxford while still in his twenties—took the lessons of Italian Renaissance architecture equally to heart; his idol was Bernini. From it he evolved what may justly be called "English Baroque," which still gladdens the gray English skies in the ornate spires and façades of Wren's churches and those of his disciples, Hawksmoor, Vanbrugh, and Archer.

A reaction to this exuberance set in around the 1720's: as Sir John Summerson puts it, "Baroque architecture has always been a blind spot in English criticism. It is strange that, whereas the fantastic element in Swift was soon accepted as a golden thread in the literature of the time, the fantasy of Vanbrugh, Hawksmoor, and Archer has always been deeply suspect." [8] How suspect it was may be seen in the denunciations of it in Pope's *Epistle to Burlington*. Here Pope, who in *The Rape of the Lock* and *The Dunciad* could devise fantasies as vivid as anyone's, takes up the cudgels on behalf of his friend, the third Earl, who, with the assistance of the architect William Kent, had begun a crusade to "return to Palladio"—the great pioneer of Italian Renaissance architecture. Pope, Burlington, and Kent won an easy victory in an England always suspicious of too much imagination, and "Palladianism" became the officially accepted architectural idiom for several decades. The casual modern viewer would probably still instinctively classify it as baroque, but it does have a heavier, more restrained effect than that of Wren and his followers. A hostile critic might even call it pedantic, and it did originate in a kind of literalist devotion to what was thought to be the principles of Andrea Palladio (and, naturally, a falling off from the spirit of Palladio's own lively architecture). Even so, it is far less pedantic than mid-Victorian Gothic or much modern architecture.

Around the middle of the century, three new movements began, one only short-lived, though fascinating while it lasted, the other two of much longer duration. The first was the craze for "chinoiserie".[9] The idealization of China by Western Europe dates from the reports of the Jesuit missionaries in China, headed by Father Matteo Ricci, in the early seventeenth century, who gave the impression of a highly civilized and extremely artistic people from whom, indeed, Western Europeans could learn a great deal (Ricci was later subjected to severe criticism by his superiors for, in effect, having let himself be converted by the Chinese, instead of converting them). This notion was, of course, grist to the Deists' mills, proof that morality and "the good life," in every sense of the term, could subsist without the aid of institutionalized Christianity. By Bayle and others Confucius came to be regarded as at least as great a moral teacher as Jesus. The idea gave rise in literature to the popularity of the "oriental tale" and "oriental letters," in which Montesquieu, Voltaire, Goldsmith, Johnson, and others allowed exotic Eastern peoples to teach Europeans rational and virtuous behavior.

In art (helped, of course, by the expansion of trade), this craze gave rise to the fashions of collecting delicate Chinese porcelain, familiar to the readers of Pope and Wycherley, of using and imitating Chinese fabrics and wallpapers, to furniture of Chinese design (associated particularly with Chippendale), and the cult of the Chinese garden. The fashion was enthusiastically propagated by the architect Sir William Chambers (interestingly, with assistance from Johnson) in his *Designs of Chinese Buildings, Furniture, etc.*, 1757. Chambers attributes to the Chinese an aesthetic of asymmetry and contrast—"sharawadgi" it was termed according to Sir William Temple's earlier *Essay on Gardens*. Not much architecture on a large scale, of course, resulted from the fashion, except Chambers's famous pagoda in Kew Gardens, and parts of George IV's fantastic palace at Brighton, but in the minor decorative arts it has continued to flourish (happily) to the present day.

The other two movements, the Gothic and Classical revivals, were to have more spectacular effects. Gothic architecture had never lapsed completely in England. Wren worked in the Gothic idiom at Oxford, and the great west towers of Westminster Abbey, which most tourists automatically think of as equally medieval with the rest of the building, were in fact built by pupils of Wren in the 1730's and 1740's. But generally, of course, "Gothick" was despised as rude and tasteless. Its revival was the result partly of the awakening of interest by seventeenth and eighteenth-century scholars in the languages, literatures, and antiquities of medieval Europe, especially northern Europe—the work of such men as Milton's friend, Junius, George Hickes, Thomas Hearne, and Thomas Gray; and partly of Horace Walpole's indefatigable, and probably neurotic, championing of the obscure, the out-of-fashion, the underdog. Few buildings in history have been given such assiduous publicity as Walpole gave his gimcrack villa at Strawberry Hill, whose plaster battlements, it was said, had to be renewed every two or three years. But they and the other Gothic trappings did something for Walpole's insecure psyche (as did his similarly Gothic novel, *The Castle of Otranto,* the first of the flourishing genre of horror stories). Perhaps the full-fledged pseudo-Gothicism of the nineteenth century did something similar for that of the Victorians. Indeed, when one considers Walpole, and William Beckford's Gothic experiments at Fonthill, and, in the next century, the names of Pugin and Ruskin, one is struck by the extent to which the Gothic revival was a literary man's rather than an architect's invention.

In the middle of the eighteenth century, the excavation of the Greco-Roman cities of Herculaneum and Pompeii provided the impetus that was eventually to result in the Classical revival of the early nineteenth century (if the student of literature is bothered by the fact that in architecture this development is contemporary with Wordsworth and Shelley rather than with Pope and Swift, he would do well to reexamine his assumptions). Massive "Classical" domes and colonnades, like those of the British Museum, the National Gallery of London, University College, London, and countless nineteenth- and twentieth-century Capitols, Parliament buildings, court houses, and post offices were to dominate public architecture for another century or more almost as much as Gothic dominated ecclesiastical architecture.

Like Victorian Gothic, the revived Classical was an antiquarian, derivative idiom in which the chief concern was to duplicate ancient techniques, and which was ultimately sterile and boring. The impulse that gave rise to the architectural idiom of Wren, Vanbrugh, Kent, and the rest, on the contrary, though it can certainly be traced back, through Bernini and Palladio, to Vitruvius and Roman architecture, and hence is also sometimes called "classical," is so in a very different sense from what was produced by Smirke, Wilkins, and other early nineteenth-century Classical revivalists. In the Renaissance and eighteenth-century works, the classical sources have been used merely as a convenient base for the products of the architect's own fertile artistic imagination, and hence it is much better to distinguish it by use of the term "baroque." The best of those who worked after the rediscovery of Greek and Roman architecture in the mid-eighteenth century was certainly Robert Adam, who, like Palladio before him, used the discoveries merely as a stimulus for evolving his own peculiar and charming style. The failure of nerve, of confidence in the contemporary artistic imagination came later, and persisted throughout the nineteenth century and much of the early twentieth.

In the occupation of bringing into existence beautiful surroundings, the subsidiary arts of interior decorating and furniture making (Chippendale, Hepplewhite, Sheraton, the Adams) reached the highest level they have known in England. So did such minor, but appealing arts as those of woodcarving, in the hands of Grinling Gibbons, ornamental ironwork, by Jean Tijou, and ceramics, by the Wedgwoods and the Chelsea potters. But most interesting of all, as reflecting a change of sensibility, was that of landscape gardening, in which a great revolt took place against the formal, or symmetrical, garden which had been the ideal throughout the Renaissance and on the Continent. There may have been some nationalist feeling involved: the supreme example of formal landscaping had recently been completed by André Le Nôtre, at Louis XIV's palace of Versailles, and was the pride of France. Students taught to think of eighteenth-century England as dominated by "classical formalism" are always surprised to learn how vigorously the English intellectuals of the time, especially Pope and Addison, rejected the conception of the symmetrical garden in favor of the natural, or free-form, landscape. To be sure, it often proved very expensive and difficult to landscape the grounds of a country seat so that they would "resemble nature"—to replant trees in asymmetrical clumps, to keep up a costly natural lawn instead of covering the walks with gravel, to construct a "ha-ha"—a ditch containing a fence below eye level, so that one's eye could have a distant vista of a natural scene with grazing sheep and cows, but without the inconvenience that the close presence of these sometimes too natural creatures would bring. But Lancelot "Capability" Brown persuaded many noble landlords to sign his contracts—he got his nickname by solemnly viewing the unimproved grounds and presently pronouncing, "Well, my lord, I see a capability in it." His best known work is the extensive park surrounding Blenheim Palace, whose "naturalness" forms a piquant setting for the unabashed and exuberant "artificiality" of Vanbrugh's baroque masterpiece. No product of eighteenth-century English taste has had more enthusiastic a reception (a fact which may cause the cynic to wonder a little about its artistic soundness): "natural" landscaping has become virtually mandatory for parks and gardens throughout the world, with the exception of the Far East, and on the Continent a favorite name for a public park is *Englische Garten*.

Painting, Engraving, Sculpture

In music, it was noted above, a strong and healthy tradition of professionalism existed continuously in England from Tudor times onward, a tradition which was not overwhelmed by the importation of innovations from Italy or France, or by the powerful genius of a Purcell or Handel, but came easily and successfully to terms with them, contributing as much as it was contributed to. In architecture, such a native tradition did not exist (or, rather, the fine Gothic tradition that had flourished up to the fifteenth century had died out); but men like Jones and Wren and Hawksmoor and Adam were artists of sufficient genius to school themselves in the Renaissance Italian tradition and use it, not merely to make uninspired copies, but as the basis for genuinely original and imaginative work. In painting, however, it is hard to think of the name of a native English painter of any importance before the eighteenth century.[10] Patrons imported mature and established artists from the Continent—chiefly from the Netherlands—for a time to execute a series of commissions, after which they returned to their native land, their English visit a relatively unimportant episode in their careers: Hans Holbein in the reign of Henry VIII, Rubens and Van Dyck under the early Stuarts. Much the same situation existed after the Restoration, except that the immigrants—Lely, Kneller, Michael Dahl—arrived at an earlier age and stayed in England permanently.

It was not until the eighteenth century that an English tradition of painting developed. But when it did, it developed with remarkable speed and strength. This was no doubt another testimonial to the age's tremendous creative energy and power of assimilation and, of course, to the wealth which made large-scale portraits of individuals and families, and views of the family's holdings, a necessity for newly rich magnates to hang on the walls of their new country seats. First-rate portraitists like Reynolds soon became wealthy men themselves.

Perhaps the chief credit for launching the "English school" of painting should go to Jonathan Richardson the Elder, not a great painter, but an excellent theorist and propagandist: his *Essay on the Theory of Painting*, which he published in 1715 at the age of fifty, made a deep impression on both Hogarth and Reynolds; the profound humanism expressed in Reynolds' *Discourses* is earlier to be found in Richardson's *Essay*. Whatever the reasons for the phenomenon, the sudden appearance of a galaxy of fine painters is remarkable: Hogarth, one of a slightly older generation, was born in 1697, Allan Ramsay in 1713, Richard Wilson in 1714, Reynolds, Gainsborough, and Stubbs in the 1720's, Romney, Joseph Wright, Benjamin West, and John Singleton Copley (it seems reasonable to include these two immigrants from America) in the 1730's. Of the younger generation, usually thought of as "Romantic," or at least "Regency," Fuseli was born in 1741, Blake and Raeburn in the 1750's, Morland and Lawrence in the 1760's, Constable and Turner in the 1770's.

The giants of the group are unquestionably Hogarth, Reynolds, and Gainsborough—in what order, their admirers will continue to dispute. Hogarth is, of course, the odd man, the sport. Handicapped, as the later artists were not, by inadequate early instruction in draughtsmanship—to provide sound early technical instruction became one of the great objects of both Hogarth and Reynolds—he perhaps suffered from an unacknowledged feeling of inferiority, which made him combative and touchy. Always playing a lone hand, he refused to defer to the authority of the great Italian masters and their English disciples, and worked out his own unique idiom.

Thackeray (who had some training in art) was probably right in including Hogarth along with various literary figures in his *English Humorists:* there is a sense in which his work is literature rather than art; although his composition and color are most skillful, it is not his line that gives delight. About most artists, this would be a damning statement; but as a composer of literary works on canvas, Hogarth is so fine that the stricture seems hardly relevant. He himself fully recognized where his strength lay, and, engraving his most popular works for wide distribution, he set himself up as the pictorial recorder and reformer of contemporary English life, especially the seamier side of it. His sequences, "The Rake's Progress," "Marriage à la Mode," "The Harlot's Progress," are pictorial novels in miniature, distinguished, as novels should be, for their sharp and objective observation of the human scene, and their careful selection of detail so as to form a valid moral commentary on it. His portraits of individuals, especially of tough, hard-bitten men of the world, Lord Lovat, Bishop Hoadly, Captain Coram, spare their subjects nothing; yet the total effect is not one of shallow cynicism; they remain intensely human and sympathetic, and even that consummate crook, Lovat, becomes pitiable in his self-deception. With more sympathetic subjects—his servants, the cast of *The Beggar's Opera,* the Graham children— he is wonderfully compassionate and understanding, without ever falling into sentimentality. The lovely epitaph on him by Samuel Johnson does him justice:

> The hand of him here torpid lies,
>   That drew th' essential form of grace;
> Here clos'd in death th' attentive eyes,
>   That saw the manners in the face.
>
> If Genius warm thee, reader, stay,
>   If merit touch thee, shed a tear;
> Be Vice and Dulness far away;
>   Great Hogarth's honour'd dust is here.

Hogarth's satiric portraits of individuals who met his disapproval, such as John Wilkes and Charles Churchill, though clever, are not transcendently so. But in his satiric scenes of everyday life, "Morning," "Noon," "Evening," and "Night," "The Election," "A Modern Midnight Conversation," and the like, he adumbrated a technique of caricature that was to develop late in the century into the fantastically grotesque idiom of such masters as Rowlandson, Gillray, and Sayers, hardly surpassed in savagery and repulsiveness by Goya and Daumier. Again, innocent students who have been told of the restraint and decorum of the century are astonished, indeed appalled, when they first encounter Rowlandson's and Gillray's apocalyptic visions of human folly and degradation.

Reynolds's reputation among literary students (if what literary students think of his art is of any consequence) has suffered from the wide publicity given to Blake's hostile comments on him. But these have as little to do with the real Reynolds as Blake's similar comments on Johnson have to do with the real Johnson. Both names serve as symbols for Blake of something he dislikes; whether the men actually embody this is another question, to which the answer is very probably "No." The fact is, of course, that Reynolds' technical skill and artistic imagination are so self-evidently great that to attempt an apology would be presumption.

Like Handel (also a lifelong bachelor) Reynolds' devotion to his art above all else verged on the miraculous. Not even the Gordon Riots could interfere with his reaching his studio on time each morning; in the last decade of his long life, his niece complained, "My uncle seems more bewitched than ever with his palettes and pencils." He "went out" in society and contributed his share to the brilliant conversation of his and his friend Johnson's circle; yet, as one reads the passages about Reynolds in Boswell, one always senses a detachment which is not there in Johnson and Burke—the main part of his mind, one feels, is back at the studio, working on a difficult canvas.

Like other great artists—like his idol Michelangelo, whose name, with typically eighteenth-century dramatic effect, he contrived to stand as the last word he uttered as President of the Royal Academy—his art improved and deepened the older he became; such masterpieces as his paintings of Lord Heathfield and Archbishop Robinson come from the later years of his working life. As with Hogarth, his finest work was his portraits of active, experienced, mature, worldly men like these; as one critic puts it, "Reynolds's work may be seen as an equation between two great traditions—that of English character in the age of Marlborough and that of the master-periods of Italian painting." But, again like Handel, small samplings of his work do not do justice to Reynolds' dazzling fecundity: as the same critic says, "He of all painters most needs to be seen in the mass; only an overall view, and long perusal of examples taken from every period of his life, can give the measure of this giant professional." [11]

Portraiture, Reynolds' genre, was one of the two great styles of painting in which the age excelled. The other was the landscape. Humanity and the English countryside were the subjects which contemporary Englishmen most wanted to see represented on their walls. Reynolds' great rival, Gainsborough (to whom Reynolds paid a noble tribute in the *Discourse* delivered to the Royal Academy after Gainsborough's death) excelled in both. Much more the solitary, unsocial artist than Reynolds— he has even been described as Romantic—possessing none of Reynolds' deep sense of responsibility to English art and the English public, he eschewed academic life, painted as he pleased (and sometimes carelessly), declined honors, and died a much poorer man than Reynolds. (Yet George III much preferred him to Reynolds, and commissioned from him many charming portraits of the Royal Family.)[12] His portraits have an intimate quality often missing in those of Reynolds, especially when Reynolds thought it incumbent on him to be allegorical. The classic contrast is that between Reynolds' imposing picture of Mrs. Siddons, the great actress of the time, in all her glory, seated on a throne as "The Tragic Muse," and Gainsborough's portrait of her in a charming blue-and-white-striped afternoon dress, as the sweet and dignified English gentlewoman she was.

Of the three great landscape painters of the century, Richard Wilson, Gainsborough, and Constable (Constable's work, of course, extended well into the nineteenth century, but began in the eighteenth), it is hard to say which is the best. Their subjects were all the same—the landscape of southern England as Jane Austen described it:

> It was a sweet view—sweet to the eye and the mind. English verdure, English culture, English comfort, seen under a sun, bright without being oppressive.[13]

Wilson sometimes attempted more rugged scenes, such as the mountains of his native Wales; one of his finest pictures is that of Mount Snowdon, surprisingly Japanese in quality. Gainsborough's and Constable's landscapes everyone knows from numerous reproductions; Wilson was neglected in his own time and later, and his genius is perhaps only now beginning to be recognized.

That the best known works of all three are English subjects, however, by no means indicates an insular attitude toward their art. All of them studied the Dutch and Italian masters—Wilson spent six years in Italy, and painted much Italian landscape—and all of them were to some extent affected by the "romantic" influence of Claude Lorrain. At the other end of the scale, hints of the later techniques of the nineteenth-century French impressionists can be detected in the freer use of light and color in Constable's later work. As so often happened, the best in English art in the century was not the result of "untutored native genius" but of the imaginative assimilation of excellence of technique wherever it was to be found. For that matter, some of the finest English landscapes—or rather townscapes—of the century were painted by the Venetian Canaletto (nearly all of whose later production was purchased for George III by his consul in Venice, Joseph Smith, and is in the English royal collection). Canaletto was persuaded to come to England for some years, and his brilliant canvases of London and the Thames valley, with their vivid blue skies and shimmering light, are the best record available of the lovely eighteenth-century city that Wordsworth knew—"Earth has not anything to show more fair."

Eighteenth-century English painters, Reynolds included, felt uneasily that they had a duty to render "the sublime," which duty they usually fulfilled by turning out from time to time vast, crowded canvases depicting historical and allegorical scenes. They fail to impress us as they presumably impressed contemporaries (not that they impressed Samuel Johnson, who averred that he would rather have a portrait of a dog that he knew than the finest historical painting in the world; and it was Johnson, ahead of his time as usual, who sneered mightily at the use by moderns of hackneyed classical mythology). Certainly Reynolds' picture of an embarrassed-looking Garrick being dragged in opposite directions by the Muse of Tragedy and the Muse of Comedy tends only to make us smile. However, Benjamin West, an immigrant from Pennsylvania, made a huge success out of the genre (for instance, his "Death of Wolfe on the Plains of Abraham") and succeeded Reynolds as President of the Royal Academy.

There is much more that could be said about the riches of eighteenth-century British painting and engraving; Blake and his friend the Swiss immigrant Fuseli, in particular, call for discussion; but it is probably better to leave them for a later volume in this series. A final note, however, must call attention to an undeservedly neglected art that flourished during the century—that of sculpture, in particular portrait sculpture. Apart from Joseph Nollekens (and his father came from Antwerp), most of its practitioners were immigrants: Caius Gabriel Cibber (sculptor of the two famous statues of "Melancholy Madness" and "Raving Madness"—as we should now say, schizophrenia and paranoia—at the gate of Bedlam, which Pope felicitously termed his son Colley's "brazen, brainless brothers"), Louis François Roubiliac, John Michael Rysbrack. As with Reynolds' portraits (and Handel's music) what strikes one about their statues and busts—Nollekens' Handel and Johnson, Roubiliac's wonderful painted terra cotta bust of Colley Cibber, Rysbrack's Queen Caroline—is their subtle insight into human psychology and their immense dramatic energy. One is sometimes tempted to advance the thesis that the dramatic impulse in the eighteenth century, denied by censorship its legitimate expression on the stage, found its outlet in the other arts, in Handel's tremendous choral climaxes, Reynolds' arresting portraits, and the bold exaggeration of feature and expression in Roubiliac's and Nollekens' portrait sculpture.

A Note on Literary and
Aesthetic Criticism and Theory

For many decades questions of eighteenth-century English artistic and literary taste and sensibility have usually been discussed in terms of two potent concepts, "neoclassicism" and "romanticism." A rough, but not too inaccurate, outline of the history of the English aesthetic from 1550 to 1850, as given in the great majority of literary histories from about 1870 onward, runs as follows: Three great movements can easily be discerned in the literary and artistic activity of the time, movements of, successively, action, reaction, then action again.[14] The English Renaissance, dated approximately 1550–1650 and centering on the reign of Elizabeth I, is characterized by boldness, adventurousness, and exuberant individualism, culminating in the great "irregular" drama and poetry of Shakespeare and the extravagant conceits of Donne. In 1660, however, as a result of the traumatic experience of the Civil War, men's minds recoiled, in literature as well as in politics, from such qualities, and sought order, decorum, regularity, and stability instead. The means by which these ends were achieved were two: first, an increased emphasis on the importance of the classical (chiefly Latin) writers, Horace, Virgil, and Juvenal in particular, as providing literary models, critical principles, and norms of social conduct for modern man; and, second, the reliance of artists and writers on rigid rules, such as the dramatic unities, for the composition of their works and a corresponding distrust of the imagination. The fact that Charles II and his court spent many years of exile at the French court before returning to England is credited with having assisted this process, influential French writers and critics of the time (Corneille, Racine, Boileau) having been infected with the neoclassical virus even earlier and more strongly.[15] Then in 1798 (though there had been foreshadowings in the shape of "pre-Romantics" such as Thomson, Gray, and the Wartons), *enfin Wordsworth vint,* along with Coleridge and Blake, to free the imagination from the shackles of these dead rules and models (and English literature lived happily ever after). To document the currency of such a picture from late nineteenth- and early twentieth-century textbooks of the history of English literature and criticism would be superlatively easy. One quotation will suffice here to illustrate it, the title of a lecture series given in the United States in 1884 by Edmund Gosse, *From Shakespeare to Pope: A History of the Decline of Romantic Poetry.*[16]

Childish as this sketch appears when presented thus baldly, and drastically as details of it have later been modified—it is encouraging to note that the concept of "pre-Romanticism," once accepted so unquestioningly, has been virtually abandoned by reputable modern literary historians[17]—its essential elements still hold a powerful sway over the minds of students. Yet it is salutary to observe how comparatively recently this pattern was imposed on the historical data.[18] The great writers of the eighteenth century, Dryden, Pope, Johnson (Swift has always been treated as an exception, sometimes even being termed a "Romantic" out of his time) were entirely unaware that they were "neoclassicists"; they did not use the term or any equivalent, nor is there any evidence that they thought of themselves as playing the role Arnold and others cast them in. Henry Hallam, in the earliest substantial literary history of the modern era, published between 1837 and 1839,[19] manages to make a thorough and perceptive survey of the literature of Europe, including England, between 1400 and 1700 without displaying any awareness of a shift from "Renaissance exuberance" to "neoclassical restraint." The history of the genesis and propagation of the concept of a "neoclassical age" needs thorough investigation. It seems safe to say, however, that it was mainly an invention of the obscure academics and journalists who, from around 1840 to 1870, wrote the pioneering textbooks of the new school subject of English literature, which was just being introduced into the curriculum of English and American colleges in the middle and late nineteenth century, and who felt a compulsion to provide a set of historical facts about the subject on which students could be examined. In short, the credentials of the concept are not so imposing that modern students need be frightened away from asking themselves whether, in spite of its wide currency, there is any compelling historical reason for accepting the hypothesis as valid.

This is not the place to enter into a detailed analysis of the question; but the student might usefully consider an alternative hypothesis that seems to fit the historical data at least as well as the "neoclassical" one—namely, that the eighteenth century, in England at least, far from representing a resurgence of reliance on previously abandoned classical rules and models, is, rather, the mid-point in a steady decline in reverence for the authority of the classical Latin and Greek writers, a decline which has been continuous from an apogee in the early Renaissance to the present, when the numbers of writers and critics who have any extensive first-hand acquaintance with the classics or regard them as in any way authoritative is small indeed. It is not surprising that Hallam failed to notice the occurrence of any "neoclassical" resurgence after 1660. He had recorded in detail that period in the early sixteenth century when "the real excellence of the ancients in literature as well as art gave rise to an enthusiastic and exclusive admiration of antiquity," the time when the test of a true intellectual was the ability to write "pure" Latin, "conformable to the standard of what is sometimes called the Augustan age, that is, of the period from Cicero to Augustus," [20] and, by comparison, the time of Dryden, Defoe, Bunyan, and Swift must have seemed a far cry indeed from such "exclusive admiration." He was aware of the great indebtedness to classical literature of earlier writers like Marlowe, Spenser, Ben Jonson, Donne, Milton, and Shakespeare himself—the fact is that allusions to the classics occur more frequently in Shakespeare's plays than in those of Dryden or in Pope's verse epistles or Johnson's essays. It is true that Dryden, Pope, and Johnson were writing for an audience who they assumed had the basic grounding in Latin literature that was the hallmark of every educated Englishman from the Renaissance down to the beginning of the twentieth century. It is also true that they enjoyed and admired Horace and Juvenal, and used them for their own purposes. But that the domination of Horace and Juvenal over the minds of eighteenth-century writers was greater than that of Seneca and Ovid over sixteenth-century writers, or that Dryden and Pope succumbed to their spell more than Shelley, say, to that of Aeschylus, or Tennyson to that of Virgil, or that either Dryden or Pope recommended the classical writers as guides for the moderns more strenuously than T. S. Eliot and Ezra Pound were later to do, would be difficult to prove. It was Pope who wrote, with sturdy independence, "Of One Who Would Not Be Buried in Westminster Abbey" (himself):

> Heroes and kings, your distance keep,
> In peace let one poor poet sleep,
> Who never flattered folks like you.
> Let Horace blush, and Virgil too.

It was Ezra Pound who wrote "Homage to Sextus Propertius."

Any study of eighteenth-century literary and aesthetic theory in England must begin by deciding for itself whether or not it will accept *a priori* the postulate that an aggressive neoclassicism (or its more fashionable modern synonym, "Augustanism") was the dominant intellectual pattern of the age. If any such study does, it will face many difficult problems when considering the work of the leading critics of the century, on which it will often have to render the verdict of "inconsistent" or "ambivalent," of wavering aimlessly between desire to adhere to the dominant theory and desire to rebel against it. Such a verdict has often been passed on both the century's greatest literary critic, Samuel Johnson, and its greatest art critic, Joshua Reynolds. The net result is to discredit their criticism, and indeed the whole body of criticism of the eighteenth century, as the work of men who fundamentally could not make up their minds, who lacked the courage of their critical convictions. If, on the other hand, they are seen as men who, though inheriting a residual legacy of authoritarianism and apriorism in critical matters from the Renaissance (which had in turn inherited it from the Middle Ages), nevertheless moved steadily and consistently in the opposite direction, and contributed greatly to the erosion of that legacy, such charges will fail. There will be no more need to be apologetic about these critics than there is about, say, another famous contemporary, Henry Cavendish, who, though reared in the medieval and Renaissance belief in the theory of phlogiston (a product, in the end, of Aristotelian physics) and never bringing himself to the point of formally renouncing this theory, nevertheless, by his "modern" experimentation with hydrogen and nitrogen, made immensely valuable contributions to the development of modern chemistry.

The fancied necessity of finding evidence in the writings of Johnson, Reynolds, and others to support the view that, at least part of the time, they were militant "neoclassicists," has frequently led to serious misreadings of their writings. Both Johnson and Reynolds were fond of using the term "general" as one of critical approbation.[21] Their modern expositors very often equate this with "abstract" and accuse them of preaching "abstractionism," though in fact Johnson never seems to have used "abstract" or "abstraction" as critical terms or said anything in favor of such a quality in imaginative writing. It is obvious, if one examines his texts without the presupposition that Johnson was a "neoclassicist," that by "general," as a term of approbation, he by no means meant "abstract." He illustrates his praise of Shakespeare's adherence to "general nature" by the example of King Claudius in *Hamlet,* and he makes it abundantly clear that it is not because Shakespeare's portrait of Claudius is an "abstract" representation of kingship that he admires it. On the contrary, he vigorously defends Shakespeare against the complaints of Voltaire and others that Claudius, in getting drunk, is much too *concrete,* too particularized, too little like the stereotype of a king. A little serious study of such passages soon convinces us that Johnson's position is precisely that of Ezra Pound when he praises Joyce's *Ulysses* and Eliot's *Prufrock:*

> James Joyce has written the best novel of the decade, and perhaps the best criticism of it has come from a Belgian who said, "All this is as true of my country as of Ireland." Eliot has a like ubiquity of application. Art does not avoid universals, it strikes at them all the harder in that it strikes though particularities. . . . [Eliot's] men in shirt-sleeves and his society ladies are not a local manifestation: they are the stuff of our modern world, and true of more countries than one.[22]

When Johnson praises "generality," he undoubtedly means "ubiquity of application" or "susceptibility of wide response," as no doubt Reynolds also does. And in the notorious passage in *Rasselas* where Imlac proclaims that the business of the poet is not to number the streaks of the tulips but "to exhibit . . . such prominent and striking features as recall the original to every mind," Johnson is surely saying no more than what Keats was later to say—that poetry should not surprise by "singularity; it should strike the reader as a wording of his own highest thoughts, and appear almost as a remembrance."

Indeed, the more one reads Johnson's remarks about how poetry should be written, the more strikingly his taste in poetry appears to resemble Wordsworth's. He detests archaic and contrived diction, the facile use of outworn mythology, unnatural inversion of normal English sentence order. Poetry, he thinks, should be communication among contemporary men in respect to contemporary issues and states of feeling, and its vehicle should be contemporary language. Gray's "images are magnified by affectation; the language is laboured into harshness. . . . His art and his struggle are too visible, and there is too little appearance of ease and nature"; Collins' "diction was often harsh, unskillfully laboured and unjudiciously selected. He affected the obsolete when it was not worthy of revival; and he puts his words out of the common order, seeming to think, with some later candidates for fame, that not to write prose is certainly to write poetry." [23] Johnson's objection to *Lycidas* is well summed up in Wordsworthian language—Milton's poem is patently *not* the spontaneous overflow of powerful feelings; and Johnson's own illustration of how an elegy should be written, "On the Death of Dr. Robert Levet," is a considerably Wordsworthian poem—even in its occasional descent into bathos, "His frame was firm, his powers were bright,/ Though now his eightieth year was nigh."

The critique of *Lycidas* is indeed an important crux in the assessment of Johnson's criticism, and to some degree of eighteenth-century criticism in general. After a century and a half of denigration, some students have begun to examine Johnson's critique seriously and to understand that, far from its being an expression of old-fashioned reactionism, it is a revolutionary document. One student has gone so far as to term it "the end of Renaissance criticism":

> Johnson was in several ways a "new man," a man of our sensibility rather than a man of the Renaissance. . . . Johnson . . . just as we today, was not very interested in the "kinds" of literature as such, and demanded that poetry accord with "nature," the accordance to be tested by "my surveys of life." He wanted genuine

passion in literature, and responded with passion to literature. He expected, as we expect, a funeral elegy to express the grief of the writer, not his adeptness at handling literary conventions; and at the end of his life, when he had lived much and suffered much, and forgotten nothing of the suffering, he found this desire for passion and above all for emotional truth in literature precisely in conflict with the Renaissance traditions which his education had affirmed. . . . Modern criticism begins with Johnson.[24]

Johnson's strictures on *Lycidas* are clarified by his two earlier *Rambler* essays on the pastoral *genre*. For him, the emotional effect of a pastoral poem comes from what we would call its realism—he defines it simply as "a poem in which any action or passion is represented by its effects upon a country life." The pastoral poetry of Theocritus and Virgil pleases him because it springs from their actual experience, in childhood and youth, of rural life in northern Italy and Sicily, and their nostalgic recollection of it after they have become city dwellers.[25] Later pastoral, like that of Spenser, Milton, and Pope, has failed because its writers have merely used a contrived rural setting as extrinsic ornament for declamation on current controversial political and religious questions, or an obituary of some recently deceased worthy, or simply to show off their own technical virtuosity; their shepherds are not countrymen whom they themselves have known, as Theocritus and Virgil did, but patently factitious stereotypes. Modern academic criticism rejects such an approach to the pastoral, and insists that we, as readers, accept it as an essentially artificial *genre* and train ourselves to sense the complex ironies implicit in the discrepancy between reality and illusion that it presents. But Johnson's ideal of the pastoral, though we may find it unacceptable, cannot be called reactionary or old-fashioned or, least of all, neoclassical. On the contrary, the ideal of presenting serious and universal human emotion in a realistic setting of "the simple life" is very modern. Crabbe, with Johnson's approval and assistance, would later attempt this; likewise Hardy, Frost, and many other late nineteenth- and early twentieth-century poets and novelists. It is a curious reflection that the work which Johnson's ideal of the pastoral most closely adumbrates is probably *Michael: A Pastoral Poem* (though he would also have approved of *The Death of the Hired Man*), and there are close resemblances between what is desiderated in *Ramblers* 36 and 37 and what is desiderated in the Preface to *Lyrical Ballads*.

The point of this long preamble is primarily to suggest that, much as eighteenth-century critical and aesthetic theory has been studied by later scholars, the usefulness of such study has too often been diminished by the attempt to fit the reading of the century's critical texts into a preconceived framework of intellectual history. The modern student should certainly at least try to approach the writings of eighteenth-century critics and aestheticians without such preconceptions, and only later, after he has familiarized himself with what these writers have actually been saying, consider whether or not there is any need to postulate such entities as "neoclassicism" and "Augustanism" to explain it. This, at least, would have been the method recommended, as it was followed by a great many of those writers themselves, products of a staunchly empiricist age. It is paradoxical, to say the least, that it has been by the exercise of a highly aprioristic procedure that the criticism of that age has been stigmatized as aprioristic.

That the century reveled in exploring the questions of what is artistically effective and why is apparent when one notes the 225 titles of books on general literary and aesthetic theory published between 1664 and 1800 which are listed in the *Cambridge Bibliography of English Literature,* followed by several hundred additional titles of works of criticism of particular genres and particular writers. "Dryden," said Johnson, "may be properly considered the father of English criticism," and certainly the contrast between the spotty and erratic history of English literary criticism before Dryden and the mighty proliferation of critics and theorists after him is striking. It would be wrong to try to explain this fact, as was once customary, by postulating an opposition between the creative imagination and the critical spirit, and asserting that the quantity of criticism produced by the eighteenth century is further proof that it was a cool, judicious age of reason, which bridled and restrained the soaring imagination—after all, as Eliot and others have pointed out, some of the greatest English critics have also been some of

the greatest English poets. The phenomenon, on the contrary, is
further proof of the century's exuberant curiosity, now ranging
through scarcely explored territory, the complex operation of
the human mind and emotions. Much of its critical effort was
directed toward expanding taste, toward developing the reader's
ability to respond to a wider range of literature—the difficult
poetry of the politically unpopular Milton (Dryden and Addison), that of Chaucer (Dryden), the folk ballads (Addison and
Percy—whom Johnson helped in preparing the *Reliques* for the
press), Hebrew poetry (Lowth), Norse literature (Gray and
others), the medieval romances, and Renaissance narrative
poetry deriving from them, such as that of Spenser, Ariosto, and
Tasso (Hurd), Middle English literature (Thomas Warton),
above all Shakespeare, the modern editing of whose works
begins with Rowe in 1709. As for cautious reliance on classical
authority, Dryden himself may be said to have promulgated the
century's declaration of critical independence in his splendid
assertion, " 'Tis not enough that Aristotle has said so, for Aristotle drew his models of tragedy from Sophocles and Euripides;
and *if he had seen ours, might have changed his mind.*" [26]

In the short space of the present volume, there is no room to
attempt even a summary of the century's vast production of "Essays on Criticism," "Essays on Taste," "Essays on Design," "Essays toward Fixing the True Standards of Wit," "Dissertations
on Genius," "Observations on Style," and the like. Of course it
may well be asked how useful it is to the student of the imaginative literature of the time to familiarize himself with all these—
to what extent they will sharpen his understanding and appreciation of the literature itself. Much of this critical and aesthetic
theorizing was written by men who were not greatly skilled, if at
all, in any of the arts: Lord Kames, for instance, was a judge of
the Scottish courts of justice, Alexander Gerard and Hugh Blair
Presbyterian divines, Archibald Alison a Scottish Episcopalian
divine (one wonders why theorizing about the nature of beauty
should have so appealed to Scottish clergymen, of all people).
And even when such theorizing is undertaken by a practitioner
of the arts, it is an old truism that, as Coleridge observed of
Wordsworth, his theory may give by no means an accurate report of his practice. An outstanding eighteenth-century illustra-

tion of this is Hogarth, who was very proud of the theory evolved in his *Analysis of Beauty* that an S-shaped curve of certain proportions ("the line of beauty") is the essential component of all artistically excellent design. But it has been pointed out that such a curve is preeminently characteristic of the rococo, which Hogarth detested, and it would be a hopeless task to try to locate the excellencies of Hogarth's own art in his use of the "line of beauty."

Aesthetics is, of course, a branch of philosophy or psychology, and the most fruitful contributions to a satisfactory theory of aesthetics were made by philosophers, or rather psychologists in the guise of philosophers, as most of the great eighteenth-century British philosophers were. If Dryden was the father of English criticism, Locke was certainly the father of eighteenth-century English aesthetic theory. Locke's great service was to reject the old Greek theory that the human mind works with inherent "logic," and to propound instead the theory of "associationism"—that we think and feel what we do largely as a result of the fortuitous associations provided by our past experience of the things we see, hear, touch, taste, and smell. A child sees a cane and trembles, not because of any logical reasoning about the nature of canes, but because in the past it has been applied vigorously to his bottom; conversely, when he sees a bon bon, he smiles. Berkeley, especially in his *New Theory of Vision,* and David Hartley, in his *Observations on Man,* push this Pavlovianism even farther; and David Hume comes to the conclusion that all "reasoning" is simply habit, the product of "conditioning" by experience. As for aesthetics, Hume declares, "Beauty is no quality in things themselves: it exists merely in the mind which contemplates them; and each mind perceives a different beauty." The simple existential act of liking or disliking comes first; afterward we try to work out a rationale to explain our doing so. That there was a nexus between such empiricist aesthetics and the practical criticism of the time is evident when we consider such a passage as Johnson's "general observation" on *Julius Caesar* (and Johnson professed no admiration of Hume): "Of this tragedy," he begins, "many particular passages deserve regard, and the contention and reconcilement of Brutus and Cassius is universally celebrated." "But," adds Johnson coolly,

"*I have never been strongly agitated in perusing it,* and think it somewhat cold and unaffecting," and this is enough to damn the work as far as Johnson is concerned.

Aesthetic theorists of the eighteenth century tend to be divided into two main classes, those who in the main concur with Locke and Hume and seek to find the causes of our liking or disliking something in the history of human experience, and those who, on the contrary, adhere to pre-Lockian psychology and postulate an "innate sense" in man which intuitively turns toward what is, in the nature of things, inherently and absolutely beautiful. The second group is not large, but a few influential eighteenth-century writers, notably Shaftesbury and, less dogmatically and more intelligently, Francis Hutcheson, stick to their Platonic guns and insist on the innate aesthetic sense which automatically responds to the true, the beautiful, and the good. The vast majority of English theorists and critics of the period fall, however, into the first category. There is Addison, whose *Spectator* essays on the imagination take an essentially psychological approach. There is Johnson, who shrewdly points out, among many other things, that the "unities" of time and place in the drama have no psychological justification, since the imagination of the spectator can quite as easily transfer him from Rome to Alexandria in the middle of a play as it transferred him from a hard theater seat in London to Rome at the beginning of it, and (in *Rambler* 60) that the source of the pleasure one gets from reading fiction or biography is what we should now call empathy. There is Burke, who finds that we are moved by "the sublime" (objects characterized by vastness, obscurity, a sense of power, and the like) when we have an "idea" of pain and danger without actually experiencing them, by contrast with our reaction to "the beautiful," whose characteristics are smallness, smoothness, delicacy, and so on. There is Lord Kames, who, though he begins by assuring us that taste is innate, nevertheless goes to great lengths to explain in associationist terms *why* some things are beautiful and others not (when you erect a "ruin" in your garden, be sure to construct it in Gothic rather than Greek style, because a Gothic ruin brings associations of time triumphing over strength, a melancholy but not unpleasing thought, whereas a Greek ruin represents the triumph of barbarity over taste, a gloomy and discouraging reflection). There are Hugh Blair (a stream running safely between banks is beautiful; a waterfall is sublime) and Archibald Alison, who is perhaps the most thoroughgoing associationist of them all—anything, he thinks, can be made affecting by association; there was, he tells us, a mathematician whose blood ran cold and whose hair stood on end when he read Newton's *Optics;* "The call of a goat among rocks," he says, "is strikingly beautiful, as expressing wildness and independence; in a farmyard, not so."

As interesting as all this may be to the student of the intellectual history of the time, it may be questioned whether much of it is actually relevant to the art of the Restoration and eighteenth century and the delight and instruction which that art is capable of affording to the modern listener, viewer, and reader. The truly great critics of the age, Dryden, Johnson and Reynolds, are also, as often happens, great executants of the arts they discuss; and Dryden and Johnson are much more critics than "metacritics"—they are concerned primarily with the concrete work before them, and very little with weaving grandiose generalizations about how the beautiful is to be defined. Reynolds, to be sure, in the fifteen presidential *Discourses* he delivered to the Royal Academy, tends to generalize more: it is a tendency inherent in the *genre* of the "presidential address," whether delivered to a gathering of artists, businessmen, university graduands, or even philological scholars.

Reynolds' *Discourses* have had an unenthusiastic reception for some time, largely, perhaps, because of Blake's witty aphorisms jotted in the margins of his copy of them. Yet the more one reads Reynolds, the more one is impressed by the seriousness and insight and the maturity and the *rightness* of so much of what he has to say. It becomes clear, for instance, as one studies the *Discourses* thoughtfully, that Reynolds is no more guilty than his friend Johnson of the most damning error that is charged against them both, that of advocating "generality," in the sense of "abstractness," in art: they are as well aware as Blake and Ezra Pound that the material of art is particularities, whatever the effect on the audience may be.[27] And after so much elaborate theorizing in a vacuum, which lesser critics of the eighteenth century (as in other centuries) were so fond of indulging in, it is reassuring to be told by Reynolds, in his thirteenth *Discourse,*

> All theories which attempt to direct or control the Art, upon any principles falsely called rational, which we form to ourselves upon supposition of what ought in reason to be the end or means of Art, independent of the known first effect produced by the objects on the imagination, must be false and delusive.

It is clear that the greatest critics of eighteenth-century England were no more under the spell of "reason" than were its greatest philosophers and greatest poets.

NOTES TO CHAPTER FOUR

1. *Studies in Oxford History, Chiefly in the Eighteenth Century* (Oxford: Oxford Historical Society, 1901), p. 28.

2. *Brideshead Revisited* (Boston: Little, Brown, 1945), p. 82.

3. Article "Architecture: Modern Architecture."

4. Margaret Whinney and Oliver Millar, *English Art, 1625–1714* (Oxford: The Clarendon Press, 1957), p. 1.

5. Perhaps it is its Welsh (Tudor) ancestry that accounts for the strong musical tradition of the British royal family, from Henry VIII, who composed songs, down through the Georges, with their devotion to Handel, and Queen Victoria, proud of having studied singing under Mendelssohn and a fine patron of contemporary music, to George V's grandson, the Earl of Harewood, a music critic and director of the Edinburgh Festival.

6. A slight break in the continuity occurred during the 1640's and 1650's, when the Puritans frowned on elaborate liturgy, and the choir of the Chapel Royal was temporarily disbanded. Yet music did not suffer as theater did. No major writer has ever been a more devoted lover of music than Milton, the son of a not undistinguished composer of madrigals and motets. Indeed, the Puritan regime has been credited with having been favorable to the development of opera, since the ban on stage plays did not extend to dramatic performances with music.

7. Although Pope and others berated Walpole as indifferent, even hostile, to the arts, the great Houghton collection was one of the finest of the time. It had a curious later history: Walpole's grandson, the third Earl of Orford, sold it to Catherine the Great of Russia, who was then assembling the Hermitage collection; then in the 1920's, the Soviet government, pressed for money, sold important pieces from the collection to Andrew Mellon, who added them to the new National Gallery of Art in Washington. Thus the great eighteenth-century Prime Minister's collection

helped to provide the nucleus for the national collections of two great world powers of the twentieth century.

Eighteenth-century British politicians seemed, in general, to choose more impressive avocations than many of their successors. Walpole's great rival, Robert Harley, Earl of Oxford, and his son were great collectors of books and manuscripts: the Harleian Miscellany, the catalogue of the Harleian Library (on both of which Samuel Johnson was employed), and the Harleian collection of manuscripts in the British Museum testify to the importance of their work. On a somewhat lower intellectual level, Godolphin, Lord Treasurer under Queen Anne, was the founding father of modern British horse racing and imported the famous Godolphin Arab, ancestor of all British thoroughbreds; Lord Townshend's important services to agriculture have already been noted in Chapter One.

8. *Georgian London* (London: Pleiades Books, 1945), p. 78.

9. William W. Appleton, *A Cycle of Cathay* (New York: Columbia University Press, 1951), is an excellent account of the history of the movement.

10. Two exceptions are the mysterious Nicholas Hilliard, painter of miniatures in the reign of Elizabeth, and William Dobson, painter of portraits in the earlier seventeenth century.

11. John Russell, "British Portrait Painters," in W. J. Turner, ed., *Aspects of British Art* (London: Collins, 1947), pp. 133–135.

12. The King may have objected, as some Johnsonians do to Reynolds' portraits of Johnson, that Reynolds fictionalized his subjects excessively. Reynolds is nearly as much responsible as Boswell for making Johnson into a quaint, eccentric, laughable figure ("Mr. Oddity"). The noble portrait of Johnson by Opie does more justice than any of Reynolds' to the grave, tender, sensitive, and deeply compassionate man that emerges from many of Johnson's writings—for instance, the elegy on the death of Dr. Levet.

13. *Emma*, Chapter 42.

14. It is probably no coincidence that this notion began to achieve currency around the same time as Macaulay's version of the Victorian theory of inevitable human progress: "We have often thought that the motion of the public mind in our country resembles that of the sea when the tide is rising. Each successive wave rushes forward, breaks, and rolls back; but the great flood is steadily coming on" (essay on Sir James Mackintosh). This was published in 1835, but of course it was not until some decades later that Macaulay's writings, in cheap editions, reached their widest audience. Macaulay and his fellow Whig politicians, as well as disseminating such historical cheer, also dabbled in literary criticism, generally with unfortunate results.

15. And of course this is a libel on the great French literature of the seventeenth century. Lytton Strachey brilliantly points out (in *Landmarks in French Literature*, Oxford University Press, 1912) how in Racine the observation of the unities effects a compression, an almost unbearable intensity of passion seldom achieved in English drama.

16. Gosse, *America: The Diary of a Visit, Winter 1884–1885*, R. L. Peters and D. G. Halliburton, eds. (West Lafayette, Indiana: Department of English, Purdue University, 1966), p. iii.

17. "What does the best verse of Coleridge, Landor, Keats, Shelley, and even Wordsworth and Byron derive from the pre-Romantics? . . . Only in a very general sense can 'Tiger, tiger, burning bright,' 'The Solitary Reaper,' and the 'Ode to a Nightingale' be rendered as the flowering of the poetry of Dyer, Thomson, the Wartons, Gray, and Collins": Raymond D. Havens, "Discontinuity in Literary Development: The Case of English Romanticism," *Studies in Philology*, XLVII (January 1950), p. 103.

18. The earliest listing of "neo-classic" in the *Oxford English Dictionary* —though, to be sure, in a very sketchy treatment—is 1881.

19. *Introduction to the Literature of Europe in the Fifteenth, Sixteenth, and Seventeenth Centuries.*

20. Hallam, I, 315–316 (2nd ed., 1843).

21. On the other hand, when Johnson uses the term "general" as one of denigration—as he frequently does—he *is* clearly using it in the sense of "abstract": e.g., of Rowe, "I know not that there can be found in his plays any deep search into nature, any accurate discriminations of kindred qualities, or nice display of passion in its progress: all is general and undefined."

22. *Instigations* (New York, 1920), p. 199; originally published in *Poetry* (Chicago), 1917.

23. After a long period in which much confusion was caused by critics who seemed to postulate that there was one language for prose and a different one for poetry, T. S. Eliot returned to the position of Johnson (and Wordsworth): "Certain qualities are to be expected of any type of good verse at any time; we may say the qualities which good verse shares with good prose. . . . One does not need to examine a great deal of the inferior verse of the eighteenth century [or any other century, one might add] to realize that the trouble with it is that it is not prosaic enough. . . . To have the virtues of good prose is the first and minimum requirement of good poetry" (Introduction of Haslewood Books edition of *London* and *The Vanity of Human Wishes*, 1930).

24. Oliver F. Sigworth, "Johnson's *Lycidas*: The End of Renaissance Criticism," *Eighteenth-Century Studies*, I (December 1967), 166–168. See also Warren L. Fleischauer, "Johnson, *Lycidas*, and the Norms of Criticism," in *Johnsonian Studies*, Magdi Wahba, ed. (Cairo, 1962).

25. "Theocritus came here [to Alexandria] late in his career. He had been born at Cos and had lived in Sicily, and he arrived full of memories that no town-dweller could share—memories of fresh air and the sun, of upland meadows and overhanging trees, of goats and sheep, of the men and the women who looked after them, and of all the charm and the coarseness that go to make up country life. He had thrown these memories into poetical form": E. M. Forster, *Alexandria: A History and a Guide* (New York: Doubleday [Anchor Books], 1961: originally published 1922), p. 35. In considering Johnson's fondness for the "authentic" pastoral of Theocritus and Virgil, it might be remembered that he too, like them, had been a country, or at least small town, dweller until he moved to the metropolis at the age of twenty-eight. Spenser, Milton, and Pope, on the other hand, were all native Londoners.

26. John Dryden, "Heads of an Answer to Rymer," written *ca.* 1678. It was Johnson who first publicized the work, printing it from Dryden's holograph, owned by Garrick, in his *Life of Dryden*.

27. Blake's most famous piece of marginalia on Reynolds is regularly garbled. It is usually reported as follows:

> "This disposition to abstractions, to generalizing and classification, is the great glory of the human mind" (Reynolds). "To generalize is to be an idiot. To particularize is the alone distinction of merit. General knowledges are those knowledges that idiots possess" (Blake).

If the source (the 1798 edition of the *Discourses*) is consulted, it will be seen that Reynolds wrote nothing of the kind. Blake's comment is on a statement attributed by Edmond Malone to Burke. Reynolds was as well aware as Blake that the achievements of the human mind which he admired most greatly were composed not of "abstractions" but of very concrete blobs and streaks of paint.

Perhaps the most perceptive treatments of Reynolds as critic that have been published are Hoyt Trowbridge, "Platonism and Sir Joshua Reynolds," *English Studies*, XXI (1939), 1–7, and Harvey D. Goldstein, "*Ut Poesis Pictura*: Reynolds on Imitation and Imagination," *Eighteenth-Century Studies*, I (Spring 1968), 213–235.

BIBLIOGRAPHICAL NOTE

I. GENERAL BIBLIOGRAPHY

The resources for the study of this complex period are so rich and varied that few readers will wish to confine themselves to the handful of works of which limited space permits mention in this note. As a guide to further reading, two bibliographical pamphlets by James L. Clifford, *Early Eighteenth-Century Literature* (revised, 1962) and *Later Eighteenth-Century Literature* (revised, 1960) distributed by the Columbia University Bookstore, New York, are recommended. They provide an excellently arranged selective list, not merely of literary texts and criticism, but of "background" works as well. The standard annual bibliography of the period, "English Literature, 1660–1800," appearing in *Philological Quarterly* each July, also provides admirable coverage of background material in political, social, ideological, and aesthetic history. The bibliographies from 1925 to 1960 have been accumulated and published in four volumes by the Princeton University Press.

II. SOCIAL HISTORY

The most useful single work for the student who wishes an accurate knowledge of the way of life in eighteenth-century Britain is A. C. Turberville (ed.), *Johnson's England,* 2 vols. (Oxford: Clarendon Press, 1933). It is a collection of 27 fascinating essays on various aspects of eighteenth-century life by experts in the field—e.g., "The Church" by Norman Sykes; "The Navy" by Admiral Sir Herbert Richmond; "The Army" by Sir John Fortescue; "London" by Dorothy George; "Architecture and the Garden" by Geoffrey Webb; "Sculpture" by Katherine Esdaile; "The Law" by Sir Frank Mac-Kinnon; book publishing by R. W. Chapman; "The Newspaper" by D. Nichol Smith. The value of the work is enhanced by 158 illustrations. A less sumptuous but still useful attempt to give a similar view is A. C. Turberville, *English Men and Manners in the Eighteenth Century* (London: Oxford University Press, 1926). Shorter but more up-to-date accounts are given by J. H. Plumb, *England in the Eighteenth Century* (Penguin Books, 1950) and Dorothy Marshall, *English People in the Eighteenth Century* (London: Longmans, 1956).

Still a classic, and delightful reading in spite of its prejudice, is the famous Chapter Three of Macaulay's *History of England* (1849), "The State of England in 1685." It is a curious paradox that for all Macaulay's and Thackeray's Victorian censure of eighteenth-century morality, they were obviously fascinated by the exuberance of the age and appreciative of it. If the modern reader can bring himself to ignore their moralizing, no more vivid introduction to the eighteenth century can be found than Macaulay's essays dealing with the period—e.g., those on Addison, Johnson, Horace Walpole, Fanny Burney, the two Pitts—and Thackeray's *Henry Esmond, The English Humorists,* and *The Four Georges.*

III. POLITICAL HISTORY

There is a great need for an up-to-date, single-volumed political history of Britain in the Restoration and eighteenth century (Dorothy Marshall's *Eighteenth Century England* [London: Longmans, 1963] is much more a social than a political history). For the period 1714–1800, the most useful single work at present available is probably V. H. H. Green, *The Hanoverians* (London: Edward Arnold, 1948). It incorporates some of the revolutionary findings of the modern school of historians of the time, led by Sir Lewis Namier, whose *The Structure of English Politics at the Accession of George III* (London: Macmillan, 1929) was the opening blast in the destruction of the older Victorian or "Whig" interpretation, exemplified in the work of Lord Macaulay, J. R. Green, W. E. H. Lecky, and G. M. Trevelyan. J. Steven Watson, *The Reign of King George III, 1760–1815* (Oxford: Clarendon Press, 1960), a volume in the Oxford History of England, is unhesitatingly recommended. J. H. Plumb, *The First Four Georges* (London: Batsford, 1956) is an amusing and, on the whole, sympathetic account of the royal family of the time. Some more specialized works are Sir Lewis Namier's essays on George III, "Monarchy and the Party System," and the "country gentlemen," in his *Personalities and Powers* (London: Hamish Hamilton, 1955); Richard Pares, *King George III and the Politicians* (Oxford: Clarendon Press, 1953); John B. Owen, *The Rise of the Pelhams* (London: Methuen, 1957); Archibald S. Foord, *His Majesty's Opposition, 1714–1830* (Oxford: Clarendon Press, 1964); J. H. Plumb, *Sir Robert Walpole* (London: Cresset, 1956–1960), 2 vols. published of a projected 3 vols.

IV. INTELLECTUAL HISTORY

No seriously comprehensive attempt to trace the controlling ideas of British thought in the eighteenth century exists, although there are studies of certain individual movements and aspects. The title of Sir Leslie Stephen's *English Thought in the Eighteenth Century* (London: Smith, Elder, 1876) is a misnomer: it is a lively and searching study of the work of a number of writers of the time, including that of the best known Deists. But there was much more to "English thought" of the time than this; moreover, when Stephen has to deal with orthodox Christian teaching, as he frequently does, it is with the bias of a militant agnostic. Basil Willey, *The Eighteenth Century Background* (London: Chatto and Windus, 1940) manages to be at the same time over-specialized and superficial. A. O. Lovejoy, *The Great Chain of Being* (Cambridge, Mass.: Harvard University Press, 1936) is a brilliant study of the history and implications of the idea of the "Great Chain," which certainly had much influence on certain Renaissance and seventeenth-century English writers. It would be wrong, however, to infer, as some students seem to have done—though Lovejoy nowhere justifies the inference—that it was widely influential in the eighteenth century. The conclusions of some recent books by literary students which attempt a facile synthesis of the "sensibility of the eighteenth century" in a simple phrase or two should be viewed with great caution.

A serious student of the thought of the time should certainly familiarize himself with British empiricist philosophy. Locke, Berkeley, and Hume prided themselves (unlike Continental philosophers) on writing in lucid colloquial prose, easily comprehensible by the ordinary educated reader, and the best introduction to their philosophy is through their own writings. The racy chapters dealing with the movement in Bertrand Russell's *History of Western Philosophy* (New York: Simon and Schuster, 1945), himself sympathetic to the empiricists and the tradition of "easy writing" in philosophy, are perhaps as good a "survey" as any for the modern student; but for something more solemn, he may consult W. R. Sorley, *A History of British Philosophy* (New York and London: Putnam, 1921), an expansion of Sorley's chapters on the subject in the *Cambridge History of English Literature*. Nor should he neglect the history of science during the period: Marjorie Nicolson's studies, such as *Science and Imagination* (Ithaca, New York: Cornell University Press, 1956) and *Mountain Gloom and Mountain Glory* (Cornell University Press, 1959), treat its impact on the creative imagination of the time.

There is no adequate account for the modern reader of what, doctrinally, Christianity in eighteenth-century Britain meant. Norman Sykes' *Church and State in Eighteenth-Century England* (Cambridge: Cambridge University Press, 1934) is a brilliant study of the Church of England in its temporal relations, which destroys the myth of its "stagnation" during this period. Bishop Stephen Neill's *Anglicanism* (Penguin Books, 1958) is a useful introduction for the beginner. But perhaps the best course for the student who wants to know the significance of Anglicanism for the eighteenth as well as other centuries is to familiarize himself with the contents of the Book of Common Prayer.

V. ARTISTIC AND AESTHETIC HISTORY

There are a number of excellent recent histories of British painting, sculpture, and architecture during the period—the relevant volumes of the Oxford History of Art (Oxford: Clarendon Press) and the Pelican History of English Art (Penguin Books), Sir John Summerson, *Georgian London* (London: Pleiades Books, 1945) and Sir Albert Richardson, *An Introduction to Georgian Architecture* (London: Art and Technics, 1949). There are also skillful recent studies of many individual artists, such as those of Hogarth by Ronald Paulson (New Haven: Yale University Press, 1965), Richard Wilson by W. G. Constable (London: Routledge and Kegan Paul, 1953), William Kent by Margaret Jourdain (London: Country Life, 1948), James Gibbs by Bryan D. G. Little (London: Batsford, 1955), and

Nicholas Hawksmoor by Kerry Downes (London: Zwemmer, 1959). There is a large literature on landscape gardening of the time (e.g., Ralph Dutton, *The English Garden* [London: Batsford, 1937]) and on other minor arts, such as interior decorating and furniture-making. W. W. Appleton, *A Cycle of Cathay* (New York: Columbia University Press, 1951) is an excellent historical account of the fashion of *chinoiserie*.

Modern appreciation of English music of the baroque age is not yet as fully developed as that of the visual arts or Continental baroque music; the standard histories (e.g., *The Oxford History of Music*, Vol. IV [Oxford: Clarendon Press, 1902; 2nd ed., 1931]) still carry a large content of Victorian and romantic suspicion of it. Perhaps the best modern study unhampered by such limitations is Paul Henry Lang's monumental *George Frideric Handel* (New York: Norton, 1966). The short volumes on Purcell by Sir Jack Westrup (1937) and Handel by E. J. Dent (1934) in the "Master Musicians" series (London: Dent; New York: Dutton) are also useful.

A convenient source-book for eighteenth-century aesthetic and literary theory is Scott Elledge (ed.), *Eighteenth-Century Critical Essays*, 2 vols. (Ithaca, New York: Cornell University Press, 1961).

❧ Index

Abbreviations: Abp = Archbishop; Bp = Bishop; Css = Countess; Mss = Marquess; Pss = Princess; Vct = Viscount.

The notes and chronological tables have not been indexed.

Visual Basic 2008 Recipes

A Problem-Solution Approach

■ ■ ■

Todd Herman, Allen Jones,
Matthew MacDonald, and Rakesh Rajan

Apress®

Visual Basic 2008 Recipes: A Problem-Solution Approach

Copyright © 2008 by Todd Herman, Allen Jones, Matthew MacDonald, Rakesh Rajan

ISBN-13 (pbk): 978-1-59059-970-9

ISBN-10 (pbk): 1-59059-970-5

ISBN-13 (electronic): 978-1-4302-0604-0

ISBN-10 (electronic): 1-4302-0604-7

Printed and bound in the United States of America 9 8 7 6 5 4 3 2 1

Lead Editor: Jonathan Gennick
Technical Reviewer: Damien Foggon
Editorial Board: Clay Andres, Steve Anglin, Ewan Buckingham, Tony Campbell, Gary Cornell, Jonathan Gennick, Matthew Moodie, Joseph Ottinger, Jeffrey Pepper, Frank Pohlmann, Ben Renow-Clarke, Dominic Shakeshaft, Matt Wade, Tom Welsh
Project Manager: Richard Dal Porto
Copy Editor: Kim Wimpsett
Associate Production Director: Kari Brooks-Copony
Production Editor: Katie Stence
Compositor: Susan Glinert Stevens
Proofreader: Liz Welch
Indexer: Broccoli Information Services
Artist: April Milne
Cover Designer: Kurt Krames
Manufacturing Director: Tom Debolski

Distributed to the book trade worldwide by Springer-Verlag New York, Inc., 233 Spring Street, 6th Floor, New York, NY 10013. Phone 1-800-SPRINGER, fax 201-348-4505, e-mail orders-ny@springer-sbm.com, or visit http://www.springeronline.com.

For information on translations, please contact Apress directly at 2855 Telegraph Avenue, Suite 600, Berkeley, CA 94705. Phone 510-549-5930, fax 510-549-5939, e-mail info@apress.com, or visit http://www.apress.com.

Apress and friends of ED books may be purchased in bulk for academic, corporate, or promotional use. eBook versions and licenses are also available for most titles. For more information, reference our Special Bulk Sales–eBook Licensing web page at http://www.apress.com/info/bulksales.

The source code for this book is available to readers at http://www.apress.com.

Once again I must praise my wife and children for their incredible patience and support while I wrote this book. My wife and dear friend, Amy, was a rock for me when I was struggling to keep my deadlines, while my daughter, Alaina, and son, Aidan, kept me laughing and reminded me why I was doing this.

Thank you, guys, for your love and support. I owe you everything.

—Todd Herman

Contents at a Glance

Contents

■CHAPTER 3 **Application Domains, Reflection, and Metadata** 97

■CHAPTER 4 **Threads, Processes, and Synchronization** 129

■CHAPTER 12   Security and Cryptography 495

■CHAPTER 13   Code Interoperability 539

About the Author

TODD HERMAN works for Berico Technologies as a senior developer as part of the intelligence community. He has been programming since he received his first computer, a Commodore 64, on his 11th birthday. His experience ranges from developing data-entry software in FoxPro for a water research laboratory to writing biometric applications in Visual Basic for NEC. He currently lives in Virginia with his wife and children, spending his free time programming, playing computer games, and watching the Sci-Fi Channel.

He recently set up a blog, which you can find at http://blogs.bericotechnologies.com/todd.

About the Technical Reviewer

DAMIEN FOGGON is a freelance developer and technical author based in Newcastle, England. When not wondering why the Falcons can never win away from home, he spends his spare time writing, playing rugby, scuba diving, or pretending that he can cook.

His next magnum opus, *Beginning ASP.NET Data Access with LINQ and ADO.NET* (take your pick of C# or VB .NET), is due out from Apress in September 2008, assuming that SQL Server 2008 actually gets released in 2008.

If he could be consistent (or interesting), his blog might not be three months out of date. You never know—you may get lucky. See for yourself at http://www.littlepond.co.uk.

Acknowledgments

I must thank Damien Foggon for, once again, performing a superb job in providing the technical editing for this book and keeping me on the correct path. I also extend my thanks to Apress for putting out remarkable material and allowing me the opportunity to throw in my two cents.

Introduction

Attempting to learn all there is to know about developing VB .NET applications using the Microsoft .NET Framework would be an incredibly daunting task. For most of us, the easiest and best approach is to dive in and start writing code. We learn through testing and experimentation, and when we run into the unknown, we search the Internet or grab a book to assist with the current subject.

Visual Basic 2008 Recipes is not a book that attempts to teach you about the inner workings of a specific subject. It is a resource book that should sit near you as you program, so you can quickly use it to reference what you need.

As you are settled in front of your computer working, you will inevitably run into a situation where you need a little guidance, as all of us do from time to time. The subject matter in this book is so comprehensive that you are bound to find at least one recipe that will fit the bill whenever you need that nudge in the right direction.

This book will not teach you everything you need to know about developing VB .NET applications in Visual Studio 2008, but it will be invaluable as a stepping-stone. Use the recipes as you need them to help move your development projects along or to give you a starting point for your own experimentation.

Note This book is based on a previously published book called *Visual Basic 2005 Recipes*. The contents were updated to reflect any changes or new additions between the 2005 and 2008 versions of Visual Studio .NET. Although some of the recipes in this book will work with .NET Framework 2.0, the main focus of this book is Visual Studio .NET and .NET Framework 3.5.

Additionally, this book was written using the final version of Visual Studio 2008 and Windows Vista Business. The code was also tested on a system running Windows XP, but please keep in mind that results may vary slightly if you are using that operating system.

CHAPTER 1

■ ■ ■

Application Development

This chapter covers some of the general features and functionality found in Visual Basic .NET 9.0 and Visual Studio 2008. The recipes in this chapter cover the following:

- Using the VB .NET command-line compiler to build console and Windows Forms applications (recipes 1-1 and 1-2)

- Creating and using code modules and libraries (recipes 1-3 and 1-4)

- Compiling and embedding a string resource file (recipe 1-5)

- Compiling applications using MSBuild.exe (recipe 1-6)

- Accessing command-line arguments from within your applications (recipe 1-7)

- Using compiler directives and attributes to selectively include code at build time (recipe 1-8)

- Manipulating the appearance of the console (recipe 1-9)

- Accessing program elements built in other languages whose names conflict with VB .NET keywords (recipe 1-10)

- Giving assemblies strong names and verifying strong-named assemblies (recipes 1-11, 1-12, 1-13, and 1-14)

- Signing an assembly with a Microsoft Authenticode digital signature (recipes 1-15 and 1-16)

- Managing the shared assemblies that are stored in the global assembly cache (recipe 1-17)

- Making your assembly more difficult to decompile (recipe 1-18)

- Understanding the basic functionality required to use Language Integrated Query (LINQ) (recipes 1-19, 1-20, 1-21, 1-22, and 1-23)

■Note All the tools discussed in this chapter ship with the Microsoft .NET Framework or the .NET Framework software development kit (SDK). The tools that are part of the .NET Framework are in the main directory for the version of the framework you are running. For example, they are in the directory C:\WINDOWS\Microsoft.NET\ Framework\v3.5 if you install version 3.5 of the .NET Framework to the default location. The .NET installation process automatically adds this directory to your environment path.

The tools provided with the SDK are in the Bin subdirectory of the directory in which you install the SDK, which is C:\Program Files\Microsoft Visual Studio 9.0\SDK\v3.5 if you chose the default path during the installation of Microsoft Visual Studio 2008. This directory is *not* added to your path automatically, so you must manually edit your path in order to have easy access to these tools. Your other option is to use the Visual Studio 2008 Command Prompt shortcut that is located under the Microsoft Visual Studio 2008/Visual Studio Tools folder in the Windows Start menu. This will launch vcvarsall.bat, which will set the right environment variables and open the command prompt. Most of the tools support short and long forms of the command-line switches that control their functionality. This chapter always shows the long form, which is more informative but requires additional typing. For the shortened form of each switch, see the tool's documentation in the .NET Framework SDK.

Also, as a final note, if you are using Windows Vista, you should be sure to run all command-line utilities using Run As Administrator, or some of them might not function properly. Doing this will still result in numerous dialog boxes requesting that you ensure you approve of the request to use administrative rights; you must respond to these dialog boxes by clicking Yes.

1-1. Create a Console Application from the Command Line

Problem

You need to use the VB .NET command-line compiler to build an application that does not require a Windows graphical user interface (GUI) but instead displays output to, and reads input from, the Windows command prompt (console).

Solution

In one of your classes, ensure you implement a Shared method named Main with one of the following signatures:

```
Public Shared Sub Main()
End Sub
Public Shared Sub Main(ByVal args As String())
End Sub
Public Shared Function Main() As Integer
End Sub
Public Shared Function Main(ByVal args As String()) As Integer
End Sub
```

Build your application using the VB .NET compiler (vbc.exe) by running the following command (where HelloWorld.vb is the name of your source code file):

```
vbc /target:exe HelloWorld.vb
```

■**Note** If you own Visual Studio, you will most often use the Console Application project template to create new console applications. However, for small applications, it is often just as easy to use the command-line compiler. It is also useful to know how to build console applications from the command line if you are ever working on a machine without Visual Studio and want to create a quick utility to automate some task.

How It Works

By default, the VB .NET compiler will build a console application unless you specify otherwise. For this reason, it's not necessary to specify the /target:exe switch, but doing so makes your intention clearer, which is useful if you are creating build scripts that will be used by others or will be used repeatedly over a period of time.

To build a console application consisting of more than one source code file, you must specify all the source files as arguments to the compiler. For example, the following command builds an application named MyFirstApp.exe from two source files named HelloWorld.vb and ConsoleUtils.vb:

```
vbc /target:exe /main:HelloWorld /out:MyFirstApp.exe HelloWorld.vb ConsoleUtils.vb
```

The /out switch allows you to specify the name of the compiled assembly. Otherwise, the assembly is named after the first source file listed—HelloWorld.vb in the example. If classes in both the HelloWorld and ConsoleUtils files contain Main methods, the compiler cannot automatically determine which method represents the correct entry point for the assembly. Therefore, you must use the compiler's /main switch to identify the name of the class that contains the correct entry point for your application. When using the /main switch, you must provide the fully qualified class name (including the namespace); otherwise, you will receive the following:

```
vbc : error BC30420: 'Sub Main' was not found in 'HelloWorld'
```

If you have a lot of VB .NET code source files to compile, you should use a response file. This simple text file contains the command-line arguments for vbc.exe. When you call vbc.exe, you give the name of this response file as a single parameter prefixed by the @ character. Here is an example:

```
vbc @commands.rsp
```

To achieve the equivalent of the previous example, commands.rsp would contain this:

```
/target:exe /main:HelloWorld /out:MyFirstApp.exe HelloWorld.vb ConsoleUtils.vb
```

For readability, response files can include comments (using the # character) and can span multiple lines. The VB .NET compiler also allows you to specify multiple response files by providing multiple parameters that are prefixed with the @ character.

The Code

The following code lists a class named ConsoleUtils that is defined in a file named ConsoleUtils.vb:

```
Imports System

Namespace Apress.VisualBasicRecipes.Chapter01
    Public Class ConsoleUtils
```

```vb
    ' This method will display a prompt and read a response from the console.
    Public Shared Function ReadString(ByVal message As String) As String

        Console.Write(message)
        Return Console.ReadLine

    End Function

    ' This method will display a message on the console.
    Public Shared Sub WriteString(ByVal message As String)

        Console.WriteLine(message)

    End Sub

    ' This method is used for testing ConsoleUtility methods.
    ' While it is not good practice to have multiple Main
    ' methods in an assembly, it sometimes can't be avoided.
    ' You specify in the compiler which Main sub routine should
    ' be used as the entry point.  For this example, this Main
    ' routine will never be executed.
    Public Shared Sub Main()

        ' Prompt the reader to enter a name.
        Dim name As String = ReadString("Please enter a name:  ")

        ' Welcome the reader to Visual Basic 2008 Recipes.
        WriteString("Welcome to Visual Basic 2008 Recipes, " & name)

    End Sub

    End Class
End Namespace
```

The HelloWorld class listed next uses the ConsoleUtils class to display the message "Hello, World" to the console (HelloWorld is contained in the HelloWorld.vb file):

```vb
Imports System

Namespace Apress.VisualBasicRecipes.Chapter01
    Public Class HelloWorld

        Public Shared Sub Main()

            ConsoleUtils.WriteString("Hello, World")
            ConsoleUtils.WriteString(vbCrLf & "Main method complete.  Press Enter.")
            Console.ReadLine()

        End Sub

    End Class
End Namespace
```

Usage

To build HelloWorld.exe from the two source files, use the following command:

```
vbc /target:exe /main:Apress.VisualBasicRecipes.Chapter01.HelloWorld ➥
/out:HelloWorld.exe ConsoleUtils.vb HelloWorld.vb
```

1-2. Create a Windows-Based Application from the Command Line

Problem

You need to use the VB .NET command-line compiler to build an application that provides a Windows Forms–based GUI.

Solution

Create a class that inherits from the `System.Windows.Forms.Form` class. (This will be your application's main form.) In one of your classes, ensure you implement a `Shared` method named `Main`. In the `Main` method, create an instance of your main form class and pass it to the `Shared` method `Run` of the `System.Windows.Forms.Application` class. Build your application using the command-line VB .NET compiler, and specify the `/target:winexe` compiler switch.

How It Works

Building an application that provides a simple Windows GUI is a world away from developing a full-fledged Windows-based application. However, you must perform certain tasks regardless of whether you are writing the Windows equivalent of "Hello, World" or the next version of Microsoft Word, including the following:

- For each form you need in your application, create a class that inherits from the `System.Windows.Forms.Form` class.

- In each of your form classes, declare members that represent the controls that will be on that form, such as buttons, labels, lists, and text boxes. These members should be declared `Private` or at least `Protected` so that other program elements cannot access them directly. If you need to expose the methods or properties of these controls, implement the necessary members in your form class, providing indirect and controlled access to the contained controls.

- Declare methods in your form class that will handle events raised by the controls contained by the form, such as button clicks or key presses when a text box is the active control. These methods should be `Private` or `Protected` and follow the standard .NET event pattern (described in recipe 15-10). It's in these methods (or methods called by these methods) where you will define the bulk of your application's functionality.

- Declare a constructor for your form class that instantiates each of the form's controls and configures their initial state (size, color, position, content, and so on). The constructor should also wire up the appropriate event handler methods of your class to the events of each control.

- Declare a Shared method named Main—usually as a member of your application's main form class. This method is the entry point for your application, and it can have the same signatures as those mentioned in recipe 1-1. In the Main method, call Application.EnableVisualStyles to allow support for themes (supported by Windows XP, Windows Server 2003, and Windows Vista), create an instance of your application's main form, and pass it as an argument to the Shared Application.Run method. The Run method makes your main form visible and starts a standard Windows message loop on the current thread, which passes the user input (key presses, mouse clicks, and so on) to your application form as events.

The Code

The Recipe01_02 class shown in the following code listing is a simple Windows Forms application that demonstrates the techniques just listed. When run, it prompts a user to enter a name and then displays a message box welcoming the user to "Visual Basic 2008 Recipes."

```
Imports System
Imports System.Windows.Forms

Namespace Apress.VisualBasicRecipes.Chapter01

    Public Class Recipe01_02
        Inherits Form

        ' Private members to hold references to the form's controls.
        Private Label1 As Label
        Private TextBox1 As TextBox
        Private Button1 As Button

        ' Constructor used to create an instance of the form and configure
        ' the form's controls.
        Public Sub New()
            ' Instantiate the controls used on the form.
            Me.Label1 = New Label
            Me.TextBox1 = New TextBox
            Me.Button1 = New Button

            ' Suspend the layout logic of the form while we configure and
            ' position the controls.
            Me.SuspendLayout()

            ' Configure Label1, which displays the user prompt.
            Me.Label1.Location = New System.Drawing.Size(16, 36)
            Me.Label1.Name = "Label1"
            Me.Label1.Size = New System.Drawing.Size(155, 16)
            Me.Label1.TabIndex = 0
            Me.Label1.Text = "Please enter your name:"

            ' Configure TextBox1, which accepts the user input.
            Me.TextBox1.Location = New System.Drawing.Point(172, 32)
            Me.TextBox1.Name = "TextBox1"
            Me.TextBox1.TabIndex = 1
            Me.TextBox1.Text = ""
```

```vb
            ' Configure Button1, which the user clicks to enter a name.
            Me.Button1.Location = New System.Drawing.Point(109, 80)
            Me.Button1.Name = "Button1"
            Me.Button1.TabIndex = 2
            Me.Button1.Text = "Enter"
            AddHandler Button1.Click, AddressOf Button1_Click

            ' Configure WelcomeForm, and add controls.
            Me.ClientSize = New System.Drawing.Size(292, 126)
            Me.Controls.Add(Me.Button1)
            Me.Controls.Add(Me.TextBox1)
            Me.Controls.Add(Me.Label1)
            Me.Name = "Form1"
            Me.Text = "Visual Basic 2008 Recipes"

            ' Resume the layout logic of the form now that all controls are
            ' configured.
            Me.ResumeLayout(False)

        End Sub

        Private Sub Button1_Click(ByVal sender As Object, ➥
ByVal e As System.EventArgs)

            ' Write debug message to the console.
            System.Console.WriteLine("User entered: " + TextBox1.Text)

            ' Display welcome as a message box.
            MessageBox.Show("Welcome to Visual Basic 2008 Recipes, " + ➥
TextBox1.Text, "Visual Basic 2008 Recipes")

        End Sub

        ' Application entry point, creates an instance of the form, and begins
        ' running a standard message loop on the current thread.  The message
        ' loop feeds the application with input from the user as events.
        Public Shared Sub Main()
            Application.EnableVisualStyles()
            Application.Run(New Recipe01_02())
        End Sub

    End Class

End Namespace
```

Usage

To build the Recipe01_02 class into an application, use this command:

```
vbc /target:winexe Recipe01-02.vb
```

The /target:winexe switch tells the compiler that you are building a Windows-based application. As a result, the compiler builds the executable in such a way that no console is created when you run your application. If you use the /target:exe switch instead of /target:winexe to build a Windows Forms application, your application will still work correctly, but you will have a console window visible while the application is running. Although this is undesirable for production-quality software, the console window is useful if you want to write debug and logging information while you're developing and testing your Windows Forms application. You can write to this console using the `Write` and `WriteLine` methods of the `System.Console` class.

Figure 1-1 shows the WelcomeForm.exe application greeting a user named John Doe. This version of the application is built using the `/target:exe` compiler switch, resulting in the visible console window in which you can see the output from the `Console.WriteLine` statement in the `button1_Click` event handler.

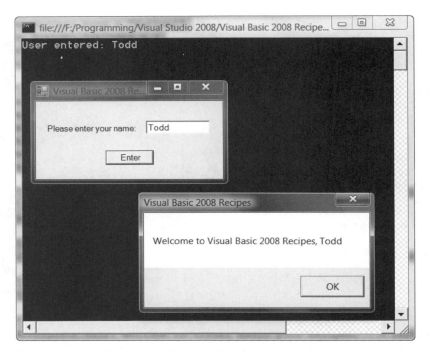

Figure 1-1. *A simple Windows Forms application*

1-3. Create and Use a Code Module from the Command Line

Problem

You need to do one or more of the following:

- Improve your application's performance and memory efficiency by ensuring the runtime loads rarely used types only when they are required.

- Compile types written in VB .NET to a form you can build into assemblies being developed in other .NET languages.

- Use types developed in another language and build them into your VB .NET assemblies.

Solution

Build your VB .NET source code into a module by using the command-line compiler and specifying the `/target:module` compiler switch. To incorporate existing modules into your assembly, use the `/addmodule` compiler switch.

How It Works

Modules are the building blocks of .NET assemblies and should not be confused with the `Module` object type block. Modules consist of a single file that contains the following:

- Microsoft Intermediate Language (MSIL) code created from your source code during compilation
- Metadata describing the types contained in the module
- Resources, such as icons and string tables, used by the types in the module

Assemblies consist of one or more modules and an assembly manifest. An *assembly manifest* is metadata that contains important information (such as the name, version, culture, and so on) regarding the assembly. If the assembly contains a single module, the module and assembly manifest are usually built into a single file for convenience. If more than one module exists, the assembly represents a logical grouping of more than one file that you must deploy as a complete unit. In these situations, the assembly manifest is either contained in a separate file or built into one of the modules. Visual Studio includes the MSIL Disassembler tool (Ildasm.exe), which lets you view the raw MSIL code for any assembly. You can use this tool to view an assembly manifest.

By building an assembly from multiple modules, you complicate the management and deployment of the assembly, but under some circumstances, modules offer significant benefits:

- The runtime will load a module only when the types defined in the module are required. Therefore, where you have a set of types that your application uses rarely, you can partition them into a separate module that the runtime will load only if necessary. This can improve performance, especially if your application is loaded across a network, and minimize the use of memory.

- The ability to use many different languages to write applications that run on the common language runtime (CLR) is a great strength of the .NET Framework. However, the VB .NET compiler can't compile your Microsoft C# or COBOL .NET code for inclusion in your assembly. To use code written in another language, you can compile it into a separate assembly and reference it. But if you want it to be an integral part of your assembly, you must build it into a module. Similarly, if you want to allow others to include your code as an integral part of their assemblies, you must compile your code as modules. When you use modules, because the code becomes part of the same assembly, members marked as `Friend` or `Protected Friend` are accessible, whereas they would not be if the code had been accessed from an external assembly.

Usage

To compile a source file named ConsoleUtils.vb (see recipe 1-1 for the contents) into a module, use the command `vbc /target:module ConsoleUtils.vb`. The result is the creation of a file named ConsoleUtils.netmodule. The .netmodule extension is the default extension for modules, and the file name is the same as the name of the VB .NET source file.

You can also build modules from multiple source files, which results in a single file containing the MSIL and metadata (the assembly manifest) for all types contained in all of the source files. The command `vbc /target:module ConsoleUtils.vb WindowsUtils.vb` compiles two source files named ConsoleUtils.vb and WindowsUtils.vb to create the module named ConsoleUtils.netmodule. The module is named after the first source file listed unless you override the name with the `/out` compiler switch. For example, the command `vbc /target:module /out:Utilities.netmodule ConsoleUtils.vb WindowsUtils.vb` creates a module named Utilities.netmodule.

To build an assembly consisting of multiple modules, you must use the `/addmodule` compiler switch. To build an executable named MyFirstApp.exe from two modules named WindowsUtils.netmodule and ConsoleUtils.netmodule and two source files named SourceOne.vb and SourceTwo.vb, use the command vbc /out:MyFirstApp.exe /target:exe /addmodule:WindowsUtils.netmodule,ConsoleUtils. netmodule SourceOne.vb SourceTwo.vb.

This command will result in an assembly that is composed of the following components:

- MyFirstApp.exe, which contains the assembly manifest as well as the MSIL for the types declared in the SourceOne.vb and SourceTwo.vb source files

- ConsoleUtils.netmodule and WindowsUtils.netmodule, which are now integral components of the multifile assembly but are unchanged by this compilation process

1-4. Create and Use a Code Library from the Command Line

Problem

You need to build a set of functionality into a reusable code library so that multiple applications can reference and reuse it.

Solution

Build your library using the command-line VB .NET compiler, and specify the /target:library compiler switch. To reference the library, use the /reference compiler switch when you build your application, and specify the names of the required libraries.

How It Works

Recipe 1-1 showed you how to build an application named MyFirstApp.exe from the two source files ConsoleUtils.vb and HelloWorld.vb. The ConsoleUtils.vb file contains the ConsoleUtils class, which provides methods to simplify interaction with the Windows console. If you were to extend the functionality of the ConsoleUtils class, you could add functionality useful to many applications. Instead of including the source code for ConsoleUtils in every application, you could build it into a library and deploy it independently, making the functionality accessible to many applications.

Usage

To build the ConsoleUtils.vb file into a library, use the command vbc /target:library ConsoleUtils.vb. This will produce a library file named ConsoleUtils.dll. To build a library from multiple source files, list the name of each file at the end of the command. You can also specify the name of the library using the /out compiler switch; otherwise, the library is named after the first source file listed. For example, to build a library named MyFirstLibrary.dll from two source files named ConsoleUtils.vb and WindowsUtils.vb, use the command vbc /out:MyFirstLibrary.dll /target:library ConsoleUtils.vb WindowsUtils.vb.

Before distributing your library, you might consider strong naming it so that no one can modify your assembly and pass it off as being the original. Strong naming your library also allows people to install it into the global assembly cache (GAC), which makes reuse much easier. (Recipe 1-12 describes how to strong name your assembly, and recipe 1-17 describes how to install a strong-named assembly into the GAC.) You might also consider signing your library with an Authenticode signature, which allows users to confirm you are the publisher of the assembly. (See recipe 1-15 for details on signing assemblies with Authenticode.)

To compile an assembly that relies on types declared within external libraries, you must tell the compiler which libraries are referenced using the /reference compiler switch. For example, to compile the HelloWorld.vb source file (from recipe 1-1) if the ConsoleUtils class is contained in the ConsoleUtils.dll library, use the command vbc /reference:ConsoleUtils.dll HelloWorld.vb. Remember these four points:

- If you reference more than one library, separate each library name with a comma or semicolon, but don't include any spaces. For example, use `/reference:ConsoleUtils.dll,WindowsUtils.dll`.

- If the libraries aren't in the same directory as the source code, use the `/libpath` switch on the compiler to specify the additional directories where the compiler should look for libraries. For example, use `/libpath:c:\CommonLibraries,c:\Dev\ThirdPartyLibs`.

- Note that additional directories can be relative to the source folder. Don't forget that at runtime, the generated assembly must be in the same folder as the application that needs it, except if you deploy it into the GAC.

- If the library you need to reference is a multifile assembly, reference the file that contains the assembly manifest. (For information about multifile assemblies, see recipe 1-3.)

1-5. Embed a Resource File in an Assembly

Problem

You need to create a string-based resource file and embed it in an assembly.

Solution

Use the Resource Generator (resgen.exe) to create a compiled resource file. You then use the `/resource` switch of the compiler to embed the file in the assembly.

■**Note** The Assembly Linker tool (al.exe) also provides functionality for working with and embedding resource files. Refer to the Assembly Linker information in the .NET Framework SDK documentation for details.

How It Works

If you need to store strings in an external file and have them accessible to your assembly, you can use a resource file. *Resources* are some form of data (a string or an image, for example) that is used by an application. A *resource file* is a repository of one or more resources that can be easily accessed.

   If you need to store only strings, you can create a simple text file that contains one or more key/value pairs in the form of `key=value`. You cannot create image resources starting from a text file.

   Once you have your text file, you compile it using the Resource Generator (resgen.exe). Using this utility, you can convert the text file into either of two types:

- An .resx file, which is an XML resource file. This file is fully documented and can be edited manually. It is also capable of supporting image resources, unlike the text file. Consult the .NET Framework SDK documentation for more details on the .resx format.

- A .resource file, which is a compiled binary file and is required if you are embedding the file into your assembly using the command-line compiler. You embed the .resource file into your assembly by using the `/resource` switch of the VB .NET compiler. The .resource file can be compiled from a .txt or .resx file.

You access the contents of the resource file by instantiating a `ResourceManager` object. The `GetString` method is used to retrieve the value for the specified string. If you have stored something other than a string such as an image in your resource file, use the `GetObject` method and cast the return value to the appropriate type.

The Code

This example borrows the code from recipe 1-2. The dialog box titles and message prompt have been removed from the code and are now contained within an external resource file. The new program uses the ResourceManager object to access the resources.

```
Imports System
Imports System.windows.forms
Imports System.Resources

Namespace Apress.VisualBasicRecipes.Chapter01
    Public Class Recipe01_05
        Inherits Form

        ' Private members to hold references to the form's controls.
        Private label1 As Label
        Private textbox1 As TextBox
        Private button1 As Button
        Private resManager As New ResourceManager("MyStrings", ➡
System.Reflection.Assembly.GetExecutingAssembly())

        ' Constructor used to create an instance of the form and configure
        ' the form's controls.
        Public Sub New()
            ' Instantiate the controls used on the form.
            Me.label1 = New Label
            Me.textbox1 = New TextBox
            Me.button1 = New Button

            ' Suspend the layout logic of the form while we configure and
            ' position the controls.
            Me.SuspendLayout()

            ' Configure label1, which displays the user prompt.
            Me.label1.Location = New System.Drawing.Size(16, 36)
            Me.label1.Name = "label1"
            Me.label1.Size = New System.Drawing.Size(155, 16)
            Me.label1.TabIndex = 0
            Me.label1.Text = resManager.GetString("UserPrompt")

            ' Configure textbox1, which accepts the user input.
            Me.textbox1.Location = New System.Drawing.Point(172, 32)
            Me.textbox1.Name = "textbox1"
            Me.textbox1.TabIndex = 1
            Me.textbox1.Text = ""

            ' Configure button1, which the user clicks to enter a name.
            Me.button1.Location = New System.Drawing.Point(109, 80)
            Me.button1.Name = "button1"
            Me.button1.TabIndex = 2
            Me.button1.Text = resManager.GetString("ButtonCaption")
            AddHandler button1.Click, AddressOf button1_Click

            ' Configure WelcomeForm, and add controls.
            Me.ClientSize = New System.Drawing.Size(292, 126)
```

```
        Me.Controls.Add(Me.button1)
        Me.Controls.Add(Me.textbox1)
        Me.Controls.Add(Me.label1)
        Me.Name = "form1"
        Me.Text = resManager.GetString("FormTitle")

        ' Resume the layout logic of the form now that all controls are
        ' configured.
        Me.ResumeLayout(False)

    End Sub

    Private Sub button1_Click(ByVal sender As Object, ➥
ByVal e As System.EventArgs)

        ' Write debug message to the console.
        System.Console.WriteLine("User entered: " + textbox1.Text)

        ' Display welcome as a message box.
        MessageBox.Show(resManager.GetString("Message") + textbox1.Text, ➥
resManager.GetString("FormTitle"))

    End Sub

    ' Application entry point, creates an instance of the form, and begins
    ' running a standard message loop on the current thread.  The message
    ' loop feeds the application with input from the user as events.
    Public Shared Sub Main()
        Application.EnableVisualStyles()
        Application.Run(New Recipe01_05())
    End Sub

    End Class
End Namespace
```

Usage

First, you must create the MyStrings.txt file that contains your resource strings:

```
;String resource file for Recipe01-05
UserPrompt=Please enter your name:
FormTitle=Visual Basic 2008 Recipes
Message=Welcome to Visual Basic 2008 Recipes,
ButtonCaption=Enter
```

You compile this file into a resource file by using the command resgen.exe MyStrings.txt Recipe01_05.MyStrings.resources. To build the example and embed the resource file, use the command vbc /resource:Recipe01_05.MyStrings.resources Recipe01-05.vb.

Notes

Using resource files from Visual Studio is a little different from using resource files from the command line. For this example, the resource file must be in the XML format (.resx) and added directly to the project. Instead of initially creating the .resource file, you can use the command resgen.exe MyStrings.txt MyStrings.resx to generate the .resx file required by Visual Studio.

1-6. Build Projects from the Command Line Using MSBuild.exe

Problem

You need to compile one or more VB .NET files from the command line, and you need to have more precise control over the build process.

Solution

Create a project file, and use the MSBuild.exe utility that ships with Visual Studio 2008. The build project should reference each VB .NET file and compile them using the VB .NET compiler (vbc.exe) via the vbc task.

How It Works

MSBuild.exe is a utility that ships with Visual Studio. It is located in the directory specific to the target framework, such as C:\Windows\Microsoft.NET\Framework\v3.5\. This utility uses an XML project file to perform specified actions on specified files. If you build an application in Visual Studio, a file with the extension .vbproj is automatically generated. This is actually an XML project file used by MSBuild.exe to build your project.

■**Note** For general information on working with XML files, please refer to Chapter 7.

The first step is creating a project file. As mentioned earlier, this is an XML file that contains key elements that MSBuild.exe interprets. The first element, which is required for any project file, is Project. This element must include the xmlns attribute set to http://schemas.microsoft.com/developer/msbuild/ 2003. The root Project element can contain any of the child elements listed in Table 1-1.

Table 1-1. *Common Child Elements*

Name	Description
Choose	Allows you to specify ItemGroup or PropertyGroup elements based on one or more condition.
Import	Imports an external project file.
ItemGroup	A group of user-defined Item elements. Each Item element represents some data to be reference elsewhere in the build project.
ProjectExtensions	Information that can be included in the build project but is ignored by MSBuild.exe.
PropertyGroup	A group of user-defined Property elements. Each Property element represents some property to be referenced elsewhere in the build project.
Target	Defines one or more Task elements. Each Task element performs some action as part of the build process.
UsingTask	Registers tasks to be made available to MSBuild.exe.

If your build project is going to reference files, your next step is to create an `ItemGroup` element with an `Item` element for each file. Item elements can be named anything, but it is best to use a name that represents what the file is. For example, if you had two VB .NET files, you might use `SourceFile`, which represents an `Item` element, as shown here:

```
<ItemGroup>
    <SourceFile Include="FileOne.vb" />
    <SourceFile Include="FileTwo.vb" />
</ItemGroup>
```

Using the same name, such as `SourceFile` used in the previous example, will group the files together. You can accomplish the same thing by putting the files on a single line and separating them with a semicolon like this:

```
<SourceFile Include="FileOne.vb;FileTwo.vb" />
```

Each `Item` element *must* contain the `Include` attribute, which is used to define the value of the element. When you need to reference a defined `Item` element, you just surround it with parentheses and precede it with the @ symbol, as in `@(SourceFile)`.

Once you have defined files, you need to do something with them. You do this by creating a `Target` element and defining any appropriate predefined `Task` elements. By default, MSBuild.exe includes several tasks, some of which are listed in Table 1-2. These tasks are defined in Microsoft.Build. Tasks.v3.5.dll and are referenced by the MSBuild.exe utility by way of the Microsoft.Common.Tasks project file, which is included for any build by default.

Table 1-2. *Common MSBuild.exe Tasks*

Name	Description
Copy	Copies the specified files to the specified location
MakeDir	Creates the specified directory
RemoveDir	Removes the specified directory
SignFile	Uses the specified certificate to sign the specified file
Message	Writes the specified message to the build log
Exec	Executes the specified application using the specified parameters
Vbc	Compiles code using the VB .NET compiler (vbc.exe)
GenerateResource	Creates resource files similar to the resgen.exe utility discussed in recipe 1-5

One of the most common tasks that will be used is the `Vbc` task. This task actually wraps vbc.exe, making it possible to compile any VB .NET files. All the parameters available to vbc.exe are available as properties to the `Vbc` task, although some of the names have changed. Table 1-3 lists some of the most common properties and their matching vbc.exe parameters.

Table 1-3. *Common Vbc Task Properties*

Vbc Task Property	Vbc.exe Parameter	Description
KeyFile	/keyfile	Specifies the cryptographic key to be used (discussed in further detail in recipe 1-9)
KeyContainer	/keycontainer	Specifies the name of the cryptographic container where the cryptographic key can be found (discussed in further detail in recipe 1-9)
References	/reference	References additional assemblies to be compiled (discussed in further detail in recipe 1-4)
TargetType	/target	Defines the format of the output file (discussed in further detail in recipes 1-1, 1-2, and 1-3)
Resources	/resources	Embeds a resource (discussed in further detail in recipe 1-5)
OutputAssembly	/out	Defines the name of the output file (discussed in further detail in recipes 1-1 and 1-3)
MainEntryPoint	/main	Specifies the location of the Sub Main routine (discussed in further detail in recipe 1-1)
AddModules	/addmodule	Imports the specified modules (discussed in further detail in recipe 1-3)

Usage

If you wanted to create a project using the files from recipe 1-1, it would look something like this:

```
<?xml version="1.0" encoding="utf-8"?>
<Project xmlns="http://schemas.microsoft.com/developer/msbuild/2003" >
  <ItemGroup>
    <SourceFile Include="ConsoleUtils.vb" />
    <SourceFile Include="HelloWorld.vb" />
  </ItemGroup>
  <Target Name="TestBuild" >
    <Vbc TargetType="exe"
        MainEntryPoint="Apress.VisualBasicRecipes.Chapter01.HelloWorld"
        OutputAssembly ="HelloWorld.exe"
        Sources="@(SourceFile)" />
  </Target>
</Project>
```

Once you have created the project file, you use MSBuild.exe to build it. MSBuild.exe includes many parameters (such as /property, /logger, and /verbosity) that can be used to fine-tune the build process. For example, we will use the simplest form, which requires only the name of the project file:

```
Msbuild.exe HelloWorld.proj
```

Executing this command will create the HelloWorld.exe file and produce results similar to the following:

```
Microsoft (R) Build Engine Version 3.5.20706.1
[Microsoft .NET Framework, Version 2.0.50727.1378]
Copyright (C) Microsoft Corporation 2007. All rights reserved.

Build started 9/1/2007 9:01:22 PM.

Build succeeded.
    0 Warning(s)
    0 Error(s)

Time Elapsed 00:00:02.42
```

Note This recipe covers only the very basics of MSBuild.exe. If you view the build project file that is automatically created by Visual Studio (as mentioned earlier), you will notice how in-depth it is. For a complete reference to the MSBuild.exe utility, refer to the online documentation at http://msdn2.microsoft.com/en-us/library/0k6kkbsd.aspx.

1-7. Access Command-Line Arguments

Problem

You need to access the arguments that were specified on the command line when your application was executed.

Solution

Use a signature for your Main method that exposes the command-line arguments as a String array. Alternatively, access the command-line arguments from anywhere in your code using the Shared members of the System.Environment class.

How It Works

Declaring your application's Main method with one of the following signatures provides access to the command-line arguments as a String array:

```
Public Shared Sub Main(ByVal args As String())
End Sub
Public Shared Function Main(ByVal args As String()) As Integer
End Sub
```

At runtime, the args argument will contain a string for each value entered on the command line after your application's name. The application's name is not included in the array of arguments.

If you need access to the command-line arguments at places in your code other than the Main method, you can process the command-line arguments in your Main method and store them for later access. However, this is not necessary since you can use the System.Environment class, which provides two Shared members that return information about the command line: CommandLine and GetCommandLineArgs. The CommandLine property returns a string containing the full command line that launched the current process. Depending on the operating system on which the application is running, path information might precede the application name. Windows Server 2003, Windows Server 2008, Windows NT 4.0, Windows 2000, Windows XP, and Windows Vista don't include path information, whereas Windows 98 and Windows ME do. The GetCommandLineArgs method returns a String array containing the command-line arguments. This array can be processed in the same way as the String array passed to the Main method, as discussed at the start of this section. Unlike the array passed to the Main method, the first element in the array returned by the GetCommandLineArgs method is the file name of the application.

■**Note** As an alternative, you can use the My.Application.CommandLineArgs method (which works identically to the GetCommandLineArgs method). We discuss the My namespace more thoroughly in Chapter 5.

The Code

To demonstrate the access of command-line arguments, the Main method in the following example steps through each of the command-line arguments passed to it and displays them to the console. The example then accesses the command line directly through the Environment class.

```
Imports System

Namespace Apress.VisualBasicRecipes.Chapter01
    Public Class Recipe01_07

        Public Shared Sub Main(ByVal args As String())

            ' Step through the command-line arguments
            For Each s As String In args
                Console.WriteLine(s)
            Next

            ' Alternatively, access the command-line arguments directly.
            Console.WriteLine(Environment.CommandLine)

            For Each s As String In Environment.GetCommandLineArgs()
                Console.WriteLine(s)
            Next

            ' Wait to continue
            Console.WriteLine(vbCrLf & "Main method complete.  Press Enter.")
            Console.ReadLine()

        End Sub

    End Class
End Namespace
```

Usage

If you execute the Recipe01-07 example using the following command:

```
Recipe01-07 "one \"two\"    three" four 'five    six'
```

the application will generate the following output on the console:

```
one "two"     three
four
'five
six'
recipe01-07   "one \"two\"      three" four 'five     six'
recipe01-07
one "two"     three
four
'five
six'

Main method complete.   Press Enter.
```

Notice that the use of double quotes (") results in more than one word being treated as a single argument, although single quotes (') do not. Also, you can include double quotes in an argument by escaping them with the backslash character (\). Finally, notice that all spaces are stripped from the command line unless they are enclosed in double quotes.

1-8. Include Code Selectively at Build Time

Problem

You need to selectively include and exclude sections of source code from your compiled assembly.

Solution

Use the #If, #ElseIf, #Else, and #End If preprocessor directives to identify blocks of code that should be conditionally included in your compiled assembly. Use the System.Diagnostics.ConditionalAttribute attribute to define methods that should be called conditionally only. Control the inclusion of the conditional code using the #Const directive in your code, or use the /define switch when you run the VB .NET compiler from the command line.

How It Works

If you need your application to function differently depending on factors such as the platform or environment on which it runs, you can build runtime checks into the logic of your code that trigger the variations in operation. However, such an approach can bloat your code and affect performance, especially if many variations need to be supported or many locations exist where evaluations need to be made.

An alternative approach is to build multiple versions of your application to support the different target platforms and environments. Although this approach overcomes the problems of code bloat and performance degradation, it would be an untenable solution if you had to maintain different source code for each version, so VB .NET provides features that allow you to build customized versions of your application from a single code base.

The #If, #ElseIf, #Else, and #End If preprocessor directives allow you to identify blocks of code that the compiler should include or exclude in your assembly at compile time. This is accomplished by evaluating the value of specified symbols. Since this happens at compile time, it may result in multiple executables being distributed. Symbols can be any literal value. They also support the use of all standard comparison and logical operators or other symbols. The #If..#End If construct evaluates #If and #ElseIf clauses only until it finds one that evaluates to true, meaning that if you define multiple symbols (winXP and win2000, for example), the order of your clauses is important. The compiler includes only the code in the clause that evaluates to true. If no clause evaluates to true, the compiler includes the code in the #Else clause.

You can also use logical operators to base conditional compilation on more than one symbol. Use parentheses to group multiple expressions. Table 1-4 summarizes the supported operators.

Table 1-4. *Logical Operators Supported by the #If . . #End If Directive*

Operator	Example	Description
NOT	#If NOT winXP	Inequality. Evaluates to true if the symbol winXP is not equal to True. Equivalent to #If NOT winXP.
AND	#If winXP AND release	Logical AND. Evaluates to true only if the symbols winXP and release are equal to True.
AndAlso	#If winXP AndAlso release	Logical AND. Works the same as the AND operator, except that the second expression (release) is not evaluated if the first expression (winXP) is False.
OR	#IF winXP OR release	Logical OR. Evaluates to true if either of the symbols winXP or release is equal to True.
OrElse	#IF winXP OrElse release	Logical OR. Works the same as the OR operator, except that the second expression (release) is not evaluated if the first expression (winXP) is True.
XOR	#IF winXP XOR release	Logical XOR. Evaluates to true if only one of the symbols, winXP or release, is equal to True.

■**Caution** You must be careful not to overuse conditional compilation directives and not to make your conditional expressions too complex; otherwise, your code can quickly become confusing and unmanageable—especially as your projects become larger.

To define a symbol, you can either include a #Const directive in your code or use the /define compiler switch. Symbols defined using #Const are active until the end of the file in which they are defined. Symbols defined using the /define compiler switch are active in all source files that are being compiled. All #Const directives must appear at the top of your source file before any code, including any Imports statements.

If you need to determine only whether a symbol has been defined, a more elegant alternative to the #If preprocessor directive is the attribute System.Diagnostics.ConditionalAttribute. If you apply ConditionalAttribute to a method, the compiler will ignore any calls to the method if the symbol specified by ConditionalAttribute is not defined, or set to False, at the calling point.

Using ConditionalAttribute centralizes your conditional compilation logic on the method declaration and means you can freely include calls to conditional methods without littering your code with #If directives. However, because the compiler literally removes calls to the conditional method from your code, your code can't have dependencies on return values from the conditional method. This means you can apply ConditionalAttribute only to subroutines.

The Code

In this example, the code assigns a different value to the local variable platformName based on whether the winVista, winXP, win2000, winNT, or Win98 symbols are defined. The head of the code defines the win2000 symbol. In addition, the ConditionalAttribute specifies that calls to the DumpState method should be included in an assembly only if the symbol DEBUG is defined during compilation. The DEBUG symbol is defined by default in debug builds.

```vb
#Const winXP = True

Imports System
Imports System.Diagnostics

Namespace APress.VisualBasicRecipes.Chapter01
    Public Class Recipe01_08

        ' Declare a string to contain the platform name
        Private Shared platformName As String
        <Conditional("DEBUG")> _
        Public Shared Sub DumpState()
            Console.WriteLine("Dump some state...")
        End Sub
        Public Shared Sub Main()

#If winVista Then       ' Compiling for Windows Vista
            platformName = "Microsoft Windows Vista"
#ElseIf winXP Then      ' Compiling for Windows XP
            platformName = "Microsoft Windows XP"
#ElseIf win2000 Then    ' Compiling for Windows 2000
            platformName = "Microsoft Windows 2000"
#ElseIf winNT Then      ' Compiling for Windows NT
            platformName = "Microsoft Windows NT"
#ElseIf win98 Then      ' Compiling for Windows 98
            platformName = "Microsoft Windows 98"
#Else                   ' Unknown platform specified
            platformName = "Unknown"
#End If

            Console.WriteLine(platformName)

            ' Call the conditional DumpState method
            DumpState()

            ' Wait to continue...
            Console.WriteLine(vbCrLf & "Main method complete.  Press Enter.")
            Console.Read()

        End Sub

    End Class
End Namespace
```

Usage

To build the example and define the symbol winVista, use the command vbc /define:winVista Recipe01-08.vb. If you compile this sample without defining the winVista symbol, the winXP symbol will be used since it was defined directly in the code. Otherwise, both winVista and winXP will be defined, but Microsoft Windows Vista will be the platformName value because of the order in which the symbols are checked.

Notes

You can apply multiple ConditionalAttribute instances to a method in order to produce logical OR behavior. Calls to the following version of the DumpState method will be compiled only if the DEBUG or TEST symbols are defined:

```
<Conditional("DEBUG"), Conditional("TEST")> _
Public Shared Sub DumpState()
    ...
End Sub
```

Achieving logical AND behavior is not as clean and involves the use of an intermediate conditional method, quickly leading to overly complex code that is hard to understand and maintain. You should be cautious with this approach, because you might end up with code in your assembly that is never called. The following is a quick example that requires the definition of both the DEBUG and TEST symbols for the DumpState functionality (contained in DumpState2) to be called:

```
<Conditional("DEBUG")> _
Public Shared Sub DumpState()
    DumpState2()
End Sub

<Conditional("TEST")> _
Public Shared Sub DumpState2()
    ...
End Sub
```

It's important to remember that you are not limited to Boolean values for your symbols. You can define a symbol with a string value, like this:

```
#Const OS = "Vista"
```

You could also do this using the command vbc /define:OS=\"winVista\" Recipe01-08.vb. You must escape quotation marks using the \ character.

To use this new symbol, the preprocessor #If..#End If construct must be changed accordingly:

```
#If OS = "winVista" Then      ' Compiling for Windows Vista
    platformName = "Microsoft Windows Vista"
#ElseIf OS = "XP" Then        ' Compiling for Windows XP
    platformName = "Microsoft Windows XP"
#ElseIf OS = "2000" Then      ' Compiling for Windows 2000
    platformName = "Microsoft Windows 2000"
#ElseIf OS = "NT" Then        ' Compiling for Windows NT
    platformName = "Microsoft Windows NT"
#ElseIf OS = "98" Then        ' Compiling for Windows 98
    platformName = "Microsoft Windows 98"
#Else                         ' Unknown platform specified
    platformName = "Unknown"
#End If
```

1-9. Manipulate the Appearance of the Console

Problem

You want to control the visual appearance of the Windows console.

Solution

Use the Shared properties and methods of the System.Console class.

How It Works

The .NET Framework includes the Console class, which gives you control over the appearance and operation of the Windows console. Table 1-5 describes the properties and methods of this class that you can use to control the console's appearance.

Table 1-5. *Properties and Methods to Control the Appearance of the Console*

Member	Description
Properties	
BackgroundColor	Gets and sets the background color of the console using one of the values from the System.ConsoleColor enumeration. Only new text written to the console will appear in this color. To make the entire console this color, call the method Clear after you have configured the BackgroundColor property.
BufferHeight	Gets and sets the buffer height in terms of rows. Buffer refers to the amount of actual data that can be displayed within the console window.
BufferWidth	Gets and sets the buffer width in terms of columns. Buffer refers to the amount of actual data that can be displayed within the console window.
CursorLeft	Gets and sets the column position of the cursor within the buffer.
CursorSize	Gets and sets the height of the cursor as a percentage of a character cell.
CursorTop	Gets and sets the row position of the cursor within the buffer.
CursorVisible	Gets and sets whether the cursor is visible.
ForegroundColor	Gets and sets the text color of the console using one of the values from the System.ConsoleColor enumeration. Only new text written to the console will appear in this color. To make the entire console this color, call the method Clear after you have configured the ForegroundColor property.
LargestWindowHeight	Returns the largest possible number of rows based on the current font and screen resolution.
LargestWindowWidth	Returns the largest possible number of columns based on the current font and screen resolution.
Title	Gets and sets text shown in the title bar.

Table 1-5. *Properties and Methods to Control the Appearance of the Console (Continued)*

Member	Description
WindowHeight	Gets and sets the physical height of the console window in terms of character rows.
WindowWidth	Gets and sets the physical width of the console window in terms of character columns.
Methods	
Clear	Clears the console.
ResetColor	Sets the foreground and background colors to their default values as configured within Windows.
SetWindowSize	Sets the width and height in terms of columns and rows.

The Code

The following example demonstrates how to use the properties and methods of the Console class to dynamically change the appearance of the Windows console:

```vbnet
Imports System

Namespace Apress.VisualBasicRecipes.Chapter01
    Public Class Recipe01_09

        Public Shared Sub Main(ByVal args As String())

            ' Display the standard console.
            Console.Title = "Standard Console"
            Console.WriteLine("Press Enter to change the console's appearance.")
            Console.ReadLine()

            ' Change the console appearance and redisplay.
            Console.Title = "Colored Text"
            Console.ForegroundColor = ConsoleColor.Red
            Console.BackgroundColor = ConsoleColor.Green
            Console.WriteLine("Press Enter to change the console's appearance.")
            Console.ReadLine()

            ' Change the console appearance and redisplay.
            Console.Title = "Cleared / Colored Console"
            Console.ForegroundColor = ConsoleColor.Blue
            Console.BackgroundColor = ConsoleColor.Yellow
            Console.Clear()
            Console.WriteLine("Press Enter to change the console's appearance.")
            Console.ReadLine()

            ' Change the console appearance and redisplay.
            Console.Title = "Resized Console"
            Console.ResetColor()
            Console.Clear()
            Console.SetWindowSize(100, 50)
```

```
            Console.BufferHeight = 500
            Console.BufferWidth = 100
            Console.CursorLeft = 20
            Console.CursorSize = 50
            Console.CursorTop = 20
            Console.CursorVisible = False
            Console.WriteLine("Main method complete.  Press Enter.")
            Console.ReadLine()

        End Sub

    End Class
End Namespace
```

1-10. Access a Program Element That Has the Same Name As a Keyword

Problem

You need to access a member of a type, but the type or member name is the same as a VB .NET keyword.

Solution

Surround all instances of the identifier name in your code with brackets ([ ]).

How It Works

The .NET Framework allows you to use software components developed in other .NET languages from within your VB .NET applications. Each language has its own set of keywords (or reserved words) and imposes different restrictions on the names programmers can assign to program elements such as types, members, and variables. Therefore, it is possible that a programmer developing a component in another language will inadvertently use a VB .NET keyword as the name of a program element. Using brackets ([ ]) enables you to use a VB .NET keyword as an identifier and overcome these possible naming conflicts.

The Code

The following code fragment creates the new Operator (perhaps a telephone operator) class. A new instance of this class is created, and its Friend property is set to True—both Operator and Friend are VB .NET keywords:

```
Public Class [Operator]
    Public [Friend] As Boolean
End Class

'  Instantiate an operator object
Dim operator1 As New [Operator]

'  Set the operator's Friend property
operator1.[Friend] = True
```

1-11. Create and Manage Strong-Named Key Pairs

Problem

You need to create public and private keys (a key pair) so that you can assign strong names to your assemblies.

Solution

Use the Strong Name tool (sn.exe) to generate a key pair and store the keys in a file or cryptographic service provider (CSP) key container.

■**Note** A CSP is an element of the Win32 CryptoAPI that provides services such as encryption, decryption, and digital signature generation. CSPs also provide key container facilities, which use strong encryption and operating system security to protect any cryptographic keys stored in the container. A detailed discussion of CSPs and CryptoAPI is beyond the scope of this book. All you need to know for this recipe is that you can store your cryptographic keys in a CSP key container and be relatively confident that it is secure as long as no one knows your Windows password. Refer to the CryptoAPI information in the platform SDK documentation for complete details.

How It Works

To generate a new key pair and store the keys in the file named MyKeys.snk, execute the command `sn -k MyKeys.snk`. (.snk is the usual extension given to files containing strong-named keys.) The generated file contains both your public and private keys. You can extract the public key using the command `sn -p MyKeys.snk MyPublicKeys.snk`, which will create MyPublicKey.snk containing only the public key. Once you have this file in hand, you can view the public key using the command `sn -tp MyPublicKeys.snk`, which will generate output similar to the (abbreviated) listing shown here:

```
Microsoft (R) .NET Framework Strong Name Utility  Version 3.5.20706.1
Copyright (c) Microsoft Corporation.  All rights reserved.

Public key is
0024000004800000940000000602000000240000525341310004000001000100c5810bb3c095d0
6de71d6cafba0b2088b45951ba76407d981d20bf1be825990619b6888d56146b9532981374df9a
fa1001b1336e262a09fa8c7d989cf4a0ad6bbe5684f9cd82cc38ba6d6707acaf13f058e22d6796
2dc72212bf797da89c08d8e65338c2972de659385472a603e00d3cc3c9f348b51d7c47a8611479
deb3f0ab

Public key token is 442a698bee81cc00
```

The public key token shown at the end of the listing is the last 8 bytes of a cryptographic hash code computed from the public key. Because the public key is so long, .NET uses the public key token for display purposes and as a compact mechanism for other assemblies to reference your public key. (Recipes 11-14 and 11-15 discuss cryptographic hash codes.)

As the name suggests, you don't need to keep the public key (or public key token) secret. When you strong name your assembly (discussed in recipe 1-12), the compiler uses your private key to generate a digital signature (an encrypted hash code) of the assembly's manifest. The compiler embeds the digital signature and your public key in the assembly so that any consumer of the assembly can verify the digital signature.

Keeping your private key secret is imperative. People with access to your private key can alter your assembly and create a new strong name—leaving your customers unaware they are using modified code. No mechanism exists to repudiate compromised strong-named keys. If your private key is compromised, you must generate new keys and distribute new versions of your assemblies that are strong named using the new keys. You must also notify your customers about the compromised keys and explain to them which versions of your public key to trust—in all, a very costly exercise in terms of both money and credibility. You can protect your private key in many ways; the approach you use will depend on several factors:

- The structure and size of your organization
- Your development and release process
- The software and hardware resources you have available
- The requirements of your customer base

■Tip Commonly, a small group of trusted individuals (the *signing authority*) has responsibility for the security of your company's strong name signing keys and is responsible for signing all assemblies just prior to their final release. The ability to delay sign an assembly (discussed in recipe 1-14) facilitates this model and avoids the need to distribute private keys to all development team members.

One feature provided by the Strong Name tool to simplify the security of strong-named keys is the use of CSP key containers. Once you have generated a key pair to a file, you can install the keys into a key container and delete the file. For example, to store the key pair contained in the file MyKeys.snk to a CSP container named StrongNameKeys, use the command sn -i MyKeys.snk StrongNameKeys. You can install only one set of keys to a single container. (Recipe 1-12 explains how to use strong-named keys stored in a CSP key container.)

An important aspect of CSP key containers is that they include user-based containers and machine-based containers. Windows security ensures users can access only their own user-based key containers. However, any user of a machine can access a machine-based container.

By default, the Strong Name tool uses machine-based key containers, meaning that anyone who can log on to your machine and who knows the name of your key container can sign an assembly with your strong-named keys. To change the Strong Name tool to use user-based containers, use the command sn -m n, and to switch to machine-based stores, use the command sn -m y. The command sn -m will display whether the Strong Name tool is currently configured to use machine-based or user-based containers.

To delete the strong-named keys from the StrongNameKeys container (as well as delete the container), use the command sn -d StrongNameKeys.

1-12. Give an Assembly a Strong Name

Problem

You need to give an assembly a strong name for several reasons:

- So it has a unique identity, which allows people to assign specific permissions to the assembly when configuring code access security policy
- So it can't be modified and passed off as your original assembly
- So it can be installed in the GAC and shared across multiple applications

Solution

When you build your assembly using the command-line VB .NET compiler, use the `/keyfile` or `/keycontainer` compiler switch to specify the location of your strong-named key pair. Use assembly-level attributes to specify optional information such as the version number and culture for your assembly. The compiler will strong name your assembly as part of the compilation process.

■**Note** If you are using Visual Studio, you can configure your assembly to be strong named by opening the project properties, selecting the Signing tab, and checking the Sign the Assembly box. You will need to specify the location of the file where your strong-named keys are stored—Visual Studio does not allow you to specify the name of a key container.

How It Works

To strong name an assembly using the VB .NET compiler, you need the following:

- A strong-named key pair contained either in a file or in a CSP key container. (Recipe 1-11 discusses how to create strong-named key pairs.)
- Compiler switches to specify the location where the compiler can obtain your strong-named key pair:
  - If your key pair is in a file, use the `/keyfile` compiler switch, and provide the name of the file where the keys are stored. For example, use `/keyfile:MyKeyFile.snk`.
  - If your key pair is in a CSP container, use the `/keycontainer` compiler switch, and provide the name of the CSP key container where the keys are stored. For example, use `/keycontainer:MyKeyContainer`.
- Optionally, specify the culture that your assembly supports by applying the attribute `System.Reflection.AssemblyCultureAttribute` to the assembly. (If you attempt to use this attribute with an executable assembly, you will receive a compile error because executable assemblies support only the neutral culture.)
- Optionally, specify the version of your assembly by applying the attribute `System.Reflection.AssemblyVersionAttribute` to the assembly.

The Code

The executable code that follows (from a file named Recipe01-09.vb) shows how to use the optional attributes (shown in bold) to specify the culture and the version for the assembly:

```
Imports System
Imports System.Reflection

<Assembly: AssemblyCulture("")>
<Assembly: AssemblyVersion("1.1.0.5")>

Namespace Apress.VisualBasicRecipes.Chapter01
    Public Class Recipe01_12

        Public Shared Sub main()
            Console.WriteLine("Welcome to Visual Basic 2008 Recipes")
```

```
          ' Wait to continue...
          Console.WriteLine(vbCrLf & "Main method complete.  Press Enter.")
          Console.Read()
       End Sub

   End Class
End Namespace
```

Usage

To create a strong-named assembly from the example code, create the strong-named keys and store them in a file named MyKeyFile using the command sn -k MyKeyFile.snk. Then install the keys into the CSP container named MyKeys using the command sn -i MyKeyFile.snk MyKeys. You can now compile the file into a strong-named assembly using the command vbc /keycontainer:MyKeys Recipe01-12.vb. If you are not using a CSP container, you can specify the specific key file using the command vbc /keyfile:MyKeyFile.snk Recipe01-12.vb.

Notes

If you use Visual Studio, you may not be able to include the optional AssemblyVersion attribute in your code. This is because the attribute may already exist for the assembly. By default, Visual Studio automatically creates a folder called MyProject. This folder stores multiple files, including AssemblyInfo.vb, which contains standard assembly attributes for the project. These can be manually edited or edited through the Assembly Information dialog box (see Figure 1-2), accessible from the Application tab of the project properties. Since the AssemblyInfo.vb file is an efficient way to store information specific to your assembly, it is actually good practice to create and use a similar file, even if you are not using Visual Studio to compile.

Figure 1-2. *The Assembly Information dialog box*

1-13. Verify That a Strong-Named Assembly Has Not Been Modified

Problem

You need to verify that a strong-named assembly has not been modified after it was built.

Solution

Use the Strong Name tool (sn.exe) to verify the assembly's strong name.

How It Works

Whenever the .NET runtime loads a strong-named assembly, the runtime extracts the encrypted hash code that's embedded in the assembly and decrypts it with the public key, which is also embedded in the assembly. The runtime then calculates the hash code of the assembly manifest and compares it to the decrypted hash code. This verification process will identify whether the assembly has changed after compilation.

If an executable assembly fails strong name verification, the runtime will display an error message or an error dialog box (depending on whether the application is a console or Windows application). If executing code tries to load an assembly that fails verification, the runtime will throw a System.IO. FileLoadException with the message "Strong name validation failed," which you should handle appropriately.

As well as generating and managing strong-named keys (discussed in recipe 1-11), the Strong Name tool allows you to verify strong-named assemblies. To verify that the strong-named assembly Recipe01-12.exe is unchanged, use the command sn -vf Recipe01-12.exe. The -v switch requests the Strong Name tool to verify the strong name of the specified assembly, and the -f switch forces strong name verification even if it has been previously disabled for the specified assembly. (You can disable strong name verification for specific assemblies using the -Vr switch, as in sn -Vr Recipe01-12.exe; see recipe 1-14 for details about why you would disable strong name verification.)

If the assembly passes strong name verification, you should see the following output:

```
Microsoft (R) .NET Framework Strong Name Utility  Version 3.5.20706.1
Copyright (c) Microsoft Corporation.  All rights reserved.

Assembly 'recipe01-12.exe' is valid
```

However, if the assembly has been modified, you will see this message:

```
Microsoft (R) .NET Framework Strong Name Utility  Version 3.5.20706.1
Copyright (c) Microsoft Corporation.  All rights reserved.

recipe01-12.exe does not represent a strongly named assembly
```

1-14. Delay Sign an Assembly

Problem

You need to create a strong-named assembly, but you don't want to give all members of your development team access to the private key component of your strong-named key pair.

Solution

Extract and distribute the public key component of your strong-named key pair. Follow the instructions in recipe 1-12 that describe how to give your assembly a strong name. In addition, specify the /delaysign switch when you compile your assembly. Disable strong name verification for the assembly using the -Vr switch of the Strong Name tool (sn.exe).

■**Note** If you are using Visual Studio, you can configure your strong-named assembly to be delay signed by opening the project properties, selecting the Signing tab, and checking the Delay Sign Only box. Doing so will prohibit your project from being run or debugged. You can get around this by skipping verification using the -Vr switch of the Strong Name tool.

How It Works

Assemblies that reference strong-named assemblies contain the public key token of the referenced assemblies. This means the referenced assembly must be strong named before it can be referenced. In a development environment in which assemblies are regularly rebuilt, this would require every developer and tester to have access to your strong-named key pair—a major security risk.

Instead of distributing the private key component of your strong-named key pair to all members of the development team, the .NET Framework provides a mechanism named *delay signing* with which you can partially strong name an assembly. The partially strong-named assembly contains the public key and the public key token (required by referencing assemblies) but contains only a placeholder for the signature that would normally be generated using the private key.

After development is complete, the signing authority (who has responsibility for the security and use of your strong-named key pair) re-signs the delay-signed assembly to complete its strong name. The signature is calculated using the private key and embedded in the assembly, making the assembly ready for distribution.

To delay sign an assembly, you need access only to the public key component of your strong-named key pair. No security risk is associated with distributing the public key, and the signing authority should make the public key freely available to all developers. To extract the public key component from a strong-named key file named MyKeyFile.snk and write it to a file named MyPublicKey.snk, use the command sn -p MyKeyFile.snk MyPublicKey.snk. If you store your strong-named key pair in a CSP key container named MyKeys, extract the public key to a file named MyPublicKey.snk using the command sn -pc MyKeys MyPublicKey.snk.

Once you have a key file containing the public key, you build the delay-signed assembly using the command-line VB .NET compiler by specifying the /delaysign compiler switch. For example, to build a delay-signed assembly using the MyPublicKey.snk public key from a source file named Recipe01-14.vb, use this command:

```
vbc /delaysign /keyfile:MyPublicKey.snk Recipe01-14.vb
```

When the runtime tries to load a delay-signed assembly, it will identify the assembly as strong named and will attempt to verify the assembly, as discussed in recipe 1-13. Because it doesn't have a digital signature, you must configure the runtime on the local machine to stop verifying the assembly's strong name using the command sn -Vr Recipe01-14.exe. Note that you need to do so on every machine on which you want to run your application.

Tip When using delay-signed assemblies, it's often useful to be able to compare different builds of the same assembly to ensure they differ only by their signatures. This is possible only if a delay-signed assembly has been re-signed using the -R switch of the Strong Name tool. To compare the two assemblies, use the command sn -D assembly1 assembly2.

Once development is complete, you need to re-sign the assembly to complete the assembly's strong name. The Strong Name tool allows you to do this without changing your source code or recompiling the assembly; however, you must have access to the private key component of the strong-named key pair. To re-sign an assembly named Recipe01-14.exe with a key pair contained in the file MyKeys.snk, use the command sn -R Recipe01-14.exe MyKeys.snk. If the keys are stored in a CSP key container named MyKeys, use the command sn -Rc Recipe01-14.exe MyKeys.

Once you have re-signed the assembly, you should turn strong name verification for that assembly back on using the -Vu switch of the Strong Name tool, as in sn -Vu Recipe01-14.exe. To enable verification for all assemblies for which you have disabled strong name verification, use the command sn -Vx. You can list the assemblies for which verification is disabled using the command sn -Vl.

1-15. Sign an Assembly with an Authenticode Digital Signature

Problem

You need to sign an assembly with Authenticode so that users of the assembly can be certain you are its publisher and the assembly is unchanged after signing.

Solution

Use the Sign Tool (signtool.exe) to sign the assembly with your software publisher certificate (SPC).

How It Works

Strong names provide a unique identity for an assembly as well as proof of the assembly's integrity, but they provide no proof as to the publisher of the assembly. The .NET Framework allows you to use Authenticode technology to sign your assemblies. This enables consumers of your assemblies to confirm that you are the publisher, as well as confirm the integrity of the assembly. Authenticode signatures also act as evidence for the signed assembly, which people can use when configuring code access security policy.

To sign your assembly with an Authenticode signature, you need an SPC issued by a recognized *certificate authority* (CA). A CA is a company entrusted to issue SPCs (along with many other types of certificates) for use by individuals or companies. Before issuing a certificate, the CA is responsible for confirming that the requesters are who they claim to be and also for making sure the requesters sign contracts to ensure they don't misuse the certificates that the CA issues them.

To obtain an SPC, you should view the Microsoft Root Certificate Program Members list at http://msdn.microsoft.com/library/default.asp?url=/library/en-us/dnsecure/html/ rootcertprog.asp. Here you will find a list of CAs, many of whom can issue you an SPC. For testing purposes, you can create a test SPC using the process described in recipe 1-16. However, you can't distribute your software signed with this test certificate. Because a test SPC isn't issued by a trusted CA, most responsible users won't trust assemblies signed with it.

Once you have an SPC, you use the Sign Tool to Authenticode sign your assembly. The Sign Tool creates a digital signature of the assembly using the private key component of your SPC and embeds the signature and the public part of your SPC in your assembly (including your public key). When verifying your assembly, the consumer decrypts the encrypted hash code using your public key, recalculates the hash of the assembly, and compares the two hash codes to ensure they are the same. As long as the two hash codes match, the consumer can be certain that you signed the assembly and that it has not changed since you signed it.

Usage

The Sign Tool provides a graphical wizard that walks you through the steps to Authenticode sign your assembly. To sign an assembly named MyAssembly.exe, run this command:

```
signtool signwizard MyAssembly.exe
```

Click Next on the introduction screen, and you will see the File Selection screen, where you must enter the name of the assembly to Authenticode sign (see Figure 1-3). Because you specified the assembly name on the command line, it is already filled in. If you are signing a multifile assembly, specify the name of the file that contains the assembly manifest. If you intend to both strong name and Authenticode sign your assembly, you must strong name the assembly first. (See recipe 1-12 for details on strong naming assemblies.)

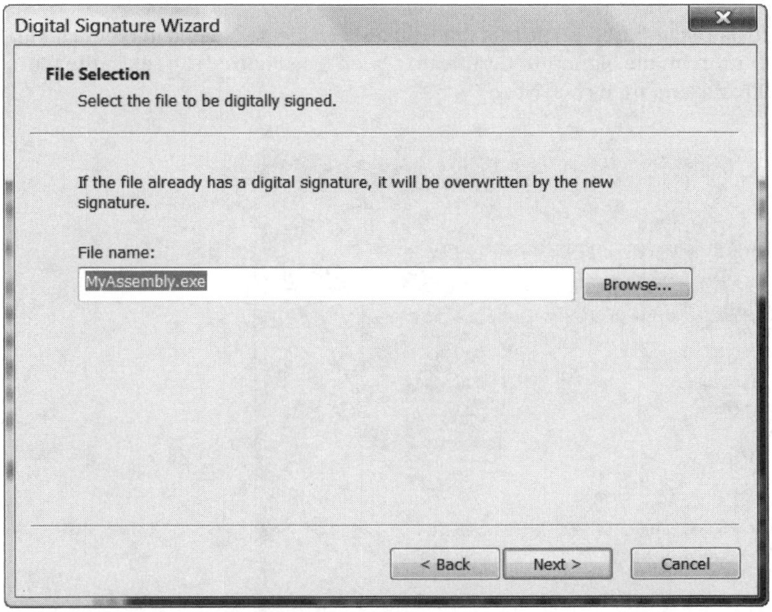

Figure 1-3. *The Sign Tool's File Selection screen*

Clicking Next takes you to the Signing Options screen (see Figure 1-4). If your SPC is in a certificate store, select the Typical radio button. If your SPC is in a file, select the Custom radio button. Then click Next.

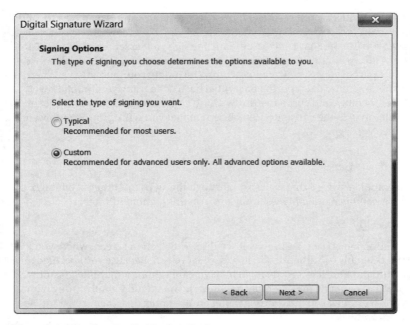

Figure 1-4. *The Sign Tool's Signing Options screen*

Assuming you want to use a file-based certificate (like the test certificate created in recipe 1-16), click the Select from File button on the Signature Certificate screen (see Figure 1-5), select the file containing your SPC certificate, and then click Next.

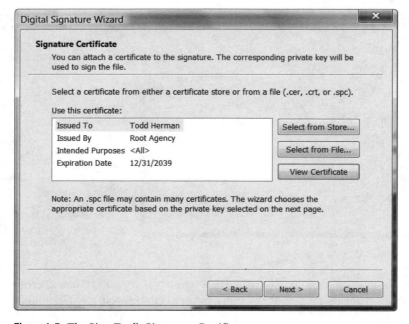

Figure 1-5. *The Sign Tool's Signature Certificate screen*

The Private Key screen allows you to identify the location of your private keys, which will either be in a file or be in a CSP key container, depending on where you created and stored them (see Figure 1-6). The example assumes they are in a file named PrivateKeys.pvk.

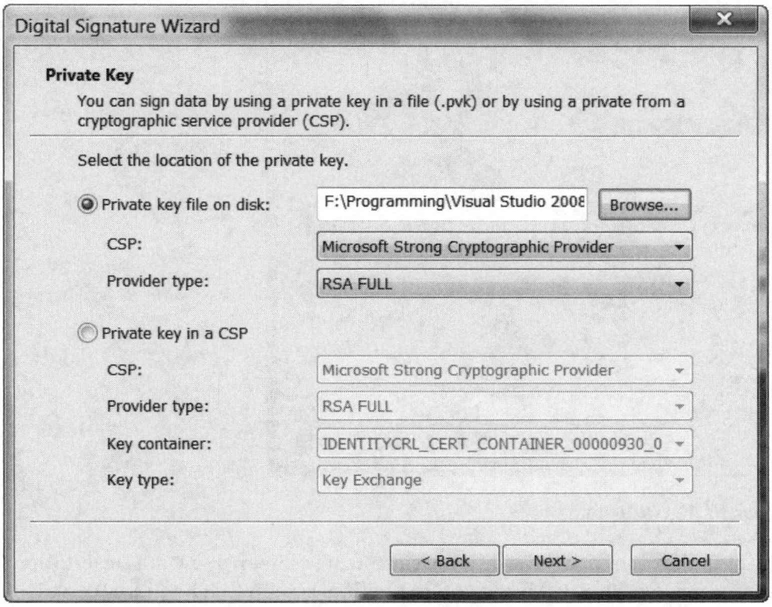

Figure 1-6. *The Sign Tool's Private Key screen*

When you click Next, if you selected to use a file, you will be prompted (see Figure 1-7) to enter a password to access the file (if required).

Figure 1-7. *Prompt for password to private key*

You can then select whether to use the sha1 or md5 hash algorithm (see Figure 1-8). The default is sha1, which is suitable for most purposes. On the Hash Algorithm screen, pick an algorithm, and then click Next.

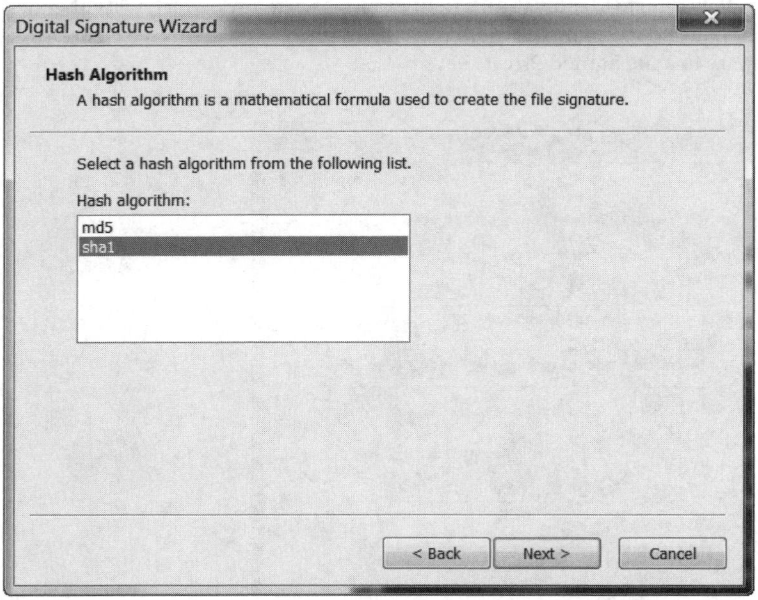

Figure 1-8. *The Sign Tool's Hash Algorithm screen*

Click Next to leave the default values on the Additional Certificates screen, the Data Description screen, and the Timestamping screen. This will bring you to the final screen (see Figure 1-9), which shows you all the previous choices you made. If everything is accurate, click Finish. If you are using a file-based private key that is password protected, you will once again be prompted to enter the password, after which the Sign Tool will Authenticode sign your assembly.

Figure 1-9. *The Sign Tool's completion screen*

Note The Sign Tool uses capicom.dll version 2.1.0.1. If an error occurs when you run signtool.exe that indicates capicom.dll is not accessible or not registered, change to the directory where capicom.dll is located (which is C:\Program Files\Common Files\Microsoft Shared\CAPICOM by default), and run the command `regsvr32 capicom.dll`.

1-16. Create and Trust a Test Software Publisher Certificate

Problem

You need to create an SPC to allow you to test the Authenticode signing of an assembly.

Solution

Use the Certificate Creation tool (makecert.exe) to create a test X.509 certificate, and use the Software Publisher Certificate Test tool (cert2spc.exe) to generate an SPC from this X.509 certificate. Trust the root test certificate using the Set Registry tool (setreg.exe).

How It Works

To create a test SPC for a software publisher named Todd Herman, create an X.509 certificate using the Certificate Creation tool. The command `makecert -n "CN=Todd Herman" -sk MyKeys TestCertificate.cer` creates a file named TestCertificate.cer containing an X.509 certificate and stores the associated private key in a CSP key container named MyKeys (which is automatically created if it does not exist). Alternatively, you can write the private key to a file by substituting the `-sk` switch with `-sv`. For example, to write the private key to a file named PrivateKeys.pvk, use the command `makecert -n " CN=Todd Herman" -sv PrivateKey.pvk TestCertificate.cer`. If you write your private key to a file, the Certificate Creation tool will prompt you to provide a password with which to protect the private key file (see Figure 1-10).

Figure 1-10. *The Certificate Creation tool requests a password when creating file-based private keys.*

The Certificate Creation tool supports many arguments, and Table 1-6 lists some of the more useful ones. You should consult the .NET Framework SDK documentation for full coverage of the Certificate Creation tool.

Table 1-6. *Commonly Used Switches of the Certificate Creation Tool*

Switch	Description
-e	Specifies the date when the certificate becomes invalid.
-m	Specifies the duration—in months—that the certificate remains valid.
-n	Specifies an X.500 name to associate with the certificate. This is the name of the software publisher that people will see when they view details of the SPC you create.
-sk	Specifies the name of the CSP key store in which to store the private key.
-ss	Specifies the name of the certificate store where the Certificate Creation tool should store the generated X.509 certificate.
-sv	Specifies the name of the file in which to store the private key.

Once you have created your X.509 certificate with the Certificate Creation tool, you need to convert it to an SPC with the Software Publisher Certificate Test tool (cert2spc.exe). To convert the certificate TestCertificate.cer to an SPC, use the command `cert2spc TestCertificate.cer TestCertificate.spc`. The Software Publisher Certificate Test tool doesn't offer any optional switches.

The final step before you can use your test SPC is to trust the root test CA, which is the default issuer of the test certificate. The Set Registry tool (setreg.exe) makes this a simple task with the command `setreg 1 true`. You can now Authenticode sign assemblies with your test SPC using the process described in recipe 1-15. When you have finished using your test SPC, you must remove trust of the root test CA using the command `setreg 1 false`.

1-17. Manage the Global Assembly Cache

Problem

You need to add or remove assemblies from the GAC.

Solution

Use the Global Assembly Cache tool (gacutil.exe) from the command line to view the contents of the GAC as well as to add and remove assemblies.

How It Works

Before you can install an assembly in the GAC, the assembly must have a strong name. (See recipe 1-12 for details on how to strong name your assemblies.) To install an assembly named SomeAssembly.dll into the GAC, use the command `gacutil /i SomeAssembly.dll`. You can install different versions of the same assembly in the GAC to meet the versioning requirements of different applications.

To uninstall the SomeAssembly.dll assembly from the GAC, use the command `gacutil /u SomeAssembly`. Notice that you don't use the .dll extension to refer to the assembly once it's installed in the GAC. This will uninstall all assemblies with the specified name. To uninstall a particular version, specify the version along with the assembly name; for example, use `gacutil /u SomeAssembly,Version=1.0.0.5`.

To view the assemblies installed in the GAC, use the command `gacutil /l`. This will produce a long list of all the assemblies installed in the GAC, as well as a list of assemblies that have been precompiled to binary form and installed in the native image (ngen) cache. To avoid searching through this

list to determine whether a particular assembly is installed in the GAC, use the command
`gacutil /l SomeAssembly`.

■**Note** The .NET Framework uses the GAC only at runtime; the VB .NET compiler won't look in the GAC to resolve any external references that your assembly references. During development, the VB .NET compiler must be able to access a local copy of any referenced shared assemblies. You can either copy the shared assembly to the same directory as your source code or use the `/libpath` switch of the VB .NET compiler to specify the directory where the compiler can find the required assemblies.

1-18. Make Your Assembly More Difficult to Decompile

Problem

You want to make sure that people cannot decompile your .NET assemblies.

Solution

The *only* way to ensure that your assembly cannot be decompiled is by not making it directly accessible. This can be accomplished using a server-based solution. If you must distribute assemblies, you have *no* way to stop people from decompiling them. The best you can do is use obfuscation and components compiled to native code to make your assemblies more difficult to decompile.

How It Works

Because .NET assemblies consist of a standardized, platform-independent set of instruction codes and metadata that describes the types contained in the assembly, they are relatively easy to decompile. This allows decompilers to generate source code that is close to your original code with ease, which can be problematic if your code contains proprietary information or algorithms that you want to keep secret.

The only way to ensure people can't decompile your assemblies is to prevent them from getting your assemblies in the first place. Where possible, implement server-based solutions such as Microsoft ASP.NET applications and web services. With the security correctly configured on your server, no one will be able to access your assemblies, and therefore they won't be able to decompile them.

When building a server solution is not appropriate, you have the following two options:

- Use an obfuscator to make it difficult to understand your code once it is decompiled. Some versions of Visual Studio include the Community Edition of an obfuscator named Dotfuscator. Obfuscators use a variety of techniques to make your assembly difficult to decompile; principal among these techniques are renaming `Private` methods and fields in such a way that it's difficult to read and understand the purpose of your code, as well as inserting control flow statements to make the logic of your application difficult to follow.

- Build the parts of your application that you want to keep secret in native DLLs or COM objects, and then call them from your managed application using P/Invoke or COM Interop. (See Chapter 14 for recipes that show you how to call unmanaged code.)

Neither approach will stop a skilled and determined person from reverse engineering your code, but both approaches will make the job significantly more difficult and deter most casual observers.

■**Note** The risks of application decompilation aren't specific to VB .NET or .NET in general. Determined people can reverse engineer any software if they have the time and the skill.

1-19. Use Implicitly Typed Variables

Problem

You need to create a strongly typed variable without explicitly declaring its type in an effort to save some development time or support LINQ, which is discussed in more detail in Chapter 6.

Solution

Ensure Option Infer is On, and then create a variable and assign it a value without using As and specifying a type.

How It Works

VB .NET 9.0 allows you to create strongly typed variables without explicitly setting their data types. You could do this in previous versions of VB .NET, if Option Strict were set to Off, but the variable was always typed as an Object. In this case, its type is automatically inferred based on its value.

To use this new functionality, Option Infer must be set to On. You can specify this setting in the Project Settings dialog box or by adding Option Infer On to the top of your code. If you create a new project in Visual Studio 2008, the project settings will have Option Infer set to On by default. Any projects that you migrate from previous Visual Studio versions will have Option Infer set to Off. If you are compiling your code using the VB compiler (vbc), you can use the /optioninfer option.

The following example demonstrates how to use type inference or implicit typing:

```
Dim name = "Todd"
Dim birthday = #7/12/1971#
Dim age = 36
Dim people = New Person() {New Person("Todd"), New Person("Amy"), ➥
New Person("Alaina"), New Person("Aidan")}
```

If you hover your cursor over any of the variables in the preceding example in the Visual Studio IDE, you will see a tool tip that shows that they are actually being strongly typed. name is *inferred* as a String, birthday is a Date, age is an Integer, and, as shown in Figure 1-11, people is an array of Person objects.

When your code is compiled to Microsoft Intermediate Language (MSIL), all variables are strongly typed. (See recipes 1-3 and 2-6 for more information about MSIL.) If you looked at this compiled MSIL code using the MSIL Disassembler tool (Ildasm.exe), you would see that it has explicitly and correctly typed each variable. The following output was taken from the Ildasm.exe results for the sample code shown previously.

```
.locals init ([0] int32 age,
    [1] valuetype [mscorlib]System.DateTime birthday,
    [2] string name,
    [3] class Apress.VisualBasicRecipes.Examples.TypeInference/Person[] people,
    [4] class Apress.VisualBasicRecipes.Examples.TypeInference/Person[] VB$t_array$S0)
```

```
Imports System
Imports System.Linq
Namespace Apress.VisualBasicRecipes.Examples

    Public Class TypeInference

        Public Class Person
            Private m_Name As String
            Public Sub New(ByVal name As String)
                m_Name = name
            End Sub
        End Class
        Public Shared Sub Main()
            Dim name = "Todd"
            Dim birthday = #7/12/1971#
            Dim age = 36
            Dim people = New Person() {New Person("Todd"), New Person("An
        End Sub       Dim people() As Apress.VisualBasicRecipes.Examples.TypeInference.Person

    End Class

End Namespace
```

Figure 1-11. *A tool tip showing inferred type*

Implicitly typing variables is an important part of creating and using LINQ queries, which are discussed in further detail in Chapters 6, 7, and 8. It is also a required component of *anonymous types*, which are discussed in recipe 1-21.

1-20. Use Object Initializers

Problem

You need to initialize the properties of a class when it is first instantiated, without relying on the class constructor or default values in an effort to save some development time or support LINQ, which is discussed in more detail in Chapter 6.

Solution

Instantiate a new class instance, and initialize any writable public fields or properties using the With keyword.

How It Works

VB .NET 9.0 includes the ability to initialize the writable public fields or properties of a class when it is first instantiated. When you use object initializers, the default constructor of the class is called automatically. This means any class you want to use object initializers for *must* have a default constructor. Any properties or fields that you do not initialize retain their default values.

Object initialization is made possible by using the With keyword. With is not new to VB .NET but was not previously usable in this manner. Here is a simple example of a class:

```vb
Public Class Person
    Private m_FirstName As String
    Private m_LastName As String

    Public Sub New()
        m_FirstName = String.Empty
        m_LastName = String.Empty
    End Sub

    Public Property FirstName() As String
        Get
            Return m_FirstName
        End Get
        Set(ByVal value As String)
            m_FirstName = value
        End Set
    End Property

    Public Property LastName() As String
        Get
            Return m_LastName
        End Get
        Set(ByVal value As String)
            m_LastName = value
        End Set
    End Property

End Class
```

In previous versions of VB .NET, you would instantiate and set property values like this:

```vb
Dim todd = New Person

With todd
    .FirstName = "Todd"
    .LastName = "Herman"
End With
```

The other option, if you had access to modify the class, is to use constructors to pass the property values. However, this method can become cumbersome quickly if you have a class with many properties. You further complicate things if you use an array, like this:

```vb
Dim people As Person() = New Person(2) {New Person, New Person, New Person}

With people(0)
    .FirstName = "Todd"
    .LastName = "Herman"
End With

With people(1)
    .FirstName = "Alaina"
    .LastName = "Herman"
End With
```

```
With people(2)
    .FirstName = "Aidan"
    .LastName = "Herman"
End With
```

Object initializers simplify this by allowing you to specify values during instantiation, like this:

```
Dim todd = New Person With {.FirstName = "Todd", .LastName = "Herman"}
```

or like this:

```
Dim people = New Person() {
                {New Person With {.FirstName = "Todd", _
                                  .LastName = "Herman"}, _
                    New Person With {.FirstName = "Amy", _
                                     .LastName = "Herman"}, _
                    New Person With {.FirstName = "Alaina", _
                                     .LastName = "Herman"}, _
                    New Person With {.FirstName = "Aidan", _
                                     .LastName = "Herman"}}
```

■Note Although it is not required, both of the preceding examples of object initialization use type inference (see recipe 1-19), rather than relying on explicit typing.

As the examples show, you use the `With` keyword followed by a comma-delimited list of fields or properties and their values. The objects being initialized and their values should be surrounded by curly braces ({}). As shown in Figure 1-12, the VB 9.0 IDE provides IntelliSense for all objects that can be initialized.

```
                    m_FirstName = value
                End Set
            End Property
        Public Property LastName() As String
            Get
                Return m_LastName
            End Get
            Set(ByVal value As String)
                m_LastName = value
            End Set
        End Property
    End Class
    Public Shared Sub Main()

        Dim todd = New Person With {.FirstName = "Todd", .LastName =
        Dim people = New Person() {New Person With {.FirstName = "Tod
                                                              "Hern
                        New Person With  FirstName      = "Amy
                                         LastName           "Hern
                        New Person With {.FirstName = "Ala
                                         .LastName = "Hern
                        New Person With {.FirstName = "Aid
```

Figure 1-12. *IntelliSense for object initializers*

Object initializers are using anonymous types (see recipe 1-21) and making LINQ queries concise and efficient.

1-21. Use Anonymous Types

Problem

You need to use a simple type class that doesn't exist without actually creating it in an effort to save some development time or support LINQ, which is discussed in more detail in Chapter 6.

Solution

Instantiate a class as you would normally, using the New keyword, but do not specify a type. You must also use object initialization (see recipe 1-20) to specify at least one property.

How It Works

When you use the New keyword to instantiate an object, you typically specify the name of the type you want to create. In VB 9.0, when you omit this name, the compiler automatically generates the class for you. This class inherits from Object and overloads the ToString, GetHashCode, and Equals methods. The overloaded version of ToString returns a string representing all the properties concatenated together. The overloaded Equals method returns True if all property comparisons are True and there are the same number of properties in the same order with the same names.

Figure 1-13 shows the MSIL Disassembler tool (Ildasm.exe) displaying the MSIL that the compiler would automatically generate for the following example (see recipes 1-3 and 2-6 for more information about MSIL):

```
Dim person = New With {.FirstName = "Todd", .LastName = "Herman"}
```

Figure 1-13. *MSIL Disassembler tool view of an anonymous type*

Creating anonymous types relies on several other new features of VB 9.0. As the name implies, the real name of an anonymous type is unknown. You will not be able to access it directly by its name and must rely on the variable used to first instantiate the class. This means you can't explicitly cast the person variable using As; you must rely on type inference (see recipe 1-19). Furthermore, an anonymous type *must* have at least one property. Properties for anonymous types are created by using object initializers (see recipe 1-20). The new version of Visual Studio fully supports the use of anonymous types by correctly displaying appropriate IntelliSense, as shown in Figure 1-14.

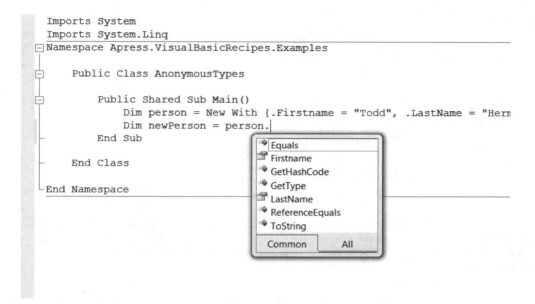

```
Imports System
Imports System.Linq
Namespace Apress.VisualBasicRecipes.Examples

    Public Class AnonymousTypes

        Public Shared Sub Main()
            Dim person = New With {.Firstname = "Todd", .LastName = "Hern
            Dim newPerson = person.
        End Sub

    End Class

End Namespace
```

Figure 1-14. *IntelliSense support for anonymous types*

Anonymous types can also infer property names from object initializers, as in this example:

```
Dim person = New With {DateTime.Now, .FirstName = "Todd", .LastName = "Herman"}
```

In this case, the anonymous type created by the compiler would have the Now, FirstName, and LastName properties.

Anonymous types are a powerful new feature available in VB 9.0 and are used extensively in LINQ queries (see Chapters 6, 7, and 8) for returning strongly typed data.

1-22. Create and Use Extension Methods

Problem

You need to extend the functionality of a class without relying on inheritance or access to the actual class.

Solution

Create the method (a Sub or Function) you want to add, and then apply the ExtensionAttribute attribute to it.

How It Works

The key to using extension methods is the attribute `ExtensionAttribute`, which is new to VB 9.0 and located in the `System.Runtime.CompilerServices` namespace. You must apply this attribute to any method that you want to use as an extension method. Furthermore, you can apply the attribute only to methods defined within a `Module`.

An extension method *extends* the functionality of a specific class without actually modifying it. The class being extended is referenced by the first parameter of the extension method. Because of this, all extension methods *must* have at least one parameter, and it *must* refer to the class being extended.

```
<System.Runtime.CompilerServices.Extension()> _
Public Function Reverse(ByVal s As String) As String

    Dim reversed As New Text.StringBuilder(s.Length)
    Dim chars As Char() = s.ToCharArray

        For count As Integer = chars.Length - 1 To 0 Step -1
            reversed.Append(chars(count))
        Next

        Return reversed.ToString

End Function
```

The `Reverse` method is an extension method because it has the `ExtensionAttribute` attribute applied to it. You also know that it extends the `String` class because the first parameter is a `String`. Using an extension method is the same as calling any other method, and the Visual Studio IDE supports this via IntelliSense, as shown in Figure 1-15.

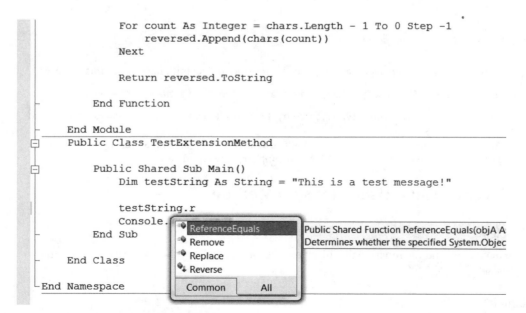

Figure 1-15. *IntelliSense support for extension methods*

In the case of the preceding example, you would create a String and then call the Reverse method, like this:

```
Dim testString As String = "This is a test message!"
Console.WriteLine(testString.Reverse())
```

This would produce the following result:

```
!egassem tset a si sihT
```

It is perfectly legitimate to call an extension method directly. When used in this manner, the first parameter of the method is used as an actual parameter. For example, you would get the same results if you changed the example to this:

```
Console.WriteLine(Reverse(testString))
```

The preceding example is fairly simple but demonstrates how easy it is to extend the functionality of a class without directly modifying it. What makes extension methods even more powerful is that they can also be used to extend base classes or even interfaces.

Extension methods are a key component of LINQ queries, which are covered in detail in Chapters 6, 7, and 8.

1-23. Create and Use Lambda Expressions

Problem

You need to use an inline function, which is a single-line function that does not require a standard function code block, in an effort to save some development time or support LINQ (discussed in more detail in Chapter 6).

Solution

Create a *lambda expression* using the Function keyword, and use it directly or pass it as an argument to a function that requires a delegate.

How It Works

To use a simple function, you typically start by creating the function. The following example takes an Integer and multiplies it by itself:

```
Private Shared Function Square(ByVal num As Integer) As Integer
    Return num * num
End Function
```

If you need to pass a function as an argument to some method, you could use a *delegate*. Delegates are used extensively by events and threading (discussed in Chapter 4) and by LINQ (discussed in Chapter 6). You accomplish this by using the Delegate keyword and using AddressOf to pass a reference to the function, as shown here:

```
Delegate Function CalculateDelegate(ByVal num As Integer) As Integer

Private Shared Sub Calculate(ByVal num As Integer, ➡
ByVal calculation As CalculateDelegate)
    Console.WriteLine(calculation(num).ToString)
End Sub
```

The previous delegate and method would be used like this:

```
Call Calculate(5, AddressOf Square)
```

In the previous example, the Calculate method will call the Square function that was passed to it, using the number 5. This will result in the number 25 being written to the console.

Everything discussed earlier is how previous versions of VB .NET handle simple functions and delegates. VB .NET 9.0 supports the same methodology but offers a very powerful alternative for small functions that return a value from a single expression. This alternative is known as the *lambda expression.*

Lambda expressions are inline functions that are based on a form of calculus with the same name. The basic concept is to take the entire function and compress it into a single line. To do this with the Square function shown earlier, you would create a statement that looks similar to this:

```
Function(num) num * num
```

The statement starts with the Function keyword that includes the list of required parameters surrounded by parentheses. This is immediately followed by the expression that must be a single line that returns some value. The previous example can be simplified by deleting the Square function and changing the execution statement to the following:

```
Call Calculate(5, Function(num) num * num)
```

This works because lambda expressions are, at their core, delegates. The compiler creates an anonymous type (see recipe 1-21) that is instantiated and used by the receiving method. Figure 1-16 shows the generated anonymous delegate as shown in the MSIL Disassembler tool (Ildasm.exe).

Figure 1-16. *MSIL Disassembler tool view of an anonymous delegate*

Lambda expressions can also be stored in a variable so it can be reused or more easily contained and passed to some method. Since VB 9.0 supports anonymous types and type inference (see recipe 1-19), you can leverage these features when using lambda expressions. For example, look at the following statement:

```
Dim calc = Function(num As Integer) num * num
```

In the previous statement, `calc` will be inferred as an anonymous delegate that meets the signature specified by the lambda expression. If you do not explicitly type the `num` parameter, then the data type for `calc` cannot be accurately inferred, resulting in an anonymous delegate whose parameters and return types are `Objects`.

To make storing lambda expressions even easier, .NET 3.5 includes the `System.Func` generic delegate. The `Func` delegate has five signatures that all include the data type of the returned value but vary depending on the number of arguments supported, which ranges from 0 to 5. With this in mind, you can change the previous example to use the `Func` delegate like this:

```
Dim calc As Func(Of Integer, Integer) = Function(num) num * num
```

The previous examples are all very basic in an attempt to simply explain the concepts of lambda expressions. The following example is a little more advanced and provides a more in-depth look at the power of lambda expressions:

```
Public Shared Sub Main()

    '  An array of numbers to be squared
    Dim numList() As Integer = {1, 2, 3, 4, 5, 6, 7, 8, 9}

    Console.WriteLine("Lambda Test:  Square an array of numbers")
    Call Calculate(numList, Function(num) num * num)
    Console.ReadLine()

End Sub

'  A method that executes the supplied function for each number
'  in the supplied array.
Private Shared Sub Calculate(ByVal nums() As Integer, ➡
ByVal calculation As Func(Of Integer, Integer))

    For Each num In nums
        '  Execute the lambda expression supplied and display the
        '  results to the console.
        Console.WriteLine(calculation(num).ToString)
    Next

End Sub
```

In this example, an array of `Integers` and a lambda expression to square numbers are passed to the `Calculate` method. The method loops through each `Integer` in the array and executes the provided lambda expression. The results would look similar to this:

```
Lambda Test:  Square an array of numbers
1
4
9
16
25
36
49
64
81
```

■**Note** LINQ (discussed in further detail in Chapter 6) relies heavily on extension methods (see recipe 1-22) that accept lambda expressions (in the form of a Func) as arguments.

CHAPTER 2

■ ■ ■

Data Manipulation

Most applications need to manipulate some form of data. The Microsoft .NET Framework provides many techniques that simplify or improve the efficiency of common data-manipulation tasks. The recipes in this chapter cover the following:

- Manipulating the contents of strings efficiently to avoid the overhead of automatic string creation due to the immutability of strings (recipe 2-1)
- Representing basic data types using different encoding schemes or as byte arrays to allow you to share data with external systems (recipes 2-2, 2-3, and 2-4)
- Validating user input and manipulating string values using regular expressions (recipes 2-5 and 2-6)
- Creating `System.DateTime` or `System.DateTimeOffset` objects from string values, such as those that a user might enter, and displaying them as formatted strings (recipe 2-7)
- Mathematically manipulating `DateTime` or `DateTimeOffset` objects in order to compare dates or add/subtract periods of time from a date (recipe 2-8)
- Converting dates and times across time zones (recipe 2-9)
- Sorting the contents of an array or an `ArrayList` collection (recipe 2-10)
- Copying the contents of a collection to an array (recipe 2-11)
- Analyzing or manipulating the contents of an array (recipe 2-12)
- Using the standard generic collection classes to instantiate a strongly typed collection (recipe 2-13)
- Using generics to define your own general-purpose container or collection class that will be strongly typed when it is used (recipe 2-14)
- Serializing object state and persisting it to a file (recipe 2-15)
- Reading user input from the Windows console (recipe 2-16)

2-1. Manipulate the Contents of a String Efficiently

Problem

You need to manipulate the contents of a `String` object and want to avoid the overhead of automatic `String` creation caused by the immutability of `String` objects.

Solution

Use the `System.Text.StringBuilder` class to perform the manipulations and convert the result to a `String` object using the `StringBuilder.ToString` method.

How It Works

`String` objects in .NET are immutable, meaning that once they are created, their content cannot be changed. If you build a string by concatenating a number of characters or smaller strings, the common language runtime (CLR) will create a completely new `String` object whenever you add a new element to the end of the existing string. Here is an example:

```
Dim testString as String
testString="Hello"
```

At this point, you have a `String` object named `testString` that contains the value "`Hello`". Since strings are immutable, adding the statement `testString=testString & " World"` will result in a new `String` object being created. The `testString` object's reference is changed to point to the newly generated string, which creates a new object that contains the value "`Hello World`". This can result in significant overhead if your application performs frequent string manipulation.

The `StringBuilder` class offers a solution by providing a character buffer and allowing you to manipulate its contents without the runtime creating a new object as a result of every change. You can create a new `StringBuilder` object that is empty or initialized with the content of an existing `String` object. You can manipulate the content of the `StringBuilder` object using overloaded methods that allow you to insert and append string representations of different data types. At any time, you can obtain a `String` representation of the current content of the `StringBuilder` object by calling `StringBuilder.ToString`.

Two important properties of `StringBuilder` control its behavior as you append new data: `Capacity` and `Length`. `Capacity` represents the size of the `StringBuilder` buffer, and `Length` represents the length of the buffer's current content. If you append new data that results in the number of characters in the `StringBuilder` object (`Length`) exceeding the capacity of the `StringBuilder` object (`Capacity`), the `StringBuilder` must allocate a new buffer to hold the data. The size of this new buffer is double the size of the previous `Capacity` value. Used carelessly, this buffer reallocation can negate much of the benefit of using `StringBuilder`. If you know the length of data you need to work with, or know an upper limit, you can avoid unnecessary buffer reallocation by specifying the capacity at creation time or setting the `Capacity` property manually. Note that 16 is the default `Capacity` property setting. When setting the `Capacity` and `Length` properties, be aware of the following behavior:

- If you set `Capacity` to a value less than the value of `Length`, the `Capacity` property throws the exception `System.ArgumentOutOfRangeException`. The same exception is also thrown if you try to raise the `Capacity` setting to more than the value of the `MaxCapacity` property. This should not be a problem except if you want to allocate more than 2 gigabytes (GB).

- If you set `Length` to a value less than the length of the current content, the content is truncated.

- If you set `Length` to a value greater than the length of the current content, the buffer is padded with spaces to the specified length. Setting `Length` to a value greater than `Capacity` automatically adjusts the `Capacity` value to be the same as the new `Length` value.

The Code

The `ReverseString` method shown in the following example demonstrates the use of the `StringBuilder` class to reverse a string. If you did not use the `StringBuilder` class to perform this operation, it would be significantly more expensive in terms of resource utilization, especially as the input string is made longer. The method creates a StringBuilder object of the correct capacity to ensure that no buffer reallocation is required during the reversal operation.

```vbnet
Imports System
Imports System.Text

Namespace Apress.VisualBasicRecipes.Chapter02

    Public Class Recipe02_01

        Public Shared Function ReverseString(ByVal str As String) As String

            ' Make sure we have a reversible string.
            If str Is Nothing Or str.Length <= 1 Then
                Return str
            End If

            ' Create a StringBuilder object with the required capacity.
            Dim revStr As StringBuilder = New StringBuilder(str.Length)

            ' Convert the string to a character array so we can easily loop
            ' through it.
            Dim chars As Char() = str.ToCharArray()

            ' Loop backward through the source string one character at a time and
            ' append each character to the StringBuilder.
            For count As Integer = chars.Length - 1 To 0 Step -1
                revStr.Append(chars(count))
            Next

            Return revStr.ToString()

        End Function

        Public Shared Sub Main()
            Console.WriteLine(ReverseString("Madam Im Adam"))

            Console.WriteLine(ReverseString("The quick brown fox jumped ➡
    over the lazy dog."))

            ' Wait to continue
            Console.WriteLine(vbCrLf & "Main method complete.  Press Enter.")
            Console.ReadLine()

        End Sub

    End Class
End Namespace
```

2-2. Encode a String Using Alternate Character Encoding

Problem

You need to exchange character data with systems that use character-encoding schemes other than UTF-16, which is the character-encoding scheme used internally by the CLR.

Solution

Use the System.Text.Encoding class and its subclasses to convert characters between different encoding schemes.

How It Works

Unicode is not the only character-encoding scheme nor is UTF-16 the only way to represent Unicode characters. When your application needs to exchange character data with external systems (particularly legacy systems) through an array of bytes, you may need to convert character data between UTF-16 and the encoding scheme supported by the other system.

The MustInherit class Encoding and its concrete subclasses provide the functionality to convert characters to and from a variety of encoding schemes. Each subclass instance supports the conversion of characters between the instance's encoding scheme and UTF-16. You obtain instances of the encoding-specific classes using the Shared factory method Encoding.GetEncoding, which accepts either the name or the code page number of the required encoding scheme.

Table 2-1 lists some commonly used character-encoding schemes and the code page number you must pass to the GetEncoding method to create an instance of the appropriate encoding class. The table also shows Shared properties of the Encoding class that provide shortcuts for obtaining the most commonly used types of encoding objects.

Table 2-1. *Character-Encoding Classes*

Encoding Scheme	Class	Create Using
ASCII	ASCIIEncoding	GetEncoding(20127) or the ASCII property
Default (current Microsoft Windows default)	Encoding	GetEncoding(0) or the Default property
UTF-7	UTF7Encoding	GetEncoding(65000) or the UTF7 property
UTF-8	UTF8Encoding	GetEncoding(65001) or the UTF8 property
UTF-16 (Big Endian)	UnicodeEncoding	GetEncoding(1201) or the BigEndianUnicode property
UTF-16 (Little Endian)	UnicodeEncoding	GetEncoding(1200) or the Unicode property

Once you have an Encoding object of the appropriate type, you convert a UTF-16 encoded Unicode string to a byte array of encoded characters using the GetBytes method. Conversely, you pass a byte array of encoded characters (such as UTF-8) to the GetString method, which will produce a UTF-16 encoded Unicode string.

The Code

The following example demonstrates how to use some encoding classes:

```vb
Imports System
Imports System.IO
Imports System.Text.Encoding

Namespace Apress.VisualBasicRecipes.Chapter02

    Public Class Recipe02_02

        Public Shared Sub Main()

            ' Create a file to hold the output.
            Using output As New StreamWriter("output.txt")
                ' Create and write a string containing the symbol for pi.
                Dim srcString As String = String.Format("Area = {0}r^2", ➥
ChrW(&H3A0))
                output.WriteLine("Source Text:  " & srcString)

                ' Write the UTF-16 encoded bytes of the source string.
                Dim utf16String As Byte() = Unicode.GetBytes(srcString)
                output.WriteLine("UTF-16 Bytes:  {0}", ➥
BitConverter.ToString (utf16String))

                ' Convert the UTF-16 encoded source string to UTF-8 and ASCII.
                Dim utf8String As Byte() = UTF8.GetBytes(srcString)
                Dim asciiString As Byte() = ASCII.GetBytes(srcString)

                ' Write the UTF-8 and ASCII encoded byte arrays.
                output.WriteLine("UTF-8 Bytes:  {0}", ➥
BitConverter.ToString (utf8string))
                output.WriteLine("ASCII Bytes:  {0}", ➥
BitConverter.ToString (asciiString))

                ' Convert UTF-8 and ASCII encoded bytes back to UTF-16 encoded
                ' string and write to the output file.
                output.WriteLine("UTF-8 Text:  {0}", UTF8.GetString(utf8String))
                output.WriteLine("ASCII Text:  {0}", ASCII.GetString(asciiString))
            End Using

            ' Wait to continue
            Console.WriteLine(vbCrLf & "Main method complete.  Press Enter.")
            Console.ReadLine()

        End Sub

    End Class
End Namespace
```

Usage

Running the code will generate a file named output.txt. If you open this file in a text editor that supports Unicode, you will see results similar to the following:

```
Source Text:  Area = r^2
UTF-16 Bytes:  41-00-72-00-65-00-61-00-20-00-3D-00-20-00-A0-03-72-00-5E-00-32-00
UTF-8 Bytes:   41-72-65-61-20-3D-20-CE-A0-72-5E-32
ASCII Bytes:   41-72-65-61-20-3D-20-3F-72-5E-32
UTF-8 Text:   Area = r^2
ASCII Text:   Area = ?r^2
```

Notice that using UTF-16 encoding, each character occupies 2 bytes, but because most of the characters are standard characters, the high-order byte is 0. (The use of little-endian byte ordering means that the low-order byte appears first.) This means that most of the characters are encoded using the same numeric values across all three encoding schemes. However, the numeric value for the symbol pi (emphasized in bold in the preceding output) is different in each of the encodings. Representing the value of pi requires more than 1 byte. UTF-8 encoding uses 2 bytes, but ASCII has no direct equivalent and so replaces pi with the code 3F. As you can see in the ASCII text version of the string, 3F is the symbol for an English question mark (?).

■**Caution** If you convert Unicode characters to ASCII or a specific code page-encoding scheme, you risk losing data. Any Unicode character with a character code that cannot be represented in the scheme will be ignored or altered.

Notes

The Encoding class also provides the Shared method Convert to simplify the conversion of a byte array from one encoding scheme to another without the need to manually perform an interim conversion to UTF-16. For example, the following statement converts the ASCII-encoded bytes contained in the asciiString byte array directly from ASCII encoding to UTF-8 encoding:

```
Dim utf8String As Byte() = Encoding.Convert(Encoding.ASCII, ➡
Encoding.UTF8, asciiString)
```

2-3. Convert Basic Value Types to Byte Arrays

Problem

You need to convert basic value types to byte arrays.

Solution

The Shared methods of the System.BitConverter class provide a convenient mechanism for converting most basic value types to and from byte arrays. An exception is the Decimal type. To convert a Decimal type to or from a byte array, you need to use a System.IO.MemoryStream object.

How It Works

The Shared method GetBytes of the BitConverter class provides overloads that take most of the standard value types and return the value encoded as an array of bytes. Support is provided for the Boolean, Char, Double, Short, Integer, Long, Single, UShort, UInteger, and ULong data types. BitConverter also provides a set of Shared methods that support the conversion of byte arrays to each of the standard value types. These are named ToBoolean, ToInt32, ToDouble, and so on. When using the BitConverter class, you may notice that some members include the values Int16, Int32, and Int64. These values are simply an alternate way of saying Short, Integer, and Long, respectively.

Unfortunately, the BitConverter class does not provide support for converting the Decimal type. Instead, write the Decimal type to a MemoryStream instance using a System.IO.BinaryWriter object, and then call the MemoryStream.ToArray method. To create a Decimal type from a byte array, create a MemoryStream object from the byte array and read the Decimal type from the MemoryStream object using a System.IO.BinaryReader instance.

The Code

The following example demonstrates how to use BitConverter to convert a Boolean type and an Integer type to and from a byte array. The second argument to each of the ToBoolean and ToInt32 methods is a zero-based offset into the byte array where the BitConverter should start taking the bytes to create the data value. The code also shows how to convert a Decimal type to a byte array using a MemoryStream object and a BinaryWriter object, as well as how to convert a byte array to a Decimal type using a BinaryReader object to read from the MemoryStream object.

```vbnet
Imports System
Imports System.IO
Namespace Apress.VisualBasicRecipes.Chapter02

    Public Class Recipe02_03

        ' Create a byte array from a decimal.
        Public Shared Function DecimalToByteArray(ByVal src As Decimal) As Byte()

            ' Create a MemoryStream as a buffer to hold the binary data.
            Using stream As New MemoryStream
                ' Create a BinaryWriter to write binary data to the stream.
                Using writer As New BinaryWriter(stream)
                    ' Write the decimal to the BinaryWriter/MemoryStream.
                    writer.Write(src)

                    ' Return the byte representation of the decimal.
                    Return stream.ToArray
                End Using
            End Using

        End Function

        ' Create a decimal from a byte array.
        Public Shared Function ByteArrayToDecimal(ByVal src As Byte()) As Decimal

            ' Create a MemoryStream containing the byte array.
            Using stream As New MemoryStream(src)
                ' Create a BinaryReader to read the decimal from the stream.
                Using reader As New BinaryReader(stream)
                    ' Read and return the decimal from the
                    ' BinaryReader/MemoryStream.
                    Return reader.ReadDecimal
                End Using
            End Using

        End Function
```

```
        Public Shared Sub Main()

            Dim b As Byte() = Nothing

            ' Convert a boolean to a byte array and display.
            b = BitConverter.GetBytes(True)
            Console.WriteLine(BitConverter.ToString(b))

            ' Convert a byte array to a boolean and display.
            Console.WriteLine(BitConverter.ToBoolean(b, 0))

            ' Convert an integer to a byte array and display.
            b = BitConverter.GetBytes(3678)
            Console.WriteLine(BitConverter.ToString(b))

            ' Convert a byte array to integer and display.
            Console.WriteLine(BitConverter.ToInt32(b, 0))

            ' Convert a decimal to a byte array and display.
            b = DecimalToByteArray(285998345545.563846696D)
            Console.WriteLine(BitConverter.ToString(b))

            ' Convert a byte array to a decimal and display.
            Console.WriteLine(ByteArrayToDecimal(b))

            ' Wait to continue
            Console.WriteLine(vbCrLf & "Main method complete.  Press Enter.")
            Console.ReadLine()

        End Sub

    End Class
End Namespace
```

Tip The `BitConverter.ToString` method provides a convenient mechanism for obtaining a `String` representation of a byte array. Calling `ToString` and passing a byte array as an argument will return a `String` object containing the hexadecimal value of each byte in the array separated by a hyphen, for example, `"34-A7-2C"`. Unfortunately, there is no standard method for reversing this process to obtain a byte array from a string with this format.

Usage

Running the code will display the following results to the console:

```
01
True
5E-0E-00-00
3678
28-38-C1-50-FD-3B-06-81-0F-00-00-00-00-00-09-00
285998345545.563846696

Main method complete.  Press Enter.
```

2-4. Base64 Encode Binary Data

Problem

You need to convert binary data into a form that can be stored as part of an ASCII text file (such as an XML file) or sent as part of a text e-mail message.

Solution

Use the Shared methods ToBase64CharArray and FromBase64CharArray of the System.Convert class to convert your binary data to and from a Base64-encoded Char array. If you need to work with the encoded data as a string value rather than as a Char array, you can use the ToBase64String and FromBase64String methods of the Convert class instead.

How It Works

Base64 is an encoding scheme that enables you to represent binary data as a series of ASCII characters so that it can be included in text files and e-mail messages in which raw binary data is unacceptable. Base64 encoding works by spreading the contents of 3 bytes of input data across 4 bytes and ensuring each byte uses only the 7 low-order bits to contain data. This means that each byte of Base64-encoded data is equivalent to an ASCII character and can be stored or transmitted anywhere ASCII characters are permitted. This process is not very efficient and can take a while to run on large amounts of data.

The ToBase64CharArray and FromBase64CharArray methods of the Convert class make it straightforward to Base64 encode and decode data. However, before Base64 encoding, you must convert your data to a byte array. Similarly, when decoding, you must convert the byte array back to the appropriate data type. (See recipe 2-2 for details on converting string data to and from byte arrays and recipe 2-3 for details on converting basic value types.) The ToBase64String and FromBase64String methods of the Convert class deal with string representations of Base64-encoded data.

The Code

The example shown here demonstrates how to Base64 encode and decode a Byte array, a Unicode String, an Integer type, and a Decimal type using the Convert class. The DecimalToBase64 and Base64ToDecimal methods rely on the ByteArrayToDecimal and DecimalToByteArray methods listed in recipe 2-3.

```
Imports System
Imports System.IO
Imports System.Text
Namespace Apress.VisualBasicRecipes.Chapter02

    Public Class Recipe02_04

        ' Create a byte array from a decimal.
        Public Shared Function DecimalToByteArray(ByVal src As Decimal) As Byte()

            ' Create a MemoryStream as a buffer to hold the binary data.
            Using stream As New MemoryStream
                ' Create a BinaryWriter to write binary data to the stream.
                Using writer As New BinaryWriter(stream)
                    ' Write the decimal to the BinaryWriter/MemoryStream.
                    writer.Write(src)
```

```vbnet
                       ' Return the byte representation of the decimal.
                      Return stream.ToArray
                  End Using
              End Using

End Function


  ' Create a decimal from a byte array.
  Public Shared Function ByteArrayToDecimal(ByVal src As Byte()) As Decimal

          ' Create a MemoryStream containing the byte array.
          Using stream As New MemoryStream(src)
              ' Create a BinaryReader to read the decimal from the stream.
              Using reader As New BinaryReader(stream)
                    ' Read and return the decimal from
                    ' the BinaryReader/MemoryStream.
                    Return reader.ReadDecimal
              End Using
          End Using

  End Function

  ' Base64 encode a Unicode string
  Public Shared Function StringToBase64(ByVal src As String) As String

          ' Get a byte representation of the source string.
          Dim b As Byte() = Encoding.Unicode.GetBytes(src)

          ' Return the Base64-encoded Unicode string.
          Return Convert.ToBase64String(b)

  End Function

  ' Decode a Base64-encoded Unicode string.
  Public Shared Function Base64ToString(ByVal src As String) As String

          ' Decode the Base64-encoded string to a byte array.
          Dim b As Byte() = Convert.FromBase64String(src)

          ' Return the decoded Unicode string.
          Return Encoding.Unicode.GetString(b)

  End Function

  ' Base64 encode a decimal
  Public Shared Function DecimalToBase64(ByVal src As Decimal) As String

          ' Get a byte representation of the decimal.
          Dim b As Byte() = DecimalToByteArray(src)

          ' Return the Base64-encoded decimal.
          Return Convert.ToBase64String(b)

  End Function
```

```vbnet
        ' Decode a Base64-encoded decimal.
        Public Shared Function Base64ToDecimal(ByVal src As String) As Decimal

            ' Decode the Base64-encoded decimal to a byte array.
            Dim b As Byte() = Convert.FromBase64String(src)

            ' Return the decoded decimal.
            Return ByteArrayToDecimal(b)

        End Function

        ' Base64 encode an integer.
        Public Shared Function IntToBase64(ByVal src As Integer) As String

            ' Get a byte representation of the integer.
            Dim b As Byte() = BitConverter.GetBytes(src)

            ' Return the Base64-encoded integer.
            Return Convert.ToBase64String(b)

        End Function

        ' Decode a Base64-encoded integer.
        Public Shared Function Base64ToInt(ByVal src As String) As Decimal

            ' Decode the Base64-encoded integer to a byte array.
            Dim b As Byte() = Convert.FromBase64String(src)

            ' Return the decoded integer.
            Return BitConverter.ToInt32(b, 0)

        End Function

        Public Shared Sub Main()

            ' Encode and decode a string
            Console.WriteLine(StringToBase64("Welcome to Visual Basic 2008 " & ➥
    "Recipes from Apress"))
            Console.WriteLine(Base64ToString("VwBlAGwAYwBvAG0AZQAgAHQAbwAg" + ➥
    "AFYAaQBzAHUAYQBsACAAQgBhAHMAaQBjACAAMgAwADAAOAAgAFIAZQBjAGkAcABlAHMAIABmA" + ➥
    "HIAbwBtACAAQQBwAHIAZQBzAHMA"))

            ' Encode and decode a decimal.
            Console.WriteLine(DecimalToBase64(285998345545.563846696D))
            Console.WriteLine(Base64ToDecimal("KDjBUPO7BoEPAAAAAAAJAA=="))

            ' Encode and decode an integer.
            Console.WriteLine(IntToBase64(35789))
            Console.WriteLine(Base64ToInt("zYsAAA=="))

            ' Wait to continue
            Console.WriteLine(vbCrLf & "Main method complete.  Press Enter.")
            Console.ReadLine()

        End Sub
```

Table 2-3. *Commonly Used Regular Expressions*

Input Type	Description	Regular Expression
Numeric input	The input consists of one or more decimal digits; for example, 5 or 5683874674.	`^\d+$`
Personal identification number (PIN)	The input consists of four decimal digits; for example, 1234.	`^\d{4}$`
Simple password	The input consists of six to eight characters; for example, ghtd6f or b8c7hogh.	`^\w{6,8}$`
Credit card number	The input consists of data that matches the pattern of most major credit card numbers; for example, 4921835221552042 or 4921-8352-2155-2042.	`^\d{4}-?\d{4}-?\d{4}-?\d{4}$`
E-mail address	The input consists of an Internet e-mail address. The `[\w-]+` expression indicates that each address element must consist of one or more word characters or hyphens; for example, somebody@adatum.com.	`^[\w-]+@([\w-]+\.)+[\w-]+$`
HTTP or HTTPS URL	The input consists of an HTTP-based or HTTPS-based URL; for example, `http://www.apress.com`.	`^https?://([\w-]+\.)+[\w-]+(/ [\w-./?%=]*)?$`

Once you know the correct regular expression syntax, create a new `System.Text.RegularExpressions.Regex` object, passing a string containing the regular expression to the `Regex` constructor. Then call the `IsMatch` method of the `Regex` object and pass the string you want to validate. `IsMatch` returns a `Boolean` value indicating whether the `Regex` object found a match in the string. The regular expression syntax determines whether the `Regex` object will match against only the full string or match against patterns contained within the string. (See the `^`, `\A`, `$`, and `\z` entries in Table 2-2.)

The Code

The `ValidateInput` method shown in the following example tests any input string to see whether it matches a specified regular expression.

```
Imports System
Imports System.Text.RegularExpressions
Namespace Apress.VisualBasicRecipes.Chapter02

    Public Class Recipe02_05


        Public Shared Function ValidateInput(ByVal expression As String, ⟶
    ByVal input As String) As Boolean

            ' Create a new Regex based on the specified regular expression.
            Dim r As New Regex(expression)

            ' Test if the specified input matches the regular expression.
            Return r.IsMatch(input)

        End Function
```

```
    Public Shared Sub Main(ByVal args As String())

        ' Test the input from the command line.  The first argument is the
        ' regular expression, and the second is the input.
        Console.WriteLine("Regular Expresion:  {0}", args(0))
        Console.WriteLine("Input:  {0}", args(1))
        Console.WriteLine("Valied = {0}", ValidateInput(args(0), args(1)))

        ' Wait to continue.
        Console.WriteLine(vbCrLf & "Main method complete.  Press Enter")
        Console.ReadLine()

    End Sub

  End Class
End Namespace
```

Usage

To execute the example, run Recipe02-05.exe, and pass the regular expression and data to test as command-line arguments. For example, to test for a correctly formed e-mail address, type the following:

```
Recipe02-05 ^[\w-]+@([\w-]+\.)+[\w-]+$ myname@mydomain.com
```

The result would be as follows:

```
Regular Expression: ^[\w-]+@([\w-]+\.)+[\w-]+$
Input: myname@mydomain.com
Valid = True
```

Notes

You can use a Regex object repeatedly to test multiple strings, but you cannot change the regular expression tested for by a Regex object. You must create a new Regex object to test for a different pattern. This is because the ValidateInput method creates a new Regex instance each time it's called. A more suitable alternative, in this case, would be to use a Shared overload of the IsMatch method, as shown in the following variant of the ValidateInput method:

```
' Alternative version of the ValidateInput method that does not create
' Regex instances.
Public Shared Function ValidateInput(ByVal expression As String, ➡
ByVal input As String) As Boolean

    ' Test if the specified input matches the regular expression.
    Return Regex.IsMatch(input, expression)

End Function
```

2-6. Use Compiled Regular Expressions

Problem

You need to minimize the impact on application performance that arises from using complex regular expressions frequently.

Solution

When you instantiate the `System.Text.RegularExpressions.Regex` object that represents your regular expression, specify the `Compiled` option of the `System.Text.RegularExpressions.RegexOptions` enumeration to compile the regular expression to Microsoft Intermediate Language (MSIL).

How It Works

By default, when you create a `Regex` object, the regular expression pattern you specify in the constructor is compiled to an intermediate form (not MSIL). Each time you use the `Regex` object, the runtime interprets the pattern's intermediate form and applies it to the target string. With complex regular expressions that are used frequently, this repeated interpretation process can have a detrimental effect on the performance of your application.

By specifying the `RegexOptions.Compiled` option when you create a `Regex` object, you force the .NET runtime to compile the regular expression to MSIL instead of the interpreted intermediary form. This MSIL is just-in-time (JIT) compiled by the runtime to native machine code on first execution, just like regular assembly code. Subsequent calls to the same `RegEx` object will use the native version that was previously compiled. You use a compiled regular expression in the same way as you use any `Regex` object; compilation simply results in faster execution.

However, a couple downsides offset the performance benefits provided by compiling regular expressions. First, the JIT compiler needs to do more work, which will introduce delays during JIT compilation. This is most noticeable if you create your compiled regular expressions as your application starts up. Second, the runtime cannot unload a compiled regular expression once you have finished with it. Unlike as with a normal regular expression, the runtime's garbage collector will not reclaim the memory used by the compiled regular expression. The compiled regular expression will remain in memory until your program terminates or you unload the application domain in which the compiled regular expression is loaded. If you plan to use a `RegEx` object only once, there is no reason to compile it. Use compiling only for situations where a `RegEx` object is used frequently.

As well as compiling regular expressions in memory, the `Shared Regex.CompileToAssembly` method allows you to create a compiled regular expression and write it to an external assembly. This means you can create assemblies containing standard sets of regular expressions, which you can use from multiple applications. To compile a regular expression and persist it to an assembly, take the following steps:

1. Create a `System.Text.RegularExpressions.RegexCompilationInfo` array large enough to hold one `RegexCompilationInfo` object for each of the compiled regular expressions you want to create.

2. Create a `RegexCompilationInfo` object for each of the compiled regular expressions. Specify values for its properties as arguments to the object constructor. The following are the most commonly used properties:

   - `Pattern`, a `String` value that specifies the pattern that the regular expression will match (see recipe 2-5 for more details)

   - `Options`, a `System.Text.RegularExpressions.RegexOptions` value that specifies options for the regular expression

   - `Name`, a `String` value that specifies the class name

   - `Namespace`, a `String` value that specifies the namespace of the class

   - `IsPublic`, a `Boolean` value that specifies whether the generated regular expression class has `Public` visibility

3. Create a System.Reflection.AssemblyName object. Configure it to represent the name of the assembly that the Regex.CompileToAssembly method will create.

4. Execute Regex.CompileToAssembly, passing the RegexCompilationInfo array and the AssemblyName object.

This process creates an assembly that contains one class declaration for each compiled regular expression—each class derives from Regex. To use the compiled regular expression contained in the assembly, instantiate the regular expression you want to use, and call its method as if you had simply created it with the normal Regex constructor. (Remember to add a reference to the assembly when you compile the code that uses the compiled regular expression classes.)

The Code

This line of code shows how to create a Regex object that is compiled to MSIL instead of the usual intermediate form:

```
Dim reg As New Regex("[\w-]+@([\w-]+\.)+[\w-]+", RegexOptions.Compiled)
```

The following example shows how to create an assembly named MyRegEx.dll, which contains two regular expressions named PinRegex and CreditCardRegex:

```
Imports System
Imports System.Reflection
Imports System.Text.RegularExpressions

Namespace Apress.VisualBasicRecipes.Chapter02

    Public Class Recipe02_06

        Public Shared Sub Main()

            ' Create the array to hold the Regex info objects.
            Dim regexInfo(1) As RegexCompilationInfo


            ' Create the RegexCompilationInfo for PinRegex.
            regexInfo(0) = New RegexCompilationInfo("^\d{4}$", ➥
RegexOptions.Compiled, "PinRegex", "Apress.VisualBasicRecipes.Chapter02", True)

            ' Create the RegexCompilationInfo for CreditCardRegex.
            regexInfo(1) = New RegexCompilationInfo( ➥
"^\d{4}-?\d{4}-?\d{4}-?\d{4}$", RegexOptions.Compiled, "CreditCardRegex", ➥
"Apress.VisualBasicRecipes.Chapter02", True)

            ' Create the AssemblyName to define the target assembly.
            Dim assembly As New AssemblyName("MyRegEx")

            ' Create the compiled regular expression.
            Regex.CompileToAssembly(regexInfo, assembly)

        End Sub

    End Class
End Namespace
```

Usage

When you want to use your new assembly, you must first add a reference to it to your project. You can do this from within the Visual Studio interface or by using the `/r:MyRegEx.dll` option of the command-line compiler.

Once you have a reference to the assembly in your project, you can easily create a reference to the compiled regular expressions contained inside, as shown in this example:

```
Dim pinRegExp As New PinRegex
```

2-7. Create Dates and Times from Strings

Problem

You need to create a `System.DateTime` or `System.DateTimeOffset` instance that represents the time and date specified in a string.

Solution

Use the `Parse`/`TryParse` or `ParseExact`/`TryParseExact` methods of the `DateTime` or `DateTimeOffset` structure.

■**Caution** Many subtle issues are associated with using the `DateTime` and `DateTimeOffset` structures to represent dates and times in your applications. Although the `Parse` and `ParseExact` methods, as well as the `TryParse` and `TryParseExact` counterparts, create `DateTime` or `DateTimeOffset` objects from strings as described in this recipe, you must be careful how you use the resulting objects within your program. See the article titled "Coding Best Practices Using DateTime in the .NET Framework" (`http://msdn.microsoft.com/netframework/default.aspx?pull=/library/en-us/dndotnet/html/datetimecode.asp`) for details about the problems you might encounter. This article does not cover the `DateTimeOffset` structure specifically, but most of it still applies since the two structures are so closely related.

How It Works

Dates and times can be represented as text in many different ways. For example, January 12 1975, 1/12/1975, and Jan-12-1975 are all possible representations of the same date, and 18:19 and 6:19 p.m. can both be used to represent the same time. The Shared `DateTime.Parse` method provides a flexible mechanism for creating `DateTime` instances from a wide variety of string representations.

The `Parse` method goes to great lengths to generate a `DateTime` object from a given string. It will even attempt to generate a `DateTime` object from a string containing partial or erroneous information and will substitute defaults for any missing values. Missing date elements default to the current date, and missing time elements default to 12:00:00 a.m. After all efforts, if `Parse` cannot create a `DateTime` object, it throws a `System.FormatException` exception.

The `Parse` method is both flexible and forgiving. However, for many applications, this level of flexibility is unnecessary. Often, you will want to ensure that `DateTime` parses only strings that match a specific format. In these circumstances, use the `ParseExact` method instead of `Parse`. The simplest overload of the `ParseExact` method takes three arguments: the time and date string to parse, a format string that specifies the structure that the time and date string must have, and an `IFormatProvider` reference that provides culture-specific information to the `ParseExact` method. If the `IFormatProvider` value is `Nothing`, the current thread's culture information is used.

The time and date must meet the requirements specified in the format string, or ParseExact will throw a System.FormatException exception. You use the same format specifiers for the format string as you use to format a DateTime object for display as a string. This means you can use both standard and custom format specifiers.

The DateTime structure also offers the TryParse and TryParseExact methods. These methods behave just like Parse and ParseExact, but they do not throw an exception if the String parameter cannot be parsed. Instead, both functions return a Boolean that determines whether the parsing was successful. If the parsing was successful, the resulting DateTime object will be saved to the ByRef parameter that was passed to the function.

The .NET Framework 3.5 introduces the new DateTimeOffset structure as an alternative to the DateTime structure. Although these structures are nearly identical, DateTimeOffset allows you to specify by how much the date and time differ from Coordinated Universal Time (UTC). The Offset property, which is read-only, is used to retrieve this value as a TimeSpan whose Hour property can range from –14 to 14.

The Code

The following example demonstrates the flexibility of the Parse method and how to use the ParseExact method. Refer to the documentation for the System.Globalization.DateTimeFormatInfo class in the .NET Framework SDK document for complete details on all available format specifiers.

```
Imports System

Namespace Apress.VisualBasicRecipes.Chapter02
    Public Class Recipe02_07

        Public Shared Sub Main(ByVal args As String())

            ' 1st January 1975 at 00:00:00
            Dim dt1 As DateTime = DateTime.Parse("Jan 1975")

            ' 12th January 1975 at 18:19:00
            Dim dt2 As DateTime = DateTime.Parse("Sunday 12 January 1975 18:19:00")

            ' 12th January 1975 at 00:00:00
            Dim dt3 As DateTime = DateTime.Parse("1,12,1975")

            ' 12th January 1975 at 18:19:00
            Dim dt4 As DateTime = DateTime.Parse("1/12/1975 18:19:00")

            ' Current Date at 18:19 showing UTC offset for local time zone
            Dim dt5 As DateTimeOffset = DateTimeOffset.Parse("6:19 PM")

            ' Current Date at 18:19 showing an offset of -8 hours from UTC.
            Dim dt6 As DateTimeOffset = DateTimeOffset.Parse("6:19 PM -8")

            ' Date set to minvalue to be used later by TryParse
            Dim dt7 As DateTime = DateTime.MinValue

            ' Display the converted DateTime objects.
            Console.WriteLine(dt1)
            Console.WriteLine(dt2)
            Console.WriteLine(dt3)
            Console.WriteLine(dt4)
```

```
                Console.WriteLine(dt5)
                Console.WriteLine(dt6)

                ' Try to parse a nondatetime string.
                If Not DateTime.TryParse("This is an invalid date", dt7) Then
                    Console.WriteLine("Unable to parse.")
                Else
                    Console.WriteLine(dt7)
                End If

                ' Parse only strings containing LongTimePattern.
                Dim dt8 As DateTime = DateTime.ParseExact("6:19:00 PM", ➥
"h:mm:ss tt", Nothing)

                ' Parse only strings containing RFC1123Pattern.
                Dim dt9 As DateTime = DateTime.ParseExact("Sun, 12 Jan 1975" & ➥
"18:19:00 GMT", "ddd, dd MMM yyyy HH'':''mm'':''ss 'GMT'", Nothing)

                ' Parse only strings containing MonthDayPattern.
                Dim dt10 As DateTime = DateTime.ParseExact("January 12", "MMMM dd", ➥
Nothing)

                ' Display the converted DateTime objects.
                Console.WriteLine(dt8)
                Console.WriteLine(dt9)
                Console.WriteLine(dt10)

                ' Wait to continue.
                Console.WriteLine(vbCrLf & "Main method complete.  Press Enter")
                Console.ReadLine()

        End Sub

    End Class
End Namespace
```

2-8. Add, Subtract, and Compare Dates and Times

Problem

You need to perform basic arithmetic operations or comparisons using dates and times.

Solution

Use the DateTime and TimeSpan structures, which support standard arithmetic and comparison operators.

How It Works

A DateTime instance represents a specific time (such as 4:15 a.m. on September 5, 1970), whereas a TimeSpan instance represents a period of time (such as 2 hours, 35 minutes). You may want to add, subtract, and compare TimeSpan and DateTime instances.

Internally, both DateTime and TimeSpan use *ticks* to represent time. A tick is equal to 100 nano-seconds. TimeSpan stores its time interval as the number of ticks equal to that interval, and DateTime stores time as the number of ticks since 12:00:00 midnight on January 1 in 0001 C.E. (C.E. stands for Common Era and is equivalent to A.D. in the Gregorian calendar.) This approach and the use of operator overloading makes it easy for DateTime and TimeSpan to support basic arithmetic and comparison operations. Table 2-4 summarizes the operator support provided by the DateTime and TimeSpan structures.

Table 2-4. *Operators Supported by DateTime and TimeSpan*

Operator	TimeSpan	DateTime
Assignment (=)	Because TimeSpan is a structure, assignment returns a copy and not a reference.	Because DateTime is a structure, assignment returns a copy and not a reference.
Addition (+)	Adds two TimeSpan instances.	Adds a TimeSpan instance to a DateTime instance.
Subtraction (-)	Subtracts one TimeSpan instance from another TimeSpan instance.	Subtracts a TimeSpan instance or a DateTime instance from a DateTime instance.
Equality (=)	Compares two TimeSpan instances and returns true if they are equal.	Compares two DateTime instances and returns true if they are equal.
Inequality (<>)	Compares two TimeSpan instances and returns true if they are not equal.	Compares two DateTime instances and returns true if they are not equal.
Greater than (>)	Determines if one TimeSpan instance is greater than another TimeSpan instance.	Determines whether one DateTime instance is greater than another DateTime instance.
Greater than or equal to (>=)	Determines if one TimeSpan instance is greater than or equal to another TimeSpan instance.	Determines whether one DateTime instance is greater than or equal to another DateTime instance.
Less than (<)	Determines whether one TimeSpan instance is less than another TimeSpan instance.	Determines whether one DateTime instance is less than another DateTime instance.
Less than or equal to (<=)	Determines whether one TimeSpan instance is less than or equal to another TimeSpan instance.	Determines whether one DateTime instance is less than or equal to another DateTime instance.
Unary negation (-)	Returns a TimeSpan instance with a negated value of the specified TimeSpan instance.	Not supported.
Unary plus (+)	Returns the TimeSpan instance specified.	Not supported.

The DateTime structure also implements the AddTicks, AddMilliseconds, AddSeconds, AddMinutes, AddHours, AddDays, AddMonths, and AddYears methods. Each of these methods, which accept a Double as opposed to a TimeSpan, allows you to add (or subtract using negative values) the appropriate element of time to a DateTime instance. These methods and the noncomparison operators listed in Table 2-4 do not modify the original DateTime; instead, they create a new instance with the modified value.

The Code

The following example demonstrates how to use operators to manipulate the DateTime, DateTimeOffset, and TimeSpan structures. The DateTimeOffset structure, first discussed in recipe 2-7, is a new structure that replicates most of the functionality available in the DateTime structure while adding the functionality to handle time zone offsets. Since these two structures are so similar, everything mentioned earlier regarding the DateTime structure applies to the DateTimeOffset structure.

```vb
Imports System

Namespace Apress.VisualBasicRecipes.Chapter02

    Public Class Recipe02_08

        Public Shared Sub Main()

            ' Create a TimeSpan representing 2.5 days.
            Dim timespan1 As New TimeSpan(2, 12, 0, 0)

            ' Create a TimeSpan representing 4.5 days.
            Dim timespan2 As New TimeSpan(4, 12, 0, 0)

            ' Create a TimeSpan representing 1 week.
            Dim oneweek As TimeSpan = timespan1 + timespan2

            ' Create a DateTime with the current date and time.
            Dim now As DateTime = DateTime.Now

            ' Create a DateTime representing 1 week ago.
            Dim past As DateTime = now - oneweek

            ' Create a DateTime representing 1 week in the future.
            Dim future As DateTime = now + oneweek

            ' Create a DateTime representing the next day using
            ' the AddDays method.
            Dim tomorrow As DateTime = now.AddDays(1)

            ' Display the DateTime instances.
            Console.WriteLine("Now      : {0}", now)
            Console.WriteLine("Past     : {0}", past)
            Console.WriteLine("Future   : {0}", future)
            Console.WriteLine("Tomorrow : {0}", tomorrow)
            Console.WriteLine(Environment.NewLine)

            ' Create various DateTimeOffset objects using the same
            ' methods demonstrated above using the DateTime structure.
            Dim nowOffset As DateTimeOffset = DateTimeOffset.Now
            Dim pastoffset As DateTimeOffset = nowOffset - oneweek
            Dim futureOffset As DateTimeOffset = nowOffset + oneweek
            Dim tomorrowoffset As DateTimeOffset = nowOffset.AddDays(1)
```

```
                    ' Change the offset used by nowOffset to -8 (which is Pacific
                    ' Standard Time).
                    Dim nowPST As DateTimeOffset = nowOffset.ToOffset(New TimeSpan(-8, ➡
0, 0))

                    ' Display the DateTimeOffset instances.
                    Console.WriteLine("Now      (with offset) : {0}", nowOffset)
                    Console.WriteLine("Past     (with offset) : {0}", pastoffset)
                    Console.WriteLine("Future   (with offset) : {0}", futureOffset)
                    Console.WriteLine("Tomorrow (with offset) : {0}", tomorrowoffset)
                    Console.WriteLine(Environment.NewLine)
                    Console.WriteLine("Now      (with offset of -8) : {0}", nowPST)

                    ' Wait to continue.
                    Console.WriteLine(vbCrLf & "Main method complete.  Press Enter")
                    Console.ReadLine()

            End Sub

        End Class

    End Namespace
```

2-9. Convert Dates and Times Across Time Zones

Problem

You need to work with dates and times in different time zones and be able to convert between them.

Solution

Use one of the conversion methods (ConvertTime, ConvertTimeBySystemTimeZoneId, ConvertTimeFromUtc, or ConvertTimeToUtc) of the new TimeZoneInfo class.

How It Works

Previous versions of .NET included the TimeZone class, which was used to represent a world time zone for a given date and time. Although this was useful, the class was severely limited because it was able to represent only the local time zone. Furthermore, conversions were limited to the local time zone and UTC.

The .NET Framework 3.5 introduces the NotInheritable TimeZoneInfo class, which adds important functionality that is missing from the TimeZone class. Table 2-5 shows some of the properties (all of which are ReadOnly) and methods of the TimeZoneInfo class.

Table 2-5. *Properties and Methods of the TimeZoneInfo Class*

Member	Description
Properties	
BaseUtcOffset	Returns a TimeSpan that represents the difference between the zone's time and Coordinated Universal Time (UTC).
DaylightName	Returns the daylight saving time name for the time zone, such as "Eastern Daylight Time" or "Pacific Daylight Time."

Table 2-5. *Properties and Methods of the TimeZoneInfo Class (Continued)*

Member	Description
DisplayName	Returns a general name for the time zone, such as "(GMT-05:00) Eastern Time (US & Canada)" or "(GMT-08:00) Pacific Time (US & Canada)."
Id	Returns the unique identifier for the time zone as defined by the operating system. In most cases, this value is the same as the StandardName.
Local	Returns an instance of a TimeZoneInfo class that represents the local time zone.
StandardName	Returns the standard name for the time zone, such as "Eastern Standard Time" or "Pacific Standard Time."
SupportsDaylightSavingTime	Returns whether any daylight saving time rules are defined for the time zone.
Utc	Returns an instance of a TimeZoneInfo class that represents the UTC time zone.
Methods	
ConvertTime	Converts the specified time to the time zone specified by the supplied TimeZoneInfo object.
ConvertTimeBySystemTimeZoneId	Converts the specified time to the time zone that corresponds to the supplied time zone identifier (see Id earlier in the table).
ConvertTimeFromUtc	Converts the specified time from UTC to the time zone specified by the supplied TimeZoneInfo object.
ConvertTimeToUtc	Converts the specified time to UTC.
CreateCustomTimeZone	Allows the creation of a new time zone.
FindSystemTimeZoneById	Returns a TimeZoneInfo object that was retrieved from the system registry using the supplied time zone identifier.
FromSerializedString	Returns a TimeZoneInfo object based on a TimeZoneInfo object that was previously serialized using the ToSerializedString method.
GetAdjustmentRules	Returns an array of AdjustmentRule objects for the current TimeZoneInfo instance. An AdjustmentRule object is typically used to specify when daylight saving time occurs.
GetSystemTimeZones	Returns a collection of TimeZoneInfo objects that were retrieved from the system registry.
GetUtcOffset	Returns a TimeSpan that represents the offset between the current TimeZoneInfo instance and UTC.
IsDaylightSavingTime	Returns True or False depending on whether the current TimeZoneInfo instance is observing daylight saving time during the specified date and time.
ToSerializedString	Returns a serialized String representation of the current TimeZoneInfo instance.

Similar to the older TimeZone class, TimeZoneInfo represents some time zone, but it is not limited to UTC or the local time zone. A TimeZoneInfo instance can refer to any time zone that is defined in the system registry. If a time zone is required that does not exist in the registry, a custom TimeZoneInfo object can be created using the CreateCustomTimeZone function. You can save and then reuse this custom time zone by using the ToSerializedString and FromSerializedString functions, respectively.

The TimeZoneInfo class does not include a constructor, and it is immutable, which means it cannot be modified once it has been instantiated. You create new instances of the TimeZoneInfo class by using one of the four available conversion methods: ConvertTime, ConvertTimeBySystemTimeZoneId, ConvertTimeFromUtc, or ConvertTimeToUtc.

The ConvertTime method includes three overloads. The first overload accepts a DateTime object (which represents the date and time to be converted) and a TimeZoneInfo object (which represents the time zone to convert the supplied data and time to). This overload returns a new DateTime object that reflects the converted date and time.

The second overload is identical to the first one mentioned earlier, but it accepts a DateTimeOffset object (refer to recipes 2-7 and 2-8 for more information), instead of a DateTime object. Also, the return type is a DateTimeOffset object.

The third overload behaves like the first, accepting a DateTime object, but it provides an extra parameter to supply a second TimeZoneInfo object. The first TimeZoneInfo parameter represents the time zone of the supplied DateTime object, while the second represents the time zone to which the supplied date and time should be converted.

The ConvertTimeBySystemTimeZoneId method is nearly identical to the ConvertTime method. They both have the three overloads that perform equivalent conversions. The only difference is that ConvertTimeBySystemTimeZoneId accepts String parameters instead of TimeZoneInfo objects. The String objects represent an identifier that is used to retrieve specific TimeZoneInfo data from the system registry and return an appropriate TimeZoneInfo instance.

The ConvertTimeFromUtc has only one version that accepts a DateTime object (which represents the date and time to be converted) and a TimeZoneInfo object (which represents the time zone to convert the supplied date and time to). This method returns the converted date and time as a DateTime object.

The last conversion method, ConvertTimeToUtc, has only two overloads. The first accepts only a DateTime object representing the date and time to convert. In this case, the method assumes the supplied date and time is in the local time zone. The second overload allows you to specify a TimeZoneInfo instance that represents the time zone of the supplied DateTime object. The converted date and time are returned as a DateTime object.

The Code

The following example demonstrates multiple ways to retrieve TimeZoneInfo objects and convert dates and times between different time zones using the different conversion methods mentioned earlier:

```
Imports System

Namespace Apress.VisualBasicRecipes.Chapter02
    Public Class Recipe02_09

        Public Shared Sub Main()

            ' Create a TimeZoneInfo object for the local time zone.
            Dim localTimeZone As TimeZoneInfo = TimeZoneInfo.Local
```

```vb
        ' Create a TimeZoneInfo object for Coordinated Universal
        ' Time (UTC).
        Dim utcTimeZone As TimeZoneInfo = TimeZoneInfo.Utc

        ' Create a TimeZoneInfo object for Pacific Standard Time (PST).
        Dim pstTimeZone As TimeZoneInfo = ➥
TimeZoneInfo.FindSystemTimeZoneById("Pacific Standard Time")

        ' Create a DateTimeOffset that represents the current time.
        Dim currentTime As DateTimeOffset = DateTimeOffset.Now

        ' Display the local time and the local time zone.
        If localTimeZone.IsDaylightSavingTime(currentTime) Then
            Console.WriteLine("Current time in the local time zone ({0}):", ➥
localTimeZone.DaylightName)
        Else
            Console.WriteLine("Current time in the local time zone ({0})", ➥
localTimeZone.StandardName)
        End If
        Console.WriteLine("  {0}", currentTime.ToString())
        Console.WriteLine(Environment.NewLine)

        ' Display the results of converting the current local time
        ' to Coordinated Universal Time (UTC).
        If utcTimeZone.IsDaylightSavingTime(currentTime) Then
            Console.WriteLine("Current time in {0}:", utcTimeZone.DaylightName)
        Else
            Console.WriteLine("Current time in {0}:", utcTimeZone.StandardName)
        End If
        Console.WriteLine("  {0}", TimeZoneInfo.ConvertTime(currentTime, ➥
utcTimeZone))
        Console.WriteLine(Environment.NewLine)

        ' Create a DateTimeOffset object that represents the current local time
        ' converted to the Pacific Stanard Time time zone.
        Dim pstDTO As DateTimeOffset = TimeZoneInfo.ConvertTime(currentTime,➥
pstTimeZone)

        ' Display the results of the conversion.
        If pstTimeZone.IsDaylightSavingTime(currentTime) Then
            Console.WriteLine("Current time in {0}:", pstTimeZone.DaylightName)
        Else
            Console.WriteLine("Current time in {0}:", pstTimeZone.StandardName)
        End If
        Console.WriteLine("  {0}", pstDTO).ToString()

        ' Display the previous results converted to Coordinated
        ' Universal Time (UTC).
        Console.WriteLine("  {0} (Converted to UTC)", ➥
TimeZoneInfo.ConvertTimeToUtc(pstDTO.DateTime, pstTimeZone))
        Console.WriteLine(Environment.NewLine)
```

```
                ' Create a DateTimeOffset that represents the current local time
                ' converted to Mountain Standard Time using the
                ' ConvertTimeBySystemTimeZoneId method.  This conversion works
                ' but it is best to create an actual TimeZoneInfo object so
                ' you have access to determine if it is daylight saving time or not.
                Dim mstDTO As DateTimeOffset = ➡
TimeZoneInfo.ConvertTimeBySystemTimeZoneId(currentTime, "Mountain Standard Time")

                ' Display the results of the conversion
                Console.WriteLine("Current time in Mountain Standard Time:")
                Console.WriteLine("  {0}", mstDTO.ToString())
                Console.WriteLine(Environment.NewLine)

                ' Wait to continue.
                Console.WriteLine(vbCrLf & "Main method complete.  Press Enter")
                Console.ReadLine()

        End Sub

    End Class
End Namespace
```

2-10. Sort an Array or an ArrayList

Problem

You need to sort the elements contained in an array or an ArrayList structure.

Solution

Use the ArrayList.Sort method to sort ArrayList objects and the Shared Array.Sort method to sort arrays.

How It Works

The simplest Sort method overload sorts the objects contained in an array or ArrayList structure as long as the objects implement the System.IComparable interface and are of the same type. All the basic data types implement IComparable. To sort objects that do not implement IComparable, you must pass the Array.Sort method an object that implements the System.Collections.IComparer interface. The IComparer implementation must be capable of comparing the objects contained within the array or ArrayList. (Recipe 15-3 describes how to implement both comparable types.)

Note Visual Studio 2008 introduces a new feature known as Language Integrate Query (LINQ). LINQ provides the functionality for querying, sorting, and converting arrays and collections. This is covered in more detail in Chapter 6.

The Code

The following example demonstrates how to use the Sort methods of the ArrayList and Array classes:

```
Imports System
Imports System.Collections

Namespace Apress.VisualBasicRecipes.Chapter02

    Public Class Recipe02_10

        Public Shared Sub Main()

            ' Create a new array and populate it.
            Dim array1 As Integer() = {4, 2, 9, 3}

            ' Sort the array.
            Array.Sort(array1)

            ' Display the contents of the sorted array.
            For Each i As Integer In array1
                Console.WriteLine(i.ToString)
            Next

            ' Create a new ArrayList and populate it.
            Dim list1 As New ArrayList(3)
            list1.Add("Amy")
            list1.Add("Alaina")
            list1.Add("Aidan")

            ' Sort the ArrayList.
            list1.Sort()


            ' Display the contents of the sorted ArrayList.
            For Each s As String In list1
                Console.WriteLine(s)
            Next

            ' Wait to continue.
            Console.WriteLine(vbCrLf & "Main method complete.  Press Enter")
            Console.ReadLine()

        End Sub

    End Class
End Namespace
```

2-11. Copy a Collection to an Array

Problem

You need to copy the contents of a collection to an array.

Solution

Use the ICollection.CopyTo method implemented by all collection classes. Alternatively, you can use the ToArray method implemented by the ArrayList, Stack, and Queue collections, as well as their respective generic versions List(Of T), Stack(Of T), and Queue(Of T). Refer to recipe 2-14 for more information regarding generics.

How It Works

The ICollection.CopyTo method and the ToArray method perform roughly the same function: they perform a copy of the elements contained in a collection to an array. Both of these methods perform only a *shallow* copy, which means that the data in memory is simply copied from one location to another rather than the target object's Copy method being called, which is referred to as a *deep copy*. The key difference is that CopyTo copies the collection's elements to an existing array, whereas ToArray creates a new array before copying the collection's elements into it.

The CopyTo method takes two arguments: an array and an index. The array is the target of the copy operation and must be of a type appropriate to handle the elements of the collection. If the types do not match, or no implicit conversion is possible from the collection element's type to the array element's type, a System.InvalidCastException exception is thrown. The index is the starting element of the array where the collection's elements will be copied. If the index is equal to or greater than the length of the array, or the number of collection elements exceeds the capacity of the array, a System.ArgumentException exception is thrown.

The ArrayList, Stack, and Queue classes and their generic versions (mentioned earlier) also implement the ToArray method, which automatically creates an array of the correct size to accommodate a copy of all the elements of the collection. If you call ToArray with no arguments, it returns an Object() array, regardless of the type of objects contained in the collection. For convenience, the ArrayList.ToArray method has an overload to which you can pass a System.Type object that specifies the type of array that the ToArray method should create. (You must still cast the returned strongly typed array to the correct type.) The layout of the array's contents depends on which collection class you are using. For example, an array produced from a Stack object will be inverted compared to the array generated by an ArrayList object.

The Code

This example demonstrates how to copy the contents of an ArrayList structure to an array using the CopyTo method and then shows how to use the ToArray method on the ArrayList object:

```
Imports System
Imports System.Collections
Namespace Apress.VisualBasicRecipes.Chapter02

    Public Class Recipe02_11

        Public Shared Sub Main()
```

```
        ' Create a new ArrayList and populate it.
        Dim list As New ArrayList(3)
        list.Add("Amy")
        list.Add("Alaina")
        list.Add("Aidan")

        ' Create a string array and use the ICollection.CopyTo method
        ' to copy the contents of the ArrayList.
        Dim array1(list.Count - 1) As String
        list.CopyTo(array1, 0)

        ' Use ArrayList.ToArray to create an object array from the
        ' contents of the collection.
        Dim array2 As Object() = list.ToArray()

        ' Use ArrayList.ToArray to create a strongly typed string
        ' array from the contents of the collection.
        Dim array3 As String() = DirectCast(list.ToArray(GetType(String)), ➥
String())

        ' Display the contents of the 3 arrays.
        Console.WriteLine("Array 1:")
        For Each s As String In array1
            Console.WriteLine(vbTab + "{0}", s)
        Next

        Console.WriteLine("Array 2:")
        For Each s As String In array2
            Console.WriteLine(vbTab + "{0}", s)
        Next

        Console.WriteLine("Array 3:")
        For Each s As String In array3
            Console.WriteLine(vbTab + "{0}", s)
        Next

        ' Wait to continue.
        Console.WriteLine(vbCrLf & "Main method complete.  Press Enter")
        Console.ReadLine()

    End Sub

  End Class
End Namespace
```

2-12. Manipulate or Evaluate the Contents of an Array

Problem

You need to perform actions on the contents of an array, such as the following:

- Determining whether an array contains any data
- Determining whether an array contains any elements that meet a specific condition

- Determining whether all elements of an array meet a specific condition
- Reversing the order of the contents

Solution

Use the appropriate methods (such as `All`, `Any`, and `Reverse`) of the `System.Linq.Enumerable` class to perform the desired action.

How It Works

The .NET Framework 3.5 introduces the `NotInheritable` class `System.Linq.Enumerable`, which contains a long list of special `Shared` methods, some of which are shown in Table 2-6, called *extension methods* (which are discussed in recipe 1-22). The majority of these methods extend the `IEnumerable(Of T)` interface, which means they can be used with any object, such as `Array`, `List(Of T)`, and `Stack(Of T)`, that implements that interface.

The methods found in the `Enumerable` class provide the underlying support for Language Integrated Query (LINQ). LINQ is a powerful new feature in Visual Studio 2008 that provides the ability to query and manipulate data stored in a variety of sources (such as databases, objects, and XML files). Although this chapter covers some of the new extension methods used by LINQ, that is not the focus of this recipe. LINQ is covered in detail in Chapter 6, so this recipe will focus on only a few of the available methods.

Table 2-6. *Some Useful Extension Methods from the Enumerable Class*

Method	Description
All	Returns `True` or `False` depending on whether all elements in the source data meet the specified condition.
Any	Returns `True` or `False` depending on whether any element in the source data meets the specified condition.
Average	Returns a numeric value representing the average of each element in the source data. This is covered in more detail in recipe 6-7.
Cast	Returns an `IEnumerable(Of T)`, where T is the specified type. Each element in the source data is converted to the specified type first. This is covered in more detail in recipe 6-15.
Concat	Returns an `IEnumerable(Of T)` containing all the elements, from both data sources specified, combined.
Contains	Returns `True` or `False` depending on whether the specified data source contains the specified data.
Distinct	Returns an `IEnumerable(Of T)` containing only the distinct, or nonrepeating, elements from the data source. This is covered in more detail in recipe 6-1.
ElementAt	Returns the element of the data source that corresponds to the specified index. This is covered in more detail in recipe 6-12.
First	Returns the first element in the data source. This is covered in more detail in recipe 6-12.
GroupBy	Returns an `IEnumerable(Of IGrouping(Of TKey, TElement))` containing data from multiple data sources grouped by the specified condition. This is covered in more detail in recipe 6-10.

Table 2-6. *Some Useful Extension Methods from the Enumerable Class (Continued)*

Method	Description
Join	Returns an IEnumerable(Of T) containing data from multiple sources joined by the specified condition. This is covered in more detail in recipe 6-11.
Last	Returns the last element in the data source. This is covered in more detail in recipe 6-12.
Max	Returns the maximum numeric value in the data source. This is covered in more detail in recipe 6-9.
Min	Returns the minimum numeric value in the data source. This is covered in more detail in recipe 6-9.
OrderBy	Returns an IOrderdedEnumerable(OF T) containing all the elements from the data source ordered by the specified key. This is covered in more detail in recipe 6-4.
Reverse	Returns an IEnumerable(OF T) containing all the elements from the source collection but in reverse order.
Select	The basis for performing queries. This is covered in more detail in recipe 6-3.
Skip	Returns an IEnumerable(Of T) containing all elements from the data source except for the number of elements specified, starting from the first. This is covered in more detail in recipe 6-13.
Sum	Returns a numeric value that represents the sum of each element in the data source. This is covered in more detail in recipe 6-7.
Take	Returns an IEnumerable(Of T) containing the specified number of elements from the data source, starting from the first. This is covered in more detail in recipe 6-13.
Where	Returns an IEnumerable(Of T) containing data from the data source that has been filtered using the specified condition. This is covered in more detail in recipe 6-5.

The All method is used to determine whether all elements in the current IEnumerable(Of T) instance meet the specified condition. The only required parameter is the condition to check for, which is represented as a *lambda expression* (see recipe 1-23). The supplied *lambda expression*, which takes the form of a Func(Of T, Boolean), is automatically run against each element in the source data. If all elements meet the set condition, True is returned.

The Any method has two versions. The first version, with no parameters, simply returns True or False depending on whether the current IEnumerable(Of T) instance contains any data. The second version resembles the All method but performs the opposite function. It takes a *lambda expression*, in the form of a Func(Of T, Boolean), but True is returned if *any* of the elements in the source data meet the specified condition.

The Reverse method returns an IEnumerable(Of T) in reverse order. No sorting is actually performed; rather, the sequence is simply reversed.

The Code

This example demonstrates how to use some of the new extension methods mentioned earlier. To make things a little easier, the sample data uses an array of anonymous types (recipe 1-21).

```vbnet
Imports System
Imports System.Collections

Namespace Apress.VisualBasicRecipes.Chapter02
    Public Class Recipe02_12

        Public Shared Sub Main()

            ' For the record, references to Battlestar Galactica
            ' are courtesy of the SciFi channel.

            ' Create sample data.  For simplicity, the data consists of an
            ' array of  anonymous types that contain three properties:
            ' Name (a String), CallSign (a String) and Age (an Integer).
            Dim galactica() = { _
                            New With {.Name = "William Adama", _
                                    .CallSign = "Husker", _
                                    .Age = 65}, _
                            New With {.Name = "Saul Tigh", _
                                    .CallSign = Nothing, _
                                    .Age = 83}, _
                            New With {.Name = "Lee Adama", _
                                    .CallSign = "Apollo", _
                                    .Age = 30}, _
                            New With {.Name = "Kara Thrace", _
                                    .CallSign = "Starbuck", _
                                    .Age = 28}, _
                            New With {.Name = "Gaius Baltar", _
                                    .CallSign = Nothing, _
                                    .Age = 42}}

            ' Variables used to store results of Any and All methods.
            Dim anyResult As Boolean
            Dim allResult As Boolean

            ' Display the contents of the galactica array.
            Console.WriteLine("Galactica Crew:")
            For Each crewMember In galactica
                Console.WriteLine("  {0}", crewMember.Name)
            Next
            Console.WriteLine(Environment.NewLine)

            ' Determine if the galactica array has any data.
            anyResult = galactica.Any

            ' Display the results of the previous test.
            Console.WriteLine("Does the array contain any data:  ")
            If anyResult Then
                Console.Write("Yes")
            Else
                Console.Write("No")
            End If
            Console.WriteLine(Environment.NewLine)
```

```vb
            ' Determine if any members have nothing set for the
            ' CallSign property, using the Any method.
            anyResult = galactica.Any(Function(crewMember) crewMember.callsign ➡
Is Nothing)

            ' Display the results of the previous test.
            Console.WriteLine("Do any crew members NOT have a callsign:  ")
            If anyResult Then
                Console.Write("Yes")
            Else
                Console.Write("No")
            End If
            Console.WriteLine(Environment.NewLine)

            ' Determine if all members of the array have an Age property
            ' greater than 40, using the All method.
            allResult = galactica.All(Function(crewMember) crewMember.Age > 40)

            ' Display the results of the previous test.
            Console.WriteLine("Are all of the crew members over 40:  ")
            If allResult Then
                Console.Write("Yes")
            Else
                Console.Write("No")
            End If
            Console.WriteLine(Environment.NewLine)

            ' Display the contents of the galactica array in reverse.
            Console.WriteLine("Galactica Crew (Reverse Order):")
            For Each crewMember In galactica.Reverse
                Console.WriteLine("  {0}", crewMember.Name)
            Next

            ' Wait to continue.
            Console.WriteLine(vbCrLf & "Main method complete.  Press Enter")
            Console.ReadLine()

        End Sub

    End Class
End Namespace
```

2-13. Use a Strongly Typed Collection

Problem

You need a collection that works with elements of a specific type so that you do not need to work with System.Object references in your code.

Solution

Use the appropriate collection class from the System.Collections.Generic namespace. When you instantiate the collection, specify the type of object the collection should contain using the generics syntax that was first introduced in .NET Framework 2.0.

How It Works

The generics functionality added to .NET Framework 2.0 and supported by specific syntax in VB
.NET 9.0 make it easy to create type-safe collections and containers (see recipe 2-14). To meet the
most common requirements for collection classes, the System.Collections.Generic namespace
contains a number of predefined generic collections, including the following:

- Dictionary
- LinkedList
- List
- Queue
- Stack

When you instantiate one of these collections, you specify the type of object that the collection
will contain by using the Of keyword with the type name in parentheses after the collection name,
such as in Dictionary(Of System.Reflection.AssemblyName). As a result, all members that add objects
to the collection expect the objects to be of the specified type, and all members that return objects
from the collection will return object references of the specified type. Using strongly typed collections and working directly with objects of the desired type simplifies development and when working
with general Object references and casting them to the desired type. It also reduces errors since the
user of generics will reveal most casting issues at compile time rather than runtime.

The Code

The following example demonstrates the use of generic collections to create a variety of collections
specifically for managing AssemblyName objects. Notice that you never need to cast to or from the
Object type.

```
Imports System
Imports System.Reflection
Imports System.Collections.Generic


Namespace Apress.VisualBasicRecipes.Chapter02

    Public Class Recipe02_13

        Public Shared Sub Main()

            ' Create an AssemblyName object for use during the example.
            Dim assembly1 As New AssemblyName("com.microsoft.crypto, " & ➥
"Culture=en, PublicKeyToken=a5d015c7d5a0b012, Version=1.0.0.0")

            ' Create and use a Dictionary of AssemblyName objects.
            Dim assemblyDictionary As New Dictionary(Of String, AssemblyName)

            assemblyDictionary.Add("Crypto", assembly1)

            Dim ass1 As AssemblyName = assemblyDictionary("Crypto")

            Console.WriteLine("Got AssemblyName from dictionary: {0}", ➥
CType(ass1, AssemblyName).ToString)
```

```
                   '  Create and use a list of AssemblyName objects.
                   Dim assemblyList As New List(Of AssemblyName)

                   assemblyList.Add(assembly1)

                   Dim ass2 As AssemblyName = assemblyList(0)

                   Console.WriteLine(vbCrLf & "Got AssemblyName from list: {0}", ➥
CType(ass2, AssemblyName).ToString)

                   '  Create and use a stack of AssemblyName objects.
                   Dim assemblyStack As New Stack(Of AssemblyName)

                   assemblyStack.Push(assembly1)

                   Dim ass3 As AssemblyName = assemblyStack.Pop

                   Console.WriteLine(vbCrLf & "Popped AssemblyName from stack: {0}", ➥
CType(ass3, AssemblyName).ToString)

                   '  Wait to continue.
                   Console.WriteLine(vbCrLf & "Main method complete.  Press Enter")
                   Console.ReadLine()

           End Sub

    End Class
End Namespace
```

2-14. Create a Generic Type

Problem

You need to create a new general-purpose type such as a collection or container that supports strong typing of the elements it contains.

Solution

Define your class using the generics syntax, first introduced in .NET Framework 2.0, provided in VB .NET 9.0.

How It Works

You can leverage the generics capabilities of VB .NET 9.0 in any class you define. This allows you to create general-purpose classes that can be used as type-safe instances by other programmers. When you declare your type, you identify it as a generic type by following the type name with a list of identifiers for the types used in the class, preceded by the Of keyword and enclosed in parentheses. Here is an example:

```
Public Class MyGeneric(Of T1, T2, T3)
End Class
```

This declaration specifies a new class named MyGenericType, which uses three generic types in its implementation (T1, T2, and T3). When implementing the type, you substitute the generic type names into the code instead of using specific type names. For example, one method might take an argument of type T1 and return a result of type T2, as shown here:

```
Public Function MyGenericMethod(ByVal arg As T1) As T2
End Function
```

When other people use your class and create an instance of it, they specify the actual types to use as part of the instantiation. Here is an example:

```
Dim obj As New MyGenericType(Of String, System.IO.Stream, String)
```

The types specified replace T1, T2, and T3 throughout the implementation, so with this instance, MyGenericMethod would actually be compiled as follows:

```
Public Function MyGenericMethod(ByVal arg As String) As Stream
End Function
```

You can also include constraints as part of your generic type definition. This allows you to make specifications such as the following:

- Only value types or only reference types can be used with the generic type.
- Only types that implement a default (empty) constructor can be used with the generic type.
- Only types that implement a specific interface can be used with the generic type.
- Only types that inherit from a specific base class can be used with the generic type.
- One generic type must be the same as another generic type (for example, T1 must be the same as T3).

For example, to specify that T1 must implement the System.IDisposable interface and provide a default constructor, that T2 must be or derive from the System.IO.Stream class, and that T3 must be the same type as T1, change the definition of MyGenericType as follows:

```
Public Class MyGenericType(Of T1 As {IDisposable}, T2 As {System.IO.Stream}, ➥
T3 As {T1})
End Class
```

The Code

The following example demonstrates a simplified bag implementation that returns those objects put into it at random. A *bag* is a data structure that can contain zero or more items, including duplicates of items, but does not guarantee any ordering of the items it contains.

```
Imports System
Imports System.Collections.Generic
Namespace Apress.VisualBasicRecipes.Chapter02

    Public Class Bag(Of T)
        '  A list to hold the bag's contents. The list must be
        '  of the same type as the bag.
        Private items As New List(Of T)

        '  A method to add an item to the bag.
        Public Sub Add(ByVal item As T)
            items.Add(item)
        End Sub
```

```vb
    '  A method to remove a random item from the bag.
    Public Function Remove() As T
        Dim item As T = Nothing

        If Not items.Count = 0 Then
            '  Determine which item to remove from the bag.
            Dim r As New Random
            Dim num As Integer = r.Next(0, items.Count)

            '  Remove the item.
            item = items(num)
            items.RemoveAt(num)
        End If

        Return item

    End Function

    '  A method to remove all items from the bag and return them
    '  as an array.
    Public Function RemoveAll() As T()

        Dim i As T() = items.ToArray()
        items.Clear()
        Return i

    End Function


End Class

Public Class Recipe02_14

    Public Shared Sub Main()

        '  Create a new bag of strings.
        Dim bag As New Bag(Of String)

        '  Add strings to the bag.
        bag.Add("Amy")
        bag.Add("Alaina")
        bag.Add("Aidan")
        bag.Add("Robert")
        bag.Add("Pearl")
        bag.Add("Mark")
        bag.Add("Karen")

        '  Take four strings from the bag and display.
        Console.WriteLine("Item 1 = {0}", bag.Remove())
        Console.WriteLine("Item 2 = {0}", bag.Remove())
        Console.WriteLine("Item 3 = {0}", bag.Remove())
        Console.WriteLine("Item 4 = {0}", bag.Remove())
        Console.WriteLine(vbCrLf)
```

```
    ' Remove the remaining items from the bag.
    Dim s As String() = bag.RemoveAll

    ' Display the remaining items.
    For i As Integer = 0 To s.Length - 1
        Console.WriteLine("Item {0} = {1}", i + 1.ToString, s(i))
    Next

    ' Wait to continue.
    Console.WriteLine(vbCrLf & "Main method complete.  Press Enter")
    Console.ReadLine()

    End Sub

    End Class
End Namespace
```

2-15. Store a Serializable Object to a File

Problem

You need to store a serializable object and its state to a file, and then deserialize it later.

Solution

Use a *formatter* to serialize the object and write it to a System.IO.FileStream object. When you need to retrieve the object, use the same type of formatter to read the serialized data from the file and deserialize the object. The .NET Framework class library includes the following formatter implementations for serializing objects to binary or SOAP format:

- System.Runtime.Serialization.Formatters.Binary.BinaryFormatter
- System.Runtime.Serialization.Formatters.Soap.SoapFormatter

How It Works

Using the BinaryFormatter and SoapFormatter classes, you can serialize an instance of any serializable type. (See recipe 15-1 for details on how to make a type serializable.) The BinaryFormatter class produces a binary data stream representing the object and its state. The SoapFormatter class produces a SOAP document. SOAP is an XML-based protocol used to exchange messages over the network. SOAP is used as the primary mechanism for communicating with web services. Refer to recipes 12-13, 12-14, and 12-15 for more information about web services.

Both the BinaryFormatter and SoapFormatter classes implement the interface System.Runtime.Serialization.IFormatter, which defines two methods: Serialize and Deserialize. The Serialize method takes a System.IO.Stream reference and a System.Object reference as arguments, serializes the Object, and writes it to the Stream. The Deserialize method takes a Stream reference as an argument, reads the serialized object data from the Stream, and returns an Object reference to a deserialized object. You must cast the returned Object reference to the correct type.

■**Caution** To call the `Serialize` and `Deserialize` methods of the `BinaryFormatter` class, your code must be granted the `SecurityPermissionFlag.SerializationFormatter` permission. To call the `Serialize` and `Deserialize` methods of the `SoapFormatter` class, your code must be granted full trust, because the `System.Runtime.Serialization.Formatters.Soap.dll` assembly in which the `SoapFormatter` class is declared does not allow partially trusted callers. Refer to recipe 13-1 for more information about assemblies and partially trusted callers.

The Code

The example shown here demonstrates how to use both `BinaryFormatter` and `SoapFormatter` to serialize a `System.Collections.ArrayList` object containing a list of people to a file. The `ArrayList` object is then deserialized from the files and the contents displayed to the console. A reference to the `System.Runtime.Serialization.Formatters.Soap` assembly may need to be added to your project before it can be used.

```
Imports System
Imports System.IO
Imports System.Collections
Imports System.Runtime.Serialization.Formatters.Soap
Imports System.Runtime.Serialization.Formatters.Binary

Namespace Apress.VisualBasicRecipes.Chapter02
    Public Class Recipe02_15

        ' Serialize an ArrayList object to a binary file.
        Private Shared Sub BinarySerialize(ByVal list As ArrayList)

            Using str As FileStream = File.Create("people.bin")
                Dim bf As New BinaryFormatter()
                bf.Serialize(str, list)
            End Using

        End Sub

        ' Deserialize an Arraylist object from a binary file.
        Private Shared Function BinaryDeserialize() As ArrayList
            Dim people As ArrayList = Nothing

            Using str As FileStream = File.OpenRead("people.bin")
                Dim bf As New BinaryFormatter()
                people = DirectCast(bf.Deserialize(str), ArrayList)
            End Using
            Return people

        End Function

        ' Serialize an ArrayList object to a SOAP file.
        Private Shared Sub SoapSerialize(ByVal list As ArrayList)
```

```vb
        Using str As FileStream = File.Create("people.soap")
            Dim sf As New SoapFormatter()
            sf.Serialize(str, list)
        End Using

    End Sub

    ' Deserialize an Arraylist object from a SOAP file.
    Private Shared Function SoapDeserialize() As ArrayList
        Dim people As ArrayList = Nothing

        Using str As FileStream = File.OpenRead("people.soap")
            Dim sf As New SoapFormatter()
            people = DirectCast(sf.Deserialize(str), ArrayList)
        End Using
        Return people

    End Function

    Public Shared Sub Main()

        ' Create and configure the ArrayList to serialize.
        Dim people As New ArrayList
        people.Add("Alex")
        people.Add("Dave")
        people.Add("Matthew")
        people.Add("Robb")

        ' Serialize the list to a file in both binary and SOAP format.
        BinarySerialize(people)
        SoapSerialize(people)

        ' Rebuild the lists of people form the binary and SOAP
        ' serializations and display them to the console.
        Dim binaryPeople As ArrayList = BinaryDeserialize()
        Dim soapPeople As ArrayList = SoapDeserialize()

        Console.WriteLine("Binary People:")
        For Each s As String In binaryPeople
            Console.WriteLine(vbTab & s)
        Next

        Console.WriteLine(vbCrLf & "SOAP People:")
        For Each s As String In soapPeople
            Console.WriteLine(vbTab & s)
        Next

        ' Wait to continue.
        Console.WriteLine(vbCrLf & "Main method complete.  Press Enter")
        Console.ReadLine()

    End Sub

    End Class
End Namespace
```

Usage

To illustrate the different results achieved using the BinaryFormatter and SoapFormatter classes, Figure 2-1 shows the contents of the people.bin file generated using the BinaryFormatter class, and Figure 2-2 shows the contents of the people.soap file generated using the SoapFormatter class.

```
00000000    00 01 00 00 00 FF FF FF   FF 01 00 00 00 00 00 00    ................
00000010    00 04 01 00 00 00 1C 53   79 73 74 65 6D 2E 43 6F    .......System.Co
00000020    6C 6C 65 63 74 69 6F 6E   73 2E 41 72 72 61 79 4C    llections.ArrayL
00000030    69 73 74 03 00 00 00 06   5F 69 74 65 6D 73 05 5F    ist....._items._
00000040    73 69 7A 65 08 5F 76 65   72 73 69 6F 6E 05 00 00    size._version...
00000050    08 08 09 02 00 00 00 04   00 00 00 04 00 00 00 10    ................
00000060    02 00 00 00 04 00 00 00   06 03 00 00 00 04 41 6C    ..............Al
00000070    65 78 06 04 00 00 00 04   44 61 76 65 06 05 00 00    ex......Dave....
00000080    00 07 4D 61 74 74 68 65   77 06 06 00 00 00 04 52    ..Matthew......R
00000090    6F 62 62 0B                                          obb.
```

Figure 2-1. *Contents of the people.bin file*

```
<SOAP-ENV:Envelope xmlns:xsi="http://www.w3.org/2001/XMLSchema-inst
<SOAP-ENV:Body>
<a1:ArrayList id="ref-1" xmlns:a1="http://schemas.microsoft.com/cl
  <_items href="#ref-2"/>
  <_size>4</_size>
  <_version>4</_version>
</a1:ArrayList>
<SOAP-ENC:Array id="ref-2" SOAP-ENC:arrayType="xsd:anyType[4]">
  <item id="ref-3" xsi:type="SOAP-ENC:string">Alex</item>
  <item id="ref-4" xsi:type="SOAP-ENC:string">Dave</item>
  <item id="ref-5" xsi:type="SOAP-ENC:string">Matthew</item>
  <item id="ref-6" xsi:type="SOAP-ENC:string">Robb</item>
</SOAP-ENC:Array>
</SOAP-ENV:Body>
</SOAP-ENV:Envelope>
```

Figure 2-2. *Contents of the people.soap file*

2-16. Read User Input from the Console

Problem

You want to read user input from the Windows console, either a line or character at a time.

Solution

Use the Read or ReadLine method of the System.Console class to read input when the user presses Enter. To read input without requiring the user to press Enter, use the Console.ReadKey method.

How It Works

The simplest way to read input from the console is to use the Shared Read or ReadLine methods of the Console class. These methods will cause your application to block, waiting for the user to enter input and press Enter. In both instances, the user will see the input characters in the console. Once the user presses Enter, the Read method will return an Integer value representing the next character of input data or –1 if no more data is available. Since Read reads only one character, it must be called repeatedly to continue capturing user input. The ReadLine method will return a string containing all the data entered or an empty string if no data was entered.

The ReadKey method provides a way to read input from the console without waiting for the user to press Enter. It waits for the user to press a key and returns a System.ConsoleKeyInfo object to the caller. By passing True as an argument to an overload of the ReadKey method, you can also prevent the key pressed by the user from being echoed to the console.

The returned ConsoleKeyInfo object contains details about the key pressed. The details are accessible through the properties of the ConsoleKeyInfo class summarized in Table 2-7.

Table 2-7. *Properties of the ConsoleKeyInfo Class*

Property	Description
Key	Gets a value of the System.ConsoleKey enumeration representing the key pressed. The ConsoleKey enumeration contains values that represent all the keys usually found on a keyboard. These include all the character and function keys; navigation and editing keys such as Home, Insert, and Delete; and more modern specialized keys such as the Windows key, media player control keys, browser activation keys, and browser navigation keys.
KeyChar	Gets a Char value containing the Unicode character representation of the key pressed. Special keys such as Insert, Delete, and F1 through F12 do not have a Unicode representation and will return Nothing.
Modifiers	Gets a bitwise combination of values from the System.ConsoleModifiers enumeration that identifies one or more modifier keys pressed simultaneously with the console key. The members of the ConsoleModifiers enumeration are Alt, Control, and Shift.

The KeyAvailable method of the Console class returns a Boolean value indicating whether input is available in the input buffer without blocking your code.

The Code

The following example reads input from the console one character at a time using the ReadKey method. If the user presses F1, the program toggles in and out of "secret" mode, where input is masked by asterisks. When the user presses Escape, the console is cleared and the input the user has entered is displayed. If the user presses Alt-X or Alt-x, the example terminates.

```
Imports System
Imports System.Collections.Generic

Namespace Apress.VisualBasicRecipes.Chapter02

    Public Class Recipe02_16
        Public Shared Sub Main()

            ' Local variable to hold the key entered by the user.
            Dim key As ConsoleKeyInfo

            ' Control whether character or asterisk is displayed.
            Dim secret As Boolean = False
```

```
             '  Character list for the user data entered.
             Dim input As New List(Of Char)
             Dim msg As String = "Enter characters and press Escape to see input." ➥
& vbCrLf & "Press F1 to enter/exit Secret mode and Alt-X to exit."

             Console.WriteLine(msg)


             '  Process input until the users presses Alt-X or Alt-x.
             Do
                 '  Read a key from the console. Intercept the key so that it is not
                 '  displayed to the console. What is displayed is determined later
                 '  depending on whether the program is in secret mode.
                 key = Console.ReadKey(True)

                 '  Switch secret mode on and off.
                 If key.Key = ConsoleKey.F1 Then
                     If secret Then
                         '  Switch secret mode off.
                         secret = False
                     Else
                         '  Switch secret mode on.
                         secret = True
                     End If
                 End If

                 If key.Key = ConsoleKey.Backspace Then
             '  Handle Backspace.
                     If input.Count > 0 Then
                         '  Backspace pressed remove the last character.
                         input.RemoveAt(input.Count - 1)

                         Console.Write(key.KeyChar)
                         Console.Write(" ")
                         Console.Write(key.KeyChar)
                     End If

                     '  Handle Escape.
                 ElseIf key.Key = ConsoleKey.Escape Then
                     Console.Clear()
                     Console.WriteLine("Input:  {0}{1}{1}", New ➥
String(input.ToArray), vbCrLf)
                     Console.WriteLine(msg)
                     input.Clear()

                     '  Handle character input.
                 ElseIf key.Key >= ConsoleKey.A And key.Key <= ConsoleKey.Z Then
                     input.Add(key.KeyChar)
```

```vbnet
            If secret Then
                Console.Write("*")
            Else
                Console.Write(key.KeyChar)
            End If

        End If


        Loop While Not key.Key = ConsoleKey.X Or Not key.Modifiers = ➥
ConsoleModifiers.Alt

        ' Wait to continue.
        Console.WriteLine("{0}{0}Main method complete.  Press Enter", vbCrLf)
        Console.ReadLine()

    End Sub

    End Class
End Namespace
```

CHAPTER 3

■ ■ ■

Application Domains, Reflection, and Metadata

When an application is run on an operating system, it is given its own private space, typically referred to as a *process*. This process ensures that different applications don't interfere with each other. The common language runtime (CLR) does the same thing within a .NET application but using *application domains*, which can be thought of as subprocesses. Although each application (including .NET applications) running in the operating system executes in a single process, .NET applications themselves can have one or more *application domains*.

A side effect, however, is that information cannot be easily shared between application domains or processes. .NET offers the perfect solution for this in the form of *reflection*, which provides a means to dynamically load information from assemblies running in different application domains. The information that can be loaded by reflection can be any available metadata (such as attributes, types, available methods, and so on) that is contained in the target assembly.

The recipes in this chapter cover the following:

- Controlling the loading of assemblies and the instantiation of types in local and remote application domains (recipes 3-1, 3-3, 3-4, and 3-7)

- Creating application domains into which you can load assemblies that are isolated from the rest of your application (recipe 3-2)

- Creating types that are guaranteed to be unable to cross application domain boundaries (recipe 3-5) and types that have the capability to cross application domain boundaries (recipe 3-6)

- Passing simple configuration data between application domains (recipe 3-8)

- Unloading application domains, which provides the only means through which you can unload assemblies at runtime (recipe 3-9)

- Inspecting and testing the type of an object using a variety of mechanisms built into the VB .NET language and capabilities provided by the objects themselves (recipes 3-10 and 3-11)

- Dynamically instantiating an object and executing its methods at runtime using reflection (recipe 3-12)

- Creating custom attributes (recipe 3-13), which allows you to associate metadata with your program elements, and inspecting the value of those custom attributes at runtime (recipe 3-14)

■**Note** An excellent reference for detailed information on all aspects of application domains and loading assemblies is *Customizing the Microsoft .NET Framework Common Language Runtime* by Steven Pratschner (Microsoft Press, 2005).

3-1. Load an Assembly into the Current Application Domain

Problem

You need to load an assembly into the current application domain at runtime.

Solution

Use the Shared Load method or the LoadFrom method of the System.Reflection.Assembly class.

■**Note** The Assembly.LoadWithPartialName method has been deprecated in .NET Framework 2.0. Instead, you should use the Assembly.Load method described in this recipe.

How It Works

Unlike with Win32, where the referenced DLLs are loaded when the process starts, the common language runtime (CLR) will automatically load the assemblies referenced by your assembly only when the metadata for their contained types is required. However, you can also explicitly instruct the runtime to load assemblies. The Load and LoadFrom methods both result in the runtime loading an assembly into the current application domain, and both return an Assembly instance that represents the newly loaded assembly. The differences between each method are the arguments you must provide to identify the assembly to load and the process that the runtime undertakes to locate the specified assembly.

The Load method provides overloads that allow you to specify the assembly to load using one of the following:

- A String containing the fully or partially qualified *display name* of the assembly
- A System.Reflection.AssemblyName containing details of the assembly
- A Byte array containing the raw bytes that constitute the assembly

A fully qualified display name contains the assembly's name (minus the extension), version, culture, and public key token, separated by commas (for example, System.Data, Version=2.0.0.0, Culture=neutral, PublicKeyToken=b77a5c561934e089). When using a fully qualified name, all four fields are mandatory. If you need to specify an assembly that doesn't have a strong name, use PublicKeyToken=null. You can also specify a partial name, but as a minimum, you must specify the assembly name (without the file extension).

In response to the Load call, the runtime undertakes an extensive process to locate and load the specified assembly. The following is a summary of this process (consult the section "How the Runtime Locates Assemblies" in the .NET Framework SDK documentation for more details):

1. If you specify a strong-named assembly, the Load method will apply the version policy and publisher policy to enable requests for one version of an assembly to be satisfied by another version. You specify the version policy in your machine or application configuration file using <bindingRedirect> elements. You specify the publisher policy in special resource assemblies installed in the global assembly cache (GAC).

2. Once the runtime has established the correct version of an assembly to use, it attempts to load strong-named assemblies from the GAC.

3. If the assembly is not strong named or is not found in the GAC, the runtime looks for applicable <codeBase> elements in your machine and application configuration files. A <codeBase> element maps an assembly name to a specific file or a uniform resource locator (URL). If the assembly is strong named, <codeBase> can refer to any location including Internet-based URLs; otherwise, <codeBase> must refer to a directory relative to the application directory. If the assembly doesn't exist at the specified location, Load throws a System.IO.FileNotFoundException.

   If no <codeBase> elements are relevant to the requested assembly, the runtime will locate the assembly using *probing*. Probing looks for the first file with the assembly's name (with either a .dll or an .exe extension) in the following locations:

   - The application root directory

   - Directories under the application root that match the assembly's name and culture

   - Directories under the application root that are specified in the private binpath using the privatePath attribute of the <Probing> element

The Load method is the easiest way to locate and load assemblies but can also be expensive in terms of processing if the runtime needs to start probing many directories for a weak-named assembly. The LoadFrom method allows you to load an assembly file specified by the supplied uniform resource identifier (URI). If the file isn't found, the runtime will throw a FileNotFoundException. The runtime won't attempt to locate the assembly in the same way as the Load method—LoadFrom provides no support for the GAC, policies, <codeBase> elements, or probing.

The Code

The following code demonstrates various forms of the Load and LoadFrom methods. Notice that unlike the Load method, LoadFrom requires you to specify the extension of the assembly file.

```
Imports System
Imports System.Reflection
Imports System.Globalization

Namespace Apress.VisualBasicRecipes.Chapter03

    Public Class Recipe03_01

        Public Shared Sub ListAssemblies()

            ' Get an array of the assemblies loaded into the current
            ' application domain.
            Dim assemblies As Assembly() = AppDomain.CurrentDomain.GetAssemblies()

            For Each a As Assembly In assemblies
                Console.WriteLine(a.GetName)
            Next

        End Sub
```

```
    Public Shared Sub Main()

        ' List the assemblies in the current application domain.
        Console.WriteLine("**** BEFORE ****")
        ListAssemblies()

        ' Load the System.Data assembly using a fully qualified display name.
        Dim name1 As String = "System.Data,Version=2.0.0.0," + ➡
"Culture=neutral,PublicKeyToken=b77a5c561934e089"
        Dim a1 As Assembly = Assembly.Load(name1)


        ' Load the System.Xml assembly using an AssemblyName.
        Dim name2 As New AssemblyName()
        name2.Name = "System.Xml"
        name2.Version = New Version(2, 0, 0, 0)
        name2.CultureInfo = New CultureInfo("")    ' Neutral culture.
        name2.SetPublicKeyToken(New Byte() {&HB7, &H7A, &H5C, &H56, ➡
&H19, &H34, &HE0, &H89})
        Dim a2 As Assembly = Assembly.Load(name2)

        ' Load the SomeAssembly assembly using a partial display name.
        Dim a3 As Assembly = Assembly.Load("SomeAssembly")

        ' Load the assembly named C:\shared\MySharedAssembly.dll.
        Dim a4 As Assembly = Assembly.LoadFrom("C:\shared\MySharedAssembly.dll")

        ' List the assemblies in the current application domain.
        Console.WriteLine("{0}{0}**** AFTER ****", vbCrLf)
        ListAssemblies()

        ' Wait to continue.
        Console.WriteLine(vbCrLf & "Main method complete.  Press Enter.")
        Console.ReadLine()

    End Sub

  End Class
End Namespace
```

3-2. Create an Application Domain

Problem

You need to create a new application domain.

Solution

Use the Shared method CreateDomain of the System.AppDomain class.

How It Works

The simplest overload of the CreateDomain method takes a single String argument specifying a human-readable name (friendly name) for the new application domain. Other overloads allow you to specify evidence and configuration settings for the new application domain. *Evidence* refers to information, such as a strong name or application path, that is used by the CLR when making security decisions. You specify evidence using a System.Security.Policy.Evidence object, and you specify configuration settings using a System.AppDomainSetup object.

The AppDomainSetup class is a container of configuration information for an application domain. Table 3-1 lists some of the properties of the AppDomainSetup class that you will use most often when creating application domains. These properties are accessible after creation through members of the AppDomain object. Some have different names, and some are modifiable at runtime; refer to the .NET Framework's software development kit (SDK) documentation on the AppDomain class for a comprehensive discussion.

Table 3-1. *Commonly Used AppDomainSetup Properties*

Property	Description
ApplicationBase	The directory where the CLR will look during probing to resolve private assemblies. Recipe 3-1 discusses probing. Effectively, ApplicationBase is the root directory for the executing application. By default, this is the directory containing the assembly. This is readable after creation using the AppDomain.BaseDirectory property.
ConfigurationFile	The name of the configuration file used by code loaded into the application domain. This is readable after creation using the AppDomain.GetData method with the key APP_CONFIG_FILE. By default, the configuration file is stored in the same folder as the application.exe file, but if you set ApplicationBase, it will be in that folder.
DisallowPublisherPolicy	Controls whether the publisher policy section of the application configuration file is taken into consideration when determining which version of a strong-named assembly to bind to. Recipe 3-1 discusses publisher policy.
PrivateBinPath	A semicolon-separated list of directories that the runtime uses when probing for private assemblies. These directories are relative to the directory specified in ApplicationBase. This is readable after application domain creation using the AppDomain.RelativeSearchPath property.

The Code

The following code demonstrates the creation and initial configuration of an application domain:

```
Imports System
Namespace Apress.VisualBasicRecipes.Chapter03

    Public Class Recipe03_02

        Public Shared Sub Main()
```

```
                  '  Instantiate an AppDomainSetup object.
                  Dim setupInfo As New AppDomainSetup

                  '  Configure the application domain setup information.
                  setupInfo.ApplicationBase = "C:\MyRootDirectory"
                  setupInfo.ConfigurationFile = "MyApp.config"
                  setupInfo.PrivateBinPath = "bin;plugins;external"

                  '  Create a new application domain passing Nothing as the evidence
                  '  argument. Remember to save a reference to the new AppDomain as
                  '  this cannot be retrieved any other way.
                  Dim newDomain As AppDomain = AppDomain.CreateDomain("My New " & ➥

"AppDomain, Nothing, setupInfo)

                  '  Wait to continue.
                  Console.WriteLine(vbCrLf & "Main method complete.  Press Enter.")
                  Console.ReadLine()

          End Sub

      End Class
End Namespace
```

▓**Note** You must maintain a reference to the AppDomain object when you create it because no mechanism exists to enumerate existing application domains from within managed code.

3-3. Execute an Assembly in a Different Application Domain

Problem

You need to execute an assembly in an application domain other than the current one.

Solution

Call the ExecuteAssembly or ExecuteAssemblyByName method of the AppDomain object that represents the application domain, and specify the file name of an executable assembly.

How It Works

If you have an executable assembly that you want to load and run in an application domain, the ExecuteAssembly or ExecuteAssemblyByName method provides the easiest solution. The ExecuteAssembly method provides four overloads. The simplest overload takes only a String containing the name of the executable assembly to run; you can specify a local file or a URL. Other ExecuteAssembly overloads allow you to specify evidence for the assembly (which affects code access security) and arguments to pass to the assembly's entry point (equivalent to command-line arguments).

The ExecuteAssembly method loads the specified assembly and executes the method defined in metadata as the assembly's entry point (usually the Main method). If the specified assembly isn't executable, ExecuteAssembly throws a System.MissingMethodException. The CLR doesn't start execution of the assembly in a new thread, so control won't return from the ExecuteAssembly method until the newly executed assembly exits. Because the ExecuteAssembly method loads an assembly using partial information (only the file name), the CLR won't use the GAC or probing to resolve the assembly. (See recipe 3-1 for more information.)

The ExecuteAssemblyByName method provides a similar set of overloads and takes the same argument types as ExecuteAssembly, but instead of just the file name of the executable assembly, it takes the display name of the assembly. (See recipe 3-1 for more information about the structure of assembly display names.) This overcomes the limitations inherent in ExecuteAssembly as a result of supplying only partial names. Here is an example of using this method:

```
Dim domain As AppDomain = AppDomain.CreateDomain("NewAppDomain")
domain.ExecuteAssemblyByName("Recipe03-03, Version=1.0.0.0, Culture=neutral, ➥
PublicKeyToken=null", Nothing, args)
```

The Code

The following code demonstrates how to use the ExecuteAssembly method to load and run an assembly. The Recipe03_03 class creates an AppDomain and executes itself in that AppDomain using the ExecuteAssembly method. This results in two copies of the Recipe03-03 assembly loaded into two different application domains.

```
Imports System
Namespace Apress.VisualBasicRecipes.Chapter03

    Public Class Recipe03_03

        Public Shared Sub Main(ByVal args As String())

            ' For the purpose of this example, if this assembly is executing
            ' in an AppDomain with the friendly name NewAppDomain, do not
            ' create a new AppDomain. This avoids an infinite loop of
            ' AppDomain creation.
            If Not AppDomain.CurrentDomain.FriendlyName = "NewAppDomain" Then
                ' Create a new application domain.
                Dim domain As AppDomain = AppDomain.CreateDomain("NewAppDomain")

                ' Execute this assembly in the new application domain and
                ' pass the array of command-line arguments.
                domain.ExecuteAssembly("Recipe03-03.exe", Nothing, args)

            End If

            ' Display the command-line arguments to the screen prefixed with
            ' the friendly name of the AppDomain.
            For Each s As String In args
                Console.WriteLine(AppDomain.CurrentDomain.FriendlyName + " : " + s)
            Next

            ' Wait to continue.
            If Not AppDomain.CurrentDomain.FriendlyName = "NewAppDomain" Then
                Console.WriteLine(vbCrLf & "Main method complete.  Press Enter.")
                Console.ReadLine()
            End If

        End Sub

    End Class
End Namespace
```

Usage

If you run `Recipe03-03` using the following command:

```
Recipe03-03 Testing AppDomains
```

you will see that the command-line arguments are listed from both the existing and new application domains:

```
NewAppDomain : Testing
NewAppDomain : AppDomains
Recipe03-03.exe : Testing
Recipe03-03.exe : AppDomains
```

3-4. Avoid Loading Unnecessary Assemblies into Application Domains

Problem

You need to pass an object reference across multiple application domain boundaries; however, to conserve memory and avoid impacting performance, you want to ensure the CLR loads only the object's type metadata into the application domains where it is required (that is, where you will actually use the object).

Solution

Wrap the object reference in a `System.Runtime.Remoting.ObjectHandle`, and unwrap the object reference only when you need to access the object.

How It Works

When you pass a marshal-by-value (MBV) object across application domain boundaries, the runtime creates a new instance of that object in the destination application domain. This means the runtime must load the assembly containing that type metadata into the application domain. Passing MBV references across intermediate application domains can result in the runtime loading unnecessary assemblies into application domains. Once loaded, these superfluous assemblies cannot be unloaded without unloading the containing application domain. (See recipe 3-9 for more information.)

The `ObjectHandle` class allows you to wrap an object reference so that you can pass it between application domains without the runtime loading additional assemblies. When the object reaches the destination application domain, you can unwrap the object reference, causing the runtime to load the required assembly and allowing you to access the object.

The Code

The following code contains some simple methods that demonstrate how to wrap and unwrap a `System.Data.DataSet` using an `ObjectHandle`:

```
Imports System
Imports System.Data
Imports System.Runtime.Remoting
```

```vbnet
Namespace Apress.VisualBasicRecipes.Chapter03

    Public Class Recipe03_04


        ' A method to wrap a DataSet.
        Public Function WrapDataset(ByVal ds As DataSet) As ObjectHandle

            ' Wrap the DataSet.
            Dim objHandle As New ObjectHandle(ds)

            ' Return the wrapped DataSet.
            Return objHandle

        End Function

        ' A method to unwrap a DataSet.
        Public Function UnwrapDataset(ByVal handle As ObjectHandle) As DataSet

            ' Unwrap the DataSet.
            Dim ds As DataSet = CType(handle.Unwrap, DataSet)

            ' Return the DataSet.
            Return ds

        End Function

    End Class
End Namespace
```

3-5. Create a Type That Cannot Cross Application Domain Boundaries

Problem

You need to create a type so that instances of the type are inaccessible to code in other application domains.

Solution

Ensure the type is nonremotable by making sure it is not serializable (no Serializable attribute) and it does not derive from the MarshalByRefObject class.

How It Works

On occasion, you will want to ensure that instances of a type cannot transcend application domain boundaries. To create a nonremotable type, ensure that it isn't serializable and that it doesn't derive (directly or indirectly) from the MarshalByRefObject class. If you take these steps, you ensure that an object's state can never be accessed from outside the application domain in which the object was instantiated—such objects cannot be used as arguments or return values in cross-application domain method calls.

Ensuring that a type isn't serializable is easy because a class doesn't inherit the ability to be serialized from its parent class. To ensure that a type isn't serializable, make sure it does not have System.SerializableAttribute applied to the type declaration.

Ensuring that a class cannot be passed by reference requires a little more attention. Many classes in the .NET class library derive directly or indirectly from MarshalByRefObject; you must be careful you don't inadvertently derive your class from one of these. Commonly used base classes that derive from MarshalByRefObject include System.ComponentModel.Component, System.IO.Stream, System.IO. TextReader, System.IO.TextWriter, System.NET.WebRequest, and System.Net.WebResponse. (Check the .NET Framework SDK documentation on MarshalByRefObject. The inheritance hierarchy for the class provides a complete list of classes that derive from it.)

3-6. Create a Type That Can Be Passed Across Application Domain Boundaries

Problem

You need to pass objects across application domain boundaries as arguments or return values.

Solution

Use marshal-by-value (MBV) or marshal-by-reference (MBR) objects.

How It Works

The .NET Remoting system (discussed in Chapter 10) makes passing objects across application domain boundaries straightforward. However, to those unfamiliar with .NET Remoting, the results can be very different from those expected. In fact, the most confusing aspect of using multiple application domains stems from the interaction with .NET Remoting and the way objects traverse application domain boundaries.

All types fall into one of three categories: nonremotable, MBV, or MBR. Nonremotable types cannot cross application domain boundaries and cannot be used as arguments or return values in cross-application domain calls. (Recipe 3-5 discusses nonremotable types.)

MBV types are serializable types. When you pass an MBV object across an application domain boundary as an argument or a return value, the .NET Remoting system serializes the object's current state, passes it to the destination application domain, and creates a new copy of the object with the same state as the original. This results in a copy of the MBV object existing in both application domains. The contents of the two instances are initially identical, but they are independent; changes made to one instance are not reflected in the other instance. This often causes confusion as you try to update the remote object but are actually updating the local copy. If you want to be able to call and change an object from a remote application domain, the object needs to be an MBR type.

MBR types are those classes that derive from System.MarshalByRefObject. When you pass an MBR object across an application domain boundary as an argument or a return value, in the destination application domain the .NET Remoting system creates a *proxy* that represents the remote MBR object. To any class in the destination application domain, the proxy looks and behaves like the remote MBR object that it represents. In reality, when a call is made against the proxy, the .NET Remoting system transparently passes the call and its arguments to the remote application domain and issues the call against the original object. Any results are passed back to the caller via the proxy. Figure 3-1 illustrates the relationship between an MBR object and the objects that access it across application domains via a proxy.

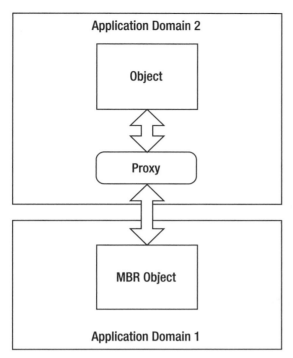

Figure 3-1. *An MBR object is accessed across application domains via a proxy.*

The Code

The following example highlights (in bold) the fundamental difference between creating classes that are passed by value (Recipe03_06MBV) and those passed by reference (Recipe03_06MBR). The code creates a new application domain and instantiates two remotable objects in it (discussed further in recipe 3-7). However, because the Recipe03_06MBV object is an MBV object, when it is created in the new application domain, it is serialized, passed across the application domain boundary, and deserialized as a new independent object in the caller's application domain. Therefore, when the code retrieves the name of the application domain hosting each object, Recipe03_06MBV returns the name of the main application domain, and Recipe03_06MBR returns the name of the new application domain in which it was created.

■**Note** This sample uses the CreateInstanceFromAndUnwrap method of the AppDomain class to create the instances of Recipe03_06MBV and Recipe03_06MBR in the new application domain. This method is covered in more detail in recipe 3-7.

```
Imports System
Namespace Apress.VisualBasicRecipes.Chapter03

    ' Declare a class that is passed by value.
    <Serializable()> _
    Public Class Recipe03_06MBV
```

```vb
        Public ReadOnly Property HomeAppDomain() As String
            Get
                Return AppDomain.CurrentDomain.FriendlyName
            End Get
        End Property

    End Class

    ' Declare a class that is passed by reference.
    Public Class Recipe03_06MBR
        Inherits MarshalByRefObject

        Public ReadOnly Property HomeAppDomain() As String
            Get
                Return AppDomain.CurrentDomain.FriendlyName
            End Get
        End Property

    End Class

    Public Class Recipe03_06
        Public Shared Sub Main(ByVal args As String())

            ' Create a new application domain.
            Dim newDomain As AppDomain = AppDomain.CreateDomain("My ➥
New AppDomain")

            ' Instantiate an MBV object in the new application domain.
            Dim mbvObject As Recipe03_06MBV = ➥
CType(newDomain.CreateInstanceFromAndUnwrap("Recipe03-06.exe", ➥
"Apress.VisualBasicRecipes.Chapter03.Recipe03_06MBV"), Recipe03_06MBV)

            ' Instantiate an MBR object in the new application domain.
            Dim mbrObject As Recipe03_06MBR = ➥
CType(newDomain.CreateInstanceFromAndUnwrap("Recipe03-06.exe", ➥
"Apress.VisualBasicRecipes.Chapter03.Recipe03_06MBR"), Recipe03_06MBR)

            ' Display the name of the application domain in which each of
            ' the objects is located.
            Console.WriteLine("Main AppDomain = {0}", ➥
AppDomain.CurrentDomain.FriendlyName)
            Console.WriteLine("AppDomain of MBV object = {0}", ➥
mbvObject.HomeAppDomain)
            Console.WriteLine("AppDomain of MBR object = {0}", ➥
mbrObject.HomeAppDomain)

            ' Wait to continue.
            Console.WriteLine(vbCrLf & "Main method complete.  Press Enter.")
            Console.ReadLine()

        End Sub

    End Class
End Namespace
```

3-7. Instantiate a Type in a Different Application Domain

Problem

You need to instantiate a type in an application domain other than the current one.

Solution

Call the `CreateInstance` method or the `CreateInstanceFrom` method of the `AppDomain` object that represents the target application domain.

How It Works

The `ExecuteAssembly` method discussed in recipe 3-3 is straightforward to use, but when you are developing sophisticated applications that use application domains, you are likely to want more control over loading assemblies, instantiating types, and invoking object members within the application domain.

The `CreateInstance` and `CreateInstanceFrom` methods provide a variety of overloads that offer fine-grained control over the process of object instantiation. The simplest overloads assume the use of a type's default constructor, but both methods implement overloads that allow you to provide arguments to use any constructor.

The `CreateInstance` method loads a named assembly into the application domain using the process described for the `Assembly.Load` method in recipe 3-1. `CreateInstance` then instantiates a named type and returns a reference to the new object wrapped in an `ObjectHandle` (described in recipe 3-4). The `CreateInstanceFrom` method also instantiates a named type and returns an `ObjectHandle`-wrapped object reference; however, `CreateInstanceFrom` loads the specified assembly file into the application domain using the process described in recipe 3-1 for the `Assembly.LoadFrom` method.

`AppDomain` also provides two convenience methods named `CreateInstanceAndUnwrap` and `CreateInstanceFromAndUnwrap` that automatically extract the reference of the instantiated object from the returned `ObjectHandle` object; you must cast the returned `Object` to the correct type.

■**Caution** Be aware that if you use `CreateInstance` or `CreateInstanceFrom` to instantiate MBV types in another application domain, the object will be created, but the returned `Object` reference won't refer to that object. Because of the way MBV objects cross application domain boundaries, the reference will refer to a copy of the object created automatically in the local application domain. Only if you create an MBR type will the returned reference refer to the object in the other application domain. (See recipe 3-6 for more details about MBV and MBR types.)

A common technique to simplify the management of application domains is to use a *controller class*. A controller class is a custom MBR type. You create an application domain and then instantiate your controller class in the application domain using `CreateInstance`. The controller class implements the functionality required by your application to manipulate the application domain and its contents. This could include loading assemblies, creating further application domains, cleaning up prior to deleting the application domain, or enumerating program elements (something you cannot normally do from outside an application domain). It is best to create your controller class in an assembly of its own to avoid loading unnecessary classes into each application domain. You should also be careful about which types you pass as return values from your controller to your main application domain to avoid loading additional assemblies.

The Code

The following code demonstrates how to use a simplified controller class named PluginManager.
When instantiated in an application domain, PluginManager allows you to instantiate classes that
implement the IPlugin interface, start and stop those plug-ins, and return a list of currently loaded
plug-ins.

```vbnet
Imports System
Imports System.Reflection
Imports System.Collections
Imports System.Collections.Generic
Imports System.Collections.Specialized

Namespace Apress.VisualBasicRecipes.Chapter03

    ' A common interface that all plug-ins must implement.
    Public Interface IPlugin

        Sub Start()
        Sub [Stop]()

    End Interface

    ' A simple IPlugin implementation to demonstrate the PluginManager
    ' controller class.
    Public Class SimplePlugin
        Implements IPlugin

        Public Sub Start() Implements IPlugin.Start
            Console.WriteLine(AppDomain.CurrentDomain.FriendlyName & ➥
": SimplePlugin starting...")
        End Sub

        Public Sub [Stop]() Implements IPlugin.Stop
            Console.WriteLine(AppDomain.CurrentDomain.FriendlyName & ➥
": SimplePlugin stopping...")
        End Sub

    End Class

    ' The controller class, which manages the loading and manipulation
    ' of plug-ins in its application domain.
    Public Class PluginManager
        Inherits MarshalByRefObject


        ' A Dictionary to hold keyed references to IPlugin instances.
        Private plugins As New Dictionary(Of String, IPlugin)

        ' Default constructor.
        Public Sub New()

        End Sub
```

```vb
       ' Constructor that loads a set of specified plug-ins on creation.
       Public Sub New(ByVal pluginList As NameValueCollection)

           ' Load each of the specified plug-ins.
           For Each plugin As String In pluginList.Keys
               Me.LoadPlugin(pluginList(plugin), plugin)
           Next

       End Sub

       ' Load the specified assembly and instantiate the specified
       ' IPlugin implementation from that assembly.
       Public Function LoadPlugin(ByVal assemblyName As String, ➡
ByVal pluginName As String)

           Try
               ' Load the named private assembly.
               Dim assembly As Assembly = Reflection.Assembly.Load(assemblyName)

               ' Create the IPlugin instance, ignore case.
               Dim plugin As IPlugin = DirectCast(assembly.CreateInstance ➡
(pluginName, True), IPlugin)

               If Not plugin Is Nothing Then
                   ' Add new IPlugin to ListDictionary
                   plugins(pluginName) = plugin

                   Return True
               Else
                   Return False
               End If
           Catch
               ' Return false on all exceptions for the purpose of
               ' this example. Do not suppress exceptions like this
               ' in production code.
               Return False
           End Try

       End Function

       Public Sub StartPlugin(ByVal plugin As String)

           Try
               ' Extract the IPlugin from the Dictionary and call Start.
               plugins(plugin).Start()
           Catch
               ' Log or handle exceptions appropriately.
           End Try

       End Sub

       Public Sub StopPlugin(ByVal plugin As String)
```

```vb
        Try
            ' Extract the IPlugin from the Dictionary and call Stop.
            plugins(plugin).Stop()
        Catch
            ' Log or handle exceptions appropriately.
        End Try

    End Sub

    Public Function GetPluginList() As ArrayList

        ' Return an enumerable list of plug-in names. Take the keys
        ' and place them in an ArrayList, which supports marshal-by-value.
        Return New ArrayList(plugins.Keys)

    End Function

End Class

Public Class Recipe03_07

    Public Shared Sub Main(ByVal args As String())

        ' Create a new application domain.
        Dim domain1 As AppDomain = AppDomain.CreateDomain("NewAppDomain1")

        ' Create a PluginManager in the new application domain using
        ' the default constructor.
        Dim manager1 As PluginManager = CType(domain1.CreateInstanceAndUnwrap ➥
("Recipe03-07", "Apress.VisualBasicRecipes.Chapter03.PluginManager"), PluginManager)

        ' Load a new plug-in into NewAppDomain1
        manager1.LoadPlugin("Recipe03-07", "Apress.VisualBasicRecipes." & ➥
 "Chapter03.SimplePlugin")

        ' Start and stop the plug-in NewAppDomain1.
        manager1.StartPlugin("Apress.VisualBasicRecipes.Chapter03.SimplePlugin")
        manager1.StopPlugin("Apress.VisualBasicRecipes.Chapter03.SimplePlugin")

        ' Create a new application domain.
        Dim domain2 As AppDomain = AppDomain.CreateDomain("NewAppDomain2")

        ' Create a ListDictionary containing a list of plug-ins to create.
        Dim pluginList As New NameValueCollection()
        pluginList("Apress.VisualBasicRecipes.Chapter03.SimplePlugin") = ➥
"Recipe03-07"

        ' Create a PluginManager in the new application domain and
        ' specify the default list of plug-ins to create.
        Dim manager2 As PluginManager = CType(domain1.CreateInstanceAndUnwrap ➥
("Recipe03-07", "Apress.VisualBasicRecipes.Chapter03.PluginManager", True, 0, ➥
Nothing, New Object() {pluginList}, Nothing, Nothing, Nothing), PluginManager)
```

```
        '  Display the list of plug-ins loaded into NewAppDomain2.
        Console.WriteLine("{0}Plugins in NewAppDomain2:", vbCrLf)

        For Each s As String In manager2.GetPluginList()
            Console.WriteLine(" - " & s)
        Next

        '  Wait to continue.
        Console.WriteLine(vbCrLf & "Main method complete.  Press Enter.")
        Console.ReadLine()

    End Sub

  End Class
End Namespace
```

Usage

If you run Recipe03-07, you should see the following:

```
NewAppDomain1: SimplePlugin starting...
NewAppDomain1: SimplePlugin stopping...

Plugins in NewAppDomain2:
 - Apress.VisualBasicRecipes.Chapter03.SimplePlugin
```

3-8. Pass Data Between Application Domains

Problem

You need a simple mechanism to pass general configuration or state data between application domains.

Solution

Use the SetData and GetData methods of the AppDomain class.

How It Works

You can pass data between application domains as arguments and return values when you invoke the methods and properties of objects that exist in other application domains. However, at times it is useful to pass data between application domains in such a way that the data is easily accessible by all code within the application domain.

Every application domain maintains a data cache that contains a set of name-value pairs. Most of the cache content reflects configuration settings of the application domain, such as the values from the AppDomainSetup object provided during application domain creation. (See recipe 3-2 for more information.) You can also use this data cache as a mechanism to exchange data between application domains or as a simple state storage mechanism for code running within the application domain.

The SetData method allows you to associate a string key with an object and store it in the application domain's data cache. The GetData method allows you to retrieve an object from the data cache using the key. If code in one application domain calls the SetData method or the GetData method to access the data cache of another application domain, the data object must support MBV or MBR semantics, or a System.Runtime.Serialization.SerializationException is thrown. (See recipe 3-6 for details on the characteristics required to allow objects to transcend application domain boundaries.)

When using the SetData or GetData methods to exchange data between application domains, you should avoid using the following keys, which are already used by the .NET Framework (refer to http://msdn2.microsoft.com/en-us/library/system.appdomain.getdata.aspx for more information):

- APP_CONFIG_FILE
- APP_NAME
- APPBASE
- APP_LAUNCH_URL
- LOADER_OPTIMIZATION
- BINPATH_PROBE_ONLY
- CACHE_BASE
- DEV_PATH
- DYNAMIC_BASE
- FORCE_CACHE_INSTALL
- LICENSE_FILE
- PRIVATE_BINPATH
- SHADOW_COPY_DIRS

The Code

The following example demonstrates how to use the SetData and GetData methods by passing a System.Collections.ArrayList between two application domains. After passing a list of pets to a second application domain for modification, the application displays the list. You will notice that the code running in the second application domain does not modify the original list because ArrayList is an MBV type, meaning that the second application domain has only a *copy* of the original list. (See recipe 3-6 for more details.)

```
Imports System
Imports System.Reflection
Imports System.collections

Namespace Apress.VisualBasicRecipes.Chapter03

    Public Class ListModifier

        Public Sub New()

            ' Get the list from the data cache.
            Dim list As ArrayList = CType(AppDomain.CurrentDomain.GetData("Pets"), ➡
ArrayList)

            ' Modify the list.
            list.Add("Turtle")

        End Sub

    End Class
```

```
    Public Class Recipe03_08

        Public Shared Sub Main()

            ' Create a new application domain.
            Dim domain As AppDomain = AppDomain.CreateDomain("Test")

            ' Create an ArrayList and populate with information.
            Dim list As New ArrayList
            list.Add("Dog")
            list.Add("Cat")
            list.Add("Fish")

            ' Place the list in the data cache of the new application domain.
            domain.SetData("Pets", list)

            ' Instantiate a ListModifier in the new application domain.
            domain.CreateInstance("Recipe03-08", "Apress.VisualBasicRecipes." & ➥
"Chapter03.ListModifier")

            ' Get the list and display its contents.
            Console.WriteLine("The list in the 'Test' application domain:")
            For Each s As String In CType(domain.GetData("Pets"), ArrayList)
                Console.WriteLine(s)
            Next
            Console.WriteLine(Environment.NewLine)

            ' Display the original list to show that it has not changed.
            Console.WriteLine("The list in the standard application domain:")
            For Each s As String In list
                Console.WriteLine(s)
            Next
            ' Wait to continue.
            Console.WriteLine(vbCrLf & "Main method complete.  Press Enter.")
            Console.ReadLine()

        End Sub

    End Class
End Namespace
```

3-9. Unload Assemblies and Application Domains

Problem

You need to unload assemblies or application domains at runtime.

Solution

You have no way to unload individual assemblies from a System.AppDomain. You can unload an entire application domain using the Shared AppDomain.Unload method, which has the effect of unloading all assemblies loaded into the application domain.

How It Works

The only way to unload an assembly is to unload the application domain in which the assembly is loaded. Unfortunately, unloading an application domain will unload all the assemblies that have been loaded into it. This might seem like a heavy-handed and inflexible approach, but with appropriate planning of your application domain, the assembly-loading structure, and the runtime dependency of your code on that application domain, it is not overly restrictive.

You unload an application domain using the Shared AppDomain.Unload method and passing it an AppDomain reference to the application domain you want to unload. You cannot unload the default application domain created by the CLR at startup.

The Unload method stops any new threads from entering the specified application domain and calls the Thread.Abort method on all threads currently active in the application domain. If the thread calling the Unload method is currently running in the specified application domain (making it the target of a Thread.Abort call), a new thread starts in order to carry out the unload operation. If a problem is encountered unloading an application domain, the thread performing the unload operation throws a System.CannotUnloadAppDomainException. Attempting to access the application domain after it has been unloaded will throw a System.AppDomainUnloadedException.

While an application domain is unloading, the CLR calls the finalization method of all objects in the application domain. Depending on the number of objects and nature of their finalization methods, this can take an arbitrary amount of time. The AppDomain.IsFinalizingForUnload method returns True if the application domain is unloading and the CLR has started to finalize contained objects; otherwise, it returns False.

The Code

This code fragment demonstrates the syntax of the Unload method:

```
'   Create a new application domain.
Dim newDomain As AppDomain = AppDomain.CreateDomain("New Domain")

'   Load assemblies into the application domain.
...

'   Unload the new application domains.
AppDomain.Unload(newDomain)
```

3-10. Retrieve Type Information

Problem

You need to obtain a System.Type object that represents a specific type.

Solution

Use one of the following:

- The GetType operator
- The Shared GetType method of the System.Type class
- The Object.GetType method of an existing instance of the type
- The GetNestedType or GetNestedTypes method of the Type class
- The GetType or GetTypes method of the Assembly class
- The GetType, GetTypes, or FindTypes method of the System.Reflection.Module class

How It Works

The Type class provides a starting point for working with types using reflection. A Type object allows you to inspect the metadata of the type, obtain details of the type's members, and create instances of the type. Because of the type's importance, the .NET Framework provides a variety of mechanisms for obtaining references to Type objects.

One method of obtaining a Type object for a specific type is to use the GetType operator shown here:

```
Dim T1 As System.Type = GetType(System.Text.StringBuilder)
```

The type name is not enclosed in quotes and must be resolvable by the compiler (meaning you must reference the assembly). Because the reference is resolved at compile time, the assembly containing the type becomes a static dependency of your assembly and will be listed as such in your assembly's manifest.

Another method that returns a Type object is Object.GetType. This method returns the type of the object that calls it. The following is an example of its usage:

```
Dim myStringBuilder As New System.Text.StringBuilder
Dim myType As System.Type = myStringBuilder.GetType()
```

You can also use the Shared method Type.GetType, which takes a string containing the type name. Because you use a string to specify the type, you can vary it at runtime, which opens the door to a world of dynamic programming opportunities using reflection (see recipe 3-12). If you specify just the type name, the runtime must be able to locate the type in an already loaded assembly. Alternatively, you can specify an assembly-qualified type name. Refer to the .NET Framework SDK documentation for the Type.GetType method for a complete description of how to structure assembly-qualified type names. Table 3-2 summarizes some other methods that provide access to Type objects.

Table 3-2. *Methods That Return Type Objects*

Method	Description
Type.GetNestedType	Gets a specified type declared as a nested type (a type that is a member of another type) within the existing Type object.
Type.GetNestedTypes	Gets an array of Type objects representing the nested types declared within the existing Type object.
Assembly.GetType	Gets a Type object for the specified type declared within the assembly.
Assembly.GetTypes	Gets an array of Type objects representing the types declared within the assembly.
Module.GetType	Gets a Type object for the specified type declared within the module. (See recipe 1-3 for a discussion of modules.)
Module.GetTypes	Gets an array of Type objects representing the types declared within the module. (See recipe 1-3 for a discussion of modules.)
Module.FindTypes	Gets a filtered array of Type objects representing the types declared within the module. The types are filtered using a delegate that determines whether each Type should appear in the final array. (See recipe 1-3 for a discussion of modules.)

The Code

The following example demonstrates how to use the GetType operator and the Type.GetType method to return a Type object for a named type and from existing objects:

```vb
Imports System
Imports System.Text

Namespace Apress.VisualBasicRecipes.Chapter03

    Public Class Recipe03_10

        Public Shared Sub Main()

            ' Obtain type information using the GetType operator.
            Dim t1 As Type = GetType(StringBuilder)

            ' Obtain type information using the Type.GetType method.
            ' Case-sensitive, return Nothing if not found.
            Dim t2 As Type = Type.GetType("System.String")

            ' Case-sensitive, throw TypeLoadException if not found.
            Dim t3 As Type = Type.GetType("System.String", True)

            ' Case-insensitive, throw TypeLoadException if not found.
            Dim t4 As Type = Type.GetType("system.string", True, True)

            ' Assembly-qualified type name.
            Dim t5 As Type = Type.GetType("System.Data.DataSet,System.Data," & _
"Version=2.0.0.0,Culture=neutral,PublicKeyToken=b77a5c561934e089")


            ' Obtain type information using the Object.GetType method.
            Dim sb As New StringBuilder
            Dim t6 As Type = sb.GetType()

            ' Display the types.
            Console.WriteLine("Type of T1:  {0}", t1.ToString)
            Console.WriteLine("Type of T2:  {0}", t2.ToString)
            Console.WriteLine("Type of T3:  {0}", t3.ToString)
            Console.WriteLine("Type of T4:  {0}", t4.ToString)
            Console.WriteLine("Type of T5:  {0}", t5.ToString)
            Console.WriteLine("Type of T6:  {0}", t6.ToString)

            ' Wait to continue.
            Console.WriteLine(vbCrLf & "Main method complete.  Press Enter.")
            Console.ReadLine()

        End Sub

    End Class
End Namespace
```

3-11. Test an Object's Type

Problem

You need to test the type of an object.

Solution

Use the inherited `Object.GetType` method to obtain a `Type` for the object. You can also use the `TypeOf` and `Is` operators to test an object's type.

How It Works

All types inherit the `GetType` method from the `Object` base class. As discussed in recipe 3-10, this method returns a `Type` reference representing the type of the object. The runtime maintains a single instance of `Type` for each type loaded, and all references for this type refer to this same object. This means you can compare two type references efficiently. For convenience, VB .NET provides the `Is` operator as a quick way to check whether an object is a specified type. In addition, `Is` will return `True` if the tested object is derived from the specified class. .NET Framework 2.0 includes the new `IsNot` operator for VB .NET. This operator is used to determine whether an object is not a specified type. Furthermore, the `Type.IsSubclassOf` method can be used to determine whether an object derives from the specified type.

When using the `TypeOf`, `Is`, and `IsNot` operators and the `IsSubClassOf` method, the specified type must be known and resolvable at compile time. A more flexible (but slower) alternative is to use the `Type.GetType` method to return a `Type` reference for a named type. The `Type` reference is not resolved until runtime, which causes a performance hit but allows you to change the type comparison at runtime based on the value of a string.

Finally, you can use the `TryCast` keyword to perform a safe cast of any object to a specified type. Unlike a standard cast that triggers a `System.InvalidCastException` if the object cannot be cast to the specified type, `TryCast` returns `Nothing`. This allows you to perform safe casts that are easy to verify, but the compared type must be resolvable at runtime.

■**Tip** The `Shared` method `GetUnderlyingType` of the `System.Enum` class allows you to retrieve the underlying type of an enumeration.

The Code

The following example demonstrates the various type-testing alternatives described in this recipe:

```
Imports System
Imports System.IO

Namespace Apress.VisualBasicRecipes.Chapter03

    Public Class Recipe03_11

        ' A method to test whether an object is an instance of a type.
        Public Shared Function IsType(ByVal obj As Object, ByVal myType ➡
As String) As Boolean
```

```vbnet
        ' Get the named type, use case-insensitive search, throw
        ' an exception if the type is not found.
        Dim t As Type = Type.GetType(myType, True, True)

        If t Is obj.GetType() Then
            Return True
        ElseIf obj.GetType.IsSubclassOf(t) Then
            Return True
        Else
            Return False
        End If

    End Function

    Public Shared Sub Main()

        ' Create a new StringReader for testing.
        Dim someObject As Object = New StringReader("This is a StringReader")

        ' Test whether someObject is a StringReader by obtaining and
        ' comparing a Type reference using the TypeOf operator.
        If someObject.GetType Is GetType(StringReader) Then
            Console.WriteLine("GetType Is: someObject is a StringReader")
        End If


        ' Test whether someObject is, or is derived from, a TextReader
        ' using the Is operator.
        If TypeOf someObject Is TextReader Then
            Console.WriteLine("TypeOf Is: someObject is a TextReader or " & ➥
"a derived class")
        End If

        ' Test whether someObject is, or is derived from, a TextReader using
        ' the Type.GetType and Type.IsSubClassOf methods.
        If IsType(someObject, "System.IO.TextReader") Then
            Console.WriteLine("GetType: someObject is, or is derived " & ➥
"from, a TextReader")
        End If

        ' Use the TryCast keyword to perform a safe cast.
        Dim reader As StringReader = TryCast(someObject, StringReader)

        If Not reader Is Nothing Then
            Console.WriteLine("TryCast: someObject is a StringReader")
        End If

        ' Wait to continue.
        Console.WriteLine(vbCrLf & "Main method complete.  Press Enter.")
        Console.ReadLine()

    End Sub

End Class
End Namespace
```

3-12. Instantiate an Object Using Reflection

Problem

You need to instantiate an object at runtime using reflection.

Solution

Obtain a Type object representing the type of object you want to instantiate, call its GetConstructor method to obtain a System.Reflection.ConstructorInfo object representing the constructor you want to use, and execute the ConstructorInfo.Invoke method.

How It Works

The first step in creating an object using reflection is to obtain a Type object that represents the type you want to instantiate. (See recipe 3-10 for details.) Once you have a Type instance, call its GetConstructor method to obtain a ConstructorInfo representing one of the type's constructors. The most commonly used overload of the GetConstructor method takes a Type array argument and returns a ConstructorInfo representing the constructor that takes the number, order, and type of arguments specified in the Type array. To obtain a ConstructorInfo representing a parameterless (default) constructor, pass an empty Type array (use the Shared field Type.EmptyTypes or New Type(0)); don't use Nothing, or GetConstructor will throw a System.ArgumentNullException. If GetConstructor cannot find a constructor with a signature that matches the specified arguments, it will return Nothing.

Once you have the desired ConstructorInfo, call its Invoke method. You must provide an Object array containing the arguments you want to pass to the constructor. If there are no arguments, pass Nothing. Invoke instantiates the new object and returns an Object reference to it, which you must cast to the appropriate type.

Reflection functionality is commonly used to implement factories in which you use reflection to instantiate concrete classes that either extend a common base class or implement a common interface. Often both an interface and a common base class are used. The abstract base class implements the interface and any common functionality, and then each concrete implementation extends the base class.

No mechanism exists to formally declare that each concrete class must implement constructors with specific signatures. If you intend third parties to implement concrete classes, your documentation must specify the constructor signature called by your factory. A common approach to avoid this problem is to use a default (empty) constructor and configure the object after instantiation using properties and methods.

The Code The following code fragment demonstrates how to instantiate a System.Text.StringBuilder object using reflection and how to specify the initial content for the StringBuilder (a String) and its capacity (an Integer):

```
Imports System
Imports System.Text
Imports System.Reflection

Namespace Apress.VisualBasicRecipes.Chapter03

    Public Class Recipe03_12

        Public Shared Function CreateStringBuilder() As StringBuilder
```

```vbnet
        ' Obtain the Type for the StringBuilder class.
        Dim type As Type = GetType(StringBuilder)

        ' Create a Type() containing Type instances for each
        ' of the constructor arguments - a String and an Integer.
        Dim argTypes As Type() = New Type() {GetType(System.String), ➥
GetType(System.Int32)}

        ' Obtain the ConstructorInfo object.
        Dim cInfo As ConstructorInfo = type.GetConstructor(argTypes)

        ' Create an Object() containing the constructor arguments.
        Dim argVals As Object() = New Object() {"Some string", 30}


        ' Create the object and cast it to a StringBuilder.
        Dim sb As StringBuilder = CType(cInfo.Invoke(argVals), StringBuilder)

        Return sb

    End Function

    End Class
End Namespace
```

The following code demonstrates a factory to instantiate objects that implement the IPlugin interface (used in recipe 3-7):

```vbnet
Imports System
Imports System.Text
Imports System.Reflection

Namespace Apress.VisualBasicRecipes.Chapter03

    ' A common interface that all plug-ins must implement.
    Public Interface IPlugin

        Property Description() As String
        Sub Start()
        Sub [Stop]()

    End Interface

    ' An abstract base class from which all plug-ins must derive.
    Public MustInherit Class AbstractPlugIn
        Implements IPlugin

        ' Hold a description for the plug-in instance.
        Private m_description As String = ""

        ' Property to get the plug-in description.
        Public Property Description() As String Implements IPlugin.Description
            Get
                Return m_description
            End Get
```

```vb
            Set(ByVal value As String)
                m_description = value
            End Set
        End Property

        ' Declare the members of the IPlugin interface as abstract.
        Public MustOverride Sub Start() Implements IPlugin.Start
        Public MustOverride Sub [Stop]() Implements IPlugin.Stop

    End Class

    ' A simple IPlugin implementation to demonstrate the PluginFactory class.
    Public Class SimplePlugin
        Inherits AbstractPlugIn


        ' Implement Start method.
        Public Overrides Sub Start()
            Console.WriteLine(Description & ": Starting...")
        End Sub
        ' Implement Stop method.
        Public Overrides Sub [Stop]()
            Console.WriteLine(Description & ": Stopping...")
        End Sub

    End Class

    ' A factory to instantiate instances of IPlugin.
    NotInheritable Class PluginFactory

        Public Shared Function CreatePlugin(ByVal assembly As String, ➥
ByVal pluginName As String, ByVal description As String) As IPlugin
            Console.WriteLine("Attempting to load plug-in")

            ' Obtain the Type for the specified plug-in.
            Dim pluginType As Type = Type.GetType(pluginName & ", " & assembly)

            ' Obtain the ConstructorInfo object.
            Dim cInfo As ConstructorInfo = pluginType.GetConstructor ➥
(Type.EmptyTypes)

            ' Create the object and cast it to IPlugin.
            Dim plugin As IPlugin = TryCast(cInfo.Invoke(Nothing), IPlugin)

            ' Configure the new IPlugin.
            plugin.Description = description

            Console.WriteLine("Plugin '{0}' [{1}] succesfully loaded.", ➥
assembly, plugin.Description)
            Console.WriteLine(Environment.NewLine)

            Return plugin

        End Function
```

```
        Public Shared Sub Main(ByVal args As String())

            ' Instantiate a new IPlugin using the PluginFactory.
            Dim plugin As IPlugin = PluginFactory.CreatePlugin("Recipe03-12",  ➥
"Apress.VisualBasicRecipes.Chapter03.SimplePlugin", "A Simple Plugin")

            plugin.Start()
            plugin.Stop()

            ' Wait to continue.
            Console.WriteLine(vbCrLf & "Main method complete.  Press Enter.")
            Console.ReadLine()

        End Sub

    End Class
End Namespace
```

3-13. Create a Custom Attribute

Problem

You need to create a custom attribute.

Solution

Create a class that derives from the abstract (MustInherit) base class System.Attribute. Implement constructors, fields, and properties to allow users to configure the attribute. Apply the System. AttributeUsageAttribute attribute to your class to define the following:

- Which program elements are valid targets of the attribute
- Whether you can apply more than one instance of the attribute to a program element
- Whether the attribute is inherited by derived types

How It Works

Attributes provide a mechanism for associating declarative information (metadata) with program elements. This metadata is contained in the compiled assembly, allowing programs to retrieve it through reflection at runtime without creating an instance of the type. (See recipe 3-14 for more details.) Other programs, particularly the CLR, use this information to determine how to interact with and manage program elements.

To create a custom attribute, derive a class from the abstract (MustInherit) base class System.Attribute. Custom attribute classes by convention should have a name ending in Attribute (but this is not essential).

A custom attribute must have at least one Public constructor; the automatically generated default constructor is sufficient. The constructor parameters become the attribute's mandatory (or positional) parameters. When you use the attribute, you must provide values for these parameters in the order they appear in the constructor. As with any other class, you can declare more than one constructor, giving users of the attribute the option of using different sets of positional parameters when applying the attribute. Any Public nonconstant writable fields and properties declared by an attribute are automatically exposed as named parameters. Named parameters are optional and are specified in the format of name-value pairs where the name is the property or field name. The following example will clarify how to specify positional and named parameters.

To control how and where a user can apply your attribute, apply the attribute `AttributeUsageAttribute` to your custom attribute class. `AttributeUsageAttribute` supports the one positional and two named parameters described in Table 3-3. The default values specify the value that is applied to your custom attribute if you do not apply `AttributeUsageAttribute` or do not specify a value for that particular parameter.

Table 3-3. *Members of the AttributeUsage Type*

Parameter	Type	Description	Default
`ValidOn`	Positional (required)	A member of the `System.AttributeTargets` enumeration that identifies the program elements on which the attribute is valid	None; you should set it to `AttributeTargets.All`
`AllowMultiple`	Named (optional)	Whether the attribute can be specified more than once for a single element	`False`
`Inherited`	Named (optional)	Whether the attribute is inherited by derived classes or overridden members	`True`

The Code

The following example shows a custom attribute named `AuthorAttribute`, which you can use to identify the name and company of the person who created an assembly or a class. `AuthorAttribute` declares a single `Public` constructor that takes a `String` containing the author's name. This means users of `AuthorAttribute` must always provide a positional `String` parameter containing the author's name. The `Company` property is `Public`, making it an optional named parameter, but the `Name` property is read-only—no `Set` accessor is declared—meaning that it isn't exposed as a named parameter.

```
Imports System
Namespace Apress.VisualBasicRecipes.Chapter03

    <AttributeUsage(AttributeTargets.Class Or AttributeTargets.Assembly, ➥
AllowMultiple:=True, Inherited:=True)> _
    Public Class AuthorAttribute
        Inherits System.Attribute

        Private m_Company As String    '  Author's company
        Private m_Name As String       '  Author's name

        '  Declare a public constructor.
        Public Sub New(ByVal name As String)
            m_Name = name
            m_Company = ""
        End Sub
```

```
    ' Declare a property to get/set the company field.
    Public Property Company() As String
        Get
            Return m_Company
        End Get

        Set(ByVal value As String)
            m_Company = value
        End Set
    End Property

    ' Declare a property to get the internal field.
    Public ReadOnly Property Name() As String
        Get
            Return m_Name
        End Get
    End Property

    End Class
End Namespace
```

Usage

The following example demonstrates how to decorate types with AuthorAttribute:

```
Imports system

'  Declare Todd as the assembly author. Assembly attributes
'  must be declared after using statements but before any other.
'  Author name is a positional parameter.
'  Company name is a named parameter.
<Assembly: Apress.VisualBasicRecipes.Chapter03.Author("Todd", Company:="The" & ➥
"Code Architects")>
Namespace Apress.VisualBasicRecipes.Chapter03

    '  Declare a class authored by Todd.
    <Author("Todd", Company:="The Code Architects")> _
    Public Class SomeClass
        '  Class implementation.
    End Class

    '  Declare a class authored by Aidan. Since the Company
    '  property is optional, we will leave it out for this test.
    <Author("Aidan")> _
    Public Class SomeOtherClass
        '  Class implementation.
    End Class
End Namespace
```

3-14. Inspect the Attributes of a Program Element Using Reflection

Problem

You need to use reflection to inspect the custom attributes applied to a program element.

Solution

All program elements, such as classes and subroutines, implement the System.Reflection. ICustomAttributeProvider interface. Call the IsDefined method of the ICustomAttributeProvider interface to determine whether an attribute is applied to a program element, or call the GetCustomAttributes method of the ICustomAttributeProvider interface to obtain objects representing the attributes applied to the program element.

How It Works

All the classes that represent program elements implement the ICustomAttributeProvider interface. This includes Assembly, Module, Type, EventInfo, FieldInfo, PropertyInfo, and MethodBase. MethodBase has two further subclasses: ConstructorInfo and MethodInfo. If you obtain instances of any of these classes, you can call the method GetCustomAttributes, which will return an Object array containing the custom attributes applied to the program element. The Object array contains only custom attributes, not those contained in the .NET Framework base class library.

The GetCustomAttributes method provides two overloads. The first takes a Boolean that controls whether GetCustomAttributes should return attributes inherited from parent classes. The second GetCustomAttributes overload takes an additional Type argument that acts as a filter, resulting in GetCustomAttributes returning only attributes of the specified type or those that derive from it.

Alternatively, you can call the IsDefined method. IsDefined provides a method that takes two arguments. The first argument is a Type object representing the type of attribute you are interested in, and the second is a Boolean that indicates whether IsDefined should look for inherited attributes of the specified type. IsDefined returns a Boolean indicating whether the specified attribute is applied to the program element and is less expensive than calling the GetCustomAttributes method, which actually instantiates the attribute objects.

The Code

The following example uses the custom AuthorAttribute declared in recipe 3-13 and applies it to the Recipe03_14 class. The Main method calls the GetCustomAttributes method, filtering the attributes so that the method returns only AuthorAttribute instances. You can safely cast this set of attributes to AuthorAttribute references and access their members without needing to use reflection.

```
Imports System
Namespace Apress.VisualBasicRecipes.Chapter03

    <Author("Aidan"), Author("Todd", Company:="The Code Architects")> _
    Public Class Recipe03_14

        Public Shared Sub Main()

            ' Get a Type object for this class.
            Dim myType As Type = GetType(Recipe03_14)
```

```vbnet
            ' Get the attributes for the type. Apply a filter so that only
            ' instances of AuthorAttributes are returned.
            Dim attrs As Object() = myType.GetCustomAttributes ➡
(GetType(AuthorAttribute), True)


            ' Enumerate the attributes and display their details.
            For Each a As AuthorAttribute In attrs
                Console.WriteLine(a.Name & ", " & a.Company)
            Next

            ' Wait to continue.
            Console.WriteLine(vbCrLf & "Main method complete.  Press Enter.")
            Console.ReadLine()

        End Sub

    End Class
End Namespace
```

CHAPTER 4

■■■

Threads, Processes, and Synchronization

One of the strengths of the Microsoft Windows operating system is that it allows many programs (processes) to run concurrently and allows each process to perform many tasks concurrently (using multiple threads). When you run an executable application, a new process is created. The process isolates your application from other programs running on the computer. The process provides the application with its own virtual memory and its own copies of any libraries it needs to run, allowing your application to execute as if it were the only application running on the machine.

Along with the process, an initial thread is created that runs your `Main` method. In single-threaded applications, this one thread steps through your code and sequentially performs each instruction. If an operation takes time to complete, such as reading a file from the Internet or doing a complex calculation, the application will be unresponsive (will *block)* until the operation is finished, at which point the thread will continue with the next operation in your program.

To avoid blocking, the main thread can create additional threads and specify which code each should start running. As a result, many threads may be running in your application's process, each running (potentially) different code and performing different operations seemingly simultaneously. In reality, unless you have multiple processors (or a single multicore processor) in your computer, the threads are not really running simultaneously. Instead, the operating system coordinates and schedules the execution of all threads across all processes; each thread is given a tiny portion (or *time slice*) of the processor's time, which gives the impression they are executing at the same time.

The difficulty of having multiple threads executing within your application arises when those threads need to access shared data and resources. If multiple threads are changing an object's state or writing to a file at the same time, your data will quickly become corrupted. To avoid problems, you must synchronize the threads to make sure they each get a chance to access the resource, but only one at a time. Synchronization is also important when waiting for a number of threads to reach a certain point of execution before proceeding with a different task and for controlling the number of threads that are at any given time actively performing a task—perhaps processing requests from client applications.

■**Note** Although it will not affect your multithreaded programming in VB .NET, it is worth noting that an operating system thread has no fixed relationship to a managed thread. The runtime host—the managed code that loads and runs the common language runtime (CLR)—controls the relationship between managed and unmanaged threads. A sophisticated runtime host, such as Microsoft SQL Server 2005, can schedule many managed threads against the same operating system thread or can perform the actions of a managed thread using different operating system threads.

This chapter describes how to control processes and threads in your own applications using the features provided by VB .NET and the Microsoft .NET Framework class library. The recipes in this chapter cover the following:

- Executing code in independent threads using features including the thread pool, asynchronous method invocation, and timers (recipes 4-1 through 4-7)

- Synchronizing the execution of multiple threads using a host of synchronization techniques, including monitors, events, mutexes, and semaphores (recipes 4-8 through 4-12)

- Terminating threads and knowing when threads have terminated (recipes 4-13 and 4-14)

- Creating thread-safe instances of the .NET collection classes (recipe 4-15)

- Starting and stopping running in new processes (recipes 4-16 and 4-17)

- Ensuring that only one instance of an application is able to run at any given time (recipe 4-18)

As you will see in this chapter, delegates are used extensively in multithreaded programs to wrap the method that a thread should execute or that should act as a callback when an asynchronous operation is complete. As in earlier versions of VB .NET, the AddressOf operator is used to instruct the compiler to generate the necessary delegate instance. As shown in recipe 1-23, a lambda expression may be used in place of a delegate.

4-1. Execute a Method Using the Thread Pool

Problem

You need to execute a task using a thread from the runtime's thread pool.

Solution

Declare a method containing the code you want to execute. The method's signature must match that defined by the System.Threading.WaitCallback delegate; that is, it must be a subroutine (not a function) and take a single Object argument. Call the Shared method QueueUserWorkItem of the System.Threading.ThreadPool class, passing it your method name. The runtime will queue your method and execute it when a thread-pool thread becomes available.

How It Works

Applications that use many short-lived threads or maintain large numbers of concurrent threads can suffer performance degradation because of the overhead associated with the creation, operation, and destruction of threads. In addition, it is common in multithreaded systems for threads to sit idle a large portion of the time while they wait for the appropriate conditions to trigger their execution. Using a thread pool provides a common solution to improve the scalability, efficiency, and performance of multithreaded systems.

The .NET Framework provides a simple thread-pool implementation accessible through the Shared members of the ThreadPool class. The QueueUserWorkItem method allows you to execute a method using a thread-pool thread by placing a work item into the queue. As a thread from the thread pool becomes available, it takes the next work item from the queue and executes it. The thread performs the work assigned to it, and when it is finished, instead of terminating, the thread returns to the thread pool and takes the next work item from the work queue.

The Code

The following example demonstrates how to use the ThreadPool class to execute a method named DisplayMessage. The example passes DisplayMessage to the thread pool twice: first with no arguments and then with a MessageInfo object, which allows you to control which message the new thread will display.

```vb
Imports System
Imports System.Threading

Namespace Apress.VisualBasicRecipes.Chapter04

    Class Recipe04_01
        ' A private class used to pass data to the DisplayMessage
        ' method when it is executed using the thread pool.
        Private Class MessageInfo
            Private m_Iterations As Integer
            Private m_Message As String

            ' A constructor that takes configuration settings for the thread.
            Public Sub New(ByVal iterations As Integer, ByVal message As String)

                m_Iterations = iterations
                m_Message = message

            End Sub

            ' Properties to retrieve configuration settings.
            Public ReadOnly Property Iterations() As Integer
                Get
                    Return m_Iterations
                End Get
            End Property

            Public ReadOnly Property Message() As String
                Get
                    Return m_Message
                End Get
            End Property

        End Class

        ' A method that conforms to the System.Threading.WaitCallback
        ' delegate signature. Displays a message to the console.
        Public Shared Sub DisplayMessage(ByVal state As Object)
            ' Safely case the state argument to a MessageInfo object.
            Dim config As MessageInfo = TryCast(state, MessageInfo)


            ' If the config argument is Nothing, no arguments were passed to
            ' the ThreadPool.QueueUserWorkItem method; use default values.
            If config Is Nothing Then
                ' Display a fixed message to the console three times.
                For count As Integer = 1 To 3
                    Console.WriteLine("A thread pool example.")
```

```vb
                                    '  Sleep for the purpose of demonstration. Avoid sleeping
                                    '  on thread-pool threads in real applications.
                                    Thread.Sleep(1000)
                            Next
                    Else
                        '  Display the specified message the specified number of times.
                        For count As Integer = 1 To config.Iterations
                            Console.WriteLine(config.Message)

                            '  Sleep for the purpose of demonstration. Avoid sleeping
                            '  on thread-pool threads in real applications.
                            Thread.Sleep(1000)
                        Next
                    End If
            End Sub

            Public Shared Sub Main()

                '  Execute DisplayMessage using the thread pool and no arguments.
                ThreadPool.QueueUserWorkItem(AddressOf DisplayMessage)

                '  Create a MessageInfo object to pass to the DisplayMessage method.
                Dim info As New MessageInfo(5, "A thread pool example with arguments.")

                '  Execute a DisplayMessage using the thread pool and providing an
                '  argument.
                ThreadPool.QueueUserWorkItem(AddressOf DisplayMessage, info)

                '  Wait to continue.
                Console.WriteLine("Main method complete.  Press Enter.")
                Console.ReadLine()

            End Sub
        End Class
End Namespace
```

Notes

Using the runtime's thread pool simplifies multithreaded programming dramatically; however, be aware that the implementation is a simple, general-purpose thread pool. Before deciding to use the thread pool, consider the following points:

- Each process has one thread pool, which supports by default a maximum of 25 concurrent threads per processor. You can change the maximum number of threads using the Shared ThreadPool.SetMaxThreads method, but some runtime hosts (IIS and SQL Server, for example) will limit the maximum number of threads and may not allow the default value to be changed at all.

- Where possible, avoid using the thread pool to execute long-running processes. The limited number of threads in the thread pool means that a handful of threads tied up with long-running processes can significantly affect the overall performance of the thread pool. Specifically, you should avoid putting thread-pool threads to sleep for any length of time.

- Thread-pool threads are background threads. You can configure threads as either foreground threads or background threads. Foreground and background threads are identical, except that a background thread will not keep an application process alive. Therefore, your application will terminate automatically when the last foreground thread of your application terminates.

- You have no control over the scheduling of thread-pool threads, and you cannot prioritize work items. The thread pool handles each work item in the sequence in which you add it to the work queue.

- Once a work item is queued, it cannot be canceled or stopped.

- Do not try to use thread-pool threads to directly update or manipulate Windows Forms controls, because they can be updated only by the thread that created them. For example, suppose that you have a form with a progress bar and a button that starts some action. When you click the button, a thread-pool thread is created to perform the action. Since the progress bar is part of the main application form, it exists on the main application's thread. Attempting to manipulate it from the thread-pool thread can cause unforeseen issues. The proper approach is to call delegate methods from the thread-pool threads and have them manipulate the interface for you. An alternative is to use the BackgroundWorker class, which encapsulates the approach of using delegates to directly access the interface.

4-2. Execute a Method Asynchronously

Problem

You need to start execution of a method and continue with other tasks while the method runs on a separate thread. After the method completes, you need to retrieve the method's return value.

Solution

Declare a delegate with the same signature as the method you want to execute. Create an instance of the delegate that references the method. Call the BeginInvoke method of the delegate instance to start executing your method. Use the EndInvoke method to determine the method's status as well as obtain the method's return value if complete.

How It Works

Typically, when you invoke a method, you do so synchronously, meaning that the calling code blocks until the method is complete. Most of the time, this is the expected, desired behavior because your code requires the operation to complete before it can continue. However, sometimes it is useful to execute a method asynchronously, meaning that you start the method in a separate thread and then continue with other operations.

The .NET Framework implements an asynchronous execution pattern that allows you to call any method asynchronously using a delegate. When you declare and compile a delegate, the compiler automatically generates two methods that support asynchronous execution: BeginInvoke and EndInvoke. When you call BeginInvoke on a delegate instance, the method referenced by the delegate is queued for asynchronous execution. BeginInvoke does not cause the code execution to wait, but rather returns immediately with an IAsyncResult instance. IAsyncResult is used when calling EndInvoke. The method referenced by BeginInvoke executes in the context of the first available thread-pool thread.

The signature of the BeginInvoke method includes the same arguments as those specified by the delegate signature, followed by two additional arguments to support asynchronous completion. These additional arguments are as follows:

- A System.AsyncCallback delegate instance that references a method that the runtime will call when the asynchronous method completes. The method will be executed by a thread-pool thread. Passing Nothing means no method is called, and you must use another mechanism (discussed later in this recipe) to determine when the asynchronous method is complete.

- A reference to an object that the runtime associates with the asynchronous operation for you. The asynchronous method does not use or have access to this object, but it is available to your code when the method completes, allowing you to associate useful state information with an asynchronous operation. For example, this object allows you to map results against initiated operations in situations where you initiate many asynchronous operations that use a common callback method to perform completion.

The EndInvoke method allows you to retrieve the return value of a method that was executed asynchronously, but you must first determine when it has finished. If your asynchronous method threw an exception, it will be rethrown so that you can handle it when you call EndInvoke. Here are the four techniques for determining whether an asynchronous method has finished:

- *Blocking* stops the execution of the current thread until the asynchronous method completes execution by calling EndInvoke. In effect, this is much the same as synchronous execution. However, you have the flexibility to decide exactly when your code enters the blocked state, giving you the opportunity to perform some additional processing before blocking.

- *Polling* involves repeatedly testing the state of an asynchronous method to determine whether it is complete by checking the IsCompleted property of the IAsyncResult returned from BeginInvoke. This is a simple technique and is not particularly efficient from a processing perspective. You should avoid tight loops that consume processor time; it is best to put the polling thread to sleep for a period using Thread.Sleep between completion tests. Because polling involves maintaining a loop, the actions of the waiting thread are limited, but you can easily update some kind of progress indicator.

- *Waiting* depends on the AsyncWaitHandle property of the IAsyncResult returned by BeginInvoke. This object derives from the System.Threading.WaitHandle class and is signaled when the asynchronous method completes. Waiting is a more efficient version of polling and also allows you to wait for multiple asynchronous methods to complete. You can specify time-out values to allow your waiting thread to notify a failure if the asynchronous method takes too long or if you want to periodically update a status indicator.

■**Caution** Even if you do not want to handle the return value of your asynchronous method, you should call EndInvoke; otherwise, you risk leaking memory each time you initiate an asynchronous call using BeginInvoke.

The Code

The following code demonstrates how to use the asynchronous execution pattern. It uses a delegate named AsyncExampleDelegate to execute a method named LongRunningMethod asynchronously. LongRunningMethod simulates a long-running method using a configurable delay (produced using Thread.Sleep). The example contains the following five methods that demonstrate the various approaches to handling asynchronous method completion:

- The BlockingExample method executes LongRunningMethod asynchronously and continues with a limited set of processing. Once this processing is complete, BlockingExample blocks until LongRunningMethod completes. To block, BlockingExample calls the EndInvoke method of the AsyncExampleDelegate delegate instance. If LongRunningMethod has already finished, EndInvoke returns immediately; otherwise, BlockingExample blocks until LongRunningMethod completes.

- The `PollingExample` method executes `LongRunningMethod` asynchronously and then enters a polling loop until `LongRunningMethod` completes. `PollingExample` tests the `IsCompleted` property of the `IAsyncResult` instance returned by `BeginInvoke` to determine whether `LongRunningMethod` is complete; otherwise, `PollingExample` calls `Thread.Sleep`.

- The `WaitingExample` method executes `LongRunningMethod` asynchronously and then waits until `LongRunningMethod` completes. `WaitingExample` uses the `AsyncWaitHandle` property of the `IAsyncResult` instance returned by `BeginInvoke` to obtain a `WaitHandle` and then calls its `WaitOne` method. Using a time-out allows `WaitingExample` to break out of waiting in order to perform other processing or to fail completely if the asynchronous method is taking too long.

- The `WaitAllExample` method executes `LongRunningMethod` asynchronously multiple times and then uses an array of `WaitHandle` objects to wait efficiently until all the methods are complete.

- The `CallbackExample` method executes `LongRunningMethod` asynchronously and passes an `AsyncCallback` delegate instance (that references the `CallbackHandler` method) to the `BeginInvoke` method. The referenced `CallbackHandler` method is called automatically when the asynchronous `LongRunningMethod` completes, leaving the `CallbackExample` method free to continue processing. It's important to note that a reference to the `AsyncExampleDelegate` is passed to the `BeginInvoke` method via the `DelegateAsyncState` parameter. If you did not pass this reference, the callback method would not have access to the delegate instance and would be unable to call `EndInvoke`.

In VB .NET, it is not necessary to implicitly create a delegate instance, such as `Dim longMethod As AsyncExampleDelegate = New AsyncExampleDelegate(AddressOf LongRunningMethod)`. Since the `AddressOf` operator does this automatically, the more efficient statement `Dim longMethod As AsyncExampleDelegate = AddressOf LongRunningMethod` is used instead.

```
Import  System
Imports System.Threading
Imports System.Collections

Namespace Apress.VisualBasicRecipes.Chapter04

    Class Recipe04_02

        '  A utility method for displaying useful trace information to the
        '  console along with details of the current thread.
        Private Shared Sub TraceMsg(ByVal currentTime As DateTime, ➥
ByVal msg As String)

            Console.WriteLine("[{0,3}/{1}] - {2} : {3}", ➥
Thread.CurrentThread.ManagedThreadId, IIf(Thread.CurrentThread.IsThreadPoolThread, ➥
"pool", "fore"), currentTime.ToString("HH:mm:ss.ffff"), msg)

        End Sub

        '  A delegate that allows you to perform asynchronous execution of
        '  LongRunningMethod.
        Public Delegate Function AsyncExampleDelegate(ByVal delay As Integer, ➥
ByVal name As String) As DateTime

        '  A simulated long-running method.
        Public Shared Function LongRunningMethod(ByVal delay As Integer, ➥
ByVal name As String) As DateTime
```

```vb
        TraceMsg(DateTime.Now, name & " example - thread starting.")

        ' Simulate time-consuming process.
        Thread.Sleep(delay)

        TraceMsg(DateTime.Now, name & " example - thread stopping.")

        ' Return the method's completion time.
        Return DateTime.Now

    End Function

    ' This method executes LongRunningMethod asynchronously and continues
    ' with other processing. Once the processing is complete, the method
    ' blocks until LongRunningMethod completes.
    Public Shared Sub BlockingExample()

        Console.WriteLine(Environment.NewLine & "*** Running Blocking " & ➥
    "Example ***")

        ' Invoke LongRunningMethod asynchronously. Pass Nothing for both the
        ' callback delegate and the asynchronous state object.
        Dim longMethod As AsyncExampleDelegate = AddressOf LongRunningMethod
        Dim asyncResult As IAsyncResult = longMethod.BeginInvoke(2000, ➥
    "Blocking", Nothing, Nothing)

        ' Perform other processing until ready to block.
        For count As Integer = 1 To 3
            TraceMsg(DateTime.Now, "Continue processing until ready to block..")

            Thread.Sleep(300)
        Next

        ' Block until the asynchronous method completes.
        TraceMsg(DateTime.Now, "Blocking until method is complete...")

        ' Obtain the completion data for the asynchronous method.
        Dim completion As DateTime = DateTime.MinValue

        Try
            completion = longMethod.EndInvoke(asyncResult)
        Catch ex As Exception
            ' Catch and handle those exceptions you would if calling
            ' LongRunningMethod directly.
        End Try

        ' Display completion information.
        TraceMsg(completion, "Blocking example complete.")

    End Sub

    ' This method executes LongRunningMethod asynchronously and then
    ' enters a polling loop until LongRunningMethod completes.
    Public Shared Sub PollingExample()
```

```
            Console.WriteLine(Environment.NewLine & "*** Running Polling " & ➥
    "Example ***")

            ' Invoke LongRunningMethod asynchronously. Pass Nothing for both the
            ' callback delegate and the asynchronous state object.
            Dim longMethod As AsyncExampleDelegate = AddressOf LongRunningMethod
            Dim asyncResult As IAsyncResult = longMethod.BeginInvoke(2000, ➥
    "Polling", Nothing, Nothing)

            ' Poll the asynchronous method to test for completion. If not
            ' complete, sleep for 300ms before polling again.
            TraceMsg(DateTime.Now, "Poll repeatedly until method is complete.")

            While Not asyncResult.IsCompleted
                TraceMsg(DateTime.Now, "Polling...")
                Thread.Sleep(300)
            End While

            ' Obtain the completion data for the asynchronous method.
            Dim completion As DateTime = DateTime.MinValue

            Try
                completion = longMethod.EndInvoke(asyncResult)
            Catch ex As Exception
                ' Catch and handle those exceptions you would if calling
                ' LongRunningMethod directly.
            End Try

            ' Display completion information.
            TraceMsg(completion, "Polling example complete.")

        End Sub

        ' This method executes LongRunningMethod asynchronously and then
        ' uses a WaitHandle to wait efficiently until LongRunningMethod
        ' completes. Use of a time-out allows the method to break out of
        ' waiting in order to update the user interface or fail if the
        ' asynchronous method is taking too long.
        Public Shared Sub WaitingExample()

            Console.WriteLine(Environment.NewLine & "*** Running Waiting " & ➥
    "Example ***")

            ' Invoke LongRunningMethod asynchronously. Pass Nothing for both the
            ' callback delegate and the asynchronous state object.
            Dim longMethod As AsyncExampleDelegate = AddressOf LongRunningMethod
            Dim asyncResult As IAsyncResult = longMethod.BeginInvoke(2000, ➥
    "Waiting", Nothing, Nothing)

            ' Wait for the asynchronous method to complete. Time-out after
            ' 300ms and display status to the console before continuing to
            ' wait.
            TraceMsg(DateTime.Now, "Waiting until method is complete.")
```

```vb
            While Not asyncResult.AsyncWaitHandle.WaitOne(300, False)
                TraceMsg(DateTime.Now, "Wait timeout...")
            End While

            ' Obtain the completion data for the asynchronous method.
            Dim completion As DateTime = DateTime.MinValue

            Try
                completion = longMethod.EndInvoke(asyncResult)
            Catch ex As Exception
                ' Catch and handle those exceptions you would if calling
                ' LongRunningMethod directly.
            End Try

            ' Display completion information.
            TraceMsg(completion, "Waiting example complete.")

        End Sub

        ' This method executes LongRunningMethod asynchronously multiple
        ' times and then uses an array of WaitHandle objects to wait
        ' efficiently until all of the methods are complete. Use of a
        ' time-out allows the method to break out of waiting in order to
        ' update the user interface or fail if the asynchronous method
        ' is taking too long.
        Public Shared Sub WaitAllExample()

            Console.WriteLine(Environment.NewLine & "*** Running WaitAll " & ➥
"Example ***")

            ' An ArrayList to hold the IAsyncResult instances for each of the
            ' asynchronous methods started.
            Dim asyncResults As New ArrayList(3)

            ' Invoke three LongRunningMethod asynchronously. Pass Nothing for
            ' both the callback delegate and the asynchronous state object. Add
            ' the IAsyncResult instance for each method to the ArrayList.
            Dim longMethod As AsyncExampleDelegate = AddressOf LongRunningMethod

            asyncResults.Add(longMethod.BeginInvoke(3000, "WaitAll 1", Nothing, ➥
Nothing))
            asyncResults.Add(longMethod.BeginInvoke(2500, "WaitAll 2", Nothing, ➥
Nothing))
            asyncResults.Add(longMethod.BeginInvoke(1500, "WaitAll 3", Nothing, ➥
Nothing))

            ' Create an array of WaitHandle objects that will be used to wait
            ' for the completion of all the asynchronous methods.
            Dim waitHandles As WaitHandle() = New WaitHandle(2) {}

            For count As Integer = 0 To 2
                waitHandles(count) = DirectCast(asyncResults(count), ➥
IAsyncResult).AsyncWaitHandle
            Next
```

```vb
    ' Wait for all three asynchronous methods to complete. Time-out
    ' after 300ms and display status to the console before continuing
    ' to wait.
    TraceMsg(DateTime.Now, "Waiting until all 3 methods are complete...")

    While Not WaitHandle.WaitAll(waitHandles, 300, False)
        TraceMsg(DateTime.Now, "WaitAll timeout...")
    End While

    ' Inspect the completion data for each method, and determine the
    ' time at which the final method completed.
    Dim completion As DateTime = DateTime.MinValue

    For Each result As IAsyncResult In asyncResults
        Try
            Dim completedTime As DateTime = longMethod.EndInvoke(result)
            If completedTime > completion Then completion = completedTime
        Catch ex As Exception
            ' Catch and handle those exceptions you would if calling
            ' LongRunningMethod directly.
        End Try
    Next

    ' Display completion information.
    TraceMsg(completion, "WaitAll example complete.")

End Sub

' This method executes LongRunningMethod asynchronously and passes
' an AsyncCallback delegate instance. The referenced CallbackHandler
' method is called automatically when the asynchronous method
' completes, leaving this method free to continue processing.
Public Shared Sub CallbackExample()

    Console.WriteLine(Environment.NewLine & "*** Running Callback" & ➡
"Example ***")

    ' Invoke LongRunningMethod asynchronously. Pass an AsyncCallback
    ' delegate instance referencing the CallbackHandler method that
    ' will be called automatically when the asynchronous method
    ' completes. Pass a reference to the AsyncExampleDelegate delegate
    ' instance as asynchronous state; otherwise, the callback method
    ' has no access to the delegate instance in order to call EndInvoke.
    Dim longMethod As AsyncExampleDelegate = AddressOf LongRunningMethod
    Dim asyncResult As IAsyncResult = longMethod.BeginInvoke(2000, ➡
"Callback", AddressOf CallbackHandler, longMethod)

    ' Continue with other processing.
    For count As Integer = 0 To 15
        TraceMsg(DateTime.Now, "Continue processing...")
        Thread.Sleep(300)
    Next

End Sub
```

```
            ' A method to handle asynchronous completion using callbacks.
            Public Shared Sub CallbackHandler(ByVal result As IAsyncResult)
                ' Extract the reference to the AsyncExampleDelegate instance
                ' from the IAsyncResult instance. This allows you to obtain the
                ' completion data.
                Dim longMethod As AsyncExampleDelegate = DirectCast(result.AsyncState, ➥
AsyncExampleDelegate)

                ' Obtain the completion data for the asynchronous method.
                Dim completion As DateTime = DateTime.MinValue

                Try
                    completion = longMethod.EndInvoke(result)
                Catch ex As Exception
                    ' Catch and handle those exceptions you would if calling
                    ' LongRunningMethod directly.
                End Try

                ' Display completion information.
                TraceMsg(completion, "Callback example complete.")

            End Sub

            <MTAThread()> _
            Public Shared Sub Main()

                ' Demonstrate the various approaches to asynchronous method completion.
                BlockingExample()
                PollingExample()
                WaitingExample()
                WaitAllExample()
                CallbackExample()

                ' Wait to continue.
                Console.WriteLine(Environment.NewLine)
                Console.WriteLine("Main method complete. Press Enter.")
                Console.ReadLine()

            End Sub
        End Class
End Namespace
```

4-3. Creating an Asynchronous Method to Update the User Interface

Problem

You need to execute, in a Windows Forms application, some method asynchronously that needs to be able to safely manipulate the user interface.

Solution

Create an instance of the System.ComponentModel.BackgroundWorker class. Perform the asynchronous action within the DoWork event handler, which is raised when you call the BackgroundWorker. RunWorkerAsync method. To allow the asynchronous method to safely interact with the user interface, include a call to the ReportProgress method (within the DoWork event handler), and handle the ProgressChanged event that it raises.

How It Works

The standard process for executing methods asynchronously is to use delegates to interact with the user interface. This process works well but requires several steps and some careful planning. The BackgroundWorker class, first introduced in .NET 2.0, encapsulates the methodology for using delegates (which is covered in detail in recipe 4-2) making it easy to use when attempting to perform asynchronous updates to an interface. Table 4-1 shows the main methods, properties, and events that make up this class.

Table 4-1. *Properties, Methods, and Events of the BackgroundWorker Class*

Member	Description
Properties	
CancellationPending	A Boolean value that indicates whether CancelAsync was called.
IsBusy	A Boolean value that indicates whether the asynchronous operation has started.
WorkerRerportsProgress	A Boolean value that indicates whether the BackgroundWorker is capable of reporting progress via the ReportProgress method.
WorkerSupportsCancellation	A Boolean value that indicates whether the BackgroundWorker is capable of supporting cancellation via the CancelAsync method.
Methods	
CancelAsync	Sets the CancellationPending property to True.
ReportProgress	Causes the ProgressChange event to be fired. Pass an Integer value, ranging from 0 to 100, to indicate the progress percentage to report.
RunWorkerAsync	Causes the DoWork event to be fired, which starts the asynchronous operation.
Events	
DoWork	Responsible for performing the asynchronous operation and is raised when the RunWorkerAsync is called.
ProgressChanged	Responsible for interacting with the user interface and is raised when the ReportProgress method is called.
RunWorkerCompleted	Responsible for performing any finalization and is raised after the DoWork event finishes.

The first step is to handle the DoWork event. This event runs asynchronously and is where your long-running method should be executed. DoWork is raised when the RunWorkerAsync method is called. This method includes an overload that takes an Object, which is used to pass some data to the asynchronous method. Code within the DoWork event handler should not interact directly with the user interface because this code is executing on a background thread.

When the DoWork event completes, the RunWorkerCompleted event is raised. If you need to return any data from the asynchronous method back to the calling routine, it should be saved to the Result property of the DoWorkEventArgs class within the DoWork event handler. This data is then passed to the Result property of the RunWorkerCompletedEventArgs class and is available for use within the RunWorkerCompleted event handler. Code within the RunWorkerCompleted event handler can safely interact with the user interface directly.

If the asynchronous method needs to be canceled, you need to call the CancelAsync method of the BackgroundWorker class. This method sets the CancellationPending property of the BackgroundWorker class to True. It is your responsibility, within the DoWork event handler, to periodically check whether CancellationPending has been set to True. If it has, you would then cancel the event by setting the Cancel property of the DoWorkEventArgs class to True. In this situation, the RunWorkerCompleted event will still be raised, but the Cancelled property of the RunWorkerCompleted-EventArgs will be set to True so you can quickly determine whether the asynchronous operation was canceled by the user. If CancelArgs is called while the BackgroundWorker.WorkerSupportsCancellation property is False, then an InvalidException is thrown.

If your asynchronous operation needs to update a control on the user interface, such as a progress bar, you would use the ReportProgress method of the BackgroundWorker class. The handler for the ProgressChanged event, which is raised by the ReportProgress method, is able to safely interact with the user interface, so any code to do so should be placed there. Both overloads of the ReportProgress method accept an Integer that are saved to the ProgressPercentage property of the ProgressChangedEventArgs class and can be quickly used to update a progress bar. One of the overloads also lets you specify the data that was initially passed to the RunWorkerAsync method. This data is saved to the UserState property of the ProgressChangedEventArgs class. If ReportProgress is called while the BackgroundWorker.WorkerReportsProgress property is False, then an InvalidException is thrown.

To have access to your BackgroundWorker instance throughout your form, you should be sure to declare it as a global variable (and using WithEvents). It may also be possible to have more than one BackgroundWorker at the same time. In this situation, you will want to cast the sender parameter of the BackgroundWorker events to a BackgroundWorker class in order to have a reference to the appropriate instance.

■**Note** The BackgroundWorker class can be manually instantiated and manipulated through code, or if you are using Visual Studio, you can drag a BackgroundWorker component from the Components tab in the Toolbox directly to your form.

The Code

The example is a simple Windows Forms application that uses the BackgroundWorker class to run a simulated long-running method asynchronously in the background without causing the user interface to freeze. The asynchronous method is started when the Start button is clicked, and it's canceled when the Cancel button is clicked. The progress bar on the form is updated via the ProgressChange event handler.

```vb
Imports System
Imports System.Windows.Forms
Imports System.ComponentModel

'  All designed code is stored in the autogenerated partial
'  class called Recipe04-03.Designer.vb.  You can see this
'  file by selecting "Show All Files" in solution explorer.
Partial Public Class Recipe04_03

    '  Instantiate the BackgroundWorker object
    Dim WithEvents worker As New BackgroundWorker

    Private Sub Recipe04_03_Load(ByVal sender As System.Object, ➥
ByVal e As System.EventArgs) Handles MyBase.Load

        worker.WorkerReportsProgress = True
        worker.WorkerSupportsCancellation = True

    End Sub

    '  Button.Click event handler for the Start button, which
    '  starts the asynchronous operation.
    Private Sub btnStart_Click(ByVal sender As System.Object, ➥
ByVal e As System.EventArgs) Handles btnStart.Click

        '  Configure the form controls.
        btnCancel.Enabled = True
        btnStart.Enabled = False
        progress.Visible = True
        progress.Maximum = 100
        progress.Value = 0

        '  Begin the background operation.
        worker.RunWorkerAsync()

    End Sub

    '  Button.Click event handler for the Cancel button, which
    '  instructs the BackgroundWorker to terminate.
    Private Sub btnCancel_Click(ByVal sender As System.Object, ➥
ByVal e As System.EventArgs) Handles btnCancel.Click

        '  Instruct the BackgroundWorker to terminate
        worker.CancelAsync()

    End Sub

    '  BackgroundWorker.DoWork event handler.  This is where the long running method
    '  that needs to run asynchronously should be executed.
    Private Sub worker_DoWork(ByVal sender As Object, ➥
ByVal e As System.ComponentModel.DoWorkEventArgs) Handles worker.DoWork
```

```vbnet
        ' Get the instance of the BackgroundWorker that raised the event.
        ' This is useful to do in case you have multiple BackgroundWorkers
        ' being handled by this event.
        Dim worker As BackgroundWorker = DirectCast(sender, BackgroundWorker)

        ' Perform a loop and pause the thread for 1 second
        ' to simulate a long running operation.
        For i As Integer = 1 To 10

            ' Check if the user requested the operation to
            ' be canceled.
            If worker.CancellationPending Then
                ' Cancel the event.
                e.Cancel = True
                Exit For
            Else
                ' Pause the thread to simulate some action occurring.
                System.Threading.Thread.Sleep(1000)

                ' Update the progress on the user interface.
                worker.ReportProgress(i * 10)
            End If
        Next

        ' Simulate returning some result back to the main thread.
        If Not e.Cancel Then e.Result = "Successful"

    End Sub

    ' BackgroundWorker.ProgressChanged event handler.  This event is used to update
    ' the user interface, such as updating a progress bar.
    Private Sub worker_ProgressChanged(ByVal sender As Object, ➥
ByVal e As System.ComponentModel.ProgressChangedEventArgs) ➥
Handles worker.ProgressChanged

        ' Update the Progress bar on the form.
        progress.Value = e.ProgressPercentage

    End Sub

    ' BackgroundWorker.RunWorkerCompleted event handler.  This event is raised once
    ' BackgroundWorker.DoWork completes and should be used for finalization.
    Private Sub worker_RunWorkerCompleted(ByVal sender As Object, ➥
ByVal e As System.ComponentModel.RunWorkerCompletedEventArgs) ➥
Handles worker.RunWorkerCompleted

        ' Check if an unhandled exception occurred in the DoWork event.
        If e.Error Is Nothing Then
            ' Check if DoWork was cancelled by the user.
            If Not e.Cancelled Then
                MessageBox.Show("Results:  " & e.Result.ToString)
            Else
                MessageBox.Show("Operation canceled by user")
            End If
```

```
        Else
            ' Display the exception.
            MessageBox.Show(e.Error.ToString)
        End If

        ' Reset form
        progress.Visible = False
        progress.Value = 0
        btnCancel.Enabled = False
        btnStart.Enabled = True

    End Sub

End Class
```

Usage

Figure 4-1 shows an example of what the recipe might look like when it is launched. When the DoWork event completes, a message box appears showing that the method finished successfully. If you click the Cancel button while the method is still executing, then it will be canceled, and the message box will appearing showing it was canceled.

Figure 4-1. *A simple Windows Forms application*

4-4. Execute a Method Periodically

Problem

You need to execute a method in a separate thread periodically.

Solution

Declare a method containing the code you want to execute periodically. The method's signature must match that defined by the System.Threading.TimerCallback delegate; in other words, it must be a subroutine (not a function) and take a single Object argument. Create a System.Threading.Timer object and pass it the method you want to execute, along with a state Object that the timer will pass to your method when the timer fires. The runtime will wait until the timer expires, and then call your method using a thread from the thread pool.

■**Tip** If you are implementing a timer in a Windows Forms application, you should consider using the System. Windows.Forms.Timer, which also provides additional support in Visual Studio that allows you to drag the timer from your Toolbox onto your application. For server-based applications where you want to signal multiple listeners each time the timer fires, consider using the System.Timers.Timer class, which notifies listeners using events.

How It Works

It is often useful to execute a method at regular intervals. For example, you might need to clean a data cache every 20 minutes. The System.Threading.Timer class makes the periodic execution of methods straightforward, allowing you to execute a method referenced by a TimerCallback delegate at specified intervals. The referenced method executes in the context of a thread from the thread pool. (See recipe 4-1 for notes on the appropriate use of thread-pool threads.)

When you create a Timer object, you specify two time intervals. The first value specifies the millisecond delay until the Timer first executes your method. Specify 0 to execute the method immediately, and specify System.Threading.Timeout.Infinite (which is –1) to create the Timer in an unstarted state. The second value specifies the interval in milliseconds; then the Timer will repeatedly call your method following the initial execution. If you specify a value of 0 or Timeout.Infinite, the Timer will execute the method only once (as long as the initial delay is not Timeout.Infinite). You can specify the time intervals as Integer, Long, UInteger, or System.TimeSpan values.

Once you have created a Timer object, you can modify the intervals used by the timer using the Change method, but you cannot change the method that is called. When you have finished with a Timer object, you should call its Dispose method to free system resources held by the timer. Disposing of the Timer object cancels any method that is scheduled for execution.

The Code

The TimerExample class shown next demonstrates how to use a Timer object to call a method named TimerHandler. Initially, the Timer object is configured to call TimerHandler after 2 seconds and then at 1-second intervals. The example allows you to enter a new millisecond interval in the console, which is applied using the Timer.Change method.

```
Imports System
Imports System.Threading

Namespace Apress.VisualBasicRecipes.Chapter04

    Class Recipe04_04

        Public Shared Sub Main()

            ' Create the state object that is passed to the TimerHandler
            ' method when it is triggered. In this case, a message to display.
            Dim state As String = "Timer fired."

            Console.WriteLine("{0} : Creating Timer.", ➡
DateTime.Now.ToString("HH:mm:ss.ffff"))

            ' Create a Timer that fires first after 2 seconds and then every
            ' second. The threadTimer object is automatically disposed at the
            ' end of the Using block.
            Using threadTimer As New Timer(AddressOf TimerTriggered, state, 2000, ➡
1000)

                Dim period As Integer

                ' Read the new timer interval from the console until the
                ' user enters 0 (zero). Invalid values use a default value
                ' of 0, which will stop the example.
```

```
            Do
                Try
                    period = Int32.Parse(Console.ReadLine())
                Catch ex As FormatException
                    period = 0
                End Try

                ' Change the timer to fire using the new interval starting
                ' immediately.
                If period > 0 Then
                    Console.WriteLine("{0} : Changing Timer Interval.", ➥
DateTime.Now.ToString("HH:mm:ss.ffff"))
                    threadTimer.Change(0, period)
                End If

            Loop While period > 0
        End Using

        ' Wait to continue.
        Console.WriteLine("Main method complete. Press Enter.")
        Console.ReadLine()

    End Sub

    Private Shared Sub TimerTriggered(ByVal state As Object)
        Console.WriteLine("{0} : {1}", DateTime.Now.ToString("HH:mm:ss.ffff"), ➥
state)
    End Sub

    End Class
End Namespace
```

4-5. Execute a Method at a Specific Time

Problem

You need to execute a method in a separate thread at a specific time.

Solution

Declare a method containing the code you want to execute. The method's signature must match that defined by the System.Threading.TimerCallback delegate; that is, it must be a subroutine (not a function) and take a single Object argument. Create a System.Threading.Timer object, and pass it the method you want to execute along with a state Object that the timer will pass to your method when the timer expires. Calculate the time difference between the current time and the desired execution time, and configure the Timer object to fire once after this period of time.

How It Works

Executing a method at a particular time is often useful. For example, you might need to back up data at 1 a.m. daily. Although primarily used for calling methods at regular intervals, the Timer object also provides the flexibility to call a method at a specific time.

When you create a Timer object, you specify two time intervals. The first value specifies the millisecond delay until the Timer first executes your method. To execute the method at a specific time, you should set this value to the difference between the current time (System.DateTime.Now) and the desired execution time. The second value specifies the interval after which the Timer will repeatedly call your method following the initial execution. If you specify a value of 0, System.Threading.Timeout. Infinite, or TimeSpan(-1), the Timer object will execute the method only once. If you need the method to execute at a specific time every day, you can easily set this value using TimeSpan.FromDays(1), which represents the number of milliseconds in 24 hours.

The Code

The following code demonstrates how to use a Timer object to execute a method at a specified time. The RunAt method calculates the TimeSpan between the current time and a time specified on the command line (in RFC1123 format) and configures a Timer object to fire once after that period of time.

```
Imports System
Imports System.Threading
Imports System.Globalization

Namespace Apress.VisualBasicRecipes.Chapter04

    Class Recipe04_05
        Public Shared Sub RunAt(ByVal execTime As DateTime)

            ' Calculate the difference between the specified execution
            ' time and the current time.
            Dim waitTime As TimeSpan = execTime - DateTime.Now

            ' Check if a time in the past was specified. If it was, set
            ' the waitTime to TimeSpan(0) which will cause the timer
            ' to execute immediately.
            If waitTime < New TimeSpan(0) Then
                Console.WriteLine("A 'Past' time was specified.")
                Console.WriteLine("Timer will fire immediately.")
                waitTime = New TimeSpan(0)
            End If

            ' Create a Timer that fires once at the specified time. Specify
            ' an interval of -1 to stop the timer executing the method
            ' repeatedly.
            Dim threadTimer As New Timer(AddressOf TimerTriggered, ➥
"Timer Triggered", waitTime, New TimeSpan(-1))

        End Sub

        Private Shared Sub TimerTriggered(ByVal state As Object)
            Console.WriteLine("{0} : {1}", DateTime.Now.ToString("HH:mm:ss.ffff"), ➥
    state)
            Console.WriteLine("Main method complete. Press Enter.")
        End Sub
```

```
      Public Shared Sub Main(ByVal args As String())

          Dim execTime As DateTime

          ' Ensure there is an execution time specified on the command line.
          If args.Length > 0 Then
              ' Convert the string to a datetime. Support only the RFC1123
              ' DateTime pattern.
              Try
                  execTime = DateTime.ParseExact(args(0), "r", Nothing)
                  Console.WriteLine("Current time    : " & ➥
DateTime.Now.ToString("r"))
                  Console.WriteLine("Execution time   : " & ➥
execTime.ToString("r"))

                  RunAt(execTime)
              Catch ex As FormatException
                  Console.WriteLine("Execution time must be of the " & ➥
"format:{0}{1}{2}", ControlChars.NewLine, ControlChars.Tab, ➥
CultureInfo.CurrentCulture.DateTimeFormat.RFC1123Pattern)
              End Try

              ' Wait to continue.
              Console.WriteLine("Waiting for Timer...")
              Console.ReadLine()
          Else
              Console.WriteLine("Specify the time you want the method to " & ➥
"execute using the format :{0}{1} {2}", ControlChars.NewLine, ControlChars.Tab, ➥
CultureInfo.CurrentCulture.DateTimeFormat.RFC1123Pattern)
          End If
      End Sub
   End Class

End Namespace
```

Usage

If you run Recipe04-05 using the following command:

```
Recipe04-05 "Sat, 22 Sep 2007 17:25:00 GMT"
```

you will see output similar to the following:

```
Current time    : Sat, 22 Sep 2007 17:23:56 GMT
Execution time   : Sat, 22 Sep 2007 17:25:00 GMT
Waiting for Timer...
17:25:00.0110 : Timer Triggered

Main method complete. Press Enter.
```

4-6. Execute a Method by Signaling a WaitHandle Object

Problem

You need to execute one or more methods automatically when an object derived from System.Threading.WaitHandle is signaled.

Solution

Declare a method containing the code you want to execute. The method's signature must match that defined by the System.Threading.WaitOrTimerCallback delegate. Using the Shared ThreadPool.RegisterWaitForSingleObject method, register the method to execute and the WaitHandle object that will trigger execution when signaled.

How It Works

You can use classes derived from the WaitHandle class to trigger the execution of a method. Using the RegisterWaitForSingleObject method of the ThreadPool class, you can register a WaitOrTimerCallback delegate instance for execution by a thread-pool thread when a specified WaitHandle-derived object enters a signaled state. You can configure the thread pool to execute the method only once or to automatically reregister the method for execution each time the WaitHandle is signaled. If the WaitHandle is already signaled when you call RegisterWaitForSingleObject, the method will execute immediately. RegisterWaitForSingleObject returns a reference to a RegistereredWaitHandle object. The Unregister method of this class can be used to cancel a registered wait operation.

The class most commonly used as a trigger is AutoResetEvent, which automatically returns to an unsignaled state after it is signaled. However, you can also use the ManualResetEvent, Mutex, and Semaphore classes, which require you to change the signaled state manually. AutoResetEvent and ManualResetEvent derive from the EventWaitHandle class, which in turn derives from WaitHandle, while Mutex and Semaphore derive directly from WaitHandle.

The Code

The following example demonstrates how to use an AutoResetEvent to trigger the execution of a method named ResetEventHandler. (The AutoResetEvent class is discussed further in recipe 4-9.)

```
Imports System
Imports System.Threading

Namespace Apress.VisualBasicRecipes.Chapter04

    Class Recipe04_06

        ' A method that is executed when the AutoResetEvent is signaled
        ' or the wait operation times out.
        Private Shared Sub ResetEventHandler(ByVal state As Object, ByVal ➥
timedOut As Boolean)

            ' Display an appropriate message to the console based on whether
            ' the wait timed out or the AutoResetEvent was signaled.
```

```vbnet
            If timedOut Then
                Console.WriteLine("{0} : Wait timed out.", ➡
DateTime.Now.ToString("HH:mm:ss.ffff"))
            Else
                Console.WriteLine("{0} : {1}", ➡
DateTime.Now.ToString("HH:mm:ss.ffff"), state)
            End If

        End Sub

        Public Shared Sub Main()

            ' Create the new AutoResetEvent in an unsignaled state.
            Dim autoEvent As New AutoResetEvent(False)


            ' Create the state object that is passed to the event handler
            ' method when it is triggered. In this case, a message to display.
            Dim state As String = "AutoResetEvent signaled."

            ' Register the ResetEventHandler method to wait for the AutoResetEvent
            ' to be signaled. Set a time-out of 3 seconds and configure the wait
            ' event to reset after activation (last argument).
            Dim handle As RegisteredWaitHandle = ➡
ThreadPool.RegisterWaitForSingleObject(autoEvent, AddressOf ResetEventHandler, ➡
state, 3000, False)

            Console.WriteLine("Press ENTER to signal the AutoResetEvent or enter" & ➡
"""CANCEL""" to unregister the wait operation.")

            While Not Console.ReadLine.ToUpper = "CANCEL"
                ' If "CANCEL" has not been entered into the console, signal
                ' the AutoResetEvent, which will cause the EventHandler
                ' method to execute. The AutoResetEvent will automatically
                ' revert to an unsignaled state.
                autoEvent.Set()
            End While

            ' Unregister the wait operation.
            Console.WriteLine("Unregistering wait operation.")
            handle.Unregister(Nothing)

            ' Wait to continue.
            Console.WriteLine("Main method complete. Press Enter.")
            Console.ReadLine()

        End Sub

    End Class
End Namespace
```

4-7. Execute a Method Using a New Thread

Problem

You need to execute code in its own thread, and you want complete control over the thread's state and operation.

Solution

Declare a method containing the code you want to execute. The method's signature must match that defined by the `System.Threading.ThreadStart` or `System.Threading.ParameterizedThreadStart` delegates. Create a new `System.Threading.Thread` object, and pass the method delegate as an argument to its constructor. Call the `Thread.Start` method to start the execution of your method.

How It Works

For maximum control and flexibility when creating multithreaded applications, you need to take a direct role in creating and managing threads. This is the most complex approach to multithreaded programming, but it is the only way to overcome the restrictions and limitations inherent in the approaches using thread-pool threads, as discussed in the preceding recipes. The `Thread` class provides the mechanism through which you create and control threads. To create and start a new thread, follow this process:

1. Define a method that matches the `ThreadStart` or `ParameterizedThreadStart` delegate. The `ThreadStart` delegate takes no arguments and must be a subroutine (not a function). This means you cannot easily pass data to your new thread. The `ParameterizedThreadStart` delegate must also be a subroutine but takes a single `Object` as an argument, allowing you to pass data to the method you want to run. The method you want to execute can be `Shared` or an instance method.

2. Create a new `Thread` object, and pass a delegate to your method as an argument to the `Thread` constructor. The new thread has an initial state of `Unstarted` (a member of the `System.Threading.ThreadState` enumeration) and is a foreground thread by default. If you want to configure it to be a background thread, you need to set its `IsBackground` property to `True`.

3. Call `Start` on the `Thread` object, which changes its state to `ThreadState.Running` and begins execution of your method. If you need to pass data to your method, include it as an argument to the `Start` call, or use the `ParameterizedThreadStart` delegate mentioned earlier. If you call `Start` more than once, it will throw a `System.Threading.ThreadStateException`.

The Code

The following code demonstrates how to execute a method in a new thread and how to pass data to the new thread.

```
Imports System
Imports System.Threading

Namespace Apress.VisualBasicRecipes.Chapter04

    Class Recipe04_07

        ' A utility method for displaying useful trace information to the
        ' console along with details of the current thread.
```

```vb
        Private Shared Sub TraceMsg(ByVal msg As String)
            Console.WriteLine("[{0,3}] - {1} : {2}", ➡
Thread.CurrentThread.ManagedThreadId, DateTime.Now.ToString("HH:mm:ss.ffff"), msg)
        End Sub

        ' A private class used to pass initialization data to a new thread.
        Private Class ThreadStartData

            ' Member variables hold initialization data for a new thread.
            Private ReadOnly m_Iterations As Integer
            Private ReadOnly m_Message As String
            Private ReadOnly m_Delay As Integer

            Public Sub New(ByVal iterations As Integer, ByVal message As String, ➡
ByVal delay As Integer)
                m_Iterations = iterations
                m_Message = message
                m_Delay = delay
            End Sub

            ' Properties provide read-only access to initialization data.
            Public ReadOnly Property Iterations()
                Get
                    Return m_Iterations
                End Get
            End Property

            Public ReadOnly Property Message()
                Get
                    Return m_Message
                End Get
            End Property

            Public ReadOnly Property Delay()
                Get
                    Return m_Delay
                End Get
            End Property

        End Class

        ' Declare the method that will be executed in its own thread. The
        ' method displays a message to the console a specified number of
        ' times, sleeping between each message for a specified duration.
        Private Shared Sub DisplayMessage(ByVal config As Object)
            Dim data As ThreadStartData = TryCast(config, ThreadStartData)

            If Not data Is Nothing Then
                For count As Integer = 0 To data.Iterations - 1
                    TraceMsg(data.Message)

                    ' Sleep for the specified period.
                    Thread.Sleep(data.Delay)
                Next
```

```
        Else
            TraceMsg("Invalid thread configuration.")
        End If

    End Sub

    Public Shared Sub Main()

        ' Create a new Thread object specifying DisplayMessage
        ' as the method it will execute.
        Dim newThread As New Thread(AddressOf DisplayMessage)

        ' Create a new ThreadStartData object to configure the thread.
        Dim config As New ThreadStartData(5, "A thread example.", 500)

        TraceMsg("Starting new thread.")

        ' Start the new thread and pass the ThreadStartData object
        ' containing the initialization data.
        newThread.Start(config)

        ' Continue with other processing.
        For count As Integer = 0 To 12
            TraceMsg("Main thread continuing processing...")
            Thread.Sleep(200)
        Next

        ' Wait to continue.
        Console.WriteLine(Environment.NewLine)
        Console.WriteLine("Main method complete. Press Enter.")
        Console.ReadLine()

    End Sub

    End Class
End Namespace
```

4-8. Synchronize the Execution of Multiple Threads Using a Monitor

Problem

You need to coordinate the activities of multiple threads to ensure the efficient use of shared resources or to ensure several threads are not updating the same shared resource at the same time.

Solution

Identify an appropriate object to use as a mechanism to control access to the shared resource/data. Use the Shared method Monitor.Enter to acquire a lock on the object, and use the Shared method Monitor.Exit to release the lock so another thread may acquire it.

How It Works

The greatest challenge in writing a multithreaded application is ensuring that the threads work in concert. This is commonly referred to as *thread synchronization* and includes the following:

- Ensuring threads access shared objects and data correctly so that they do not cause corruption

- Ensuring threads execute only when they are meant to and cause minimum overhead when they are idle

The most commonly used synchronization mechanism is the System.Threading.Monitor class. The Monitor class allows a single thread to obtain an exclusive lock on an object by calling the Shared method Monitor.Enter. By acquiring an exclusive lock prior to accessing a shared resource or data, you ensure that only one thread can access the resource concurrently. Once the thread has finished with the resource, release the lock to allow another thread to access it. A block of code that enforces this behavior is often referred to as a *critical section*.

■Note Monitors are managed-code synchronization mechanisms that do not rely on any specific operating system primitives. This ensures your code is portable should you want to run it on a non-Windows platform. This is in contrast to the synchronization mechanisms discussed in recipes 4-9, 4-10, and 4-11, which rely on Win32 operating system–based synchronization objects.

You can use any object to act as the lock; it is common to use the keyword Me to obtain a lock on the current object, but it is better to use a separate object dedicated to the purpose of synchronization. The key point is that all threads attempting to access a shared resource must try to acquire the *same* lock. Other threads that attempt to acquire a lock using Monitor.Enter on the same object will block (enter a WaitSleepJoin state) and are added to the lock's *ready queue* until the thread that owns the lock releases it by calling the Shared method Monitor.Exit. When the owning thread calls Exit, one of the threads from the ready queue acquires the lock. We say "one of the threads" because threads are not necessarily executed in any specific order. If the owner of a lock does not release it by calling Exit, all other threads will block indefinitely. Therefore, it is important to place the Exit call within a Finally block to ensure that it is called even if an exception occurs. To ensure threads do not wait indefinitely, you can specify a time-out value when you call Monitor.Enter.

■Tip Because Monitor is used so frequently in multithreaded applications, VB .NET provides language-level support through the Synclock statement, which the compiler translates to the use of the Monitor class. A block of code encapsulated in a Synclock statement is equivalent to calling Monitor.Enter when entering the block and Monitor.Exit when exiting the block. In addition, the compiler automatically places the Monitor.Exit call in a Finally block to ensure that the lock is released if an exception is thrown.

Using Monitor.Enter and Monitor.Exit is often all you will need to correctly synchronize access to a shared resource in a multithreaded application. However, when you are trying to coordinate the activation of a pool of threads to handle work items from a shared queue, Monitor.Enter and Monitor.Exit will not be sufficient. In this situation, you want a potentially large number of threads to wait efficiently until a work item becomes available without putting unnecessary load on the central processing unit (CPU). This is where you need the fine-grained synchronization control provided by the Monitor.Wait, Monitor.Pulse, and Monitor.PulseAll methods.

The thread that currently owns the lock can call Monitor.Wait, which will release the lock and place that thread on the lock's *wait queue*. Threads in a wait queue also have a state of WaitSleepJoin and will continue to block until a thread that owns the lock calls either the Monitor.Pulse method or the Monitor.PulseAll method. Monitor.Pulse moves one of the waiting threads from the wait queue to the ready queue, and Monitor.PulseAll moves all threads. Once a thread has moved from the wait queue to the ready queue, it can acquire the lock the next time the lock is released. It is important to understand that threads on a lock's wait queue *will not* acquire a released lock; they will wait indefinitely until you call Monitor.Pulse or Monitor.PulseAll to move them to the ready queue.

So, in practice, when your pool threads are inactive, they sit in the wait queue. As a new work item arrives, a dispatcher obtains the lock and calls Monitor.Pulse, moving one worker thread to the ready queue, where it will obtain the lock as soon as the dispatcher releases it. The worker thread takes the work item, releases the lock, and processes the work item. Once the worker thread has finished with the work item, it again obtains the lock in order to take the next work item, but if there is no work item to process, the thread calls Monitor.Wait and goes back to the wait queue.

The Code

The following example demonstrates how to synchronize access to a shared resource (the console) and the activation of waiting threads using the Monitor.Wait, Monitor.Pulse, and Monitor.PulseAll methods. The example starts three worker threads that take work items from a queue and processes them. These threads initially have no work items and are put into a wait state using Monitor.Wait. When the user presses Enter the first two times, work items (strings in the example) are added to the work queue, and Monitor.Pulse is called to release one waiting thread for each work item. The third time the user presses Enter, Monitor.PulseAll is called, releasing all waiting threads and allowing them to terminate.

```
Imports System
Imports System.Threading
Imports System.Collections.Generic

Namespace Apress.VisualBasicRecipes.Chapter04

    Class Recipe04_08

        ' Declare an object for synchronization of access to the console.
        ' A shared object is used because you are using it in shared methods.
        Private Shared consoleGate As New Object

        ' Declare a Queue to represent the work queue.
        Private Shared workQueue As New Queue(Of String)

        ' Declare a flag to indicate to activated threads that they should
        ' terminate and not process more work items.
        Private Shared workItemsProcessed As Boolean = False

        ' A utility method for displaying useful trace information to the
        ' console along with details of the current thread.
        Private Shared Sub TraceMsg(ByVal msg As String)

            SyncLock consoleGate
                Console.WriteLine("[{0,3}/{1}] - {2} : {3}", ➥
Thread.CurrentThread.ManagedThreadId, IIf(Thread.CurrentThread.IsThreadPoolThread, ➥
"pool", "fore"), DateTime.Now.ToString("HH:mm:ss.ffff"), msg)
            End SyncLock

        End Sub
```

```vb
' Declare the method that will be executed by each thread to process
' items from the work queue.
Private Shared Sub ProcessWorkItems()

    ' A local variable to hold the work item taken from the work queue.
    Dim workItem As String = Nothing

    TraceMsg("Thread started, processing items from the queue...")

    ' Process items from the work queue until termination is signaled.
    While Not workItemsProcessed
        ' Obtain the lock on the work queue.
        Monitor.Enter(workQueue)

        Try
            ' Pop the next work item and process it, or wait if none
            ' are available.
            If workQueue.Count = 0 Then
                TraceMsg("No work items, waiting...")

                ' Wait until Pulse is called on the workQueue object.
                Monitor.Wait(workQueue)
            Else
                ' Obtain the next work item.
                workItem = workQueue.Dequeue
            End If
        Catch
        Finally
            ' Always release the lock.
            Monitor.Exit(workQueue)
        End Try

        ' Process the work item if one was obtained.
        If Not workItem Is Nothing Then
            ' Obtain a lock on the console and display a series
            ' of messages.
            SyncLock consoleGate
                For i As Integer = 0 To 4
                    TraceMsg("Processing " & workItem)
                    Thread.Sleep(200)
                Next
            End SyncLock

            ' Reset the status of the local variable.
            workItem = Nothing
        End If
    End While

    ' This will be reached only if workItemsProcessed is true.
    TraceMsg("Terminating.")
End Sub
```

```
Public Shared Sub Main()

    TraceMsg("Starting worker threads.")

    ' Add an initial work item to the work queue.
    SyncLock workQueue
        workQueue.Enqueue("Work Item 1")
    End SyncLock

    ' Create and start three new worker threads running the
    ' ProcessWorkItems method.
    For count As Integer = 1 To 3
        Dim newThread As New Thread(AddressOf ProcessWorkItems)
        newThread.Start()
    Next

    Thread.Sleep(1500)

    ' The first time the user presses Enter, add a work item and
    ' activate a single thread to process it.
    TraceMsg("Press Enter to pulse one waiting thread.")
    Console.ReadLine()

    ' Acquire a lock on the workQueue object.
    SyncLock workQueue
        ' Add a work item.
        workQueue.Enqueue("Work Item 2.")

        ' Pulse 1 waiting thread.
        Monitor.Pulse(workQueue)
    End SyncLock

    Thread.Sleep(2000)

    ' The second time the user presses Enter, add three work items and
    ' activate three threads to process them.
    TraceMsg("Press Enter to pulse three waiting threads.")
    Console.ReadLine()

    ' Acquire a lock on the workQueue object.
    SyncLock workQueue
        ' Add work items to the work queue, and activate worker threads.
        workQueue.Enqueue("Work Item 3.")
        Monitor.Pulse(workQueue)
        workQueue.Enqueue("Work Item 4.")
        Monitor.Pulse(workQueue)
        workQueue.Enqueue("Work Item 5.")
        Monitor.Pulse(workQueue)
    End SyncLock

    Thread.Sleep(3500)
```

```
        ' The third time the user presses Enter, signal the worker threads
        ' to terminate and activate them all.
        TraceMsg("Press Enter to pulse all waiting threads.")
        Console.ReadLine()

        ' Acquire a lock on the workQueue object.
        SyncLock workQueue
            ' Signal that threads should terminate.
            workItemsProcessed = True

            ' Pulse all waiting threads.
            Monitor.PulseAll(workQueue)
        End SyncLock

        Thread.Sleep(1000)


        ' Wait to continue.
        TraceMsg("Main method complete. Press Enter.")
        Console.ReadLine()

    End Sub

    End Class
End Namespace
```

4-9. Synchronize the Execution of Multiple Threads Using an Event

Problem

You need a mechanism to synchronize the execution of multiple threads in order to coordinate their activities or access to shared resources.

Solution

Use the EventWaitHandle, AutoResetEvent, and ManualResetEvent classes from the System.Threading namespace.

How It Works

The EventWaitHandle, AutoResetEvent, and ManualResetEvent classes provide similar functionality. The EventWaitHandle class is the base class from which the AutoResetEvent and ManualResetEvent classes are derived. EventWaitHandle inherits directly from System.Threading.WaitHandle and allows you to create named events. All three event classes allow you to synchronize multiple threads by manipulating the state of the event between two possible values: *signaled* and *unsignaled.*

Threads requiring synchronization call Shared or inherited methods of the WaitHandle abstract base class (summarized in Table 4-2) to test the state of one or more event objects. If the events are signaled when tested, the thread continues to operate unhindered. If the events are unsignaled, the thread enters a WaitSleepJoin state, blocking until one or more of the events become signaled or when a given time-out expires.

Table 4-2. *WaitHandle Methods for Synchronizing Thread Execution*

Method	Description
WaitOne	Causes the calling thread to enter a WaitSleepJoin state and wait for a specific WaitHandle derived object to be signaled. You can also specify a time-out value. The WaitingExample method in recipe 4-2 demonstrates how to use the WaitOne method.
WaitAny	A Shared method that causes the calling thread to enter a WaitSleepJoin state and wait for any one of the objects in a WaitHandle array to be signaled. You can also specify a time-out value.
WaitAll	A Shared method that causes the calling thread to enter a WaitSleepJoin state and wait for all the WaitHandle objects in a WaitHandle array to be signaled. You can also specify a time-out value. The WaitAllExample method in recipe 4-2 demonstrates how to use the WaitAll method.
SignalAndWait	A Shared method that causes the calling thread to signal a specified event object and then wait on a specified event object. The signal and wait operations are carried out as an atomic operation. You can also specify a time-out value.

The key differences between the three event classes are how they transition from a signaled to an unsignaled state and their visibility. Both the AutoResetEvent and ManualResetEvent classes are local to the process in which they are declared. To signal an AutoResetEvent class, call its Set method, which will release only one thread that is waiting on the event. The AutoResetEvent class will then automatically return to an unsignaled state. The code in recipe 4-6 demonstrates how to use an AutoResetEvent class.

The ManualResetEvent class must be manually switched back and forth between signaled and unsignaled states using its Set and Reset methods. Calling Set on a ManualResetEvent class will set it to a signaled state, releasing all threads that are waiting on the event. Only by calling Reset does the ManualResetEvent class become unsignaled.

You can configure the EventWaitHandle class to operate in a manual or automatic reset mode, making it possible to act like either the AutoResetEvent class or the ManualResetEvent class. When you create the EventWaitHandle, you pass a value of the System.Threading.EventResetMode enumeration to configure the mode in which the EventWaitHandle will function; the two possible values are AutoReset and ManualReset. The unique benefit of the EventWaitHandle class is that it is not constrained to the local process. When you create an EventWaitHandle class, you can associate a name with it that makes it accessible to other processes, including nonmanaged Win32 code. This allows you to synchronize the activities of threads across process and application domain boundaries and synchronize access to resources that are shared by multiple processes. To obtain a reference to an existing named EventWaitHandle, call one of the available constructors of the Shared method EventWaitHandle. OpenExisting, and specify the name of the event.

The Code

The following example demonstrates how to use a named EventWaitHandle in manual mode that is initially signaled. A thread is spawned that waits on the event and then displays a message to the console—repeating the process every 2 seconds. When you press Enter, you toggle the event between a signaled and an unsignaled state. This example uses the Join keyword to cause the application's execution to wait until the thread terminates. Join is covered in more detail in recipe 4-13.

```
Imports System
Imports System.Threading

Namespace Apress.VisualBasicRecipes.Chapter04

    Class Recipe04_09

        ' Boolean to signal that the second thread should terminate.
        Public Shared terminate As Boolean = False

        ' A utility method for displaying useful trace information to the
        ' console along with details of the current thread.
        Private Shared Sub TraceMsg(ByVal msg As String)
            Console.WriteLine("[{0,3}] - {1} : {2}", ➥
Thread.CurrentThread.ManagedThreadId, DateTime.Now.ToString("HH:mm:ss.ffff"), msg)
        End Sub

        ' Declare the method that will be executed on the separate thread.
        ' The method waits on the EventWaitHandle before displaying a message
        ' to the console and then waits two seconds and loops.
        Private Shared Sub DisplayMessage()

            ' Obtain a handle to the EventWaitHandle with the name "EventExample".
            Dim eventHandle As EventWaitHandle = ➥
EventWaitHandle.OpenExisting("EventExample")

            TraceMsg("DisplayMessage Started.")

            While Not terminate
                ' Wait on the EventWaitHandle, time-out after two seconds. WaitOne
                ' returns true if the event is signaled; otherwise, false. The
                ' first time through, the message will be displayed immediately
                ' because the EventWaitHandle was created in a signaled state.
                If eventHandle.WaitOne(2000, True) Then
                    TraceMsg("EventWaitHandle In Signaled State.")
                Else
                    TraceMsg("WaitOne Time Out -- EventWaitHandle In" & ➥
"Unsignaled State.")
                End If
                Thread.Sleep(2000)
            End While

            TraceMsg("Thread Terminating.")
        End Sub

        Public Shared Sub Main()

            ' Create a new EventWaitHandle with an initial signaled state, in
            ' manual mode, with the name "EventExample".
            Using eventHandle As New EventWaitHandle(True, ➥
```

```vbnet
            EventResetMode.ManualReset, "EventExample")
                        ' Create and start a new thread running the DisplayMessage
                        ' method.
                        TraceMsg("Starting DisplayMessageThread.")
                        Dim newThread As New Thread(AddressOf DisplayMessage)
                        newThread.Start()

                        ' Allow the EventWaitHandle to be toggled between a signaled and
                        ' unsignaled state up to three times before ending.
                        For count As Integer = 1 To 3
                            ' Wait for Enter to be pressed.
                            Console.ReadLine()


                            ' You need to toggle the event. The only way to know the
                            ' current state is to wait on it with a 0 (zero) time-out
                            ' and test the result.
                            If eventHandle.WaitOne(0, True) Then
                                TraceMsg("Switching Event To UnSignaled State.")

                                ' Event is signaled, so unsignal it.
                                eventHandle.Reset()
                            Else
                                TraceMsg("Switching Event To Signaled State.")

                                ' Event is unsignaled, so signal it.
                                eventHandle.Set()
                            End If
                        Next

                        ' Terminate the DisplayMessage thread, and wait for it to
                        ' complete before disposing of the EventWaitHandle.
                        terminate = True
                        eventHandle.Set()
                        newThread.Join(5000)

                End Using

                ' Wait to continue.
                Console.WriteLine(Environment.NewLine)
                Console.WriteLine("Main method complete. Press Enter.")
                Console.ReadLine()

            End Sub

        End Class
End Namespace
```

4-10. Synchronize the Execution of Multiple Threads Using a Mutex

Problem

You need to coordinate the activities of multiple threads (possibly across process boundaries) to ensure the efficient use of shared resources or to ensure several threads are not updating the same shared resource at the same time.

Solution

Use the System.Threading.Mutex class.

How It Works

The Mutex has a similar purpose to the Monitor discussed in recipe 4-8—it provides a means to ensure only a single thread has access to a shared resource or section of code at any given time. However, unlike the Monitor, which is implemented fully within managed code, the Mutex is a wrapper around an operating system synchronization object. This means you can use a Mutex to synchronize the activities of threads across process boundaries, even with threads running in nonmanaged Win32 code. If you need to open an existing mutex, you can use the OpenExisting or one of the constructor overloads that lets you specify a name.

Like the EventWaitHandle, AutoResetEvent, and ManualResetEvent classes discussed in recipe 4-9, the Mutex is derived from System.Threading.WaitHandle and enables thread synchronization in a similar fashion. A Mutex is in either a signaled state or an unsignaled state. A thread acquires ownership of the Mutex at construction or by using one of the methods listed earlier in Table 4-2. If a thread has ownership of the Mutex, the Mutex is unsignaled, meaning other threads will block if they try to acquire ownership. Ownership of the Mutex is released by the owning thread calling the Mutex.ReleaseMutex method, which signals the Mutex and allows another thread to acquire ownership. A thread may acquire ownership of a Mutex any number of times without problems, but it must release the Mutex an equal number of times to free it and make it available for another thread to acquire. If the thread with ownership of a Mutex terminates normally, the Mutex automatically becomes signaled, allowing another thread to acquire ownership.

The Code

The following example demonstrates how to use a named Mutex to limit access to a shared resource (the console) to a single thread at any given time. This example uses the Join keyword to cause the application's execution to wait until the thread terminates. Join is covered in more detail in recipe 4-13.

```
Imports System
Imports System.Threading

Namespace Apress.VisualBasicRecipes.Chapter04

    Class Recipe04_10

        ' Boolean to signal that the second thread should terminate.
        Public Shared terminate As Boolean = False
```

```vb
    ' A utility method for displaying useful trace information to the
    ' console along with details of the current thread.
    Private Shared Sub TraceMsg(ByVal msg As String)
        Console.WriteLine("[{0,3}] - {1} : {2}", ➡
Thread.CurrentThread.ManagedThreadId, DateTime.Now.ToString("HH:mm:ss.ffff"), msg)
    End Sub

    ' Declare the method that will be executed on the separate thread.
    ' In a loop the method waits to obtain a Mutex before displaying a
    ' a message to the console and then waits one second before releasing
    ' the Mutex.
    Private Shared Sub DisplayMessage()

        ' Obtain a handle to the Mutex with the name MutexExample.
        ' Do not attempt to take ownership immediately.
        Using newMutex As New Mutex(False, "MutexExample")
            TraceMsg("Thread Started.")

            While Not terminate
                ' Wait on the Mutex.
                newMutex.WaitOne()


                TraceMsg("Thread owns the Mutex.")
                Thread.Sleep(1000)
                TraceMsg("Thread releasing the Mutex.")

                ' Release the Mutex.
                newMutex.ReleaseMutex()

                ' Sleep a little to give another thread a good chance of
                ' acquiring the Mutex.
                Thread.Sleep(100)
            End While
            TraceMsg("Thread terminating.")
        End Using

    End Sub

    Public Shared Sub Main()

        TraceMsg("Starting threads -- press Enter to terminate.")

        ' Create and start three new threads running the
        ' DisplayMessage method.
        Dim thread1 As New Thread(AddressOf DisplayMessage)
        Dim thread2 As New Thread(AddressOf DisplayMessage)
        Dim thread3 As New Thread(AddressOf DisplayMessage)

        thread1.Start()
        thread2.Start()
        thread3.Start()
```

```
'   Wait for Enter to be pressed.
    Console.ReadLine()

'   Terminate the DisplayMessage threads, and wait for them to
'   complete before disposing of the Mutex.
    terminate = True
    thread1.Join(5000)
    thread2.Join(5000)
    thread3.Join(5000)

'   Wait to continue.
    Console.WriteLine(Environment.NewLine)
    Console.WriteLine("Main method complete. Press Enter.")
    Console.ReadLine()

        End Sub

    End Class
End Namespace
```

4-11. Synchronize the Execution of Multiple Threads Using a Semaphore

Problem

You need to control the number of threads that can access a shared resource or section of code concurrently.

Solution

Use the System.Threading.Semaphore class.

How It Works

The Semaphore is another synchronization class derived from the System.Threading.WaitHandle class. The purpose of the Semaphore is to allow a specified maximum number of threads to access a shared resource or section of code concurrently.

As with the other synchronization classes derived from WaitHandle (discussed in recipes 4-9 and 4-10), a Semaphore is either in a signaled state or in an unsignaled state. Threads wait for the Semaphore to become signaled using the methods described earlier in Table 4-2. The Semaphore maintains a count of the active threads it has allowed through and automatically switches to an unsignaled state once the maximum number of threads is reached. The Release method of the Semaphore object is used to signal the Semaphore, allowing other waiting threads the opportunity to act. A thread may acquire ownership of the Semaphore more than once, reducing the maximum number of threads that can be active concurrently, and must call Release the same number of times to fully release it. To make things a little easier, the Release method includes an overload that allows you to specify the number of threads that should be released.

The Code

The following example demonstrates how to use a named Semaphore to limit access to a shared resource (the console) to two threads at any given time. The code is similar to that used in recipe 4-10 but substitutes a Semaphore for the Mutex. This example uses the Join keyword to cause the application's execution to wait until the thread terminates. Join is covered in more detail in recipe 4-13.

```vb
Imports System
Imports System.Threading

Namespace Apress.VisualBasicRecipes.Chapter04

    Class Recipe04_11

        ' Boolean to signal that the second thread should terminate.
        Public Shared terminate As Boolean = False


        ' A utility method for displaying useful trace information to the
        ' console along with details of the current thread.
        Private Shared Sub TraceMsg(ByVal msg As String)
            Console.WriteLine("[{0,3}] - {1} : {2}", ➡
Thread.CurrentThread.ManagedThreadId, DateTime.Now.ToString("HH:mm:ss.ffff"), msg)
        End Sub

        ' Declare the method that will be executed on the separate thread.
        ' In a loop the method waits to obtain a Semaphore before displaying a
        ' a message to the console and then waits one second before releasing
        ' the Semaphore.
        Private Shared Sub DisplayMessage()

            ' Obtain a handle to the Semaphore, created in main, with the name
            ' SemaphoreExample. Do not attempt to take ownership immediately.
            Using sem As Semaphore = Semaphore.OpenExisting("SemaphoreExample")
                TraceMsg("Thread Started.")

                While Not terminate
                    ' Wait on the Semaphore.
                    sem.WaitOne()

                    TraceMsg("Thread owns the Semaphore.")
                    Thread.Sleep(1000)
                    TraceMsg("Thread releasing the Semaphore.")

                    ' Release the Semaphore.
                    sem.Release()

                    ' Sleep a little to give another thread a good chance of
                    ' acquiring the Semaphore.
                    Thread.Sleep(100)
                End While
                TraceMsg("Thread terminating.")
            End Using

        End Sub


        Public Shared Sub Main()
```

```
    ' Create a new Semaphore with the name SemaphoreExample.
    Using sem As New Semaphore(2, 2, "SemaphoreExample")
        TraceMsg("Starting threads -- press Enter to terminate.")

        ' Create and start three new threads running the
        ' DisplayMessage method.
        Dim thread1 As New Thread(AddressOf DisplayMessage)
        Dim thread2 As New Thread(AddressOf DisplayMessage)
        Dim thread3 As New Thread(AddressOf DisplayMessage)

        thread1.Start()
        thread2.Start()
        thread3.Start()

        ' Wait for Enter to be pressed.
        Console.ReadLine()

        ' Terminate the DisplayMessage threads, and wait for them to
        ' complete before disposing of the Semaphore.
        terminate = True
        thread1.Join(5000)
        thread2.Join(5000)
        thread3.Join(5000)

    End Using

    ' Wait to continue.
    Console.WriteLine(Environment.NewLine)
    Console.WriteLine("Main method complete. Press Enter.")
    Console.ReadLine()

  End Sub

 End Class
End Namespace
```

4-12. Synchronize Access to a Shared Data Value

Problem

You need to ensure operations on a numeric data value are executed atomically so that multiple threads accessing the value do not cause errors or corruption.

Solution

Use the Shared members of the System.Threading.Interlocked class.

How It Works

The Interlocked class contains several Shared methods that perform some simple arithmetic and comparison operations on a variety of data types and ensure the operations are carried out atomically. Table 4-3 summarizes the methods and the data types on which they can be used. Note that the methods use the ByRef keyword on their arguments to allow the method to update the value of the actual value type variable passed in. If an operation (such as subtraction) you want to perform is not supported by the Interlocked class, you will need to implement your own synchronization using the other approaches described in this chapter.

Table 4-3. *Interlocked Methods for Synchronizing Data Access*

Method	Description
Add	Adds two Integer or Long values and sets the value of the first argument to the sum of the two values.
CompareExchange	Compares two values; if they are the same, sets the first argument to a specified value. This method has overloads to support the comparison and exchange of Integer, Long, Single, Double, Object, and System.IntPtr.
Decrement	Decrements an Integer or Long value.
Exchange	Sets the value of a variable to a specified value. This method has overloads to support the exchange of Integer, Long, Single, Double, Object, and System.IntPtr.
Increment	Increments an Integer or Long value.

The Code

The following simple example demonstrates how to use the methods of the Interlocked class. The example does not demonstrate Interlocked in the context of a multithreaded program and is provided only to clarify the syntax and effect of the various methods.

```
Imports System
Imports System.threading

Namespace Apress.VisualBasicRecipes.Chapter04

    Class Recipe04_12

        Public Shared Sub Main()

            Dim firstInt As Integer = 2500
            Dim secondInt As Integer = 8000

            Console.WriteLine("firstInt initial value = {0}", firstInt)
            Console.WriteLine("secondInt initial value = {0}", secondInt)

            ' Decrement firstInt in a thread-safe manner. This is
            ' the thread-safe equivalent of firstInt = firstInt - 1.
            Interlocked.Decrement(firstInt)

            Console.WriteLine(Environment.NewLine)
            Console.WriteLine("firstInt after decrement = {0}", firstInt)

            ' Increment secondInt in a thread-safe manner. This is
            ' the thread-safe equivalent of secondInt = secondInt + 1.
            Interlocked.Increment(secondInt)
```

```
Console.WriteLine("secondInt after increment = {0}", secondInt)

' Add the firstInt and secondInt values, and store the result
' in firstInt. This is the thread-safe equivalent of firstInt
' = firstInt + secondInt.
Interlocked.Add(firstInt, secondInt)

Console.WriteLine(Environment.NewLine)
Console.WriteLine("firstInt after Add = {0}", firstInt)
Console.WriteLine("secondInt after Add = {0}", secondInt)

' Exchange the value of firstInt with secondInt. This is the
' thread-safe equivalent of secondInt = firstInt.
Interlocked.Exchange(secondInt, firstInt)

Console.WriteLine(Environment.NewLine)
Console.WriteLine("firstInt after Exchange = {0}", firstInt)
Console.WriteLine("secondInt after Exchange = {0}", secondInt)

' Compare firstInt with secondInt, and if they are equal, set
' firstInt to 5000. This is the thread-safe equivalent of
' if firstInt = secondInt then firstInt = 5000.
Interlocked.CompareExchange(firstInt, 5000, secondInt)

Console.WriteLine(Environment.NewLine)
Console.WriteLine("firstInt after CompareExchange = {0}", firstInt)
Console.WriteLine("secondInt after CompareExchange = {0}", secondInt)

' Wait to continue.
Console.WriteLine(Environment.NewLine)
Console.WriteLine("Main method complete. Press Enter.")
Console.ReadLine()

    End Sub

  End Class
End Namespace
```

4-13. Know When a Thread Finishes

Problem

You need to know when a thread has finished.

Solution

Use the IsAlive property or the Join method of the Thread class.

How It Works

The easiest way to test whether a thread has finished executing is to test the Thread.IsAlive property. The IsAlive property returns True if the thread has been started but has not terminated or been aborted. The IsAlive property provides a simple test to see whether a thread has finished executing, but commonly you will need one thread to wait for another thread to complete its processing. Instead of testing IsAlive in a loop, which is inefficient, you can use the Thread.Join method.

Join causes the calling thread to block until the referenced thread terminates, at which point the calling thread will continue. You can optionally specify an Integer or a TimeSpan value that specifies the time, after which the Join operation will time out and execution of the calling thread will resume. If you specify a time-out value, Join returns True if the thread terminated and returns False if Join timed out.

The Code

The following example executes a second thread and then calls Join (with a time-out of 2 seconds) to wait for the second thread to terminate. Because the second thread takes about 5 seconds to execute, the Join method will always time out, and the example will display a message to the console. The example then calls Join again without a time-out and blocks until the second thread terminates.

```
Imports System
Imports System.threading

Namespace Apress.VisualBasicRecipes.Chapter04

    Class Recipe04_13

        Private Shared Sub DisplayMessage()

            ' Display a message to the console 5 times.
            For count As Integer = 1 To 5
                Console.WriteLine("{0} : DisplayMessage thread", ➥
DateTime.Now.ToString("HH:mm:ss.ffff"))

                ' Sleep for 1 second.
                Thread.Sleep(1000)
            Next
        End Sub

        Public Shared Sub Main()

            ' Create a new Thread to run the DisplayMessage method.
            Dim newThread As New Thread(AddressOf DisplayMessage)

            Console.WriteLine("{0} : Starting DisplayMessage thread.", ➥
DateTime.Now.ToString("HH:mm:ss.ffff"))

            ' Start the DisplayMessage thread.
            newThread.Start()

            ' Block until the DisplayMessage thread finishes, or time-out after
            ' 2 seconds.
            If Not newThread.Join(2000) Then
                Console.WriteLine("{0} : Join timed out !!", ➥
DateTime.Now.ToString("HH:mm:ss.ffff"))
            End If
```

```
    ' Block again until the DisplayMessage thread finishes with
    ' no time-out.
    newThread.Join()

    ' Wait to continue.
    Console.WriteLine("Main method complete. Press Enter.")
    Console.ReadLine()

  End Sub

End Class
End Namespace
```

4-14. Terminate the Execution of a Thread

Problem

You need to terminate an executing thread without waiting for it to finish on its own accord.

Solution

Call the Abort method of the Thread object you want to terminate.

How It Works

It is better to write your code so that you can signal to a thread that it should shut down and allow it to terminate naturally. Recipes 4-8, 4-9, and 4-10 demonstrate this technique (using a Boolean flag). However, sometimes you will want a more direct method of terminating an active thread.

Calling Abort on an active Thread object terminates the thread by throwing a System.Threading. ThreadAbortException in the code that the thread is running. You can pass an object as an argument to the Abort method, which is accessible to the aborted thread through the ExceptionState property of the ThreadAbortException. When called, Abort returns immediately, but the runtime determines exactly when the exception is thrown, so you cannot assume the thread has terminated when Abort returns. You should use the techniques described in recipe 4-13 if you need to determine when the aborted thread is actually finished.

The aborted thread's code can catch the ThreadAbortException to perform cleanup, but the runtime will automatically throw the exception again when exiting the Catch block to ensure that the thread terminates. So, you should not write code after the Catch block because it will never execute. However, calling the Shared Thread.ResetAbort in the Catch block will cancel the abort request and exit the Catch block, allowing the thread to continue executing. Once you abort a thread, you cannot restart it by calling Thread.Start.

■Tip An alternative to using the Abort method is to use a member variable. The thread should check the variable when appropriate. When you need to, set this variable to instruct the thread to end gracefully. This method offers a little more control than Abort.

The Code

The following example creates a new thread that continues to display messages to the console until you press Enter, at which point the thread is terminated by a call to Thread.Abort.

```vb
Imports System
Imports System.Threading

Namespace Apress.VisualBasicRecipes.Chapter04

    Class Recipe04_14

        Private Shared Sub Displaymessage()

            Try
                While True
                    ' Display a message to the console.
                    Console.WriteLine("{0} : DisplayMessage thread active", ➡
DateTime.Now.ToString("HH:mm:ss.ffff"))

                    ' Sleep for 1 second.
                    Thread.Sleep(1000)
                End While
            Catch ex As ThreadAbortException
                ' Display a message to the console.
                Console.WriteLine("{0} : DisplayMessage thread terminating - {1}", ➡
DateTime.Now.ToString("HH:mm:ss.ffff"), DirectCast(ex.ExceptionState, String))

                ' Call Thread.ResetAbort here to cancel the abort request.
            End Try

            ' This code is never executed unless Thread.ResetAbort is
            ' called in the previous catch block.
            Console.WriteLine("{0} : nothing is called after the catch block", ➡
DateTime.Now.ToString("HH:mm:ss.ffff"))

        End Sub

        Public Shared Sub Main()

            ' Create a new Thread to run the DisplayMessage method.
            Dim newThread As New Thread(AddressOf Displaymessage)

            Console.WriteLine("{0} : Starting DisplayMessage thread - press " & ➡
"Enter to terminate.", DateTime.Now.ToString("HH:mm:ss.ffff"))

            ' Start the DisplayMessage thread.
            newThread.Start()

            ' Wait until Enter is pressed and terminate the thread.
            System.Console.ReadLine()

            newThread.Abort("User pressed Enter")

            ' Block again until the DisplayMessage thread finishes.
            newThread.Join()
```

```
        ' Wait to continue.
        Console.WriteLine("Main method complete. Press Enter.")
        Console.ReadLine()

    End Sub

    End Class
End Namespace
```

4-15. Create a Thread-Safe Collection Instance

Problem

You need multiple threads to be able to safely access the contents of a collection concurrently.

Solution

Use SyncLock statements in your code to synchronize thread access to the collection, or to access the collection through a thread-safe wrapper.

How It Works

By default, the standard collection classes from the System.Collections, System.Collections. Specialized, and System.Collections.Generic namespaces will support multiple threads reading the collection's content concurrently. However, if more than one of these threads tries to modify the collection, you will almost certainly encounter problems. This is because the operating system can interrupt the actions of the thread while modifications to the collection have been only partially applied. This leaves the collection in an indeterminate state, which could cause another thread accessing the collection to fail, return incorrect data, or corrupt the collection.

■**Note** Using thread synchronization introduces a performance overhead. Making collections non-thread-safe by default provides better performance for the vast majority of situations where multiple threads are not used.

The most commonly used collections from the System.Collections namespace implement a Shared method named Synchronized; this includes only the ArrayList, Hashtable, Queue, SortedList, and Stack classes. The Synchronized method takes a collection object of the appropriate type as an argument and returns an object that provides a synchronized wrapper around the specified collection object. The wrapper object is returned as the same type as the original collection, but all the methods and properties that read and write the collection ensure that only a single thread has access to the initial collection content concurrently. You can test whether a collection is thread-safe using the IsSynchronized property. Once you get the wrapper, you should neither access the initial collection nor create a new wrapper; both result in a loss of thread safety.

The collection classes such as HybridDictionary, ListDictionary, and StringCollection from the System.Collections.Specialized namespace do not implement a Synchronized method. To provide thread-safe access to instances of these classes, you must implement manual synchronization using the Object returned by their SyncRoot property. This property and IsSynchronized are both defined by the ICollection interface that is implemented by all collection classes from System. Collections and System.Collections.Specialized (except BitVector32). You can therefore synchronize all your collections in a fine-grained way.

However, the classes in the System.Collections.Generic namespace provide no built-in synchronization mechanisms, leaving it to you to implement thread synchronization manually using the techniques discussed in this chapter.

Caution Often you will have multiple collections and data elements that are related and need to be updated atomically. In these instances, you should not use the synchronization mechanisms provided by the individual collection classes. This approach will introduce synchronization problems, such as deadlocks and race conditions. You must decide which collections and other data elements need to be managed atomically and use the techniques described in this chapter to synchronize access to these elements as a unit.

The Code

The following code snippet shows how to create a thread-safe Hashtable instance:

```
' Create a standard Hashtable.
Dim hUnsync As New Hashtable

' Create a synchronized wrapper.
Dim hSync = Hashtable.Synchronized(hUnsync)
```

The following code snippet shows how to create a thread-safe NameValueCollection. Notice that the NameValueCollection class derives from the NameObjectCollectionBase class, which uses an explicit interface implementation to implement the ICollection.SyncRoot property. As shown, you must cast the NameValueCollection to an ICollection instance before you can access the SyncRoot property. Casting is not necessary with other specialized collection classes such as HybridDictionary, ListDictionary, and StringCollection, which do not use explicit interface implementation to implement SyncRoot.

```
' Create a NameValueCollection.
Dim nvCollection As New NameValueCollection

' Obtain a lock on the NameValue collection before modification.
SyncLock DirectCast(nvCollection, ICollection).SyncRoot
    ...
End SyncLock
```

4-16. Start a New Process

Problem

You need to execute an application in a new process.

Solution

Call one of the Shared Start method overloads of the System.Diagnostics.Process class. Specify the configuration details of the process you want to start as individual arguments to the Start method or in a System.Diagnostics.ProcessStartInfo object that you pass to the Start method.

How It Works

The Process class provides a managed representation of an operating system process and offers a simple mechanism through which you can execute both managed and unmanaged applications. The Process class implements five Shared overloads of the Start method, which you use to start a new process. All these methods return a Process object that represents the newly started process. Two of these overloads are methods that allow you to specify only the path and arguments to pass to the new process. For example, the following statements both execute Notepad in a new process:

```
' Execute notepad.exe with no command-line arguments.
Process.Start("notepad.exe")

' Execute notepad.exe passing the name of the file to open as a
' command-line argument.
Process.Start("notepad.exe", "SomeFile.txt")
```

Two other overloads allow you to specify the name of a Windows user who the process should run as. You must specify the username, password, and Windows domain. The password is specified as a System.Security.SecureString for added security. (See recipe 13-18 for more information about the SecureString class.) Here is an example:

```
Dim mySecureString As New System.Security.SecureString

' Obtain a password and place it in SecureString (see recipe 13-18).

' Execute notepad.exe with no command-line arguments.
Process.Start("notepad.exe", "Todd", mySecureString, "MyDomain")

' Execute notepad.exe passing the name of the file to open as a
' command-line argument.
Process.Start("notepad.exe", "SomeFile.txt", "Todd", mySecureString, "MyDomain")
```

The remaining Shared overload requires you to create a ProcessStartInfo object configured with the details of the process you want to run. Using the ProcessStartInfo object provides greater control over the behavior and configuration of the new process. Table 4-4 summarizes some of the commonly used properties of the ProcessStartInfo class.

Table 4-4. *Properties of the ProcessStartInfo Class*

Property	Description
Arguments	The command-line arguments to pass to the new process.
Domain	A String containing the Windows domain name to which the user belongs.
ErrorDialog	If Process.Start cannot start the specified process, it will throw a System.ComponentModel.Win32Exception. If ErrorDialog is True, Start displays an error dialog box to the user before throwing the exception.
FileName	The path, or just the name if it is in the same directory as the executable, of the application to start. You can also specify any type of file for which you have configured an application association. For example, you could specify a file with a .doc or an .xls extension, which would cause Microsoft Word or Microsoft Excel to run.
LoadUserProfile	A Boolean indicating whether the user's profile should be loaded from the registry when the new process is started. This is used if you need to access information from the HKEY_CURRENT_USER registry key.

Table 4-4. *Properties of the ProcessStartInfo Class (Continued)*

Property	Description
Password	A SecureString containing the password of the user.
UserName	A String containing the name of the user to use when starting the process.
WindowStyle	A member of the System.Diagnostics.ProcessWindowStyle enumeration, which controls how the window is displayed. Valid values include Hidden, Maximized, Minimized, and Normal.
WorkingDirectory	The fully qualified name of the initial directory for the new process.

It is also possible to create and view information on processes running on a remote computer. This is accomplished by creating an instance of a Process class and specifying the target computer name. You can also use the Shared methods GetProcessById, GetProcessByName and GetProcesses. Each method returns a Process object (or an array of Process objects) and has an overload that takes the name of the target computer.

When finished with a Process object, you should dispose of it in order to release system resources—call Close, call Dispose, or create the Process object within the scope of a Using statement.

■**Note** Disposing of a Process object does not affect the underlying system process, which will continue to run.

The Code

The following example uses Process to execute Notepad in a maximized window and open a file named C:\Temp\file.txt. After creation, the example calls the Process.WaitForExit method, which blocks the calling thread until a process terminates or a specified time-out expires. This method returns True if the process ends before the time-out and returns False otherwise.

```
Imports System
Imports System.Diagnostics

Namespace Apress.VisualBasicRecipes.Chapter04

    Class Recipe04_16

        Public Shared Sub Main()

            ' Create a ProcessStartInfo object and configure it with the
            ' information required to run the new process.
            Dim startInfo As New ProcessStartInfo

            startInfo.FileName = "notepad.exe"
            startInfo.Arguments = "file.txt"
            startInfo.WorkingDirectory = "C:\Temp"
            startInfo.WindowStyle = ProcessWindowStyle.Maximized
            startInfo.ErrorDialog = True
```

```
        ' Declare a new process object.
        Dim newProcess As Process

        Try
            ' Start the new process.
            newProcess = Process.Start(startInfo)

            ' Wait for the new process to terminate before exiting.
            Console.WriteLine("Waiting 30 seconds for process to finish.")

            If newProcess.WaitForExit(30000) Then
                Console.WriteLine("Process terminated.")
            Else
                Console.WriteLine("Timed out waiting for process to end.")
            End If
        Catch ex As Exception
            Console.WriteLine("Could not start process.")
            Console.WriteLine(ex)
        End Try

        ' Wait to continue.
        Console.WriteLine(Environment.NewLine)
        Console.WriteLine("Main method complete. Press Enter.")
        Console.ReadLine()

    End Sub

    End Class
End Namespace
```

4-17. Terminate a Process

Problem

You need to terminate a process such as an application or a service.

Solution

Obtain a Process object representing the operating system process you want to terminate. For Windows-based applications, call Process.CloseMainWindow to send a close message to the application's main window. For Windows-based applications that ignore CloseMainWindow, or for non-Windows-based applications, call the Process.Kill method.

How It Works

If you start a new process from managed code using the Process class (discussed in recipe 4-16), you can terminate the process using the Process object that represents the new process. You can also obtain Process objects that refer to other currently running processes using the Shared methods of the Process class summarized in Table 4-5.

As mentioned in recipe 4-16, you can obtain a Process object that refers to a process running on a remote computer. However, you can only view information regarding remote processes. The Kill and CloseMainWindow methods work only on local processes.

Table 4-5. *Methods for Obtaining Process References*

Method	Description
GetCurrentProcess	Returns a Process object representing the currently active process.
GetProcessById	Returns a Process object representing the process with the specified ID. This is the process ID (PID) you can get using Windows Task Manager.
GetProcesses	Returns an array of Process objects representing all currently active processes.
GetProcessesByName	Returns an array of Process objects representing all currently active processes with a specified friendly name. The friendly name is the name of the executable excluding file extension or path; for example, a friendly name could be notepad or calc.

Once you have a Process object representing the process you want to terminate, you need to call either the CloseMainWindow method or the Kill method. The CloseMainWindow method posts a WM_CLOSE message to a Windows-based application's main window. This method has the same effect as if the user had closed the main window using the system menu, and it gives the application the opportunity to perform its normal shutdown routine. CloseMainWindow will not terminate applications that do not have a main window or applications with a disabled main window—possibly because a modal dialog box is currently displayed. Under such circumstances, CloseMainWindow will return False.

CloseMainWindow returns True if the close message was successfully sent, but this does not guarantee that the process is actually terminated. For example, applications used to edit data typically give the user the opportunity to save unsaved data if a close message is received. The user usually has the chance to cancel the close operation under such circumstances. This means CloseMainWindow will return True, but the application will still be running once the user cancels. You can use the Process.WaitForExit method to signal process termination and the Process.HasExited property to test whether a process has terminated. Alternatively, you can use the Kill method.

The Kill method simply terminates a process immediately; the user has no chance to stop the termination, and all unsaved data is lost. Kill is the only option for terminating Windows-based applications that do not respond to CloseMainWindow and for terminating non-Windows-based applications.

The Code

The following example starts a new instance of Notepad, waits 5 seconds, and then terminates the Notepad process. The example first tries to terminate the process using CloseMainWindow. If CloseMainWindow returns False, or the Notepad process is still running after CloseMainWindow is called, the example calls Kill and forces the Notepad process to terminate. You can force CloseMainWindow to return False by leaving the File Open dialog box open.

```
Imports System
Imports System.Threading
Imports System.Diagnostics

Namespace Apress.VisualBasicRecipes.Chapter04

    Class Recipe04_17

        Public Shared Sub Main()
```

```vb
            ' Create a new Process and run notepad.exe.
            Using newProcess As Process = Process.Start("notepad.exe", ➡
 "C:\SomeFile.txt")
                ' Wait for 5 seconds and terminate the notepad process.
                Console.WriteLine("Waiting 5 seconds before terminating " & ➡
"notepad.exe.")
                Thread.Sleep(5000)

                ' Terminate notepad process.
                Console.WriteLine("Terminating Notepad with CloseMainWindow.")

                ' Try to send a close message to the main window.
                If Not newProcess.CloseMainWindow Then
                    ' Close message did not get sent - Kill Notepad.
                    Console.WriteLine("CloseMainWindow returned false - " & ➡
"terminating Notepad with Kill.")
                    newProcess.Kill()
                Else
                    ' Close message sent successfully. Wait for 2 seconds
                    ' for termination confirmation before resorting to kill.
                    If Not newProcess.WaitForExit(2000) Then
                        Console.WriteLine("CloseMaineWindow failed to " & ➡
"terminate - terminating Notepad with Kill.")
                        newProcess.Kill()
                    End If
                End If
            End Using

            ' Wait to continue.
            Console.WriteLine("Main method complete. Press Enter.")
            Console.ReadLine()

        End Sub

    End Class
End Namespace
```

4-18. Ensure That Only One Instance of an Application Can Execute Concurrently

Problem

You need to ensure that a user can have only one instance of an application running concurrently.

Solution

Create a named System.Threading.Mutex object, and have your application try to acquire ownership of it at startup.

How It Works

The Mutex provides a mechanism for synchronizing the execution of threads across process boundaries and also provides a convenient mechanism through which to ensure that only a single instance of an application is running concurrently. By trying to acquire ownership of a named Mutex at startup and exiting if the Mutex cannot be acquired, you can ensure that only one instance of your application is running. Refer to recipe 4-10 for further information on the Mutex class.

The Code

This example uses a Mutex named MutexExample to ensure that only a single instance of the example can execute.

```
Imports System
Imports System.Threading

Namespace Apress.VisualBasicRecipes.Chapter04

    Class Recipe04_18

        Public Shared Sub Main()

            ' A Boolean that indicates whether this application has
            ' initial ownership of the Mutex.
            Dim ownsMutex As Boolean

            ' Attempts to create and take ownership of a Mutex named
            ' MutexExample.
            Using newMutex As New Mutex(True, "MutexExample", ownsMutex)
                ' If the application owns the Mutex it can continue to execute;
                ' otherwise, the application should exit.
                If ownsMutex Then
                    Console.WriteLine("This application currently owns the " & _
"mutex named MutexExample. Additional instances of this application will not " & _
"run until you release the mutex by pressing Enter.")


                    Console.ReadLine()

                    ' Release the mutex.
                    newMutex.ReleaseMutex()
                Else
                    Console.WriteLine("Another instance of this application " & _
"already owns the mutex named MutexExample. This instance of the application " & _
"will terminate.")
                End If
            End Using

            ' Wait to continue.
            Console.WriteLine("Main method complete. Press Enter.")
            Console.ReadLine()

        End Sub
    End Class

End Namespace
```

Note If you do not construct the Mutex in a Using statement and encapsulate the body of your application in the body of the Using block as shown in this example, in long-running applications, the garbage collector may dispose of the Mutex if it is not referenced after initial creation. This will result in releasing the Mutex and allowing additional instances of the application to execute concurrently. In these circumstances, you should include the statement System.GC.KeepAlive(mutex) to ensure the reference to the Mutex class is not garbage collected. Thanks to Michael A. Covington for highlighting this possibility.

CHAPTER 5

■ ■ ■

Files, Directories, and I/O

The Microsoft .NET Framework I/O classes fall into two basic categories. First are the classes that retrieve information from the file system and allow you to perform file system operations such as copying files and moving directories. Two examples are the FileInfo and the DirectoryInfo classes. The second, and possibly more important, category includes a broad range of classes that allow you to read and write data from all types of streams. Streams can correspond to binary or text files, a file in an isolated store, a network connection, or even a memory buffer. In all cases, the way you interact with a stream is the same.

The primary namespace for .NET Framework I/O operations is System.IO; however, .NET offers VB .NET programmers another option in the form of the My object. My, located in the Microsoft.VisualBasic assembly, is a highly versatile object that encapsulates common functionality, including I/O operations, into several root classes. These classes provide quick and easy access to common functionality. Table 5-1 lists the main root classes of My.

Table 5-1. *Main Root Objects of My*

Object	Description
Application	Provides access to information and methods related to the current application.
Computer	Provides access to information and methods for various computer-related objects. This object contains the following child objects: Audio, Clipboard, Clock, FileSystem, Info, Keyboard, Mouse, Network, Ports, and Registry.
Forms	Provides access to information and methods related to the forms contained in your project.
Resources	Provides access to information and methods related to any resources contained in your project.
Settings	Provides access to information and methods related to your application settings.
User	Provides access to information and methods related to the current user.
WebServices	Provides access to information and methods related to any web services contained in your application.

The classes available to the My object are determined by the current project. For example, if you are creating a web control or web site, the My.Forms class will not be accessible. Refer to the .NET Framework software development kit (SDK) documentation for more details on the availability of My classes and for instructions on how this availability can be customized by using special compiler constants.

This chapter describes how to use the various file system and stream-based classes provided by the System.IO namespace and the My.Microsoft.VisualBasic.FileSystem class.

The recipes in this chapter cover the following:

- Retrieving or modifying information about a file, directory, or drive (recipes 5-1, 5-2, 5-4, 5-5, and 5-17)

- Copying, moving, and deleting files and directories (recipe 5-3)

- Showing a directory tree in a Microsoft Windows-based application and use the common file dialog boxes (recipes 5-6 and 5-18)

- Reading and writing text and binary files (recipes 5-7 and 5-8)

- Parsing formatted text files (recipe 5-9)

- Reading files asynchronously (recipe 5-10)

- Searching for specific files and test files for equality (recipes 5-11 and 5-12)

- Working with strings that contain path information (recipes 5-13, 5-14, and 5-15)

- Creating temporary files and files in a user-specific isolated store (recipes 5-16 and 5-19)

- Monitoring the file system for changes (recipe 5-20)

- Writing to COM ports (recipe 5-21)

- Generating random filenames (recipe 5-22)

- Retrieving or modifying the access control lists (ACLs) of a file or directory (recipe 5-23)

5-1. Retrieve Information About a File, Directory, or Drive

Problem

You need to retrieve information about a file, directory, or drive.

Solution

Create a new System.IO.FileInfo, System.IO.DirectoryInfo, or System.IO.DriveInfo object, depending on the type of resource about which you need to retrieve information. Supply the path of the resource to the constructor, and then you will be able to retrieve information through the properties of the class.

How It Works

To create a FileInfo, DirectoryInfo, or DriveInfo object, you supply a relative or fully qualified path to the constructor. You can also use the GetFileInfo, GetDirectoryInfo, and GetDriveInfo Shared methods of the My.Computer.FileSystem. These methods return an instance of a FileInfo, DirectoryInfo, and DriveInfo object, respectively. You can retrieve information through the corresponding object properties. Table 5-2 lists some of the key members and methods of these objects.

Table 5-2. *Key Members for Files, Directories, and Drives*

Member	Applies To	Description
Exists	FileInfo and DirectoryInfo	Returns True or False, depending on whether a file or a directory exists at the specified location.
Attributes	FileInfo and DirectoryInfo	Returns one or more flag values from the System.IO.FileAttributes enumeration, which represents the attributes of the file or the directory.
CreationTime, LastAccessTime, and LastWriteTime	FileInfo and DirectoryInfo	Return System.DateTime instances that describe when a file or a directory was created, last accessed, and last updated, respectively.
FullName and Name	FileInfo and DirectoryInfo	Returns a string that represents the full path of the directory or file or just the file name (with extension), respectively.
Extension	FileInfo	Returns a string representing the extension for the file.
IsReadOnly	FileInfo	Returns True or False, depending on whether a file is read-only.
Length	FileInfo	Returns the file size as a number of bytes.
DirectoryName and Directory	FileInfo	DirectoryName returns the name of the parent directory as a string. Directory returns a full DirectoryInfo object that represents the parent directory and allows you to retrieve more information about it.
Parent and Root	DirectoryInfo	Return a DirectoryInfo object that represents the parent or root directory.
CreateSubdirectory	DirectoryInfo	Creates a directory with the specified name in the directory represented by the DirectoryInfo object. It also returns a new DirectoryInfo object that represents the subdirectory.
GetDirectories	DirectoryInfo	Returns an array of DirectoryInfo objects, with one element for each subdirectory contained in this directory.
GetFiles	DirectoryInfo	Returns an array of FileInfo objects, with one element for each file contained in this directory.
DriveType	DriveInfo	Returns a DriveType enumeration value that represents the type of the specified drive; for example, Fixed or CDRom.
AvailableFreeSpace	DriveInfo	Returns a Long that represents the free space available in the drive.
GetDrives	DriveInfo	Returns an array of DriveInfo objects that represents the logical drives in the computer.

The following are a few points to note while working with these objects:

- FileInfo and DirectoryInfo classes derive from the abstract FileSystemInfo class, which defines common methods such as CreationTime, Exists, and so on. The DriveInfo class does not inherit from this base class, so it does not provide some of the common members available in the other two classes.

- The full set of properties FileInfo and DirectoryInfo objects expose is read the first time you interrogate any property. If the file or directory changes after this point, you must call the Refresh method to update the properties. However, this is not the case for DriveInfo; each property access asks the file system for an up-to-date value.

- Specifying an invalid path, directory, or drive when using the corresponding My.Computer. FileSystem methods will throw the appropriate exception. When using the FileInfo, DirectoryInfo, or DriveInfo classes directly, you will not encounter an error if you specify an invalid path. Instead, you will receive an object that represents an entity that does not exist— its Exists (or IsReady property for DriveInfo) property will be False. You can use this object to manipulate the entity. However, if you attempt to read most other properties, exceptions such as FileNotFoundException, DirectoryNotFoundException, and so on, will be thrown.

The Code

The following console application takes a file path from a command-line argument, and then displays information about the file, the containing directory, and the drive.

```
Imports System
Imports System.IO

Namespace Apress.VisualBasicRecipes.Chapter05

    Public Class Recipe05_01
        Public Shared Sub Main(ByVal args As String)

            If args.Length > 0 Then
                '  Display file information.
                Dim file As FileInfo = New FileInfo(args(0))

                Console.WriteLine("Checking file: " & file.Name)
                Console.WriteLine("File exists: " & file.Exists.ToString)

                If file.Exists Then
                    Console.Write("File created: ")
                    Console.WriteLine(file.CreationTime.ToString)
                    Console.Write("File last updated: ")
                    Console.WriteLine(file.LastWriteTime.ToString)
                    Console.Write("File last accessed: ")
                    Console.WriteLine(file.LastAccessTime.ToString)
                    Console.Write("File size: ")
                    Console.WriteLine(file.Length.ToString)
                    Console.Write("File attribute list: ")
                    Console.WriteLine(file.Attributes.ToString)
                End If
                Console.WriteLine()
```

```vbnet
    ' Display directory information.
    Dim dir As DirectoryInfo = file.Directory

    Console.WriteLine("Checking directory: " & dir.Name)
    Console.WriteLine("In directory: " & dir.Parent.Name)
    Console.Write("Directory exists: ")
    Console.WriteLine(dir.Exists.ToString)

    If dir.Exists Then
        Console.Write("Directory created: ")
        Console.WriteLine(dir.CreationTime.ToString)
        Console.Write("Directory last updated: ")
        Console.WriteLine(dir.LastWriteTime.ToString)
        Console.Write("Directory last accessed: ")
        Console.WriteLine(dir.LastAccessTime.ToString)
        Console.Write("Directory attribute list: ")
        Console.WriteLine(file.Attributes.ToString)
        Console.Write("Directory contains: ")
        Console.WriteLine(dir.GetFiles().Length.ToString & " files")
    End If
    Console.WriteLine()

    ' Display drive information.
    Dim drv As DriveInfo = New DriveInfo(file.FullName)

    Console.Write("Drive: ")
    Console.WriteLine(drv.Name)

    If drv.IsReady Then
        Console.Write("Drive type: ")
        Console.WriteLine(drv.DriveType.ToString)
        Console.Write("Drive format: ")
        Console.WriteLine(drv.DriveFormat.ToString)
        Console.Write("Drive free space: ")
        Console.WriteLine(drv.AvailableFreeSpace.ToString)
    End If

    ' Wait to continue.
    Console.WriteLine(Environment.NewLine)
    Console.WriteLine("Main method complete. Press Enter.")
    Console.ReadLine()

Else
    Console.WriteLine("Please supply a filename.")
End If

End Sub

    End Class
End Namespace
```

Instead of explicitly creating the FileInfo, DirectoryInfo, and DriveInfo class instances, you can also use the appropriate Shared methods of the My.Computer.FileSystem class, as shown in the following examples.

```
' Display file information.
Dim file As FileInfo = My.Computer.FileSystem.GetFileInfo(args(0))

' Display directory information.
Dim dir As DirectoryInfo = ➥
My.Computer.FileSystem.GetDirectoryInfo(file.Directory.ToString)

' Display drive information.
Dim drv As DriveInfo = My.Computer.FileSystem.GetDriveInfo(file.FullName)
```

Usage

If you execute the command Recipe05-01.exe c:\windows\win.ini, you might expect the following output:

```
Checking file: win.ini
File exists: True
File created: 11/2/2006 6:23:31 AM
File last updated: 7/29/2007 5:10:17 PM
File last accessed: 11/2/2006 6:23:31 AM
File size (bytes): 219
File attribute list: Archive

Checking directory: windows
In directory: c:\
Directory exists: True
Directory created: 11/2/2006 7:18:34 AM
Directory last updated: 9/24/2007 6:06:52 PM
Directory last accessed: 9/24/2007 6:06:52 PM
Directory attribute list: Archive
Directory contains: 46 files

Drive: c:\
Drive type: Fixed
Drive format: NTFS
Drive free space: 45285109760

Main method complete. Press Enter.
```

▨**Note** Instead of using the instance methods of the FileInfo and DirectoryInfo classes, you can use the Shared File and Directory classes (note that a class corresponding to the DriveInfo class does not exist). The methods of the File and Directory classes, found in the System.IO namespace, expose most of the same functionality, but they require you to submit the file name or path with every method invocation. In cases where you need to perform multiple operations with the same file or directory, using the FileInfo and DirectoryInfo classes will be faster, because they will perform security checks only once. Also note that you could obtain the list of all logical drives in the computer by using the Shared DriveInfo.GetDrives method.

5-2. Set File and Directory Attributes

Problem

You need to test or modify file or directory attributes.

Solution

Create a System.IO.FileInfo object for a file or a System.IO.DirectoryInfo object for a directory and use the bitwise And, Or, and Xor operators to modify the value of the Attributes property.

How It Works

The FileInfo.Attributes and DirectoryInfo.Attributes properties represent file attributes such as archive, system, hidden, read-only, compressed, and encrypted. (Refer to the MSDN reference for the full list.) Because a file can possess any combination of attributes, the Attributes property accepts a combination of enumerated values. To individually test for a single attribute or change a single attribute, you need to use bitwise arithmetic.

Note The Attributes setting is made up (in binary) of a series of ones and zeros, such as 00010011. Each 1 represents an attribute that is present, while each 0 represents an attribute that is not. When you use a bitwise And operation, it compares each individual digit against each digit in the enumerated value. For example, if you bitwise And a value of 00100001 (representing an individual file's archive and read-only attributes) with the enumerated value 00000001 (which represents the read-only flag), the resulting value will be 00000001—it will have a 1 only where it can be matched in both values.

The Code

The following example takes a read-only test file and checks for the read-only attribute.

```
Imports System
Imports system.IO

Namespace Apress.VisualBasicRecipes.Chapter05

    Public Class Recipe05_02
        Public Shared Sub Main()

            ' This file has the archive and read-only attributes.
            Dim file As New FileInfo("data.txt")

            ' This displays the string "ReadOnly, Archive".
            Console.WriteLine(file.Attributes.ToString)
            Console.WriteLine(Environment.NewLine)
```

```
                    ' This test fails, because other attributes are set.
                    If file.Attributes = FileAttributes.ReadOnly Then
                        Console.WriteLine("File is read-only (faulty test).")
                    End If

                    ' This test succeeds, because it filters out just the
                    ' read-only attributes.
                    If file.Attributes And FileAttributes.ReadOnly = ➡
FileAttributes.ReadOnly Then
                        Console.WriteLine("File is read-only (correct test).")
                    End If

                    ' Wait to continue.
                    Console.WriteLine(Environment.NewLine)
                    Console.WriteLine("Main method complete. Press Enter.")
                    Console.ReadLine()

            End Sub

    End Class
End Namespace
```

When setting an attribute, you must use bitwise arithmetic, as demonstrated in the following example. In this case, it's needed to ensure that you don't inadvertently clear the other attributes.

```
' This adds just the read-only attribute.
file.Attributes = file.Attributes Or FileAttributes.ReadOnly

' This removes just the read-only attibute.
file.Attributes = file.Attributes Xor FileAttributes.ReadOnly
```

5-3. Copy, Move, or Delete a File or a Directory

Problem

You need to copy, move, or delete a file or directory.

Solution

You have two main options for manipulating files and directories. One option is to create a System. IO.FileInfo object for a file or a System.IO.DirectoryInfo object for a directory, supplying the path in the constructor. You can then use the object's methods to copy, move, and delete the file or directory. Alternatively, you can use the My.Computer.FileSystem class and its Shared methods.

How It Works

The FileInfo, DirectoryInfo, and My.Computer.FileSystem classes include a host of valuable methods for manipulating files and directories. Table 5-3 shows methods for the FileInfo class, Table 5-4 shows methods for the DirectoryInfo class, and Table 5-5 shows methods for the My.Computer. FileSystem class.

Table 5-3. *Key Instance Methods for Manipulating a FileInfo Object*

Method	Description
CopyTo	Copies a file to the new path and file name specified as a parameter. It also returns a new FileInfo object that represents the new (copied) file. You can supply an optional additional parameter of True to allow overwriting.
Create and CreateText	Create creates the specified file and returns a FileStream object that you can use to write to it. CreateText performs the same task, but returns a StreamWriter object that wraps the stream. For more information about writing files, see recipes 5-7 and 5-8.
Open, OpenRead, OpenText, and OpenWrite	Open opens a file and allows you to specify the mode (Open, Append, and so on), access type (Read, Write, and so on), and sharing options. OpenRead and OpenText open a file in read-only mode, returning a FileStream or StreamReader object. OpenWrite opens a file in write-only mode, returning a FileStream object. For more information about reading files, see recipes 5-7 and 5-8.
Delete	Removes the file, if it exists.
Encrypt and Decrypt	Encrypt/decrypt a file using the current account. This applies to NTFS file systems only.
MoveTo	Moves the file to the new path and file name specified as a parameter. MoveTo can also be used to rename a file without changing its location.
Replace	Replaces contents of a file by the current FileInfo object. This method could also take a backup copy of the replaced file.

Table 5-4. *Key Instance Methods for Manipulating a DirectoryInfo Object*

Method	Description
Create	Creates the specified directory. If the path specifies multiple directories that do not exist, they will all be created at once.
CreateSubdirectory	Creates a directory with the specified path in the directory represented by the DirectoryInfo object. If the path specifies multiple directories that do not exist, they will all be created at once. It also returns a new DirectoryInfo object that represents the last directory in the specified path.
Delete	Removes the directory, if it exists. If you want to delete a directory that contains files or other directories, you must use the overloaded Delete method that accepts a parameter named Recursive and set it to True.
MoveTo	Moves the directory (contents and all) to a new path. MoveTo can also be used to rename a directory without changing its location.

Table 5-5. *Key Shared Methods for Manipulating Files and Directories with the My.Computer.FileSystem Object*

Method	Description
CopyDirectory and CopyFile	Copies a directory (and all its contents) or a file to the new path specified.
CreateDirectory	Creates a new directory with the specified name and path. If the path specifies multiple directories that do not exist, they will all be created at once.
DeleteDirectory and DeleteFile	Deletes the specified directory (and all its contents) or file. Both methods offer the Recycle parameter, which determines if files are deleted permanently or sent to the Recycle Bin. DeleteDirectory has a parameter named OnDirectoryNotEmpty to determine whether all contents should be deleted.
MoveDirectory and MoveFile	Moves a directory (and all its contents) or a file to the new path specified.
OpenTextFieldParser	Opens a file and returns a TextFieldParser object. The TextFieldParser class is contained in the Microsoft.VisualBasic.FileIO namespace and is used to parse the contents of a text file. For more information about parsing, see recipe 5-9.
OpenTextFileReader and OpenTextFileWriter	Opens the specified file and returns either a StreamReader or StreamWriter as appropriate. For more information about reading and writing files, see recipes 5-7 and 5-8.

The Code

One useful feature that is missing from the DirectoryInfo class is a copy method. The following example contains a helper function that can copy any directory and its contents.

```
Imports System
Imports system.IO

Namespace Apress.VisualBasicRecipes.Chapter05

    Public Class Recipe05_03

        Public Shared Sub Main(ByVal args As String())

            If args.Length = 2 Then
                Dim sourceDir As New DirectoryInfo(args(0))
                Dim destinationDir As New DirectoryInfo(args(1))

                CopyDirectory(sourceDir, destinationDir)

                ' Wait to continue.
                Console.WriteLine(Environment.NewLine)
                Console.WriteLine("Main method complete. Press Enter.")
                Console.ReadLine()
```

```
            Else
                Console.WriteLine("USAGE:   " & " Recipe05_03 [sourcePath] " & ➥
"[destinationPath]")
            End If

        End Sub

        Public Shared Sub CopyDirectory(ByVal source As DirectoryInfo, ➥
ByVal destination As DirectoryInfo)

            If Not destination.Exists Then
                Console.WriteLine("Creating the destination folder {0}", ➥
destination.FullName)
                destination.Create()
            End If

            ' Copy all files.
            Dim files As FileInfo() = source.GetFiles

            For Each file As FileInfo In files
                Console.WriteLine("Copying the {0} file...", file.Name)
                file.CopyTo(Path.Combine(destination.FullName, file.Name))
            Next

            ' Process subdirectories.
            Dim dirs As DirectoryInfo() = source.GetDirectories

            For Each dir As DirectoryInfo In dirs
                ' Get destination directory.
                Dim destinationDir As String = Path.Combine(destination.FullName, ➥
dir.Name)

                ' Call CopyDirectory recursively.
                CopyDirectory(dir, New DirectoryInfo(destinationDir))
            Next

        End Sub

    End Class
End Namespace
```

While the recipe contains examples of useful methods in the `FileInfo` and `DirectoryInfo` classes, your time would be best spent using the `Shared My.Computer.FileSystem.CopyDirectory` method. This would replace the entire preceding example with the following line of code.

```
My.Computer.FileSystem.CopyDirectory("SomeSourceDirectory", "SomeTargetDirectory")
```

Usage

If you executed the command `Recipe05-03.exe c:\nvidia c:\temp`, you would see results similar to the following (assuming the source directory exists and contains data):

```
Creating the destination folder c:\temp
Creating the destination folder c:\temp\WinVista
Creating the destination folder c:\temp\WinVista\163.69
Creating the destination folder c:\temp\WinVista\163.69\English
Copying the data1.cab file...
Copying the data1.hdr file...
Copying the data2.cab file...
Copying the DPInst.ex_ file...
...
Copying the setup.ini file...
Copying the setup.inx file...
Copying the setup.iss file...
Copying the setup.skin file...

Main method complete. Press Enter.
```

5-4. Calculate the Size of a Directory

Problem

You need to calculate the size of all files contained in a directory (and, optionally, its subdirectories).

Solution

Examine all the files in a directory and add together their FileInfo.Length properties. Use recursive logic to include the size of files in contained subdirectories.

How It Works

The DirectoryInfo class does not provide any property that returns size information. However, you can easily calculate the size of all files contained in a directory by adding together each file's size, which is contained in the FileInfo.Length property.

The Code

The following example calculates the size of a directory and optionally examines subdirectories recursively.

```
Imports System
Imports system.IO

Namespace Apress.VisualBasicRecipes.Chapter05

    Public Class Recipe05_04
        Public Shared Sub Main(ByVal args As String())

            If args.Length > 0 Then
                Dim dir As New DirectoryInfo(args(0))

                Console.WriteLine("Total size: " & ➡
```

```
CalculateDirectorySize(dir, True).ToString & " bytes.")

                    ' Wait to continue.
                    Console.WriteLine(Environment.NewLine)
                    Console.WriteLine("Main method complete. Press Enter.")
                    Console.ReadLine()

            Else
                Console.WriteLine("Please supply a directory path.")
            End If

        End Sub

        Public Shared Function CalculateDirectorySize(ByVal dir As DirectoryInfo, ➥
ByVal includeSubDirs As Boolean) As Long

            Dim totalSize As Long = 0

            ' Examine all contained files.
            Dim files As FileInfo() = dir.GetFiles

            For Each currentFile As FileInfo In files
                totalSize += currentFile.Length
            Next

            ' Examine all contained directories.
            If includeSubDirs Then
                Dim dirs As DirectoryInfo() = dir.GetDirectories

                For Each currentDir As DirectoryInfo In dirs
                    totalSize += CalculateDirectorySize(currentDir, True)
                Next
            End If

            Return totalSize

        End Function

    End Class
End Namespace
```

Usage

To use the application, you execute it and pass in a path to the directory for which you want to see the total size. For example, to see the size of the help directory located under the Windows directory, you would use Recipe05-04.exe c:\windows\help, which would produce results similar to the following:

```
Total size: 106006151 bytes.

Main method complete. Press Enter.
```

5-5. Retrieve Version Information for a File

Problem

You want to retrieve file version information, such as the publisher of a file, its revision number, associated comments, and so on.

Solution

Use the Shared GetVersionInfo method of the System.Diagnostics.FileVersionInfo class.

How It Works

The .NET Framework allows you to retrieve file information without resorting to the Windows API. Instead, you simply need to use the FileVersionInfo class and call the GetVersionInfo method with the file name as a parameter. You can then retrieve extensive information through the FileVersionInfo properties.

The Code

The FileVersionInfo properties are too numerous to list here, but the following code snippet shows an example of what you might retrieve.

```
Imports System
Imports system.Diagnostics

Namespace Apress.VisualBasicRecipes.Chapter05

    Public Class Recipe05_05
        Public Shared Sub Main(ByVal args As String())

            If args.Length > 0 Then
                Dim info As FileVersionInfo = ➥
FileVersionInfo.GetVersionInfo(args(0))

                ' Display version information.
                Console.WriteLine("Checking File: " & info.FileName)
                Console.WriteLine("Product Name: " & info.ProductName)
                Console.WriteLine("Product Version: " & info.ProductVersion)
                Console.WriteLine("Company Name: " & info.CompanyName)
                Console.WriteLine("File Version: " & info.FileVersion)
                Console.WriteLine("File Description: " & info.FileDescription)
                Console.WriteLine("Original Filename: " & info.OriginalFilename)
                Console.WriteLine("Legal Copyright: " & info.LegalCopyright)
                Console.WriteLine("InternalName: " & info.InternalName)
                Console.WriteLine("IsDebug: " & info.IsDebug)
                Console.WriteLine("IsPatched: " & info.IsPatched)
                Console.WriteLine("IsPreRelease: " & info.IsPreRelease)
                Console.WriteLine("IsPrivateBuild: " & info.IsPrivateBuild)
                Console.WriteLine("IsSpecialBuild: " & info.IsSpecialBuild)
```

```
                    '  Wait to continue.
                    Console.WriteLine(Environment.NewLine)
                    Console.WriteLine("Main method complete. Press Enter.")
                    Console.ReadLine()

                Else
                    Console.WriteLine("Please supply a filename.")
                End If

            End Sub

        End Class
    End Namespace
```

Usage

If you run the command Recipe05-05 c:\windows\explorer.exe, the example produces results similar to the following:

```
Checking File: c:\windows\explorer.exe
Product Name: Microsoftr Windowsr Operating System
Product Version: 6.0.6000.16386
Company Name: Microsoft Corporation
File Version: 6.0.6000.16386 (vista_rtm.061101-2205)
File Description: Windows Explorer
Original Filename: EXPLORER.EXE.MUI
Legal Copyright: c Microsoft Corporation. All rights reserved.
InternalName: explorer
IsDebug: False
IsPatched: False
IsPreRelease: False
IsPrivateBuild: False
IsSpecialBuild: False

Main method complete. Press Enter.
```

5-6. Show a Just-in-Time Directory Tree in the TreeView Control

Problem

You need to display a directory tree in a TreeView control. However, filling the directory tree structure at startup is too time-consuming.

Solution

Fill the first level of directories in the TreeView control and add a hidden dummy node to each directory branch. React to the TreeView.BeforeExpand event to fill in subdirectories in a branch just before it's displayed.

How It Works

You can use recursion to build an entire directory tree. However, scanning the file system in this way can be slow, particularly for large drives. For this reason, professional file management software programs (including Windows Explorer) use a different technique. They query the necessary directory information when the user requests it.

The TreeView control is particularly well suited to this approach because it provides a BeforeExpand event that fires before a new level of nodes is displayed. You can use a placeholder (such as an asterisk or empty TreeNode) in all the directory branches that are not filled in. This allows you to fill in parts of the directory tree as they are displayed.

To use this type of solution, you need the following three ingredients:

- A Fill method that adds a single level of directory nodes based on a single directory. You will use this method to fill directory levels as they are expanded.

- A basic Form.Load event handler that uses the Fill method to add the first level of directories for the drive.

- A TreeView.BeforeExpand event handler that reacts when the user expands a node and calls the Fill method if this directory information has not yet been added.

The Code

The following shows the code for this solution. The automatically generated code for the form designer is not included here, but it is included with this book's downloadable code.

```vb
Imports System
Imports System.IO

'  All design code is stored in the autogenerated partial
'  class called DirectoryTree.Designer.vb. You can see this
'  file by selecting Show All Files in Solution Explorer.
Partial Public Class DirectoryTree

    Private Sub DirectoryTree_Load(ByVal sender As System.Object, ➥
ByVal e As System.EventArgs) Handles MyBase.Load


        '  Set the first node.
        Dim rootNode As New TreeNode("C:\")
        treeDirectory.Nodes.Add(rootNode)

        '  Fill the first level and expand it.
        Fill(rootNode)
        treeDirectory.Nodes(0).Expand()

    End Sub

    Private Sub treeDirectory_BeforeExpand(ByVal sender As Object, ➥
ByVal e As System.Windows.Forms.TreeViewCancelEventArgs) Handles ➥
treeDirectory.BeforeExpand
```

```
        '  If a dummy node is found, remove it and read the
        '  real directory list.
        If e.Node.Nodes(0).Text = "*" Then
            e.Node.Nodes.Clear()
            Fill(e.Node)
        End If

    End Sub

    Private Sub Fill(ByVal dirNode As TreeNode)

        Dim dir As New DirectoryInfo(dirNode.FullPath)

        '  An exception could be thrown in this code if you don't
        '  have sufficient security permissions for a file or directory.
        '  You can catch and then ignore this exception.

        For Each dirItem As DirectoryInfo In dir.GetDirectories
            '  Add a node for the directory.
            Dim newNode As New TreeNode(dirItem.Name)
            dirNode.Nodes.Add(newNode)
            newNode.Nodes.Add("*")
        Next

    End Sub
End Class
```

Figure 5-1 shows the directory tree in action.

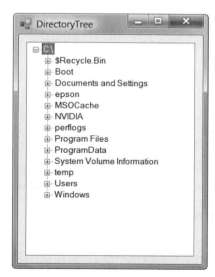

Figure 5-1. *A directory tree with the TreeView*

If you prefer to use the My object, you can replace the use of the DirectoryInfo class with the My.Computer.FileSystem class. The following replacement Fill method is an example of how to do this.

```
Private Sub Fill(ByVal dirNode As TreeNode)

    ' An exception could be thrown in this code if you don't
    ' have sufficient security permissions for a file or directory.
    ' You can catch and then ignore this exception.
    For Each dir As String In ➡
My.Computer.FileSystem.GetDirectories(dirNode.FullPath)
        ' Add a node for the directory.
        Dim newNode As New TreeNode(Path.GetFileName(dir))
        dirNode.Nodes.Add(newNode)
        newNode.Nodes.Add("*")
    Next

End Sub
```

5-7. Read and Write a Text File

Problem

You need to write data to a sequential text file using ASCII, Unicode (UTF-16), or UTF-8 encoding.

Solution

Create a new System.IO.FileStream object that references the file. To write the file, wrap the FileStream in a System.IO.StreamWriter and use the overloaded Write method. To read the file, wrap the FileStream in a System.IO.StreamReader and use the Read or ReadLine method. The File class also provides the Shared CreateText and OpenText methods for writing and reading UTF-8 files. Another alternative is to use the OpenTextFileReader and OpenTextFileWriter methods of the My.Computer.FileSystem class. These methods open a file and return a StreamReader or StreamWriter, respectively.

How It Works

The .NET Framework allows you to write or read text with any stream by using the StreamWriter and StreamReader classes. When writing data with the StreamWriter, you use the StreamWriter.Write method. This method is overloaded to support all the common VB .NET data types, including strings, chars, integers, floating-point numbers, decimals, and so on. However, the Write and WriteLine methods always convert the supplied data to text. Unlike Write, the WriteLine method places each value on a separate line, so you should use it if you want to be able to easily convert the text back to its original data type.

The way a string is represented depends on the encoding you use. The most common encodings are listed in Table 5-6.

The .NET Framework provides a class for each type of encoding in the System.Text namespace. When using StreamReader and StreamWriter, you can specify the encoding or simply use the default UTF-8 encoding.

■Note The Encoding class also offers the Default property, which represents the encoding for your operating system's base character encoding table.

Table 5-6. *Common Encodings*

Encoding	Description	Represented By
ASCII	Encodes each character in a string using 7 bits. ASCII-encoded data cannot contain extended Unicode characters. When using ASCII encoding in .NET, the bits will be padded and the resulting byte array will have 1 byte for each character.	ASCII property of the System.Text.Encoding class
UTF-7 Unicode	Uses 7 bits for ordinary ASCII characters and multiple 7-bit pairs for extended characters. This encoding is primarily for use with 7-bit protocols such as mail, and it is not regularly used.	UTF7 property of the System.Text.Encoding class
UTF-8 Unicode	Uses 8 bits for ordinary ASCII characters and multiple 8-bit pairs for extended characters. The resulting byte array will have 1 byte for each character (provided there are no extended characters).	UTF8 property of the System.Text.Encoding class
Full Unicode (or UTF-16)	Represents each character in a string using 16 bits. The resulting byte array will have 2 bytes for each character.	Unicode property of the System.Text.Encoding class
UTF-32 Unicode	Represents each character in a string using 32 bits. The resulting byte array will have 4 bytes for each character.	UTF32 property of the System.Text.Encoding class

When reading information, you use the Read or ReadLine method of StreamReader. The Read method reads a single character, or the number of characters you specify, and returns the data as an Integer that represents the character read or the number of characters read, respectively. The ReadLine method returns a string with the content of an entire line. The ReadToEnd method will return a string with the content starting from the current position to the end of the stream. An alternative to the ReadToEnd method is the Shared ReadAllText method of the My.Computer.FileSystem and System.IO.File classes.

The Code

The following console application writes and then reads a text file.

```
Imports System
Imports System.IO
Imports System.Text

Namespace Apress.VisualBasicRecipes.Chapter05

    Public Class Recipe05_07
        Public Shared Sub Main()

            ' Create a new file.
            Using fs As New FileStream("test.txt", FileMode.Create)
                ' Create a writer and specify the encoding. The
                ' default (UTF-8) supports special Unicode characters,
```

```vbnet
                            '  but encodes all standard characters in the same way as
                            '  ASCII encoding.
                            Using w As New StreamWriter(fs, Encoding.UTF8)

                                '  Write a decimal, string, special Unicode character
                                '  and char.
                                w.WriteLine(CDec(124.23))
                                w.WriteLine("Test string")
                                w.WriteLine("δ")      'Produced by pressing ALT+235
                                w.WriteLine("!"c)

                            End Using
                        End Using

                        Console.WriteLine("Press Enter to read the information.")
                        Console.ReadLine()

                        '  Open the file in read-only mode.
                        Using fs As New FileStream("test.txt", FileMode.Open)
                            Using r As New StreamReader(fs, Encoding.UTF8)
                                '  Read the data and convert it to the appropriate data type.
                                Console.WriteLine(Decimal.Parse(r.ReadLine))
                                Console.WriteLine(r.ReadLine)
                                Console.WriteLine(Char.Parse(r.ReadLine))
                                Console.WriteLine(Char.Parse(r.ReadLine))
                            End Using
                        End Using

                        '  Wait to continue.
                        Console.WriteLine(Environment.NewLine)
                        Console.WriteLine("Main method complete. Press Enter.")
                        Console.ReadLine()

                End Sub

        End Class
End Namespace
```

Note In the previous example, if you change the encoding from UTF8 to ASCII when creating the text file, the extended character will be displayed as a question mark. This is because ASCII does not include that extended character as part of its character set.

If you prefer to use the My object, you can use the OpenTextFileReader and OpenTextFileWriter methods of the My.Computer.FileSystem class. These methods do not require a FileStream object, which makes the code a little simpler, as shown in the following example.

```vbnet
'  Open and write to a file.
Using w As StreamWriter = My.Computer.FileSystem.OpenTextFileWriter("test.txt", ➡
False, Encoding.UTF8)
    '  Write a decimal, string, special Unicode character
    '  and char.
```

```
    w.WriteLine(CDec(124.23))
    w.WriteLine("Test string")
    w.WriteLine("")      'Produced by pressing ALT+235     w.WriteLine("!"c)
End Using


' Open and read from the file.
Using r As StreamReader = My.Computer.FileSystem.OpenTextFileReader("test.txt", ➥
Encoding.UTF8)
    ' Read the data and convert it to the appropriate data type.
    Console.WriteLine(Decimal.Parse(r.ReadLine))
    Console.WriteLine(r.ReadLine)
    Console.WriteLine(Char.Parse(r.ReadLine))
    Console.WriteLine(Char.Parse(r.ReadLine))
End Using
```

5-8. Read and Write a Binary File

Problem

You need to write data to a binary file, with strong data typing.

Solution

Create a new `System.IO.FileStream` object that references the file. To write the file, wrap the `FileStream` in a `System.IO.BinaryWriter` and use the overloaded `Write` method. To read the file, wrap the `FileStream` in a `System.IO.BinaryReader` and use the `Read` method that corresponds to the expected data type.

How It Works

The .NET Framework allows you to write or read binary data with any stream by using the `BinaryWriter` and `BinaryReader` classes. When writing data with the `BinaryWriter`, you use the `Write` method. This method is overloaded to support all the common VB .NET data types, including strings, chars, integers, floating-point numbers, decimals, and so on. The information will then be encoded as a series of bytes and written to the file. You can configure the encoding used for strings, which defaults to UTF-8, by using an overloaded constructor that accepts a `System.Text.Encoding` object, as described in recipe 5-7.

You must be particularly fastidious with data types when using binary files. This is because when you retrieve the information, you must use one of the strongly typed `Read` methods from the `BinaryReader`, unless you intend to read the file character by character. For example, to retrieve decimal data, you use `ReadDecimal`. To read a string, you use `ReadString`. (The `BinaryWriter` always records the length of a string when it writes it to a binary file to prevent any possibility of error.)

The Code

The following console application writes and then reads a binary file.

```
Imports System
Imports System.IO


Namespace Apress.VisualBasicRecipes.Chapter05

    Public Class Recipe05_08
        Public Shared Sub Main()
```

```
    ' Create a new file and writer.
    Using fs As New FileStream("test.bin", FileMode.Create)
        Using w As New BinaryWriter(fs)
            ' Write a decimal, 2 strings, a special Unicode character
            ' and a char.
            w.Write(CDec(124.23))
            w.Write("Test string")
            w.Write("Test string 2")
            w.Write("δ"c)     'Produced by pressing ALT+235
            w.Write("!"c)
        End Using
    End Using
    Console.WriteLine("Press Enter to read the information.")
    Console.ReadLine()

    ' Open the file in read-only mode.
    Using fs As New FileStream("test.bin", FileMode.Open)
        ' Display the raw information in the file.
        Using sr As New StreamReader(fs)
            Console.WriteLine(sr.ReadToEnd)
            Console.WriteLine()
        End Using

        ' Reposition the FileStream so we can reuse it.
        fs.Position = 0

        ' Read the data and convert it to the appropriate data type.
        Using br As New BinaryReader(fs)
            Console.WriteLine(br.ReadDecimal)
            Console.WriteLine(br.ReadString)
            Console.WriteLine(br.ReadString)
            Console.WriteLine(br.ReadChar)
            Console.WriteLine(br.ReadChar)
        End Using
    End Using

    ' Wait to continue.
    Console.WriteLine(Environment.NewLine)
    Console.WriteLine("Main method complete. Press Enter.")
    Console.ReadLine()

End Sub

End Class
End Namespace
```

5-9. Parse a Delimited Text File

Problem

You need to parse the contents of a delimited text file.

Solution

Create and configure a new `Microsoft.VisualBasic.FileIO.TextFieldParser` object that references the file you need to parse. Loop through the file until the `EndOfData` property is `True`. Use the `ReadFields` method to return an array of strings representing one row of parsed data from the file.

How It Works

The `TextFieldParser` class can be found in the `Microsoft.VisualBasic.FileIO` namespace. You can either use one of its constructors to create an instance directly or use the `Shared My.Computer.FileSystem.OpenTextFieldParser` method to return an instance. Some of the more important properties and methods of this class are listed in Table 5-7.

Table 5-7. *Key Properties and Methods of the TextFieldParser Class*

Property or Method	Description
CommentTokens	An array of strings that indicates which lines in the file are comments. Commented lines are skipped.
Delimiters	An array of strings that defines the delimiters used in the text file. TextFieldType must be set to FieldType.Delimited to use this property.
EndOfData	Returns True if there is no more data to be parsed.
ErrorLine	Returns the actual line in the file that threw the last MalformedLineException.
ErrorLineNumber	Returns the line number that threw the last MalformedLineException.
FieldWidths	An array of integers that defines the widths of each field. TextFieldType must be set to FieldType.FixedWidth to use this property.
HasFieldsEnclosedInQuotes	Indicates whether some fields are enclosed in quotation marks. This is True by default.
TextFieldType	Indicates the type of file from the FieldType enumeration (Delimited or FixedWidth) that is being parsed. This is set to Delimited by default.
ReadFields	Reads and parses all fields for the current row and returns the data as an array of strings. The pointer is then moved to the next row. If a field cannot be parsed, a MalformedLineException is thrown.
SetDelimiters	Sets the Delimiters property to the value or values specified. The single parameter for this method is a parameter array, so you can supply a comma-separated list of values rather than an actual array.
SetFieldWidths	Sets the FieldWidths property to the value or values specified. The single parameter for this method is a parameter array, so you can supply a comma-separated list of values rather than an actual array.

Once you have an instance, you need to configure it according to the file you need to parse. If your file is delimited, set the `TextFieldType` property to `Delimited` and set the `Delimiters` property to the appropriate delimiters. If the file is fixed width, set the TextFieldType property to FixedWidth and set the FieldWidths property to the appropriate widths. Use the CommentTokens property to instruct the parser to skip rows that are comments and do not contain any data to be parsed.

Use the ReadFields method to parse the current row, return an array of strings containing each field parsed, and move the file pointer to the next row. If a field cannot be parsed, a MalformedLineException is thrown. You can then use the ErrorLine and ErrorLineNumber properties of the TextFieldParser class to obtain information about which line and field caused the exception.

The Code

The following example creates a sample comma-delimited log file. The file is then read and parsed, using the TextFieldParser class. The fields contained in the file are written to the console.

```
Imports System
Imports System.IO
Imports Microsoft.VisualBasic.FileIO

Namespace Apress.VisualBasicRecipes.Chapter05

    Public Class Recipe05_09

        Public Shared Sub Main()

            ' Create the sample log file.
            Using w As StreamWriter = ➡
My.Computer.FileSystem.OpenTextFileWriter("SampleLog.txt", ➡
 False, System.Text.Encoding.UTF8)

                ' Write sample log records to the file. The parser
                ' will skip blank lines. Also, the TextFieldParser
                ' can be configured to ignore lines that are comments.
                w.WriteLine("# In this sample log file, comments " & ➡
"start with a # character. The")
                w.WriteLine("# parser, when configured correctly, " & ➡
"will ignore these lines.")
                w.WriteLine("")
                w.WriteLine("{0},INFO,""{1}""", DateTime.Now, ➡
"Some informational text.")
                w.WriteLine("{0},WARN,""{1}""", DateTime.Now, ➡
"Some warning message.")
                w.WriteLine("{0},ERR!,""{1}""", DateTime.Now, ➡
"[ERROR] Some exception has occurred.")
                w.WriteLine("{0},INFO,""{1}""", DateTime.Now, ➡
"More informational text.")
                w.WriteLine("{0},ERR!,""{1}""", DateTime.Now, ➡
"[ERROR] Some exception has occurred.")

            End Using

            Console.WriteLine("Press Enter to read and parse the information.")
            Console.ReadLine()
```

```vbnet
            ' Open the file in and parse the data into a
            ' TextFieldParser object.
            Using logFile As TextFieldParser = ➥
My.Computer.FileSystem.OpenTextFieldParser("SampleLog.txt")

                Console.WriteLine("Parsing text file.")
                Console.WriteLine(Environment.NewLine)

                ' Write header information to the console.
                Console.WriteLine("{0,-29} {1} {2}", "Date/Time in RFC1123", ➥
"Type", "Message")

                ' Configure the parser. For this recipe, make sure
                ' HasFieldsEnclosedInQuotes is True.
                logFile.TextFieldType = FieldType.Delimited
                logFile.CommentTokens = New String() {"#"}
                logFile.Delimiters = New String() {","}
                logFile.HasFieldsEnclosedInQuotes = True

                Dim currentRecord As String()

                ' Loop through the file until we reach the end.
                Do While Not logFile.EndOfData
                    Try
                        ' Parse all the fields into the currentRow
                        ' array. This method automatically moves
                        ' the file pointer to the next row.
                        currentRecord = logFile.ReadFields

                        ' Write the parsed record to the console.
                        Console.WriteLine("{0:r} {1} {2}", ➥
DateTime.Parse(currentRecord(0)), currentRecord(1), currentRecord(2))
                    Catch ex As MalformedLineException
                        ' The MalformedLineException is thrown by the
                        ' TextFieldParser anytime a line cannot be
                        ' parsed.
                        Console.WriteLine("An exception occurred attempting " & ➥
"to parse this row:  ", ex.Message)
                    End Try
                Loop
            End Using


        ' Wait to continue.
        Console.WriteLine(Environment.NewLine)
        Console.WriteLine("Main method complete. Press Enter.")
        Console.ReadLine()

    End Sub

    End Class
End Namespace
```

5-10. Read a File Asynchronously

Problem

You need to read data from a file without blocking the execution of your code. This technique is commonly used if the file is stored on a slow backing store (such as a networked drive in a wide area network).

Solution

Create a separate class that will read the file asynchronously. Start reading a block of data using the FileStream.BeginRead method and supply a callback method. When the callback is triggered, retrieve the data by calling FileStream.EndRead, process it, and read the next block asynchronously with BeginRead.

How It Works

The FileStream includes basic support for asynchronous use through the BeginRead and EndRead methods. Using these methods, you can read a block of data on one of the threads provided by the .NET Framework thread pool, without needing to directly use the threading classes in the System. Threading namespace.

When reading a file asynchronously, you choose the amount of data that you want to read at a time. Depending on the situation, you might want to read a very small amount of data at a time (for example, if you are copying it block by block to another file) or a relatively large amount of data (for example, if you need a certain amount of information before your processing logic can start). You specify the block size when calling BeginRead, and you pass a buffer where the data will be placed. Because the BeginRead and EndRead methods need to be able to access many of the same pieces of information, such as the FileStream, the buffer, the block size, and so on, it's usually easiest to encapsulate your asynchronous file reading code in a single class.

The Code

The following example demonstrates reading a file asynchronously. The AsyncProcessor class provides a public StartProcess method, which starts an asynchronous read. Every time the read operation finishes, the OnCompletedRead callback is triggered and the block of data is processed. If there is more data in the file, a new asynchronous read operation is started. AsyncProcessor reads 2 kilobytes (2,048 bytes) at a time.

```
Imports System
Imports System.IO
Imports System.Threading

Namespace Apress.VisualBasicRecipes.Chapter05

    Public Class AsyncProcessor

        Private inputStream As Stream

        ' The buffer that will hold the retrieved data.
        Private buffer As Byte()

        ' The amount that will be read in one block (2KB).
        Private m_BufferSize As Integer = 2048
```

```vb
        Public ReadOnly Property BufferSize() As Integer
            Get
                Return m_BufferSize
            End Get
        End Property

        Public Sub New(ByVal fileName As String, ByVal size As Integer)

            m_BufferSize = size
            buffer = New Byte(m_BufferSize) {}

            ' Open the file, specifying true for asynchronous support.
            inputStream = New FileStream(fileName, FileMode.Open, FileAccess.Read, ➡
    FileShare.Read, m_BufferSize, True)

        End Sub

        Public Sub StartProcess()

            ' Start the asynchronous read, which will fill the buffer.
            inputStream.BeginRead(buffer, 0, buffer.Length, ➡
    AddressOf OnCompletedRead, Nothing)

        End Sub

        Private Sub OnCompletedRead(ByVal asyncResult As IAsyncResult)

            ' One block has been read asynchronously. Retrieve
            ' the data.
            Dim bytesRead As Integer = inputStream.EndRead(asyncResult)

            ' If no bytes are read, the stream is at the end of the file.
            If bytesRead > 0 Then
                ' Pause to simulate processing this block of data.
                Console.WriteLine("{0}[ASYNC READER]: Read one block.", ➡
    ControlChars.Tab)
                Thread.Sleep(20)

                ' Begin to read the next block asynchronously.
                inputStream.BeginRead(buffer, 0, buffer.Length, ➡
    AddressOf OnCompletedRead, Nothing)
            Else
                ' End the operation.
                Console.WriteLine("{0}[ASYNC READER]: Complete.", ControlChars.Tab)
                inputStream.Close()
            End If

        End Sub

    End Class
End Namespace
```

Usage

The following example shows a console application that uses `AsyncProcessor` to read a 2-megabyte file.

```vbnet
Imports System
Imports System.IO
Imports System.Threading

Namespace Apress.VisualBasicRecipes.Chapter05

    Public Class Recipe05_10

        Public Shared Sub Main(ByVal args As String())
            ' Create a 2 MB test file.
            Using fs As New FileStream("test.txt", FileMode.Create)
                fs.SetLength(2097152)
            End Using

            ' Start the asynchronous file processor on another thread.
            Dim asyncIO As New AsyncProcessor("test.txt", 2048)
            asyncIO.StartProcess()

            ' At the same time, do some other work.
            ' In this example, we simply loop for 10 seconds.
            Dim startTime As DateTime = DateTime.Now


            While DateTime.Now.Subtract(startTime).TotalSeconds < 10
                Console.WriteLine("[MAIN THREAD]: Doing some work.")

                ' Pause to simulate a time-consuming operation.
                Thread.Sleep(100)
            End While

            Console.WriteLine("[MAIN THREAD]: Complete.")
            Console.ReadLine()

            ' Remove the test file.
            File.Delete("test.txt")
        End Sub

    End Class
End Namespace
```

The following is an example of the output you will see when you run this test.

```
[MAIN THREAD]: Doing some work.
        [ASYNC READER]: Read one block.
        [ASYNC READER]: Read one block.
[MAIN THREAD]: Doing some work.
        [ASYNC READER]: Read one block.
        [ASYNC READER]: Read one block.
        [ASYNC READER]: Read one block.
        [ASYNC READER]: Read one block.
[MAIN THREAD]: Doing some work.
```

```
[ASYNC READER]: Read one block.
[ASYNC READER]: Read one block.
[ASYNC READER]: Read one block.
. . .
```

5-11. Find Files That Match a Wildcard Expression

Problem

You need to process multiple files based on a filter expression (such as *.dll or mysheet20??.xls).

Solution

Use the overloaded version of the System.IO.DirectoryInfo.GetFiles method that accepts a filter expression and returns an array of FileInfo objects. For searching recursively across all subdirectories, use the overloaded version that accepts the SearchOption enumeration.

How It Works

The DirectoryInfo and Directory objects both provide a way to search the directories for files that match a specific filter expression. These search expressions can use the standard ? and * wildcards. You can use a similar technique to retrieve directories that match a specified search pattern by using the overloaded DirectoryInfo.GetDirectories method. The GetFiles method, used in several other recipes in this chapter to retrieve a list of files, includes an overload that lets you specify that you want to search recursively using the SearchOption.AllDirectories enumeration constant.

As an alternative, you can also use the Shared GetFiles method of the My.Computer.FileSystem class. This method returns only strings representing the full path of the file, rather than FileInfo objects. As with the System.IO.DirectoryInfo.GetFiles method, you can use an overload to search recursively using the SearchOptions.SearchAllSubDirectories enumeration constant. This method also allows you to search for multiple file extensions at once.

The Code

The following example retrieves the names of all the files in a specified directory that match a specified filter string. The directory and filter expression are submitted as command-line arguments. The code then iterates through the retrieved FileInfo collection of matching files and displays the name and size of each one.

```vb
Imports System
Imports System.IO

Namespace Apress.VisualBasicRecipes.Chapter05

    Public Class Recipe05_11
        Public Shared Sub Main(ByVal args As String())

            If args.Length = 2 Then
                Dim dir As New DirectoryInfo(args(0))
                Dim files As FileInfo() = dir.GetFiles(args(1))
```

```
        ' Display the name of all the files.
        For Each file As FileInfo In files
            Console.Write("Name: " & file.Name + "  ")
            Console.WriteLine("Size: " & file.Length.ToString)
        Next

        ' Wait to continue.
        Console.WriteLine(Environment.NewLine)
        Console.WriteLine("Main method complete. Press Enter.")
        Console.ReadLine()

    Else
        Console.WriteLine("USAGE:  Recipe05-11 [directory]" & ➡
"[filterExpression]")
        End If

    End Sub

    End Class
End Namespace
```

Usage

If you run the command Recipe05-11 c:\ *.sys, the example produces the following output:

```
Name: config.sys  Size: 10
Name: hiberfil.sys  Size: 2147016704
Name: pagefile.sys  Size: 2460942336

Main method complete. Press Enter.
```

5-12. Test Two Files for Equality

Problem

You need to quickly compare the content of two files and determine whether it matches exactly.

Solution

Calculate the hash code of each file using the System.Security.Cryptography.HashAlgorithm class, and then compare the hash codes.

How It Works

You might compare file content in a number of ways. For example, you could examine a portion of the file for similar data, or you could read through each file byte by byte, comparing each byte as you go. Both of these approaches are valid, but in some cases, it's more convenient to use a *hash code* algorithm.

A hash code algorithm generates a small (typically about 20 bytes) binary fingerprint for a file. While it's *possible* for different files to generate the same hash codes, that is statistically unlikely to occur. In fact, even a minor change (for example, modifying a single bit in the source file) has an approximately 50-percent chance of independently changing each bit in the hash code. For this reason, hash codes are often used in security code to detect data tampering. (Hash codes are discussed in more detail in recipes 13-14, 13-15, and 13-16.)

To create a hash code, you must first create a HashAlgorithm object, typically by calling the Shared HashAlgorithm.Create method. This defaults to using the sha1 algorithm but provides an overload allowing other algorithms to be provided. You then call the HashAlgorithm.ComputeHash, method, passing in a byte array or string representing the data to be hashed. The hashed data is returned in a byte array.

The Code

The following example demonstrates a simple console application that reads two file names that are supplied as arguments and uses hash codes to test the files for equality. The hashes are compared by converting them into strings. Alternatively, you could compare them by iterating over the byte array and comparing each value. That approach would be slightly faster, but because the overhead of converting 20 bytes into a string is minimal, it's not required.

```
Imports System
Imports System.IO
Imports System.Security.Cryptography

Namespace Apress.VisualBasicRecipes.Chapter05

    Public Class Recipe05_12
        Public Shared Sub Main(ByVal args As String())

            If args.Length = 2 Then
                Console.WriteLine("comparing {0} and {1}", args(0), args(1))

                ' Create the hashing object.
                Using hashAlg As HashAlgorithm = HashAlgorithm.Create
                    Using fsA As New FileStream(args(0), FileMode.Open), ➡
fsB As New FileStream(args(1), FileMode.Open)
                        ' Calculate the hash for the files.
                        Dim hashBytesA As Byte() = hashAlg.ComputeHash(fsA)
                        Dim hashBytesB As Byte() = hashAlg.ComputeHash(fsB)

                        ' Compare the hashes.
                        If BitConverter.ToString(hashBytesA) = ➡
BitConverter.ToString(hashBytesB) Then
                            Console.WriteLine("Files match.")
                        Else
                            Console.WriteLine("No match.")
                        End If

                    End Using

                    ' Wait to continue.
                    Console.WriteLine(Environment.NewLine)
                    Console.WriteLine("Main method complete. Press Enter.")
                    Console.ReadLine()

                End Using
```

```
        Else
            Console.WriteLine("USAGE:  Recipe05-12 [fileName] [fileName]")
        End If

    End Sub

  End Class
End Namespace
```

Usage

You use this recipe by executing it and passing in a parameter for each file to compare: `Recipe05-12 c:\SomeFile.txt c:\SomeOtherFile.txt`. If the files are equal, "Files Match" will be displayed on the console. Otherwise, "No Match" will be displayed.

5-13. Manipulate Strings Representing File Names

Problem

You want to retrieve a portion of a path or verify that a file path is in a normal (standardized) form.

Solution

Process the path using the `System.IO.Path` class. You can use `Path.GetFileName` to retrieve a file name from a path, `Path.ChangeExtension` to modify the extension portion of a path string, and `Path.Combine` to create a fully qualified path without worrying about whether your directory includes a trailing directory separation (\) character.

How It Works

File paths are often difficult to work with in code because of the many different ways to represent the same directory. For example, you might use an absolute path (C:\Temp), a UNC path (\\MyServer\\MyShare\temp), or one of many possible relative paths (C:\Temp\MyFiles\..\ or C:\Temp\MyFiles\..\..\temp).

The easiest way to handle file system paths is to use the `Shared` methods of the `Path` class to make sure you have the information you expect. For example, here is how to take a file name that might include a qualified path and extract just the file name:

```
Dim filename As String = "..\System\MyFile.txt"
filename = Path.GetFileName(filename)

' Now filename = "MyFile.txt"
```

And here is how you might append the file name to a directory path using the `Path.Combine` method:

```
Dim filename As String = "..\..\myfile.txt"
Dim fullPath As String = "c:\Temp"

filename = Path.GetFileName(filename)
fullPath = Path.Combine(fullPath, filename)

' fullPath is now "c:\Temp\myfile.txt"
```

The advantage of this approach is that a trailing backslash (\) is automatically added to the path name if required. The Path class also provides the following useful Shared methods for manipulating path information:

- GetExtension returns just the extension of the file in the string. If there is no extension, an empty string is returned.

- ChangeExtension modifies the current extension of the file in a string. If no extension is specified, the current extension will be removed.

- GetDirectoryName returns all the directory information, which is the text between the first and last directory separators (\).

- GetFileNameWithoutExtension is similar to GetFileName, but it omits the extension.

- GetFullPath has no effect on an absolute path, and it changes a relative path into an absolute path using the current directory. For example, if C:\Temp\ is the current directory, calling GetFullPath on a file name such as test.txt returns C:\Temp\test.txt.

- GetPathRoot retrieves a string with the root (for example, "C:\"), provided that information is in the string. For a relative path, it returns Nothing.

- HasExtension returns True if the path ends with an extension.

- IsPathRooted returns True if the path is an absolute path and False if it's a relative path.

The My.Computer.FileSystem offers two Shared methods that also work with paths. The CombinePath method is the equivalent of Path.Combine. The GetParentPath method, similar to the GetDirectoryName method, returns the path of the parent folder for the path specified.

Note In most cases, an exception will be thrown if you try to supply an invalid path to one of these methods (for example, paths that include illegal characters). However, path names that are invalid because they contain a wildcard character (* or ?) will not cause the methods to throw an exception. You could use the Path.GetInvalidPathChars or Path.GetInvalidFileNameChars method to obtain an array of characters that are illegal in path or file names, respectively.

5-14. Determine Whether a Path Is a Directory or a File

Problem

You have a path (in the form of a string), and you want to determine whether it corresponds to a directory or a file.

Solution

Test the path with the Directory.Exists and File.Exists methods.

How It Works

The System.IO.Directory and System.IO.File classes both provide a Shared Exists method. The Directory.Exists method returns True if a supplied relative or absolute path corresponds to an existing directory, even a shared folder with an UNC name. File.Exists returns True if the path corresponds to an existing file.

As an alternative, you can use the Shared FileExists and DirectoryExists methods of the My.Computer.FileSystem class. These methods work in the same way as the Exists method of the System.IO.Directory and System.IO.File classes.

The Code

The following example demonstrates how you can quickly determine whether a path corresponds to a file or directory.

```
Imports System
Imports System.IO

Namespace Apress.VisualBasicRecipes.Chapter05

    Public Class Recipe05_14
        Public Shared Sub Main(ByVal args As String())

            For Each arg As String In args
                Console.Write(arg)

                If Directory.Exists(arg) Then
                    Console.WriteLine(" is a directory.")
                ElseIf File.Exists(arg) Then
                    Console.WriteLine(" is a file.")
                Else
                    Console.WriteLine(" does not exist.")
                End If
            Next

            ' Wait to continue.
            Console.WriteLine(Environment.NewLine)
            Console.WriteLine("Main method complete. Press Enter.")
            Console.ReadLine()

        End Sub

    End Class
End Namespace
```

Usage

You use this recipe by executing it and passing in a parameter representing a path to a file or a directory: Recipe05-14 c:\SomeFile or Recipe05-14 c:\SomeDirectory. A message notifying you whether the path refers to a directory or a file will be displayed.

5-15. Work with Relative Paths

Problem

You want to set the current working directory so that you can use relative paths in your code.

Solution

Use the Shared GetCurrentDirectory and SetCurrentDirectory methods of the System.IO.Directory class.

How It Works

Relative paths are automatically interpreted in relation to the current working directory, which is the path of the current application by default. You can retrieve the current working directory by calling Directory.GetCurrentDirectory or change it using Directory.SetCurrentDirectory. In addition, you can use the Shared GetFullPath method of the System.IO.Path class to convert a relative path into an absolute path using the current working directory.

The Code

The following is a simple example that demonstrates working with relative paths.

```
Imports System
Imports System.IO

Namespace Apress.VisualBasicRecipes.Chapter05

    Public Class Recipe05_15
        Public Shared Sub Main()

            Console.WriteLine("Using: " & Directory.GetCurrentDirectory())
            Console.WriteLine("The relative path for 'file.txt' will " & ➥
"automatically become: '" & Path.GetFullPath("file.txt") & "'")
            Console.WriteLine()

            Console.WriteLine("Changing current directory to c:\")
            Directory.SetCurrentDirectory("C:\")

            Console.WriteLine("Now the relative path for 'file.txt' will " & ➥
"automatically become: '" & Path.GetFullPath("file.txt") & "'")

            ' Wait to continue.
            Console.WriteLine(Environment.NewLine)
            Console.WriteLine("Main method complete. Press Enter.")
            Console.ReadLine()

        End Sub

    End Class

End Namespace
```

Usage

The output for this example might be the following (if you run the application in the directory C:\temp).

```
Using: c:\temp
The relative path 'file.txt' will automatically become 'c:\temp\file.txt'

Changing current directory to c:\
The relative path 'file.txt' will automatically become 'c:\file.txt'
```

■**Caution** If you use relative paths, it's recommended that you set the working path at the start of each file interaction. Otherwise, you could introduce unnoticed security vulnerabilities that could allow a malicious user to force your application into accessing or overwriting system files by tricking it into using a different working directory.

5-16. Create a Temporary File

Problem

You need to create a file that will be placed in the user-specific temporary directory and will have a unique name, so that it will not conflict with temporary files generated by other programs.

Solution

Use the `Shared GetTempFileName` method of the `System.IO.Path` class, which returns a path made up of the user's temporary directory and a randomly generated file name.

How It Works

You can use a number of approaches to generate temporary files. In simple cases, you might just create a file in the application directory, possibly using a GUID or a timestamp in conjunction with a random value as the file name. However, the `Path` class provides a helper method that can save you some work. It creates a file with a unique file name in the current user's temporary directory. On Windows Vista, this is a folder similar to C:\Users\[username]\AppData\Local\Temp, while on Windows XP it is similar to C:\Documents and Settings\[username]\Local Settings\temp by default.

The Code

The following example demonstrates creating a temporary file.

```
Imports System
Imports System.IO

Namespace Apress.VisualBasicRecipes.Chapter05

    Public Class Recipe05_16
        Public Shared Sub Main()

            Dim tempFile As String = Path.GetTempFileName

            Console.WriteLine("Using " & tempFile)
```

```
    Using fs As New FileStream(tempFile, FileMode.Open)
        ' Write some data
    End Using

    ' Now delete the file.
    File.Delete(tempFile)

    ' Wait to continue.
    Console.WriteLine(Environment.NewLine)
    Console.WriteLine("Main method complete. Press Enter.")
    Console.ReadLine()

End Sub

    End Class
End Namespace
```

5-17. Get the Total Free Space on a Drive

Problem

You need to examine a drive and determine how many bytes of free space are available.

Solution

Use the `DriveInfo.AvailableFreeSpace` property.

How It Works

The `DriveInfo` class provides members that let you find out the drive type, free space, and many other details of a drive. In order to create a new `DriveInfo` object, you need to pass the drive letter or the drive root string to the constructor, such as `'C'` or `"C:\"` for creating a `DriveInfo` instance representing the C drive of the computer. You could also retrieve the list of logical drives available by using the Shared `Directory.GetLogicalDrives` method, which returns an array of strings, each containing the root of the drive, such as `"C:\"`. For more details on each drive, you create a `DriveInfo` instance, passing either the root or the letter corresponding to the logical drive. If you need a detailed description of each logical drive, call the `DriveInfo.GetDrives` method, which returns an array of `DriveInfo` objects, instead of using `Directory.GetLogicalDrives`.

■**Note** A `System.IO.IOException` exception is thrown if you try to access an unavailable network drive.

The Code

The following console application shows the available free space using the `DriveInfo` class for the given drive or for all logical drives if no argument is passed to the application.

```
Imports System
Imports System.IO

Namespace Apress.VisualBasicRecipes.Chapter05
```

```
Public Class Recipe05_17

    Public Shared Sub Main(ByVal args As String())

        If args.Length = 1 Then
            Dim drive As New DriveInfo(args(0))

            Console.Write("Free space in {0}-drive (in kilobytes): ", args(0))
            Console.WriteLine(drive.AvailableFreeSpace / 1024)
        Else
            For Each drive As DriveInfo In DriveInfo.GetDrives

                Try
                    Console.WriteLine("Free space in {0}-drive " & ➥
"(in kilobytes):  {1}", drive.RootDirectory, drive.AvailableFreeSpace / ➥
1024.ToString)
                Catch ex As IOException
                    Console.WriteLine(drive)
                End Try

            Next
        End If

        '  Wait to continue.
        Console.WriteLine(Environment.NewLine)
        Console.WriteLine("Main method complete. Press Enter.")
        Console.ReadLine()

    End Sub

    End Class
End Namespace
```

Note In addition to the AvailableFreeSpace property, DriveInfo also defines a TotalFreeSpace property. The difference between these two properties is that AvailableFreeSpace takes into account disk quotas.

Usage

You use this tool by executing it and passing in one or more drive letters for which you want to return the size, such as Recipe05-17 C:. If you run it without passing any parameters, it will attempt to return the size information for all drives on the system and generate results similar to the following:

```
A:\
Free space in C:\-drive (in kilobytes):   44094956
Free space in D:\-drive (in kilobytes):   0
E:\
Free space in F:\-drive (in kilobytes):   144671240

Main method complete. Press Enter.
```

5-18. Show the Common File Dialog Boxes

Problem

You need to show the standard Windows dialog boxes for opening and saving files and for selecting a folder.

Solution

Use the OpenFileDialog, SaveFileDialog, and FolderBrowserDialog classes in the System.Windows. Forms namespace. Call the ShowDialog method to display the dialog box, examine the return value to determine whether the user clicked Open or Cancel, and retrieve the selection from the FileName or SelectedPath property.

How It Works

The .NET Framework provides objects that wrap many of the standard Windows dialog boxes, including those used for saving and selecting files and directories. Each dialog box is appropriately formatted for the current operating system. The dialog box classes all inherit from System.Windows.Forms. CommonDialog and include the following:

- OpenFileDialog, which allows the user to select a file, as shown in Figure 5-2. The file name and path are provided to your code through the FileName property (or the FileNames collection, if you have enabled multiple file select by setting Multiselect to True). Additionally, you can use the Filter property to set the file format choices and set CheckFileExists. Filter lets you limit the file types that are displayed, and CheckFileExists ensures that only an existing file can be specified.

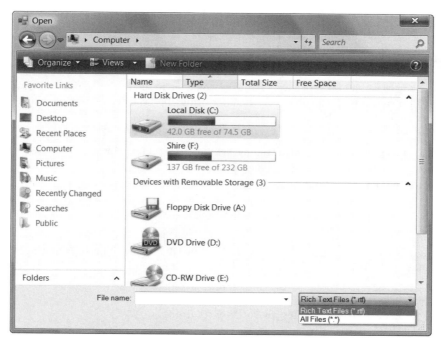

Figure 5-2. *OpenFileDialog shows the Open dialog box.*

- SaveFileDialog, which allows the user to specify a new file. This dialog box looks nearly identical to the OpenFileDialog shown in Figure 5-2 earlier but with appropriate captions. The file name and path are provided to your code through the FileName property. You can also use the Filter property to set the file format choices, and set the CreatePrompt and OverwritePrompt Boolean properties to instruct .NET to display a confirmation if the user selects a new file or an existing file, respectively.

- FolderBrowserDialog, which allows the user to select (and optionally create) a directory, as shown in Figure 5-3. The selected path is provided through the SelectedPath property, and you can specify whether a Make New Folder button should appear using the ShowNewFolderButton property.

Figure 5-3. *FolderBrowserDialog shows the Browse for Folder dialog box.*

When using OpenFileDialog or SaveFileDialog, you need to set the filter string, which specifies the allowed file extensions. If you do not set the filter string, the Type drop-down list will be empty, and all files will be shown in the dialog box.

The filter string is separated with the pipe character (|) in this format:

```
[Text label] | [Extension list separated by semicolons] | [Text label]
| [Extension list separated by semicolons] |  . . .
```

You can also set the Title (form caption) and the InitialDirectory.

The Code

The following code shows a Windows-based application that allows the user to load documents into a RichTextBox, edit the content, and then save the modified document. When opening and saving a document, the OpenFileDialog and SaveFileDialog classes are used.

```
' All designed code is stored in the autogenerated partial
' class called MainForm.Designer.vb. You can see this
' file by selecting Show All Files in Solution Explorer.
Partial Public Class MainForm
```

```
    Private Sub mnuOpen_Click(ByVal sender As Object, ByVal e As System.EventArgs) ➡
Handles mnuOpen.Click

        Dim dlg As New OpenFileDialog

        dlg.Filter = "Rich Text Files (*.rtf)|*.RTF|All Files (*.*)|*.*"
        dlg.CheckFileExists = True
        dlg.InitialDirectory = Application.StartupPath

        If dlg.ShowDialog = Windows.Forms.DialogResult.OK Then
            rtDoc.LoadFile(dlg.FileName)
            rtDoc.Enabled = True
        End If

    End Sub

    Private Sub mnuSave_Click(ByVal sender As Object, ByVal e As System.EventArgs) ➡
Handles mnuSave.Click

        Dim dlg As New SaveFileDialog

        dlg.Filter = "Rich Text Files (*.rtf)|*.RTF" & ➡
"All Files (*.*)|*.*"
        dlg.InitialDirectory = Application.StartupPath

        If dlg.ShowDialog = Windows.Forms.DialogResult.OK Then
            rtDoc.SaveFile(dlg.FileName)
        End If

    End Sub

    Private Sub mnuExit_Click(ByVal sender As Object, ByVal e As System.EventArgs) ➡
Handles mnuExit.Click

        Me.Close()

    End Sub
End Class
```

5-19. Use an Isolated Store

Problem

You need to store data in a file, but your application does not have the required `FileIOPermission` for the local hard drive.

Solution

Use the `IsolatedStorageFile` and `IsolatedStorageFileStream` classes from the `System.IO.IsolatedStorage` namespace. These classes allow your application to write data to a file in a user-specific directory without needing permission to access the local hard drive directly.

How It Works

The .NET Framework includes support for isolated storage, which allows you to read and write to a user-specific or machine-specific virtual file system that the common language runtime (CLR) manages. When you create isolated storage files, the data is automatically serialized to a unique location in the user profile path. In Windows Vista, the profile path is typically something like C:\Users\ [username]\AppData\Local\IsolatedStorage\, while in Windows XP, it is similar to C:\Documents and Settings\[username]\Local Settings\Application Data\isolated storage\).

One reason you might use isolated storage is to give a partially trusted application limited ability to store data. For example, the default CLR security policy gives local code unrestricted FileIOPermission, which allows it to open or write to any file. Code that you run from a remote server on the local intranet is automatically assigned fewer permissions. It lacks the FileIOPermission, but it has the IsolatedStoragePermission, giving it the ability to use isolated stores. (The security policy also limits the maximum amount of space that can be used in an isolated store.) Another reason you might use an isolated store is to better secure data. For example, data in one user's isolated store will be restricted from another non-administrative user.

By default, each isolated store is segregated by user and assembly. That means that when the same user runs the same application, the application will access the data in the same isolated store. However, you can choose to segregate it further by application domain, so that multiple AppDomain instances running in the same application receive different isolated stores.

The files are stored as part of a user's profile, so users can access their isolated storage files on any workstation they log on to if roaming profiles are configured on your local area network. (In this case, the store must be specifically designated as a roaming store by applying the IsolatedStorageFile. Roaming flag when it's created.) By letting the .NET Framework and the CLR provide these levels of isolation, you can relinquish some responsibility for maintaining the separation between files, and you do not need to worry as much that programming oversights or misunderstandings will cause loss of critical data.

The Code

The following example shows how you can access isolated storage.

```vb
Imports System
Imports System.IO
Imports System.IO.IsolatedStorage

Namespace Apress.VisualBasicRecipes.Chapter05

    Public Class Recipe05_19
        Public Shared Sub Main(ByVal args As String())

            ' Create the store for the current user.
            Using store As IsolatedStorageFile = ➥
IsolatedStorageFile.GetUserStoreForAssembly
                ' Create a folder in the root of the isolated store.
                store.CreateDirectory("MyFolder")

                ' Create a file in the isolated store.
                Using fs As New IsolatedStorageFileStream("MyFile.txt", ➥
FileMode.Create, store)
                    Dim w As New StreamWriter(fs)

                    ' You can now write to the file as normal.
                    w.WriteLine("Test")
                    w.Flush()
```

```
        End Using

        Console.WriteLine("Current size: " & store.CurrentSize.ToString)
        Console.WriteLine("Scope: " & store.Scope.ToString)
        Console.WriteLine("Contained files include:")

        Dim files As String() = store.GetFileNames("*.*")
        For Each file As String In files
            Console.WriteLine(file)
        Next

    End Using

    ' Wait to continue.
    Console.WriteLine(Environment.NewLine)
    Console.WriteLine("Main method complete. Press Enter.")
    Console.ReadLine()

    End Sub

    End Class
End Namespace
```

The following demonstrates using multiple AppDomain instances running in the same application to receive different isolated stores.

```
' Access isolated storage for the current user and assembly
' (which is equivalent to the first example).
store = IsolatedStorageFile.GetStore(IsolatedStorageScope.User Or ➥
IsolatedStorageScope.Assembly, Nothing, Nothing)

' Access isolated storage for the current user, assembly,
' and application domain.  In other words, this data is
' accessible only by the current AppDomain instance.
store = IsolatedStorageFile.GetStore(IsolatedStorageScope.User Or ➥
IsolatedStorageScope.Assembly Or IsolatedStorageScope.Domain, Nothing, Nothing)
```

The preceding use of GetStore is equivalent to calling the GetUserStoreForDomain method of the IsolatedStorageFile class.

5-20. Monitor the File System for Changes

Problem

You need to react when a file system change is detected in a specific path (such as a file modification or creation).

Solution

Use the System.IO.FileSystemWatcher component, specify the path or file you want to monitor, and handle the Error, Created, Deleted, Renamed, and Changed events as needed.

How It Works

When linking together multiple applications and business processes, it's often necessary to create a program that waits idly and becomes active only when a new file is received or changed. You can create this type of program by scanning a directory periodically, but you face a key trade-off. The more often you scan, the more system resources you waste. The less often you scan, the longer it will take to detect a change. The solution is to use the FileSystemWatcher class to react directly to Windows file events.

To use FileSystemWatcher, you must create an instance and set the following properties:

- Path indicates the directory you want to monitor.

- Filter indicates the types of files you are monitoring.

- NotifyFilter indicates the type of changes you are monitoring.

FileSystemWatcher raises four key events: Created, Deleted, Renamed, and Changed. All of these events provide information through their FileSystemEventArgs parameter, including the name of the file (Name), the full path (FullPath), and the type of change (ChangeType). The Renamed event provides a RenamedEventArgs instance, which derives from FileSystemEventArgs, and adds information about the original file name (OldName and OldFullPath).

By default, the FileSystemWatcher is disabled. To start it, you must set the FileSystemWatcher. EnableRaisingEvents property to True. If you ever need to disable it, just set the property to False.

The Created, Deleted, and Renamed events require no configuration. However, if you want to use the Changed event, you need to use the NotifyFilter property to indicate the types of changes you want to watch. Otherwise, your program might be swamped by an unceasing series of events as files are modified.

The NotifyFilter property, which defaults to LastWrite, FileName, and DirectoryName, can be set using any combination of the following values from the System.IO.NotifyFilters enumeration:

- Attributes

- CreationTime

- DirectoryName

- FileName

- LastAccess

- LastWrite

- Security

- Size

The FileSystemWatcher is capable of detecting many file- or folder-related actions at once. It does this by creating and using threads from the ThreadPool to handle the appropriate events. As events occur, they are queued in an internal buffer. If this buffer overflows, some of the events may be lost. This overflow fires the Error event. You should handle this event to log or resolve this issue if it arises.

The Code

The following example shows a console application that handles Created and Deleted events, and tests these events by creating a test file.

```
Imports System
Imports System.IO
Imports System.Windows.Forms
```

```vb
Namespace Apress.VisualBasicRecipes.Chapter05

    Public Class Recipe05_20
        Public Shared Sub Main()

            Using watch As New FileSystemWatcher

                watch.Path = Application.StartupPath
                watch.Filter = "*.*"
                watch.IncludeSubdirectories = True

                ' Attach the event handlers.
                AddHandler watch.Created, AddressOf OnCreatedOrDeleted
                AddHandler watch.Deleted, AddressOf OnCreatedOrDeleted
                watch.EnableRaisingEvents = True

                Console.WriteLine("Press Enter to create a file.")
                Console.ReadLine()

                If File.Exists("test.bin") Then
                    File.Delete("test.bin")
                End If

                ' Create test.bin file.
                Using fs As New FileStream("test.bin", FileMode.Create)
                    ' Do something here...
                End Using

                Console.WriteLine("Press Enter to terminate the application.")
                Console.ReadLine()

            End Using

            ' Wait to continue.
            Console.WriteLine(Environment.NewLine)
            Console.WriteLine("Main method complete. Press Enter.")
            Console.ReadLine()

        End Sub

        ' Fires when a new file is created or deleted in the directory
        ' that is being monitored.
        Private Shared Sub OnCreatedOrDeleted(ByVal sender As Object, ➥
ByVal e As FileSystemEventArgs)

            ' Display the notification information.
            Console.WriteLine("{0}NOTIFICATION: {1} was {2}", ControlChars.Tab, ➥
e.FullPath, e.ChangeType.ToString)
            Console.WriteLine()

        End Sub

    End Class
End Namespace
```

5-21. Access a COM Port

Problem

You need to send data directly to a serial port.

Solution

Use the `System.IO.Ports.SerialPort` class. This class represents a serial port resource and defines methods that enable communication through it.

How It Works

The .NET Framework defines a `System.IO.Ports` namespace that contains several classes. The central class is `SerialPort`. A `SerialPort` instance represents a serial port resource and provides methods that let you communicate through it. The `SerialPort` class also exposes properties that let you specify the port, baud rate, parity, and other information. If you need a list of the available COM ports, the `SerialPort` class provides the `GetPortNames` method, which returns a string array containing the names of each port.

As an alternative, the `My` object contains the `My.Computer.Ports` class, which can be used to work with ports. This class contains the `Shared SerialPortNames` property and the `Shared OpenSerialPort` method. `SerialPortNames` is equivalent to the `GetPortNames` method, but it returns a `ReadOnlyCollection(Of String)`, which is a read-only collection of strings. `OpenSerialPort` returns a `SerialPort` instance. This method has several overloads that let you correctly configure the returned instance.

The Code

The following example demonstrates a simple console application that lists all available COM ports and then writes a string to the first available one.

```
Imports System
Imports System.IO.Ports

Namespace Apress.VisualBasicRecipes.Chapter05

    Public Class Recipe05_21
        Public Shared Sub Main()

            ' Enumerate each of the available COM ports
            ' on the computer.
            Console.WriteLine("Available Ports on this computer:")
            For Each portName As String In SerialPort.GetPortNames
                Console.WriteLine("PORT: " & portName)
            Next
            Console.WriteLine()


            ' For this example, lets just grab the first item from
            ' the array returned by the GetPortNames method.
            Dim testPort As String = SerialPort.GetPortNames(0)
            Using port As New SerialPort(testPort)
```

```
            ' Set the properties.
            port.BaudRate = 9600
            port.Parity = Parity.None
            port.ReadTimeout = 10
            port.StopBits = StopBits.One

            ' Write a message into the port.
            port.Open()
            port.Write("Hello world!")
            port.Close()

            Console.WriteLine("Wrote to the {0} port.", testPort)

        End Using

        ' Wait to continue.
        Console.WriteLine(Environment.NewLine)
        Console.WriteLine("Main method complete. Press Enter.")
        Console.ReadLine()

    End Sub

    End Class
End Namespace
```

5-22. Get a Random File Name

Problem

You need to get a random name for creating a folder or a file.

Solution

Use the Path.GetRandomFileName method, which returns a random name.

How It Works

The System.IO.Path class includes a GetRandomFileName method that generates a random string that can be used for creating a new file or folder. The difference between GetRandomFileName and GetTempFileName (discussed in recipe 5-16) of the Path class is that GetRandomFileName just returns a random string and does not create a file, whereas GetTempFileName creates a new 0-byte temporary file and returns the path to the file.

5-23. Manipulate the Access Control Lists of a File or Directory

Problem

You want to modify the access control list (ACL) of a file or directory in the computer.

Solution

Use the `GetAccessControl` and `SetAccessControl` methods of the `File` or `Directory` class.

How It Works

The .NET Framework includes support for ACLs for resources such as I/O, registry, and threading classes. You can retrieve and apply the ACL for a resource by using the `GetAccessControl` and `SetAccessControl` methods defined in the corresponding resource classes. For example, the `File` and `Directory` classes define both these methods, which let you manipulate the ACLs for a file or directory.

To add or remove an ACL-associated right of a file or directory, you need to first retrieve the `FileSecurity` or `DirectorySecurity` object currently applied to the resource using the `GetAccessControl` method. Once you retrieve this object, you need to perform the required modification of the rights, and then apply the ACL back to the resource using the `SetAccessControl` method. Table 5-8 shows a list of the common methods used for adding and removing ACL permissions.

Table 5-8. *Key Methods for Adding and Removing ACLs*

Method	Description
AddAccessRule	Adds the permissions specified.
ResetAccessRule	Adds the permissions specified. If the specified permission already exists, it will be replaced.
RemoveAccessRule	Removes all of the permissions that match the specified rule.
RemoveAccessRuleAll	Removes all permissions for the user referenced in the specified rule.
RemoveAccessRuleSpecific	Removes the permissions specified.

The Code

The following example demonstrates the effect of denying Everyone Read access to a temporary file, using a console application. An attempt to read the file after a change in the ACL triggers a security exception.

```
Imports System
Imports System.IO
Imports System.Security.AccessControl


Namespace Apress.VisualBasicRecipes.Chapter05
    Public Class Recipe05_23

        Public Shared Sub Main()
            Dim fileName As String

            ' Create a new file and assign full control to 'Everyone'.
            Console.WriteLine("Press any key to write a new file...")
            Console.ReadKey(True)
```

```vb
        fileName = Path.GetRandomFileName
        Using testStream As New FileStream(fileName, FileMode.Create)
            ' Do something...
        End Using
        Console.WriteLine("Created a new file {0}.", fileName)
        Console.WriteLine()

        ' Deny 'Everyone' access to the file.
        Console.WriteLine("Press any key to deny 'Everyone' access " & ➥
"to the file.")
        Console.ReadKey(True)

        SetRule(fileName, "Everyone", FileSystemRights.Read, ➥
AccessControlType.Deny)

        Console.WriteLine("Removed access rights of 'Everyone'.")
        Console.WriteLine()

        ' Attempt to access the file.
        Console.WriteLine("Press any key to attempt to access the file...")
        Console.ReadKey(True)

        Dim stream As FileStream
        Try
            stream = New FileStream(fileName, FileMode.Create)
        Catch ex As Exception
            Console.WriteLine("Exception thrown : ")
            Console.WriteLine(ex.ToString)
        Finally
            If stream IsNot Nothing Then
                stream.Close()
                stream.Dispose()
            End If
        End Try

        ' Wait to continue.
        Console.WriteLine(Environment.NewLine)
        Console.WriteLine("Main method complete. Press Enter.")
        Console.ReadLine()

    End Sub

    Private Shared Sub SetRule(ByVal filePath As String, ByVal account As ➥
String, ByVal rights As FileSystemRights, ByVal controlType As AccessControlType)

        ' Get a FileSecurity object that represents the
        ' current security settings.
        Dim fSecurity As FileSecurity = File.GetAccessControl(filePath)

        ' Update the FileSystemAccessRule with the new
        ' security settings.
        fSecurity.ResetAccessRule(New FileSystemAccessRule(account, rights, ➥
controlType))
```

```
        ' Set the new access settings.
        File.SetAccessControl(filePath, fSecurity)

    End Sub

  End Class
End Namespace
```

CHAPTER 6

■■■

Language Integrated Query (LINQ)

A key element of almost any application is data. Inevitably, data needs to be listed, sorted, analyzed, or displayed in some fashion. It is the nature of what we, as programmers, do. We accomplish this by manually performing the appropriate operations and relying on the current functionality provided by the existing .NET Framework. We also rely heavily on the use of external data sources, such as SQL Server or XML files.

Before LINQ, writing code to query a data source required the query to be sent to the data source as a string where it would be executed. This resulted in a separation of functionality and control between the application and the data. The .NET Framework has always provided functionality (such as ADO.NET) that made things fairly painless, but it required that developers have intimate knowledge of the data source and its respective query language to be able to accomplish their goals.

Most developers have become used to working with data in this manner and have adapted appropriately. Language Integrated Query (LINQ, pronounced "link") has positioned itself to resolve this situation and is one of the major new additions to the .NET Framework 3.5.

LINQ, at its core, is a set of features that, when used together, provide the ability to query any data source. Data can be easily queried and joined from multiple and varying data sources, such as joining data gathered from a SQL Server database and an XML file. The initial release of VB 9.0 includes several APIs that extend LINQ and provide support for the most common data sources, as listed in Table 6-1. LINQ was designed to be easily extended, which you can take advantage of to create full query support for any other data sources not covered by the included APIs.

Table 6-1. *APIs That Extend LINQ*

Name	Namespace	Supported Data Source
LINQ to Objects	`System.Linq`	Objects that inherit from `IEnumerable` or `IEnumerable(Of T)` (covered in this chapter)
LINQ to XML	`System.Xml.Linq`	XML documents (covered in Chapter 7)
LINQ to SQL	`System.Data.Linq`	SQL Server databases (covered in Chapter 8)
LINQ to DataSet	`System.Data`	ADO.NET datasets (covered in Chapter 8)
LINQ to Entities	`System.Data.Objects`	Entity Data Model (EDM) objects[a] (not covered in this book)

[a] *EDM will be released as an addition to Visual Studio 2008 sometime in 2008.*

The primary intent of this chapter is to cover the basic functionality and techniques that make up LINQ, focusing on LINQ to Objects. The recipes in this chapter cover the following:

- Querying data in a collection and controlling what data is returned (recipes 6-1, 6-2, and 6-3)
- Sorting and filtering data in collections (recipes 6-4 and 6-5)
- Performing aggregate operations (such as Min and Max) on collections (recipe 6-6 through recipe 6-9)
- Grouping and joining data in one or more collections (recipes 6-10 and 6-11)
- Retrieving a subset of data from a collection (recipes 6-12)
- Using paging to display the contents of a collection (recipe 6-13)
- Comparing and combining two collections (recipe 6-14)
- Casting a collection to a specific type (recipe 6-15)

■Note LINQ relies heavily on the following functionality introduced in version 3.5 of the .NET Framework: implicit typing, object initializers, anonymous types, extension methods, and lambda expressions. To better understand this chapter, you should first review the recipes in Chapter 1 that cover these new concepts.

6-1. Query a Generic Collection

Problem

You need to query data that is stored in a collection that implements IEnumerable(Of T).

Solution

Create a general LINQ query, using the From clause, to iterate through the data stored in the target collection.

How It Works

LINQ to Objects, represented by the System.Linq namespace, extends the core LINQ framework and provides the mechanisms necessary to query data stored in objects that inherit IEnumerable(Of T). Querying IEnumerable objects is also supported but requires an extra step, which is covered in recipe 6-2.

A standard query consists of one or more query operators that query the given data source and return the specified results. If you have any familiarity with Structured Query Language (SQL), which LINQ closely resembles, you will quickly recognize these standard operators. Here is an example query, assuming names is an IEnumerable(Of String):

```
Dim query = From name In names
```

This query uses the From clause, which designates the source of the data. This clause is structured like a For...Next loop where you specify a variable to be used as the iterator (in the case, name) and the source (in this case, names). As you can see by the example, you do not need to specify the data type for the iterator because it is inferred based on the data type of the source. It is possible to reference more than one data source in a single From clause, which would then allow you to query on each source or a combination of both (see recipe 6-11 for more details).

It is important to note that the previous example does not actually do anything. After that line of code executes, `query` is an `IEnumerable(Of T)` that contains only information and instructions that define the query. The query will not be executed until you actually iterate through the results. Most queries work in this manner, but it is possible to force the query to execute immediately.

Like `name`, the data type for the results (`query`) is also being inferred. The data type depends on what is being returned by the actual query. In this case, that would be an `IEnumerable(Of String)` since `name` is a `String`. When creating queries, you are not required to use type inference. You could have used the following:

```
Dim query As IEnumerable(Of String) = From name As String In names Select name
```

Although that would work, type inference makes the query appear much cleaner and easier to follow. Since the example returns a sequence of values, you execute the query by iterating through it using a `For...Next` loop, as shown here:

```
For Each name in query
    ...
Next
```

If you need to ensure that duplicate data in the source is not part of the results, then you can add the `Distinct` clause to the end of your query. Any duplicate items in the source collection will be skipped when the query is executed. If you did this to the previous example, it would look like this:

```
Dim query = From name In names Distinct
```

Both of the previous example queries use what is known as *query syntax*, which is distinguished by the use of query clauses (such as `From` or `Distinct`). Query syntax is used primarily for appearance and ease of use. When the code is compiled, however, this syntax is translated to and compiled as *method syntax*.

Behind all query operators (clauses) is an actual method. The exception to this rule is the `From` clause, which simply translates to the `For...Next` loop shown previously. These methods are actually extension methods that extend `IEnumberable(Of T)` and are found in the `System.Linq.Enumerable` class. The previous example would be compiled as this:

```
Dim query = names.Distinct
```

Query syntax is much easier to understand and appears cleaner in code, especially with longer or more advanced queries. However, with some query operators, method syntax can give you more fine-tuned control over the operation itself or the results.

The Code

The following example queries the array of `Process` objects returned from the `Process.GetProcess` function and displays them to the console:

```
Imports System
Imports System.Linq
Imports System.Diagnostics

Namespace Apress.VisualBasicRecipes.Chapter06
    Public Class Recipe06_01

        Public Shared Sub Main()
```

```
'  Build the query to return information for all
'  processes running on the current machine.  The
'  data will be returned as instances of the Process
'  class.
Dim procsQuery = From proc In Process.GetProcesses

'  Run the query generated earlier and iterate
'  through the results.
For Each proc In procsQuery
    Console.WriteLine(proc.ProcessName)
Next

'  Wait to continue.
Console.WriteLine()
Console.WriteLine("Main method complete.  Press Enter.")
Console.ReadLine()

        End Sub

    End Class
End Namespace
```

6-2. Query a Nongeneric Collection

Problem

You need to query data that is stored in a collection that implements IEnumerable, such as an ArrayList, rather than IEnumerable(Of T).

Solution

Create a standard LINQ query, such as the one described in recipe 6-1, but strongly type the iterator variable used in the From clause.

How It Works

LINQ queries support collections that implement IEnumerable(Of T) by default. Nongeneric collections, such as an ArrayList, are not supported by default because the extension methods that make up the standard query clauses do not extend IEnumerable. A typical query, assuming names implements IEnumerable(Of T), looks something like this:

```
Dim query = From name In names
```

If names were an ArrayList, the query would not function properly because name is not strongly typed, which would result in query being an IEnumerable(Of Object) rather than the appropriate IEnumerable(OF String). This is because of the inability to infer the type of a collection that implements IEnumerable. However, you can make the query work by ensuring that the iterator is strongly typed, as shown here:

```
Dim query = From name As String In names
```

In the previous case, however, specifying the wrong type will cause an InvalidCast exception to be thrown. An alternate solution is to simply convert the IEnumerable object to an object that inherits IEnumerable(Of T), which is demonstrated in recipe 6-15.

6-3. Control Query Results

Problem

You need to control (or transform) the results of a query in order to do either of the following:

- Limit the amount of information returned.
- Change the names of the properties returned.

Solution

Create a standard LINQ query, such as the one described in recipe 6-1, and use the Select clause to specify the exact value or values you need to return.

How It Works

Recipe 6-1 covered how to create a basic query using the From clause, such as the following:

```
Dim query = From book In books
```

This is the most basic form a query can take, and it simply returns all the results. In this case, assuming books is a collection of Book objects, the results of the query would be an IEnumerable(Of Book) collection containing all the Book objects stored in books. Returning all the resulting data in this manner might be fine for most queries, but there are many situations where you may need to alter, or even limit, the data that is returned. You can accomplish this by using the Select clause.

■**Note** As mentioned in recipe 6-1, LINQ closely resembles SQL. One of the main differences between LINQ and SQL, however, is that with LINQ the From clause precedes the Select clause. This format forces the data source to be specified first, which allows IntelliSense and type inference to work appropriately.

The Select clause is responsible for specifying what data is returned by the query. You are not forced to return just the iterator or a single field of the iterator, if it were a class. You can return calculated data or even an anonymous type that contains properties based on data from the iterator. If multiple items are used in the Select clause, then a new anonymous type is created and returned, with each item being a property of the new class. If the Select clause is omitted from a query, the query defaults to returning all iterators that were part of the From clause. Here are a few examples:

- `Dim query = From book In books Select book`: This would return a collection of all the book objects currently stored in the books collection, which would be the same results if the Select clause had been completely omitted.

- `Dim query = From book In books Select book.Title`: This would return only the Title property for each book object result in query that is an IEnumerable(Of String), assuming Title is a String.

- `Dim query = From book In books Select BookName=book.Title,PublishDate=book.date`: This would return a collection of anonymous types that have BookName and PublishDate properties.

As mentioned in recipe 6-1, the use of a query clause is referred to as *query syntax*. Although it does not look as clean, it is possible to directly use the Select extension method, which is what the Select clause is translated to when it is compiled. This example is the *method syntax* for the last query syntax example shown earlier:

```
Dim query = books.Select(Function(book) New With {.Name = book.Title, ➡
PublishDate=book.Date})
```

As you see, the Select method accepts a lambda expression that specifies what results should be returned. The .NET Framework will apply the specified expression to each object in the books collection, returning the proper information each time. The Select method includes an overload that passes the index of the current item to the lambda expression.

The Code

The following example queries the array of processes returned from the Process.GetProcess function. The Select clause transforms the data into an anonymous type that consists of three properties: Id, ProcessName, and MemUsed.

```
Imports System
Imports System.Linq
Imports System.Diagnostics

Namespace Apress.VisualBasicRecipes.Chapter06
    Public Class Recipe06_03

        Public Shared Sub Main()

            ' Build the query to return information for all
            ' processes running on the current machine.  The
            ' data will be returned in the form of anonymous
            ' types with Id, Name, and MemUsed properties.
            Dim procInfoQuery = From proc In Process.GetProcesses _
                            Select proc.Id, Name = proc.ProcessName, ➡
MemUsed = proc.WorkingSet64

            ' Run the query generated earlier and iterate
            ' through the results.
            For Each proc In procInfoQuery
                Console.WriteLine("[{0,5}] {1,-20} - {2}", proc.Id, ➡
proc.Name, proc.MemUsed)
            Next

            ' Wait to continue.
            Console.WriteLine()
            Console.WriteLine("Main method complete.  Press Enter.")
            Console.ReadLine()

        End Sub

    End Class
End Namespace
```

6-4. Sort Data Using LINQ

Problem

You need to ensure that the results of a query are sorted appropriately, or you just need to sort the elements in a collection or array.

Solution

Create a standard LINQ query, such as the one described in recipe 6-1, and use the Order By clause to ensure that the data is ordered correctly.

How It Works

If you are familiar with query languages, you should recognize the Order By clause. It is used to specify how the data returned from a query is sorted. The Order By clause also supports the optional Ascending and Descending keywords, which specify in which direction the data is sorted. If omitted, Ascending is used by default. An Order By clause might look something like this:

```
Order By book.Title Ascending
```

The Order By clause always comes after the From clause, but it can come before *or* after the Select clause. Placing the Order By clause before or after the Select clause will allow you to sort on the iterator used by the From clause. However, if you want to sort on the data returned by the Select clause, then Order By must come after Select.

You can sort on multiple fields by separating them with commas, like this:

```
Order By bool.Title, book.Price Descending
```

As mentioned in recipe 6-1, the use of query clauses is referred to as *query syntax*. Here is a complete example of query syntax that uses the Order By clause:

```
Dim query = From book In books _
            Select Name = book.Title, book.Author _
            Order By Author, Name
```

When this statement is compiled, it is first translated to *method syntax*. The Order By clause is translated to a call to the OrderBy or ThenBy (or corresponding OrderByDescending or ThenByDescending) extension method. If you are sorting by only one field, you would use only OrderBy or OrderByDescending. The ThenBy methods are identical to the OrderBy methods and are used to chain multiple sort statements. The previous example, when translated to method syntax, looks like this:

```
Dim query2 = books.Select(Function(book) New With ➡
{.Name = book.Title, book.Author}) _
              .OrderBy(Function(book) book.Author) _
              .ThenBy(Function(book) book.Name)
```

The OrderBy and ThenBy methods both accept a lambda expression that is used to specify what field to sort by. The OrderBy and ThenBy methods both include overloads that allow you to specify a specific IComparer(Of T) (see recipe 14-3) to be used, if the default comparer is not sufficient.

The Code

The following example queries the array of processes returned from the Process.GetProcess function. The Select clause transforms the data into an anonymous type that consists of a Name property and an Id property. The Order By clause is then used to sort the results by Name and then by Id.

```
Imports System
Imports System.Linq
Imports System.Diagnostics

Namespace Apress.VisualBasicRecipes.Chapter06
    Public Class Recipe06_04

        Public Shared Sub Main()

            ' Build the query to return information for all
            ' processes running on the current machine.  The
            ' data will be returned in the form of anonymous
            ' types with Id and Name properties ordered by Name
            ' and by Id.
            Dim procInfoQuery = From proc In Process.GetProcesses _
                                Select proc.Id, Name = proc.ProcessName _
                                Order By Name, Id

            ' Run the query generated earlier and iterate
            ' through the results.
            For Each proc In procInfoQuery
                Console.WriteLine("{0,-20} [{1,5}]", proc.Name, proc.Id)
            Next

            ' Wait to continue.
            Console.WriteLine()
            Console.WriteLine("Main method complete.  Press Enter.")
            Console.ReadLine()

        End Sub

    End Class
End Namespace
```

6-5. Filter Data Using LINQ

Problem

You need to query data that is stored in a collection, but you need to apply some constraint, or *filter*, to the data in order to limit the scope of the query.

Solution

Create a standard LINQ query, such as the ones described in the previous recipes, and use the Where clause to specify how the data should be filtered.

How It Works

While the Select clause (see recipe 6-3) is responsible for transforming or returning data from a LINQ query, the Where clause is responsible for filtering what data is available to be returned. If you are familiar with SQL, the LINQ Where clause is virtually indistinguishable from the like-named clause in SQL. A Boolean expression, which is used to perform the data filtering, precedes the Where clause. As with the Order By clause (see recipe 6-4), the Where clause can also come before or after the Select clause depending on whether you need to filter against a property returned by Select.

The following example will return all book elements, stored in the books collection, that have a Price value greater than or equal to 49.99. Any standard Boolean expression can be used with the Where clause to further refine the data that is actually queried.

```
Dim query = From book In books _
            Where book.Price >= 49.99
```

As mentioned in each of the previous recipes, the previous example uses what is called *query syntax* because it is actually using query clauses rather than the underlying methods. All queries are translated to *method syntax* as they are being compiled. For instance, this query:

```
Dim query = From book In books _
            Select Name = book.Title, book.Author, Cost = book.Price _
            Where Cost >= 49.99
```

would be translated to the following:

```
Dim query = books.Select(Function(book) New With {.Name = book.Title, ➡
book.Author, .Cost = book.Price}) _
                .Where(Function(book) book.Cost >= 49.99)
```

As you may have come to expect, the Where method accepts a lambda expression that provides the Boolean expression that will be applied to each element of the data source. The Where method includes an overload that passes the index of the current item to the lambda expression.

The Code

The following example queries the array of processes returned from the Process.GetProcess function. The Where clause is used to limit the results to only those processes that have more than five megabytes of memory allocated.

```
Imports System
Imports System.Linq
Imports System.Diagnostics

Namespace Apress.VisualBasicRecipes.Chapter06
    Public Class Recipe06_05

        Public Shared Sub Main()

            ' Build the query to return information for all
            ' processes running on the current machine that
            ' have more than 5MB of physical memory allocated.
            ' The data will be returned in the form of anonymous
            ' types with Id, Name, and MemUsed properties.
```

```
                    Dim procInfoQuery = From proc In Process.GetProcesses _
                                Where proc.WorkingSet64 > (1024 * 1024) * 5 _
                                Select proc.Id, Name = proc.ProcessName, ➡
MemUsed = proc.WorkingSet64


                    '  Run the query generated earlier and iterate
                    '  through the results.
                    For Each proc In procInfoQuery
                        Console.WriteLine("{0,-20} [{1,5}] - {2}", proc.ProcessName, ➡
proc.Id, proc.WorkingSet64)
                    Next

                    '  Wait to continue.
                    Console.WriteLine()
                    Console.WriteLine("Main method complete.  Press Enter.")
                    Console.ReadLine()

            End Sub

        End Class
End Namespace
```

6-6. Perform General Aggregate Operations

Problem

You need to perform some calculation, such as computing the minimum or sum, on a series of data stored in a collection or array.

Solution

Create a LINQ query, similar to those described in the previous recipes, and use an Aggregate clause to perform any necessary calculations.

How It Works

The Aggregate clause is used to perform some calculation over a series of data. It is the only clause that can be used in place of the From clause (recipe 6-1), and it is used in a similar manner. Using the Aggregate clause forces the immediate execution of the query and returns a single object, rather than a collection that needs to be enumerated through.

The first part of the Aggregate clause is identical to the format of the From clause. You define the name for the iterator and the source of the data, like this:

```
Aggregate book In books
```

The Aggregate clause requires using the Into clause, which contains one or more expressions that specify the aggregate operation that should be performed. To complete the partial example, you would add the Into clause, like this:

```
Aggregate book In books
Into <some expression>
```

<some expression> represents a calculation that you would need to perform over the entire data source. To help perform the most common aggregate functions, the .NET Framework 3.5 includes

the following methods: Count, Min, Max, Average, and Sum. These methods are used within the Into clause and are covered in more detail in recipes 6-7 through 6-9.

A situation may arise where you need to perform an aggregate operation (such as calculating standard deviation) that does not currently have a method directly associated with it. In this situation, you have the option of using the Aggregate method directly (using method syntax) rather than the clause (which would be query syntax). When a query is compiled, it is first translated from query to method syntax. As an example, the following statement would re-create the functionality accomplished by the Count method, if it did not already exist:

```
Dim result = books.Aggregate(0, Function(currentCount, book) currentCount + 1)
```

This statement would return the total count of all elements in the books collection. The first parameter (0) represents the initial value, or *seed*. If this value is not supplied, then the method defaults to using the first element of the data source as the initial value. The second parameter (or first if you did not supply a seed value) is a lambda expression that performs the specified calculation.

The first parameter passed to the lambda expression represents the current aggregate value, which is the current count of elements in the previous example. The second represents the current element within the data source. The value returned by the expression will become the new value passed into the lambda expression during the next iteration.

Please keep in mind that the previous example is just a simple demonstration of method syntax for the Aggregate operation. To accomplish the same functionality, you could just use the Count method of the collection (as in books.Count).

6-7. Perform Average and Sum Calculations

Problem

You need to calculate the average or sum of a series of values stored in a collection or array.

Solution

Create an Aggregate query, covered in recipe 6-6, and use the Average or Sum function, within the Into clause, to perform the required calculation.

How It Works

Recipe 6-6 details how to use the Aggregate...Into clause. This clause is used to perform some calculation over a series of data. The Into clause is used to specify the calculation that is to be performed.

To calculate the average of a series of values, you would use the Average function, like this:

```
Dim avg = Aggregate book In books _
        Into Average(book.Price)
```

This will return a single value that represents the average Price value of all the book objects in the collection. If the data source implements the ICollection(Of T) interface, which is the base class for all generic collections, then you must specify a parameter that represents the property value that should be aggregated (as in the earlier example). If, however, the data source does not implement the ICollection(Of T) interface, such as a String array, then the Average clause does not require any parameters.

As stated in previous recipes, the query is translated to *method syntax* when it is compiled. The Average method, used in query or method syntax, supports all major numeric data types (Decimal, Int32, Int64, Single, and Double). If a parameter is passed, such as book.Price in the previous example, it is defined by a lambda expression. Here is the method syntax equivalent for the example:

```
Dim avg = books.Average(Function(book) book.Price)
```

To calculate the sum of a series of values, you would use the Sum function, like this:

```
Dim total = Aggregate book In books _
            Into Sum(book.Price)
```

This will return a single value that represents the sum of all Price values in the collection. As with the Average function mentioned earlier, you do not need to specify any parameters if the data source does not implement ICollection(Of T).

The Sum method, used in query or method syntax, supports all major numeric data types (Decimal, Int32, Int64, Single, and Double). If a parameter is passed, such as book.Price in the previous example, it is compiled as a lambda expression. Here is the method syntax equivalent for the example:

```
Dim total = books.Sum(Function(book) book.Price)
```

The Code

The following example queries the array of processes returned from the Process.GetProcess function. The Aggregate...Into clause is used to calculate the average and sum of the allocated physical memory for each process. The data is returned as an anonymous type that contains the AverageMemory and TotalMemory properties.

```
Imports System
Imports System.Linq
Imports System.Diagnostics

Namespace Apress.VisualBasicRecipes.Chapter06
    Public Class Recipe06_07

        Public Shared Sub Main()

            '  Build the query to return the average and total
            '  physical memory used by all of the processes
            '  running on the current machine.  The data is returned
            '  as an anonymous type that contains the aggregate data.
            Dim aggregateData = Aggregate proc In Process.GetProcesses _
                            Into AverageMemory = Average(proc.WorkingSet64), _
                                 TotalMemory = Sum(proc.WorkingSet64)

            '  Display the formatted results on the console.
            Console.WriteLine("Average Allocated Physical Memory:  {0,6} MB", ➥
(aggregateData.AverageMemory / (1024 * 1024)).ToString("#.00"))
            Console.WriteLine("Total Allocated Physical Memory  :  {0,6} MB", ➥
(aggregateData.TotalMemory / (1024 * 1024)).ToString("#.00"))

            '  Wait to continue.
            Console.WriteLine()
            Console.WriteLine("Main method complete.  Press Enter.")
            Console.ReadLine()

        End Sub

    End Class
End Namespace
```

6-8. Perform Count Operations

Problem

You need to count the number of elements within a collection or array.

Solution

Create an `Aggregate` query, covered in recipe 6-6, and use the `Count` or `LongCount` function, within the `Into` clause.

How It Works

Recipe 6-6 details the use of the `Aggregate...Into` clause. This clause is used to perform some calculation over a series of data. The `Into` clause is used to specify the calculation that is to be performed.

If you need to count all the elements in a series, you use either the `Count` or `LongCount` function, such as this:

```
Dim cnt = Aggregate book In books _
          Into Count(book.Price = 49.99)
```

This will return an `Integer` value that represents the count of all elements whose `Price` value is equal to 49.99. The `LongCount` function works identically but returns the resulting value as a `Long`. If the data source implements the `ICollection(Of T)` interface, which is the base class for all generic collections, then you must specify a parameter that represents the property value that should be aggregated (as in the previous example). If, however, the data source does not implement the `ICollection(Of T)` interface, such as a `String` array, then the `Count` clause does not require any parameters.

As stated in previous recipes, the query is translated to method syntax when it is compiled. If an expression is supplied, such as `book.Price = 49.99` in the earlier example, it is defined by an underlying lambda expression. Here is the method syntax equivalent for the example:

```
Dim cnt = books.Count(Function(book) book.Price = 49.99)
```

The Code

The following example queries the array of processes returned from the `Process.GetProcess` function and orders them by the `ProcessName` property. The `Aggregate...Into` clause is used to count the number of thread objects contained in the `Process.Threads` collection for each process. The `Select` clause transforms the data into a series of anonymous types that have the `ProcessName` and `ThreadCount` properties.

```
Imports System
Imports System.Linq
Imports System.Diagnostics

Namespace Apress.VisualBasicRecipes.Chapter06
    Public Class Recipe06_08

        Public Shared Sub Main()
```

```vbnet
        ' Build the query to return information for all
        ' processes running on the current machine. The
        ' Process.Threads collection, for each process, will
        ' be counted using the Count method.  The data will
        ' be returned as anonymous types containing the name
        ' of the process and the number of threads.
        Dim query = From proc In Process.GetProcesses _
                    Order By proc.ProcessName _
                    Aggregate thread As ProcessThread In proc.Threads _
                    Into ThreadCount = Count(thread.Id) _
                    Select proc.ProcessName, ThreadCount

        ' Run the query generated earlier and iterate through
        '  the results.
        For Each proc In query
            Console.WriteLine("The {0} process has {1} threads.", ➥
proc.ProcessName, proc.ThreadCount.ToString)
        Next

        ' Wait to continue.
        Console.WriteLine()
        Console.WriteLine("Main method complete.  Press Enter.")
        Console.ReadLine()

    End Sub

    End Class
End Namespace
```

6-9. Perform Min and Max Calculations

Problem

You need to calculate the minimum or maximum value contained in a series of values stored in a collection or array.

Solution

Create an Aggregate query, covered in recipe 6-6, and use the Min or Max function, within the Into clause, to perform the required calculation.

How It Works

Recipe 6-6 details the use of the Aggregate...Into clause. This clause is used to perform some calculation over a series of numeric data. The Into clause is used to specify the calculation that is to be performed.

To calculate the minimum value in a series of values, you would use the Min function, like this:

```vbnet
Dim minPrice = Aggregate book In books _
               Into Min(book.Price)
```

This will return a single value that represents the minimum Price value for all the book objects in the collection. As mentioned in the previous aggregate method recipes, if the data source implements the ICollection(Of T) interface, which is the base class for all generic collections, then you must specify a parameter that represents the property value that should be aggregated (as in the earlier example). If, however, the data source does not implement the ICollection(Of T) interface, such as a String array, then the Count clause does not require any parameters.

As stated in previous recipes, the query is translated to method syntax when it is compiled. The Min method, used in query or method syntax, supports all major numeric data types (Decimal, Int32, Int64, Single, and Double). If a parameter is passed, such as book.Price in the previous example, it is defined by a lambda expression. Here is the method syntax equivalent for the example:

```
Dim minPrice = books.Min(Function(book) book.Price)
```

To calculate the maximum value of a series of values, you would use the Max function, like this:

```
Dim maxPrice = Aggregate book In books _
          Into Max(book.Price)
```

This will return a single value that represents the maximum Price value in the collection. As with the Min function mentioned earlier, you do not need to specify any parameters if the data source is a series of simple data types.

The Max method, used in query or method syntax, supports all major numeric data types (Decimal, Int32, Int64, Single, and Double). If a parameter is passed, such as book.Price in the earlier example, it is compiled as a lambda expression. Here is the method syntax equivalent for the example:

```
Dim maxPrice = books.Max(Function(book) book.Price)
```

The Code

The following example queries the array of processes returned from the Process.GetProcess function. The Aggregate...Into clause is used to calculate the minimum and maximum physical memory allocated for each process. The data is returned as an anonymous type that contains the MinMemory and MaxMemory properties.

```
Imports System
Imports System.Linq
Imports System.Diagnostics

Namespace Apress.VisualBasicRecipes.Chapter06
    Public Class Recipe06_09

        Public Shared Sub Main()

            ' Build the query to return the minimum and maximum
            ' physical memory allocated by all of the processes
            ' running on the current machine.  The data is returned
            ' as an anonymous types that contain the aggregate data.
            Dim aggregateData = Aggregate proc In Process.GetProcesses _
                        Into MinMemory = Min(proc.WorkingSet64), _
                            MaxMemory = Max(proc.WorkingSet64)
```

```
                    ' Display the formatted results on the console.
                    Console.WriteLine("Minimum Allocated Physical Memory:   {0,6} MB", ➡
            (aggregateData.MinMemory / (1024 * 1024)).ToString("#.00"))
                    Console.WriteLine("Maximum Allocated Physical Memory:   {0,6} MB", ➡
            (aggregateData.MaxMemory / (1024 * 1024)).ToString("#.00"))

                    ' Wait to continue.
                    Console.WriteLine()
                    Console.WriteLine("Main method complete.   Press Enter.")
                    Console.ReadLine()

            End Sub

        End Class
End Namespace
```

6-10. Group Query Results

Problem

You need to query data that is stored in a collection or array, but you need group the data in some hierarchical format.

Solution

Create a standard LINQ query, such as the ones described in the previous recipes, and use the Group By clause to specify how the data should be organized.

How It Works

The Group By clause is used to organize the data returned from a query in a hierarchical format, meaning that data is returned as groups of elements or even groups of grouped elements. The format for the first portion of the clause is Group *fields* By *key fields*, where *fields* is a list of fields that will be included with the grouped data and *key fields* represents how the data is actually grouped. If no *fields* are supplied, then all available properties are included with the grouped data.

The second portion of the clause is similar to the Aggregate clause (recipe 6-6) in that it uses the Into clause and expects one or more aggregate expressions. Any included aggregate expression will be applied to the grouped data. If you need to return that actual grouped data, rather than just aggregate values, you can use the Group keyword with the Into clause. If needed, you can specify an alias for the grouped data.

Here is an example query:

```
Dim query = From book In books _
            Group book.Price By book.Author _
            Into Count = Count(), AveragePrice = Average(Price)
```

When this query is executed, it returns a collection of anonymous types that includes the Count and AveragePrice properties. The Count property represents the count of all book elements in each Author group, and the AveragePrice property represents the average price of all the books in each group. Since only aggregate data was returned, there is no hierarchical data that needs to be iterated through.

The previous example shows a basic demonstration of the Group By clause that returns grouped elements. The following is a more advanced example that returns groups of grouped elements:

```
Dim query = From book In books _
            Order By book.Author _
            Group book.Title, book.Price By book.Author _
            Into Booklist = Group
```

This query returns the `Title` and `Price` properties for each book belonging to the specified `Author`. The data returned is a collection of anonymous types that includes an `Author` property, which is the key that was used to group the data, and a `BookList` property, which is a collection of anonymous types that represents the data in the group. To correctly iterate through this hierarchical data, you would look through both collections, like this:

```
For Each currentAuthor In query
    For Each book In currentAuthor.BookList
        ...
    Next
Next
```

As mentioned in earlier recipes in this chapter, *query syntax* refers to the use of clauses to build a query. It provides a very clean and user-friendly format, as demonstrated by the previous examples. However, when a query is compiled, it is translated to the appropriate underlying methods, which are referred to as *method syntax*. Here is what the translated version of the first example would look like:

```
Dim query = books.GroupBy(Function(book) book.Author, _
                          Function(book) book.Price, _
                          Function(author, priceList) _
                                New With {.Key = author, _
                                          .Count = priceList.Count, _
                                          .AveragePrice = priceList.Average})
```

The `GroupBy` method has overloads that let you specify a specific `IComparer(Of T)` (recipe 14-3) to use. There are also overloads that let you specify a lambda expression that is used to identify the elements to be grouped or a lambda expression that is used to transform the resulting data.

The Code

The following example queries the array of processes returned from the `Process.GetProcess` function. The `Where` clause is used to return data only if a group has more than one process.

```
Imports System
Imports System.Linq
Imports System.Diagnostics

Namespace Apress.VisualBasicRecipes.Chapter06
    Public Class Recipe06_10

        Public Shared Sub Main()

            ' Build the query to return information for all processes
            ' running on the current machine and group them based
            ' on the mathematical floor of the allocated physical
            ' memory.  The count, maximum, and minimum values for each
            ' group are calculated and returned as properties of the
            ' anonymous type.  Data is returned only for groups that
            ' have more than one process.
```

```
            Dim query = From proc In Process.GetProcesses _
                        Order By proc.ProcessName _
                        Group By MemGroup = Math.Floor((proc.WorkingSet64 / ➡
(1024 * 1024))) _
                        Into Count = Count(), Max = Max(proc.WorkingSet64), ➡
 Min = Min(proc.WorkingSet64) _
                        Where Count > 1 _
                        Order By MemGroup


            '  Run the query generated earlier and iterate through the
            '  results.
            For Each result In query
                Console.WriteLine("Physical Allocated Memory Group:  {0} MB", ➡
result.MemGroup)
                Console.WriteLine("# of processes that have this amount of " & ➡
"memory allocated:  {0}", result.Count)
                Console.WriteLine("Minimum amount of physical memory" & ➡
" allocated:                {0} ({1})", result.Min, (result.Min / ➡
(1024 * 1024)).ToString("#.00"))
                Console.WriteLine("Maximum amount of physical memory" & ➡
" allocated:                {0} ({1})", result.Max, (result.Max / ➡
(1024 * 1024)).ToString("#.00"))
                Console.WriteLine()
            Next


            '  Wait to continue.
            Console.WriteLine()
            Console.WriteLine("Main method complete.  Press Enter.")
            Console.ReadLine()


        End Sub


    End Class
End Namespace
```

6-11. Query Data from Multiple Collections

Problem

You need to execute a query based on the combined data from multiple collections.

Solution

Create a standard LINQ query, such as the ones described by the previous recipes in this chapter, and use the Join clause to join the data from multiple sources.

How It Works

If you have any experience with SQL, or other query languages, you will most likely recognize the need to join data from multiple sources. One of the most popular join functions available to Microsoft T-SQL is INNER JOIN, which returns only the elements from the first source that match elements in the second.

The .NET Framework 3.5 supplies the Join clause, which provides functionality equivalent to an inner join. Here is an example:

```
Dim query = From book In books _
            Join stockInfo In stock _
            On book.ISBN Equals stockInfo.ISBN _
            Order By book.ISBN
```

The first portion of the Join clause is similar to the From clause (recipe 6-1) in that you supply a variable and a data source. In this case, the variable supplied is used later in the clause as a reference to the source. The second portion uses the On and Equals clauses to specify the two keys that need to be compared from the two data sources. For the record, the first data source is specified in the From clause, while the second is specified in the Join clause.

The results of this query would be a collection of anonymous types, ordered by the ISBN property. The anonymous type contains a book property and a stockInfo property, which represent the book and stock classes that were joined based on their ISBN properties.

Note It is possible to perform a basic join operation without actually using the Join clause. You can accomplish this by specifying multiple data sources within the From clause and by using the Where clause to specify the appropriate keys. Although this works, it is suggested you use the Join clause to perform this operation appropriately.

Here is another example query that uses the Join clause:

```
Dim query2 = From book In books _
             Join stockInfo In stock _
             On book.ISBN Equals stockInfo.ISBN _
             Order By book.ISBN _
             Select ID = book.ISBN, BookName = book.Title, stockInfo.Quantity
```

This example is similar to the previous example, but it demonstrates how you can still use the Select clause to transform the results of the query into a specific format. In this case, the resulting anonymous types would have ID, BookName, and Quantity properties.

As mentioned in previous recipes in this chapter, the clauses used in the previous query would be converted to their underlying method calls during compilation. The method syntax equivalent of the example is as follows:

```
Dim query = books.Join(stock, _
                  Function(book) book.ISBN, _
                  Function(stockinfo) stockinfo.ISBN, _
                  Function(book, stockInfo) New With _
                                      {.ID = book.ISBN, _
                                       .BookName = book.Title, _
                                       stockInfo.Quantity}) _
              .OrderBy(Function(item) item.ID)
```

The first parameter of the Join method represents the inner data source to which the outer source will be joined. The next parameter is a lambda expression that specifies the key in the outer data source, while the parameter following it specifies the matching key in the inner data source. The last parameter is also a lambda expression that receives instances of both sources and allows you to transform the results, similar to the Select method (recipe 6-3). The Join method also offers an overload that lets you specify your own IEqualityComparer(Of T).

■**Note** Although it is not covered in this recipe, the .NET Framework 3.5 also provides the Group Join clause, which performs similar functionality to the Join clause but groups the data (like the Group By clause) as well. Consult the documentation for more details on Group Join.

The Code

The following example creates an array of String objects that contains the names of processes that should be monitored on the local computer. This array is joined to the array of processes returned from the Process.GetProcess function using the ProcessName property.

```
Imports System
Imports System.Linq
Imports System.Diagnostics

Namespace Apress.VisualBasicRecipes.Chapter06
    Public Class Recipe06_11

        Public Shared Sub Main()

            ' Store a list of processes that will be monitored or
            ' that information should be gathered for.
            Dim processesToMonitor = New String() {"explorer", _
                                                   "iexplore", _
                                                   "lsass", _
                                                   "rundll32", _
                                                   "services", _
                                                   "winlogon", _
                                                   "svchost"}

            ' Build the query to return information for all of the
            ' processes that should be monitored by joining them to
            ' the list of all processes running on the current
            ' computer.  The count, maximum, and minimum values for each
            ' group are calculated and returned as properties of the
            ' anonymous type.  Data is returned only for groups that
            ' have more than one process.
            Dim query = From proc In Process.GetProcesses _
                    Order By proc.ProcessName _
                    Join myProc In processesToMonitor _
                    On proc.ProcessName Equals myProc _
                    Select Name = proc.ProcessName, proc.Id, ➥
PhysicalMemory = proc.WorkingSet64

            ' Run the query generated earlier and iterate through the
            ' results.
            For Each proc In query
                Console.WriteLine("{0,-10} ({1,5}) - Allocated Physical " & ➥
"Memory: {2,5} MB", proc.Name, proc.Id, (proc.PhysicalMemory / ➥
(1024 * 1024)).ToString("#.00"))
            Next
```

```
        ' Wait to continue.
        Console.WriteLine()
        Console.WriteLine("Main method complete.  Press Enter.")
        Console.ReadLine()

    End Sub

  End Class
End Namespace
```

6-12. Returning Specific Elements of a Collection

Problem

You need to retrieve a specific element or groups of elements from a collection.

Solution

Call any of the partitioning methods listed in Table 6-2, such as `First` or `Single`, to return the desired element from the collection.

How It Works

Not all of the extension methods found in the `System.Linq.Enumerable` namespace relate directly to a query clause, such as those covered in the previous recipes of this chapter. The methods listed in Table 6-2 fall in this category and provide functionality to extract a single element from a collection. If you use any of these methods as part of a query, the query will execute immediately.

Table 6-2. *Common Partitioning Methods*

Method	Description
ElementAt	Returns the item at the specified index in the collection. Since the collection is zero-based, the first element is at index 0.
Single	Returns the only item in the collection.
First	Returns the first item in the collection.
Last	Returns the last item in the collection.

```
Dim myBook = books.ElementAt(3)
```

The previous example demonstrates a use of the `ElementAt` method, which allows you to specify, in the form of an `Integer`, the zero-based index of the element you want to retrieve. An `ArgumentOutOfRangeException` is thrown if you specify an index that does not exist.

```
Dim myBook = books.Single
```

The previous code demonstrates how to use the `Single` method, which returns the *only* element that is in the collection. An `InvalidOperationException` is thrown if the collection contains more than one element. This method includes an overload, which lets you specify a condition in the form of a *lambda expression*, such as the following:

```
Dim myBook = books.Single(Function(book) book.Price = 59.99)
```

Used in this manner, the Single method will return the *only* element that meets the given condition. Again, an InvalidOperationException is thrown if more than one element meets the provided condition.

```
Dim theFirstBook = books.First
```

The previous code demonstrates the First method, which returns the first element in the collection. An InvalidOperationException would be thrown if the collection contained no elements. As with the Single method, you can also specify a lambda expression to be used as a condition. The first element that meets the condition will be returned.

```
Dim theLastBook = books.Last
```

The previous code demonstrates the Last method, which returns the last element in the collection. An InvalidOperationException would be thrown if the collection contained no elements. As with the Single and First methods, you can also specify a lambda expression to be used as a condition. The last element that meets the condition will be returned.

Each of the methods described earlier has a matching method that ends with OrDefault, such as SingeOrDefault and LastOrDefault. In cases where the collection is empty, these methods would return a default value (which is Nothing for reference types) instead of throwing an exception.

6-13. Display Collection Data Using Paging

Problem

You need to segment data from a collection into *pages*.

Solution

Create a standard query that uses both the Skip and Take clauses to segment the data into appropriately sized pages, and then execute the query in a loop, changing the parameters used with Skip and Take to retrieve and display each page.

How It Works

It is common to divide large amounts of data into manageable chunks, or *pages*. This is accomplished with LINQ by using a combination of the Skip and Take clauses.

The Skip clause forces the query to skip the specified number of elements, starting from the beginning of the data source. The following example would skip the first three elements of the books collection and then return the rest:

```
Dim query = From book In books Skip 3
```

The Take clause is the exact opposite. It returns the specified number of elements, starting from the beginning of the data source, and then skips the rest. The following is an example that returns only the first three elements of the books collections:

```
Dim query = From book In books Take 3
```

Together, both of these clauses are used to simulate paging. This is accomplished by skipping and taking data, using the Skip and Take clauses, in specific sizes within a loop.

The Code

The following example uses LINQ to query the processes that are using more than 5 MB of memory. A page, which consists of ten items, is retrieved by using Skip and Take as described in this recipe. The example loops through each page, displaying the data until there is no more.

```vb
Imports System
Imports System.Linq
Imports System.Diagnostics

Namespace Apress.VisualBasicRecipes.Chapter06
    Public Class Recipe06_13

        ' This field holds the size of our pages.
        Private Shared pageSize As Integer = 10
        Private Const FIVE_MB = 3 * (1024 * 1024)
        Public Shared Sub Main()

            ' Use LINQ to retrieve a List(Of Process) List of
            ' processes that are using more then 5MB of memory.  The
            ' ToList method is used to force the query to execute immediately
            ' and save the results in the procs variable so they can be reused.
            Dim procs = (From proc In Process.GetProcesses.ToList _
                         Where proc.WorkingSet64 > FIVE_MB _
                         Order By proc.ProcessName _
                         Select proc).ToList

            Dim totalPages As Integer

            ' Determine the exact number of pages of information
            ' available for display.
            totalPages = Math.Floor(procs.Count / pageSize)
            If procs.Count Mod pageSize > 0 Then totalPages += 1


            Console.WriteLine("LIST OF PROCESSES WITH MEMORY USAGE OVER 5 MB:")
            Console.WriteLine("")

            ' Loop and display each page of data.
            For i = 0 To totalPages - 1
                Console.WriteLine("PAGE {0} OF {1}", i + 1.ToString(), ➥
totalPages.ToString())

                ' Query the procs collection and return a single page
                ' of processes using the Skip and Take clauses.
                Dim currentPage = From proc In procs _
                                  Skip i * pageSize Take pageSize

                ' Loop through all the process records for the current page.
                For Each proc In currentPage
                    Console.WriteLine("{0,-20} - {1,5} MB", proc.ProcessName, ➥
(proc.WorkingSet64 / (1024 * 1024)).ToString("#.00"))
                Next
```

```
            ' Check whether there are any more pages.
            If Not i = totalPages - 1 Then
                Console.WriteLine("Press Enter for the next page.")
                Console.ReadLine()
            End If
        Next

        Console.WriteLine("No more data available.  Press Enter to end.")
        Console.ReadLine()

    End Sub

End Class
End Namespace
```

Notes

Although they weren't needed for this recipe, both the Skip and Take clauses can use the While clause (Skip While and Take While). The While clause allows you to specify a condition rather than simply supplying an Integer value. This means elements will be taken or skipped depending on whether the condition has been met. It is important to note that the operation will end the first time the condition is False. Here is an example:

```
Dim query = From book In books _
            Order By book.Price Descending _
            Take While book.Price >= 49.99
```

As mentioned in the other recipes in this chapter, the previous query is written in *query syntax* because it uses the more stylized query clauses similar to those found in T-SQL. However, when the query is compiled, it is first translated to the underlying methods. The following is the equivalent method syntax for the example query:

```
Dim query = books.OrderByDescending(Function(book) book.Price) _
                .TakeWhile(Function(book) book.Price >= 49.99)
```

The Take and Skip methods take an Integer that represents the number of elements in the collection to take or skip, respectively. TakeWhile and SkipWhile, however, take a lambda expression that supplies the condition that must be met for elements to be taken or skipped. Both of these methods include overloads that pass the corresponding elements' index to the lambda expression.

6-14. Compare and Combine Collections

Problem

You need to quickly compare or combine the contents of two collections.

Solution

Call the Except, Intersect, or Union method to perform the appropriate action. If you need to combine the data, use the Concat method.

How It Works

Most of the functionality supported by LINQ is directly related to building queries. The `System.Linq.Enumerable` class, which is where the extension methods used by LINQ are located, contains additional supporting methods. Although these methods don't have query clauses directly associated with them, they can still be used with queries since they return objects that inherit `IEnumerable(Of T)`.

Four examples of these methods are `Except`, `Intersect`, `Union`, and `Concat`. `Except`, `Intersect`, and `Union` provide the functionality to allow two collections to be compared in a specific manner resulting in a new collection, while `Concat` simply combines them. Using any of these methods as part of a query will force the query to execute immediately.

The `Except` method, shown next, compares two collections and returns all elements from the prime source that were not found in the supplied collection:

```
Dim missingBooks = myBooks.Except(yourBooks)
```

The `Intersect` method, shown next, compares two collections and returns all elements that match in both:

```
Dim sameBooks = myBooks.Intersect(yourBooks)
```

The `Union` method, shown next, compares two collections and returns the combination of all elements from both sources. This method will *not* return duplicate elements.

```
Dim combinedBooks = myBooks.Union(yourBooks)
```

The `Concat` method, shown next, performs the same overall functionality as `Union`, but all the elements (including duplicates) are returned:

```
Dim allBooks = myBooks.Concat(yourBooks)
```

■**Note** Each of the four methods mentioned include an overload that allows you to specify your own `IEqualityComparer(Of T)` to use. If one is not supplied, the default equality comparer for each particular object is used.

The Code

The following example demonstrates how to use the four LINQ-related extension methods discussed:

```
Imports System
Imports System.Linq
Imports System.Diagnostics

Namespace Apress.VisualBasicRecipes.Chapter06
    Public Class Recipe06_14

        Public Shared Sub Main()

            ' Array to hold a set of strings.
            Dim myWishList = New String() {"XBox 360", _
                                "Rolex", _
                                "Serenity", _
                                "iPod iTouch", _
                                "Season 3 of BSG", _
                                "Dell XPS", _
                                "Halo 3"}
```

```vbnet
          ' An array holding a second set of strings.
          Dim myShoppingCart = New String() {"Shrek", _
                                          "Swatch (Green)", _
                                          "Sony Walkman", _
                                          "XBox 360", _
                                          "Season 3 of The Golden Girls", _
                                          "Serenity"}

          ' Returns elements from myWishList that are NOT in
          ' myShoppingCart.
          Dim result1 = myWishList.Except(myShoppingCart)

          Console.WriteLine("Items in the wish list that were not in the " & ➥
    "shopping cart:")
          For Each item In result1
              Console.WriteLine(item)
          Next
          Console.WriteLine()

          ' Returns elements that are common in both myWishList
          ' and myShoppingCart.
          Dim result2 = myWishList.Intersect(myShoppingCart)

          Console.WriteLine("Matching items from both lists:")
          For Each item In result2
              Console.WriteLine(item)
          Next
          Console.WriteLine()

          ' Returns all elements from myWishList and myShoppingCart
          ' without duplicates.
          Dim result3 = myWishList.Union(myShoppingCart)

          Console.WriteLine("All items from both lists (no duplicates):")
          For Each item In result3
              Console.WriteLine(item)
          Next
          Console.WriteLine()

          ' Returns all elements from myWishList and myShoppingCart
          ' including duplicates
          Dim result4 = myWishList.Concat(myShoppingCart)

          Console.WriteLine("All items from both lists (with duplicates):")
          For Each item In result4
              Console.WriteLine(item)
          Next

          ' Wait to continue.
          Console.WriteLine()
          Console.WriteLine("Main method complete.  Press Enter.")
          Console.ReadLine()
```

```
        End Sub

    End Class
End Namespace
```

6-15. Cast a Collection to a Specific Type

Problem

You need to convert a nongeneric collection, such as an ArrayList, into a generic collection so it will be capable of fully supporting LINQ.

Solution

Use the Cast or OfType extension method to cast the target collection to the specified type.

How It Works

As noted in several other recipes in this chapter, the System.Linq.Enumerable class contains all the extension methods that make up LINQ to Objects. Although the vast majority of these methods extend IEnumerable(Of T), a few of them actually extend IEnumerable. Two of the most important methods that are designed this way are Cast and OfType. Since these methods extend IEnumerable, it provides a mechanism to easily convert a collection (such as an ArrayList) to an IEnumerable(Of T) type so it can fully support LINQ.

Recipe 6-2 covered the basics of using an ArrayList, or any other IEnumerable type, with LINQ by strongly typing the iterator used in the From clause. What it didn't cover is that when this type of query is compiled, it actually makes a call to the Cast method to return an IEnumerable(Of T) object. This method goes through the source collection attempting to cast each object to the specified data type. The end result is an appropriately typed generic collection that now fully supports LINQ. If an element of the collection cannot be cast to the specified type, an InvalidCastException will be thrown.

The other method that provides casting functionality is OfType. This method works similarly to the Cast method, but it simply skips elements that cannot be cast rather than throwing an exception.

The Code

The following example demonstrates how to convert a nongeneric collection, which is one that doesn't inherit from IEnumerable(Of T), into one that does so it can fully support LINQ:

```vb
Imports System
Imports System.Linq
Imports System.Diagnostics

Namespace Apress.VisualBasicRecipes.Chapter06

    Public Class Recipe06_15

        Public Class Tool
            Public Name As String
        End Class

        Public Class Clothes
            Public Name As String
        End Class
```

```vbnet
Public Shared Sub Main()

    ' From Example - NonGeneric Collection
    Dim employeeList As New ArrayList

    employeeList.Add("Todd")
    employeeList.Add("Alex")
    employeeList.Add("Joe")
    employeeList.Add("Todd")
    employeeList.Add("Ed")
    employeeList.Add("David")
    employeeList.Add("Mark")

    ' You can't normally use standard query operators on
    ' an ArrayList (IEnumerable) unless you strongly type
    ' the From clause.  Strongly typing the From clause
    ' creates a call to the Cast function, shown below.
    Dim queryableList = employeeList.Cast(Of String)()
    Dim query = From name In queryableList

    For Each name In query
        Console.WriteLine(name)
    Next
    Console.WriteLine()

    Dim shoppingCart As New ArrayList

    shoppingCart.Add(New Clothes With {.Name = "Shirt"})
    shoppingCart.Add(New Clothes With {.Name = "Socks"})
    shoppingCart.Add(New Tool With {.Name = "Hammer"})
    shoppingCart.Add(New Clothes With {.Name = "Hat"})
    shoppingCart.Add(New Tool With {.Name = "Screw Driver"})
    shoppingCart.Add(New Clothes With {.Name = "Pants"})
    shoppingCart.Add(New Tool With {.Name = "Drill"})

    ' Attempting to iterate through the results would generate
    ' an InvalidCastException because some items cannot be
    ' cast to the appropriate type.  However, some items
    ' may be cast prior to hitting the exception.
    Dim queryableList2 = shoppingCart.Cast(Of Clothes)()

    Console.WriteLine("Cast (using Cast) all items to 'Clothes':")
    Try
        For Each item In queryableList2
            Console.WriteLine(item.Name)
        Next
    Catch ex As Exception
        Console.WriteLine(ex.Message)
    End Try
    Console.WriteLine()
```

```vb
    ' OfType is similar to cast but wouldn't cause the
    ' exception as shown in the previous example.  Only
    ' the items that can be successfully cast will be returned.
    Dim queryableList3 = shoppingCart.OfType(Of Clothes)()

    Console.WriteLine("Cast (using OfType) all items to 'Clothes':")
    For Each item In queryableList3
        Console.WriteLine(item.Name)
    Next
    Console.WriteLine()

    Console.WriteLine()
    Console.WriteLine("Main method complete.  Press Enter.")
    Console.ReadLine()

End Sub

End Class
End Namespace
```

CHAPTER 7

■ ■ ■

LINQ to XML and XML Processing

Extensible Markup Language (XML) has become an integral part of operating systems and application development. Many components or features in Visual Studio such as serialization, web services, and configuration files all use XML behind the scenes. When you need to manipulate XML directly, you will need to work with the System.Xml namespace.

Common XML tasks include parsing an XML file, validating it against a schema, applying an XSL transform to create a new document or Hypertext Markup Language (HTML) page, and searching intelligently with XPath.

.NET Framework 3.5 introduces LINQ to XML, which contains an updated version of the XML Document Object Model (DOM) used in earlier versions of .NET. As the name implies, LINQ to XML also provides LINQ support for XML. Language Integrated Query (LINQ) is a powerful new querying functionality that is covered in depth in Chapter 6.

The recipes in this chapter mainly focus on the changes and new additions that surround LINQ to XML rather than how things were handled previously using the standard DOM classes (such as XmlDocument). If you find yourself in the position where you are maintaining code that uses these older classes, you can use the included recipes to upgrade, or you can refer to other resources, such as *Visual Basic Recipes 2005* from Apress (the previous version of this book) or *Beginning XML, Fourth Edition (Programmer to Programmer)* from Wrox.

The recipes in this chapter cover the following:

- Creating and loading XML files (recipes 7-1 and 7-2)

- Manipulating the contents of XML files (recipes 7-3, 7-4, and 7-5)

- Querying an XML document by using LINQ (recipe 7-6), by using namespaces (recipe 7-7), or by using XPath (recipe 7-8)

- Joining multiple XML files (recipe 7-9)

- Converting an XML file to a delimited file, and vice versa (recipe 7-10)

- Validating an XML document against an XML schema (recipe 7-11)

- Serializing an object to XML (recipe 7-12), creating an XML schema for a class (recipe 7-13), and generating the source code for a class based on an XML schema (recipe 7-14)

- Transforming an XML document to another document using an XSL Transformations (XSLT) style sheet (recipe 7-15)

■**Note** The recipes in this chapter rely heavily on LINQ, which is fully covered in Chapter 6. For that reason, it is suggested that you read through all those recipes prior to working with this chapter.

7-1. Create an XML Document

Problem

You need to create some XML data and save it to a file.

Solution

Use XML literals to create a System.Xml.Linq.XElement object, and then use the Save method to save the XML tree to a file.

How It Works

The .NET Framework provides several different ways to process XML documents. The one you use depends on the programming task you are attempting to accomplish. The .NET Framework 3.5 includes classes that provide the functionality to manipulate and query XML files. Although all previous versions of .NET supported similar functionality, the new LINQ to XML classes, the most common of which can be found in Table 7-1, have greatly enhanced its support of the W3C Document Object Model (DOM). The DOM dictates how XML documents are structured and manipulated; you can find detailed specifications at http://www.w3c.org/DOM.

Table 7-1. *Common LINQ to XML Classes*

Class	Description
XAttribute	Represents an attribute.
XDocument	Represents a complete XML tree. This class derives from XContainer, which is the base class for all XML elements that can have child elements.
XElement	Represents an XML element and is the basic construct used for representing XML trees. This class also derives from XContainer.
XName	Represents attribute and element names.
XNode	Represents the base class for XML nodes (such as comments or elements).

The primary class used for creating and representing XML trees is the XElement class. This class provides all the functionally necessary to add, remove, or change elements and attributes. Performing these actions in earlier versions of .NET was tedious because you were forced to create the XML tree element by element, like this:

```
Using fs As New FileStream("sample.xml", FileMode.Create)
    Using w As XmlWriter = XmlWriter.Create(fs)
        w.WriteStartDocument()
        w.WriteStartElement("Products")
        w.WriteStartElement("Product")
        w.WriteAttributeString("id", "1001")
        w.WriteElementString("ProductName", "Visual Basic 2008 Recipes")
        w.WriteElementString("ProductPrice", "49.99")
        w.WriteEndElement()
```

```
      w.Flush()
    End Using
End Using
```

This example will produce the sample.xml file, which looks similar to the following:

```
<?xml version="1.0" encoding="utf-8"?>
<Products>
  <Product id="1001">
    <ProductName>Visual Basic 2008 Recipes</ProductName>
    <ProductPrice>49.99</ProductPrice>
  </Product>
</Products>
```

The .NET Framework 3.5 still supports these same methods, but with the introduction of LINQ to XML, there is really no reason to use them because the new functionality is much more efficient and looks cleaner. The constructor for XElement can accept XElement or XAttribute objects as parameters. This allows you to create an entire XML tree in one statement by nesting the creation of each as the appropriate XElement or XAttribute parameter, as shown here:

```
Dim xmlTree As XElement = _
  New XElement("Products", _
    New XElement("Product", _
      New XAttribute("id", "1001"), _
      New XElement("ProductName", "Visual Basic 2008 Recipes"), _
      New XElement("ProductPrice", "49.99")))


xmlTree.Save("products.xml")
```

This code, referred to as *functional construction*, produces an XML file identical to the one produced using the older methods. *Functional construction* is a much more refined approach to creating XML trees. You simply create new instances of XElement and XAttribute objects as required to build the complete tree. Since an XElement object can refer to one or more elements, xmlTree contains the full XML tree and can be easily saved using the Save method or written directly to the screen using ToString.

Visual Studio 2008 provides Visual Basic developers with an even easier way to create and work with XML using XML literals and embedded expressions. XML literals literally refers to writing XML directly in your code, such as the following:

```
Dim xmlTree = <Products>
                <Product id="1001">
                  <ProductName>Visual Basic 2008 Recipes</ProductName>
                  <ProductPrice>49.99</ProductPrice>
                </Product>
              </Products>
```

This example is identical to the previous one, but we're sure you see the benefits. Actually, when compiled, this code is actually first translated to functional construction. Furthermore, using XML literals allows you to use embedded expressions as well. If you are familiar with ASP.NET, you may already be familiar with embedded expressions, which allow you to embed code within a markup language. For example, if you had the product ID stored in a variable named productID, you could rewrite the previous code like this:

```
Dim xmlTree = <Products>
                <Product id=<%= productID %>>
                  <ProductName>Visual Basic 2008 Recipes</ProductName>
                  <ProductPrice>49.99</ProductPrice>
                </Product>
              </Products>
```

This example reveals the true power of what LINQ to XML now offers. With the use of XML literals and embedded expressions and LINQ, you can easily create sophisticated XML files.

As mentioned earlier, the most commonly used class for working with XML is XElement. However, you can also use the XDocument class (which is covered in more detail in recipe 7-2). Both classes are similar, but XDocument supports the extra information (such as comments and processing instructions) that XElement doesn't.

The Code

The following code creates an XML tree using literals and embedded expressions. The root of the tree, <Employees>, is created using an XML literal. An embedded expression, in the form of a LINQ query, is used to create each child <Employee> node. The LINQ query retrieves all the Employee objects from employeeList and transforms them, using more literals and embedded expressions, into the <Employee> nodes.

```
Imports System
Imports System.Xml.Linq

Namespace Apress.VisualBasicRecipes.Chapter07

    Public Class Recipe07_01

        Public Class Employee
            Public EmployeeID As Integer
            Public FirstName As String
            Public LastName As String
            Public Title As String
            Public HireDate As DateTime
            Public HourlyWage As Double
        End Class

        Public Shared Sub Main()

            ' Create a List to hold employees
            Dim employeeList = New Employee() _
                    {New Employee With {.EmployeeID = 1, _
                                        .FirstName = "Joed", _
                                        .LastName = "McCormick", _
                                        .Title = "Airline Pilot", _
                                        .HireDate = DateTime.Now.AddDays(-25), _
                                        .HourlyWage = 100.0}, _
```

```vbnet
                        New Employee With {.EmployeeID = 2, _
                                .FirstName = "Kia", _
                                .LastName = "Nakamura", _
                                .Title = "Super Genius", _
                                .HireDate = DateTime.Now.AddYears(-10), _
                                .HourlyWage = 999.99}, _
                        New Employee With {.EmployeeID = 3, _
                                .FirstName = "Romi", _
                                .LastName = "Brady", _
                                .Title = "Quantum Physicist", _
                                .HireDate = DateTime.Now.AddMonths(-15), _
                                .HourlyWage = 120.0}, _
                        New Employee With {.EmployeeID = 4, _
                                .FirstName = "Leah", _
                                .LastName = "Clooney", _
                                .Title = "Molecular Biologist", _
                                .HireDate = DateTime.Now.AddMonths(-10), _
                                .HourlyWage = 100.75}}

        ' Use XML literals to create the XML tree.
        ' Embedded expressions are used, with LINQ, to
        ' query the employeeList collection and build
        ' each employee node.
        Dim employees = _
            <Employees>
                <%= From emp In employeeList _
                    Select _
                    <Employee id=<%= emp.EmployeeID %>>
                        <Name><%= emp.FirstName & " " & emp.LastName %></Name>
                        <Title><%= emp.Title %></Title>
                        <HireDate><%= emp.HireDate.ToString("MM/dd/yyyy") ➡
%></HireDate>

                        <HourlyRate><%= emp.HourlyWage %></HourlyRate>
                    </Employee> _
                %>
            </Employees>

        ' Save the XML tree to a file and then display it on
        ' the screen.
        employees.Save("Employees.xml")
        Console.WriteLine(employees.ToString())

        ' Wait to continue.
        Console.WriteLine()
        Console.WriteLine("Main method complete.  Press Enter.")
        Console.ReadLine()

    End Sub
End Class

End Namespace
```

7-2. Load an XML File into Memory

Problem

You need to load the contents of an XML file into memory.

Solution

Use the Load method of the XElement or XDocument class.

How It Works

Recipe 7-1 covered XElement, the primary LINQ to XML class for working with XML trees. Although this class is extremely powerful, it does not provide properties or methods for working with all aspects of a full XML document, such as comments or processing instructions. To work with this extended information, you must rely on the XDocument class.

Although the XElement class can contain any number of child elements, the XDocument class, which represents the very top level of an XML document itself, can have only one child element. This one element, accessed by the Root property, is an XElement that contains the rest of the XML tree.

The XElement and XDocument classes both include the Parse and Load methods. The Parse method is used to parse the contents of a String to an XElement or XDocument object. Both classes support an overload of the method that allows you to specify how white spaces should be handled. The Load method allows you to load the complete contents of an XML file into an XDocument object or just the XML tree into an XElement object. Overloads of this method let you specify the target file as a String representing the path to the file, a TextReader instance, or an XmlReader instance.

The Code

The following code loads the contents of the Employees.xml file and displays the document declaration and root element on the screen:

```
Imports System
Imports System.Xml.Linq

Namespace Apress.VisualBasicRecipes.Chapter07

    Public Class Recipe07_02

        Public Shared Sub Main()

            ' Load the Employees.xml and store the contents into an
            ' XDocument object.
            Dim xmlDoc As XDocument = XDocument.Load("Employees.xml")

            ' Display the XML files declaration information.
            Console.WriteLine("The document declaration is '{0}'", ➥
xmlDoc.Declaration.ToString)

            ' Display the name of the root element in the loaded
            ' XML tree.  The Root property returns the top-level
            ' XElement, the Name property returns the XName class
            ' associated with Root and LocalName returns the name
            ' of the element as a string).
```

```
            Console.WriteLine("The root element is '{0}'", ➡
xmlDoc.Root.Name.LocalName)

            ' Wait to continue.
            Console.WriteLine()
            Console.WriteLine("Main method complete.  Press Enter.")
            Console.ReadLine()

        End Sub

    End Class
End Namespace
```

7-3. Insert Elements into an XML Document

Problem

You need to modify an XML document by inserting new data.

Solution

Use one of the available add methods (Add, AddAfterSelf, AddBeforeSelf, or AddFirst) of the XElement class, passing in an instance of the XElement or XAttribute object to create.

How It Works

The XElement class provides the following methods for inserting new elements and attributes into an existing XML tree:

- Add adds the specified element(s) or attribute(s) to the current XElement. The element(s) or attribute(s) are added at the end of any existing ones.

- AddAfterSelf and AddBeforeSelf add the specified element(s) or attribute(s) before or after the current XElement.

- AddFirst adds the specified element(s) at the top of the elements in the current element.

Each method accepts either a single XElement or XAttribute object or a collection of them, represented as an IEnumerable(Of XElement) or IEnumerable(Of XAttribute), respectively. You can specify what data to add using any of the methods discussed in the previous recipes, such as *functional construction* and *XML literals*. Also, you must keep mindful of what you are attempting to add and where you are trying to add it when using AddAfterSelf, AddBeforeSelf, and AddFirst. You will receive an exception if you attempt to use these methods to add XAttribute objects to XElement objects that refer to nodes or content. They should be used only for adding XAttribute objects to XAttribute objects and XElement objects to XElement objects.

The Code

The following example loads the contents of an XML file and then uses the XElement.Add method to add new elements and an attribute before displaying the contents.

Note This recipe uses shortcuts known as *axis properties*. Refer to recipe 7-6 for more information about axis properties and how they are used.

```vb
Imports System
Imports System.Xml.Linq

Namespace Apress.VisualBasicRecipes.Chapter07

    Public Class Recipe07_03

        Public Shared Sub Main()

            ' Load the Employees.xml and store the contents into an
            ' XElement object.
            Dim employees As XElement = XElement.Load("Employees.xml")

            ' Get the maximum value for the ID attribute.  The element
            ' axis property (<>) and the attribute axis property (@) are
            ' used to access the id attribute.
            Dim maxId As Integer = Aggregate ele In employees.<Employee> _
                            Into Max(CInt(ele.@id))

            ' Create the new Employee node using functional construction.
            Dim newEmployee = <Employee id=<%= maxId + 1 %>>
                            <Name>Robb Matthews</Name>
                            <Title>Super Hero</Title>
                            <HireDate>07/15/2006</HireDate>
                            <HourlyRate>59.95</HourlyRate>
                        </Employee>

            ' Add the new node to the bottom of the XML tree.
            employees.Add(newEmployee)

            ' Loop through all the Employee nodes and insert
            ' the new 'TerminationDate' node and the 'Status' attribute.
            For Each ele In employees.<Employee>
                ele.Add(<TerminationDate></TerminationDate>)
                ele.Add(New XAttribute("Status", ""))
            Next

            ' Display the XML on the console.
            Console.WriteLine(employees.ToString())

            ' Wait to continue.
            Console.WriteLine()
            Console.WriteLine("Main method complete.  Press Enter.")
            Console.ReadLine()

        End Sub

    End Class
End Namespace
```

7-4. Change the Value of an Element or Attribute

Problem

You need to modify an XML document by changing the value of an element or attribute.

Solution

Use one of the available set methods (`SetValue`, `SetAttributeValue`, or `SetElementValue`) of the `XElement` class.

How It Works

The `XElement` class provides the following methods for changing the value of elements and attributes in an existing XML tree:

- `SetValue` converts the specified value to a `String` and then assigns it to the `Value` property of the current `XElement` instance. This method is also available to the `XAttribute` class.

- `SetAttributeValue` converts the specified value to a `String` and then assigns it to the `Value` property of the attribute specified by the provided `XName` parameter.

- `SetElementValue` converts the specified value to a `String` and then assigns it to the `Value` property of the element specified by the provided `XName` parameter.

`SetAttributeValue` and `SetElementValue` both take an `XName` parameter to specify which element or attribute should be set. The `XName` class, which represents an element or attributes name and/or namespace, has no constructor but implicitly converts strings to `XName` objects. This means you need to pass only a string containing the name of the target, and it will automatically generate an appropriate `XName` instance.

Both of these methods also have added functionality built into them. If you specify the value as `Nothing`, then the specified element or attribute will be deleted from the XML tree. If you specify a target that does not exist, the element or attribute will be created and assigned the provided value.

All of the methods mentioned set the `Value` property of the target element or attribute. It is also possible to assign a value directly to this property without using any of the other supplied methods.

The Code

This code loads the contents of an XML file and then uses the `XElement.SetValue` method to change the contents:

```
Imports System
Imports System.Xml.Linq

Namespace Apress.VisualBasicRecipes.Chapter07

    Public Class Recipe07_04

        Public Shared Sub Main()

            ' Load the Employees.xml and store the contents into an
            ' XElement object.
            Dim employees As XElement = XElement.Load("Employees.xml")
```

```
            ' Query the XML Tree and get the Name and Hourly Rate elements.
            Dim beforeQuery = From ele In employees.<Employee> _
                            Select Name = ele.<Name>.Value, Wage = ➥
CDbl(ele.<HourlyRate>.Value)

            ' Display the employee names and their hourly rate.
            Console.WriteLine("Original hourly wages:")
            For Each ele In beforeQuery
                Console.WriteLine("{0} gets paid ${1} an hour.", ele.Name, ➥
ele.Wage.ToString())
            Next
            Console.WriteLine()

            ' Loop through all the HourlyRate elements, setting them to
            ' the new payrate, which is the old rate * 5%.
            Dim currentPayRate As Double = 0
            For Each ele In employees.<Employee>.<HourlyRate>
                currentPayRate = (ele.Value) + ((ele.Value) * 0.05)
                ele.SetValue(currentPayRate)
            Next

            ' Query the XML Tree and get the Name and Hourly Rate elements.
            Dim afterQuery = From ele In employees.<Employee> _
                            Select Name = ele.<Name>.Value, Wage = ➥
CDbl(ele.<HourlyRate>.Value)

            ' Display the employee names and their new hourly rate.
            Console.WriteLine("Hourly Wages after 5% increase:")
            For Each ele In afterQuery
                Console.WriteLine("{0} gets paid ${1} an hour.", ele.Name, ➥
ele.Wage.ToString("##.##"))
            Next

            ' Wait to continue.
            Console.WriteLine()
            Console.WriteLine("Main method complete.  Press Enter.")
            Console.ReadLine()

        End Sub

    End Class
End Namespace
```

7-5. Remove or Replace Elements or Attributes

Problem

You need to modify an XML document by completely removing or replacing certain attributes or elements.

Solution

Use one of the available replace or remove methods of the XElement class.

How It Works

The XElement class provides the following methods for replacing or removing elements or attributes in an existing XML tree:

- RemoveAll removes all elements (nodes and attributes) from the element represented by the current XElement instance.

- RemoveAttributes removes all the attributes from the element represented by the current XElement instance.

- ReplaceAll removes all the elements (nodes and attributes) from the element represented by the current XElement instance and replaces them with the element (or collection of elements) provided.

- ReplaceAttributes removes all the attributes from the element represented by the current XElement instance and replaces them with the attribute (or collection of attributes) provided.

- ReplaceNodes removes all nodes (elements, comments, processing instructions, and so on) from the element represented by the current XElement instance and replaces them with the nodes provided.

- ReplaceWith removes the node represented by the XElement instance and replaces it with the provided node or nodes.

All of the methods listed here are in the XElement class. If you are working with an XAttribute instance, you can use the Remove method to delete the current attribute. You also have the option to use the SetAttributeValue or SetElementValue method (covered in recipe 7-4) to remove the specified attribute or element by passing a value of Nothing.

■Caution You must be very careful when removing or replacing elements within a loop. Many of the available methods that return a collection of objects (such as Elements or Descendants) actually perform LINQ queries and use deferred execution (discussed in detail in Chapter 6). This means that data could be in the process of being queried as it is being deleting, which can cause unexpected results. In these situations, you should use the ToList extension method, available to all IEnumberable(Of T) objects, to force the query that runs in the background to execute immediately rather than be deferred.

The Code

This code loads the contents of an XML file and then uses the XElement.SetElementValue method to remove all the HireDate elements. The example also demonstrates the use of the Remove method by removing the fourth Employee node.

```
Imports System
Imports System.Xml.Linq

Namespace Apress.VisualBasicRecipes.Chapter07

    Public Class Recipe07_05

        Public Shared Sub Main()

            ' Load the Employees.xml and store the contents into an
            ' XElement object.
            Dim employees As XElement = XElement.Load("Employees.xml")
```

```
' Remove the 4th Employee element.
employees.<Employee>.ElementAt(3).Remove()

' Loop through all the Employee elements and remove
' the HireDate element.
For Each ele In employees.<Employee>.ToList
    ele.SetElementValue("HireDate", Nothing)
Next

Console.WriteLine(employees.ToString)

' Wait to continue.
Console.WriteLine()
Console.WriteLine("Main method complete.  Press Enter.")
Console.ReadLine()

    End Sub

  End Class
End Namespace
```

7-6. Query an XML Document Using LINQ

Problem

You need to filter the contents of or find specific elements in an XML document.

Solution

Use any of the query clauses available in System.Xml.Linq.

How It Works

LINQ allows you to execute sophisticated queries on collections that derive from IEnumerable(Of T). The main class used to manipulate XML, XElement, includes several methods (such as Elements, Descendants, and Attributes) that return IEnumerable collections of the appropriate type.

To make things easier and cleaner, LINQ to XML supports the use of shortcuts known as *axis properties*, which are new to VB .NET 9. The XElement class has three main axis properties available that correlate to either the Elements, Attributes, or Descendants method.

The Elements method returns an IEnumerable(Of XElement). For example, currentElement. Elements("MyElement") would return all the MyElement child elements of the currentElement element. The axis property shortcut is simply using the name of the element surrounded by <>. The previous example updated to use the shortcut would be currentElement.<MyElement>.

The Attributes method returns an IEnumerable(Of XAttribute). For example, currentElement. Attributes("MyAttribute") would return all the MyAttribute attributes for the currentElement element. The axis property shortcut is the symbol @ followed by the attribute name. The previous example updated to use the shortcut would be currentElement.@id. If the attribute name includes any spaces or other VB .NET illegal characters (such as a hyphen), it must be surrounded by <>. For example, since hyphens are illegal characters, an attribute named first-name would have to be referenced like this: currentElement.@<first-name>.

The Descendants method returns an IEnumerable(Of XElement). For example, currentElement. Descendants("Name") would return all the Name child elements for the currentElement element, no matter how deep in the tree they are. The axis property shortcut is the ellipsis (...) followed by the element name surrounded by <>. The previous example updated to use the shortcut would be currentElement...<Name>.

The Code

This code loads the contents of an XML file and then uses LINQ to perform several queries on the contents:

```
Imports System
Imports System.Xml.Linq

Namespace Apress.VisualBasicRecipes.Chapter07

    Public Class Recipe07_06

        Public Shared Sub Main()

            ' Load the Employees.xml file and store the contents into
            ' an XElement object.
            Dim employees As XElement = XElement.Load("Employees.xml")

            ' Get the count of all employees hired this year.
            Dim cnt = Aggregate ele In employees.<Employee> _
                    Where CDate(ele.<HireDate>.Value).Year = Now.Year _
                    Into Count()

            Console.WriteLine("{0} employees were hired this year.", cnt)
            Console.WriteLine()

            ' Query for all of the employees that make (HourlyRate) more than
            ' $100 an hour.  An anonymous type is returned containing the
            ' id, Name, and Pay properties  that correspond to the id attribute
            ' and the Name and HourlyRate elements, respectively.
            Dim query = From ele In employees.<Employee> _
                    Where CDbl(ele.<HourlyRate>.Value) >= 100 _
                    Select ele.@id, ele.<Name>.Value, Pay = ➥
CDbl(ele.<HourlyRate>.Value) _
                    Order By Name

            Console.WriteLine("Employees who make more than $100 an hour:")
            For Each emp In query
                Console.WriteLine("[{0,-2}] {1,-25} ${2,-6}", emp.id, emp.Name, ➥
emp.Pay.ToString("##.00"))
            Next

            ' Wait to continue.
            Console.WriteLine()
            Console.WriteLine("Main method complete.  Press Enter.")
            Console.ReadLine()

        End Sub

    End Class
End Namespace
```

7-7. Query for Elements in a Specific XML Namespace

Problem

You need to filter the contents of or find specific elements in an XML document that belong to a specific XML namespace.

Solution

Define any appropriate namespaces, and then perform your query using any of the clauses available in `System.Xml.Linq`, ensuring that you specify the appropriate namespace to use.

How It Works

As with the .NET Framework itself, XML namespaces are used to separate elements into groups. Every `XElement` object in an XML tree contains an `XName` object, which in turn contains an `XNamespace` object. If you have XML that contains information from multiple sources or related to multiple entities, using namespaces provides an appropriate mechanism for dividing the information logically rather than physically separating it.

XML namespaces begin with the `xmlns` key and a value. All children elements of the element that you specified a namespace for default to belonging to that namespace. You also have the option of specifying an alias that represents the full namespace. Here is an example of the `www.MyCompany.com` namespace that uses an alias of `mc`:

```
Dim xmlTree = <Root xmlns:mc="www.MyCompany.com"/>
```

All elements in a tree belong to the namespace specified by its parent or to the default namespace. A default namespace is specified in the normal manner described earlier but without the use of an alias. If a parent node specifies more than one namespace, then you should use the namespace alias to specify to which namespace each element belongs. If you do not do this, the default namespace, or the first default namespace in the case that more than one has been specified, will be used. Here is another example:

```
Dim xmlTree = <Root xmlns="www.MyCompany.com" xmlns:yc="www.YourCompany.com">
                <Child1>Child 1</Child1>
                <yc:Child2>Child 2</yc:Child2>
              </Root>
```

In this example, the `Child1` node belongs to the default (`www.MyCompany.com`) namespace, while the `Child2` node belongs to the `yc` (or `www.YourCompany.com`) namespace.

If you are manipulating or creating XML trees that include namespaces, you can make your work easier by using the `Imports` statement to include these namespaces. This statement is the same statement you use to import .NET namespaces into your code. This will allow you to specify one or more namespaces that your XML data will use. If you had first imported the namespaces from the previous example, you could have left it out of your actual XML. The updated example would look similar to this:

```
Imports <xmlns="www.MyCompany.com">
Imports <xmlns:yc="www.YourCompany.com">

Dim xmlTree = <Root>
                <Child1>Child 1</Child1>
                <yc:Child2>Child 2</yc:Child2>
              </Root>
```

Since each XElement object includes the namespace as an XNamespace instance, the saved data will include the appropriate namespace declarations. However, you must be careful when using namespaces with the imports statement. If a default namespace, one without an alias defined, were not declared, then only the namespace that was directly used (yc) would end up being declared in the resulting XML document. To ensure this doesn't happen, you should always define your default namespace (or at least the alias) within the root node.

If you need to retrieve the name of an element, you should use the Name property, which returns an instance of the XName class. By default, this will return the combination of the element's local name and its namespace. To just get the element name, you should use the LocalName property. To get the namespace, you use the Namespace property, which returns an instance of an XNamespace class. You can also use the GetXmlNamespace method, which will return an XNamespace instance based on the provided alias.

The Code

This code loads the contents of an XML file and then queries for any elements that belong to the defined namespaces:

```
Imports System
Imports System.Xml.Linq
Imports <xmlns:gfh="www.GenuisesForHire.com">
Imports <xmlns:tfh="www.TempsForHire.com">

Namespace Apress.VisualBasicRecipes.Chapter07

    Public Class Recipe07_07

        Public Shared Sub Main()

            ' Load the Employees.xml file and store the contents into
            ' an XElement object.
            Dim employees As XElement = XElement.Load("EmployeesWithNS.xml")

            ' Build the query to get all nodes that are in the
            ' www.GenuisesForHire.com namespace.
            Dim gfhEmployees = From ele In employees.Descendants _
                           Order By ele.<Name>.Value() _
                           Where (ele.Name.Namespace = GetXmlNamespace(gfh)) _
                           Select ele.<Name>.Value()

            ' Execute the query and display the results.
            Console.WriteLine("All 'Geniuses For Hire' employees:")
            For Each emp In gfhEmployees
                Console.WriteLine(emp)
            Next
            Console.WriteLine()

            ' Build the query to get all nodes that are in the
            ' www.TempsForHire.com namespace.
            Dim tfhEmployees = From ele In employees.Descendants _
                           Order By ele.<Name>.Value() _
                           Where (ele.Name.Namespace = GetXmlNamespace(tfh)) _
                           Select ele.<Name>.Value()
```

```
                        '  Execute the query and display the results.
                        Console.WriteLine("All 'Temps For Hire' employees:")
                        For Each emp In tfhEmployees
                            Console.WriteLine(emp)
                        Next

                        '  Wait to continue.
                        Console.WriteLine()
                        Console.WriteLine("Main method complete.  Press Enter.")
                        Console.ReadLine()

                End Sub

        End Class
End Namespace
```

7-8. Query an XML Document Using XPath

Problem

You need to search an XML document for nodes using advanced search criteria.

Solution

Execute an XPath expression using the XPathSelectElement or XPathSelectElements extension method of the System.Xml.XPath.Extensions class.

How It Works

The Extensions class defines two extension methods that allow you to perform XPath searches on an XNode: XPathSelectElement and XPathSelectElements. These methods operate on all contained child nodes. You can easily search on the entire XML tree by calling either of the methods from XDocument. Root or an instance of XElement that reflects the top level of the tree. You can also search on only a portion of the XML tree depending on the contents of your source XElement instance.

The Code

As an example, consider the following employees.xml document, which represents a list of employees and tasks assigned to them (only one employee is shown). This document includes text and numeric data, nested elements, and attributes, so it provides a good way to test simple XPath expressions.

```
<?xml version="1.0" encoding="utf-8"?>
<Employees>
  <Employee id="1">
    <Name>Todd Herman</Name>
    <Title>Software Engineer</Title>
    <HireDate>10/19/2007</HireDate>
    <HourlyRate>19.95</HourlyRate>
    <Tasks>
```

```
      <Task id="1">
        <Name>Task 1</Name>
        <Description>Description of Sample Task 1</Description>
        <Status>Open</Status>
      </Task>
    </Tasks>
  </Employee>
</Employees>
```

Basic XPath syntax uses a pathlike notation. For example, if you are searching from the Employees root node, the path /Employee/Tasks/Task indicates a <Task> element that is nested inside a <Tasks> element, which, in turn, is nested in a parent <Employee> element. This is an absolute path. This recipe uses an XPath absolute path to find the name of every task assigned to an employee. It then performs the same query using LINQ to highlight some of the differences between XPath and LINQ.

```vb
Imports System
Imports System.Xml.Linq
Imports System.Xml.XPath

Namespace Apress.VisualBasicRecipes.Chapter07

    Public Class Recipe07_08

        Public Shared Sub Main()

            ' Load the Employees.xml and store the contents into an
            ' XElement object.
            Dim employees As XElement = XElement.Load("EmployeesAndTasks.xml")

            ' Use XPath to get the tasks for each employee.
            Dim xpathQuery = employees.XPathSelectElements("/Employee/Tasks/Task")

            ' Loop through the query results and display the information
            ' to the screen.
            For Each task In xpathQuery
                Console.WriteLine("{0,-15} - {1} ({2})", ➥
task.Parent.Parent.<Name>.Value, task.<Name>.Value, task.<Description>.Value)
            Next
            Console.WriteLine()

            ' Use LINQ to get the tasks for each employee and order them
            ' by the employee's name.
            Dim linqQuery = From task In employees.<Employee>...<Task> _
                            Select EmployeeName = task.Parent.Parent.<Name>.Value, _
                                   TaskName = task.<Name>.Value, _
                                   task.<Description>.Value _
                            Order By EmployeeName


            ' Execute the query and loop through the results, displaying the
            ' Information to the screen.
            For Each task In linqQuery
                Console.WriteLine("{0,-15} - {1} ({2})", task.EmployeeName, ➥
task.TaskName, task.Description)
            Next
```

```
                    '  Wait to continue.
                    Console.WriteLine()
                    Console.WriteLine("Main method complete.  Press Enter.")
                    Console.ReadLine()

            End Sub

        End Class
End Namespace
```

Notes

XPath provides a rich and powerful search syntax, details of which can be found at http://www.w3.org/TR/xpath. However, XPath is yet another query language that needs to be learned. If you are familiar and comfortable with XPath, then you should feel free to use it because LINQ to XML fully supports it. If you are not, your best bet is to stick with using LINQ.

LINQ, which is covered in great detail in Chapter 6, provides the same functionality provided by XPath but in a more embedded and concise manner. XPath expressions are not compiled (they are just strings), so finding errors can be difficult while LINQ is compiled and can alert you to potential problems. Furthermore, LINQ provides more sophisticated query functionality and is strongly typed while XPath is not.

7-9. Join and Query Multiple XML Documents

Problem

You need to perform queries based on the combination of two XML documents that have a common key.

Solution

Use either the Join or Group Join query clause available in System.Xml.Linq.

How It Works

LINQ allows you to perform SQL-like queries on various data sources, such as XML. These queries support the ability to join multiple data sources based on a common key using the Join or Group Join clause.

Recipe 7-6 mentions how you can perform in-depth queries on XML data using the LINQ to XML API, and recipe 6-11 covers the Join and Group Join LINQ clauses in detail.

The Code

The following code loads the contents of two XML files (employees.xml and tasks.xml) and uses the Group Join LINQ clause to query and join them based on each employee's ID:

```
Imports System
Imports System.Xml.Linq

Namespace Apress.VisualBasicRecipes.Chapter07
    Public Class Recipe07_09

        Public Shared Sub Main()
```

```vb
' Load the Employees.xml and Tasks.xml files
' and store the contents into XElement objects.
Dim employees As XElement = XElement.Load("Employees.xml")
Dim tasks As XElement = XElement.Load("Tasks.xml")

' Build a query to join the two XML trees on the employee's
' Id.  TaskList will represent the collection of task
' elements.
Dim query = From emp In employees.<Employee> _
            Group Join task In tasks.<Task> _
            On emp.@id Equals task.@empId _
            Into TaskList = Group _
            Select EmployeeName = emp.<Name>.Value, _
                TaskList

' Execute the query and loop through the results, displaying
' them on the console.
For Each emp In query
    ' Display the employee's name.
    Console.WriteLine("Tasks for {0}:", emp.EmployeeName)

    ' Now loop through the task list
    For Each task In emp.TaskList
        Console.WriteLine("{0} - {1}", task.<Name>.Value, ➥
task.<Status>.Value)
    Next
    Console.WriteLine()
Next
Console.WriteLine()

' Wait to continue.
Console.WriteLine()
Console.WriteLine("Main method complete.  Press Enter.")
Console.ReadLine()

        End Sub

    End Class
End Namespace
```

7-10. Convert an XML File to a Delimited File (and Vice Versa)

Problem

You need to convert the contents of an XML file to a text file with delimited fields or convert a text file with delimited fields to an XML file.

Solution

To transform XML data to a delimited text file, use a LINQ query to retrieve and data and project it into an appropriate format. To transform the delimited text file to an XML tree, read and parse the data while creating the necessary XML nodes using *XML literals* and embedded expressions.

How It Works

LINQ to XML gives you the power to quickly and easily transform XML data to and from different formats by altering or transforming XML nodes within a LINQ query. If you need to transform the data in an existing XML tree into another format, you simply use LINQ (which is covered in great detail in Chapter 6) to query the information and use the Select clause to project the data into the desired format.

It is just as easy to transform data from other sources into XML by either looping through that data or performing a LINQ query, where applicable. While looping through the data, via either method, use XML literals along with embedded expressions (covered in recipe 7-1) to construct the new XML tree.

The Code

This recipe first loads the Employees.xml file into memory and performs a query on the data using LINQ, returning the data as fields surrounded by quotes and delimited by commas. This information is then saved and displayed to the screen.

Next, the recipe takes the newly created delimited file and opens it into a TextFieldParser object (which is covered in recipe 5-9) where it is read and parsed and finally built into an XML tree using XML literals and embedded expressions.

```vb
Imports System
Imports System.IO
Imports System.Text
Imports System.Xml.Linq
Imports Microsoft.VisualBasic.FileIO

Namespace Apress.VisualBasicRecipes.Chapter07
    Public Class Recipe07_10

        Public Shared Sub Main(ByVal args As String())

            ' Call the subroutine to convert an XML tree to
            ' a delimited text file.
            Call XMLToFile(args(0))

            ' Call the subroutine to convert a delimited text
            ' file to an XML tree.
            Call FileToXML()


            ' Wait to continue.
            Console.WriteLine()
            Console.WriteLine("Main method complete.  Press Enter.")
            Console.ReadLine()

        End Sub

        Private Shared Sub XMLToFile(ByVal xmlFile As String)

            ' Load the Employees.xml file and store the contents into
            ' an XElement object.
            Dim employees As XElement = XElement.Load(xmlFile)
```

```vb
    ' Create a StringBuilder that will be used to hold
    ' the delimited text.
    Dim delimitedData As New StringBuilder

    ' Create a query to convert the XML data into fields delimited
    ' by quotes and commas.
    Dim xmlData = _
        From emp In employees.<Employee> _
            Select _
            String.Format("""{0}"",""{1}"",""{2}"",""{3}"",""{4}""", _
                emp.@id, emp.<Name>.Value, _
                emp.<Title>.Value, emp.<HireDate>.Value, _
                emp.<HourlyRate>.Value)

    ' Execute the query and store the contents into the
    ' StringBuilder.
    For Each row In xmlData
        delimitedData.AppendLine(row)
    Next

    ' Display the contents to the screen and save it to the data.txt
    ' file.
    Console.WriteLine(delimitedData.ToString)
    File.WriteAllText("data.txt", delimitedData.ToString)

End Sub

Private Shared Sub FileToXML()

    ' Create the XElement object that will be used to build
    ' the XML data.
    Dim xmlTree As XElement

    ' Open the data.text file and parse it into a TextFieldParser
    ' object.
    Using parser As TextFieldParser = _
        My.Computer.FileSystem.OpenTextFieldParser("data.txt")

        ' Configure the TextFieldParser to ensure it understands
        ' that the fields are enclosed in quotes and delimited
        ' with commas.
        parser.TextFieldType = FieldType.Delimited
        parser.Delimiters = New String() {","}
        parser.HasFieldsEnclosedInQuotes = True

        ' Create the root of our XML tree.
        xmlTree = <Employees></Employees>

        Dim currentRow As String()

        ' Loop through the file until the end is reached.
        Do While Not parser.EndOfData
```

```
                        '  Parse the fields out for the current row.
                        currentRow = parser.ReadFields

                        '  Create each employee node and add it to the tree.
                        '  Each node is created using embedded expressions
                        '  that contain the appropriate field data that was
                        '  previously parsed.
                        xmlTree.Add(<Employee id=<%= currentRow(0) %>>
                                        <Name><%= currentRow(1) %></Name>
                                        <Title><%= currentRow(2) %></Title>
                                        <HireDate><%= currentRow(3) %></HireDate>
                                        <HourlyRate><%= currentRow(4) %></HourlyRate>
                                    </Employee>)
                    Loop

                End Using

                '  Display the new XML tree to the screen.
                Console.WriteLine(xmlTree)

        End Sub

    End Class

End Namespace
```

Usage

If you execute the command Recipe07-10.exe Employees.xml, the sample XML file will first be converted to a delimited file that will look like this:

```
"1","Joed McCormick","Airline Pilot","09/29/2007","100"
"2","Kai Nakamura","Super Genius","10/24/1997","999.99"
"3","Romi Doshi","Actress","07/24/2006","120"
"4","Leah Clooney","Molecular Biologist","12/24/2006","100.75"
```

The conversion from the previous delimited data back to an XML file results in the following:

```
<Employees>
  <Employee id="2">
    <Name>Joed McCormick</Name>
    <Title>Airline Pilot</Title>
    <HireDate>09/29/2007</HireDate>
    <HourlyRate>100</HourlyRate>
  </Employee>
  <Employee id="2">
    <Name>Kai Nakamura</Name>
    <Title>Super Genius</Title>
    <HireDate>10/24/1997</HireDate>
    <HourlyRate>999.99</HourlyRate>
  </Employee>
  <Employee id="3">
    <Name>Romi Doshi</Name>
```

```
      <Title>Actress</Title>
      <HireDate>07/24/2006</HireDate>
      <HourlyRate>120</HourlyRate>
    </Employee>
    <Employee id="4">
      <Name>Leah Clooney</Name>
      <Title>Molecular Biologist</Title>
      <HireDate>12/24/2006</HireDate>
      <HourlyRate>100.75</HourlyRate>
    </Employee>
</Employees>
```

7-11. Validate an XML Document Against a Schema

Problem

You need to validate the content of an XML document by ensuring that it conforms to an XML schema.

Solution

Since LINQ to XML has not added any new or direct support for working with XML schemas, you need to rely on the more general functionality found in the System.Xml namespace. To use XML schemas, you should call XmlReader.Create and supply an XmlReaderSettings object that indicates you want to perform validation. Then move through the document one node at a time by calling XmlReader.Read, catching any validation exceptions. To find all the errors in a document without catching exceptions, handle the ValidationEventHandler event on the XmlReaderSettings object given as a parameter to XmlReader.

Although LINQ to XML has not added any functionality related to this subject, it is important to note that you can use the XNode.CreateReader method to create an XmlReader based on XElement or XDocument instances.

How It Works

An XML schema defines the rules that a given type of XML document must follow. The schema includes rules that define the following:

- The elements and attributes that can appear in a document

- The data types for elements and attributes

- The structure of a document, including which elements are children of other elements

- The order and number of child elements that appear in a document

- Whether elements are empty, can include text, or require fixed values

XML Schema Definition (XSD) documents are actually just XML documents that use a special namespace (namespaces are covered more in recipe 7-7), which is defined as xmlns:xsd="http://www.w3.org/2001/XMLSchema". At its most basic level, XSD defines the elements that can occur in an XML document. You use a separate predefined element (named <element>) in the XSD document to indicate each element that is required in the target document. The type attribute indicates the data type. This recipe uses the employee list first presented in recipe 7-1.

Here is an example for an employee name:

```
<xsd:element name="Name" type="xsd:string" />
```

And here is an example for the employee hourly rate element:

```
<xsd:element name="HourlyRate" type="xsd:decimal" />
```

The basic schema data types are defined at http://www.w3.org/TR/xmlschema-2. They map closely to .NET data types and include String, Integer, Long, Decimal, Single, DateTime, Boolean, and Base64Binary—to name a few of the most frequently used types.

Both the EmployeeName and HourlyRate are *simple types* because they contain only character data. Elements that contain nested elements are called *complex types*. You can nest them together using a <sequence> tag, if order is important, or an <all> tag, if it is not. Here is how you might model the <employee> element in the employee list. Notice that attributes are always declared after elements, and they are not grouped with a <sequence> or <all> tag because the order is not important:

```
<xsd:complexType name="Employee">
  <xsd:sequence>
    <xsd:element name="Name" type="xsd:string" />
    <xsd:element name="Title" type="xsd:string" />
    <xsd:element name="HireDate" type="xsd:date" />
    <xsd:element name="HourlyRate" type="xsd:decimal" />
  </xsd:sequence>
  <xsd:attribute name="id" type="xsd:integer" />
</xsd:complexType>
```

By default, a listed element can occur exactly one time in a document. You can configure this behavior by specifying the maxOccurs and minOccurs attributes. Here is an example that allows an unlimited number of products in the catalog:

```
<xsd:element name="Employee" type="Employee" maxOccurs="unbounded" />
```

Here is the complete schema for the product catalog XML:

```
<?xml version="1.0" encoding="utf-8"?>
<xsd:schema xmlns:xsd="http://www.w3.org/2001/XMLSchema">
  <!-- Define the Employee Complex type-->
  <xsd:complexType name="Employee">
    <xsd:sequence>
      <xsd:element name="Name" type="xsd:string" />
      <xsd:element name="Title" type="xsd:string" />
      <xsd:element name="HireDate" type="xsd:date" />
      <xsd:element name="HourlyRate" type="xsd:decimal" />
    </xsd:sequence>
    <xsd:attribute name="id" type="xsd:integer" />
  </xsd:complexType>

  <!-- This is the structure that the document must match -->
  <xsd:element name="Employees">
    <xsd:complexType>
      <xsd:sequence>
        <xsd:element name="Employee" type="Employee" maxOccurs="unbounded" />
      </xsd:sequence>
    </xsd:complexType>
  </xsd:element>
</xsd:schema>
```

The XmlReader class can enforce these schema rules, provided you explicitly request a validating reader when you use the XmlReader.Create method. (Even if you do not use a validating reader, an exception will be thrown if the reader discovers XML that is not *well formed*, such as an illegal character, improperly nested tags, and so on.)

Once you have created your validating reader, the validation occurs automatically as you read through the document. As soon as an error is found, the XmlReader raises a ValidationEventHandler event with information about the error on the XmlReaderSettings object given at creation time. If you want, you can handle this event and continue processing the document to find more errors. If you do not handle this event, an XmlException will be raised when the first error is encountered, and processing will be aborted.

The Code

The following example shows a utility class that displays all errors in an XML document when the ValidateXml method is called. Errors are displayed in a console window, and a final Boolean variable is returned to indicate the success or failure of the entire validation operation.

```
Imports System
Imports System.Xml
Imports System.Xml.Schema

Namespace Apress.VisualBasicRecipes.Chapter07

    Public Class ConsoleValidator

        ' Set to true if at least one error exists.
        Private failed As Boolean

        Public Function ValidateXML(ByVal xmlFileName As String, ➡
ByVal schemaFileName As String)

            ' Set the type of validation.
            Dim settings As New XmlReaderSettings
            settings.ValidationType = ValidationType.Schema

            ' Load the schema file.
            Dim schemas As New XmlSchemaSet
            settings.Schemas = schemas

            ' When loading the schema, specify the namespace it validates
            ' and the location of the file.  Use Nothing to use the
            ' target Namespace specified in the schema.
            schemas.Add(Nothing, schemaFileName)

            ' Specify an event handler for validation errors.
            AddHandler settings.ValidationEventHandler, ➡
AddressOf HandleValidationEvents

            ' Create the validating reader.
            Dim validator As XmlReader = XmlReader.Create(xmlFileName, settings)

            failed = False
            Try
                ' Read all XML data.
                While validator.Read()
                End While
```

```vb
                Catch ex As Exception
                    ' This happens if the XML document includes illegal characters
                    ' or tags that aren't properly nested or closed.
                    Console.WriteLine("A critical XML error has occurred.")
                    Console.WriteLine(ex.Message)
                    failed = True
                Finally
                    validator.Close()
                End Try

                Return Not failed

            End Function

            Private Sub HandleValidationEvents(ByVal sender As Object, ➥
        ByVal args As ValidationEventArgs)

                failed = True

                ' Display the validation error.
                Console.WriteLine("Validation error: " & args.Message)
                Console.WriteLine()

            End Sub

        End Class
    End Namespace
```

Here is how you would use the class to validate the product catalog:

```vb
    Public Class Recipe07_11

        Public Shared Sub Main(ByVal args As String())

            Dim xmlValidator As New ConsoleValidator
            Console.WriteLine("Validating Employees.xml")

            Dim success As Boolean = ➥
        xmlValidator.ValidateXML(args(0), args(1))

            If Not success Then
                Console.WriteLine("Validation failed.")
            Else
                Console.WriteLine("Validation succeeded.")
            End If
            Console.ReadLine()

        End Sub

    End Class
```

Usage

If the document is valid, no messages will appear, and the `success` variable will be set to true. But consider what happens if you use a document that breaks schema rules, such as the following InvalidEmployees.xml file:

```xml
<?xml version="1.0" encoding="utf-8"?>
<Employees>
  <Employee id="1">
    <Name>Joed McCormick</Name>
    <HireDate>2007-09-29</HireDate>
    <HourlyRate>100</HourlyRate>
  </Employee>
  <Employee id="1" badAttribute="bad" >
    <Name>Kai Nakamura</Name>
    <Title>Super Genius</Title>
    <HireDate>10/24/1997</HireDate>
    <HourlyRate>999.99</HourlyRate>
  </Employee>
  <Employee id="3">
    <Name>Romi Doshi</Name>
    <Title>Actress</Title>
    <HireDate>2006-07-24</HireDate>
    <HourlyRate>120</HourlyRate>
  </Employee>
  <Employee id="4">
    <Name>Leah Clooney</Name>
    <Title>Molecular Biologist</Title>
    <HireDate>2006-12-24</HireDate>
    <HourlyRate>100.75</HourlyRate>
  </Employee>
  <Unknown />
</Employees>
```

If you run the example using `Recipe07-11.exe InvalidEmployees.xml Employees.xsd`, the sample file will not validate, and the output will indicate each error, as shown here:

```
Validating Employees.xml
Validation error: The element 'Employee' has invalid child element 'HireDate'. L
ist of possible elements expected: 'Title'.

Validation error: The 'badAttribute' attribute is not declared.

Validation error: The 'HireDate' element is invalid - The value '10/24/1997' is
invalid according to its datatype 'http://www.w3.org/2001/XMLSchema:date' - The
string '10/24/1997' is not a valid XsdDateTime value.

Validation error: The element 'Employees' has invalid child element 'Unknown'. L
ist of possible elements expected: 'Employee'.

Validation failed.
```

■Note For more in-depth information regarding XML schemas, refer to `http://www.w3.org/xml/schema.html`.

7-12. Use XML Serialization with Custom Objects

Problem

You need to use XML as a serialization format. However, you don't want to process the XML directly in your code. Instead, you want to interact with the data using custom objects.

Solution

Use the `System.Xml.Serialization.XmlSerializer` class to transfer data from your object to XML, and vice versa. You can also mark up your class code with attributes to customize its XML representation.

How It Works

The `XmlSerializer` class allows you to convert objects to XML data, and vice versa. This process is used natively by web services and provides a customizable serialization mechanism that does not require a single line of custom code. The `XmlSerializer` class is even intelligent enough to correctly create arrays when it finds nested elements.

The only requirements for using `XmlSerializer` are as follows:

- The `XmlSerializer` serializes only properties and `Public` variables.

- The classes you want to serialize must include a default zero-argument constructor. The `XmlSerializer` uses this constructor when creating the new object during deserialization.

- All class properties must be readable *and* writable. This is because `XmlSerializer` uses the property `Get` accessor to retrieve information and the property `Set` accessor to restore the data after deserialization.

To use XML serialization, you must first mark up your data objects with attributes that indicate the desired XML mapping. You can find these attributes in the `System.Xml.Serialization` namespace. The attributes are as follows:

- `XmlRoot` specifies the name of the root element of the XML file. By default, `XmlSerializer` will use the name of the class. You can apply this attribute to the class declaration.

- `XmlElement` indicates the element name to use for a property or `Public` variable. By default, `XmlSerializer` will serialize properties and `Public` variables using their names.

- `XmlArray` indicates that a property or `Public` variable is an array of elements. `XmlArrayItem` is used to specify the name used for each item in the array.

- `XmlAttribute` indicates that a property or `Public` variable should be serialized as an attribute, not an element, and specifies the attribute name.

- `XmlEnum` configures the text that should be used when serializing enumerated values. If you don't use `XmlEnum`, the name of the enumerated constant will be used.

- `XmlIgnore` indicates that a property or `Public` variable should not be serialized.

The Code

As an example, consider an updated version of the employee list first shown in recipe 7-1. You can represent this XML document using `EmployeeRoster` and `Employee` objects. Here's the class code that you might use:

```vb
Imports System
Imports System.IO
Imports System.Xml
Imports System.Xml.Serialization

Namespace Apress.VisualBasicRecipes.Chapter07

    <XmlRoot("EmployeeRoster")> _
    Public Class EmployeeRoster

        ' Use the date data type (and ignore the time portion
        ' in the serialized XML).
        <XmlElement(ElementName:="LastUpdated", datatype:="date")> _
        Public LastUpdated As DateTime

        ' Configure the name of the tag that holds all employees
        ' and the name of the employee tag itself.
        <XmlArray("Employees"), XmlArrayItem("Employee")> _
        Public Employees As Employee()

        Public Sub New()
        End Sub

        Public Sub New(ByVal update As DateTime)

            Me.LastUpdated = update

        End Sub

    End Class

    Public Class Employee

        <XmlElement("Name")> _
        Public Name As String = String.Empty

        <XmlElement("Title")> _
        Public Title As String = String.Empty

        <XmlElement(ElementName:="HireDate", datatype:="date")> _
        Public HireDate As DateTime = Date.MinValue

        <XmlElement("HourlyRate")> _
        Public HourlyRate As Decimal = 0

        <XmlAttribute(AttributeName:="id", DataType:="integer")> _
        Public Id As String = String.Empty
```

```vb
            Public Sub New()
            End Sub

            Public Sub New(ByVal employeeName As String, ➡
    ByVal employeeTitle As String, ByVal employeeHireDate As DateTime,➡
    ByVal employeeHourlyRate As Decimal)

                Me.Name = employeeName
                Me.Title = employeeTitle
                Me.HireDate = employeeHireDate
                Me.HourlyRate = employeeHourlyRate

            End Sub

        End Class

    End Namespace
```

Notice that these classes use the XML serialization attributes to rename element names, indicate data types that are not obvious, and specify how <Employee> elements will be nested in the <EmployeeRoster>.

Using these custom classes and the XmlSerializer object, you can translate XML into objects, and vice versa. The following is the code you would need to create a new Employee object, serialize the results to an XML document, deserialize the document back to an object, and then display the XML document:

```vb
Imports System
Imports System.IO
Imports System.Xml
Imports System.Xml.Serialization

Namespace Apress.VisualBasicRecipes.Chapter07

    Public Class Recipe07_12

        Public Shared Sub Main()

            ' Create the employee roster.
            Dim roster = New EmployeeRoster(DateTime.Now)
            Dim employees = New Employee() _
                {New Employee With {.Id = 1, .Name = "Joed McCormick", _
                                    .Title = "Airline Pilot", _
                                    .HireDate = DateTime.Now.AddDays(-25), _
                                    .HourlyRate = 100.0}, _
                    New Employee With {.Id = 2, .Name = "Kai Nakamura", _
                                    .Title = "Super Genius", _
                                    .HireDate = DateTime.Now.AddYears(-10), _
                                    .HourlyRate = 999.99}, _
                    New Employee With {.Id = 3, .Name = "Romi Doshi", _
                                    .Title = "Actress", _
                                    .HireDate = DateTime.Now.AddMonths(-15), _
                                    .HourlyRate = 120.0}, _
```

```vb
                    New Employee With {.Id = 4, .Name = "Leah Clooney", _
                                       .Title = "Molecular Biologist", _
                                       .HireDate = DateTime.Now.AddMonths(-10), _
                                       .HourlyRate = 100.75}}


        roster.Employees = employees

        ' Serialize the order to a file.
        Dim serializer As New XmlSerializer(GetType(EmployeeRoster))
        Dim fs As New FileStream("EmployeeRoster.xml", FileMode.Create)

        serializer.Serialize(fs, roster)
        fs.Close()

        roster = Nothing

        ' Deserialize the order from the file.
        fs = New FileStream("EmployeeRoster.xml", FileMode.Open)
        roster = DirectCast(serializer.Deserialize(fs), EmployeeRoster)

        ' Serialize the order to the console window.
        serializer.Serialize(Console.Out, roster)
        Console.ReadLine()

    End Sub

  End Class
End Namespace
```

7-13. Create a Schema for a .NET Class

Problem

You need to create an XML schema based on one or more VB .NET classes. This will allow you to validate XML documents before deserializing them with the XmlSerializer.

Solution

Use the XML Schema Definition Tool (xsd.exe) command-line utility included with the .NET Framework. Specify the name of your assembly as a command-line argument, and add the /t:[TypeName] parameter to indicate the types for which you want to generate a schema.

How It Works

Recipe 7-12 demonstrated how to use the XmlSerializer to serialize .NET objects to XML and deserialize XML into .NET objects. But if you want to use XML as a way to interact with other applications, business processes, or non–.NET Framework applications, you'll need an easy way to validate the XML before you attempt to deserialize it. You will also need to define an XML schema document that defines the structure and data types used in your XML format so that other applications can work with it. One quick solution is to generate an XML schema using the xsd.exe command-line utility.

The xsd.exe utility is included with the .NET Framework. If you have installed the SDK for Microsoft Visual Studio 2008, you will find it in a directory such as C:\Program Files\Microsoft Visual Studio 9.0\SDK\v3.5\Bin. The xsd.exe utility can generate schema documents from compiled assemblies. You simply need to supply the filename and indicate the class that represents the XML document with the / t:[TypeName] parameter.

Usage

As an example, consider the EmployeeRoster and Employee classes shown in recipe 7-12. You could create the XML schema for a product catalog with the following command line:

```
xsd Recipe7-12.exe /t:EmployeeRoster
```

You need to specify only the EmployeeRoster class on the command line because the Employee class is referenced by the EmployeeRoster and will be included automatically. The generated schema in this example will represent a complete employee list, with contained employees. It will be given the default filename schema0.xsd. You can now use the validation technique shown in recipe 7-11 to test whether the XML document can be successfully validated with the schema.

7-14. Generate a Class from a Schema

Problem

You need to create one or more VB .NET classes based on an XML schema. You can then create an XML document in the appropriate format using these objects and the XmlSerializer.

Solution

Use the xsd.exe command-line utility included with the .NET Framework. Specify the name of your schema file as a command-line argument, and add the /c parameter to indicate you want to generate class code.

How It Works

Recipe 7-13 introduced the xsd.exe command-line utility, which you can use to generate schemas based on class definitions. The reverse operation—generating VB .NET source code based on an XML schema document—is also possible. This is primarily useful if you want to write a certain format of XML document but you do not want to manually create the document by writing individual nodes with the XmlDocument class or the XmlWriter class. Instead, by using xsd.exe, you can generate a set of full .NET objects. You can then serialize these objects to the required XML representation using the XmlSerializer, as described in recipe 7-12.

To generate source code from a schema, you simply need to supply the filename of the schema document and add the /c parameter to indicate you want to generate the required classes.

Usage

As an example, consider the schema you generated in recipe 7-13. You can generate VB .NET code for this schema with the following command line:

```
xsd EmployeeRoster.xsd /c /language:vb
```

This will generate one VB .NET file (EmployeeRoster.vb) with two classes: Employee and EmployeeRoster. These classes are similar to the ones created in recipe 7-12, except that the class member names match the XML document exactly. Optionally, you can add the /f parameter. If you do, the generated classes will be composed of Public fields. If you do not, the generated classes will use Public properties instead (which simply wrap Private fields).

7-15. Perform an XSL Transform

Problem

You need to transform an XML document into another document using an XSLT style sheet.

Solution

Use the System.Xml.Xsl.XslCompiledTransform class. Load the XSLT style sheet using the XslCompiledTransform.Load method, and generate the output document by using the Transform method and supplying a source XML document.

How It Works

XSLT (or XSL transforms) is an XML-based language designed to transform one XML document into another document. You can use XSLT to create a new XML document with the same data but arranged in a different structure or to select a subset of the data in a document. You can also use it to create a different type of structured document. XSLT is commonly used in this manner to format an XML document into an HTML page.

The Code

This recipe transforms the EmployeeRoster.xml document shown in recipe 7-12 into an HTML document with a table and then displays the results.

Essentially, every XSLT style sheet consists of a set of templates. Each template matches some set of elements in the source document and then describes the contribution that the matched element will make to the resulting document. To match the template, the XSLT document uses XPath expressions, as described in recipe 7-8.

The employee style sheet contains two template elements (as children of the root stylesheet element). The first template matches the root EmployeeRoster element. When the XSLT processor finds an EmployeeRoster element, it outputs the HTML elements necessary to start the HTML document and the text result of an XPath expression. It then starts a table with appropriate column headings and inserts some data about the client using the value-of command, which inserts the value of the specified element as text.

Next, the apply-templates command branches off and performs the processing of any contained Employee elements. This is required because there might be multiple Employee elements. Each Employee element is matched using the XPath expression Employees/Employee. The root EmployeeRoster node is not specified because it is the current node. Finally, the initial template writes the HTML elements necessary to end the HTML document.

The following is what the finished XLST looks like:

```
<?xml version="1.0" encoding="UTF-8" ?>
<xsl:stylesheet xmlns:xsl="http://www.w3.org/1999/XSL/Transform" version="1.0">
  <xsl:template match="EmployeeRoster">
    <html>
      <body>
        <p>
          Employee Roster(Last update on <b>
            <xsl:value-of select="LastUpdated"/>
          </b>)
        </p>
        <table border="1">
          <td>ID</td>
          <td>Name</td>
          <td>Hourly Rate</td>
          <xsl:apply-templates select="Employees/Employee"/>
        </table>
      </body>
    </html>
  </xsl:template>

  <xsl:template match="Employees/Employee">
    <tr>
      <td>
        <xsl:value-of select="@id"/>
      </td>
      <td>
        <xsl:value-of select="Name"/>
      </td>
      <td>
        <xsl:value-of select="HourlyRate"/>
      </td>
    </tr>
  </xsl:template>
</xsl:stylesheet>
```

If you execute this transform on the sample EmployeeRoster.xml file shown in recipe 7-12, you will end up with an HTML document similar to the following:

```
<html>
  <body>
    <p> Employee Roster(Last update on <b>2007-10-26</b>)</p>
    <table border="1">
      <td>ID</td>
      <td>Name</td>
      <td>Hourly Rate</td>
      <tr>
        <td>1</td>
        <td>Joed McCormick</td>
        <td>100</td>
      </tr>
```

```
    <tr>
      <td>2</td>
      <td>Kai Nakamura</td>
      <td>999.99</td>
    </tr>
    <tr>
      <td>3</td>
      <td>Romi Doshi</td>
      <td>120</td>
    </tr>
    <tr>
      <td>4</td>
      <td>Leah Clooney</td>
      <td>100.75</td>
    </tr>
  </table>
 </body>
</html>
```

To apply an XSLT style sheet in .NET, you use the `XslCompiledTransform` class. (Do not confuse this class with the similar `XslTransform` class—it still works, but it was deprecated in .NET Framework 2.0.)

The following code shows a Windows-based application that programmatically applies the transformation and then displays the transformed file in a window using the `WebBrowser` control:

```vb
Imports System
Imports System.Windows.Forms
Imports System.Xml.Xsl


' All designed code is stored in the autogenerated partial
' class called TransformXML.Designer.vb. You can see this
' file by selecting Show All Files in Solution Explorer.
Partial Public Class TransformXml

    Private Sub TransformXml_Load(ByVal sender As Object, ➡
ByVal e As System.EventArgs) Handles Me.Load

        Dim transform As New XslCompiledTransform

        ' Load the XSLT style sheet.
        transform.Load("Xml2Html.xslt")

        ' Transform EmployeeRoster.xml into Employees.html using
        ' the previously generated style sheet.
        transform.Transform("EmployeeRoster.xml", "EmployeeRoster.html")

        Browser.Navigate(Application.StartupPath & "\EmployeeRoster.html")

    End Sub

End Class
```

Figure 7-1 shows the application results.

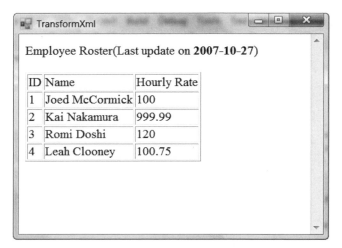

Figure 7-1. *The style sheet output for EmployeeRoster.xml*

■**Note** For more in-depth information regarding XSLT, refer to `http://www.w3.org/tr/xslt`.

Notes

Although XSLT style sheets allow you to transform XML files to another format, you are still required to know and understand how to write and format the file. Recipe 7-10 demonstrates how LINQ can also be used to transform an XML file. LINQ could also have been used with this recipe to generate an equivalent HTML file.

CHAPTER 8

■ ■ ■

Database Access

In the Microsoft .NET Framework, access to a wide variety of data sources is enabled through a group of classes collectively named Microsoft ADO.NET. Each type of data source is supported through the provision of a data provider. Each data provider contains a set of classes that not only implement a standard set of interfaces (defined in the System.Data namespace) but also provide functionality unique to the data source they support. These classes include representations of connections, commands, properties, data adapters, and data readers through which you interact with a data source.

■Note ADO.NET is an extensive subsection of the .NET Framework class library and includes a great deal of advanced functionality. For comprehensive coverage of ADO.NET, read David Sceppa's excellent book *Programming Microsoft ADO.NET 2.0 Core Reference* (Microsoft Press, 2006) or *Pro ADO.NET 2.0* (Apress, 2005). Although these books target .NET 2.0, they are still excellent resources.

Table 8-1 lists the data providers included as standard with the .NET Framework.

Table 8-1. *.NET Framework Data Provider Implementations*

Data Provider	Description
.NET Framework Data Provider for ODBC	Provides connectivity (via COM Interop) to any data source that implements an ODBC interface. This includes Microsoft SQL Server, Oracle, and Microsoft Access databases. Data provider classes are contained in the System.Data.Odbc namespace and have the prefix Odbc.
.NET Framework Data Provider for OLE DB	Provides connectivity (via COM Interop) to any data source that implements an OLE DB interface. This includes Microsoft SQL Server, MSDE, Oracle, and Jet databases. Data provider classes are contained in the System.Data.OleDb namespace and have the prefix OleDb.
.NET Framework Data Provider for Oracle	Provides optimized connectivity to Oracle databases via Oracle client software version 8.1.7 or later. Data provider classes are contained in the System.Data.OracleClient namespace and have the prefix Oracle.

Table 8-1. *.NET Framework Data Provider Implementations (Continued)*

Data Provider	Description
.NET Framework Data Provider for SQL Server	Provides optimized connectivity to Microsoft SQL Server version 7 and later (including MSDE) by communicating directly with the SQL Server data source, without the need to use ODBC or OLE DB. Data provider classes are contained in the System.Data.SqlClient namespace and have the prefix Sql.
.NET Compact Framework Data Provider for SQL Server Compact Edition	Provides connectivity to Microsoft SQL Server 2005 Compact Edition. Data provider classes are contained in the System.Data.SqlServerCe namespace and have the prefix SqlCe.

Language Integrated Query (LINQ), which is new to .NET 3.5, provides the functionality necessary to perform queries on any supported data source. For databases, this functionality is provided by the LINQ to ADO.NET API, which is located in the System.Data.Linq namespace.

LINQ to ADO.NET consists of LINQ to Datasets and LINQ to SQL. LINQ to Datasets provides several extension methods that make it easier to convert the contents of a DataTable to an IEnumerable(Of DataRow) collection. LINQ to SQL provides the necessary tools (such as the Object Relational Designer) to create object classes that represent and map directly to database tables.

This chapter describes some of the most commonly used aspects of ADO.NET. The recipes in this chapter cover the following:

- Creating, configuring, opening, and closing database connections (recipe 8-1)

- Employing connection pooling to improve the performance and scalability of applications that use database connections (recipe 8-2)

- Creating and securely storing database connection strings (recipes 8-3 and 8-4)

- Executing SQL commands and stored procedures and using parameters to improve their flexibility (recipes 8-5 and 8-6)

- Processing the results returned by database queries either as a set of rows or as XML (recipes 8-7 and 8-8)

- Executing database operations asynchronously, which allows your main code to continue with other tasks while the database operation executes in the background (recipe 8-9)

- Writing generic ADO.NET code that can be configured to work against any relational database for which a data provider is available (recipe 8-10)

- Accessing a database using mapped object classes (recipe 8-11 and recipe08-12)

- Discovering all instances of SQL Server (2000, 2005 and 2008) available on a network (recipe 8-13)

■**Note** Unless otherwise stated, the recipes in this chapter have been written to use SQL Server 2005 Express Edition running on the local machine and use the AdventureWorks sample database provided by Microsoft. To run the examples against your own database, ensure the AdventureWorks sample is installed and that the recipe's connection string reflects the name of your server instead of .\sqlexpress. You can find AdventureWorksDB.msi, the installation file for the AdventureWorks sample database, at http://www.codeplex.com/MSFTDBProdSamples/Release/ProjectReleases.aspx?ReleaseId=4004. You'll find a link called *Release Notes*, which contains instructions on installing and configuring the samples, in the same location.

8-1. Connect to a Database

Problem

You need to open a connection to a database.

Solution

Create a connection object appropriate to the type of database to which you need to connect. Configure the connection object by setting its ConnectionString property. Open the connection by calling the connection object's Open method.

How It Works

The first step in database access is to open a connection to the database. All connection objects inherit from the MustInherit System.Data.Common.DbConnection class. This class implements the System.Data.IDbConnection interface. The DbConnection class represents a database connection, and each data provider includes a unique implementation. Here is the list of the implementations for the five standard data providers:

- System.Data.Odbc.OdbcConnection

- System.Data.OleDb.OleDbConnection

- System.Data.OracleClient.OracleConnection

- System.Data.SqlClient.SqlConnection

- System.Data.SqlServerCe.SqlCeConnection

You configure a connection object using a connection string. A connection string is a set of semicolon-separated name-value pairs. You can supply a connection string either as a constructor argument or by setting a connection object's ConnectionString property before opening the connection. Each connection class implementation requires that you provide different information in the connection string. Refer to the ConnectionString property documentation for each implementation to see the values you can specify. Possible settings include the following:

- The name of the target database server

- The name of the database to open initially

- Connection time-out values

- Connection-pooling behavior (see recipe 8-2)

- Authentication mechanisms to use when connecting to secured databases, including the provision of a username and password if needed

Once configured, call the connection object's Open method to open the connection to the database. You can then use the connection object to execute commands against the data source (discussed in recipe 8-3). The properties of a connection object also allow you to retrieve information about the state of a connection and the settings used to open the connection. When you're finished with a connection, you should always call its Close method to free the underlying database connection and system resources. IDbConnection extends System.IDisposable, meaning that each connection class implements the Dispose method. Dispose automatically calls Close, making the Using statement a very clean and efficient way of using connection objects in your code.

You achieve optimum scalability by opening your database connection as late as possible and closing it as soon as you have finished. This ensures that you do not tie up database connections for long periods, so you give all the code the maximum opportunity to obtain a connection. This is especially important if you are using connection pooling.

The Code

The following example demonstrates how to use both the SqlConnection and OleDbConnection classes to open a connection to a Microsoft SQL Server database running on the local machine that uses integrated Windows security.

```
Imports System
Imports System.Data
Imports System.Data.SqlClient
Imports System.Data.OleDb

Namespace Apress.VisualBasicRecipes.Chapter08

    Public Class Recipe08_01

        Public Shared Sub SqlConnectionExample()

            ' Configure an empty SqlConnection object.
            Using con As New SqlConnection

                ' Configure the SqlConnection object's connection string.
                con.ConnectionString = "Data Source=.\sqlexpress;Database=" & ➥
"AdventureWorks;Integrated Security=SSPI;"

                ' Open the database connection.
                con.Open()

                ' Display the information about the connection.
                If con.State = ConnectionState.Open Then
                    Console.WriteLine("SqlConnection Information:")
                    Console.WriteLine("  Connection State = " & con.State)
                    Console.WriteLine("  Connection String = " & ➥
con.ConnectionString)
                    Console.WriteLine("  Database Source = " & con.DataSource)
                    Console.WriteLine("  Database = " & con.Database)
                    Console.WriteLine("  Server Version = " & con.ServerVersion)
                    Console.WriteLine("  Workstation Id = " & con.WorkstationId)
                    Console.WriteLine("  Timeout = " & con.ConnectionTimeout)
                    Console.WriteLine("  Packet Size = " & con.PacketSize)
                Else
                    Console.WriteLine("SqlConnection failed to open.")
                    Console.WriteLine("  Connection State = " & con.State)
                End If

                ' Close the database connection.
                con.Close()

            End Using

        End Sub
```

```vb
    Public Shared Sub OleDbConnectionExample()

        ' Configure an empty SqlConnection object.
        Using con As New OleDbConnection

            ' Configure the SqlConnection object's connection string.
            con.ConnectionString = "Provider=SQLOLEDB;Data Source=" & ➡
".\sqlexpress;Initial Catalog=AdventureWorks;Integrated Security=SSPI;"

            ' Open the database connection.
            con.Open()

            ' Display the information about the connection.
            If con.State = ConnectionState.Open Then
                Console.WriteLine("OleDbConnection Information:")
                Console.WriteLine("  Connection State = " & con.State)
                Console.WriteLine("  Connection String = " & ➡
con.ConnectionString)
                Console.WriteLine("  Database Source = " & con.DataSource)
                Console.WriteLine("  Database = " & con.Database)
                Console.WriteLine("  Server Version = " & con.ServerVersion)
                Console.WriteLine("  Timeout = " & con.ConnectionTimeout)
            Else
                Console.WriteLine("OleDbConnection failed to open.")
                Console.WriteLine("  Connection State = " & con.State)
            End If

            ' Close the database connection.
            con.Close()

        End Using

    End Sub

    Public Shared Sub Main()

        ' Open connection using SqlConnection.
        SqlConnectionExample()
        Console.WriteLine(Environment.NewLine)

        ' Open connection using OleDbConnection.
        OleDbConnectionExample()
        Console.WriteLine(Environment.NewLine)

        ' Wait to continue.
        Console.WriteLine(Environment.NewLine)
        Console.WriteLine("Main method complete.  Press Enter.")
        Console.ReadLine()

    End Sub

  End Class

End Namespace
```

8-2. Use Connection Pooling

Problem

You need to use a pool of database connections to improve application performance and scalability.

Solution

Configure the connection pool using settings in the connection string of a connection object.

How It Works

Connection pooling significantly reduces the overhead associated with creating and destroying database connections. Connection pooling also improves the scalability of solutions by reducing the number of concurrent connections a database must maintain. Many of these connections sit idle for a significant portion of their lifetimes.

With connection pooling, the first time you create a connection, the .NET Framework checks the pool to see whether a connection is available. If the pool hasn't yet reached its limit, a new connection will be created and added to it. The next time you attempt to use a connection with the identical connection string, instead of a new connection being created and opened, the existing connection in the pool is used. When you close the connection, it is returned to the pool until it is needed again. Once created, a pool exists until your process terminates.

The SQL Server and Oracle data providers encapsulate connection-pooling functionality that they enable by default. One connection pool exists for each unique connection string you specify when you open a new connection. Each time you open a new connection with a connection string that you used previously, the connection is taken from the existing pool. Only if you specify a different connection string will the data provider create a new connection pool. You can control some characteristics of your pool using the connection string settings described in Table 8-2.

Table 8-2. *Connection String Settings That Control Connection Pooling*

Setting	Description
Connection Lifetime	Specifies the maximum time in seconds that a connection is allowed to live in the pool before it's closed. The age of a connection is tested only when the connection is returned to the pool. This setting is useful for minimizing pool size if the pool is not heavily used and also ensures optimal load balancing is achieved in clustered database environments. The default value is 0, which means connections exist for the life of the current process.
Connection Reset	Supported only by the SQL Server data provider. Specifies whether connections are reset as they are taken from the pool. A value of True (the default) ensures a connection's state is reset but requires an additional communication with the database.
Max Pool Size	Specifies the maximum number of connections that should be in the pool. Connections are created and added to the pool as required until this value is reached. If a request for a connection is made but there are no free connections, the calling code will block until a connection becomes available or times out. The default value is 100.

Table 8-2. *Connection String Settings That Control Connection Pooling*

Setting	Description
Min Pool Size	Specifies the minimum number of connections that should be in the pool. On pool creation, this number of connections is created and added to the pool. During periodic maintenance or when a connection is requested, connections are added to the pool to ensure the minimum number of connections is available. The default value is 0.
Pooling	Set to False to obtain a nonpooled connection. The default value is True.

The Code

The following example demonstrates the configuration of a connection pool that contains a minimum of 5 and a maximum of 15 connections. Connections expire after 10 minutes (600 seconds) and are reset each time a connection is obtained from the pool. The example also demonstrates how to use the Pooling setting to obtain a connection object that is not from a pool. This is useful if your application uses a single long-lived connection to a database.

```
Imports System
Imports System.Data.SqlClient

Namespace Apress.VisualBasicRecipes.Chapter08

    Public Class Recipe08_02

        Public Shared Sub Main()

            ' Obtain a pooled connection.
            Using con As New SqlConnection

                ' Configure the SqlConnection object's connection string.
                con.ConnectionString = "Data Source=.\sqlexpress;Database=" & ➥
"AdventureWorks;Integrated Security=SSPI;Min Pool Size=5;Max Pool Size=15;" & ➥
"Connection Reset=True;Connection Lifetime=600;"

                ' Open the database connection.
                con.Open()

                ' Access the database...

                ' Close the database connection.
                ' This returns the connection to the pool for reuse.
                con.Close()

                ' At the end of the using block, the Dispose calls Close
                ' which returns the connection to the pool for reuse.
            End Using

            ' Obtain a nonpooled connection.
            Using con As New SqlConnection
```

```
                 ' Configure the SqlConnection object's connection string.
                 con.ConnectionString = "Data Source=.\sqlexpress;Database=" & ➥
      "AdventureWorks;Integrated Security=SSPI;Pooling=False;"

                 ' Open the database connection.
                 con.Open()

                 ' Access the database...

                 ' Close the database connection.
                 con.Close()

             End Using

             ' Wait to continue.
             Console.WriteLine(Environment.NewLine)
             Console.WriteLine("Main method complete.  Press Enter.")
             Console.ReadLine()

         End Sub

     End Class
 End Namespace
```

Notes

The ODBC and OLE DB data providers also support connection pooling, but they do not implement connection pooling within managed .NET classes, and you do not configure the pool in the same way as you do for the SQL Server and Oracle data providers. ODBC connection pooling is managed by the ODBC Driver Manager and configured using the ODBC Data Source Administrator tool in the Control Panel. OLE DB connection pooling is managed by the native OLE DB implementation. The most you can do is disable pooling by including the setting OLE DB Services=-4; in your connection string.

The SQL Server CE data provider does not support connection pooling, because SQL Server CE supports only a single concurrent connection.

8-3. Create a Database Connection String Programmatically

Problem

You need to programmatically create or modify a syntactically correct connection string by working with its component parts or by parsing a given connection string.

Solution

Use the System.Data.Common.DbConnectionStringBuilder class or one of its strongly typed subclasses that form part of an ADO.NET data provider.

How It Works

Connection strings are String objects that contain a set of configuration parameters in the form of name-value pairs separated by semicolons. These configuration parameters instruct the ADO.NET infrastructure how to open a connection to the data source you want to access and how to handle the life cycle of connections to that data source. As a developer, you will often simply define your connection string by hand and store it in a configuration file (see recipe 8-4). However, at times, you may want to build a connection string from component elements entered by a user, or you may want to parse an existing connection string into its component parts to allow you to manipulate it programmatically. The DbConnectionStringBuilder class and the classes derived from it provide both these capabilities.

DbConnectionStringBuilder is a class used to create connection strings from name-value pairs or to parse connection strings, but it does not enforce any logic on which configuration parameters are valid. Instead, each data provider (except the SQL Server CE data provider) includes a unique implementation derived from DbConnectionStringBuilder that accurately enforces the configuration rules for a connection string of that type. Here is the list of available DbConnectionStringBuilder implementations for standard data providers:

- System.Data.Odbc.OdbcConnectionStringBuilder
- System.Data.OleDb.OleDbConnectionStringBuilder
- System.Data.OracleClient.OracleConnectionStringBuilder
- System.Data.SqlClient.SqlConnectionStringBuilder

Each of these classes exposes properties for getting and setting the possible parameters for a connection string of that type. To parse an existing connection string, pass it as an argument when creating the DbConnectionStringBuilder-derived class, or set the ConnectionString property. If this string contains a keyword not supported by the type of connection, an ArgumentException exception is thrown.

The Code

The following example demonstrates the use of the SqlConnectionStringBuilder class to parse and construct SQL Server connection strings:

```
Imports System
Imports System.Data.SqlClient

Namespace Apress.VisualBasicRecipes.Chapter08

    Public Class Recipe08_03

        Public Shared Sub Main()

            ' Configure the SqlConnection object's connection string.
            Dim conString As String = "Data Source=.\sqlexpress;Database=" & ➥
"AdventureWorks;Integrated Security=SSPI;Min Pool Size=5;Max Pool Size=15; " & ➥
"Connection Lifetime=600;"

            ' Parse the SQL Server connection string and display the component
            ' configuration parameters.
            Dim sb1 As New SqlConnectionStringBuilder(conString)

            Console.WriteLine("Parsed SQL Connection String Parameters:")
            Console.WriteLine("  Database Source = " & sb1.DataSource)
            Console.WriteLine("  Database = " & sb1.InitialCatalog)
            Console.WriteLine("  Use Integrated Security = " & ➥
sb1.IntegratedSecurity)
```

```
Console.WriteLine("  Min Pool Size = " & sb1.MinPoolSize)
Console.WriteLine("  Max Pool Size = " & sb1.MaxPoolSize)
Console.WriteLine("  Lifetime = " & sb1.LoadBalanceTimeout)

' Build a connection string from component parameters and display it.
Dim sb2 As New SqlConnectionStringBuilder(conString)

sb2.DataSource = ".\sqlexpress"
sb2.InitialCatalog = "AdventureWorks"
sb2.IntegratedSecurity = True
sb2.MinPoolSize = 5
sb2.MaxPoolSize = 15
sb2.LoadBalanceTimeout = 600

Console.WriteLine(Environment.NewLine)
Console.WriteLine("Constructed connection string:")
Console.WriteLine("  " & sb2.ConnectionString)

' Wait to continue.
Console.WriteLine(Environment.NewLine)
Console.WriteLine("Main method complete.  Press Enter.")
Console.ReadLine()

    End Sub

End Class
End Namespace
```

8-4. Store a Database Connection String Securely

Problem

You need to store a database connection string securely.

Solution

Store the connection string in an encrypted section of the application's configuration file.

> **Note** Protected configuration—the .NET Framework feature that lets you encrypt configuration information—relies on the key storage facilities of the Data Protection API (DPAPI) to store the secret key used to encrypt the configuration file. This solves the very difficult problem of code-based secret key management. Refer to recipe 12-18 for more information about the DPAPI.

How It Works

Database connection strings often contain secret information, or at the very least information that would be valuable to someone trying to attack your system. As such, you should not store connection strings in plain text; it is also not sufficient to hard-code them into the application code. Strings embedded in an assembly can easily be retrieved using a disassembler. The .NET Framework, since 2.0, contains a number of classes and capabilities that make storing and retrieving encrypted connection strings in your application's configuration trivial.

Unencrypted connection strings are stored in the machine or application configuration file in the <connectionStrings> section in the format shown here:

```
<configuration>
    <connectionStrings>
        <add name="ConnectionString1" connectionString="Data Source=➥
.\sqlexpress;Database=AdventureWorks;Integrated Security=SSPI;Min Pool Size=5; ➥
Max Pool Size=15;Connection Reset=True;Connection Lifetime=600;"
            providerName="System.Data.SqlClient" />
    </connectionStrings>
</configuration>
```

The easiest way to read this connection string is to use the indexed ConnectionStrings property of the System.Configuration.ConfigurationManager class. Specifying the name of the connection string you want as the property index will return a System.Configuration.ConnectionStringSettings object. The ConnectionString property gets the connection string, and the ProviderName property gets the provider name that you can use to create a data provider factory (see recipe 8-10). You can also assign an arbitrary name to the ConnectionStringSettings instance using the Name property. This process will work regardless of whether the connection string has been encrypted or written in plain text.

To write a connection string to the application's configuration file, you must first obtain a System.Configuration.Configuration object, which represents the application's configuration file. The easiest way to do this is by calling the System.Configuration.ConfigurationManager. OpenExeConfiguration method. You should then create and configure a new System.Configuration. ConnectionStringSettings object to represent the stored connection string. You should provide a name, connection string, and data provider name for storage. Add the ConnectionStringSettings object to the Configuration's ConnectionStringsSection collection, available through the Configuration.ConnectionStrings property. Finally, save the updated file by calling the Configuration.Save method.

To encrypt the connection strings section of the configuration file, before saving the file, you must configure the ConnectionStringsSection collection. To do this, call the ConnectionStringsSection.SectionInformation.ProtectSection method and pass it a string containing the name of the protected configuration provider to use: either RsaProtectedConfigurationProvider or DPAPIProtectedConfigurationProvider. To disable encryption, call the SectionInformation.Unprotect method.

■**Note** To use the classes from the System.Configuration namespace discussed in this recipe, you must add a reference to the System.Configuration.dll assembly when you build your application.

The Code

The following example demonstrates the writing of an encrypted connection string to the application's configuration file and the subsequent reading and use of that connection string:

```
Imports System
Imports System.Configuration
Imports System.Data.SqlClient
```

```vb
Namespace Apress.VisualBasicRecipes.Chapter08

    Public Class Recipe08_04

        Private Shared Sub WriteEncryptedConnectionStringSection(ByVal name As ➥
    String, ByVal constring As String, ByVal provider As String)

                ' Get the configuration file for the current application.  Specify
                ' the ConfigurationUserLevel.None argument so that we get the
                ' configuration settings that apply to all users.
                Dim config As Configuration = ➥
    ConfigurationManager.OpenExeConfiguration(ConfigurationUserLevel.None)

                ' Get the connectionStrings section from the configuration file.
                Dim section As ConnectionStringsSection = config.ConnectionStrings

                ' If the connectionString section does not exist, create it.
                If section Is Nothing Then
                    section = New ConnectionStringsSection
                    config.Sections.Add("connectionSettings", section)
                End If

                ' If it is not already encrypted, configure the connectionStrings
                ' section to be encrypted using the standard RSA Protected
                ' Configuration Provider.
                If Not section.SectionInformation.IsProtected Then
                    ' Remove this statement to write the connection string in clear
                    ' text for the purpose of testing.
                    section.SectionInformation.ProtectSection ➥
    ("RsaProtectedConfigurationProvider")
                End If

                ' Create a new connection string element and add it to the
                ' connection string configuration section.
                Dim cs As New ConnectionStringSettings(name, constring, provider)
                section.ConnectionStrings.Add(cs)

                ' Force the connection string section to be saved whether
                ' it was modified or not.
                section.SectionInformation.ForceSave = True

                ' Save the updated configuration file.
                config.Save(ConfigurationSaveMode.Full)

        End Sub

        Public Shared Sub main()

                ' The connection string information to be written to the
                ' configuration file.
                Dim conName As String = "ConnectionString1"
                Dim conString As String = "Data Source=.\sqlexpress;Database=" & ➥
    "AdventureWorks;Integrated Security=SSPI;Min Pool Size=5;Max Pool Size=5;" & ➥
    "Connection Reset=True;Connection Lifetime=600;"
```

```
        Dim providerName As String = "System.Data.SqlClient"

        ' Write the new connection string to the application's
        ' configuration file.
        WriteEncryptedConnectionStringSection(conName, conString, providerName)

        ' Read the encrypted connection string settings from the
        ' application's configuration file.
        Dim cs2 As ConnectionStringSettings = ➥
ConfigurationManager.ConnectionStrings("ConnectionString1")

        ' Use the connections string to create a new SQL Server connection.
        Using con As New SqlConnection(cs2.ConnectionString)
            ' Issue database commands/queries...
        End Using

        ' Wait to continue.
        Console.WriteLine(Environment.NewLine)
        Console.WriteLine("Main method complete.  Press Enter.")
        Console.ReadLine()

    End Sub

  End Class
End Namespace
```

Notes

The example in this recipe uses the OpenExeConfiguration method to open the configuration file for the application. It accepts a ConfigurationUserLevel enumerator value, which is set to None to get the configuration settings for all users. If you need to access user-specific settings, you should use the PerUserRoaming or PerUserRoamingAndLocal value. PerUserRoaming refers to the current user's roaming configuration settings. PerUserRoamingAndLocal refers to the user's local settings.

8-5. Execute a SQL Command or Stored Procedure

Problem

You need to execute a SQL command or stored procedure on a database.

Solution

Create a command object appropriate to the type of database you intend to use. Configure the command object by setting its CommandType and CommandText properties. Execute the command using the ExecuteNonQuery, ExecuteReader, or ExecuteScalar method, depending on the type of command and its expected results.

How It Works

All command objects inherit the MustInherit System.Data.Common.DbCommand class, which implements the System.Data.IDbCommand interface. The DbCommand class represents a database command,

and each data provider includes a unique implementation. Here is the list of the implementations for the five standard data providers:

- `System.Data.Odbc.OdbcCommand`
- `System.Data.OleDb.OleDbCommand`
- `System.Data.OracleClient.OracleCommand`
- `System.Data.SqlClient.SqlCommand`
- `System.Data.SqlServerCe.SqlCeCommand`

To execute a command against a database, you must have an open connection (discussed in recipe 8-1) and a properly configured command object appropriate to the type of database you are accessing. You can create command objects directly using a constructor, but a simpler approach is to use the `CreateCommand` factory method of a connection object. The `CreateCommand` method returns a command object of the correct type for the data provider and configures it with the appropriate information (such as `CommandTimeout` and `Connection`) obtained from the connection you used to create the command. Before executing the command, you must configure the properties described in Table 8-3, which are common to all command implementations.

Table 8-3. *Common Command Object Properties*

Property	Description
CommandText	A `String` containing the text of the SQL command to execute or the name of a stored procedure. The content of the `CommandText` property must be compatible with the value you specify in the `CommandType` property.
CommandTimeout	An `Integer` that specifies the number of seconds to wait for the command to return before timing out and raising an exception. Defaults to 30 seconds.
CommandType	A value of the `System.Data.CommandType` enumeration that specifies the type of command represented by the command object. For most data providers, valid values are `StoredProcedure`, when you want to execute a stored procedure, and `Text`, when you want to execute a SQL text command. If you are using the OLE DB data provider, you can specify `TableDirect` when you want to return the entire contents of one or more tables. Refer to the .NET Framework SDK documentation for more details. Defaults to `Text`.
Connection	A `DbConnection` instance that provides the connection to the database on which you will execute the command. If you create the command using the `IDbConnection.CreateCommand` method, this property will be automatically set to the `DbConnection` instance from which you created the command.
Parameters	A `System.Data.DbParameterCollection` instance containing the set of parameters to substitute into the command. This property is optional. (See recipe 8-6 for details on how to use parameters.)
Transaction	A `System.Data.DbTransaction` instance representing the transaction into which to enlist the command. If the connection object used to create this method specified a transaction, this property will be automatically set to that instance. This property is optional. (See the .NET Framework SDK documentation for details about transactions.)

Once you have configured your command object, you can execute it in a number of ways, depending on the nature of the command, the type of data returned by the command, and the format in which you want to process the data:

- To execute a command that does not return database data (such as UPDATE, INSERT, DELETE, or CREATE TABLE), call ExecuteNonQuery. For the UPDATE, INSERT, and DELETE commands, the ExecuteNonQuery method returns an Integer that specifies the number of rows affected by the command. For commands that don't return rows, such as CREATE TABLE, ExecuteNonQuery returns the value –1.

- To execute a command that returns a result set, such as a SELECT statement or stored procedure, use the ExecuteReader method. ExecuteReader returns a DbDataReader instance (discussed in recipe 8-7) through which you have access to the result data. When the ExecuteReader command returns, the connection cannot be used for any other commands while the IDataReader is open. Most data providers also allow you to execute multiple SQL commands in a single call to the ExecuteReader method, as demonstrated in the example in this recipe, which also shows how to access each result set.

- If you want to execute a query but need only the value from the first column of the first row of result data, use the ExecuteScalar method. The value is returned as an Object reference that you must cast to the correct type.

■**Note** The IDbCommand implementations included in the Oracle and SQL data providers implement additional command execution methods. Recipe 8-8 describes how to use the ExecuteXmlReader method provided by the SqlCommand class. Refer to the .NET Framework's SDK documentation, at http://msdn2.microsoft.com/ en-us/library/system.data.oracleclient.oraclecommand(vs.90).aspx, for details on the additional ExecuteOracleNonQuery and ExecuteOracleScalar methods provided by the OracleCommand class.

The Code

The following example demonstrates the use of command objects to update a database record, return records from a query, and obtain a scalar value. Recipe 8-6 covers the use of stored procedures.

```
Imports System
Imports System.Data
Imports System.Data.SqlClient

Namespace Apress.VisualBasicRecipes.Chapter08

    Public Class Recipe08_05

        Public Shared Sub ExecuteNonQueryExample(ByVal con As IDbConnection)

            ' Create and configure a new command.
            Dim com As IDbCommand = con.CreateCommand
            com.CommandType = CommandType.Text
            com.CommandText = "UPDATE HumanResources.Employee SET Title = " & ➥
"'Production Supervisor' WHERE EmployeeID = 24;"

            ' Execute the command and process the result.
            Dim result As Integer = com.ExecuteNonQuery
```

```vbnet
            If result = 1 Then
                Console.WriteLine("Employee title updated.")
            ElseIf result > 1 Then
                Console.WriteLine("{0} employee titles updated.", result)
            Else
                Console.WriteLine("Employee title not updated.")
            End If

    End Sub

    Public Shared Sub ExecuteReaderExample(ByVal con As IDbConnection)

        ' Create and configure a new command.
        Dim com As IDbCommand = con.CreateCommand
        com.CommandType = CommandType.Text
        com.CommandText = "SET ROWCOUNT 10;SELECT " &
"Production.Product.Name, Production.Product.ListPrice FROM " &
"Production.Product ORDER BY Production.Product.ListPrice DESC;SET ROWCOUNT 0;"

        ' Execute the command and process the results.
        Using reader As IDataReader = com.ExecuteReader

            While reader.Read
                ' Display the product details.
                Console.WriteLine("  {0} = {1}", reader("Name"), ➥
reader("ListPrice"))
            End While

        End Using

    End Sub

    Public Shared Sub ExecuteScalarExample(ByVal con As IDbConnection)

        ' Create and configure a new command.
        Dim com As IDbCommand = con.CreateCommand
        com.CommandType = CommandType.Text
        com.CommandText = "SELECT COUNT(*) FROM HumanResources.Employee;"

        ' Execute the command and cast the result.
        Dim result As Integer = CInt(com.ExecuteScalar)

        Console.WriteLine("Employee count = " & result)

    End Sub

    Public Shared Sub Main()

        ' Create a new SqlConnection object.
        Using con As New SqlConnection

            ' Configure the SqlConnection object's connection string.
            con.ConnectionString = "Data Source=.\sqlexpress;Database=" & ➥
"AdventureWorks;Integrated Security=SSPI;"
```

```
        '  Open the database connection and execute the example
        '  commands through the connection.
        con.Open()

        ExecuteNonQueryExample(con)
        Console.WriteLine(Environment.NewLine)

        ExecuteReaderExample(con)
        Console.WriteLine(Environment.NewLine)

        ExecuteScalarExample(con)
        Console.WriteLine(Environment.NewLine)

        '  Close the database connection.
        con.Close()

      End Using

      '  Wait to continue.
      Console.WriteLine(Environment.NewLine)
      Console.WriteLine("Main method complete.  Press Enter.")
      Console.ReadLine()

    End Sub

  End Class
End Namespace
```

Notes

The example in this recipe demonstrates how to use a command object to execute a few different SQL statements against a database. Since the statements are sent to the server as strings, they are not compiled or interpreted as anything by the .NET compiler. This means syntax checking or errors in the statement are not performed, which makes diagnosing problems more difficult. Furthermore, you are forced to know how to use Structured Query Language (SQL).

As mentioned in the introduction to this chapter, .NET 3.5 introduces Language Integrated Query (LINQ), which provides a structured and interpreted language for querying various data sources. LINQ to ADO.NET encompasses LINQ to Datasets and LINQ to SQL, which allow LINQ to be used with databases. Using LINQ limits the need-to-know SQL, and since it is compiled as part of the language, it supports IntelliSense as well as syntax and error checking. LINQ is covered in greater detail in Chapter 6.

To use LINQ to Datasets, you would first need to fill a DataTable or DataSet (an object that can contain multiple tables and represents a disconnected database) with data from the database. One the data has been loaded, the AsEnumerable extension method (see recipe 1-22 for extension methods) is used to return the table as an IEnumerable(Of DataRow) collection. The LINQ to Objects API (also covered in Chapter 6) provides querying functionality for any object that inherits from IEnumerable(Of T).

LINQ to SQL provides the means to create .NET class objects that represent, and directly map to, specific tables in a database. Any changes or queries made against the class objects are converted to the appropriate query language (such as SQL) and sent to the server where they are executed. Recipe 8-12 and recipe 8-13 cover the two main ways to create these objects.

8-6. Use Parameters in a SQL Command or Stored Procedure

Problem

You need to set the arguments of a stored procedure or use parameters in a SQL query to improve flexibility.

Solution

Create parameter objects appropriate to the type of command object you intend to execute. Configure the parameter objects' data types, values, and directions and add them to the command object's parameter collection using the `DbCommand.Parameters.Add` method.

How It Works

All command objects support the use of parameters, so you can do the following:

- Set the arguments of stored procedures.
- Receive stored procedure return values.
- Substitute values into SQL queries at runtime.

All parameter objects inherit the `MustInherit System.Data.Common.DbParameter` class, which implements the `System.Data.IDataParameter` interface. The `DbParameter` class represents a parameter, and each data provider includes a unique implementation. Here is the list of the implementations for the five standard data providers:

- `System.Data.Odbc.OdbcParameter`
- `System.Data.OleDb.OleDbParameter`
- `System.Data.OracleClient.OracleParameter`
- `System.Data.SqlClient.SqlParameter`
- `System.Data.SqlServerCe.SqlCeParameter`

To use parameters with a text command, you must identify where to substitute the parameter's value within the command. The ODBC, OLE DB, and SQL Server CE data providers support positional parameters; the location of each argument is identified by a question mark (?). For example, the following command identifies two locations to be substituted with parameter values:

```
UPDATE HumanResources.Employee SET Title = ? WHERE EmployeeId = ?
```

The SQL Server and Oracle data providers support named parameters, which allow you to identify each parameter location using a name preceded by the at symbol (@). Named parameters are very useful when you need to use the same parameter in multiple locations because you need to create only one parameter object for it. Here is the equivalent command using named parameters:

```
UPDATE HumanResources.Employee SET Title = @title WHERE EmployeeId = @id
```

To specify the parameter values to substitute into a command, you must create parameter objects of the correct type and add them to the command object's parameter collection accessible through the `Parameters` property. You can add named parameters in any order, but you must add positional parameters in the same order they appear in the text command. When you execute your command, the value of each parameter is substituted into the command before it is executed against the data source. You can create parameter objects in the following ways:

- Use the CreateParameter method of the command object.

- Use the Parameters.Add method of the command object.

- Use System.Data.Common.DbProviderFactory.

- Directly create parameter objects using constructors and configure them using constructor arguments or through setting their properties. (This approach ties you to a specific database provider.)

A parameter object's properties describe everything about a parameter that the command object needs to use the parameter object when executing a command against a data source. Table 8-4 describes the properties that you will use most frequently when configuring parameters.

When using parameters to execute stored procedures, you must provide parameter objects to satisfy each argument required by the stored procedure, including both input and output arguments. If a stored procedure has a return value, the parameter to hold the return value (with a Direction property equal to ReturnValue) must be the first parameter added to the parameter collection.

Table 8-4. *Commonly Used Parameter Properties*

Property	Description
DbType	A value of the System.Data.DbType enumeration that specifies the type of data contained in the parameter. Commonly used values include String, Int32, DateTime, and Currency. Since this property is flagged as MustOverride, the specific providers will override it to return more appropriate information, such as the SqlDbType enumeration that is returned from the SqlParameter class. The specific provider class will typically also supply an appropriately named DbType property that returns the type specific to the provider, such as the SqlDbType property of the SqlParameter class.
Direction	A value from the System.Data.ParameterDirection enumeration that indicates the direction in which the parameter is used to pass data. Valid values are Input, InputOutput, Output, and ReturnValue. The default is Input.
IsNullable	A Boolean that indicates whether the parameter accepts Nothing values. The default is False.
ParameterName	A String containing the name of the parameter.
Value	An Object containing the value of the parameter.

The Code

The following example demonstrates the use of parameters in SQL queries. The ParameterizedCommandExample method demonstrates the use of parameters in a SQL Server UPDATE statement. The ParameterizedCommandExample method's arguments include an open SqlConnection, an Integer, and a String. The values of the two strings are substituted into the UPDATE command using parameters. The StoredProcedureExample method demonstrates the use of parameters to call a stored procedure.

Since not all providers support named parameters, this example specifically uses SQL objects. Instead of using DbConnection, DbCommand, and DataParameter, it uses the specific classes SqlConnection, SqlCommand, and SqlParameter, respectively.

The appropriate data type, for the parameter, is assigned using the SqlParameter.SqlDbType property. As Table 8-4 mentions, you could also have used the DbType property, which is overridden by the SqlParameter class, to return the same information as the SqlDbType property.

```vb
Imports System
Imports System.Data
Imports System.Data.SqlClient

Namespace Apress.VisualBasicRecipes.Chapter08

    Public Class Recipe08_06

        Public Shared Sub ParameterizedCommandExample(ByVal con As ➥
SqlConnection, ByVal employeeID As Integer, ByVal title As String)

            ' Create and configure a new command containing 2 named parameters.
            Using com As SqlCommand = con.CreateCommand

                com.CommandType = CommandType.Text
                com.CommandText = "UPDATE HumanResources.Employee SET Title " & ➥
"= @title WHERE EmployeeID = @id;"

                ' Create a SqlParameter object for the title parameter.
                Dim p1 As SqlParameter = com.CreateParameter
                p1.ParameterName = "@title"
                p1.SqlDbType = SqlDbType.VarChar
                p1.Value = title
                com.Parameters.Add(p1)

                ' Use a shorthand syntax to add the id parameter.
                com.Parameters.Add("@id", SqlDbType.Int).Value = employeeID

                ' Execute the command and process the result.
                Dim result As Integer = com.ExecuteNonQuery

                If result = 1 Then
                    Console.WriteLine("Employee {0} title updated to {1}", ➥
employeeID, title)
                ElseIf result > 1 Then
                    ' Indicates multiple records were affected.
                    Console.WriteLine("{0} records for employee {1} had " & ➥
"the title updated to {2}", result, employeeID, title)
                Else
                    Console.WriteLine("Employee {0} title not updated.", employeeID)
                End If

            End Using

        End Sub

        Public Shared Sub StoredProcedureExample(ByVal con As SqlConnection, ➥
ByVal managerID As Integer)

            ' Create and configure a new command containing 2 named parameters.
            Using com As SqlCommand = con.CreateCommand

                com.CommandType = CommandType.StoredProcedure
                com.CommandText = "uspGetManagerEmployees"
```

```vb
        ' Create the required SqlParameter object.
        com.Parameters.Add("@ManagerID", SqlDbType.Int).Value = managerID

        ' Execute the command and process the result.
        Dim result As Integer = com.ExecuteNonQuery

        Using reader As SqlDataReader = com.ExecuteReader
            Console.WriteLine("Employees managed by manager #{0}.", ➥
managerID.ToString)

            While reader.Read
                ' Display the product details.
                Console.WriteLine("  {0}, {1} ({2})", ➥
reader("LastName"), reader("FirstName"), reader("employeeID"))
            End While

        End Using

    End Using

End Sub

Public Shared Sub Main()

    ' Create a new SqlConnection object.
    Using con As New SqlConnection

        ' Configure the SqlConnection object's connection string.
        con.ConnectionString = "Data Source=.\sqlexpress;Database=" & ➥
"AdventureWorks;Integrated Security=SSPI;"

        ' Open the database connection and execute the example
        ' commands through the connection.
        con.Open()

        ParameterizedCommandExample(con, 16, "Production Technician")
        Console.WriteLine(Environment.NewLine)

        StoredProcedureExample(con, 185)
        Console.WriteLine(Environment.NewLine)

        ' Close the database connection.
        con.Close()

    End Using

    ' Wait to continue.
    Console.WriteLine(Environment.NewLine)
    Console.WriteLine("Main method complete.  Press Enter.")
    Console.ReadLine()

End Sub

    End Class
End Namespace
```

8-7. Process the Results of a SQL Query Using a Data Reader

Problem

You need to process the data contained in the System.Data.DbDataReader class instance returned when you execute the DbCommand.ExecuteReader method (see recipe 8-5).

Solution

Use the members of the DbDataReader class to move through the rows in the result set sequentially and access the individual data items contained in each row.

How It Works

The DbDataReader class represents a data reader, which is a forward-only, read-only mechanism for accessing the results of a SQL query. This is a MustInherit class that implements both the System.Data.IDataReader and System.Data.IDataRecord interfaces. Each data provider includes a unique DbDataReader implementation. Here is the list of the implementations for the five standard data providers:

- System.Data.Odbc.OdbcDataReader
- System.Data.OleDb.OleDbDataReader
- System.Data.OracleClient.OracleDataReader
- System.Data.SqlClient.SqlDataReader
- System.Data.SqlServerCe.SqlCeDataReader

Together, the IDataReader and IDataRecord interfaces supply the functionality that provides access to both the data and the structure of the data contained in the result set. Table 8-5 describes some of the commonly used members of the IDataReader and IDataRecord interfaces.

Table 8-5. *Commonly Used Members of Data Reader Classes*

Member	Description
Property	
FieldCount	Gets the number of columns in the current row.
HasRows	Returns True if the DbDataReader has any rows and False if it doesn't.
IsClosed	Returns True if the DbDataReader is closed and False if it's currently open.
Item	Returns an Object representing the value of the specified column in the current row. Columns can be specified using a zero-based integer index or a string containing the column name. You must cast the returned value to the appropriate type. This is the indexer for the IDataRecord interface.
Method	
GetDataTypeName	Gets the name of the data source data type as a String for a specified column.
GetFieldType	Gets a System.Type instance representing the data type of the value contained in the column specified using a zero-based integer index.

Table 8-5. *Commonly Used Members of Data Reader Classes*

Member	Description
GetName	Gets the name of the column specified by using a zero-based integer index.
GetOrdinal	Gets the zero-based column ordinal for the column with the specified name.
GetSchemaTable	Returns a System.Data.DataTable instance that contains metadata describing the columns contained in the DbDataReader.
IsDBNull	Returns True if the value in the specified column contains a data source null value; otherwise, it returns False.
NextResult	If the DbDataReader includes multiple result sets because multiple statements were executed, NextResult moves to the next set of results. This method returns True or False, indicating whether or not there are more results. By default, the DbDataReader is positioned on the first result set.
Read	Advances the reader to the next record. This method returns True or False, indicating whether or not there are more records. The reader always starts prior to the first record.

In addition to those members listed in Table 8-5, the data reader provides a set of methods for retrieving typed data from the current row. Each of the following methods takes an integer argument that identifies the zero-based index of the column from which the data should be returned: GetBoolean, GetByte, GetBytes, GetChar, GetChars, GetDateTime, GetDecimal, GetDouble, GetFloat, GetGuid, GetInt16, GetInt32, GetInt64, GetString.

The SQL Server and Oracle data readers also include methods for retrieving data as data source–specific data types. For example, the SqlDataReader includes methods such as GetSqlByte, GetSqlDecimal, and GetSqlMoney, and the OracleDataReader includes methods such as GetOracleLob, GetOracleNumber, and GetOracleMonthSpan. Refer to the .NET Framework SDK documentation for more details.

When you have finished with a data reader, you should always call its Close method so that you can use the database connection again. DbDataReader extends System.IDisposable, meaning that each data reader class implements the Dispose method. Dispose automatically calls Close, making the Using statement a very clean and efficient way of using data readers.

The Code

The following example demonstrates the use of a data reader to process the contents of two result sets returned by executing a batch query containing two SELECT queries. The first result set is enumerated and displayed to the console. The second result set is inspected for metadata information, which is then displayed.

```
Imports System
Imports System.Data
Imports System.Data.SqlClient

Namespace Apress.VisualBasicRecipes.Chapter08

    Public Class Recipe08_07

        Public Shared Sub Main()
```

```vb
                ' Create a new SqlConnection object.
                Using con As New SqlConnection

                    ' Configure the SqlConnection object's connection string.
                    con.ConnectionString = "Data Source=.\sqlexpress;Database=" & ➥
"AdventureWorks;Integrated Security=SSPI"

                    ' Create and configure a new command.
                    Using com As SqlDbCommand = con.CreateCommand

                        com.CommandType = CommandType.Text
                        com.CommandText = "SELECT e.BirthDate,c.FirstName," & ➥
"c.LastName FROM HumanResources.Employee e INNER JOIN Person.Contact c ON " & ➥
"e.EmployeeID"=c.ContactID ORDER BY e.BirthDate;SELECT * FROM " & ➥
"humanResources.Employee"

                        ' Open the database connection and execute the example
                        ' commands through the connection.
                        con.Open()

                        ' Execute the command and obtain a DataReader.
                        Using reader As SqlDataReader = com.ExecuteReader

                            ' Process the first set of results and display the
                            ' content of the result set.
                            Console.WriteLine("Employee Birthdays (By Age).")

                            While reader.Read
                                Console.WriteLine("  {0,18:D} - {1} {2}", ➥
reader.GetDateTime(0), reader("FirstName"), reader(2))
                            End While
                            Console.WriteLine(Environment.NewLine)

                            ' Process the second set of results and display details
                            ' about the columns and data types in the result set.
                            If (reader.NextResult()) Then
                                reader.NextResult()
                                Console.WriteLine("Employee Table Metadata.")
                                For field As Integer = 0 To reader.FieldCount - 1
                                    Console.WriteLine(" Column Name:{0} Type:{1}", ➥
reader.GetName(field), reader.GetDataTypeName(field))
                                Next
                            End If

                        End Using

                        ' Close the database connection.
                        con.Close()

                    End Using

                End Using

                ' Wait to continue.
```

```
            Console.WriteLine(Environment.NewLine)
            Console.WriteLine("Main method complete.  Press Enter.")
            Console.ReadLine()

        End Sub

    End Class
End Namespace
```

8-8. Obtain an XML Document from a SQL Server Query

Problem

You need to execute a query against a SQL Server 2000 (or later) database and retrieve the results as XML.

Solution

Specify the FOR XML clause in your SQL query to return the results as XML. Execute the command using the ExecuteXmlReader method of the System.Data.SqlClient.SqlCommand class, which returns a System.Xml.XmlReader object through which you can access the returned XML data.

How It Works

SQL Server 2000 (and later versions) provides direct support for XML. You simply need to add the clause FOR XML AUTO to the end of a SQL query to indicate that the results should be returned as XML. By default, the XML representation is not a full XML document. Instead, it simply returns the result of each record in a separate element, with all the fields as attributes. For example, this query:

```
SELECT DepartmentID, [Name] FROM HumanResources.Department FOR XML AUTO
```

returns XML with the following structure:

```
<HumanResources.Department DepartmentID="12" Name="Document Control" />
<HumanResources.Department DepartmentID="1" Name="Engineering" />
<HumanResources.Department DepartmentID="16" Name="Executive" />
```

Alternatively, you can add the ELEMENTS keyword to the end of a query to structure the results using nested elements rather than attributes. For example, this query:

```
SELECT DepartmentID, [Name] FROM HumanResources.Department FOR XML AUTO, ELEMENTS
```

returns XML with the following structure:

```
<HumanResources.Department>
  <DepartmentID>12</DepartmentID>
  <Name>Document Control</Name>
</HumanResources.Department>
<HumanResources.Department>
  <DepartmentID>1</DepartmentID>
  <Name>Engineering</Name>
</HumanResources.Department>
<HumanResources.Department>
  <DepartmentID>16</DepartmentID>
  <Name>Executive</Name>
</HumanResources.Department>
```

▪**Tip** You can also fine-tune the format using the FOR XML EXPLICIT syntax. For example, this allows you to convert some fields to attributes and others to elements. Refer to SQL Server Books Online, http://msdn2. microsoft.com/en-us/library/ms189068.aspx, for more information.

When the ExecuteXmlReader command returns, the connection cannot be used for any other commands while the XmlReader is open. You should process the results as quickly as possible, and you must always close the XmlReader. Instead of using the XmlReader to access the data sequentially, you can read the XML data into an XElement or XDocument class (both of which are located in the System.Xml.Linq namespace). This way, all the data is retrieved into memory, and the database connection can be closed. You can then continue to interact with the XML document. (Chapter 7, which covers LINQ to XML, contains numerous examples on using the XDocument and XElement classes.)

The Code

The following example demonstrates how to retrieve results as XML using the FOR XML clause and the ExecuteXmlReader method:

```
Imports System
Imports System.Xml
Imports System.Data
Imports System.Data.SqlClient

Namespace Apress.VisualBasicRecipes.Chapter08

    Public Class Recipe08_08

        Public Shared Sub ConnectedExample()

            ' Create a new SqlConnection object.
            Using con As New SqlConnection

                ' Configure the SqlConnection object's connection string.
                con.ConnectionString = "Data Source=.\sqlexpress;Database=" & ➥
"AdventureWorks;Integrated Security=SSPI;"

                ' Create and configure a new command that includes the
                ' FOR XML AUTO clause.
                Using com As SqlCommand = con.CreateCommand

                    com.CommandType = CommandType.Text
                    com.CommandText = "SELECT DepartmentID, [Name], " & ➥
"GroupName FROM HumanResources.Department FOR XML AUTO"

                    ' Open the database connection.
                    con.Open()

                    ' Execute the command and retrieve and XmlReader to access
                    ' the results.
                    Using reader As XmlReader = com.ExecuteXmlReader

                        ' Loop through the reader.
                        While reader.Read
```

```vb
                                ' Make sure we are dealing with an actual element of
                                ' some type.
                                If reader.NodeType = XmlNodeType.Element Then

                                    ' Create an XElement object based on the current
                                    ' contents of the reader.
                                    Dim currentEle As XElement = ➥
XElement.ReadFrom(reader)

                                    ' Display the name of the current element and list
                                    ' any attributes that it may have.
                                    Console.WriteLine("Element: {0}", currentEle.Name)
                                    If currentEle.HasAttributes Then
                                        For i As Integer = 0 To ➥
currentEle.Attributes.Count - 1

                                            Console.Write(" {0}: {1}", ➥
currentEle.Attributes()(i).Name, currentEle.Attributes()(i).Value)
                                        Next
                                    End If
                                End If
                            End While

                End Using

                ' Close the database connection.
                con.Close()

            End Using
        End Using

    End Sub

    Public Shared Sub DisconnectedExample()

        ' This will be used to create the new XML document.
        Dim doc As New XDocument

        ' Create a new SqlConnection object.
        Using con As New SqlConnection

            ' Configure the SqlConnection object's connection string.
            con.ConnectionString = "Data Source=.\sqlexpress;Database=" & ➥
"AdventureWorks;Integrated Security=SSPI;"

            ' Create and configure a new command that includes the
            ' FOR XML AUTO clause.
            Using com As SqlCommand = con.CreateCommand

                com.CommandType = CommandType.Text
                com.CommandText = "SELECT DepartmentID, [Name], " & ➥
"GroupName FROM HumanResources.Department FOR XML AUTO;"

                ' Open the database connection.
                con.Open()
```

```vb
                        ' Execute the command and retrieve and XmlReader to access
                        ' the results.
                    Using reader As XmlReader = com.ExecuteXmlReader
                            ' Create the parent element for the results.
                        Dim root As XElement = <Results></Results>

                            ' Loop through the reader and add each node as a
                            ' child to the root.
                        While reader.Read

                                ' We need to make sure we are only dealing with
                                ' some form of an Element.
                            If reader.NodeType = XmlNodeType.Element Then
                                Dim newChild As XNode = XElement.ReadFrom(reader)
                                root.Add(newChild)
                            End If

                        End While

                            ' Finally, add the root element (and all of its children)
                            ' to the new XML document.
                        doc.Add(root)

                    End Using

                        ' Close the database connection.
                    con.Close()

                End Using
            End Using

            ' Process the disconnected XmlDocument.
            Console.WriteLine(doc.ToString)

        End Sub

        Public Shared Sub Main()

            ConnectedExample()
            Console.WriteLine(Environment.NewLine)

            DisconnectedExample()
            Console.WriteLine(Environment.NewLine)

            ' Wait to continue.
            Console.WriteLine(Environment.NewLine)
            Console.WriteLine("Main method complete.  Press Enter.")
            Console.ReadLine()

        End Sub

    End Class
End Namespace
```

8-9. Perform Asynchronous Database Operations Against SQL Server

Problem

You need to execute a query or command against a SQL Server database as a background task while your application continues with other processing.

Solution

Use the `BeginExecuteNonQuery`, `BeginExecuteReader`, or `BeginExecuteXmlReader` method of the `System.Data.SqlClient.SqlCommand` class to start the database operation as a background task. These methods all return a `System.IAsyncResult` object that you can use to determine the operation's status or use thread synchronization to wait for completion. Use the `IAsyncResult` object and the corresponding `EndExecuteNonQuery`, `EndExecuteReader`, or `EndExecuteXmlReader` method to obtain the result of the operation.

■**Note** Only the `SqlCommand` class supports the asynchronous operations described in this recipe. The equivalent command classes for the Oracle, SQL Server CE, ODBC, and OLE DB data providers do not provide this functionality.

How It Works

You will usually execute operations against databases synchronously, meaning that the calling code blocks until the operation is complete. Synchronous calls are most common because your code will usually require the result of the operation before it can continue. However, sometimes it's useful to execute a database operation asynchronously, meaning that you start the method in a separate thread and then continue with other operations.

The `SqlCommand` class implements the asynchronous execution pattern similar to that discussed in recipe 4-2. As with the general asynchronous execution pattern described in recipe 4-2, the arguments of the asynchronous execution methods (`BeginExecuteNonQuery`, `BeginExecuteReader`, and `BeginExecuteXmlReader`) are the same as those of the synchronous variants (`ExecuteNonQuery`, `ExecuteReader`, and `ExecuteXmlReader`), but they take the following two additional arguments to support asynchronous completion:

- A `System.AsyncCallback` delegate instance that references a method that the runtime will call when the asynchronous operation completes. The method is executed in the context of a thread-pool thread. Passing `Nothing` means that no method is called and you must use another completion mechanism (discussed later in this recipe) to determine when the asynchronous operation is complete.

- An `Object` reference that the runtime associates with the asynchronous operation. The asynchronous operation does not use or have access to this object, but it's available to your code when the operation completes, allowing you to associate useful state information with an asynchronous operation. For example, this object allows you to map results against initiated operations in situations where you initiate many asynchronous operations that use a common callback method to perform completion.

The `EndExecuteNonQuery`, `EndExecuteReader`, and `EndExecuteXmlReader` methods allow you to retrieve the return value of an operation that was executed asynchronously, but you must first determine when it has finished. Here are the four techniques for determining whether an asynchronous method has finished:

- *Blocking*: This method stops the execution of the current thread until the asynchronous operation completes execution. In effect, this is much the same as synchronous execution. However, you do have the flexibility to decide exactly when your code enters the blocked state, giving you the opportunity to carry out some additional processing before blocking.

- *Polling*: This method involves repeatedly testing the state of an asynchronous operation to determine whether it's complete. This is a simple technique and is not particularly efficient from a processing perspective. You should avoid tight loops that consume processor time. It's best to put the polling thread to sleep for a period using Thread.Sleep between completion tests. Because polling involves maintaining a loop, the actions of the waiting thread are limited, but you can easily update some kind of progress indicator.

- *Waiting*: This method uses an object derived from the System.Threading.WaitHandle class to signal when the asynchronous method completes. Waiting is a more efficient version of polling and in addition allows you to wait for multiple asynchronous operations to complete. You can also specify time-out values to allow your waiting thread to fail if the asynchronous operation takes too long or if you want to periodically update a status indicator.

- *Callback*: This is a method that the runtime calls when an asynchronous operation completes. The calling code does not need to take any steps to determine when the asynchronous operation is complete and is free to continue with other processing. Callbacks provide the greatest flexibility but also introduce the greatest complexity, especially if you have many concurrently active asynchronous operations that all use the same callback. In such cases, you must use appropriate state objects to match completed methods against those you initiated.

The Code

Recipe 4-2 provides examples of all the completion techniques summarized in the preceding list. The following example demonstrates the use of an asynchronous call to execute a stored procedure on a SQL Server database. The code uses a callback to process the returned result set.

```
Imports System
Imports System.Data
Imports System.Threading
Imports System.Data.SqlClient

Namespace Apress.VisualBasicRecipes.Chapter08

    Public Class Recipe08_09

        ' A method to handle asynchronous completion using callbacks.
        Public Shared Sub CallBackHandler(ByVal result As IAsyncResult)

            ' Obtain a reference to the SqlCommand used to initiate the
            ' asynchronous operation.
            Using cmd As SqlCommand = TryCast(result.AsyncState, SqlCommand)
                ' Obtain the result of the stored procedure.
                Using reader As SqlDataReader = cmd.EndExecuteReader(result)
```

```vbnet
                        ' Display the results of the stored procedure to the console.
                        ' To ensure the program is thread safe, SyncLock is used
                        ' to stop more than one thread from accessing the console
                        ' at the same time.
                        SyncLock Console.Out
                            Console.WriteLine("Bill of Materials:")
                            Console.WriteLine("ID        Description       Quantity" & _
    "   ListPrice")

                            While reader.Read
                                ' Display the record details.
                                Console.WriteLine("{0}    {1}    {2}    {3}", _
    reader("ComponentID"), reader("ComponentDesc"), reader("TotalQuantity"), _
    reader("ListPrice"))
                            End While

                        End SyncLock

                    End Using
                End Using

            End Sub

        Public Shared Sub Main()

                ' Create a new SqlConnection object.
                Using con As New SqlConnection

                    ' Configure the SqlConnection object's connection string.
                    ' You must specify Asynchronous Processing=True to support
                    ' asynchronous operations over the connection.
                    con.ConnectionString = "Data Source=.\sqlexpress;Database=" & _
    "AdventureWorks;Integrated Security=SSPI;Asynchronous Processing=true;"

                    ' Create and configure a new command to run a stored procedure.
                    Using cmd As SqlCommand = con.CreateCommand

                        cmd.CommandType = CommandType.StoredProcedure
                        cmd.CommandText = "uspGetBillOfMaterials"

                        ' Create the required SqlParameter objects.
                        cmd.Parameters.Add("@StartProductID", SqlDbType.Int).Value = 771
                        cmd.Parameters.Add("@CheckDate", _
    SqlDbType.DateTime).Value = DateTime.Parse("07/10/2000")

                        ' Open the database connection and execute the command
                        ' asynchronously.  Pass the reference to the SqlCommand
                        ' used to initiate the asynchronous operation.
                        con.Open()
                        cmd.BeginExecuteReader(AddressOf CallBackHandler, cmd)
                    End Using
```

```
                        '  Continue with other processing.
                        For count As Integer = 1 To 10
                            SyncLock Console.Out
                                Console.WriteLine("{0} : Continue processing...", ➥
DateTime.Now.ToString("HH:mm:ss.ffff"))
                            End SyncLock
                            Thread.Sleep(500)
                        Next

                        '  Close the database connection.
                        con.Close()

                        '  Wait to continue.
                        Console.WriteLine(Environment.NewLine)
                        Console.WriteLine("Main method complete.  Press Enter.")
                        Console.ReadLine()

                End Using
            End Sub

        End Class
    End Namespace
```

8-10. Write Database-Independent Code

Problem

You need to write code that can be configured to work against any relational database supported by an ADO.NET data provider.

Solution

Program to the ADO.NET data provider base classes that inherit the main interfaces, such as IDbConnection, in the System.Data namespace. Unlike the concrete implementations, such as SqlConnection, the base classes do not rely on features and data types that are unique to specific database implementations. Use factory classes and methods to instantiate the data provider objects you need to use.

How It Works

Using a specific data provider implementation (the SQL Server data provider, for example) simplifies your code and may be appropriate if you need to support only a single type of database or require access to specific features provided by that data provider, such as the asynchronous execution for SQL Server detailed in recipe 8-9. However, if you program your application against a specific data provider implementation, you will need to rewrite and test those sections of your code if you want to use a different data provider at some point in the future.

Table 8-6 contains a summary of the main interfaces you must program against when writing generic ADO.NET code that will work with any relational database's data provider. The table also explains how to create objects of the appropriate type that implement the interface. Many of the recipes in this chapter demonstrate the use of ADO.NET data provider interfaces over specific implementation, as highlighted in the table.

Table 8-6. *Data Provider Interfaces*

Interface	Description	Demonstrated In
IDbConnection	Represents a connection to a relational database. You must program the logic to create a connection object of the appropriate type based on your application's configuration information or use the CreateConnection factory method of the MustInherit DbProviderFactory class (discussed in this recipe).	Recipes 8-1 and 8-5
IDbCommand	Represents a SQL command that is issued to a relational database. You can create IDbCommand objects of the appropriate type using the IDbConnection.CreateCommand or CreateCommand factory method of the MustInherit DbProviderFactory class.	Recipes 8-5 and 8-6
IDataParameter	Represents a parameter to an IDbCommand object. You can create IDataParameter objects of the correct type using the DbType property and the IDbCommand.CreateParameter, IDbCommand.Parameters.Add, or CreateParameter factory method of the MustInherit DbProviderFactory class.	Recipe 8-6
IDataReader	Represents the result set of a database query and provides access to the contained rows and columns. An object of the correct type will be returned when you call the IDbCommand.ExecuteReader method.	Recipes 8-5 and 8-7
IDataAdapter	Represents the set of commands used to fill a System.Data.DataSet from a relational database and to update the database based on changes to the DataSet. You must program the logic to create a data adapter object of the appropriate type based on your application's configuration information or use the CreateAdapter factory method of the MustInherit DbProviderFactory class.	(Not covered)

The System.Data.Common.DbProviderFactory class was first introduced in NET Framework 2.0 and provides a set of factory methods for creating all types of data provider objects, making it useful for implementing generic database code. Most important, DbProviderFactory provides a mechanism for obtaining an initial IDbConnection instance, which is the critical starting point to writing generic ADO.NET code. Each of the standard data provider implementations (except the SQL Server CE data provider) includes a unique factory class derived from DbProviderFactory. Here is the list of DbProviderFactory subclasses:

- System.Data.Odbc.OdbcFactory

- System.Data.OleDb.OleDbFactory

- System.Data.OracleClient.OracleClientFactory

- System.Data.SqlClient.SqlClientFactory

■**Note** It's important to understand that there is no common data type for parameters. You are forced to use DbType, and you are responsible for understanding the mapping between your generic provider and your data source.

You can obtain an instance of the appropriate DbProviderFactory subclass using the DbProviderFactories class, which is effectively a factory of factories. Each data provider factory is described by configuration information in the machine.config file similar to that shown here for the SQL Server data adapter. This can be changed or overridden by application-specific configuration information if required.

```
<configuration>
 <system.data>
   <DbProviderFactories>
     <add name="SqlClient Data Provider" invariant="System.Data.SqlClient" ➥
description=".Net Framework Data Provider for SqlServer" type= ➥
"System.Data.SqlClient.SqlClientFactory, System.Data, Version=2.0.0.0, ➥
Culture=neutral, PublicKeyToken=b77a5c561934e089" />
     <add name="Odbc Data Provider" ... />
     <add name="OleDb Data Provider" ... />
     <add name="OracleClient Data Provider" ... />
     <add name="SQL Server CE Data ... />
   </DbProviderFactories>
 </system.data>
</configuration>
```

You can enumerate the available data provider factories by calling DbProviderFactories. GetFactoryClasses, which returns a System.Data.DataTable containing the following columns:

- Name, which contains a human-readable name for the provider factory. This is taken from the name attribute in the configuration information.

- Description, which contains a human-readable description for the provider factory. This is taken from the description attribute of the configuration information.

- InvariantName, which contains the unique name used to refer to the data provider factory programmatically. This is taken from the invariant attribute of the configuration information.

- AssemblyQualifiedName, which contains the fully qualified name of the DbProviderFactory class for the data provider. This is taken from the type attribute of the configuration information.

Normally, you would allow the provider to be selected at install time, or the first time the application was run, and then store the settings as user or application configuration data. The most important piece of information is the InvariantName, which you pass to the DbProviderFactories. GetFactory method to obtain the DbProviderFactory implementation you will use to create your IDbConnection instances.

■Note Prior to .NET Framework 2.0, it was difficult to write generic ADO.NET code because each data provider implemented its own exception class that did not extend a common base class. Since .NET Framework 2.0, the System.Data.Common.DbException class has been added as the base class of all data provider-specific exceptions, making the generic handling of database exceptions a reality.

The Code

The following example demonstrates the enumeration of all data providers configured for the local machine and application. It then uses the DbProviderFactories class to instantiate a DbProviderFactory object (actually a SqlClientFactory) from which it creates the appropriate

IDbConnection. It then uses the factory methods of the data provider interfaces to create other required objects, resulting in code that is completely generic.

```vb
Imports System
Imports System.Data
Imports System.Data.Common

Namespace Apress.VisualBasicRecipes.Chapter08

    Public Class Recipe08_10

        Public Shared Sub Main()

            ' Obtain the list of ADO.NET data providers registered in the
            ' machine and application configuration file.
            Using providers As DataTable = DbProviderFactories.GetFactoryClasses

                ' Enumerate the set of data providers and display details.
                Console.WriteLine("Available ADO.NET Data Providers:")

                For Each prov As DataRow In providers.Rows
                    Console.WriteLine(" Name:{0}", prov("Name"))
                    Console.WriteLine("   Description:{0}", ➥
prov("Description"))
                    Console.WriteLine("   Invariant Name:{0}", ➥
prov("InvariantName"))
                Next

            End Using

            ' Obtain the DbProviderFactory for SQL Server.  The provider to use
            ' could be selected by the user or read from a configuration file.
            ' In this case, we simply pass the invariant name.
            Dim factory As DbProviderFactory = ➥
DbProviderFactories.GetFactory("System.Data.SqlClient")

            ' Use the DbProviderFactory to create the initial IDbConnection, and
            ' then the data provider inteface factory methods for other objects.
            Using con As IDbConnection = factory.CreateConnection

                ' Normally, read the connection string from secure storage.
                ' See recipe 8-2.  In this case, use a default value.
                con.ConnectionString = "Data Source=.\sqlexpress;Database=" & ➥
"AdventureWorks;Integrated Security=SSPI;"

                ' Create and configure a new command.
                Using com As IDbCommand = con.CreateCommand

                    com.CommandType = CommandType.Text
                    com.CommandText = "SET ROWCOUNT 10;SELECT prod.Name, " & ➥
"inv.Quantity FROM Production.Product prod INNER JOIN " & ➥
"Production.ProductInventory inv ON prod.ProductID = inv.ProductID " & ➥
"ORDER BY inv.Quantity DESC;"
```

```vb
                        '  Open the connection.
                        con.Open()

                        '  Execute the command and process the results.
                        Using reader As IDataReader = com.ExecuteReader

                            Console.WriteLine(Environment.NewLine)
                            Console.WriteLine("Quantity of the Ten Most Stocked " & ➥
"Products:")

                            While reader.Read
                                '  Display the product details.
                                Console.WriteLine("  {0} = {1}", reader("Name"), ➥
reader("Quantity"))
                            End While

                        End Using

                        '  Close the database connection.
                        con.Close()

                    End Using
                End Using

                '  Wait to continue.
                Console.WriteLine(Environment.NewLine)
                Console.WriteLine("Main method complete.  Press Enter.")
                Console.ReadLine()

            End Sub

        End Class
    End Namespace
```

8-11. Create a Database Object Model

Problem

You need to create objects that map directly to tables in a relational database.

Solution

Use the Object Relational Designer (O/R Designer) to automatically generate .NET classes that map directly to tables within the target database.

How It Works

LINQ to SQL, the Language Integrated Query (see Chapter 6) API, provides integrated query support for databases. It accomplishes this by using object classes, created in any .NET language, that tightly map to tables in a database. Instead of creating string-based commands to collect or change data in a database, as shown in the earlier recipes in this chapter, you simply change property values or create new instances of the mapped object classes.

Although the object classes can be created manually by using the various attributes located in the System.Data.Linq.Mapping namespace, this could be very error-prone and time-consuming. To assist in this process, Visual Studio 2008 includes the Object Relational Designer, which is capable of automatically generated the object classes for you.

The first step in using the O/R Designer to create your object classes is to add it to your project. You do this by selecting Project ➤ Add New Item, which will open the Add New Item dialog box (see Figure 8-1). From the template list, select LINQ to SQL Classes, and change the default name to something that makes sense for your project. Once you are finished, click the Add button.

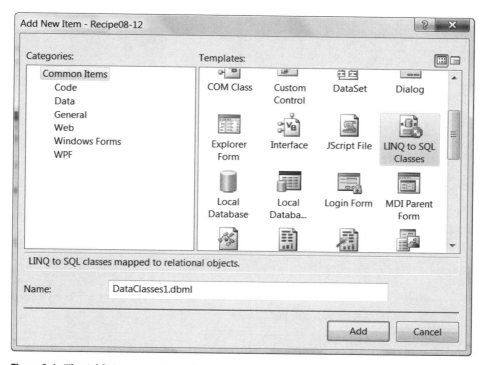

Figure 8-1. *The Add New Item dialog box*

A few things happen when you first add the O/R Designer component to your project. To see everything, you should make sure your project is selected and click the Show All Files icon in the Solution Explorer. This will reveal any hidden files within the currently selected project.

You will immediately notice that the newly added .dbml item is really a group that contains a .dbml.layout file and a .designer.vb file. The .dbml file is an XML file that contains all metadata- and database-specific information, while the .dbml.layout, which is also XML, is just placement and configuration data used by the designer. The .designer.vb file is the code file that contains all the automatically generated class objects. At this point, the object contains only the data context class that inherits from System.Data.Linq.DataContext. This class represents the primary bridge between the class objects and the database.

Double-clicking the .dbml item will open the O/R Designer, allowing you to begin adding objects to it. Now you are ready to add tables to the designer. To do this, open the Server Explorer window, and select the connection folder that contains the tables you want to add. Once your connection has been successfully established, display the list of available tables, and drag the desired ones to the designer (see Figure 8-2).

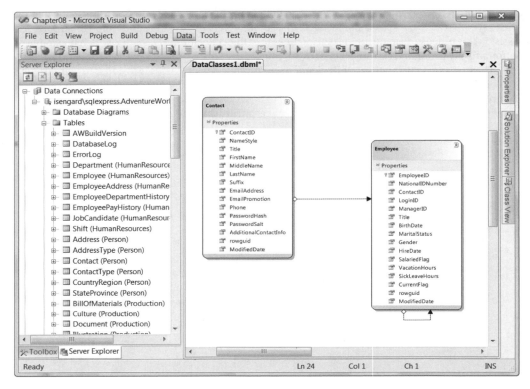

Figure 8-2. *The O/R Designer*

■**Note** Currently, the O/R Designer supports only SQL Server.

The designer will display a class diagram for each table added. The first time you add a table to the designer, a new project setting containing the connection information will automatically be added to the app.config file for your project. The automatically generated data context class will also be updated to include a constructor that will use this new setting to connect to the database. Also, a new class for each table added will be generated.

Each class object, or entity, maps directly to a table in the database, while each property maps to columns in the table. Any stored procedures or user-defined functions will be functions in the entity class. Special attributes from the System.Data.Linq.Mapping namespace are used to tag each element and instruct how they map back to the database. Even relationships that exist in the database are reflected in the new object model as *associations*.

Once the objects have been created, using them is very straightforward. You just need to understand that instances of each object represent a row in the table. To create a new row, create a new instance of that object. To change the value of a column in a table, change the property. The SubmitChanges method of the DataContext class is used to persist any changes to the database. All you need to get started is a new instance of the generated data context class that will make the connection to the database for you and be used as a bridge.

Note You can also use SQLMetal.exe, a command-line utility to generate the object classes. This is covered in recipe 8-12.

The Code

The following example demonstrates how to retrieve data from the database and perform a basic query on it, all using the classes automatically generated by the O/R Designer:

```vb
Imports System
Imports System.Data.Linq

Namespace Apress.VisualBasicRecipes.Chapter08

    Public Class Recipe08_11

        Shared Sub Main()

            ' Create an instance of the DataContext that was
            ' created by the O/R Designer.
            Dim dbContext = New AdventureWorksDataContext()

            ' Create a query to return the name and HireDate for
            ' each employee that was hired prior to the year 2000.
            ' Note that you can easily access a related table (Contact)
            ' without having to perform any joins.
            Dim Query = From emp In dbContext.Employees _
                        Where emp.HireDate.Year < 2000 _
                        Select Name = emp.Contact.LastName & ", " & ➡
emp.Contact.FirstName, _
                            emp.HireDate _
                        Order By Name

            ' Execute the query and display the results.
            For Each emp In Query
                Console.WriteLine("{0} was hired on {1}", emp.Name, ➡
emp.HireDate.ToString("MM/dd/yyy"))
            Next

            ' Wait to continue.
            Console.WriteLine(Environment.NewLine)
            Console.WriteLine("Main method complete.  Press Enter.")
            Console.ReadLine()

        End Sub

    End Class
End Namespace
```

8-12. Generate Data Object Classes from the Command Line

Problem

You need to create objects that map directly to tables in a relational database, but you do not have access to Visual Studio 2008 or can't use the O/R Designer for some reason.

Solution

Use SqlMetal.exe to automatically generate .NET classes that map directly to tables within the target database.

How It Works

Recipe 8-11 covers the basics on using the new Object Relational Designer (O/R Designer) to create a set of object classes that model a relational database. Since a situation may arise where you need to perform this same functionality from the command line, Visual Studio 2008 also includes the SqlMetal.exe utility.

SqlMetal.exe is distributed with Visual Studio 2008 and is located in a directory similar to C:\Windows\Microsoft.NET\Framework\v3.5. To use it, just execute it and pass in any appropriate parameters (see Table 8-7 for a list of the main ones).

Table 8-7. *Main SqlMetal.exe Parameters*

Parameter	Description
/server:	Used to specify the SQL server to connect to.
/database:	Used to specify the actual database to connect to.
/user	Used to specify a name to use to log on to the database. SqlMetal.exe defaults to using Windows authentication if no user or password is provided.
/password	Used to specify a password to use to log on to the database. SqlMetal.exe defaults to using Windows authentication if no user or password is provided.
/views	Instructs the utility to extract all views.
/functions	Instructs the utility to extract all functions.
/sprocs	Instructs the utility to extract all stored procedures.
/dbml:	Instructs the utility to generate a .dbml file that can be opened with the O/R Designer.
/code:	Instructs the utility to generate source code.
/map:	Instructs the utility to generate an XML mapping file.
/language:	Used to specify what language should be used for generated code.

Usage

In its simplest form, you need to supply only the server and a database to target:

```
Sqlmetal /server:.\sqlexpress /database:AdventureWorks
```

However, since no target was specified, the results will be displayed as XML on the screen. In most situations, this is not desired, so you should specify a target, like this:

```
Sqlmetal /server:.\sqlexpress /database:AdventureWorks /dbml:AdventureWorks.dbml
```

This command will create a .dbml file that can be easily opened and edited within Visual Studio 2008 using the O/R Designer (see Figure 8-3) that was covered in recipe 8-11.

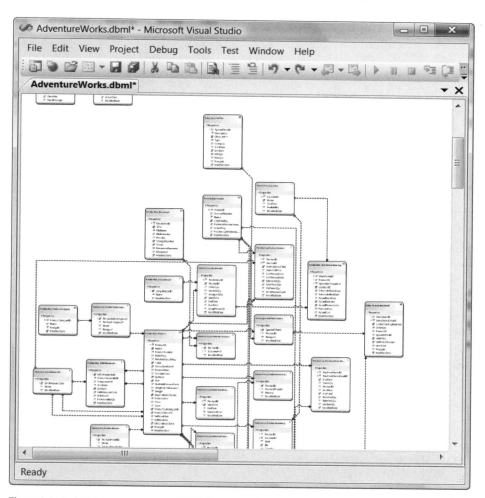

Figure 8-3. *SqlMetal.exe-generated DBML viewed in the O/R Designer*

8-13. Discover All Instances of SQL Server on Your Network

Problem

You need to obtain a list of all instances of SQL Server 2000 or SQL Server 2005 that are accessible on the network.

Solution

Use the GetDataSources method of the System.Data.Sql.SqlDataSourceEnumerator class.

■**Note** Your code needs to be granted FullTrust to be able to execute the GetDataSources method.

How It Works

The SqlDataSourceEnumerator class makes it easy to enumerate the SQL Server instances accessible on the network. Since this class does not have an accessible constructor, you must use the Shared property SqlDataSourceEnumerator.Instance to return an instance of the class. You then use the GetDataSources method to return a System.Data.DataTable that contains a set of System.Data.DataRow objects. Each DataRow represents a single SQL Server instance and contains the following columns:

- ServerName, which contains the name of the server where the SQL Server instance is hosted.

- InstanceName, which contains the name of the SQL Server instance or the empty string if the SQL Server is the default instance.

- IsClustered, which indicates whether the SQL Server instance is part of a cluster.

- Version, which contains the version of the SQL Server instance (8.00.x for SQL Server 2000, 9.00.x for SQL Server 2005, or 10.00.x for SQL Server 2008).

The Code

The following example demonstrates the use of the SqlDataSourceEnumerator class to discover and display details of all SQL Server instances accessible (and visible) on the network:

```
Imports System
Imports System.Data
Imports System.Data.Sql

Namespace Apress.VisualBasicRecipes.Chapter08

    Public Class Recipe08_13

        Public Shared Sub Main()

            ' Obtain the DataTable of SQL Server instances.
            Using sqlSources As DataTable = ➥
SqlDataSourceEnumerator.Instance.GetDataSources()

                ' Enumerate the set of SQL Servers and display details.
                Console.WriteLine("Discover SQL Server Instances:")
```

```
        For Each source As DataRow In sqlSources.Rows
            Console.WriteLine(" Server Name:{0}", source("ServerName"))
            Console.WriteLine(" Instance Name:{0}", source("InstanceName"))
            Console.WriteLine(" Is Clustered:{0}", source("IsClustered"))
            Console.WriteLine(" Version:{0}", source("Version"))
            Console.WriteLine(Environment.NewLine)
        Next

    End Using

    ' Wait to continue.
    Console.WriteLine(Environment.NewLine)
    Console.WriteLine("Main method complete.  Press Enter.")
    Console.ReadLine()

    End Sub

  End Class
End Namespace
```

CHAPTER 9

■■■

Windows Forms

The Microsoft .NET Framework includes a rich set of classes for creating traditional Windows-based applications in the System.Windows.Forms namespace. These range from basic controls such as the TextBox, Button, and MainMenu classes to specialized controls such as TreeView, LinkLabel, and NotifyIcon. In addition, you will find all the tools you need to manage Multiple Document Interface (MDI) applications, integrate context-sensitive help, and even create multilingual user interfaces— all without needing to resort to the complexities of the Win32 API.

The traditional model for developing these Windows-based applications has not fundamentally changed since .NET was first released. The .NET Framework 3.0, initially released with Windows Vista, has made a formidable attempt to change the model with the introduction of Windows Presentation Foundation (WPF).

WPF allows the development of highly sophisticated user interfaces using an enhanced design model that allows a much deeper control of all elements and their appearance. Furthermore, an attempt has been made to separate the user interface design from the code. Similar to how ASP .NET applications are designed, the front end (or user interface) for WPF applications is created using Extensible Application Markup Language (XAML, pronounced "zammel"). The back end is all handled by managed code.

Visual Studio 2008 includes a detailed WPF designer that is similar to the Windows Forms designer. Other designers (Microsoft Expression Designer, Microsoft XAML Pad, and so on) that let you visually create XAML-based WPF applications are also available. It is important to note that WPF applications can be completely written in managed code rather than using XAML. This, however, goes against the underlying concept of WPF and would force you to create user interfaces without a designer (since they currently output only XAML).

Since the topic of this book is Visual Basic (and not XAML), the in-depth subject of WPF and XAML is best handled by other sources such as the *Pro WPF with VB 2008: Windows Presentation Foundation .NET 3.5* by Matthew MacDonald (Apress, 2008), *Foundations of WPF: An Introduction to Windows Presentation Foundation* by Laurence Moroney (Apress, 2006), or *Applications = Code + Markup* (Microsoft Press) by Charles Petzold. Therefore, this chapter will concentrate on tips and timesaving techniques to assist with building the more traditional Windows-based applications.

■**Note** Most of the recipes in this chapter use control classes, which are defined in the System.Windows. Forms namespace. When introducing these classes, the full namespace name is not indicated. In other words, System.Windows.Forms is assumed.

The recipes in this chapter cover the following:

- Adding controls to a form programmatically at runtime so that you can build forms dynamically instead of building static forms only in the Visual Studio forms designer (recipe 9-1)

- Linking arbitrary data objects to controls to provide an easy way to associate data with a control without needing to maintain additional data structures (recipe 9-2)

- Processing all the controls on a form in a generic way (recipe 9-3)

- Tracking all the forms and MDI forms in an application (recipes 9-4 and 9-5)

- Saving user-based and computer-based configuration information for Windows Forms applications using the mechanisms built into the .NET Framework and Windows (recipe 9-6)

- Forcing a list box to always display the most recently added item so that users do not need to scroll up and down to find it (recipe 9-7)

- Assisting input validation by restricting what data a user can enter into a textbox and implementing a component-based mechanism for validating user input and reporting errors (recipes 9-8 and 9-16)

- Implementing a custom autocomplete combo box so that you can make suggestions for completing words as users type data (recipe 9-9)

- Allowing users to sort a list view based on the values in any column (recipe 9-10)

- Quickly laying out all the controls on a form (recipe 9-11)

- Providing multilingual support in your Windows Forms application (recipe 9-12)

- Creating forms that cannot be moved and create borderless forms that can be moved (recipes 9-13 and 9-14)

- Creating an animated system tray icon for your application (recipe 9-15)

- Supporting drag-and-drop functionality in your Windows Forms application (recipe 9-17)

- Providing context-sensitive help to the users of your Windows Forms application (recipe 9-18)

- Displaying web-based information within your Windows application and allowing users to browse the Web from within your application (recipe 9-19)

- Creating a basic WPF application using VB .NET (recipe 9-20)

- Forcing a Windows Vista application to request administrative privileges using UAC (recipe 9-21)

■**Note** Visual Studio, with its advanced design and editing capabilities, provides the easiest and most productive way to develop Windows Forms applications. Therefore, the recipes in this chapter—unlike those in most other chapters—rely heavily on the use of Visual Studio. Instead of focusing on the library classes that provide the required functionality or looking at the code generated by Visual Studio, these recipes focus on how to achieve the recipe's goal using the Visual Studio user interface and the code that you must write manually to complete the required functionality.

9-1. Add a Control Programmatically

Problem

You need to add a control to a form at runtime, not design time.

Solution

Create an instance of the appropriate control class. Then add the control object to a form or a container control by calling `Controls.Add` on the container. (The container's `Controls` property returns a `ControlCollection` instance.)

How It Works

In a .NET form-based application, there is really no difference between creating a control at design time and creating it at runtime. When you create controls at design time (using a tool such as Microsoft Visual Studio), the necessary code is added to your form class. Visual Studio places this code in a separate source file using the partial type functionality. You can use the same code in your application to create controls on the fly. Just follow these steps:

1. Create an instance of the appropriate control class.

2. Configure the control properties accordingly (particularly the size and position coordinates).

3. Add the control to the form or another container. Every control implements a read-only `Controls` property that returns a `ControlCollection` containing references to all of its child controls. To add a child control, invoke the `Controls.Add` method.

4. If you need to handle the events for the new control, you can wire them up to existing methods.

If you need to add multiple controls to a form or container, you should call `SuspendLayout` on the parent control before adding the dynamic controls, and then call `ResumeLayout` once you have finished. This temporarily disables the layout logic used to position controls and will allow you to avoid significant performance overheads and weird flickering if many controls are being added.

The Code

The following example demonstrates the dynamic creation of a list of checkboxes. One checkbox is added for each item in a `String` array. All the checkboxes are added to a panel that has its `AutoScroll` property set to `True`, which gives basic scrolling support to the checkbox list.

```
Imports System
Imports System.Windows.Forms


'   All designed code is stored in the autogenerated partial
'   class called Recipe09-01.Designer.vb.  You can see this
'   file by selecting Show All Files in Solution Explorer.
Partial Public Class Recipe09_01

    Private Sub Recipe09_01_Load(ByVal sender As Object, ➥
ByVal e As System.EventArgs) Handles Me.Load

        '  Create an array of strings to use as the labels for
        '  the dynamic checkboxes.
        Dim colors As String() = {"Red", "Green", "Black", "Blue", "Purple", ➥
"Pink", "Orange", "Cyan"}

        '  Suspend the panel's layout logic while multiple controls
        '  are added.
        panel1.SuspendLayout()
```

```
    ' Specify the Y coordinate of the topmost checkbox in the list.
    Dim topPosition As Integer = 10

    ' Create one new checkbox for each name in the list of colors
    For Each color As String In colors
        ' Create a new checkbox.
        Dim newCheckBox As New CheckBox

        ' Configure the new checkbox.
        newCheckBox.Top = topPosition
        newCheckBox.Left = 10
        newCheckBox.Text = color

        ' Set the Y coordinate of the next checkbox.
        topPosition += 30

        ' Add the checkbox to the panel contained by the form.
        panel1.Controls.Add(newCheckBox)
    Next

    ' Resume the form's layout logic now that all controls
    ' have been added.
    Me.ResumeLayout()

End Sub

End Class
```

Usage

Figure 9-1 shows how the example will look when run.

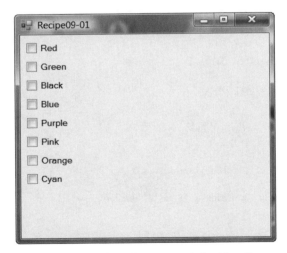

Figure 9-1. *A dynamically generated checkbox list*

9-2. Link Data to a Control

Problem

You need to link an object to a specific control (perhaps to store some arbitrary information that relates to a given display item).

Solution

Store a reference to the object in the Tag property of the control.

How It Works

Every class that derives from Control inherits a Tag property. The Tag property is not used by the control or the .NET Framework. Instead, it's reserved as a convenient storage place for application-specific information. In addition, some other classes not derived from Control also provide a Tag property. Useful examples include the ListViewItem, TreeNode, and MenuItem classes.

Because the Tag property is defined as an Object type, you can use it to store any value type or reference type, from a simple number or string to a custom object you have defined. When retrieving data from the Tag property, you must cast the Object to the correct type before use.

The Code

The following example adds a list of file names (as ListViewItem objects) to a ListView control. The corresponding System.IO.FileInfo object for each file is stored in the Tag property of its respective ListViewItem. When a user double-clicks one of the file names, the code retrieves the FileInfo object from the Tag property and displays the file name and size using the MessageBox Shared method Show.

```
Imports System
Imports System.IO
Imports System.Windows.Forms

'  All designed code is stored in the autogenerated partial
'  class called Recipe09-02.Designer.vb.  You can see this
'  file by selecting Show All Files in Solution Explorer.
Partial Public Class Recipe09_02

    Private Sub Recipe09_02_Load(ByVal sender As Object, ➥
ByVal e As System.EventArgs) Handles Me.Load

        ' Get all the files in the root directory
        Dim rootDirectory As New DirectoryInfo("C:\")
        Dim files As FileInfo() = rootDirectory.GetFiles

        ' Display the name of each file in the ListView.
        For Each file As FileInfo In files
            Dim item As ListViewItem = listView1.Items.Add(file.Name)
            item.ImageIndex = 0

            ' Associate each FileInfo object with its ListViewItem.
            item.Tag = file
        Next

    End Sub
```

```
    Private Sub listView1_ItemActivate(ByVal sender As Object, ➥
ByVal e As System.EventArgs) Handles listView1.ItemActivate

        ' Get information from the linked FileInfo object and display
        ' it using a MessageBox.
        Dim item As ListViewItem = DirectCast(sender, ListView).SelectedItems(0)
        Dim file As FileInfo = DirectCast(item.Tag, FileInfo)
        Dim info As String = String.Format("{0} is {1} bytes.", file.FullName, ➥
file.Length)

        MessageBox.Show(info, "File Information")

    End Sub

End Class
```

Usage

Figure 9-2 shows how the example will look when run.

Figure 9-2. *Storing data in the Tag property*

9-3. Process All the Controls on a Form

Problem

You need to perform a generic task with all the controls on the form. For example, you may need to retrieve or clear their Text property, change their color, or resize them.

Solution

Iterate recursively through the collection of controls. Interact with each control using the properties and methods of the base Control class.

How It Works

You can iterate through the controls on a form using the ControlCollection object obtained from the Controls property. The ControlCollection includes all the controls that are placed directly on the form surface. However, if any of these controls are container controls (such as GroupBox, Panel, or TabPage), they might contain more controls. Thus, it's necessary to use recursive logic that searches the Controls collection of every control on the form.

The Code

The following example demonstrates the use of recursive logic to find every TextBox on a form and clears the text they contain. When a button is clicked, the code tests each control on the form to determine whether it is a TextBox by using the TypeOf keyword in conjunction with the Is operator.

```vb
Imports System
Imports System.IO
Imports System.Windows.Forms

' All designed code is stored in the autogenerated partial
' class called Recipe09-03.Designer.vb.  You can see this
' file by selecting Show All Files in Solution Explorer.
Partial Public Class Recipe09_03

    Private Sub cmdProcessAll_Click(ByVal sender As System.Object, ➡
ByVal e As System.EventArgs) Handles cmdProcessAll.Click

        ProcessControls(Me)

    End Sub

    Private Sub ProcessControls(ByVal ctrl As Control)

        ' Ignore the control unless it's a text box.
        If TypeOf (ctrl) Is TextBox Then
            ctrl.Text = ""
        End If

        ' Process controls recursively.  This is required
        ' if controls contain other controls (for
        ' example, if you use panels, group boxes, or other
        ' container controls).
        For Each ctrlChild As Control In ctrl.Controls
            ProcessControls(ctrlChild)
        Next

    End Sub

End Class
```

9-4. Track the Visible Forms in an Application

Problem

You need access to all the open forms that are currently owned by an application.

Solution

Iterate through the `FormCollection` object that you get from the `Shared` property `OpenForms` of the `Application` object.

How It Works

Since .NET Framework 2.0, Windows Forms applications automatically keep track of the open forms that they own. This information is accessed through the `Application.OpenForms` property, which returns a `FormCollection` object containing a `Form` object for each form the application owns. You can iterate through the `FormCollection` to access all `Form` objects or obtain a single `Form` object using its name (`Form.Name`) or its position in the `FormCollection` as an index.

The `My` object (see Chapter 5 for more information) provides an identical `OpenForms` property in the `My.Application` class. It also provides quick-and-easy design-time access to each form in the current project via the `My.Forms` class.

The Code

The following example demonstrates the use of the `Application.OpenForms` property and the `FormCollection` it returns to manage the active forms in an application. The example allows you to create new forms with specified names. A list of active forms is displayed when you click the Refresh List button. When you click the name of a form in the list, it is made the active form.

Because of the way the `FormCollection` works, more than one form may have the same name. If duplicate forms have the same name, the first one found will be activated. If you try to retrieve a `Form` using a name that does not exist, `Nothing` is returned. The following is the code for the application's main form:

```
Imports System
Imports System.Windows.Forms

' All designed code is stored in the autogenerated partial
' class called Recipe09-04.Designer.vb.  You can see this
' file by selecting Show All Files in Solution Explorer.
Public Class Recipe09_04

    Private Sub Recipe09_04_Load(ByVal sender As System.Object, ➥
ByVal e As System.EventArgs) Handles MyBase.Load

        ' Refresh the list to display the initial set of forms.
        RefreshForms()

    End Sub
```

```vb
    ' A button click event handler to create a new child form.
    Private Sub btnNewForm_Click(ByVal sender As System.Object, ➡
ByVal e As System.EventArgs) Handles btnNewForm.Click

        ' Create a new child form and set its name as specified.
        ' If no name is specified, use a default name.
        Dim child As New Recipe09_04Child

        If Me.txtFormName.Text Is String.Empty Then
            child.Name = "Child Form"
        Else
            child.Name = txtFormName.Text
        End If

        ' Show the new child form.
        child.Show()

    End Sub

    ' List selection event handler to activate the selected form based on
    ' its name.
    Private Sub listForms_SelectedIndexChanged(ByVal sender As Object, ➡
ByVal e As System.EventArgs) Handles listForms.SelectedIndexChanged

        ' Activate the selected form using its name as the index into the
        ' collection of active forms.  If there are duplicate forms with the
        ' same name, the first one found will be activated.
        Dim selectedForm As Form = Application.OpenForms(listForms.Text)

        ' If the form has been closed, using its name as an index into the
        ' FormCollection will return Nothing.  In this instance, update the
        ' list of forms.
        If selectedForm IsNot Nothing Then
            ' Activate the selected form.
            selectedForm.Activate()
        Else
            ' Display a message and refresh the form list.
            MessageBox.Show("Form closed; refreshing list...", "Form Closed")
            RefreshForms()
        End If

    End Sub

    ' A button click event handler to initiate a refresh of the list of
    ' active forms.
    Private Sub btnRefresh_Click(ByVal sender As System.Object, ➡
ByVal e As System.EventArgs) Handles btnRefresh.Click

        RefreshForms()

    End Sub
```

```
'  A method to perform a refresh of the list of active forms.
Private Sub RefreshForms()

    '  Clear the list and repopulate from the Application.OpenForms
    '  property.
    listForms.Items.Clear()

    For Each f As Form In Application.OpenForms
        listForms.Items.Add(f.Name)
    Next

End Sub

End Class
```

The following is the code for the child forms that is created when the New Form button is clicked:

```
Imports System
Imports System.Windows.Forms

'  class called Recipe09-04Child.Designer.vb.  You can see this
'  file by selecting Show All Files in Solution Explorer.
Partial Public Class Recipe09_04Child

    '  A button click event handler to close the child form.
    Private Sub btnClose_Click(ByVal sender As System.Object, ➥
ByVal e As System.EventArgs) Handles btnClose.Click

        Close()

    End Sub

    '  Display the name of the form when it is painted.
    Private Sub Recipe09_04Child_Paint(ByVal sender As Object, ➥
ByVal e As System.Windows.Forms.PaintEventArgs) Handles Me.Paint

        '  Display the name of the form.
        lblFormName.Text = Name

    End Sub

End Class
```

9-5. Find All MDI Child Forms

Problem

You need to find all the forms that are currently being displayed in an MDI application.

Solution

Iterate through the forms returned by the MdiChildren collection property of the MDI parent.

How It Works

The .NET Framework includes two convenient shortcuts for managing the forms open in MDI applications: the MdiParent and MdiChildren properties of the Form class. The MdiParent property of any MDI child returns a Form representing the containing parent window. The MdiChildren property returns an array containing all of the MDI child forms.

The Code

The following example presents an MDI parent window that allows you to create new MDI children by clicking the New item on the File menu. Each child window contains a label, which displays the date and time when the MDI child was created, and a button. When the button is clicked, the event handler walks through all the MDI child windows and displays the label text that each one contains. Notice that when the example enumerates the collection of MDI child forms, it converts the generic Form reference to the derived Recipe09_05Child form class so that it can use the LabelText property. The following is the Recipe09_05Parent class:

```vb
Imports System
Imports System.Windows.Forms


'  All designed code is stored in the autogenerated partial
'  class called Recipe09-05Parent.Designer.vb.  You can see this
'  file by selecting Show All Files in Solution Explorer.
Partial Public Class Recipe09_05Parent

    '  When the New menu item is clicked, create a new MDI child.
    Private Sub mnuNew_Click(ByVal sender As System.Object, ➥
ByVal e As System.EventArgs) Handles mnuNew.Click

        Dim frm As New Recipe09_05Child

        frm.MdiParent = Me
        frm.Show()

    End Sub

End Class
```

The following is the Recipe09_05Child class:

```vb
Imports System
Imports System.Windows.Forms


'  All designed code is stored in the autogenerated partial
'  class called Recipe09-05Child.Designer.vb.  You can see this
'  file by selecting Show All Files in Solution Explorer.
Partial Public Class Recipe09_05Child

    '  A property to provide easy access to the label data.
    Public ReadOnly Property LabelText() As String
        Get
            Return label.Text
        End Get
    End Property
```

```
'  When a button on any of the MDI child forms is clicked, display the
'  contents of each form by enumerating the MdiChildren collection.
Private Sub cmdShowAllWindows_Click(ByVal sender As System.Object, ➥
ByVal e As System.EventArgs) Handles cmdShowAllWindows.Click

        For Each frm As Form In Me.MdiParent.MdiChildren
            ' Cast the generic Form to the Recipe07_05Child derived class
            '  type.
            Dim child As Recipe09_05Child = DirectCast(frm, Recipe09_05Child)
            MessageBox.Show(child.LabelText, frm.Text)
        Next

    End Sub

    '  Set the MDI child form's label to the current date/time.
    Private Sub Recipe09_05Child_Load(ByVal sender As Object, ➥
ByVal e As System.EventArgs) Handles Me.Load

        label.Text = DateTime.Now.ToString

    End Sub

End Class
```

Usage

Figure 9-3 shows how the example will look when run.

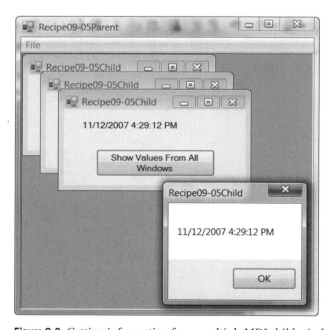

Figure 9-3. *Getting information from multiple MDI child windows*

9-6. Save Configuration Settings for a Form

Problem

You need to store configuration settings for a form so that they are remembered the next time that the form is shown.

Solution

Use the Application Settings functionality, which is configurable at design time in Visual Studio.

How It Works

The Application Settings functionality, first introduced in .NET Framework 2.0, provides an easy-to-use mechanism through which you can save application and user settings used to customize the appearance and operation of a Windows Forms application. You configure Application Settings through the Properties panel of each Windows control (including the main Windows Form) in your application. By expanding the ApplicationSettings property and clicking the ellipsis (the three dots) to the right of (PropertyBinding), you can review and configure Application Settings for each property of the active control. See Figure 9-4 for an example.

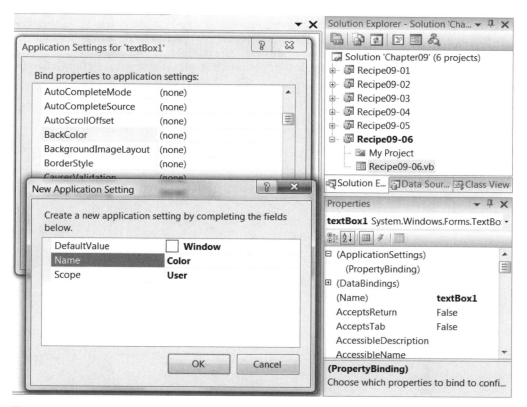

Figure 9-4. *Configuring Application Settings in Visual Studio*

When you configure a new application setting for a control's property, you must assign it a name, a default value, and a scope:

- The name allows you to both access the setting programmatically and reuse the application setting across multiple controls.

- The default value is used if the application cannot obtain a value from a configuration file at runtime.

- The scope is either User or Application.

Settings with an Application scope are stored in the application's configuration file (usually located in the same folder as the application assembly) and are read-only. The benefit of an Application scope is that you can change configuration settings by editing the configuration file without needing to recompile the application. Settings with a User scope are read-write by default and are stored in a file located in an *isolated store* (see recipe 5-19 for information about isolated stores).

When you configure your application to use Application Settings, Visual Studio actually autogenerates a wrapper class that provides access to the configuration file information, regardless of whether it is scoped as Application or User. This class, named MySettings, is in the Settings.Designer. vb file, which can be found in your project's My Project folder. This folder also contains the Settings. settings file. When you open this file in Visual Studio, it will display a dialog box that allows you to easily edit your application's settings. You will see these files only if you have turned on the Show All Files option in the Solution Explorer.

The My.Settings class contains properties with names matching each of the Application Setting names you configured for your controls' properties. The controls will automatically read their configuration at startup, but you should store configuration changes prior to terminating your application by calling the My.Settings.Save method. You can also configure this to occur automatically by checking the Save My.Settings on Shutdown option in the Application section of your project's properties, as shown in Figure 9-5.

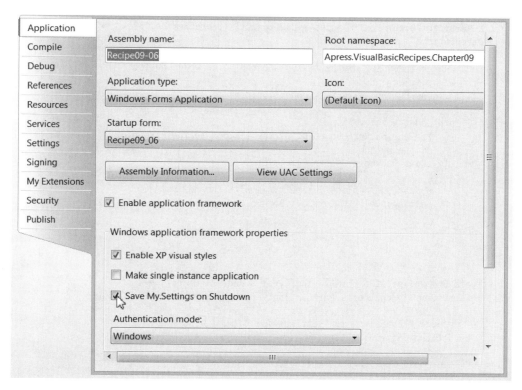

Figure 9-5. *Automatically saving settings on shutdown*

The Code

The following example shows how to update and save application settings, which are `Size` and `Color` in this case, at runtime:

```
Imports System
Imports System.ComponentModel
Imports System.Windows.Forms

'  All designed code is stored in the autogenerated partial
'  class called Recipe09-06.Designer.vb.  You can see this
'  file by selecting Show All Files in Solution Explorer.
Partial Public Class Recipe09_06

    Private Sub Recipe09_06_Load(ByVal sender As Object, ➥
ByVal e As System.EventArgs) Handles Me.Load

        Me.Size = My.Settings.Size

    End Sub
```

```
    Private Sub Button_Click(ByVal sender As System.Object, ➡
ByVal e As System.EventArgs) Handles redButton.Click, blueButton.Click, ➡
greenButton.Click

        ' Change the color of the textbox depending on which button
        ' was clicked.
        Dim btn As Button = TryCast(sender, Button)

        If btn IsNot Nothing Then
            ' Set the background color of the textbox to the ForeColor
            ' of the button.
            textBox1.BackColor = btn.ForeColor

            ' Update the application settings with the new value.
            My.Settings.Color = textBox1.BackColor

        End If

    End Sub

    Private Sub Recipe09_06_FormClosing(ByVal sender As Object, ➡
ByVal e As System.Windows.Forms.FormClosingEventArgs) Handles Me.FormClosing

        ' Update the application settings for Form.
        My.Settings.Size = Me.Size

        ' Store all application settings.
        My.Settings.Save()

    End Sub

End Class
```

9-7. Force a List Box to Scroll to the Most Recently Added Item

Problem

You need to scroll a list box programmatically so that the most recently added items are visible.

Solution

Set the ListBox.TopIndex property, which sets the first visible list item.

How It Works

In some cases, you might have a list box that stores a significant amount of information or one that you add information to periodically. Often, the most recent information, which is added at the end of the list, is more important than the information at the top of the list. One solution is to scroll the list box so that recently added items are visible. The ListBox.TopIndex property enables you to do this by allowing you to specify which item is visible at the top of the list.

The Code

The following sample form includes a list box and a button. Each time the button is clicked, 20 items are added to the list box. Each time new items are added, the code sets the `ListBox.TopIndex` property and forces the list box to display the most recently added items. To provide better feedback, the same line is also selected.

```vb
Imports System
Imports System.Windows.Forms

'  All designed code is stored in the autogenerated partial
'  class called Recipe09-07.Designer.vb.  You can see this
'  file by selecting Show All Files in Solution Explorer.
Partial Public Class Recipe09_07

    Private counter As Integer = 0

    ' Button click event handler adds 20 new items to the ListBox.
    Private Sub cmdTest_Click(ByVal sender As Object, ➡
ByVal e As System.EventArgs) Handles cmdTest.Click

        ' Add 20 items.
        For i As Integer = 1 To 20
            counter += 1
            listBox1.Items.Add("Item " & counter.ToString())
        Next

        ' Set the TopIndex property of the ListBox to ensure the
        ' most recently added items are visible.  SelectedIndex
        ' is then used to select the new item.
        listBox1.TopIndex = listBox1.Items.Count - 1
        listBox1.SelectedIndex = listBox1.Items.Count - 1

    End Sub

End Class
```

9-8. Restrict a Text Box to Accepting Only Specific Input

Problem

You need to create a text box that will accept only the specified characters or keystrokes.

Solution

Use the `MaskedTextBox` control, and set the `Mask` property to configure the input that is acceptable.

How It Works

One way to ensure user input is valid is to prevent invalid data from being entered in the first place. The `MaskedTextBox` control facilitates this approach. The `MaskedTextBox.Mask` property takes a string that specifies the input mask for the control. This mask determines what type of input a user can enter at each point in the control's text area. If the user enters an incorrect character, the control will beep if the BeepOnError property is True, and the MaskInputRejected event is raised so that you can customize the handling of incorrect input.

■Note The MaskedTextBox control will not solve all your user-input validation problems. Although it does make some types of validation easy to implement, without customization, it will not ensure some common validation requirements are met. For example, you can specify that only numeric digits can be input, but you cannot specify that they must be less than a specific value, and you cannot control the overall characteristics of the input value.

The Code

The following example demonstrates the use of the MaskedTextBox control. A series of buttons allows you to change the active mask on the MaskedTextBox control and experiment with the various masks. Notice that the control automatically tries to accommodate existing content with the new mask when the mask is changed. If the content is not allowed with the new mask, the control is cleared.

```
Imports System
Imports System.Windows.Forms

'  All designed code is stored in the autogenerated partial
'  class called Recipe09-08.Designer.vb.  You can see this
'  file by selecting Show All Files in Solution Explorer.
Partial Public Class Recipe09_08

    Private Sub btnTime_Click(ByVal sender As System.Object, ➡
ByVal e As System.EventArgs) Handles btnTime.Click

        ' Set the input mask to that of a short time.
        Me.mskTextBox.UseSystemPasswordChar = False
        Me.mskTextBox.Mask = "00:00"
        Me.lblActiveMask.Text = Me.mskTextBox.Mask
        Me.mskTextBox.Focus()

    End Sub

    Private Sub btnDecimal_Click(ByVal sender As System.Object, ➡
ByVal e As System.EventArgs) Handles btnDecimal.Click

        ' Set the input mask to that of a decimal.
        Me.mskTextBox.UseSystemPasswordChar = False
        Me.mskTextBox.Mask = "999,999.00"
        Me.lblActiveMask.Text = Me.mskTextBox.Mask
        Me.mskTextBox.Focus()

    End Sub
```

```
    Private Sub btnDate_Click(ByVal sender As System.Object, ➡
ByVal e As System.EventArgs) Handles btnDate.Click

        ' Set the input mask to that of a short date.
        Me.mskTextBox.UseSystemPasswordChar = False
        Me.mskTextBox.Mask = "00/00/0000"
        Me.lblActiveMask.Text = Me.mskTextBox.Mask
        Me.mskTextBox.Focus()

    End Sub

    Private Sub btnUSZip_Click(ByVal sender As System.Object, ➡
ByVal e As System.EventArgs) Handles btnUSZip.Click

        ' Set the input mask to that of a US ZIP code.
        Me.mskTextBox.UseSystemPasswordChar = False
        Me.mskTextBox.Mask = "00000-9999"
        Me.lblActiveMask.Text = Me.mskTextBox.Mask
        Me.mskTextBox.Focus()

    End Sub

    Private Sub btnUKPost_Click(ByVal sender As System.Object, ➡
ByVal e As System.EventArgs) Handles btnUKPost.Click

        ' Set the input mask to that of a UK postcode.
        Me.mskTextBox.UseSystemPasswordChar = False
        Me.mskTextBox.Mask = ">LCCC 9LL"
        Me.lblActiveMask.Text = Me.mskTextBox.Mask
        Me.mskTextBox.Focus()

    End Sub

    Private Sub btnPinNumber_Click(ByVal sender As System.Object, ➡
ByVal e As System.EventArgs) Handles btnPinNumber.Click

        ' Set the input mask to that of a secret pin.
        Me.mskTextBox.UseSystemPasswordChar = True
        Me.mskTextBox.Mask = "0000"
        Me.lblActiveMask.Text = Me.mskTextBox.Mask
        Me.mskTextBox.Focus()

    End Sub

End Class
```

9-9. Use an Autocomplete Combo Box

Problem

You want to create a combo box that automatically completes what the user is typing based on the item list.

Solution

You can implement a basic autocomplete combo box by creating a custom control that overrides the `OnKeyPress` and `OnTextChanged` methods of the `ComboBox` object.

How It Works

An autocomplete control has many different variations. For example, the control may fill in values based on a list of recent selections (as Microsoft Excel does when you are entering cell values), or the control might display a drop-down list of near matches (as Microsoft Internet Explorer does when you are typing a URL). You can create a basic autocomplete combo box by handling the `KeyPress` and `TextChanged` events or by creating a custom class that derives from `ComboBox` and overrides the `OnKeyPress` and `OnTextChanged` methods.

Although the approach in this recipe gives you complete control over how the autocomplete functionality is implemented, the `ComboBox` control includes some built-in autocomplete functionality. Using this built-in functionality is easy and based on using the `AutoCompleteSource` and `AutoCompleteMode` properties.

The Code

The following example contains an `AutoCompleteComboBox` control that derives from `ComboBox`. The `AutoCompleteComboBox` control supports autocompletion by overriding the `OnKeyPress` and `OnTextChanged` methods. In the `OnKeyPress` method, the combo box determines whether an autocomplete replacement should be made. If the user pressed a character key (such as a letter), the replacement can be made, but if the user pressed a control key (such as the backspace key, the cursor keys, and so on), no action should be taken. The `OnTextChanged` method performs the actual replacement after the key processing is complete. This method looks up the first match for the current text in the list of items and then adds the rest of the matching text. After the text is added, the combo box selects the characters between the current insertion point and the end of the text. This allows the user to continue typing and replace the autocomplete text if it is not what the user wants.

```
Imports System
Imports System.Windows.Forms

Public Class AutoCompleteCombobox
    Inherits ComboBox

    ' A private member to track if a special key is pressed, in
    ' which case, any text replacement operation will be skipped.
    Private controlKey As Boolean = False

    ' Determine whether a special key was pressed.
    Protected Overrides Sub OnKeyPress(ByVal e As KeyPressEventArgs)
```

```
    '  First call the overridden base class method.
    MyBase.OnKeyPress(e)

    '  Clear the text if the Escape key is pressed.
    If e.KeyChar = ChrW(Keys.Escape) Then
        '  Clear the text.
        Me.SelectedIndex = -1
        Me.Text = ""
        controlKey = True
    ElseIf Char.IsControl(e.KeyChar) Then
        '  Don't try to autocomplete when control key is pressed.
        controlKey = True
    Else
        '  Noncontrol keys should trigger autocomplete.
        controlKey = False
    End If

End Sub

'  Perform the text substitution.
Protected Overrides Sub OnTextChanged(ByVal e As System.EventArgs)

    '  First call the overridden base class method.
    MyBase.OnTextChanged(e)

    If Not Me.Text = "" And Not controlKey Then
        '  Search the current contents of the combo box for a
        '  matching entry.
        Dim matchText As String = Me.Text
        Dim match As Integer = Me.FindString(matchText)

        '  If a matching entry is found, insert it now.
        If Not match = -1 Then
            Me.SelectedIndex = match

            '  Select the added text so it can be replaced
            '  if the user keeps trying.
            Me.SelectionStart = matchText.Length
            Me.SelectionLength = Me.Text.Length - Me.SelectionStart
        End If
    End If

End Sub

End Class
```

Usage

The following code demonstrates the use of the AutoCompleteComboBox by adding it to a form and filling it with a list of words. In this example, the control is added to the form manually, and the list of words is retrieved from a text file named words.txt. As an alternative, you could compile the AutoCompleteComboBox class to a separate class library assembly and then add it to the Visual Studio Toolbox so you could add it to forms at design time.

```
Imports System
Imports System.IO
Imports System.Drawing
Imports System.Windows.Forms

'  All designed code is stored in the autogenerated partial
'  class called Recipe09-09.Designer.vb.  You can see this
'  file by selecting Show All Files in Solution Explorer.
Partial Public Class Recipe09_09

    Private Sub Recipe09_09_Load(ByVal sender As Object, ➡
ByVal e As System.EventArgs) Handles Me.Load
        '  Add the AutoCompleteComboBox to the form.
        Dim combo As New AutoCompleteCombobox

        combo.Location = New Point(10, 10)
        Me.Controls.Add(combo)

        '  Read the list of words from the file words.txt and add them
        '  to the AutoCompleteComboBox.
        Using fs As New FileStream("..\..\Names.txt", FileMode.Open)
            Using r As New StreamReader(fs)
                While r.Peek > -1
                    Dim name As String = r.ReadLine
                    combo.Items.Add(name)
                End While
            End Using
        End Using

    End Sub

End Class
```

Figure 9-6 shows how the AutoCompleteComboBox will look when the example is run.

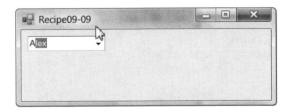

Figure 9-6. *An autocomplete combo box*

9-10. Sort a List View by Any Column

Problem

You need to sort a list view, but the built-in ListView.Sort method sorts based on only the first column.

Solution

Create a type that implements the System.Collections.IComparer interface and can sort ListViewItem objects. The IComparer type can sort based on any ListViewItem criteria you specify. Set the ListView. ListViewItemSorter property with an instance of the IComparer type before calling the ListView. Sort method.

How It Works

The ListView control provides a Sort method that orders items alphabetically based on the text in the first column. If you want to sort based on other column values or order items numerically, you need to create a custom implementation of the IComparer interface that can perform the work. The IComparer interface defines a single method named Compare, which takes two Object arguments and determines which one should be ordered first. Full details of how to implement the IComparer interface are available in recipe 14-3.

The Code

The following example demonstrates how to create an IComparer implementation named ListViewItemComparer. This class relies on the Compare method of String and Decimal to perform appropriate comparisons. The ListViewItemComparer class also implements two additional properties: Column and Numeric. The Column property identifies the column that should be used for sorting. The Numeric property is a Boolean flag that can be set to True if you want to perform number-based comparisons instead of alphabetic comparisons. The numeric sorting is applied when the users clicks the first column.

When the user clicks a column heading, the example creates a ListViewItemComparer instance, configures the column to use for sorting, and assigns the ListViewItemComparer instance to the ListView.ListViewItemSorter property before calling the ListView.Sort method.

```
Imports System
Imports System.Collections
Imports System.Windows.Forms


'  All designed code is stored in the autogenerated partial
'  class called Recipe09-10.Designer.vb.  You can see this
'  file by selecting Show All Files in Solution Explorer.
Partial Public Class Recipe09_10

    Private Sub listView1_ColumnClick(ByVal sender As Object, ➥
ByVal e As System.Windows.Forms.ColumnClickEventArgs) Handles listView1.ColumnClick

        ' Create and/or configure the ListViewItemComparer to sort based on
        ' the column that was clicked.
        Dim sorter As ListViewItemComparer = ➥
TryCast(listView1.ListViewItemSorter, ListViewItemComparer)

        If sorter Is Nothing Then
            ' Create a new ListViewItemComparer.
            sorter = New ListViewItemComparer(e.Column)

            ' Use Decimal comparison for the first column.
            If e.Column = 0 Then
                sorter.Numeric = True
```

```vb
        Else
            sorter.Numeric = False
        End If

        listView1.ListViewItemSorter = sorter
    Else
        ' Use Decimal comparison for the first column.
        If e.Column = 0 Then
            sorter.Numeric = True
        Else
            sorter.Numeric = False
        End If

        ' Configure the existing ListViewItemComparer.
        If sorter.Column = e.Column Then
            sorter.Descending = Not sorter.Descending
        Else
            sorter.Column = e.Column
            sorter.Descending = False
        End If
    End If

    ' Sort the ListView.
    listView1.Sort()

End Sub

End Class

Public Class ListViewItemComparer
    Implements IComparer

    ' Private members to configure comparer logic.
    Private m_Column As Integer
    Private m_Numeric As Boolean = False
    Private m_Descending As Boolean = False

    ' Property to get/set the column to use for comparison.
    Public Property Column() As Integer
        Get
            Return m_Column
        End Get
        Set(ByVal value As Integer)
            m_Column = Value
        End Set
    End Property

    ' Property to get/set whether numeric comparison is required
    ' as opposed to the standard alphabetic comparison.
    Public Property Numeric() As Boolean
        Get
            Return m_Numeric
        End Get
```

```vb
            Set(ByVal value As Boolean)
                m_Numeric = Value
            End Set
    End Property


    ' Property to get/set whether we are sorting in descending
    ' order or not.
    Public Property Descending() As Boolean
        Get
            Return m_Descending
        End Get
        Set(ByVal Value As Boolean)
            m_Descending = Value
        End Set
    End Property


    Public Sub New(ByVal columnIndex As Integer)
        m_Column = columnIndex
    End Sub


    Public Function Compare(ByVal x As Object, ByVal y As Object) ➡
As Integer Implements System.Collections.IComparer.Compare

        ' Convert the arguments to ListViewItem objects.
        Dim itemX As ListViewItem = TryCast(x, ListViewItem)
        Dim itemY As ListViewItem = TryCast(y, ListViewItem)

        ' Handle the logic for a Nothing reference as dictated by the
        ' IComparer interface.  Nothing is considered less than
        ' any other value.
        If itemX Is Nothing And itemY Is Nothing Then
            Return 0
        ElseIf itemX Is Nothing Then
            Return -1
        ElseIf itemY Is Nothing Then
            Return 1
        End If

        ' Short-circuit condition where the items are references
        ' to the same object.
        If itemX Is itemY Then Return 0

        ' Determine if numeric comparison is required.
        If Numeric Then
            ' Convert column text to numbers before comparing.
            ' If the conversion fails, just use the value 0.
            Dim itemXVal, itemYVal As Decimal

            If Not Decimal.TryParse(itemX.SubItems(Column).Text, itemXVal) Then
                itemXVal = 0
            End If
```

```
            If Not Decimal.TryParse(itemY.SubItems(Column).Text, itemYVal) Then
                itemYVal = 0
            End If

            If Descending Then
                Return Decimal.Compare(itemYVal, itemXVal)
            Else
                Return Decimal.Compare(itemXVal, itemYVal)
            End If
        Else
            ' Keep the column text in its native string format
            ' and perform an alphabetic comparison.
            Dim itemXText As String = itemX.SubItems(Column).Text
            Dim itemYText As String = itemY.SubItems(Column).Text

            If Descending Then
                Return String.Compare(itemYText, itemXText)
            Else
                Return String.Compare(itemXText, itemYText)
            End If
        End If

    End Function

End Class
```

9-11. Lay Out Controls Automatically

Problem

You have a large set of controls on a form and you want them arranged automatically.

Solution

Use the FlowLayoutPanel container to dynamically arrange the controls using a horizontal or vertical flow, or use the TableLayoutPanel container to dynamically arrange the controls in a grid.

How It Works

The FlowLayoutPanel and TableLayoutPanel containers simplify the design-time and runtime layout of the controls they contain. At both design time and runtime, as you add controls to one of these panels, the panel's logic determines where the control should be positioned, so you do not need to determine the exact location.

With the FlowLayoutPanel container, the FlowDirection and WrapContents properties determine where controls are positioned. FlowDirection controls the order and location of controls, and it can be set to LeftToRight (the default), TopDown, RightToLeft, or BottomUp. The WrapContents property controls whether controls run off the edge of the panel or wrap around to form a new line of controls. The default is to wrap controls.

With the `TableLayoutPanel` container, the `RowCount` and `ColumnCount` properties control how many rows and columns are currently in the panel's grid. The default for both of these properties is 0, which means there are no rows or columns. The `GrowStyle` property determines how the grid grows to accommodate more controls once it is full, and it can be set to `AddRows` (the default), `AddColumns`, or `FixedSize` (which means the grid cannot grow).

Figure 9-7 shows the design-time appearance of both a `TableLayoutPanel` container and a `FlowLayoutPanel` container. The `TableLayoutPanel` panel is configured with three rows and three columns. The `FlowLayoutPanel` panel is configured to wrap contents and use left-to-right flow direction.

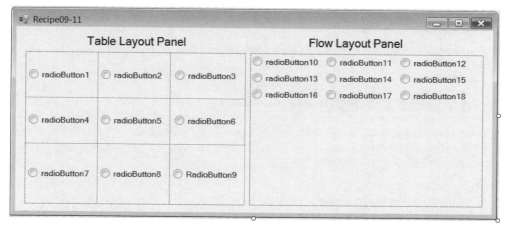

Figure 9-7. *Using a FlowLayoutPanel panel and a TableLayoutPanel panel*

9-12. Make a Multilingual Form

Problem

You need to create a localizable form that can be deployed in more than one language.

Solution

Store all locale-specific information in resource files, which are compiled into satellite assemblies.

How It Works

The .NET Framework includes built-in support for localization through its use of resource files. The basic idea is to store information that is locale-specific (for example, button text) in a resource file. You can create resource files for each culture you need to support and compile them into satellite assemblies. When you run the application, .NET will automatically use the correct satellite assembly based on the locale settings of the current user/computer.

You can read to and write from resource files manually; they are XML files (see recipe 1-17 for more information about resource files). However, Visual Studio also includes extensive design-time support for localized forms. It works like this:

1. Set the Localizable property of a Form to True using the Properties window.

2. Set the Language property of the form to the locale for which you want to enter information, as shown in Figure 9-8. Then configure the localizable properties of all the controls on the form. Instead of storing your changes in the designer-generated code for the form, Visual Studio will actually create a new resource file to hold your data.

Figure 9-8. *Selecting a language for localizing a form*

3. Repeat step 2 for each language you want to support. Each time you enter a new locale for the form's Language property, a new resource file will be generated. If you select Project ➤ Show All Files from the Visual Studio menu, you will find these resource files under your form's folder, as shown in Figure 9-9. If you change the Language property to a locale you have already configured, your previous settings will reappear, and you will be able to modify them.

You can now compile and test your application on differently localized systems. Visual Studio will create a separate directory and satellite assembly for each resource file in the project. You can select Project ➤ Show All Files from the Visual Studio menu to see how these files are arranged, as shown in Figure 9-9.

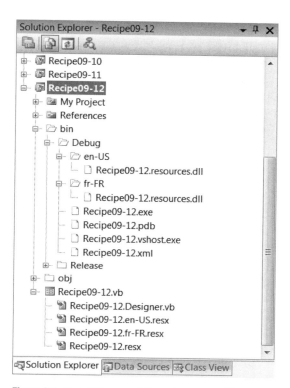

Figure 9-9. *Satellite assembly and resource files structure*

The Code

Although you do not need to manually code any of the localization functionality, as a testing shortcut, you can force your application to adopt a specific culture by modifying the Thread.CurrentUICulture property of the application thread. However, you must modify this property before the form has loaded.

```
Imports System
Imports System.Threading
Imports System.Globalization
Imports System.Windows.Forms


'  All designed code is stored in the autogenerated partial
'  class called Recipe09-12.Designer.vb.  You can see this
'  file by selecting Show All Files in Solution Explorer.
Partial Public Class Recipe09_12

    Public Shared Sub Main()

        Thread.CurrentThread.CurrentUICulture = New CultureInfo("fr-FR")
        Application.Run(New Recipe09_12)

    End Sub

End Class
```

Usage

Figure 9-10 shows both the English and French versions of the example. As you can see, both the language and the layout of the form are different depending on the current locale.

Figure 9-10. *English and French localizations*

9-13. Create a Form That Cannot Be Moved

Problem

You want to create a form that occupies a fixed location on the screen and cannot be moved.

Solution

Make a borderless form by setting the FormBorderStyle property of the Form class to the value FormBorderStyle.None.

How It Works

You can create a borderless form by setting the FormBorderStyle property of a Form to None. Border-less forms cannot be moved. However, as their name implies, they also lack any kind of border. If you want a border, you will need to add it yourself, either by writing manual drawing code or by using a background image.

One other approach to creating an immovable form does provide a basic control-style border. First, set the ControlBox, MinimizeBox, and MaximizeBox properties of the form to False. Then set the Text property to an empty string. The form will have a raised gray border or black line (depending on the FormBorderStyle option you use), similar to a button. Figure 9-11 shows both types of immovable forms.

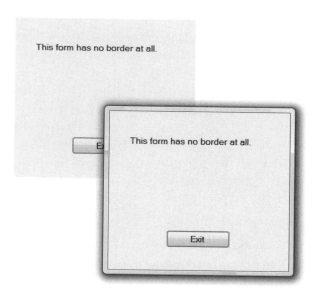

Figure 9-11. *Two types of forms that cannot be moved*

9-14. Make a Borderless Form Movable

Problem

You need to create a borderless form that can be moved. This might be the case if you are creating a custom window that has a unique look (for example, for a visually rich application such as a game or a media player).

Solution

Create another control that responds to the MouseDown, MouseUp, and MouseMove events and programmatically moves the form.

How It Works

Borderless forms omit a title bar, which makes it impossible for a user to move them. You can compensate for this shortcoming by adding a control to the form that serves the same purpose. For example, Figure 9-12 shows a form that includes a label to support dragging. The user can click this label and then drag the form to a new location on the screen while holding down the mouse button. As the user moves the mouse, the form moves correspondingly, as though it were "attached" to the mouse pointer.

Figure 9-12. *A movable borderless form*

To implement this solution, take the following steps:

1. Create a form-level Boolean variable that tracks whether the form is currently being dragged.

2. When the label is clicked, the code sets the flag to indicate that the form is in drag mode. At the same time, the current mouse position is recorded. You add this logic to the event handler for the Label.MouseDown event.

3. When the user moves the mouse over the label, the form is moved correspondingly, so that the position of the mouse over the label is unchanged. You add this logic to the event handler for the Label.MouseMove event.

4. When the user releases the mouse button, the dragging mode is switched off. You add this logic to the event handler for the Label.MouseUp event.

The Code

The following example creates a borderless form that a user can move by clicking a form control and dragging the form:

```vb
Imports System
Imports System.Windows.Forms

' All designed code is stored in the autogenerated partial
' class called Recipe09-14.Designer.vb.  You can see this
' file by selecting Show All Files in Solution Explorer.
Partial Public Class Recipe09_14

    ' Boolean member tracks whether the form is in drag mode.
    ' If it is, mouse movements over the label will be translated
    ' into form movements.
    Private dragging As Boolean

    ' Stores the offset where the label is clicked.
    Private pointClicked As Point
```

```vbnet
' MouseDown event handler for the label initiates the dragging process.
Private Sub lblDrag_MouseDown(ByVal sender As Object,➡
ByVal e As MouseEventArgs) Handles lblDrag.MouseDown

    If e.Button = Windows.Forms.MouseButtons.Left Then
        ' Turn the drag mode on and store the point clicked.
        dragging = True
        pointClicked = New Point(e.X, e.Y)
    Else
        dragging = False
    End If

End Sub

' MouseMove event handler for the label processes dragging movements if
' the form is in drag mode.
Private Sub lblDrag_MouseMove(ByVal sender As Object, ➡
ByVal e As MouseEventArgs) Handles lblDrag.MouseMove

    If dragging Then

        Dim pointMoveTo As Point

        ' Find the current mouse position in screen coordinates.
        pointMoveTo = Me.PointToScreen(New Point(e.X, e.Y))

        ' Compensate for the position of the control clicked.
        pointMoveTo.Offset(-pointClicked.X, -pointClicked.Y)

        ' Move the form.
        Me.Location = pointMoveTo

    End If

End Sub

' MouseUp event handler for the label switches off drag mode.
Private Sub lblDrag_MouseUp(ByVal sender As Object, ➡
ByVal e As System.Windows.Forms.MouseEventArgs) Handles lblDrag.MouseUp
    dragging = False
End Sub

Private Sub cmdClose_Click(ByVal sender As System.Object, ➡
ByVal e As System.EventArgs) Handles cmdClose.Click
    Me.Close()
End Sub

End Class
```

9-15. Create an Animated System Tray Icon

Problem

You need to create an animated system tray icon (perhaps to indicate the status of a long-running task).

Solution

Create and show a `NotifyIcon` control. Use a timer that fires periodically (every second or so) and updates the `NotifyIcon.Icon` property.

How It Works

The .NET Framework makes it easy to show a system tray icon with the `NotifyIcon` component. You simply need to add this component to a form and supply an icon by setting the `Icon` property. Optionally, you can add a linked context menu through the `ContextMenu` property. The `NotifyIcon` component automatically displays its context menu when it's right-clicked. You can animate a system tray icon by swapping the icon periodically.

The Code

The following example uses eight icons, each of which shows a moon graphic in a different stage of fullness. By moving from one image to another, the illusion of animation is created.

```
Imports System
Imports System.Windows.Forms

'  All designed code is stored in the autogenerated partial
'  class called Recipe09-15.Designer.vb.  You can see this
'  file by selecting Show All Files in Solution Explorer.
Partial Public Class Recipe09_15

    '  An array to hold the set of Icons used to create the
    '  animation effect.
    Private images As Icon() = New Icon(8) {}

    '  An integer to identify the current icon to display.
    Dim offset As Integer = 0

    Private Sub Recipe09_15_Load(ByVal sender As Object, ➥
ByVal e As System.EventArgs) Handles Me.Load

        '  Load the basic set of eight icons.
        images(0) = New Icon("moon01.ico")
        images(1) = New Icon("moon02.ico")
        images(2) = New Icon("moon03.ico")
        images(3) = New Icon("moon04.ico")
        images(4) = New Icon("moon05.ico")
        images(5) = New Icon("moon06.ico")
        images(6) = New Icon("moon07.ico")
        images(7) = New Icon("moon08.ico")

    End Sub
```

```
    Private Sub timer_Elapsed(ByVal sender As Object, ➡
ByVal e As System.Timers.ElapsedEventArgs) Handles timer.Elapsed

        ' Change the icon.  This event handler fires once every
        ' second (500ms).
        notifyIcon.Icon = images(offset)
        offset += 1
        If offset > 7 Then offset = 0

    End Sub

End Class
```

9-16. Validate an Input Control

Problem

You need to alert the user of invalid input in a control, such as a TextBox.

Solution

Use the ErrorProvider component to display an error icon next to the offending control. Check for errors before allowing the user to continue.

How It Works

You can perform validation in a Windows-based application in a number of ways. One approach is to refuse any invalid character as the user presses a key by using a MaskedTextBox control, as shown in recipe 9-8. Another approach is to respond to control validation events and prevent users from changing focus from one control to another if an error exists. A less invasive approach is to simply flag the offending control in some way so that the user can review all the errors at once. You can use this approach by adding the ErrorProvider component to your form.

The ErrorProvider is a special property extender component that displays error icons next to invalid controls. You show the error icon next to a control by using the ErrorProvider.SetError method and specifying the appropriate control and a string error message. The ErrorProvider will then show a warning icon to the right of the control. When the user hovers the mouse above the warning icon, the detailed message appears. To clear an error, just pass an empty string to the SetError method.

You need to add only one ErrorProvider component to your form, and you can use it to display an error icon next to any control. To add the ErrorProvider, drag it on the form or into the component tray, or create it manually in code.

The Code

The following example checks the value that a user has entered into a text box whenever the text box loses focus. The code validates this text box using a regular expression that checks to see whether the value corresponds to the format of a valid e-mail address (see recipe 2-5 for more details on regular expressions). If validation fails, the ErrorProvider is used to display an error message. If the text is valid, any existing error message is cleared from the ErrorProvider. Finally, the Click event handler for the OK button steps through all the controls on the form and verifies that none of them has errors before allowing the example to continue. In this example, an empty text box is allowed, although it would be a simple matter to perform additional checks when the OK button is clicked for situations where empty text boxes are not acceptable.

```vb
Imports System
Imports System.Windows.Forms
Imports System.Text.RegularExpressions

' All designed code is stored in the autogenerated partial
' class called Recipe09-16.Designer.vb.  You can see this
' file by selecting Show All Files in Solution Explorer.
Partial Public Class Recipe09_16

    ' Button click event handler ensures the ErrorProvider is not
    ' reporting any error for each control before proceeding.
    Private Sub Button1_Click(ByVal sender As System.Object, ➥
ByVal e As System.EventArgs) Handles Button1.Click

        Dim errorText As String = String.Empty
        Dim invalidInput As Boolean = False

        For Each ctrl As Control In Me.Controls
            If Not errProvider.GetError(ctrl) = String.Empty Then
                errorText += "  * " & errProvider.GetError(ctrl) & ➥
ControlChars.NewLine
                invalidInput = True
            End If
        Next

        If invalidInput Then
            MessageBox.Show(String.Format("This form contains the " & ➥
"following unresolved errors:{0}{0}{1}", ControlChars.NewLine, errorText, ➥
"Invalid Input", MessageBoxButtons.OK, MessageBoxIcon.Warning))
        Else
            Me.Close()
        End If

    End Sub

    ' When the TextBox loses focus, check that the contents are a valid
    ' e-mail address.
    Private Sub txtEmail_Leave(ByVal sender As Object, ➥
ByVal e As System.EventArgs) Handles txtEmail.Leave

        ' Create a regular expression to check for valid e-mail addresses.
        Dim emailRegEx As Regex

        emailRegEx = New Regex("^[\w-]+@([\w]+\.)+[\w]+$")

        ' Validate the text from the control that raised the event.
        Dim ctrl As Control = DirectCast(sender, Control)

        If emailRegEx.IsMatch(ctrl.Text) Or ctrl.Text = String.Empty Then
            errProvider.SetError(ctrl, String.Empty)
```

```
        Else
            errProvider.SetError(ctrl, "This is not a valid email address.")
        End If

    End Sub

End Class
```

Usage

Figure 9-13 shows how the `ErrorProvider` control indicates an input error for the `TextBox` control when the example is run.

Figure 9-13. *A validated form with the ErrorProvider*

9-17. Use a Drag-and-Drop Operation

Problem

You need to use the drag-and-drop feature to exchange information between two controls (possibly in separate windows or in separate applications).

Solution

Start a drag-and-drop operation using the `DoDragDrop` method of the `Control` class, and then respond to the `DragEnter` and `DragDrop` events.

How It Works

A drag-and-drop operation allows the user to transfer information from one place to another by clicking an item and dragging it to another location. A drag-and-drop operation consists of the following three basic steps:

1. The user clicks a control, holds down the mouse button, and begins dragging. If the control supports the drag-and-drop feature, it sets aside some information.

2. The user drags the mouse over another control. If this control accepts the dragged type of content, the mouse cursor changes to the special drag-and-drop icon (arrow and page). Otherwise, the mouse cursor becomes a circle with a line drawn through it.

3. When the user releases the mouse button, the data is sent to the control, which can then process it appropriately.

To support drag-and-drop functionality, you must handle the DragEnter, DragDrop, and (typically) MouseDown events. To start a drag-and-drop operation, you call the source control's DoDragDrop method. At this point, you submit the data and specify the type of operations that will be supported (copying, moving, and so on). Controls that can receive dragged data must have the AllowDrop property set to True. These controls will receive a DragEnter event when the mouse drags the data over them. At this point, you can examine the data that is being dragged, decide whether the control can accept the drop, and set the DragEventArgs.Effect property accordingly. The final step is to respond to the DragDrop event in the destination control, which occurs when the user releases the mouse button.

The DragEventArgs.Data property, which is an IDataObject, represents the data that is being dragged or dropped. IDataObject is an interface for transferring general data objects. You get the data by using the GetData method. The GetDataPresent method, which accepts a String or Type, is used to determine the type of data represented by the IDataObject.

The Code

The following example allows you to drag content between two text boxes, as well as to and from other applications that support drag-and-drop operations:

```
Imports System
Imports System.Windows.Forms

'  All designed code is stored in the autogenerated partial
'  class called Recipe09-17.Designer.vb.  You can see this
'  file by selecting Show All Files in Solution Explorer.
Partial Public Class Recipe09_17

    Private Sub TextBox_DragDrop(ByVal sender As Object, ➥
ByVal e As DragEventArgs) Handles TextBox1.DragDrop, TextBox2.DragDrop

        Dim txt As TextBox = DirectCast(sender, TextBox)
        txt.Text = DirectCast(e.Data.GetData(DataFormats.Text), String)

    End Sub

    Private Sub TextBox_DragEnter(ByVal sender As Object, ➥
ByVal e As DragEventArgs) Handles TextBox1.DragEnter, TextBox2.DragEnter

        If e.Data.GetDataPresent(DataFormats.Text) Then
            e.Effect = DragDropEffects.Copy
        Else
            e.Effect = DragDropEffects.None
        End If

    End Sub

    Private Sub TextBox_MouseDown(ByVal sender As Object, ➥
ByVal e As MouseEventArgs) Handles TextBox1.MouseDown, TextBox2.MouseDown

        Dim txt As TextBox = DirectCast(sender, TextBox)
        txt.SelectAll()
        txt.DoDragDrop(txt.Text, DragDropEffects.Copy)

    End Sub

End Class
```

9-18. Use Context-Sensitive Help

Problem

You want to display a specific help file topic depending on the currently selected control.

Solution

Use the `HelpProvider` component, and set the `HelpKeyword` and `HelpNavigator` extended properties for each control.

How It Works

The .NET Framework provides support for context-sensitive help through the `HelpProvider` class. The `HelpProvider` class is a special extender control. You add it to the component tray of a form, and it extends all the controls on the form with a few additional properties, including `HelpNavigator` and `HelpKeyword`. For example, Figure 9-14 shows a form that has two controls and a `HelpProvider` named `helpProvider1`. The `ListBox` control, which is currently selected, has several help-specific properties that are provided through the `HelpProvider`.

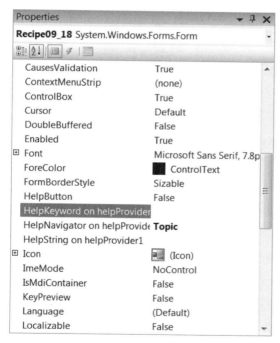

Figure 9-14. *The HelpProvider extender properties*

To use context-sensitive help with `HelpProvider`, follow these three steps:

1. Set the `HelpProvider.HelpNamespace` property with the name of the help file (for example, myhelp.chm).

2. For every control that requires context-sensitive help, set the `HelpNavigator` extender property to `HelpNavigator.Topic`.

3. For every control that requires context-sensitive help, set the `HelpKeyword` extender property with the name of the topic that should be linked to this control. (The topic names are specific to the help file and can be configured in your help-authoring tools.)

If the user presses the F1 key while a control has focus, the help file will be launched automatically, and the linked topic will be displayed in the help window. If the user presses F1 while positioned on a control that does not have a linked help topic, the help settings for the containing control will be used (for example, a group box or a panel). If there are no containing controls or the containing control does not have any help settings, the form's help settings will be used. You can also use the `HelpProvider` methods to set or modify context-sensitive help mapping at runtime.

9-19. Display a Web Page in a Windows-Based Application

Problem

You want to display a web page and provide web-navigation capabilities within your Windows Forms application.

Solution

Use the `WebBrowser` control to display the web page and other standard controls like buttons and text boxes to allow the user to control the operation of the `WebBrowser`.

■**Caution** The `WebBrowser` control is a managed wrapper around the `WebBrowser` ActiveX control, which is the same component used by Internet Explorer. This means that if you use a `Main` method, it must be annotated with the `STAThread` attribute. Furthermore, the component is very resource-intensive and should be disposed of correctly.

How It Works

The `WebBrowser` control, first introduced in .NET Framework 2.0, makes it a trivial task to embed highly functional web browser capabilities into your Windows applications. The `WebBrowser` control is responsible for displaying web pages and maintaining page history, but it does not provide any controls for user interaction. Instead, the `WebBrowser` control exposes properties and events that you can manipulate programmatically to control the operation of the `WebBrowser`. This approach makes the `WebBrowser` control highly flexible and adaptable to almost any situation. Table 9-1 summarizes some of the commonly used `WebBrowser` members related to web navigation.

You can also use the `WebBrowser.DocumentText` property to set (or get) the currently displayed HTML contents of the `WebBrowser`. To manipulate the contents using the Document Object Model (DOM), get an `HtmlDocument` instance via the `Document` property.

Table 9-1. *Commonly Used Members of the WebBrowser Control*

Member	Description
Property	
AllowNavigation	Controls whether the WebBrowser can navigate to another page after its initial page has been loaded
CanGoBack	Indicates whether the WebBrowser currently holds back page history, which would allow the GoBack method to succeed
CanGoForward	Indicates whether the WebBrowser currently holds forward page history, which would allow the GoForward method to succeed
IsBusy	Indicates whether the WebBrowser is currently busy downloading a page
Url	Holds the URL of the currently displayed/downloading page
Method	
GoBack	Displays the previous page in the page history, if there is one
GoForward	Displays the next page in the page history, if there is one
GoHome	Displays the home page of the current user as configured in Internet Explorer
Navigate	Displays the web page at the specified URL
Stop	Stops the current WebBrowser activity
Event	
DocumentCompleted	Signals that the active download has completed and the document is displayed in the WebBrowser

The Code

The following example uses the WebBrowser control to allow users to navigate to a web page whose address is entered into a TextBox. Buttons also allow users to move forward and backward through page history and navigate directly to their personal home page.

```vb
Imports System
Imports System.Windows.Forms


' All designed code is stored in the autogenerated partial
' class called Recipe09-19.Designer.vb.  You can see this
' file by selecting Show All Files in Solution Explorer.
Partial Public Class Recipe09_19

    Private Sub goButton_Click(ByVal sender As System.Object, ➥
ByVal e As System.EventArgs) Handles goButton.Click

        ' Navigate to the URL specified in the textbox.
        webBrowser1.Navigate(textURL.Text)

    End Sub
```

```vb
    Private Sub backButton_Click(ByVal sender As System.Object, ➥
ByVal e As System.EventArgs) Handles backButton.Click

        ' Go to the previous page in the WebBrowser history.
        webBrowser1.GoBack()

    End Sub

    Private Sub homeButton_Click(ByVal sender As System.Object, ➥
ByVal e As System.EventArgs) Handles homeButton.Click

        ' Navigate to the current user's home page.
        webBrowser1.GoHome()

    End Sub

    Private Sub forwardButton_Click(ByVal sender As System.Object, ➥
ByVal e As System.EventArgs) Handles forwardButton.Click

        ' Go to the next page in the WebBrowser history.
        webBrowser1.GoForward()

    End Sub

    Private Sub Recipe09_19_Load(ByVal sender As Object, ➥
ByVal e As System.EventArgs) Handles Me.Load

        ' Navigate to the Apress home page when the application first
        ' loads.
        webBrowser1.Navigate("http://www.apress.com")

    End Sub

    ' Event handler to perform general interface maintenance once a
    ' document has been loaded into the WebBrowser.
    Private Sub webBrowser1_DocumentCompleted(ByVal sender As Object, ➥
ByVal e As WebBrowserDocumentCompletedEventArgs) ➥
Handles webBrowser1.DocumentCompleted

        ' Update the content of the TextBox to reflect the current URL.
        textURL.Text = webBrowser1.Url.ToString

        ' Enable or disable the Back button depending on whether the
        ' WebBrowser has back history
        If webBrowser1.CanGoBack Then
            backButton.Enabled = True
        Else
            backButton.Enabled = False
        End If
```

```
' Enable or disable the Forward button depending on whether the
' WebBrowser has forward history.
If webBrowser1.CanGoForward Then
    forwardButton.Enabled = True
Else
    forwardButton.Enabled = False
End If

    End Sub

End Class
```

9-20. Create a Windows Presentation Foundation Application

Problem

You need to create a Windows Presentation Foundation (WPF) application using only managed code (no XAML).

Solution

Create an instance of the System.Windows class, and use an instance of the System.Windows.Application to display it.

How It Works

As mentioned in the introduction to this chapter, WPF is a new format for creating Windows-based applications that uses an approach similar to ASP.NET. The front end is written using XAML, and many tools are available for visually designing it and outputting XAML. The back end is handled by managed code.

Although what we've just described is how WPF is meant to be used, it is still possible to create a WPF application completely using managed code. This would allow you to benefit from the new and powerful functionality available to WPF applications without having to learn a new language. However, the downside is that you will be unable to visually design your applications because none of the designers currently provides managed code output.

Two primary objects are required for any WPF application: System.Windows.Window and System.Windows.Application. The Window object, similar to the Form object in Windows Forms applications, is the visible representation of your application. There can be more than one Window, but your application will end when the last one is closed. The Application object is invisible but is the underlying object to any WPF application. Every WPF application must have one, and only one, Application object.

To create a WPF application using managed code, you must first ensure that you have a reference to the following primary APIs: PresentationCore, PresentationFramework, and WindowsBase. The most basic application requires only that you create a Window and Application instance. You then call the Run method of the Application class, which starts the application.

The Code

The following example creates a simple WPF application with a button. The form is centered on the screen and closed when the button is clicked.

```vb
Imports System
Imports System.Windows
Imports System.Windows.Controls

Namespace Apress.VisualBasicRecipes.Chapter09

    Class Recipe09_20
        Inherits System.Windows.Window

        Public Shared Sub Main()

            Dim app As New Application
            app.Run(New Recipe09_20)

        End Sub

        Public Sub New()

            Dim btn As New Button

            Title = "Recipe09-20"

            Width = 300
            Height = 300
            Left = SystemParameters.PrimaryScreenWidth / 2 - Width / 2
            Top = SystemParameters.PrimaryScreenHeight / 2 - Height / 2

            AddHandler btn.Click, AddressOf ButtonClick

            btn.Content = "Click To Close"
            btn.Width = 150
            btn.Height = 50
            btn.ToolTip = "Close this WPF form"

            Content = btn

        End Sub

        Private Sub ButtonClick(ByVal sender As Object, ByVal e As RoutedEventArgs)

            Close()

        End Sub

    End Class
End Namespace
```

Usage

Figure 9-15 shows what the Windows Presentation Foundation application looks like when it is executed.

Figure 9-15. *A sample WPF application*

9-21. Run a Windows Vista Application with Elevated Rights

Problem

Your Vista application requires administrator rights to execute.

Solution

Create an application manifest with the `requestedExecutionLevel` element set to `requireAdministrator`, and then embed the manifest into your application.

■**Note** Using the manifest solution is supported only in Windows Vista because it pertains to its User Account Control (UAC) feature. If you are not using Vista, the manifest will be ignored, and you will want to use impersonation to force your application to run under a different user's account.

How It Works

Windows Vista institutes a new security model, in which everything is executed under the rights of a normal user, even if launched by an administrator. To work around this, a feature known as User Account Control (UAC) was added. If you have used Windows Vista and encountered a dialog box requesting elevated permissions, then you have most likely encountered the UAC.

To support the UAC, your application must include a special manifest file that defines the UAC options. Figure 9-16 shows a typical properties screen for a Visual Studio 2008 project, which now includes the View UAC Settings button. Clicking this button will display the manifest that will be embedded in your application.

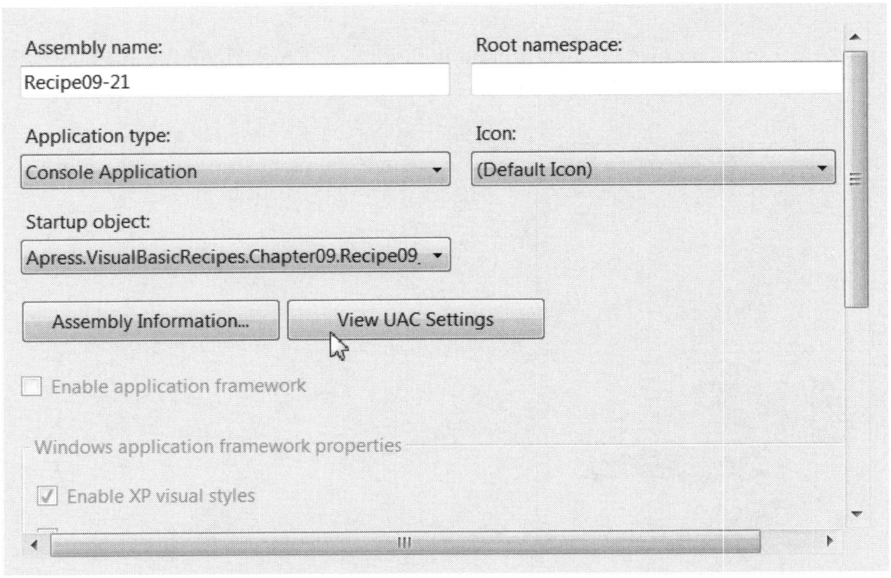

Figure 9-16. *View UAC Settings*

The manifest is an XML file that looks like this:

```xml
<?xml version="1.0" encoding="utf-8"?>
<asmv1:assembly manifestVersion="1.0" xmlns="urn:schemas-microsoft-com:asm.v1" ➡
xmlns:asmv1="urn:schemas-microsoft-com:asm.v1" ➡
xmlns:asmv2="urn:schemas-microsoft-com:asm.v2" ➡
xmlns:xsi="http://www.w3.org/2001/XMLSchema-instance">
  <assemblyIdentity version="1.0.0.0" name="MyApplication.app"/>
  <trustInfo xmlns="urn:schemas-microsoft-com:asm.v2">
    <security>
      <requestedPrivileges xmlns="urn:schemas-microsoft-com:asm.v3">
        <!-- UAC Manifest Options
            If you want to change the Windows User Account Control level replace the
            requestedExecutionLevel node with one of the following.

        <requestedExecutionLevel  level="asInvoker" />
        <requestedExecutionLevel  level="requireAdministrator" />
        <requestedExecutionLevel  level="highestAvailable" />

            If you want to utilize File and Registry Virtualization for backward
            compatibility then delete the requestedExecutionLevel node.
        -->
        <requestedExecutionLevel level="asInvoker" />
      </requestedPrivileges>
    </security>
  </trustInfo>
</asmv1:assembly>
```

To make your application require administrator access, ensure that the `level` attribute of the `requestedExecutionLevel` property is set to `requireAdministrator`. Once you compile your application, the manifest will be embedded into it. This will be shown by the small shield image that will automatically become part of your application's icon.

When you attempt to run the application within Visual Studio 2008, the dialog box shown in Figure 9-17 will be displayed. This dialog box informs you that your application requires administrator rights. If you agree, Visual Studio 2008 will be restarted with administrator rights (as shown in the title bar). If Visual Studio 2008 was already running under elevated administrator rights, you will not see the dialog box.

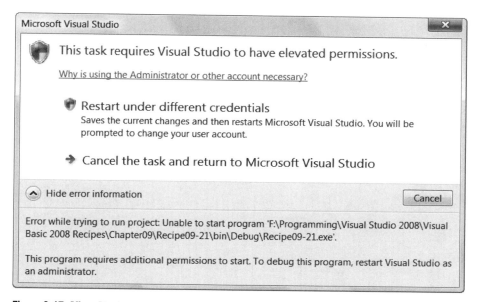

Figure 9-17. *View UAC Settings*

When you attempt to run the application from within Windows, the standard UAC dialog box will be displayed, requesting approval for elevated access. The application will not execute unless you allow the elevation of rights.

CHAPTER 10

■ ■ ■

Multimedia

Multimedia is an expansive subject that covers sound, video, graphics, and printing. The aim of this chapter is to briefly touch on each main topic. If you want more detailed information, refer to books devoted to the subject, such as *Pro .NET 2.0 Graphics Programming* by Eric White (Apress, 2005) or *Pro .NET 2.0 Windows Forms and Custom Controls in VB 2005* by Matthew MacDonald (Apress, 2006).

The .NET Framework provides direct support for most multimedia functionality. The System. Drawing namespace provides support for manipulating two-dimensional drawings. Most of the classes in this namespace, such as Drawing2D and Graphics, wrap GDI32.dll and USER32.dll. These libraries provide the native Graphics Device Interface (GDI) functionality in the Windows application programming interface (API). They also make it easier to draw complex shapes, work with coordinates and transforms, and process images. The Printing namespace, which contains classes related to printing, is also part of the System.Drawing namespace. This namespace uses GDI support for drawing text or images to a Document object. Although this class does provide support for enumerating and collecting information for installed printers, it is limited to local printers, and it does not support all information, such as print jobs.

The System.Media namespace provides support for playing basic sounds, such as WAV files. If you want to show a video file or play more sophisticated audio files, such as MP3s, you will need to look beyond the .NET Framework.

For even more enhanced functionality, the .NET Framework 3.0 introduced Windows Presentation Foundation (WPF). This version of the framework, which was initially released with the release of Windows Vista, is responsible for much of the graphical effects used by it. WPF, as mentioned in the previous chapter, is a new model for creating Windows applications. The interfaces are created using Extensible Application Markup Language (XAML) while events are handled by managed code (such as VB .NET). This is similar to how ASP.NET applications work where HTML is used for the interface.

WPF also provides more enhanced support for graphics, including 3D support, and playing video and audio files. For more detailed information, you should refer to any available books on the subject, such as *Applications = Code + Markup* by Charles Petzoid (Microsoft Press, 2006) or *Pro WPF: Windows Presentation Foundation in .NET 3.0* by Matthew MacDonald (Apress, 2007).

This chapter presents recipes that show you how to use built-in .NET features and, where necessary, native Win32 libraries via P/Invoke or COM Interop. The recipes in this chapter cover the following:

- Finding the fonts installed in your system (recipe 10-1)
- Performing hit testing with shapes (recipe 10-2)
- Creating an irregularly shaped form or control (recipe 10-3)
- Creating a sprite that can be moved around (recipe 10-4)

- Displaying an image that can be made to scroll (recipe 10-5)

- Capturing an image of the desktop (recipe 10-6)

- Enabling double buffering to increase performance while redrawing (recipe 10-7)

- Creating a thumbnail for an existing image (recipe 10-8)

- Playing a beep or a system-defined sound (recipe 10-9), playing a WAV file (recipe 10-10), playing a non-WAV file such as an MP3 file (recipe 10-11), and playing a video with DirectShow (recipe 10-12)

- Retrieving information about the printers installed in the machine (recipe 10-13), printing a simple document (recipe 10-14), printing a document that has multiple pages (recipe 10-15), printing wrapped text (recipe 10-16), showing a print preview (recipe 10-17), and managing print jobs (recipe 10-18)

■Note Although it is possible to create Windows Presentation Foundation (WPF) applications using VB .NET, it is more appropriate to use XAML, as intended. For this reason, this chapter does not contain any WPF recipes.

10-1. Find All Installed Fonts

Problem

You need to retrieve a list of all the fonts installed on the current computer.

Solution

Create a new instance of the `System.Drawing.Text.InstalledFontCollection` class, which contains a collection of `FontFamily` objects representing all the installed fonts.

How It Works

The `InstalledFontCollection` class allows you to retrieve information about currently installed fonts, via the `Families` property. The `Families` property is provided by the `MustInherit FontCollection` class which `InstalledFontCollection` derives from.

The Code

The following code shows a form that iterates through the font collection when it is first created. Every time it finds a font, it creates a new `Label` control that will display the font name in the given font face (at a size of 14 points). The `Label` is added to a `Panel` control named pnlFonts with `AutoScroll` set to `True`, allowing the user to scroll through the list of available fonts.

```
Imports System
Imports System.Drawing
Imports System.Windows.Forms
Imports System.Drawing.text

' All designed code is stored in the autogenerated partial
' class called Recipe10-01.Designer.vb.  You can see this
' file by selecting Show All Files in Solution Explorer.
```

```vbnet
Partial Public Class Recipe10_01

    Private Sub Recipe10_01_Load(ByVal sender As Object, ➥
ByVal e As System.EventArgs) Handles Me.Load

        ' Create the font collection.
        Using fontFamilies As New InstalledFontCollection

            ' Iterate through all font families
            Dim offset As Integer = 10

            For Each family As FontFamily In fontFamilies.Families

                Try
                    ' Create a label that will display text in this font.
                    Dim fontLabel As New Label

                    fontLabel.Text = family.Name
                    fontLabel.Font = New Font(family, 14)
                    fontLabel.Left = 10
                    fontLabel.Width = pnlFonts.Width
                    fontLabel.Top = offset

                    ' Add the label to a scrollable Panel.
                    pnlFonts.Controls.Add(fontLabel)
                    offset += 30
                Catch ex As ArgumentException
                    ' An ArgumentException will be thrown if the selected
                    ' font does not support regular style (the default used
                    ' when creating a font object).  For this example, we
                    ' will display an appropriate message in the list.
                    Dim fontLabel As New Label

                    fontLabel.Text = ex.Message
                    fontLabel.Font = New Font("Arial", 10, FontStyle.Italic)
                    fontLabel.ForeColor = Color.Red
                    fontLabel.Left = 10
                    fontLabel.Width = 500
                    fontLabel.Top = offset

                    ' Add the label to a scrollable Panel.
                    pnlFonts.Controls.Add(fontLabel)
                    offset += 30
                End Try

            Next

        End Using

    End Sub
End Class
```

Usage

Figure 10-1 shows results similar to what you will see when you run the recipe.

Figure 10-1. *A list of installed fonts*

10-2. Perform Hit Testing with Shapes

Problem

You need to detect whether a user clicks inside a shape.

Solution

Test the point where the user clicked with methods such as Rectangle.Contains and Region.IsVisible (in the System.Drawing namespace) or GraphicsPath.IsVisible (in the System.Drawing.Drawing2D namespace), depending on the type of shape.

How It Works

Often, if you use GDI+ to draw shapes on a form, you need to be able to determine when a user clicks in a given shape. You can determine this using a Rectangle and a Point. A Rectangle is defined by its height, width, and upper-left coordinates, which are reflected by the Height, Width, X, and Y properties. A Point, which is an X and Y coordinate, represents a specific location on the screen. The .NET Framework provides three methods to help with this task:

- The Rectangle.Contains method, which takes a point and returns true if the point is inside a given rectangle. In many cases, you can retrieve a rectangle for another type of object. For example, you can use Image.GetBounds to retrieve the invisible rectangle that represents the image boundaries. The Rectangle structure is a member of the System.Drawing namespace.

- The GraphicsPath.IsVisible method, which takes a point and returns true if the point is inside the area defined by a closed GraphicsPath. Because a GraphicsPath can contain multiple lines, shapes, and figures, this approach is useful if you want to test whether a point is contained inside a nonrectangular region. The GraphicsPath class is a member of the System.Drawing. Drawing2D namespace.

- The Region.IsVisible method, which takes a point and returns true if the point is inside the area defined by a Region. A Region, like the GraphicsPath, can represent a complex nonrect-angular shape. Region is a member of the System.Drawing namespace.

The Code

The following example shows a form that creates a Rectangle and a GraphicsPath. By default, these two shapes are given light blue backgrounds. However, an event handler responds to the Form. MouseMove event, checks to see whether the mouse pointer is in one of these shapes, and updates the shape's background to bright pink if the pointer is there.

Note that the highlighting operation takes place directly inside the MouseMove and Paint event handlers. The painting is performed only if the current selection has changed. For simpler code, you could invalidate the entire form every time the mouse pointer moves in or out of a region and handle *all* the drawing in the Form.Paint event handler, but this would lead to more drawing and generate additional flicker as the entire form is repainted.

```
Imports System
Imports System.Drawing
Imports System.Windows.Forms
Imports System.Drawing.Drawing2D

'  All designed code is stored in the autogenerated partial
'  class called Recipe10-02.Designer.vb.  You can see this
'  file by selecting Show All Files in Solution Explorer.
Partial Public Class Recipe10_02

    ' Define the shapes used on this form.
    Private path As GraphicsPath
    Private rect As Rectangle

    ' Define the flags that track where the mouse pointer is.
    Private inPath As Boolean = False
    Private inRectangle As Boolean = False

    ' Define the brushes used for painting the shapes.
    Private highlightBrush As Brush = Brushes.HotPink
    Private defaultBrush As Brush = Brushes.LightBlue

    Private Sub Recipe10_02_Load(ByVal sender As Object, ➥
ByVal e As System.EventArgs) Handles Me.Load

        ' Create the shapes that will be displayed.
        path = New GraphicsPath
        path.AddEllipse(10, 10, 100, 60)
        path.AddCurve(New Point() {New Point(50, 50), New Point(10, 33), ➥
New Point(80, 43)})
        path.AddLine(50, 120, 250, 80)
        path.AddLine(120, 40, 110, 50)
        path.CloseFigure()

        rect = New Rectangle(100, 170, 220, 170)

    End Sub
```

```vb
    Private Sub Recipe10_02_MouseMove(ByVal sender As Object, ➡
ByVal e As System.Windows.Forms.MouseEventArgs) Handles Me.MouseMove

        Using g As Graphics = Me.CreateGraphics
            ' Perform hit testing with rectangle.
            If rect.Contains(e.X, e.Y) Then
                If Not inRectangle Then
                    inRectangle = True

                    ' Highlight the rectangle.
                    g.FillRectangle(highlightBrush, rect)
                    g.DrawRectangle(Pens.Black, rect)
                End If
            ElseIf inRectangle Then
                inRectangle = False

                ' Restore the unhighlighted rectangle.
                g.FillRectangle(defaultBrush, rect)
                g.DrawRectangle(Pens.Black, rect)
            End If

            ' Perform hit testing with path.
            If path.IsVisible(e.X, e.Y) Then
                If Not inPath Then
                    inPath = True

                    ' Highlight the path.
                    g.FillPath(highlightBrush, path)
                    g.DrawPath(Pens.Black, path)
                End If
            ElseIf inPath Then
                inPath = False

                ' Restore the unhighlighted path.
                g.FillPath(defaultBrush, path)
                g.DrawPath(Pens.Black, path)
            End If

        End Using

    End Sub

    Private Sub Recipe10_02_Paint(ByVal sender As Object, ➡
ByVal e As System.Windows.Forms.PaintEventArgs) Handles Me.Paint

        Dim g As Graphics = e.Graphics

        ' Paint the shapes according to the current selection.
        If inPath Then
            g.FillPath(highlightBrush, path)
            g.FillRectangle(defaultBrush, rect)
        ElseIf inRectangle Then
            g.FillRectangle(highlightBrush, rect)
            g.FillPath(defaultBrush, path)
```

```
        Else
            g.FillPath(defaultBrush, path)
            g.FillRectangle(defaultBrush, rect)
        End If

        g.DrawPath(Pens.Black, path)
        g.DrawRectangle(Pens.Black, rect)

    End Sub

End Class
```

Usage

Figure 10-2 shows the application in action.

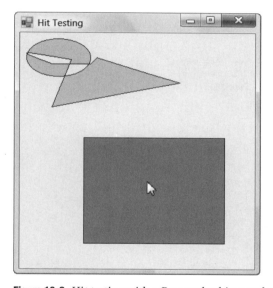

Figure 10-2. *Hit testing with a Rectangle object and a GraphicsPath object*

10-3. Create an Irregularly Shaped Control

Problem

You need to create a nonrectangular form or control.

Solution

Create a new System.Drawing.Region object that has the shape you want for the form, and assign it to the Form.Region or Control.Region property.

How It Works

To create a nonrectangular form or control, you first need to define the shape you want. The easiest approach is to use the System.Drawing.Drawing2D.GraphicsPath object, which can accommodate any combination of ellipses, rectangles, closed curves, and even strings. You can add shapes to a GraphicsPath instance using methods such as AddEllipse, AddRectangle, AddClosedCurve, and AddString. Once you are finished defining the shape you want, you can create a Region object from this GraphicsPath—just pass the GraphicsPath to the Region class constructor. Finally, you can assign the Region to the Form.Region property or the Control.Region property.

The Code

The following example creates an irregularly shaped form (shown in Figure 10-3) using two curves made of multiple points, which are converted into a closed figure using the GraphicsPath. CloseAllFigures method.

```
Imports System
Imports System.Drawing
Imports System.Windows.Forms
Imports System.Drawing.Drawing2D
'  All designed code is stored in the autogenerated partial
'  class called Recipe10-03.Designer.vb.  You can see this
'  file by selecting Show All Files in Solution Explorer.
Partial Public Class Recipe10_03

    Private Sub Recipe10_03_Load(ByVal sender As Object, ➡
ByVal e As System.EventArgs) Handles Me.Load

        Dim path As New GraphicsPath
        Dim pointsA As Point() = New Point() {New Point(0, 0), ➡
New Point(40, 60), New Point(Me.Width - 100, 10)}
        Dim pointsB As Point() = New Point() {New Point(Me.Width - 40, ➡
Me.Height - 60), New Point(Me.Width, Me.Height), New Point(10, Me.Height)}

        path.AddCurve(pointsA)
        path.AddCurve(pointsB)

        path.CloseAllFigures()

        Me.Region = New Region(path)

    End Sub

    Private Sub cmdClose_Click(ByVal sender As System.Object, ➡
ByVal e As System.EventArgs) Handles cmdClose.Click

        Me.Close()

    End Sub

End Class
```

Usage

When you run the application, you will see results similar to Figure 10-3.

■Note Another method for creating nonrectangular forms (not controls) is using the BackgroundImage and TransparencyKey properties available in the Form class. However, this method could cause display problems when monitors are set to a color depth greater than 24-bit. For more information about this topic, refer to the Microsoft Knowledge Base article at http://support.microsoft.com/kb/822495.

Figure 10-3. *A nonrectangular form*

For an example that demonstrates a nonrectangular control, refer to recipe 10-4.

10-4. Create a Movable Sprite

Problem

You need to create a shape the user can manipulate on a form, perhaps by dragging it, resizing it, or otherwise interacting with it.

Solution

Create a custom control, and override the painting logic to draw a shape. Assign your shape to the Control.Region property. You can then use this Region to perform hit testing, which is demonstrated in recipe 10-2.

How It Works

If you need to create a complex user interface that incorporates many custom-drawn elements, you need a way to track these elements and allow the user to interact with them. The easiest approach in .NET is to create a dedicated control by deriving a class from System.Windows.Forms.Control. You can then customize the way this control appears and operates by adding the appropriate functionality to the appropriate events. For example, if the control needs to respond in a certain way when it is selected, you may want to add the needed functionality to the MouseEnter, MouseLeave, MouseUp, or MouseDown event.

The Code

The following example shows a control that represents a simple ellipse shape on a form. All controls are associated with a rectangular region on a form, so the EllipseShape control generates an ellipse that fills these boundaries (provided through the Control.ClientRectangle property). Once the shape has been generated, the Control.Region property is set according to the bounds on the ellipse. This ensures events such as MouseMove, MouseDown, Click, and so on, will occur only if the mouse is over the ellipse, not the entire client rectangle.

Here is the full EllipseShape code:

```vb
Imports System
Imports System.Drawing
Imports System.Drawing.Drawing2D

'  All designed code is stored in the autogenerated partial
'  class called EllipseShape.Designer.vb.  You can see this
'  file by selecting Show All Files in Solution Explorer.
Public Class EllipseShape
    Inherits System.Windows.Forms.Control

    Dim path As GraphicsPath = Nothing

    Private Sub RefreshPath()

        ' Create the GraphicsPath for the shape (in this case
        ' an ellipse that fits inside the full control area)
        ' and apply it to the control by setting the Region
        ' property.
        path = New GraphicsPath
        path.AddEllipse(Me.ClientRectangle)
        Me.Region = New Region(path)

    End Sub

    Protected Overrides Sub OnPaint(ByVal e As System.Windows.Forms.PaintEventArgs)

        MyBase.OnPaint(e)

        If path IsNot Nothing Then
            e.Graphics.SmoothingMode = SmoothingMode.AntiAlias
            e.Graphics.FillPath(New SolidBrush(Me.BackColor), path)
            e.Graphics.DrawPath(New Pen(Me.ForeColor, 4), path)
        End If

    End Sub
```

```
    Private Sub EllipseShape_Resize(ByVal sender As Object, ➥
ByVal e As System.EventArgs) Handles Me.Resize

        RefreshPath()
        Me.Invalidate()

    End Sub

End Class
```

You could define the `EllipseShape` control in a separate class library assembly so you could add it to the Visual Studio .NET Toolbox and use it at design time. However, even without taking this step, it is easy to create a simple test application. The following Windows Forms application creates two ellipses and allows the user to drag both of them around the form, simply by holding the mouse down and moving the pointer:

```
Imports System
Imports System.Drawing
Imports System.Windows.Forms

'  All designed code is stored in the autogenerated partial
'  class called Recipe10-04.Designer.vb.  You can see this
'  file by selecting Show All Files in Solution Explorer.
Partial Public Class Recipe10_04

    '  Tracks when drag mode is on.
    Private isDraggingA As Boolean = False
    Private isDraggingB As Boolean = False

    '  The ellipse shape controls.
    Private ellipseA, ellipseB As EllipseShape

    Private Sub Recipe10_04_Load(ByVal sender As Object, ➥
ByVal e As System.EventArgs) Handles Me.Load

        '  Create and configure both ellipses.
        ellipseA = New EllipseShape
        ellipseA.Width = 100
        ellipseA.Height = 100
        ellipseA.Top = 30
        ellipseA.Left = 30
        ellipseA.BackColor = Color.Red
        Me.Controls.Add(ellipseA)

        ellipseB = New EllipseShape
        ellipseB.Width = 100
        ellipseB.Height = 100
        ellipseB.Top = 130
        ellipseB.Left = 130
        ellipseB.BackColor = Color.LightSteelBlue
        Me.Controls.Add(ellipseB)
```

```vb
        ' Attach both ellipses to the same set of event handlers.
        AddHandler ellipseA.MouseDown, AddressOf Ellipse_MouseDown
        AddHandler ellipseA.MouseUp, AddressOf Ellipse_MouseUp
        AddHandler ellipseA.MouseMove, AddressOf Ellipse_MouseMove

        AddHandler ellipseB.MouseDown, AddressOf Ellipse_MouseDown
        AddHandler ellipseB.MouseUp, AddressOf Ellipse_MouseUp
        AddHandler ellipseB.MouseMove, AddressOf Ellipse_MouseMove

    End Sub

    Private Sub Ellipse_MouseDown(ByVal sender As Object, ByVal e As MouseEventArgs)

        If e.Button = Windows.Forms.MouseButtons.Left Then
            ' Get the ellipse that triggered this event.
            Dim ctrl As Control = DirectCast(sender, Control)
            ctrl.Tag = New Point(e.X, e.Y)

            If ctrl Is ellipseA Then
                isDraggingA = True
            Else
                isDraggingB = True
            End If
        End If

    End Sub

    Private Sub Ellipse_MouseUp(ByVal sender As Object, ByVal e As MouseEventArgs)

        isDraggingA = False
        isDraggingB = False

    End Sub

    Private Sub Ellipse_MouseMove(ByVal sender As Object, ByVal e As MouseEventArgs)

        ' Get the ellipse that triggered this event.
        Dim ctrl As Control = DirectCast(sender, Control)

        If (isDraggingA And (ctrl Is ellipseA)) Or (isDraggingB And ➥
(ctrl Is ellipseB)) Then

            ' Get the offset.
            Dim pnt As Point = DirectCast(ctrl.Tag, Point)

            ' Move the control.
            ctrl.Left = e.X + ctrl.Left - pnt.X
            ctrl.Top = e.Y + ctrl.Top - pnt.Y

        End If

    End Sub

End Class
```

Usage

Figure 10-4 shows the user about to drag an ellipse.

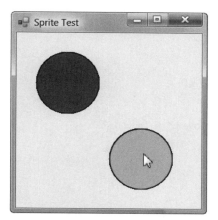

Figure 10-4. *Dragging custom shape controls on a form*

10-5. Create a Scrollable Image

Problem

You need to create a scrollable picture.

Solution

Leverage the automatic scroll capabilities of the System.Windows.Forms.Panel control by setting Panel.AutoScroll to True and placing a System.Windows.Forms.PictureBox control with the image content inside the Panel.

How It Works

The Panel control has built-in scrolling support, as shown in recipe 10-1. If you place any controls in it that extend beyond its bounds and you set Panel.AutoScroll to True, the panel will show scroll bars that allow the user to move through the content. This works particularly well with large images. You can load or create the image in memory, assign it to a picture box (which has no intrinsic support for scrolling), and then show the picture box inside the panel. The only consideration you need to remember is to make sure you set the picture box dimensions equal to the full size of the image you want to show.

The Code

The following example creates an image that represents a document. The image is generated as an in-memory bitmap, and several lines of text are added using the Graphics.DrawString method. The image is then bound to a picture box, which is shown in a scrollable panel.

```vb
Imports System
Imports System.Drawing
Imports System.Windows.Forms

'  All designed code is stored in the autogenerated partial
'  class called Recipe10-05.Designer.vb.  You can see this
'  file by selecting Show All Files in Solution Explorer.
Public Class Recipe10_05

    Private Sub Recipe10_05_Load(ByVal sender As Object, ➥
ByVal e As System.EventArgs) Handles Me.Load

        Dim text As String = "The quick brown fox jumps over the lazy dog."

        Using fnt As New Font("Tahoma", 14)

            '  Create an in-memory bitmap.
            Dim bmp As New Bitmap(600, 600)

            Using g As Graphics = Graphics.FromImage(bmp)

                g.FillRectangle(Brushes.White, New Rectangle(0, 0, bmp.Width, ➥
bmp.Height))

                '  Draw several lines of text on the bitmap.
                For i As Integer = 1 To 10
                    g.DrawString(text, fnt, Brushes.Black, 50, 50 + i * 60)
                Next

            End Using

            '  Display the bitmap in the picture box.
            pictureBox1.BackgroundImage = bmp
            pictureBox1.Size = bmp.Size

        End Using

    End Sub

End Class
```

Usage

When you run the application, you will get results similar to those shown in Figure 10-5.

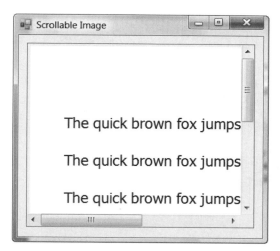

Figure 10-5. *Adding scrolling support to custom content*

10-6. Perform a Screen Capture

Problem

You need to take a snapshot of the current desktop.

Solution

Use the CopyFromScreen method of the Graphics class to copy screen contents.

How It Works

The Graphics class now includes CopyFromScreen methods that copy color data from the screen onto the drawing surface represented by a Graphics object. This method requires you to pass the source and destination points and the size of the image to be copied.

The Code

The following example captures the screen and displays it in a picture box. It first creates a new Bitmap object and then invokes CopyFromScreen to draw onto the Bitmap. After drawing, the image is assigned to the picture box.

```
Imports System
Imports System.Drawing
Imports System.Windows.Forms
```

```
'  All designed code is stored in the autogenerated partial
'  class called Recipe10-06.Designer.vb.  You can see this
'  file by selecting Show All Files in Solution Explorer.
Partial Public Class Recipe10_06

    Private Sub cmdCapture_Click(ByVal sender As System.Object, ➥
ByVal e As System.EventArgs) Handles cmdCapture.Click

        Dim screenCapture As New Bitmap(Screen.PrimaryScreen.Bounds.Width, ➥
Screen.PrimaryScreen.Bounds.Height)

        Using g As Graphics = Graphics.FromImage(screenCapture)
            g.CopyFromScreen(0, 0, 0, 0, screenCapture.Size)
        End Using

        pictureBox1.Image = screenCapture

    End Sub

End Class
```

Usage

When you run the application and click the Capture button, you will get results similar to those shown in Figure 10-6.

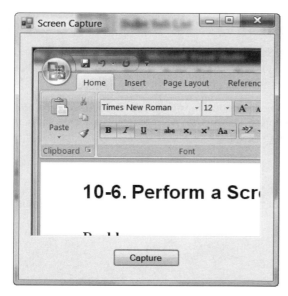

Figure 10-6. *Capturing the screen contents*

10-7. Use Double Buffering to Increase Redraw Speed

Problem

You need to optimize drawing for a form or an authored control that is frequently refreshed, and you want to reduce flicker.

Solution

Set the `DoubleBuffered` property of the form to `True`.

How It Works

In some applications, you need to repaint a form or control frequently. This is commonly the case when creating animations. For example, you might use a timer to invalidate your form every second. Your painting code could then redraw an image at a new location, creating the illusion of motion. The problem with this approach is that every time you invalidate the form, Windows repaints the window background (clearing the form) and then runs your painting code, which draws the graphic element by element. This can cause substantial onscreen flicker.

Double buffering is a technique you can implement to reduce this flicker. With double buffering, your drawing logic writes to an in-memory bitmap, which is copied to the form at the end of the drawing operation in a single, seamless repaint operation. Flickering is reduced dramatically.

.NET Framework 2.0 introduced a default double buffering mechanism for forms and controls. You can enable this by setting the `DoubleBuffered` property of your form or control to `True` or by using the `SetStyle` method.

The Code

The following example sets the `DoubleBuffered` property of the form to `True` and shows an animation of an image alternately growing and shrinking on the page. The drawing logic takes place in the `Form.Paint` event handler, and a timer invalidates the form in a preset interval so that the image can be redrawn. The user can choose whether to enable double buffering through a checkbox on the form. Without double buffering, the form flickers noticeably. When double buffering is enabled, however, the image grows and shrinks with smooth, flicker-free animation.

```
Imports System
Imports System.Drawing
Imports System.Windows.Forms
Imports System.Drawing.Drawing2D

' All designed code is stored in the autogenerated partial
' class called Recipe10-07.Designer.vb.  You can see this
' file by selecting Show All Files in Solution Explorer.
Partial Public Class Recipe10_07

    ' Track the image size and the type of animation
    ' (expanding or shrinking).
    Private isShrinking As Boolean = False
    Private imageSize As Integer = 0

    ' Store the logo that will be painted on the form.
    Private img As Image
```

```vb
    Private Sub Recipe10_07_Load(ByVal sender As Object, ➥
ByVal e As System.EventArgs) Handles Me.Load

        ' Load the logo image from the file.
        img = Image.FromFile("test.jpg")

        ' Start the time that invalidates the form.
        tmrRefresh.Start()

    End Sub

    Private Sub tmrRefresh_Tick(ByVal sender As Object, ➥
ByVal e As System.EventArgs) Handles tmrRefresh.Tick

        ' Change the desired image size according to the animation mode.
        If isShrinking Then
            imageSize -= 1
        Else
            imageSize += 1
        End If

        ' Change the sizing direction if it nears the form border.
        If imageSize > (Me.Width - 150) Then
            isShrinking = True
        ElseIf imageSize < 1 Then
            isShrinking = False
        End If

        Me.Invalidate()

    End Sub

    Private Sub Recipe10_07_Paint(ByVal sender As Object, ➥
ByVal e As System.Windows.Forms.PaintEventArgs) Handles Me.Paint

        Dim g As Graphics

        g = e.Graphics
        g.SmoothingMode = SmoothingMode.HighQuality

        ' Draw the background.
        g.FillRectangle(Brushes.Yellow, New Rectangle(New Point(0, 0), ➥
Me.ClientSize))

        ' Draw the logo image.
        g.DrawImage(img, 50, 50, 50 + imageSize, 50 + imageSize)

    End Sub

    Private Sub chkUseDoubleBuffering_CheckedChanged(ByVal sender As Object, ➥
ByVal e As System.EventArgs) Handles chkUseDoubleBuffering.CheckedChanged
```

```
        Me.DoubleBuffered = chkUseDoubleBuffering.Checked

    End Sub

End Class
```

10-8. Show a Thumbnail for an Image

Problem

You need to show thumbnails (small representations of pictures) for the images in a directory.

Solution

Read the image from the file using the `Shared FromFile` method of the `System.Drawing.Image` class. You can then retrieve a thumbnail using the `Image.GetThumbnailImage` method.

How It Works

The `Image` class provides the functionality for generating thumbnails through the `GetThumbnailImage` method. You simply need to pass the width and height of the thumbnail you want (in pixels), and the `Image` class will create a new `Image` object that fits these criteria. Antialiasing is used when reducing the image to ensure the best possible image quality, although some blurriness and loss of detail is inevitable. (*Antialiasing* is the process of removing jagged edges, often in resized graphics, by adding shading with an intermediate color.) In addition, you can supply a notification callback, allowing you to create thumbnails asynchronously.

When generating a thumbnail, it is important to ensure that the aspect ratio remains constant. For example, if you reduce a 200×100 picture to a 50×50 thumbnail, the width will be compressed to one quarter and the height will be compressed to one half, distorting the image. To ensure that the aspect ratio remains constant, you can change either the width or the height to a fixed size and then adjust the other dimension proportionately.

■**Note** If you attempt to load a file that is not a supported image type, you will receive an `OutOfMemoryException`. This is important to know because it is not the error you might expect to receive in this situation.

The Code

The following example reads a bitmap file and generates a thumbnail that is not greater than 200×200 pixels while preserving the original aspect ratio:

```
Imports System
Imports System.Drawing
Imports System.Windows.Forms

' All designed code is stored in the autogenerated partial
' class called Recipe10-08.Designer.vb.  You can see this
' file by selecting Show All Files in Solution Explorer.
Partial Public Class Recipe10_08
```

```
      Private thumbNail As Image
      Private Sub Recipe10_08_Load(ByVal sender As Object, ➥
ByVal e As System.EventArgs) Handles Me.Load

         Using img As Image = Image.FromFile("test.jpg")

            Dim thumbnailWidth As Integer = 0
            Dim thumbnailHeight As Integer = 0

            ' Adjust the largest dimension to 200 pixels.
            ' This ensures that a thumbnail will not be larger than
            ' 200x200 pixel square for each one.
            If img.Width > img.Height Then
               thumbnailWidth = 200
               thumbnailHeight = Convert.ToInt32((CSng(200) / img.Width) * ➥
img.Height)
            Else
               thumbnailHeight = 200
               thumbnailWidth = Convert.ToInt32((CSng(200) / img.Height) * ➥
img.Height)
            End If

            thumbNail = img.GetThumbnailImage(thumbnailWidth, thumbnailHeight, ➥
Nothing, IntPtr.Zero)

         End Using

      End Sub

      Private Sub Recipe10_08_Paint(ByVal sender As Object, ➥
ByVal e As System.Windows.Forms.PaintEventArgs) Handles Me.Paint

         e.Graphics.DrawImage(thumbNail, 10, 10)

      End Sub

End Class
```

10-9. Play a Simple Beep or System Sound

Problem

You need to play a simple system-defined beep or sound.

Solution

Use the managed Beep method of the Console class or the Play method of the SystemSound class.

How It Works

Overloads of the `Console.Beep` method, introduced in .NET Framework 2.0, let you play a beep with the default frequency and duration or with a frequency and duration you specify. Frequency is represented in hertz (and must range from 37 to 32,767), and the duration is represented in milliseconds. Internally, these methods invoke the `Beep` Win32 function and use the computer's internal speaker. Thus, if the computer does not have an internal speaker, no sound will be produced.

The `System.Media` namespace contains the following classes for playing sound files:

- The `SystemSound` class represents a Windows sound event, such as an asterisk, beep, question, and so on. It also defines a `Play` method, which lets you play the sound associated with it.

- The `SystemSounds` class defines properties that let you obtain the `SystemSound` instance of a specific Windows sound event. For example, it defines an `Asterisk` property that returns a `SystemSound` instance associated with the asterisk Windows sound event.

- The `SoundPlayer` class lets you play WAV files. For more information about how to play a WAV file using this class, refer to recipe 10-10.

As an alternative for playing system sounds, you can also use the `My` namespace (refer to Chapter 5 for further details). `My` includes the `My.Computer.Audio` class, which contains the Shared `PlaySystemSound` method for playing system sounds. It takes a `SystemSound` object as its parameter.

The Code

The following example plays two different beeps and the asterisk sound in succession, using the `Console` and `SystemSound` classes:

```
Imports System
Imports System.Windows.Forms
Imports System.Media

'  All designed code is stored in the autogenerated partial
'  class called Recipe10-09.Designer.vb.  You can see this
'  file by selecting Show All Files in Solution Explorer.
Partial Public Class Recipe10_09

    Private Sub Recipe10_09_Load(ByVal sender As Object, ➥
ByVal e As System.EventArgs) Handles Me.Load

        ' Play a beep with default frequency and
        ' duration (800 and 200, respectively)
        Console.Beep()

        ' Play a beep with frequency as 200 and duration as 300.
        Console.Beep(200, 300)

        ' Play the sound associated with the Asterisk event.
        SystemSounds.Asterisk.Play()

    End Sub

End Class
```

The following shows how to use the `My` namespace to play the system sound:

```
My.Computer.Audio.PlaySystemSound(SystemSounds.Asterisk)
```

10-10. Play a WAV File

Problem

You need to play a WAV file.

Solution

Create a new instance of the `System.Media.SoundPlayer` class, pass the location or stream of the WAV file, and invoke the `Play` method.

How It Works

The `System.Media` namespace, first introduced in .NET Framework 2.0, contains a `SoundPlayer` class. `SoundPlayer` contains constructors that let you specify the location of a WAV file or its stream. Once you have created an instance, you just need to invoke the `Play` method to play the file. The `Play` method creates a new thread to play the sound and is thus asynchronous (unless a stream is used). For playing the sound synchronously, use the `PlaySync` method. Note that `SoundPlayer` supports only the WAV format.

Before a file is played, it is loaded into memory. You can load a file in advance by invoking the `Load` or `LoadSync` method, depending on whether you want the operation to be asynchronous or synchronous.

The `My.Computer.Audio` class provides an alternative for playing WAV files. This class consists of the `Shared` methods `Play`, `PlaySystemSound` (refer to recipe 10-9), and `Stop`. The `Play` method, the equivalent of the `SoundPlayer.Play` method, uses the `PlayMode` parameter to configure how the sound is played. `PlayMode` is an `AudioPlayMode` enumerated type that can be set to `Background` (plays the sound asynchronously), `BackgroundLoop` (plays the sound asynchronously and loops until the `Stop` method is called), and `WaitToComplete` (plays the sound synchronously).

The Code

The following example shows a simple form that allows users to open any WAV file and play it:

```
Imports System
Imports System.Windows.Forms
Imports System.Media

'  All designed code is stored in the autogenerated partial
'  class called Recipe10-10.Designer.vb.  You can see this
'  file by selecting Show All Files in Solution Explorer.
Partial Public Class Recipe10_10

    Private Sub cmdOpen_Click(ByVal sender As System.Object, ➥
ByVal e As System.EventArgs) Handles cmdOpen.Click

        '  Allow the user to choose a file.
        Dim openDialog As New OpenFileDialog

        openDialog.Filter = "WAV Files|*.wav|All Files|*.*"

        If openDialog.ShowDialog = Windows.Forms.DialogResult.OK Then
            Dim player As New SoundPlayer(openDialog.FileName)
```

```
        Try
            player.Play()
        Catch ex As Exception
            MessageBox.Show("An error occurred while playing media.")
        Finally
            player.Dispose()
        End Try
    End If

End Sub
```

End Class

To use the `My` namespace, remove references to the `Player` object and replace `Player.Play()` with this:

```
My.Computer.Audio.Play(openDialog.FileName)
```

10-11. Play a Sound File

Problem

You need to play a non-WAV format audio file such as an MP3 file.

Solution

Use the ActiveMovie COM component included with Windows Media Player, which supports WAV and MP3 audio.

How It Works

The ActiveMovie Quartz library provides a COM component that can play various types of audio files, including the WAV and MP3 formats. The Quartz type library is provided through quartz.dll and is included as a part of Microsoft DirectX with Media Player and the Windows operating system.

The first step for using the library is to generate an interop class that can manage the interaction between your .NET application and the unmanaged Quartz library. You can generate a C# class with this interop code using the Type Library Importer utility (Tlbimp.exe) and the following command line, where `[WindowsDir]` is the path for your installation of Windows:

```
tlbimp [WindowsDir]\system32\quartz.dll /out:QuartzTypeLib.dll
```

Alternatively, you can generate the interop class using Visual Studio by adding a reference. To do this, right-click your project in Solution Explorer, choose Add Reference from the context menu, select the COM tab, and scroll down to select ActiveMovie Control Type Library. If you cannot find the component in the list, you can browse to the file quartz.dll (shown in the previous path) and add the reference that way or just use the previous method to create the library yourself.

Once the interop class has been generated and referenced by your project, you can work with the `IMediaControl` interface. You can specify the file you want to play using `RenderFile`, and you can control playback using methods such as `Run`, `Stop`, and `Pause`. The actual playback takes place on a separate thread, so it will not block your code.

Although the .NET Framework will eventually release any references to a COM object and collect the memory it uses, it is best practice to do this yourself as soon as it is no longer needed. Managed code does not access COM objects directly but instead uses a *runtime callable wrapper* (RCW). The RCW acts as a proxy between managed code and a referenced COM object. The `Shared` method `ReleaseComObject`, from the `System.Runtime.InteropServices.Marshal` class, properly destroys the RCW and the COM object it used.

The Code

The following example shows a simple form that allows you to open any audio file and play it. The COM object is destroyed using `ReleaseComObject`.

You can also use the Quartz library to show movie files, as demonstrated in recipe 10-12.

```
Imports System
Imports System.Windows.Forms
Imports QuartzTypeLib

'  All designed code is stored in the autogenerated partial
'  class called Recipe10-11.Designer.vb.  You can see this
'  file by selecting Show All Files in Solution Explorer.
Partial Public Class Recipe10_11

    Dim graphManager As QuartzTypeLib.FilgraphManager

    Private Sub cmdOpen_Click(ByVal sender As System.Object, ➥
ByVal e As System.EventArgs) Handles cmdOpen.Click

        '  Allow the user to choose a file.
        Dim openDialog As New OpenFileDialog

        openDialog.Filter = "Media FIles|*.wav;*.mp3;*.mp2;*.wma|All Files|*.*"

        If openDialog.ShowDialog = Windows.Forms.DialogResult.OK Then
            '  Access the IMediaControl interface.
            graphManager = New QuartzTypeLib.FilgraphManager
            Dim mc As QuartzTypeLib.IMediaControl = DirectCast(graphManager, ➥
QuartzTypeLib.IMediaControl)

            '  Specify the file.
            mc.RenderFile(openDialog.FileName)

            Try
                mc.Run()
            Catch ex As Exception
                MessageBox.Show("An error occurred while playing media.")
            End Try

        End If

    End Sub

    Private Sub Recipe10_11_FormClosing(ByVal sender As Object, ➥
ByVal e As System.Windows.Forms.FormClosingEventArgs) Handles Me.FormClosing
```

```
        If graphManager IsNot Nothing Then
            ' Destroy the COM object (QuartzTypeLib) that we are using.
            System.Runtime.InteropServices.Marshal.ReleaseComObject(graphManager)
        End If

    End Sub

End Class
```

10-12. Show a Video with DirectShow

Problem

You need to play a video file (such as an MPEG, an AVI, or a WMV file) in a Windows Forms application.

Solution

Use the ActiveMovie COM component included with Windows Media Player. Bind the video output to a picture box on your form by setting the IVideoWindow.Owner property to the PictureBox.Handle property.

How It Works

Although the .NET Framework does not include any managed classes for interacting with video files, you can leverage the functionality of DirectShow using the COM-based Quartz library included with Windows Media Player and the Windows operating system. For information about creating an interop assembly for the Quartz type library, refer to recipe 10-11.

Once you have created the interop assembly, you can use the IMediaControl interface to load and play a movie. This is essentially the same technique demonstrated in recipe 10-11 with audio files. However, if you want to show the video window inside your application interface (rather than in a separate stand-alone window), you must also use the IVideoWindow interface. The core FilgraphManager object can be cast to both the IMediaControl interface and the IVideoWindow interface (several other interfaces are also supported, such as IBasicAudio, which allows you to configure balance and volume settings). With the IVideoWindow interface, you can bind the video output to a control on your form, such as a Panel or a PictureBox. To do so, set the IVideoWindow.Owner property to the handle for the control, which you can retrieve using the Control.Handle property. Then call IVideoWindow. SetWindowPosition to set the window size and location. You can call this method to change the video size during playback (for example, if the form is resized).

The Code

The following example shows a simple form that allows users to open any video file and play it back in the provided picture box. The picture box is anchored to all sides of the form, so it changes size as the form resizes. The code responds to the PictureBox.SizeChanged event to change the size of the corresponding video window. Also, the reference to the QuartzTypeLib is destroyed using ReleaseComObject (discussed in recipe 10-11) when the form is closed.

```
Imports System
Imports System.Drawing
Imports System.Windows.Forms
Imports QuartzTypeLib
```

```vb
' All designed code is stored in the autogenerated partial
' class called Recipe10-12.Designer.vb.  You can see this
' file by selecting Show All Files in Solution Explorer.
Partial Public Class Recipe10_12

    ' Define the constants used for specifying the window style.
    Private Const WS_CHILD As Integer = &H40000000
    Private Const WS_CLIPCHILDREN As Integer = &H2000000

    ' Hold a form-level reference to the QuartzTypeLib.FilgraphManager
    ' object.
    Private graphManager As FilgraphManager

    ' Hold a form-level reference to the media control interface,
    ' so the code can control playback of the currently loaded
    ' movie.
    Private mc As IMediaControl = Nothing

    ' Hold a form-level reference to the video window in case it
    ' needs to be resized.
    Private videoWindow As IVideoWindow = Nothing

    Private Sub cmdOpen_Click(ByVal sender As System.Object, ➡
ByVal e As System.EventArgs) Handles cmdOpen.Click

        ' Allow the user to choose a file.
        Dim openDialog As New OpenFileDialog

        openDialog.Filter = "Media Files|*.mpg;*.avi;*.wma;*.mov;" & ➡
"*.wav;*.mp2;*.mp3|All Files|*.*"

        If openDialog.ShowDialog = Windows.Forms.DialogResult.OK Then

            ' Stop the playback for the current movie, if it exists.
            If mc IsNot Nothing Then mc.Stop()

            ' Load the movie file.
            graphmanager = New FilgraphManager
            graphmanager.RenderFile(openDialog.FileName)

            ' Attach the view to a picture box on the form.
            Try
                videoWindow = DirectCast(graphmanager, IVideoWindow)
                videoWindow.Owner = pictureBox1.Handle.ToInt32
                videoWindow.WindowStyle = WS_CHILD Or WS_CLIPCHILDREN
                videoWindow.SetWindowPosition(pictureBox1.ClientRectangle.Left, ➡
pictureBox1.ClientRectangle.Top, pictureBox1.ClientRectangle.Width, ➡
pictureBox1.ClientRectangle.Height)
```

```
        Catch ex As Exception
            '  An error can occur if the file does not have a video
            '  source (for example, an MP3 file).
            '  You can ignore this error and still allow playback to
            '  continue (without any visualization).
        End Try

        '  Start the playback (asynchronously).
        mc = DirectCast(graphmanager, IMediaControl)
        mc.Run()

    End If

End Sub

Private Sub pictureBox1_SizeChanged(ByVal sender As Object, ➥
ByVal e As System.EventArgs) Handles pictureBox1.SizeChanged

    If videoWindow IsNot Nothing Then

        Try
            videoWindow.SetWindowPosition(pictureBox1.ClientRectangle.Left, ➥
pictureBox1.ClientRectangle.Top, pictureBox1.ClientRectangle.Width, ➥
pictureBox1.ClientRectangle.Height)
        Catch ex As Exception
            '  Ignore the exception thrown when resizing the form
            '  when the file does not have a video source.
        End Try

    End If

End Sub

Private Sub Recipe10_12_FormClosed(ByVal sender As Object, ➥
ByVal e As System.Windows.Forms.FormClosedEventArgs) Handles Me.FormClosed

    '  Destroy the COM object (QuartzTypeLib) that we are using.
    If graphManager IsNot Nothing Then
        System.Runtime.InteropServices.Marshal.ReleaseComObject(graphManager)
    End If

End Sub

End Class
```

Usage

Figure 10-7 shows an example of the output you will see.

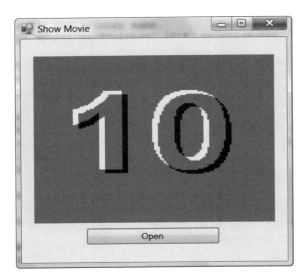

Figure 10-7. *Playing a video file*

10-13. Retrieve Information About Installed Printers

Problem

You need to retrieve a list of available printers.

Solution

Read the names in the InstalledPrinters collection of the System.Drawing.Printing.PrinterSettings class.

How It Works

The PrinterSettings class encapsulates the settings for a printer and information about the printer. For example, you can use the PrinterSettings class to determine supported paper sizes, paper sources, and resolutions and check for the ability to print color or double-sided (*duplexed*) pages. In addition, you can retrieve default page settings for margins, page orientation, and so on.

The PrinterSettings class provides a Shared InstalledPrinters string collection, which includes the name of every printer installed on the computer. If you want to find out more information about the settings for a specific printer, create a PrinterSettings instance, and set the PrinterName property accordingly.

The Code

The following code shows a console application that finds all the printers installed on a computer and displays information about the paper sizes and the resolutions supported by each one.

You do not need to take this approach when creating an application that provides printing features. As you will see in recipe 10-14, you can use the PrintDialog class to prompt the user to choose a printer and its settings. The PrintDialog class can automatically apply its settings to the appropriate PrintDocument without any additional code.

```vb
Imports System
Imports System.Drawing.Printing

Namespace Apress.VisualBasicRecipes.Chapter10

    Public Class Recipe10_13

        Public Shared Sub Main()

            For Each printerName As String In PrinterSettings.InstalledPrinters

                ' Display the printer name.
                Console.WriteLine("Printer: {0}", printerName)

                ' Retrieve the printer settings.
                Dim printer As New PrinterSettings
                printer.PrinterName = printerName

                ' Check that this is a valid printer.
                ' (This step might be required if you read the printer name
                ' from a user-supplied value or a registry or configuration
                ' file setting.)
                If printer.IsValid Then
                    ' Display the list of valid resolutions.
                    Console.WriteLine("Supported Resolutions:")

                    For Each resolution As PrinterResolution In ➥
printer.PrinterResolutions
                        Console.WriteLine("  {0}", resolution)
                    Next
                    Console.WriteLine()

                    ' Display the list of valid paper sizes.
                    Console.WriteLine("Supported Paper Sizes:")

                    For Each size As PaperSize In printer.PaperSizes
                        If System.Enum.IsDefined(size.Kind.GetType, size.Kind) Then
                            Console.WriteLine("  {0}", size)
                        End If
                    Next
                    Console.WriteLine()
                End If
            Next
            Console.ReadLine()
        End Sub
    End Class

End Namespace
```

Usage

When you run this recipe, you will results similar to the following:

```
Printer: EPSON al-cx11 advanced
Supported Resolutions:
  [PrinterResolution High]
  [PrinterResolution Medium]
  [PrinterResolution Low]
  [PrinterResolution Draft]
  [PrinterResolution X=300 Y=300]
  [PrinterResolution X=600 Y=600]

Supported Paper Sizes:
  [PaperSize A4 210 x 297 mm Kind=A4 Height=1169 Width=827]
  [PaperSize B4 257 x 364 mm Kind=B4 Height=1433 Width=1012]
  [PaperSize B5 182 x 257 mm Kind=B5 Height=1012 Width=717]
. . .
```

Note You can print a document in almost any type of application. However, your application must include a reference to the System.Drawing.dll assembly. If you are using a project type in Visual Studio that would not normally have this reference (such as a console application), you must add it.

10-14. Print a Simple Document

Problem

You need to print text or images.

Solution

Create a PrintDocument, and write a handler for the PrintDocument.PrintPage event that uses the DrawString and DrawImage methods of the Graphics class to print data to the page.

How It Works

The .NET Framework uses an asynchronous event-based printing model. To print a document, you create a System.Drawing.Printing.PrintDocument instance, configure its properties, and then call its Print method, which schedules the print job. The common language runtime (CLR) will then fire the BeginPrint, PrintPage, and EndPrint events of the PrintDocument class on a new thread. You handle these events and use the provided System.Drawing.Graphics object to output data to the page. Graphics and text are written to a page in the same way as you draw to a window using GDI+. However, you might need to track your position on a page, because every Graphics class method requires explicit coordinates that indicate where to draw.

You configure printer settings through the PrintDocument.PrinterSettings and PrintDocument.DefaultPageSettings properties. The PrinterSettings property returns a full PrinterSettings object (as described in recipe 10-13), which identifies the printer that will be used. The DefaultPageSettings property provides a full PageSettings object that specifies printer resolution, margins, orientation, and so on. You can configure these properties in code, or you can use the System.Windows.Forms.PrintDialog class to let the user make the changes using the standard Windows Print dialog box, shown in Figure 10-8. In the Print dialog box, the user can select a printer and choose the number of copies. The user can also click the Properties button to configure advanced settings such as page layout and printer resolution. Finally, the user can either accept or cancel the print operation by clicking OK or Cancel.

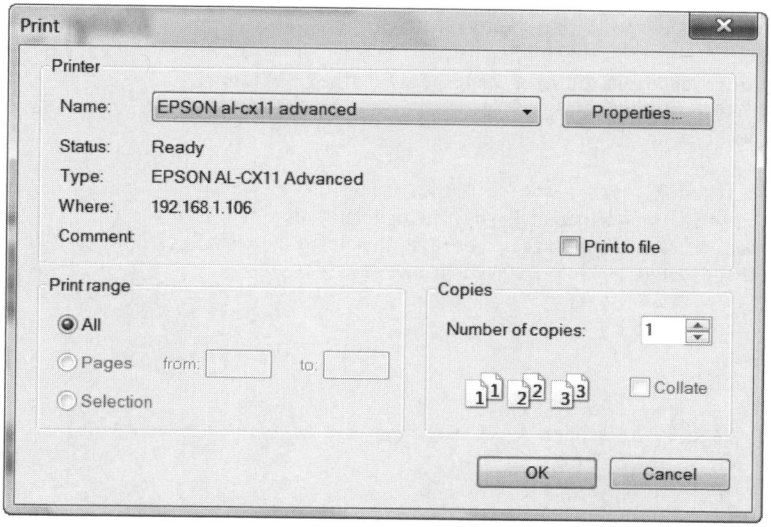

Figure 10-8. *Using the PrintDialog class*

Before using the PrintDialog class, you must explicitly attach it to a PrintDocument object by setting the PrintDialog.Document property. Then any changes the user makes in the Print dialog box will be automatically applied to the PrintDocument object.

The Code

The following example provides a form with a single button. When the user clicks the button, the application creates a new PrintDocument, allows the user to configure print settings, and then starts an asynchronous print operation (provided the user clicks OK). An event handler responds to the PrintPage event and writes several lines of text and an image.

This example has one limitation: it can print only a single page. To print more complex documents and span multiple pages, you will probably want to create a specialized class that encapsulates the document information, the current page, and so on, as described in recipe 10-15.

```
Imports System
Imports System.Drawing
Imports System.Windows.Forms
Imports System.Drawing.Printing
Imports System.IO

'  All designed code is stored in the autogenerated partial
'  class called Recipe10-14.Designer.vb.  You can see this
'  file by selecting Show All Files in Solution Explorer.
Partial Public Class Recipe10_14
```

```
    Private Sub cmdPrint_Click(ByVal sender As System.Object, ➥
ByVal e As System.EventArgs) Handles cmdPrint.Click

        ' Create the document and attach an event handler.
        Dim doc As New PrintDocument

        AddHandler doc.PrintPage, AddressOf Doc_PrintPage

        ' Allow the user to choose a printer and specify other settings.
        Dim dlgSettings As New PrintDialog
        dlgSettings.Document = doc

        ' If the user clicked OK, print the document.
        If dlgSettings.ShowDialog = Windows.Forms.DialogResult.OK Then
            ' This method returns immediately, before the print job starts.
            ' The PrintPage event will fire asynchronously.
            doc.Print()
        End If

    End Sub

    Private Sub Doc_PrintPage(ByVal sender As Object, ByVal e As PrintPageEventArgs)

        ' Determine the font.
        Using fnt As New Font("Arial", 30)
            ' Determine the position on the page. In this case,
            ' we read the margin settings (although there is
            ' nothing that prevents your code from going outside
            ' the margin bounds).
            Dim x As Single = e.MarginBounds.Left
            Dim y As Single = e.MarginBounds.Top

            ' Determine the height of a line (based on the font used).
            Dim lineHeight As Single = Font.GetHeight(e.Graphics)

            ' Print five lines of text.
            For i As Integer = 1 To 5
                ' Draw the text with a black brush, using the
                ' font and coordinates we have determined.
                e.Graphics.DrawString("This is line " & i.ToString, Font, ➥
Brushes.Black, x, y)

                ' Move down the equivalent spacing of one line.
                y += lineheight
            Next
            y += lineHeight

            ' Draw an image.
            e.Graphics.DrawImage(Image.FromFile(Path.Combine(➥
Application.StartupPath,"test.jpg")), x, y)

        End Using
    End Sub

End Class
```

10-15. Print a Multipage Document

Problem

You need to print complex documents with multiple pages and possibly print several different documents at once.

Solution

Place the information you want to print into a custom class that derives from `PrintDocument`, and in the `PrintPage` event handler, set the `PrintPageEventArgs.HasMorePages` property to `True` as long as pages are remaining.

How It Works

The `PrintDocument.PrintPage` event is triggered to let you to print only a single page. If you need to print more pages, you need to set the `PrintPageEventArgs.HasMorePages` property to `True` in the `PrintPage` event handler. As long as `HasMorePages` is set to `True`, the `PrintDocument` class will continue firing `PrintPage` events. However, it is up to you to track which page you are on, what data should be placed on each page, and what is the last page for which `HasMorePage` is not set to `True`. To facilitate this tracking, it is a good idea to create a custom class.

The Code

The following example shows a class called `TextDocument`. This class inherits from `PrintDocument` and adds three properties. `Text` stores an array of text lines, `PageNumber` reflects the last printed page, and `Offset` indicates the last line that was printed from the `Text` array.

```
Public Class TextDocument
    Inherits PrintDocument

    Private m_Text As String()
    Private m_PageNumber As Integer
    Private m_Offset As Integer

    Public Sub New(ByVal txt As String())

        Me.Text = txt

    End Sub

    Public Property Text() As String()
        Get
            Return m_Text
        End Get
        Set(ByVal value As String())
            m_Text = value
        End Set
    End Property
```

```
    Public Property PageNumber() As Integer
        Get
            Return m_PageNumber
        End Get
        Set(ByVal value As Integer)
            m_PageNumber = value
        End Set
    End Property

    Public Property Offset() As Integer
        Get
            Return m_Offset
        End Get
        Set(ByVal value As Integer)
            m_Offset = value
        End Set
    End Property

End Class
```

Depending on the type of material you are printing, you might want to modify this class. For example, you could store an array of image data, some content that should be used as a header or footer on each page, font information, or even the name of a file from which you want to read the information. Encapsulating the information in a single class makes it easier to print more than one document at the same time. This is especially important because the printing process runs in a new dedicated thread. As a consequence, the user is able to keep working in the application and therefore update your data while the pages are printing. So, this dedicated class should contain a copy of the data to print to avoid any concurrency problems.

The code that initiates printing is the same as in recipe 10-14, but now it creates a TextDocument instance instead of a PrintDocument instance. The PrintPage event handler keeps track of the current line and checks whether the page has space before attempting to print the next line. If a new page is needed, the HasMorePages property is set to True and the PrintPage event fires again for the next page. If not, the print operation is deemed complete. This simple code sample also takes into account whether a line fits on the page, according to the height (see recipe 10-16).

The full form code is as follows:

```
Imports System
Imports System.Drawing
Imports System.Windows.Forms
Imports System.Drawing.Printing

'  All designed code is stored in the autogenerated partial
'  class called Recipe10-15.Designer.vb.  You can see this
'  file by selecting Show All Files in Solution Explorer.
Partial Public Class Recipe10_15

    Private Sub cmdPrint_Click(ByVal sender As System.Object, ➥
ByVal e As System.EventArgs) Handles cmdPrint.Click

        ' Create a document with 100 lines.
        Dim printText As String() = New String(100) {}
```

```vb
        For i As Integer = 1 To 100
            printText(i) = i.ToString
            printText(i) += ": The quick brown fox jumps over the lazy dog."
        Next

        Dim doc As New TextDocument(printText)

        AddHandler doc.PrintPage, AddressOf Doc_PrintPage

        Dim dlgSettings As New PrintDialog
        dlgSettings.Document = doc

        ' If the user clicked OK, print the document.
        If dlgSettings.ShowDialog = Windows.Forms.DialogResult.OK Then
            ' This method returns immediately, before the print job starts.
            ' The PrintPage event will fire asynchronously.
            doc.Print()
        End If

    End Sub

    Private Sub Doc_PrintPage(ByVal sender As Object, ByVal e As PrintPageEventArgs)

        ' Retrieve the document that sent this event.
        Dim doc As TextDocument = DirectCast(sender, TextDocument)

        ' Determine the font and determine the line height.
        Using fnt As New Font("Arial", 10)
            Dim lineHeight As Single = Font.GetHeight(e.Graphics)

            ' Create variables to hold position on the page.
            Dim x As Single = e.MarginBounds.Left
            Dim y As Single = e.MarginBounds.Top

            ' Increment the page counter (to reflect the page that
            ' is about to be printed).
            doc.PageNumber += 1

            ' Print all the information that can fit on the page.
            ' This loop ends when the next line would go over the
            ' bottom margin or there are no more lines to print.
            While ((y + lineHeight) < e.MarginBounds.Bottom And ➥
doc.Offset <= doc.Text.GetUpperBound(0))
                e.Graphics.DrawString(doc.Text(doc.Offset), Font, ➥
Brushes.Black, x, y)

                ' Move to the next line of data.
                doc.Offset += 1

                ' Move the equivalent of one line down the page.
                y += lineHeight
            End While
```

```
            If doc.Offset < doc.Text.GetUpperBound(0) Then
                ' There is still at least one more page. Signal
                ' this event to fire again.
                e.HasMorePages = True
            End If

        End Using
    End Sub

End Class
```

10-16. Print Wrapped Text

Problem

You need to parse a large block of text into distinct lines that fit on one page.

Solution

Use the Graphics.DrawString method overload that accepts a bounding rectangle.

How It Works

Often, you will need to break a large block of text into separate lines that can be printed individually on a page. The .NET Framework can perform this task automatically, provided you use a version of the Graphics.DrawString method that accepts a bounding rectangle. You specify a rectangle that represents where you want the text to be displayed. The text is then wrapped automatically to fit within those confines.

The Code

The following code demonstrates this approach, using the bounding rectangle that represents the printable portion of the page. It prints a large block of text from a text box on the form.

```
Imports System
Imports System.Drawing
Imports System.Windows.Forms
Imports System.Drawing.Printing

'  All designed code is stored in the autogenerated partial
'  class called Recipe10-16.Designer.vb.  You can see this
'  file by selecting Show All Files in Solution Explorer.
Partial Public Class Recipe10_16

    Private Sub cmdPrint_Click(ByVal sender As System.Object, ➥
ByVal e As System.EventArgs) Handles cmdPrint.Click

        ' Create the document and attach an event handler.
        Dim text As String = "Windows Server 2003 builds on the core strengths " & _
        "of the Windows family of operating systems--security, manageability, " & _
        "reliability, availability, and scalability. Windows Server 2003 " & _
        "provides an application environment to build, deploy, manage, and " & _
        "run XML web services. Additionally, advances in Windows Server 2003 " & _
```

```
                "provide many benefits for developing applications."

                Dim doc As New ParagraphDocument(text)
                AddHandler doc.PrintPage, AddressOf Doc_PrintPage

                ' Allow the user to choose a printer and specify other settings.
                Dim dlgsettings As New PrintDialog
                dlgsettings.Document = doc

                ' If the user clicked OK, print the document.
                If dlgsettings.ShowDialog = Windows.Forms.DialogResult.OK Then
                    doc.Print()
                End If

        End Sub

        Private Sub Doc_PrintPage(ByVal sender As Object, ByVal e As PrintPageEventArgs)

                ' Retrieve the document that sent this event.
                Dim doc As ParagraphDocument = DirectCast(sender, ParagraphDocument)

                ' Define the font and text.
                Using fnt As New Font("Arial", 35)
                    e.Graphics.DrawString(doc.Text, Font, Brushes.Black, ➡
        e.MarginBounds, StringFormat.GenericDefault)
                End Using

        End Sub

End Class

Public Class ParagraphDocument
        Inherits PrintDocument

        Private m_Text As String

        Public Sub New(ByVal txt As String)
            Me.Text = txt
        End Sub

        Public Property Text() As String
            Get
                Return m_Text
            End Get
            Set(ByVal value As String)
                m_Text = value
            End Set
        End Property

End Class
```

10-17. Show a Dynamic Print Preview

Problem

You need to use an onscreen preview that shows how a printed document will look.

Solution

Use `PrintPreviewDialog` or `PrintPreviewControl` (both of which are found in the `System.Windows.Forms` namespace).

How It Works

The .NET Framework provides two elements of user interface that can take a `PrintDocument` instance, run your printing code (such as the code demonstrated in recipe 10-15), and use it to generate a graphical onscreen preview:

- The `PrintPreviewDialog`, which shows a preview in a stand-alone form
- The `PrintPreviewControl`, which shows a preview in a control that can be embedded in one of your own custom forms

To use a stand-alone print preview form, create a `PrintPreviewDialog` object, assign its `Document` property, and call the `Show` method:

```
Dim dlgPreview As New PrintPreviewDialog
dlgPreview.Document = doc
dlgPreview.Show()
```

The Print Preview window (shown in Figure 10-9) provides all the controls the user needs to move from page to page, zoom in, and so on. The window even provides a print button that allows the user to send the document directly to the printer. You can tailor the window to some extent by modifying the `PrintPreviewDialog` properties.

Figure 10-9. *Using the PrintPreviewDialog control*

You can also add a `PrintPreviewControl` control to any of your forms to show a preview alongside other information. In this case, you do not need to call the `Show` method. As soon as you set the `PrintPreviewControl.Document` property, the preview is generated. To clear the preview, set the `Document` property to `Nothing`. To refresh the preview, reassign the `Document` property. `PrintPreviewControl` shows only the preview pages, not any additional controls. However, you can add your own controls for zooming, tiling multiple pages, and so on. You simply need to adjust the `PrintPreviewControl` properties accordingly.

The Code

As an example, consider the form shown in Figure 10-10. It incorporates a `PrintPreviewControl` and allows the user to select a zoom setting.

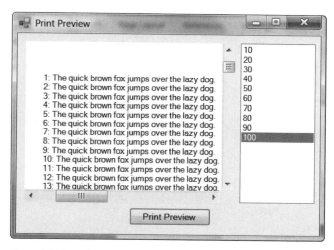

Figure 10-10. *Using the PrintPreviewControl in a custom window*

Here is the complete form code:

```vb
Imports System
Imports System.Drawing
Imports System.Windows.Forms
Imports System.Drawing.Printing

' All designed code is stored in the autogenerated partial
' class called Recipe10-17.Designer.vb.  You can see this
' file by selecting Show All Files in Solution Explorer.
Partial Public Class Recipe10_17

    Private doc As PrintDocument
    Private Sub Recipe10_17_Load(ByVal sender As Object, ➥
ByVal e As System.EventArgs) Handles Me.Load

        ' Set the allowed zoom settings.
        For i As Integer = 1 To 10
            lstZoom.Items.Add((i * 10).ToString)
        Next
```

```
        ' Create a document with 100 lines.
        Dim printText As String() = New String(100) {}

        For i As Integer = 1 To 100
            printText(i) = i.ToString
            printText(i) += ": The quick brown fox jumps over the lazy dog."
        Next

        Dim doc As New TextDocument(printText)

        AddHandler doc.PrintPage, AddressOf Doc_PrintPage

        ' Set the Zoom list to "100"
        lstZoom.Text = "100"

        ' Configure the PrintPreviewControl to show the page at 100%
        ' (Zoom = 1), and two pages vertically (Rows = 2).  Finally,
        ' we assign the doc variable to the Document property.
        PrintPreviewControl.Zoom = 1
        printPreviewControl.Rows = 2
        printPreviewControl.Document = doc

    End Sub

    Private Sub cmdPrint_Click(ByVal sender As System.Object, ➥
ByVal e As System.EventArgs) Handles cmdPrint.Click

        ' Set the zoom.
        PrintPreviewControl.Zoom = Single.Parse(lstZoom.Text) / 100

        ' Rebind the PrintDocument to refresh the preview.
        PrintPreviewControl.Document = doc

    End Sub

    Private Sub Doc_PrintPage(ByVal sender As Object, ByVal e As PrintPageEventArgs)

        ' Retrieve the document that sent this event.
        Dim doc As TextDocument = DirectCast(sender, TextDocument)

        ' Determine the font and determine the line height.
        Using fnt As New Font("Arial", 10)
            Dim lineHeight As Single = Font.GetHeight(e.Graphics)

            ' Create variables to hold position on page.
            Dim x As Single = e.MarginBounds.Left
            Dim y As Single = e.MarginBounds.Top

            ' Increment the page counter (to reflect the page that
            ' is about to be printed).
            doc.PageNumber += 1
```

```
                ' Print all the information that can fit on the page.
                ' This loop ends when the next line would go over the
                ' margin bounds, or there are no more lines to print.
                While ((y + lineHeight) < e.MarginBounds.Bottom And doc.Offset <= ➡
doc.Text.GetUpperBound(0))
                        e.Graphics.DrawString(doc.Text(doc.Offset), Font, ➡
Brushes.Black, x, y)

                        ' Move to the next line of data.
                        doc.Offset += 1

                        ' Move the equivalent of one line down the page.
                        y += lineHeight
                End While

                If doc.Offset < doc.Text.GetUpperBound(0) Then
                        ' There is still at least one more page.  Signal
                        ' this event to fire again.
                        e.HasMorePages = True
                End If

        End Using
    End Sub

End Class

' (TextDocument class code omitted. See recipe 10-15.)
```

10-18. Manage Print Jobs

Problem

You need to pause or resume a print job or a print queue.

Solution

Use Windows Management Instrumentation (WMI). You can retrieve information from the print queue using a query with the Win32_PrintJob class, and you can use the Pause and Resume methods of the WMI Win32_PrintJob and Win32_Printer classes to manage the queue.

How It Works

WMI allows you to retrieve a vast amount of system information using a query-like syntax. One of the tasks you can perform with WMI is to retrieve a list of outstanding print jobs, along with information about each one. You can also perform operations such as printing and resuming a job or all the jobs for a printer. To use WMI, you need to add a reference to the System.Management.dll assembly.

The Code

The following code shows a Windows application that interacts with the print queue. It performs a WMI query to get a list of all the outstanding print jobs on the computer and displays the job Name for each one in a list box. When the user selects the item, a more complete WMI query is performed, and additional details about the print job are displayed in a text box. Finally, the user can click the Pause/Resume button after selecting a job to change its status.

Remember that Windows permissions might prevent you from pausing or resuming print jobs created by another user. In fact, permissions might even prevent you from retrieving status information and could cause a security exception to be thrown.

```vb
Imports System
Imports System.Drawing
Imports System.Windows.Forms
Imports System.Management
Imports System.Collections
Imports System.text

'  All designed code is stored in the autogenerated partial
'  class called Recipe10-18.Designer.vb.  You can see this
'  file by selecting Show All Files in Solution Explorer.
Partial Public Class Recipe10_18

    Private Sub cmdRefresh_Click(ByVal sender As System.Object, ➡
ByVal e As System.EventArgs) Handles cmdRefresh.Click

        Call GetJobs()

    End Sub

    Private Sub Recipe10_18_Load(ByVal sender As Object, ➡
ByVal e As System.EventArgs) Handles Me.Load

        Call GetJobs()

    End Sub

    '  This helper method attempts to bind directly to the
    '  specified WMI job.  If successful, the found job is
    '  returned.
    Private Function GetSelectedJob(ByVal jobName As String) As ManagementObject

        Try
            '  Select the matching print job.
            Dim job As New ManagementObject("Win32_PrintJob=""" & jobName & """")
            job.Get()

            Return job
        Catch ex As Exception
            '  The job could not be found.  It has most likely already completed.
            Return Nothing
        End Try

    End Function

    '  This helper method performs a WMI query and returns all
    '  of the current WMI jobs.
    Private Sub GetJobs()
```

```vb
        ' Select all the outstanding print jobs.
        Dim query As String = "SELECT * FROM Win32_PrintJob"

        Using jobQuery As New ManagementObjectSearcher(query)
            Using jobs As ManagementObjectCollection = jobQuery.Get()
                ' Add the jobs in the queue to the list box.
                lstJobs.Items.Clear()
                txtJobInfo.Text = ""

                For Each job As ManagementObject In jobs
                    lstJobs.Items.Add(job("Name"))
                Next
            End Using
        End Using

    End Sub

    Private Sub lstJobs_SelectedIndexChanged(ByVal sender As Object, ➥
ByVal e As System.EventArgs) Handles lstJobs.SelectedIndexChanged

        Dim job As ManagementObject = GetSelectedJob(lstJobs.Text)

        If job Is Nothing Then
            txtJobInfo.Text = ""
            Exit Sub
        End If

        ' Display job information.
        Dim jobInfo As New StringBuilder

        jobInfo.AppendFormat("Document: {0}", job("Document").ToString)
        jobInfo.Append(Environment.NewLine)
        jobInfo.AppendFormat("DriverName: {0}", job("DriverName").ToString)
        jobInfo.Append(Environment.NewLine)
        jobInfo.AppendFormat("Status: {0}", job("Status").ToString)
        jobInfo.Append(Environment.NewLine)
        jobInfo.AppendFormat("Owner: {0}", job("Owner").ToString)
        jobInfo.Append(Environment.NewLine)
        jobInfo.AppendFormat("PagesPrinted: {0}", job("PagesPrinted").ToString)
        jobInfo.Append(Environment.NewLine)
        jobInfo.AppendFormat("TotalPages: {0}", job("TotalPages").ToString)

        If job("JobStatus") IsNot Nothing Then
            txtJobInfo.Text += Environment.NewLine
            txtJobInfo.Text += "JobStatus: " & job("JobStatus").ToString
        End If

        If job("StartTime") IsNot Nothing Then
            jobInfo.Append(Environment.NewLine)
            jobInfo.AppendFormat("StartTime: {0}", job("StartTime").ToString)
        End If
        txtJobInfo.Text = jobInfo.ToString

    End Sub
```

```vbnet
    Private Sub cmdPause_Click(ByVal sender As System.Object, ➥
ByVal e As System.EventArgs) Handles cmdPause.Click

        If lstJobs.SelectedIndex = -1 Then Exit Sub

        Dim job As ManagementObject = GetSelectedJob(lstJobs.Text)

        If job Is Nothing Then Exit Sub

        ' Ensure that the job is not already paused (1).
        If Not (CInt(job("StatusMask") And 1)) = 1 Then
            ' Attempt to pause the job.
            Dim returnValue As Integer = CType(job.InvokeMethod("Pause", ➥
Nothing), Integer)

            ' Display information about the return value.
            If returnValue = 0 Then
                MessageBox.Show("Successfully paused job.")
            ElseIf returnValue = 5 Then
                MessageBox.Show("Access denied.")
            Else
                MessageBox.Show("Unrecognized return value when pausing job.")
            End If
        End If

    End Sub

    Private Sub cmdResume_Click(ByVal sender As System.Object, ➥
ByVal e As System.EventArgs) Handles cmdResume.Click

        If lstJobs.SelectedIndex = -1 Then Exit Sub

        Dim job As ManagementObject = GetSelectedJob(lstJobs.Text)

        If job Is Nothing Then Exit Sub

        ' Check to ensure that the job is actually paused (1).
        If (CInt(job("StatusMask") And 1)) = 1 Then
            ' Attempt to resume the job.
            Dim returnValue As Integer = CType(job.InvokeMethod("Resume", ➥
Nothing), Integer)

            ' Display information about the return value.
            If returnValue = 0 Then
                MessageBox.Show("Successfully resumed job.")
            ElseIf returnValue = 5 Then
                MessageBox.Show("Access denied.")
            Else
                MessageBox.Show("Unrecognized return value when resuming job.")
            End If

        End If

    End Sub
End Class
```

Usage

Figure 10-11 shows an example of running this application.

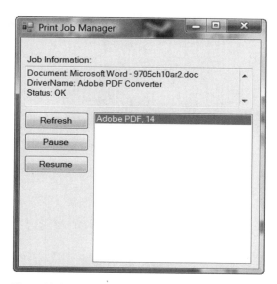

Figure 10-11. *Retrieving information from the print queue*

▓**Note** Other WMI methods you might use in a printing scenario include `AddPrinterConnection`, `SetDefaultPrinter`, `CancelAllJobs`, and `PrintTestPage`, all of which work with the `Win32_Printer` class. For more information about WMI, refer to `http://www.microsoft.com/whdc/system/pnppwr/wmi/default.mspx`.

CHAPTER 11

■■■

Networking and Remoting

The Microsoft .NET Framework includes a full set of classes for network programming. These classes support everything from socket-based programming with Transmission Control Protocol/Internet Protocol (TCP/IP) to downloading files and HTML pages from the Web over Hypertext Transfer Protocol (HTTP). Not only do these networking classes provide you with a rich set of tried-and-tested tools to use in your own distributed applications, they are also the foundation on which two high-level distributed programming models integral to the .NET Framework are built: remoting and web services.

Although remoting and web services share many similarities (for example, they both abstract cross-process and cross-machine calls as method invocations on remote objects), they also have fundamental differences. Web services are built using cross-platform standards and are based on the concept of XML messaging. Web services are executed by the ASP.NET runtime, which means they gain ASP.NET features such as output caching. This also means that web services are fundamentally stateless. Overall, web services are best suited when you need to cross platform boundaries (for example, with a Java client calling an ASP.NET web service) or trust boundaries (for example, in business-to-business transactions). Although web services are extremely useful and powerful, since they are built on ASP .NET, which is not covered in this book, they will not be covered in this chapter.

Remoting is a .NET-specific technology for distributed objects and is the successor to Distributed Component Object Model (DCOM). It's ideal for in-house systems in which all applications are built on the .NET platform, such as the backbone of an internal order-processing system. Remoting allows for different types of communication, including leaner binary messages and more efficient TCP/IP connections, which aren't supported by web services. In addition, remoting is the only technology that supports stateful objects and bidirectional communication through callbacks. It's also the only technology that allows you to send custom .NET objects over the wire.

Although not covered in detail in this chapter, it is extremely important to mention Windows Communication Foundation (WCF). WCF was first introduced in the .NET Framework 3.0 and represents a central framework that encompasses most communication functionality (such as the ones mentioned earlier) that previously were handled by various, unrelated namespaces. For more in-depth coverage of WCF, you can refer to other specific resources such as *Windows Communication Foundation Unleashed* by Craig McMurty, et al. (SAMS, 2007) or *Pro WCF: Practical Microsoft SOA Implementation (Pro)* by Chris Peiris and Dennis Mulder (Apress, 2007).

The recipes in this chapter cover the following:

- Obtaining configuration and network statistic information about the network interfaces on a computer, as well as detecting when network configuration changes occur (recipes 11-1 and 11-2)

- Downloading files from File Transfer Protocol (FTP) and HTTP servers (recipes 11-3, 11-4, and 11-6)

- Responding to HTTP requests from within your application (recipe 11-5)

- Sending e-mail messages with attachments using Simple Mail Transfer Protocol (SMTP) (recipe 11-7)

- Using the Domain Name System (DNS) to resolve a host name into an Internet Protocol (IP) address (recipe 11-8)

- Pinging an IP address to determine whether it is accessible and calculating round-trip communication speeds by sending it an Internet Control Message Protocol (ICMP) Echo request (recipe 11-9)

- Communicating between programs through the direct use of TCP in both synchronous and asynchronous communication models (recipes 11-10 and 11-11)

- Communicating between processes using named pipes (recipe 11-13)

- Creating remotable objects and registering them with the .NET Framework's remoting infrastructure (recipes 11-14 and 11-15)

- Hosting a remote object in Internet Information Services (IIS) (recipe 11-16)

- Controlling the lifetime and versioning of remotable objects (recipes 11-17 and 11-18)

- Consuming a Real Simple Syndication (RSS) feed (recipe 11-17)

11-1. Obtain Information About the Local Network Interface

Problem

You need to obtain information about the network adapters and network configuration of the local machine.

Solution

Call the Shared method GetAllNetworkInterfaces of the System.Net.NetworkInformation. NetworkInterface class to get an array of objects derived from the abstract class NetworkInterface. Each object represents a network interface available on the local machine. Use the members of each NetworkInterface object to retrieve configuration information and network statistics for that interface.

How It Works

The System.Net.NetworkInformation namespace, which was first introduced in .NET Framework 2.0, provides easy access to information about network configuration and statistics that was not readily available to .NET applications previously.

The primary means of retrieving network information are the properties and methods of the NetworkInterface class. You do not instantiate NetworkInterface objects directly. Instead, you call the Shared method NetworkInterface.GetAllNetworkInterfaces, which returns an array of NetworkInterface objects. Each object represents a single network interface on the local machine. You can then obtain network information and statistics about the interface using the NetworkInterface members described in Table 11-1.

■**Tip** The System.Net.NetworkInformation.IPGlobalProperties class (first introduced in .NET Framework 2.0) also provides access to useful information about the network configuration of the local computer.

Table 11-1. *Members of the NetworkInterface Class*

Member	Description
Properties	
Description	Gets a String that provides a general description of the interface.
Id	Gets a String that contains the unique identifier of the interface.
IsReceiveOnly	Gets a Boolean indicating whether the interface can only receive or can both send and receive data.
Name	Gets a String containing the name of the interface.
NetworkInterfaceType	Gets a value from the System.Net.NetworkInformation. NetworkInterfaceType enumeration that identifies the type of interface. Common values include Ethernet, FastEthernetT, and Loopback.
OperationalStatus	Gets a value from the System.Net.NetworkInformation. OperationalStatus enumeration that identifies the status of the interface. Common values include Down and Up.
Speed	Gets a Long that identifies the speed (in bits per second) of the interface as reported by the adapter, not based on dynamic calculation.
SupportsMulticast	Gets a Boolean indicating whether the interface is enabled to receive multicast packets.
Methods	
GetIPProperties	Returns a System.Net.NetworkInformation.IPInterfaceProperties object that provides access to the TCP/IP configuration information for the interface. Properties of the IPInterfaceProperties object provide access to WINS, DNS, gateway, and IP address configuration.
GetIPv4Statistics	Returns a System.Net.NetworkInformation.IPv4InterfaceStatistics object that provides access to the TCP/IP v4 statistics for the interface. The properties of the IPv4InterfaceStatistics object provide access to information about bytes sent and received, packets sent and received, discarded packets, and packets with errors.
GetPhysicalAddress	Returns a System.Net.NetworkInformation.PhysicalAddress object that provides access to the physical address of the interface. You can obtain the physical address as a Byte array using the method PhysicalAddress.GetAddressBytes or as a String using PhysicalAddress. ToString.
Supports	Returns a Boolean indicating whether the interface supports a specified protocol. You specify the protocol using a value from the System. Net.NetworkInformation.NetworkInterfaceComponent enumeration. Possible values include IPv4 and IPv6.

The NetworkInterface class also provides two other Shared members that you will find useful:

- The Shared property LoopbackInterfaceIndex returns an Integer identifying the index of the loopback interface within the NetworkInterface array returned by GetAllNetworkInterfaces.

- The Shared method GetIsNetworkAvailable returns a Boolean indicating whether any network connection is available; that is, has an OperationalStatus value of Up.

The Code

The following example uses the members of the NetworkInterface class to display information about all the network interfaces on the local machine:

```
Imports System
Imports System.Net.NetworkInformation

Namespace Apress.VisualBasicRecipes.Chapter11
    Public Class Recipe11_01

        Public Shared Sub Main()

            ' Only proceed if there is a network available.
            If NetworkInterface.GetIsNetworkAvailable Then
                ' Get the set of all NetworkInterface objects for the local
                ' machine.
                Dim interfaces As NetworkInterface() = ➥
NetworkInterface.GetAllNetworkInterfaces

                ' Iterate through the interfaces and display information.
                For Each ni As NetworkInterface In interfaces
                    ' Report basic interface information.
                    Console.WriteLine("Interface Name: {0}", ni.Name)
                    Console.WriteLine("    Description: {0}", ni.Description)
                    Console.WriteLine("    ID: {0}", ni.Id)
                    Console.WriteLine("    Type: {0}", ni.NetworkInterfaceType)
                    Console.WriteLine("    Speed: {0}", ni.Speed)
                    Console.WriteLine("    Status: {0}", ni.OperationalStatus)

                    ' Report physical address.
                    Console.WriteLine("    Physical Address: {0}", ➥
ni.GetPhysicalAddress().ToString)

                    ' Report network statistics for the interface.
                    Console.WriteLine("    Bytes Sent: {0}", ➥
ni.GetIPv4Statistics().BytesSent)
                    Console.WriteLine("    Bytes Received: {0}", ➥
ni.GetIPv4Statistics.BytesReceived)

                    ' Report IP configuration.
                    Console.WriteLine("    IP Addresses:")
                    For Each addr As UnicastIPAddressInformation In ➥
ni.GetIPProperties.UnicastAddresses
                        Console.WriteLine("        - {0} (lease expires {1})", ➥
addr.Address, DateTime.Now.AddSeconds(addr.DhcpLeaseLifetime))
```

```
                Next
                Console.WriteLine(Environment.NewLine)

            Next
        Else
            Console.WriteLine("No network available.")
        End If


        ' Wait to continue.
        Console.WriteLine(Environment.NewLine)
        Console.WriteLine("Main method complete.  Press Enter.")
        Console.ReadLine()

    End Sub

    End Class
End Namespace
```

11-2. Detect Changes in Network Connectivity

Problem

You need a mechanism to check whether changes to the network occur during the life of your application.

Solution

Add handlers to the Shared NetworkAddressChanged and NetworkAvailabilityChanged events implemented by the System.Net.NetworkInformation.NetworkChange class. The My object also offers a shared NetworkAvailabilityChanged event. This event is implemented by the My.Computer.Network class, which is part of the Microsoft.VisualBasic.Devices namespace. (See Chapter 5 for more information about the My object.)

How It Works

The NetworkChange class provides an easy-to-use mechanism that allows applications to be aware of changes to network addresses and general network availability. This allows your applications to adapt dynamically to the availability and configuration of the network.

The NetworkAvailabilityChanged event fires when a change occurs to general network availability. The NetworkAvailabilityChangedEventHandler delegate is used to handle this event and is passed a NetworkAvailabilityEventArgs object when the event fires. The NetworkAvailabilityEventArgs. IsAvailable property returns a Boolean value indicating whether the network is available or unavailable following the change.

The NetworkAvailabilityChanged event, of the My object, works in the same way as the matching event in the NetworkChange class. This version of the event uses the NetworkAvailableEventHandler delegate to handle this event, but its event arguments parameter is a NetworkAvailableEventArgs object. Also, the property for retrieving network availability is named IsNetworkAvailable.

The NetworkAddressChanged event fires when the IP address of a network interface changes. An instance of the NetworkAddressChangedEventHandler delegate is required to handle these events. No event-specific arguments are passed to the event handler, which must call

NetworkInterface.GetAllNetworkInterfaces (discussed in recipe 11-1) to determine what has changed and to take appropriate action. The My object does not offer an equivalent for this event.

The Code

The following example demonstrates how to use handlers that catch NetworkAddressChanged and NetworkAvailabilityChanged events and then displays status information to the console:

```
Imports System
Imports System.Net.NetworkInformation

Namespace Apress.VisualBasicRecipes.Chapter11
    Public Class Recipe11_02

        ' Declare a method to handle NetworkAvailabilityChanged events.
        Private Shared Sub NetworkAvailabilityChanged(ByVal sender As Object, ➥
ByVal e As NetworkAvailabilityEventArgs)

            '  Report whether the network is now available or unavailable.
            If e.IsAvailable Then
                Console.WriteLine("Network Available")
            Else
                Console.WriteLine("Network Unavailable")
            End If

        End Sub

        ' Declare a method to handle NetworkAddressChanged events.
        Private Shared Sub NetworkAddressChanged(ByVal sender As Object, ➥
ByVal e As EventArgs)

            Console.WriteLine("Current IP Addresses:")

            '  Iterate through the interfaces and display information.
            For Each ni As NetworkInterface In ➥
NetworkInterface.GetAllNetworkInterfaces
                For Each addr As UnicastIPAddressInformation In ➥
ni.GetIPProperties.UnicastAddresses
                    Console.WriteLine("        - {0} (lease expires {1})", ➥
addr.Address, DateTime.Now.AddSeconds(addr.DhcpLeaseLifetime))
                Next
            Next

        End Sub

        Public Shared Sub Main()

            '  Add the handlers to the NetworkChange events.
            AddHandler NetworkChange.NetworkAvailabilityChanged, ➥
AddressOf NetworkAvailabilityChanged
            AddHandler NetworkChange.NetworkAddressChanged, ➥
AddressOf NetworkAddressChanged
```

```
' Wait to continue.
Console.WriteLine(Environment.NewLine)
Console.WriteLine("Press Enter to stop waiting for network events.")
Console.ReadLine()

End Sub

End Class
End Namespace
```

To use the My object equivalent of the NetworkAvailabilityChanged event, replace the NetworkAvailabilityChanged handler with the following:

```
' Declare a method to handle NetworkAvailabilityChanged events.
Private Shared Sub NetworkAvailabilityChanged(ByVal sender As Object, ➥
ByVal e As Microsoft.VisualBasic.Devices.NetworkAvailableEventArgs)

    ' Report whether the network is now available or unavailable.
    If e.IsNetworkAvailable Then
        Console.WriteLine("Network Available")
    Else
        Console.WriteLine("Network Unavailable")
    End If

End Sub
```

You also need to replace the current call to AddHandler with this:

```
AddHandler My.Computer.Network.NetworkAvailabilityChanged, AddressOf ➥
NetworkAvailabilityChanged
```

11-3. Download Data over HTTP or FTP

Problem

You need a quick, simple way to download data from the Internet using HTTP or FTP.

Solution

Use the methods of the System.Net.WebClient class or the DownloadFile method of the My.Computer. Network class. (Refer to Chapter 5 for more information about the My object.)

How It Works

The .NET Framework provides several mechanisms for transferring data over the Internet. One of the easiest approaches is to use the System.Net.WebClient class. WebClient provides many high-level methods that simplify the transfer of data by specifying the source as a uniform resource identifier (URI); Table 11-2 summarizes them. The URI can specify that a file (file://), FTP (ftp://), HTTP ((http://), or HTTPS (https://) protocol be used to download the resource.

Table 11-2. *Data Download Methods of the WebClient Class*

Method	Description
OpenRead	Returns a System.IO.Stream that provides access to the data from a specified URI.
OpenReadAsync	Same as OpenRead, but performs the data transfer using a thread-pool thread so that the calling thread does not block. Add an event handler to the OpenReadCompleted event to receive notification that the operation has completed.
DownloadData	Returns a Byte array that contains the data from a specified URI.
DownloadDataAsync	Same as DownloadData, but performs the data transfer using a thread-pool thread so that the calling thread does not block. Add an event handler to the DownloadDataCompleted event to receive notification that the operation has completed.
DownloadFile	Downloads data from a specified URI and saves it to a specified local file.
DownloadFileAsync	Same as DownloadFile, but performs the data transfer using a thread-pool thread so that the calling thread does not block. Add an event handler to the DownloadFileCompleted event to receive notification that the operation has completed.
DownloadString	Returns a String that contains the data from a specified URI.
DownloadStringAsync	Same as DownloadString, but performs the data transfer using a thread-pool thread so that the calling thread does not block. Add an event handler to the DownloadStringCompleted event to receive notification that the operation has completed.

The asynchronous download methods allow you to download data as a background task using a thread from the thread pool (discussed in recipe 4-1). When the download is finished or fails, the thread calls the appropriate event on the WebClient object, which you can handle using a method that matches the signature of the System.ComponentModel.AsyncCompletedEventHandler delegate if you don't want to derive a type from WebClient and override the virtual method. However, the WebClient object can handle only a single concurrent asynchronous download, making a WebClient object suitable for the background download of large single sets of data but not for the download of many files concurrently. (You could, of course, create multiple WebClient objects to handle multiple downloads.) You can cancel the outstanding asynchronous download using the method CancelAsync.

■**Tip** The WebClient class derives from System.ComponentModel.Component, so you can add it to the Visual Studio 2008 Form Designer Toolbox in order to allow you to easily set the properties or define the event handlers in a Windows Forms–based application.

If you need to download only a file, the My object also offers a DownloadFile method. As with the matching method in the WebClient class, you can specify a String or Uri for the address parameter. The My version of the method lets you specify a username and password or a System.Net.ICredential object, while the WebClient version requires you to use the Credentials property of the class, which accepts only an ICredential object. Unlike with the WebClient version, you can also specify a time-out using the connectionTimeout parameter or show a non-modal progress dialog box (which includes a Cancel button) using the showUI parameter.

The Code

The following example downloads a specified resource from a URI as a string and, since it is an
HTML page, parses it for any fully qualified URLs that refer to GIF files. It then downloads each of
these files to the local hard drive.

```vb
Imports System
Imports System.IO
Imports System.Net
Imports System.Text.RegularExpressions

Namespace Apress.VisualBasicRecipes.Chapter11
    Public Class Recipe11_03

        Public Shared Sub Main()

            ' Specify the URI of the resource to parse.
            Dim remoteUri As String = "http://www.msdn.com"

            ' Create a WebClient to perform the download.
            Dim client As New WebClient

            Console.WriteLine("Downloading {0}", remoteUri)

            ' Perform the download getting the resource as a string.
            Dim str As String = client.DownloadString(remoteUri)

            ' Use a regular expression to extract all fully qualified
            ' URIs that refer to GIF files.
            Dim matches As MatchCollection = Regex.Matches(str, ➥
"http\S+[^-,;:?]\.gif")

            ' Try to download each referenced GIF file.
            For Each expMatch As Match In matches
                For Each grp As Group In expMatch.Groups
                    ' Determine the local filename.
                    Dim downloadedFile As String = ➥
grp.Value.Substring(grp.Value.LastIndexOf("/") + 1)

                    Try
                        ' Download and store the file.
                        Console.WriteLine("Downloading {0} to file {1}", ➥
grp.Value, downloadedFile)

                        client.DownloadFile(New Uri(grp.Value), downloadedFile)
                    Catch ex As Exception
                        Console.WriteLine("Failed to download {0}", grp.Value)
                    End Try
                Next
            Next

            ' Wait to continue.
            Console.WriteLine(Environment.NewLine)
            Console.WriteLine("Main method complete.  Press Enter.")
            Console.ReadLine()
```

```
        End Sub

    End Class
End Namespace
```

■Note The regular expression used in the example is simple and is not designed to cater to all possible URL structures. Recipes 2-5 and 2-6 discuss regular expressions.

Changing the code sample to use the My version of DownloadFile is as simple as replacing client.DownloadFile with My.Computer.Network.DownloadFile.

Notes

You may also want to upload data to resources specified as a URI, although this technique is not as commonly used as the other approaches discussed in this recipe. The WebClient class also provides the following methods for performing uploads that are equivalent to the download methods discussed previously:

- OpenWrite
- OpenWriteAsync
- UploadData
- UploadDataAsync
- UploadFile
- UploadFileAsync
- UploadString
- UploadStringAsync

Not to be outdone, My offers the UploadFile method, which is used in a similar fashion to the DownloadFile method.

11-4. Download a File and Process It Using a Stream

Problem

You need to retrieve a file from a web site, but you do not want to save it directly to the hard drive, or you do not have permission to do so. Instead, you need to process the data in your application directly in memory.

Solution

Use the System.Net.WebRequest class to create your request, the System.Net.WebResponse class to retrieve the response from the web server, and some form of reader (typically a System.IO.StreamReader for HTML or text data, or a System.IO.BinaryReader for a binary file) to parse the response data.

■ Note You could also use the OpenRead method of the System.Net.WebClient class to open a stream. However, the additional capabilities of the WebRequest and WebResponse classes give you more control over the operation of the network request.

How It Works

Opening and downloading a stream of data from the Web using the WebRequest and WebResponse classes takes the following four basic steps:

1. Use the Shared method Create of the WebRequest class to specify the page you want. This method returns a WebRequest-derived object, depending on the type of URI you specify. For example, if you use an HTTP or HTTPS URI (with the scheme http:// or https://), you will create an HttpWebRequest instance. If you use a file system URI (with the scheme file://), you will create a FileWebRequest instance. You can also use an FTP URI (with the scheme ftp://), which will create an FtpWebRequest.
2. Use the GetResponse method of the WebRequest object to return a WebResponse object for the page. If the request times out, a System.Net.WebException will be thrown. You can configure the time-out for the network request through the WebRequest.Timeout property in milliseconds (the default value is 10000).
3. Create a StreamReader or a BinaryReader that wraps the stream returned by the WebResponse.GetResponseStream method. In some cases, you might have to use other means to wrap the returning stream, such as the Image.FromStream method.
4. Perform any steps you need to with the stream contents.

The Code

The following example retrieves and displays a graphic and the HTML content of a web page.

```
Imports System
Imports System.Net
Imports System.IO
Imports System.Drawing
Imports System.Windows.Forms

'  All designed code is stored in the autogenerated partial
'  class called Recipe11-04.Designer.vb. You can see this
'  file by selecting Show All Files in Solution Explorer.
Public Class Recipe11_04

    Private Sub Recipe11_04_Load(ByVal sender As Object, ➥
ByVal e As System.EventArgs) Handles Me.Load

        Dim picUri As String = "http://www.apress.com/img/img05/Hex_RGB4.jpg"
        Dim htmlUri As String = "http://www.apress.com"

        '  Create the requests.
        Dim requestPic As WebRequest = WebRequest.Create(picUri)
        Dim requestHtml As WebRequest = WebRequest.Create(htmlUri)
```

```
'  Get the responses. This takes the most significant amount of
'  time, particularly if the file is large, because the whole
'  response is retrieved.
Dim responsePic As WebResponse = requestPic.GetResponse
Dim responseHtml As WebResponse = requestHtml.GetResponse

'  Read the image from the response stream.
picturebox1.Image = Image.FromStream(responsePic.GetResponseStream)

'  Read the text from the response stream.
Using r As New StreamReader(responseHtml.GetResponseStream)
    textbox1.text = r.ReadToEnd
End Using

    End Sub

End Class
```

Usage

Running the example will display, as shown in Figure 11-1, the image and HTML data retrieved from the target locations.

Figure 11-1. *Downloading content from the Web using a stream*

11-5. Respond to HTTP Requests from Your Application

Problem

You want your application to be able to respond to HTTP requests programmatically.

Solution

Use the System.Net.HttpListener class, which was first introduced in .NET Framework 2.0.

■**Note** Your application must be running on Windows XP Service Pack 2 (or later) or Windows 2003 (or later) to use the HttpListener class; otherwise, a System.PlatformNotSupportedException will be thrown when you try to instantiate it. Check the Boolean returned by the Shared property HttpListener.IsSupported to see whether support is available.

How It Works

The HttpListener class provides an easy-to-use mechanism through which your programs can accept and respond to HTTP requests. To use the HttpListener class, follow these steps:

1. Instantiate an HttpListener object.

2. Configure the URI prefixes that the HttpListener object will handle using the Prefixes property. A URI prefix is a string that represents the starting portion of a URI, which consists of the schema type (such as http:// or https://), a host, and optionally a path and port. The Prefixes property returns a System.Net.HttpListenerPrefixCollection collection to which you can add URI prefixes using the Add method. Each prefix must end with a forward slash (/), or a System.ArgumentException is thrown. If you specify a URL prefix that is already being handled, a System.Net.HttpListenerException is thrown. When a client makes a request, the request will be handled by the listener configured with the prefix that most closely matches the client's requested URL.

3. Start the HttpListener object by calling its Start method. You must call Start before the HttpListener object can accept and process HTTP requests.

4. Accept client requests using the GetContext method of the HttpListener object. The GetContext method will block the calling thread until a request is received and then returns a System.Net. HttpListenerContext object. Alternatively, you can use the BeginGetContext and EndGetContext methods to listen for requests on a thread-pool thread. When a request is received, the System. AsynchCallback delegate specified as the argument to the BeginGetContext method will be called and passed the HttpListenerContext object. Regardless of how it is obtained, the HttpListenerContext objects implements three read-only properties critical to the handling of a client request:

   - The Request property returns a System.Net.HttpListenerRequest through which you can access details of the client's request.

   - The Response property returns a System.Net.HttpListenerResponse through which you can configure the response to send to the client.

   - The User property returns an instance of a type implementing System.Security.Principal. IPrincipal, which you can use to obtain identity, authentication, and authorization information about the user associated with the request.

5. Configure the HTTP response through the members of the HttpListenerResponse object accessible through the HttpListenerContext.Response property.

6. Send the response by calling the Close method of the HttpListenerResponse object.

7. Once you have finished processing HTTP requests, call Stop on the HttpListener object to stop accepting more requests and pause the listener. Call Close to shut down the HttpListener object, which will wait until all outstanding requests have been processed, or call Abort to terminate the HttpListener object without waiting for requests to be complete.

■**Note** When using the HttpListener class, be sure you are running as a system administrator because higher-level rights are required to use it. If you are running under Windows Vista, you have the option of configuring the User Access Control (UAC) settings (refer to recipe 9-21 for more information on this) to ensure your application appropriately demands administrative rights.

The Code

The following example demonstrates how to use the HttpListener class to process HTTP requests. The example starts listening for five requests concurrently using the asynchronous BeginGetContext method and handles the response to each request by calling the RequestHandler method. Each time a request is handled, a new call is made to BeginGetContext so that you always have the capacity to handle up to five requests.

To open a connection to the example from your browser, enter the URL http://localhost:19080/ VisualBasicRecipes/ or http://localhost:20000/Recipe11-05/, and you will see the response from the appropriate request handler.

```vb
Imports System
Imports System.IO
Imports System.Net
Imports System.Text
Imports System.Threading

Namespace Apress.VisualBasicRecipes.Chapter11
    Public Class Recipe11_05

        ' Configure the maximum number of requests that can be
        ' handled concurrently.
        Private Shared maxRequestHandlers As Integer = 5

        ' An integer used to assign each HTTP request handler a unique
        ' identifier.
        Private Shared requestHandlerID As Integer = 0

        ' The HttpListener is the class that provides all the
        ' capabilities to receive and process HTTP requests.
        Private Shared listener As HttpListener

        Public Shared Sub Main()

            ' Quit gracefully if this feature is not supported.
            If Not HttpListener.IsSupported Then
                Console.WriteLine("You must be running this example on Windows" & ➡
" XP SP2, Windows Server 2003, or higher to create an HttpListener.")

                Exit Sub
            End If

            ' Create the HttpListener.
            listener = New HttpListener
```

```vbnet
        ' Configure the URI prefixes that will map to the HttpListener.
        listener.Prefixes.Add("http://localhost:19080/VisualBasicRecipes/")
        listener.Prefixes.Add("http://localhost:20000/Recipe11-05/")

        ' Start the HttpListener before listening for incoming requests.
        Console.WriteLine("Starting HTTP Server")
        listener.Start()
        Console.WriteLine("HTTP Server started")
        Console.WriteLine(Environment.NewLine)

        ' Create a number of asynchronous request handlers up to
        ' the configurable maximum. Give each a unique identifier.
        For count As Integer = 1 To maxRequestHandlers
            listener.BeginGetContext(AddressOf RequestHandler, ➥
  "RequestHandler_" & Interlocked.Increment(requestHandlerID))
        Next

        ' Wait for the user to stop the HttpListener.
        Console.WriteLine("Press Enter to stop the HTTP Server.")
        Console.ReadLine()

        ' Stop accepting new requests.
        listener.Stop()

        ' Terminate the HttpListener without processing current requests.
        listener.Abort()

        ' Wait to continue.
        Console.WriteLine(Environment.NewLine)
        Console.WriteLine("Main method complete.  Press Enter.")
        Console.ReadLine()

    End Sub

    ' A method to asynchronously process individual requests
    ' and send responses.
    Private Shared Sub RequestHandler(ByVal result As IAsyncResult)

        Console.WriteLine("{0}: Activated.", result.AsyncState)

        Try
            ' Obtain the HttpListenerContext for the new request.
            Dim context As HttpListenerContext = listener.EndGetContext(result)

            Console.WriteLine("{0}: Processing HTTP Request from {1} ({2}).", ➥
  result.AsyncState, context.Request.UserHostName, context.Request.RemoteEndPoint)

            ' Build the response using a StreamWriter feeding the
            ' Response.OutputStream.
            Dim sw As New StreamWriter(context.Response.OutputStream, ➥
  Encoding.UTF8)
```

```vb
            sw.WriteLine("<html>")
            sw.WriteLine("<head>")
            sw.WriteLine("<title>Visual Basic Recipes</title>")
            sw.WriteLine("</head>")
            sw.WriteLine("<body>")
            sw.WriteLine("Recipe 11-05: " & result.AsyncState)
            sw.WriteLine("</body>")
            sw.WriteLine("</html>")
            sw.Flush()

            ' Configure the response.
            context.Response.ContentType = "text/html"
            context.Response.ContentEncoding = Encoding.UTF8

            ' Close the response to send it to the client.
            context.Response.Close()

            Console.WriteLine("{0}: Sent HTTP response.", result.AsyncState)
        Catch ex As ObjectDisposedException
            Console.WriteLine("{0}: HttpListener disposed--shutting down.", ➥
result.AsyncState)
        Finally
            ' Start another handler unless the HttpListener is closing.
            If listener.IsListening Then
                Console.WriteLine("{0}: Creating new request handler.", ➥
result.AsyncState)

                listener.BeginGetContext(AddressOf RequestHandler, ➥
"RequestHandler_" & Interlocked.Increment(requestHandlerID))
            End If
        End Try

    End Sub

    End Class
End Namespace
```

11-6. Get an HTML Page from a Site That Requires Authentication

Problem

You need to retrieve a file from a web site, but the web site requires that you provide credentials for the purpose of authentication.

Solution

Use the System.Net.WebRequest and System.Net.WebResponse classes as described in recipe 11-4. Before making the request, configure the WebRequest.Credentials and WebRequest.Certificates properties with the necessary authentication information.

■**Tip** You could also use the `System.Net.WebClient` class (discussed in recipe 11-3). It also has `Credentials` and `Certificates` properties that allow you to associate user credentials with a web request.

How It Works

Some web sites require user authentication information. When connecting through a browser, this information might be submitted transparently (for example, on a local intranet site that uses Integrated Windows authentication), or the browser might request this information with a login dialog box. When accessing a web page programmatically, your code needs to submit this information. The approach you use depends on the type of authentication implemented by the web site:

- If the web site is using basic or digest authentication, you can transmit a username and password combination by manually creating a new `System.Net.NetworkCredential` object, which implements the `ICredentials` and `ICredentialsByHost` interfaces, and assigning it to the `WebRequest.Credentials` property. With digest authentication, you may also supply a domain name.

- If the web site is using Integrated Windows authentication, you can take the same approach and manually create a new `System.Net.NetworkCredential` object. Alternatively, you can retrieve the current user login information from the `System.Net.CredentialCache` object using the `DefaultCredentials` property.

- If the web site requires a client certificate, you can load the certificate from a file using the `System.Security.Cryptography.X509Certificates.X509Certificate2` class and add that to the `HttpWebRequest.ClientCertificates` collection. Since the base `WebRequest` class does not have the `ClientCertifcates` collection, you must explicitly cast it to an `HttpWebRequest` object.

- You can load an X.509 certificate from a certificate store using the class `System.Security.Cryptography.X509Certificates.X509Store` defined in the `System.Security` assembly. You can either find a certificate in the store programmatically using the `X509Store.Certificates.Find` method or present users with a Windows dialog box and allow them to select the certificate. To present a dialog box, pass a collection of X.509 certificates contained in an `X509Certificate2Collection` object to the `SelectFromCollection` method of the `System.Security.Cryptography.X509Certificates.X509Certificate2UI` class.

The Code

The following example demonstrates all four of the basic approaches described previously. Note that you need to add a reference to the `System.Security` assembly.

```
Imports System
Imports System.Net
Imports System.Security.Cryptography.X509Certificates

Namespace Apress.VisualBasicRecipes.Chapter11
    Public Class Recipe11_06

        Public Shared Sub Main()

            ' Create a WebRequest that authenticates the user with a
            ' username and password combination over basic authentication.
            Dim requestA As WebRequest = WebRequest.Create("http:" & ➥
```

```vbnet
"//www.somesite.com")
            requestA.Credentials = New NetworkCredential("username", "password")

            ' Create a WebRequest that authenticates the current user
            ' with Integrated Windows authentication.
            Dim requestB As WebRequest = WebRequest.Create("http:" & ➥
"//www.somesite.com")
            requestB.Credentials = CredentialCache.DefaultCredentials

            ' Create a WebRequest that authenticates the user with a client
            ' certificate loaded from a file.
            Dim requestC As HttpWebRequest = ➥
DirectCast(WebRequest.Create("http://www.somesite.com"), HttpWebRequest)
            Dim cert1 = X509Certificate.CreateFromCertFile("..\..\" & ➥
"TestCertificate.cer")
            requestC.ClientCertificates.Add(cert1)

            ' Create a WebRequest that authenticates the user with a client
            ' certificate loaded from a certificate store. Try to find a
            ' certificate with a specific subject, but if it is not found,
            ' present the user with a dialog so he can select the certificate
            ' to use from his personal store.
            Dim requestD As HttpWebRequest = ➥
DirectCast(WebRequest.Create("http://www.somesite.com"), HttpWebRequest)
            Dim store As New X509Store
            Dim certs As X509Certificate2Collection = ➥
store.Certificates.Find(X509FindType.FindBySubjectName, "Todd Herman", False)

            If certs.Count = 1 Then
                requestD.ClientCertificates.Add(certs(0))
            Else
                certs = X509Certificate2UI.SelectFromCollection( ➥
store.Certificates,"Select Certificate", "Select the certificate to use for " & ➥
"authentication.", X509SelectionFlag.SingleSelection)

                If Not certs.Count = 0 Then
                    requestD.ClientCertificates.Add(certs(0))
                End If
            End If

            ' Now issue the request and process the responses...

        End Sub

    End Class
End Namespace
```

11-7. Send E-mail Using SMTP

Problem

You need to send e-mail using an SMTP server.

Solution

Use the SmtpClient and MailMessage classes in the System.Net.Mail namespace.

How It Works

An instance of the SmtpClient class provides the mechanism through which you communicate with the SMTP server. You configure the SmtpClient using the properties described in Table 11-3.

Table 11-3. *Properties of the SmtpClient Class*

Property	Description
ClientCertificates	Gets a System.Security.Cryptography.X509Certificates. X509CertificatesCollection to which you add the certificates to use for communicating with the SMTP server (if required).
Credentials	Gets or sets an implementation of the System.Net. ICredentialsByHost interface that represents the credentials to use to gain access to the SMTP server. The CredentialCache and NetworkCredential classes implement the ICredentialsByHost interface. Use NetworkCredential if you want to specify a single set of credentials and CredentialCache if you want to specify more than one.
EnableSsl	Gets or sets a Boolean value that indicates whether the SmtpClient should use Secure Sockets Layer (SSL) to communicate with the SMTP server. The default value is False.
Host	Gets or sets a String containing the host name or IP address of the SMTP server to use to send e-mail.
Port	Gets or sets an Integer value containing the port number to connect to on the SMTP server. The default value is 25.
Timeout	Gets or sets an Integer value containing the time-out in milliseconds when attempting to send e-mail. The default is 100 seconds.
UseDefaultCredentials	Gets or sets a Boolean value indicating whether the default user credentials are used when communicating with the SMTP server. If true, the credentials passed to the SMTP server are automatically obtained from the Shared property CredentialCache. DefaultCredentials. The default value is False.

■**Tip** You can specify default settings for the SmtpClient in the <mailSettings> section of your machine or application configuration files. Configurable default values include the host, port, username, password, and whether or not the default credentials should be used.

Mail messages are represented by MailMessage objects, which you instantiate and then configure using the members summarized in Table 11-4.

Table 11-4. *Properties of the MailMessage Class*

Property	Description
Attachments	Gets or sets a System.Net.Mail.AttachmentCollection containing the set of attachments for the e-mail message. A System.Net.Mail.Attachment object represents each attachment. You can create Attachment objects from files or streams, and you can configure the encoding and content type for each attachment.
Bcc	Gets or sets a System.Net.Mail.MailAddressCollection containing the blind carbon copy addresses for the e-mail message. The MailAddressCollection contains one or more MailAddress objects.
Body	Gets or sets a String value that contains the body text of the e-mail message.
BodyEncoding	Gets or sets a System.Text.Encoding object that specifies the encoding for the body of the e-mail message. The default value is Nothing, resulting in a default encoding of us-ascii, which is equivalent to the Encoding object returned by the Shared property Encoding.ASCII.
CC	Gets or sets a System.Net.Mail.MailAddressCollection containing the carbon copy addresses for the e-mail message. The MailAddressCollection contains one or more MailAddress objects.
From	Gets or sets a System.Net.Mail.MailAddress containing the from address for the e-mail message.
IsBodyHtml	Gets or sets a Boolean value identifying whether the body of the e-mail message contains HTML.
ReplyTo	Gets or sets a System.Net.Mail.MailAddress containing the reply address for the e-mail message.
Subject	Gets or sets a String containing the subject for the e-mail message.
SubjectEncoding	Gets or sets a System.Text.Encoding object that specifies the encoding used to encode the subject of the e-mail subject. The default value is Nothing, resulting in a default encoding of us-ascii, which is equivalent to the Encoding object returned by the Shared property Encoding.ASCII.
To	Gets or sets a System.Net.Mail.MailAddressCollection containing the destination addresses for the e-mail message. The MailAddressCollection contains one or more MailAddress objects.

Once you have configured the SmtpClient, you can send your MailMessage objects using the SmtpClient.Send method, which will cause your code to block until the send operation is completed or fails. Alternatively, you can send mail using a thread from the thread pool by calling the SendAsync method. When you call SendAsync, your code will be free to continue other processing while the e-mail is sent. Add an event handler to the SendCompleted event to receive notification that the asynchronous send has completed.

The Code

The following example demonstrates how to use the SmtpClient class to send an e-mail message with multiple attachments to a set of recipients whose e-mail addresses are specified as command-line arguments.

```
Imports System
Imports System.Net
Imports System.Net.Mail

Namespace Apress.VisualBasicRecipes.Chapter11
    Public Class Recipe11_07

        Public Shared Sub Main(ByVal args As String())

            ' Create and configure the SmtpClient that will send the mail.
            ' Specify the host name of the SMTP server and the port used
            ' to send mail.
            Dim client As New SmtpClient("mail.somecompany.com", 25)

            ' Configure the SmtpClient with the credentials used to connect
            ' to the SMTP server.
            client.Credentials = New NetworkCredential("user@somecompany.com", ➥
"password")

            ' Create the MailMessage to represent the e-mail being sent.
            Using msg As New MailMessage

                ' Configure the e-mail sender and subject.
                msg.From = New MailAddress("author@visual-basic-recipes.com")
                msg.Subject = "Greetings from Visual Basic Recipes"

                ' Configure the e-mail body.
                msg.Body = "This is a message from Recipe 11-07 of Visual " & ➥
"Basic Recipes.  Attached is the source file and the binary for the recipe."

                ' Attach the files to the e-mail message and set their MIME type.
                msg.Attachments.Add(New Attachment("..\..\Recipe11-07.vb", ➥
"text/plain"))
                msg.Attachments.Add(New Attachment("Recipe11-07.exe", ➥
"application/octet-stream"))

                ' Iterate through the set of recipients specified on the
                ' command line. Add all addresses with the correct structure
                ' as recipients.
                For Each arg As String In args
                    ' Create a MailAdress from each value on the command line
                    ' and add it to the set of recipients.
```

```
                        Try
                            msg.To.Add(New MailAddress(arg))
                        Catch ex As FormatException
                            ' Proceed to the next specified recipient.
                            Console.WriteLine("{0}: Error -- {1}", arg, ex.Message)
                            Continue For
                        End Try

                        ' Send the message.
                        client.Send(msg)
                    Next

                End Using

                ' Wait to continue.
                Console.WriteLine(Environment.NewLine)
                Console.WriteLine("Main method complete.  Press Enter.")
                Console.ReadLine()

            End Sub

        End Class
    End Namespace
```

11-8. Resolve a Host Name to an IP Address

Problem

You want to determine the IP address for a computer based on its fully qualified domain name by performing a DNS query.

Solution

Use the method GetHostEntry of the System.Net.Dns class, and pass the computer's fully qualified domain name as a string parameter.

How It Works

On the Internet, the human-readable names that refer to computers are mapped to IP addresses, which is what TCP/IP requires in order to communicate between computers. For example, the name www.apress.com might be mapped to the IP address 65.19.150.100. To determine the IP address for a given name, the computer contacts a DNS server. The name or IP address of the DNS server contacted is configured as part of a computer's network configuration.

The entire process of name resolution is transparent if you use the System.Net.Dns class, which allows you to retrieve the IP address for a host name by calling GetHostEntry.

The Code

The following example retrieves the IP addresses of all computers whose fully qualified domain names are specified as command-line arguments:

```
Imports System
Imports System.Net
```

```vb
Namespace Apress.VisualBasicRecipes.Chapter11
    Public Class Recipe11_08

        Public Shared Sub Main(ByVal args As String())

            For Each comp As String In args

                Try
                    ' Retrieve the DNS entry for the specified computer.
                    Dim dnsEntry As IPHostEntry = Dns.GetHostEntry(comp)

                    ' The DNS entry may contain more than one IP address. Iterate
                    ' through them and display each one along with the type of
                    ' address (AddressFamily).
                    For Each address As IPAddress In dnsEntry.AddressList
                        Console.WriteLine("{0} = {1} ({2})", comp, address, ➥
address.AddressFamily)
                    Next
                Catch ex As Exception
                    Console.WriteLine("{0} = Error ({1})", comp, ex.Message)
                End Try
            Next

            ' Wait to continue.
            Console.WriteLine(Environment.NewLine)
            Console.WriteLine("Main method complete.  Press Enter.")
            Console.ReadLine()

        End Sub

    End Class
End Namespace
```

Note The `IPAddress` class fully supports both IPv4 and IPv6.

Usage

Running the example with the following command line:

recipe11-08 www.apress.com www.microsoft.com localhost somejunk

will produce the following output. Notice that multiple IP addresses are returned for some host names.

```
www.apress.com = 65.19.150.101 (InterNetwork)
www.microsoft.com = 207.46.192.254 (InterNetwork)
www.microsoft.com = 207.46.19.190 (InterNetwork)
www.microsoft.com = 207.46.19.254 (InterNetwork)
www.microsoft.com = 207.46.193.254 (InterNetwork)
localhost = 127.0.0.1 (InterNetwork)
somejunk = Error (No such host is known)
```

11-9. Ping an IP Address

Problem

You want to check to see whether a computer is online and accessible and gauge its response time.

Solution

Send a ping message. This message is sent using the ICMP, accessible through the Send method of the System.Net.NetworkInformation.Ping class.

How It Works

A ping message contacts a device at a specific IP address, passing it a test packet, and requests that the remote device respond by echoing back the packet. To gauge the connection latency between two computers, you can measure the time taken for a ping response to be received.

■**Caution** Many commercial web sites do not respond to ping requests because they represent an unnecessary processing overhead and are often used in denial of service attacks. The firewall that protects the site will usually filter out ping requests before they reach the specified destination. This will cause your ping request to time out.

The Ping class allows you to send ping messages using the Send method. The Send method provides a number of overloads, which allow you to specify the following:

- The IP address or host name of the target computer. You can specify this as a String or a System.Net.IPAddress object.

- The number of milliseconds to wait for a response before the request times out (specified as an Integer). The default is set to 5000.

- A System.Net.NetworkInformation.PingOptions object that specifies time-to-live and fragmentation options for the transmission of the ping message.

The Send method will return a System.Net.NetworkInformation.PingReply object. The Status property of the PingReply will contain a value from the System.Net.NetworkInformation.IPStatus enumeration from which you can determine the result of the ping request. The most common values will be Success and TimedOut. If the host name you pass to the Send method cannot be resolved, Send will throw an exception, but you must look at the InnerException to determine the cause of the problem.

The Ping class also provides a SendAsync method that performs the ping request using a thread-pool thread so that the calling thread does not block. When the ping is finished or fails because of a time-out, the thread raises the PingCompleted event on the Ping object, which you can handle using a method that matches the signature of the System.Net.NetworkInformation. PingCompletedEventHandler delegate. However, the Ping object can handle only a single concurrent request; otherwise, it will throw a System.InvalidOperationException.

■**Tip** The Ping class derives from System.ComponentModel.Component, so you can add it to the Visual Studio 2008 Form Designer Toolbox. This will allow you to easily set the properties or define the event handlers in a Windows Forms–based application.

The Code

The following example pings the computers whose domain names or IP addresses are specified as command-line arguments.

```vbnet
Imports System
Imports System.Net.NetworkInformation

Namespace Apress.VisualBasicRecipes.Chapter11
    Public Class Recipe11_09

        Public Shared Sub Main(ByVal args As String())

            ' Create an instance of the Ping class.
            Using png As New Ping
                Console.WriteLine("Pinging:")

                For Each comp As String In args

                    Try
                        Console.Write("    {0}...", comp)

                        ' Ping the specified computer with a time-out of 100ms.
                        Dim reply As PingReply = png.Send(comp, 100)

                        If reply.Status = IPStatus.Success Then
                            Console.WriteLine("Success - IP Address:{0} " & ➡
"Time:{1}ms", reply.Address, reply.RoundtripTime)
                        Else
                            Console.WriteLine(reply.Status.ToString)
                        End If

                    Catch ex As Exception
                        Console.WriteLine("Error ({0})", ex.InnerException.Message)
                    End Try

                Next

            End Using

            ' Wait to continue.
            Console.WriteLine(Environment.NewLine)
            Console.WriteLine("Main method complete.  Press Enter.")
            Console.ReadLine()

        End Sub

    End Class
End Namespace
```

Usage

Running the example with the following command line:

```
recipe11-09 www.apress.com www.google.com localhost somejunk
```

will produce the following output:

```
Pinging:
    www.apress.com...TimedOut
    www.google.com...Success - IP Address: 64.233.169.99 Time:122ms
    localhost...Success - IP Address:127.0.0.1 Time:0ms
    somejunk...Error (No such host is known)
```

11-10. Communicate Using TCP

Problem

You need to send data between two computers on a network using a TCP/IP connection.

Solution

One computer (the server) must begin listening using the System.Net.Sockets.TcpListener class. Another computer (the client) connects to it using the System.Net.Sockets.TcpClient class. Once a connection is established, both computers can communicate using the System.Net.Sockets. NetworkStream class.

How It Works

TCP is a reliable, connection-oriented protocol that allows two computers to communicate over a network. It provides built-in flow control, sequencing, and error handling, which make it reliable and easy to program.

To create a TCP connection, one computer must act as the server and start listening on a specific endpoint. (An *endpoint* is a combination of an IP address and a port number.) The other computer must act as a client and send a connection request to the endpoint on which the first computer is listening. Once the connection is established, the two computers can take turns exchanging messages. The .NET Framework makes this process easy through its stream abstraction. Both computers simply write to and read from a System.Net.Sockets.NetworkStream to transmit data.

■**Note** Even though a TCP connection always requires a server and a client, an individual application could be both. For example, in a peer-to-peer application, one thread is dedicated to listening for incoming requests (acting as a server), and another thread is dedicated to initiating outgoing connections (acting as a client). In the examples in this chapter, the client and server are provided as separate applications and are placed in separate subdirectories.

Once a TCP connection is established, the two computers can send any type of data by writing it to the NetworkStream. However, it's a good idea to begin designing a networked application by defining the application-level protocol that clients and servers will use to communicate. This protocol includes constants that represent the allowable commands, ensuring that your application code doesn't include hard-coded communication strings.

The Code

In this recipe's example, the defined protocol is basic. You would add more constants depending on the type of application. For example, in a file transfer application, you might include a client message for requesting a file. The server might then respond with an acknowledgment and return file details such as the file size. These constants should be compiled into a separate class library assembly, which must be referenced by both the client and server. Here is the code for the shared protocol:

```
Namespace Apress.VisualBasicRecipes.Chapter11

    Public Class Recipe11_10Shared

        Public Const AcknowledgeOK As String = "OK"
        Public Const AcknowledgeCancel = "Cancel"
        Public Const Disconnect As String = "Bye"
        Public Const RequestConnect As String = "Hello"

    End Class

End Namespace
```

The following code is a template for a basic TCP server. It listens on a fixed port, accepts the first incoming connection using the TcpListener.AcceptTcpClient method, and then waits for the client to request a disconnect. At this point, the server could call the AcceptTcpClient method again to wait for the next client, but instead it simply shuts down.

```
Imports System
Imports System.IO
Imports System.Net
Imports System.Net.Sockets

Namespace Apress.VisualBasicRecipes.Chapter11

    Public Class Recipe11_10Server

        Public Shared Sub Main()

            ' Create a new listener on port 8000.
            Dim listener As New TcpListener(IPAddress.Parse("127.0.0.1"), 8000)

            Console.WriteLine("About to initialize port.")
            listener.Start()
            Console.WriteLine("Listening for a connection...")

            Try
                ' Wait for a connection request, and return a TcpClient
                ' initialized for communication.
                Using client As TcpClient = listener.AcceptTcpClient
                    Console.WriteLine("Connection accepted.")

                    ' Retrieve the network stream.
                    Dim stream As NetworkStream = client.GetStream()
```

```
                            ' Create a BinaryWriter for writing to the stream.
                            Using w As New BinaryWriter(stream)
                                ' Create a BinaryReader for reading from the stream.
                                Using r As New BinaryReader(stream)

                                    If r.ReadString = Recipe11_10Shared.RequestConnect Then
                                        w.Write(Recipe11_10Shared.AcknowledgeOK)
                                        Console.WriteLine("Connection completed.")

                                        While Not r.ReadString = ➥
Recipe11_10Shared.Disconnect
                                        End While

                                        Console.WriteLine(Environment.NewLine)
                                        Console.WriteLine("Disconnect request received.")
                                    Else
                                        Console.WriteLine("Can't complete connection.")
                                    End If

                                End Using
                            End Using
                        End Using

                        Console.WriteLine("Connection closed.")

                    Catch ex As Exception
                        Console.WriteLine(ex.ToString)
                    Finally
                        ' Close the underlying socket (stop listening for
                        ' new requests).
                        listener.Stop()
                        Console.WriteLine("Listener stopped.")
                    End Try

                    ' Wait to continue.
                    Console.WriteLine(Environment.NewLine)
                    Console.WriteLine("Main method complete.  Press Enter.")
                    Console.ReadLine()

                End Sub

        End Class
End Namespace
```

The following code is a template for a basic TCP client. It contacts the server at the specified IP address and port. In this example, the loopback address (127.0.0.1) is used, which always points to the local computer. Keep in mind that a TCP connection requires two ports: one at the server end and one at the client end. However, only the server port to connect to needs to be specified. The outgoing client port can be chosen dynamically at runtime from the available ports, which is what the TcpClient class will do by default.

```
Imports System
Imports System.IO
Imports System.Net
Imports System.Net.Sockets
```

```vb
Namespace Apress.VisualBasicRecipes.Chapter11
    Public Class Recipe11_10Client

        Public Shared Sub Main()

            Dim client As New TcpClient

            Try

                Console.WriteLine("Attempting to connect to the server on " & ➥
"port 8000.")
                client.Connect(IPAddress.Parse("127.0.0.1"), 8000)
                Console.WriteLine("Connection established.")

                ' Retrieve the network stream.
                Dim stream As NetworkStream = client.GetStream()

                ' Create a BinaryWriter for writing to the stream.
                Using w As New BinaryWriter(stream)
                    ' Create a BinaryReader for reading from the stream.
                    Using r As New BinaryReader(stream)

                        ' Start a dialogue.
                        w.Write(Recipe11_10Shared.RequestConnect)

                        If r.ReadString = Recipe11_10Shared.AcknowledgeOK Then
                            Console.WriteLine("Connected.")
                            Console.WriteLine("Press Enter to disconnect.")
                            Console.ReadLine()
                            Console.WriteLine("Disconnecting...")
                            w.Write(Recipe11_10Shared.Disconnect)
                        Else
                            Console.WriteLine("Connection not completed.")
                        End If

                    End Using
                End Using

            Catch ex As Exception
                Console.WriteLine(ex.ToString)
            Finally
                ' Close the connection socket.
                client.Close()
                Console.WriteLine("Port closed.")
            End Try

            ' Wait to continue.
            Console.WriteLine(Environment.NewLine)
            Console.WriteLine("Main method complete.  Press Enter.")
            Console.ReadLine()

        End Sub

    End Class
End Namespace
```

Usage

Here's a sample connection transcript on the server side:

```
About to initialize port.
Listening for a connection...
Connection accepted.
Connection completed.

Disconnect request received.
Connection closed.
Listener stopped.
```

And here's a sample connection transcript on the client side:

```
Attempting to connect to the server on port 8000.
Connection established.
Connected.
Press Enter to disconnect.

Disconnecting...
Port closed.
```

11-11. Create a Multithreaded TCP Server That Supports Asynchronous Communications

Problem

You need to handle multiple network requests concurrently or perform a network data transfer as a background task while your program continues with other processing.

Solution

Use the `AcceptTcpClient` method of the `System.Net.Sockets.TcpListener` class to accept connections. Every time a new client connects, start a new thread to handle the connection. Alternatively, use the `TcpListener.BeginAcceptTcpClient` to accept a new client connection on a thread-pool thread using the asynchronous execution pattern (discussed in recipe 4-2).

To start a background task to handle the asynchronous sending of data, you can use the `BeginWrite` method of the `System.Net.Sockets.NetworkStream` class and supply a callback method—each time the callback is triggered, send more data.

How It Works

A single TCP endpoint (IP address and port) can serve multiple connections. In fact, the operating system takes care of most of the work for you. All you need to do is create a worker object on the server that will handle each connection on a separate thread. The `TcpListener.AcceptTcpClient` method returns a `TcpClient` when a connection is established. This should be passed off to a threaded worker object so that the worker can communicate with the remote client.

Alternatively, call the `TcpListener.BeginAcceptTcpClient` method to start an asynchronous operation using a thread-pool thread that waits in the background for a client to connect. `BeginAcceptTcpClient` follows the asynchronous execution pattern, allowing you to wait for the operation to complete or specify a callback that the .NET runtime will call when a client connects. (See recipe 4-2 for details on the options available.) Whichever mechanism you use, once

BeginAcceptTcpClient has completed, call EndAcceptTcpClient to obtain the newly created TcpClient object.

To exchange network data asynchronously, you can use the NetworkStream class, which includes basic support for asynchronous communication through the BeginRead and BeginWrite methods. Using these methods, you can send or receive a block of data on one of the threads provided by the thread pool, without blocking your code. When sending data asynchronously, you must send raw binary data (an array of bytes). It's up to you to choose the amount you want to send or receive at a time.

One advantage of this approach when sending files is that the entire content of the file does not have to be held in memory at once. Instead, it is retrieved just before a new block is sent. Another advantage is that the server can abort the transfer operation easily at any time.

The Code

The following example demonstrates various techniques for handling network connections and communications asynchronously. The server (Recipe11-11Server) starts a thread-pool thread listening for new connections using the TcpListener.BeginAcceptTcpClient method and specifying a callback method to handle the new connections. Every time a client connects to the server, the callback method obtains the new TcpClient object and passes it to a new threaded ClientHandler object to handle client communications.

The ClientHandler object waits for the client to request data and then sends a large amount of data (read from a file) to the client. This data is sent asynchronously, which means ClientHandler could continue to perform other tasks. In this example, it simply monitors the network stream for messages sent from the client. The client reads only a third of the data before sending a disconnect message to the server, which terminates the remainder of the file transfer and drops the client connection.

Here is the code for the shared protocol:

```
Namespace Apress.VisualBasicRecipes.Chapter11

    Public Class Recipe11_11Shared

        Public Const AcknowledgeOK As String = "OK"
        Public Const AcknowledgeCancel = "Cancel"
        Public Const Disconnect As String = "Bye"
        Public Const RequestConnect As String = "Hello"
        Public Const RequestData = "Data"

    End Class

End Namespace
```

Here is the server code:

```
Imports System
Imports System.IO
Imports System.Net
Imports System.Threading
Imports System.Net.Sockets

Namespace Apress.VisualBasicRecipes.Chapter11
    Public Class Recipe11_11Server
```

```vb
    ' A flag used to indicate whether the server is shutting down.
    Private Shared m_Terminate As Boolean
    Public Shared ReadOnly Property Terminate() As Boolean
        Get
            Return m_Terminate
        End Get
    End Property

    ' A variable to track the identity of each client connection.
    Private Shared ClientNumber As Integer = 0

    ' A single TcpListener will accept all incoming client connections.
    Private Shared listener As TcpListener

    Public Shared Sub Main()

        ' Create a 100KB test file for use in the example. This file will
        ' be sent to clients that connect.
        Using fs As New FileStream("test.bin", FileMode.Create)
            fs.SetLength(100000)
        End Using

        Try
            ' Create a TcpListener that will accept incoming client
            ' connections on port 8000 of the local machine.
            listener = New TcpListener(IPAddress.Parse("127.0.0.1"), 8000)

            Console.WriteLine("Starting TcpListener...")

            ' Start the TcpListener accepting connections.
            m_Terminate = False
            listener.Start()

            ' Begin asynchronously listening for client connections. When a
            ' new connection is established, call the ConnectionHandler method
            ' to process the new connection.
            listener.BeginAcceptTcpClient(AddressOf ConnectionHandler, Nothing)

            ' Keep the server active until the user presses Enter.
            Console.WriteLine("Server awaiting connections.  Press Enter " & _
    "to stop server.")
            Console.ReadLine()

        Finally
            ' Shut down the TcpListener. This will cause any outstanding
            ' asynchronous requests to stop and throw an exception in
            ' the ConnectionHandler when EndAcceptTcpClient is called.
            ' A more robust termination synchronization may be desired here,
            ' but for the purpose of this example, ClientHandler threads
            ' are all background threads and will terminate automatically when
            ' the main thread terminates. This is suitable for our needs.
            Console.WriteLine("Server stopping...")
            m_Terminate = True
            If listener IsNot Nothing Then listener.Stop()
```

```vbnet
        End Try

        ' Wait to continue.
        Console.WriteLine(Environment.NewLine)
        Console.WriteLine("Main method complete.  Press Enter.")
        Console.ReadLine()

    End Sub

    ' A method to handle the callback when a connection is established
    ' from a client. This is a simple way to implement a dispatcher
    ' but lacks the control and scalability required when implementing
    ' full-blown asynchronous server applications.
    Private Shared Sub ConnectionHandler(ByVal result As IAsyncResult)

        Dim client As TcpClient = Nothing

        ' Always end the asynchronous operation to avoid leaks.
        Try
            ' Get the TcpClient that represents the new client connection.
            client = listener.EndAcceptTcpClient(result)
        Catch ex As ObjectDisposedException
            ' The server is shutting down and the outstanding asynchronous
            ' request calls the completion method with this exception.
            ' The exception is thrown when EndAcceptTcpClient is called.
            ' Do nothing and return.
            Exit Sub
        End Try

        Console.WriteLine("Dispatcher:  New connection accepted.")

        ' Begin asynchronously listening for the next client
        ' connection.
        listener.BeginAcceptTcpClient(AddressOf ConnectionHandler, Nothing)

        If client IsNot Nothing Then
            ' Determine the identifier for the new client connection.
            Interlocked.Increment(ClientNumber)

            Dim clientName As String = "Client " & ClientNumber.ToString

            Console.WriteLine("Dispatcher: Creating client handler ({0})", ➥
clientName)

            ' Create a new ClientHandler to handle this connection.
            Dim blah As New ClientHandler(client, clientName)

        End If

    End Sub

End Class
```

```vbnet
' A class that encapsulates the logic to handle a client connection.
Public Class ClientHandler

    ' The TcpClient that represents the connection to the client.
    Private client As TcpClient

    ' A name that uniquely identifies this ClientHandler.
    Private clientName As String

    ' The amount of data that will be written in one block (2KB).
    Private bufferSize As Integer = 2048

    ' The buffer that holds the data to write.
    Private buffer As Byte()

    ' Used to read data from the local file.
    Private testFile As FileStream

    ' A signal to stop sending data to the client.
    Private stopDataTransfer As Boolean

    Public Sub New(ByVal cli As TcpClient, ByVal cliID As String)

        Me.buffer = New Byte(bufferSize) {}
        Me.client = cli
        Me.clientName = cliID

        ' Create a new background thread to handle the client connection
        ' so that we do not consume a thread-pool thread for a long time
        ' and also so that it will be terminated when the main thread ends.
        Dim newThread As New Thread(AddressOf ProcessConnection)
        newThread.IsBackground = True
        newThread.Start()

    End Sub

    Private Sub ProcessConnection()

        Using client

            ' Create a BinaryReader to receive messages from the client. At
            ' the end of the using block, it will close both the BinaryReader
            ' and the underlying NetworkStream.
            Using reader As New BinaryReader(client.GetStream)

                If reader.ReadString = Recipe11_11Shared.RequestConnect Then

                    ' Create a BinaryWriter to send messages to the client.
                    ' At the end of the using block, it will close both the
                    ' BinaryWriter and the underlying NetworkStream.
                    Using writer As New BinaryWriter(client.GetStream)

                        writer.Write(Recipe11_11Shared.AcknowledgeOK)
                        Console.WriteLine(clientName & ": Connection " & ➡
"established.")
```

```
                    Dim message As String = ""

                    While Not message = Recipe11_11Shared.Disconnect

                        Try
                            ' Read the message from the client.
                            message = reader.ReadString
                        Catch ex As Exception
                            ' For the purpose of the example,
                            ' any exception should be taken
                            ' as a client disconnect.
                            message = Recipe11_11Shared.Disconnect
                        End Try

                        If message = Recipe11_11Shared.RequestData Then

                            Console.WriteLine(clientName & ":" & ➥
"Requested data.", "Sending...")

                            ' The filename could be supplied by the client,
                            ' but in this example, a test file is
                            ' hard-coded.
                            testFile = New FileStream("test.bin", ➥
FileMode.Open, FileAccess.Read)

                            ' Send the file size. This is how the client
                            ' knows how much to read.
                            writer.Write(testFile.Length.ToString)

                            ' Start an asynchronous send operation.
                            stopDataTransfer = False
                            StreamData(Nothing)
                        ElseIf message = Recipe11_11Shared.Disconnect Then
                            Console.WriteLine(clientName & ": Client " & ➥
"disconnecting...")

                            stopDataTransfer = True
                        Else
                            Console.WriteLine(clientName & ": Unknown " & ➥
"command.")
                        End If
                    End While
                End Using
            Else
                Console.WriteLine(clientName & ": Could not establish " & ➥
"connection.")
            End If
        End Using
    End Using
    Console.WriteLine(clientName & ": Client connection closed.")

End Sub
```

```vb
        Private Sub StreamData(ByVal asyncResult As IAsyncResult)

            ' Always complete outstanding asynchronous operations to avoid
            ' leaks.
            If asyncResult IsNot Nothing Then

                Try
                    client.GetStream.EndWrite(asyncResult)
                Catch ex As Exception
                    ' For the purpose of the example, any exception obtaining
                    ' or writing to the network should just terminate the
                    ' download.
                    testFile.Close()
                    Exit Sub
                End Try

            End If

            ' Check if the code has been triggered to stop.
            If Not stopDataTransfer And Not Recipe11_11Server.Terminate Then
                ' Read the next block from the file.
                Dim bytesRead As Integer = testFile.Read(buffer, 0, buffer.Length)

                ' If no bytes are read, the stream is at the end of the file.
                If bytesRead > 0 Then
                    Console.WriteLine(clientName & ": Streaming next block.")

                    ' Write the next block to the network stream.
                    client.GetStream.BeginWrite(buffer, 0, buffer.Length, ➡
AddressOf StreamData, Nothing)
                Else
                    ' End the operation.
                    Console.WriteLine(clientName & ": File streaming complete.")
                    testFile.Close()
                End If
            Else
                ' Client disconnected.
                Console.WriteLine(clientName & ": Client disconnected.")
                testFile.Close()
            End If

        End Sub
    End Class

End Namespace
```

And here is the client code:

```vb
Imports System
Imports System.IO
Imports System.Net
Imports System.Net.Sockets

Namespace Apress.VisualBasicRecipes.Chapter11
    Public Class Recipe11_11Client
```

```vb
        Public Shared Sub Main()

            Using client As New TcpClient

                Console.WriteLine("Attempting to connect to the server on " & ➥
    "port 8000.")

                    ' Connect to the server.
                    client.Connect(IPAddress.Parse("127.0.0.1"), 8000)

                    ' Create a BinaryWriter for writing to the stream.
                    Using writer As New BinaryWriter(client.GetStream)

                        ' Start a dialogue.
                        writer.Write(Recipe11_11Shared.RequestConnect)

                        ' Create a BinaryReader for reading from the stream.
                        Using reader As New BinaryReader(client.GetStream)

                            If reader.ReadString = Recipe11_11Shared.AcknowledgeOK Then
                                Console.WriteLine("Connection established.  Press " & ➥
    "Enter to download data.")
                                Console.ReadLine()

                                ' Send message requesting data to server.
                                writer.Write(Recipe11_11Shared.RequestData)

                                ' The server should respond with the size of
                                ' the data it will send. Assume it does.
                                Dim fileSize As Integer = ➥
    Integer.Parse(reader.ReadString())

                                ' Only get part of the data, then carry out a
                                ' premature disconnect.
                                For i As Integer = 1 To fileSize / 3
                                    Console.Write(client.GetStream.ReadByte)
                                Next

                                Console.WriteLine(Environment.NewLine)
                                Console.WriteLine("Press Enter to disconnect.")
                                Console.ReadLine()
                                Console.WriteLine("Disconnecting...")

                                writer.Write(Recipe11_11Shared.Disconnect)
                            Else
                                Console.WriteLine("Connection not completed.")
                            End If

                        End Using
                    End Using
            End Using
```

```
            '  Wait to continue.
            Console.WriteLine(Environment.NewLine)
            Console.WriteLine("Main method complete.  Press Enter.")
            Console.ReadLine()

        End Sub

    End Class
End Namespace
```

11-12. Communicate Using UDP

Problem

You need to send data between two computers on a network using a UDP stream.

Solution

Use the `System.Net.Sockets.UdpClient` class, and use two threads: one to send data and the other to receive it.

How It Works

UDP is a connectionless protocol that doesn't include any flow control or error checking. Unlike TCP, UDP shouldn't be used where reliable communication is required. However, because of its lower overhead, UDP is often used for "chatty" applications where it is acceptable to lose some messages. For example, imagine you want to create a network in which individual clients send information about the current temperature at their locations to a server every few minutes. You might use UDP in this case because the communication frequency is high and the damage caused by losing a packet is trivial (because the server can just continue to use the last received temperature reading).

The Code

The application shown in the following code uses two threads: one to receive messages and one to send them. The application stops when the user presses the Enter key without any text to send. Notice that UDP applications cannot use the `NetworkStream` abstraction that TCP applications can. Instead, they must convert all data to a stream of bytes using an encoding class, as described in recipe 2-2.

```
Imports System
Imports System.Text
Imports System.Net
Imports System.Net.Sockets
Imports System.Threading

Namespace Apress.VisualBasicRecipes.Chapter11
    Public Class Recipe11_12

        Private Shared localPort As Integer

        Public Shared Sub Main()
```

```vbnet
' Define the endpoint where messages are sent.
Console.Write("Connect to IP: ")
Dim ip As String = Console.ReadLine
Console.Write("Connect to port: ")
Dim port As Integer = Int32.Parse(Console.ReadLine)

Dim remoteEndPoint As New IPEndPoint(IPAddress.Parse(ip), port)

' Define the local endpoint (where messages are received).
Console.Write("Local port for listening: ")
localPort = Int32.Parse(Console.ReadLine)

' Create a new thread for receiving incoming messages.
Dim receiveThread As New Thread(AddressOf ReceiveData)
receiveThread.IsBackground = True
receiveThread.Start()

Using client As New UdpClient
    Console.WriteLine("Type message and press Enter to send:")

    Try
        Dim txt As String

        Do
            txt = Console.ReadLine

            ' Send the text to the remote client.
            If Not txt.Length = 0 Then
                ' Encode the data to binary using UTF8 encoding.
                Dim data As Byte() = Encoding.UTF8.GetBytes(txt)

                ' Send the text to the remote client.
                client.Send(data, data.Length, remoteEndPoint)
            End If
        Loop While Not txt.Length = 0
    Catch ex As Exception
        Console.WriteLine(ex.ToString)
    Finally
        client.Close()
    End Try
End Using

' Wait to continue.
Console.WriteLine(Environment.NewLine)
Console.WriteLine("Main method complete.  Press Enter.")
Console.ReadLine()

End Sub

Private Shared Sub ReceiveData()
```

```
Using client As New UdpClient(localPort)
    ' This is an endless loop, but since it is running in
    ' a background thread, it will be destroyed when the
    ' application (the main thread) ends.
    While True

        Try
            ' Receive bytes.
            Dim anyIP As New IPEndPoint(IPAddress.Any, 0)
            Dim data As Byte() = client.Receive(anyIP)

            ' Convert bytes to text using UTF8 encoding.
            Dim txt As String = Encoding.UTF8.GetString(data)

            ' Display the retrieved text.
            Console.WriteLine(">> " & txt)

        Catch ex As Exception
            Console.WriteLine(ex.ToString)
        End Try

    End While
End Using

    End Sub

End Class
End Namespace
```

Usage

To test this application, load two instances at the same time. On computer A, specify the IP address and port for computer B. On computer B, specify the IP address and port for computer A. You can then send text messages back and forth at will. You can test this application with clients on the local computer using the loopback alias 127.0.0.1, provided you use different listening ports. For example, imagine a situation with two UDP clients, client A and client B. Here's a sample transcript for client A:

```
Connect to IP: 127.0.0.1
Connect to port: 8001
Local port for listening: 8080
Type message and press Enter to send:
Hi there!
```

And here's the corresponding transcript for client B (with the received message):

```
Connect to IP: 127.0.0.1
Connect to port: 8080
Local port for listening: 8001
Type message and press Enter to send:
>> Hi there!
```

11-13. Communicate Using Named Pipes

Problem

You need to send data between two processes on the same computer (or remote computers) using a named pipes connection.

Solution

One computer (the server) must create the server using the NamedPipeServerStream class and wait for connections clients using the WaitForConnection method. Another computer (the client) establishes a connection to the server pipe by creating an instance of the NamedPipeClientStream and using the Connect method.

How It Works

A pipe represents a line of communications between two processes, which may or may not be on the same machine. These pipes come in two main forms: anonymous and named. Anonymous pipes, represented by the AnonymousPipeServerStream and AnonymousPipeClientStream classes, work in the same way that named pipes work, but they are not named and support only one-way communication. Named pipes, represented by NamedPipeServerStream and NamedPipeClientStream, are created with a specific name and can be set to send, receive, or send and receive data. System.IO.Pipes is new to .NET Framework 3.5 and is the parent namespace for all the classes related to pipes.

You create a new named pipe server by creating a new instance of the NamedPipeServerStream class, which inherits from the PipeStream base class (which inherits from Stream). When creating the named pipe server, you must specify a name to use. You can also specify the direction of the pipe as In, Out, or InOut. The server waits for a client connection by calling the WaitForConnection method.

You create a new named pipe client, using the NamedPipeClientStream class, in the same manner that the server was created, specifying the name of the server pipe itself. By default, the localhost will be used as the target system that contains the server pipe. A connection is established by calling the Connect method.

Once a connection has been established, all communications are easily handled using StreamReader and StreamWriter objects that are instantiated using the appropriate client or server instance of the named pipe.

The Code

The following is a basic example of a named pipe server, named TestPipeServer. The pipe is opened to support both input and output so it can receive as well as send data. It waits for incoming client connections by calling the WaitForConnection method and then relies on a StreamReader and StreamWriter to interact across the pipe.

```
Imports System
Imports System.IO
Imports System.Net
Imports System.Net.Sockets
Imports System.IO.Pipes

Namespace Apress.VisualBasicRecipes.Chapter11
    Public Class Recipe11_13Server

        Public Shared Sub Main()
```

```vbnet
            Dim namedPipeServer As NamedPipeServerStream = Nothing
            Dim w As StreamWriter = Nothing
            Dim r As StreamReader = Nothing

            Try
                ' Create the named server pipe and configure it to support both
                ' input and output.
                namedPipeServer = New NamedPipeServerStream("TestPipeServer", ➡
PipeDirection.InOut)
                Console.WriteLine("Waiting for client connection...")

                ' Wait for clients to connect to the named pipe.
                namedPipeServer.WaitForConnection()
                Console.WriteLine("Connection established with client.")

                ' Create a StreamReader for reading from the stream.
                r = New StreamReader(namedPipeServer)

                ' Create a StreamWriter for writing to the stream.
                w = New StreamWriter(namedPipeServer)
                w.AutoFlush = True

                Console.WriteLine("From Client: {0}", r.ReadLine())

                ' Send a couple messages to the client pipe.
                w.WriteLine("Welcome to the server.  Please send me " & ➡
"some information.")
                w.WriteLine("Send the string 'DONE' when you are done.")

                ' Keep reading information from the pipe until the text
                ' "DONE" is sent.
                Dim msg As String
                Do
                    msg = r.ReadLine()
                    Console.WriteLine("From Client: {0}", msg)
                Loop Until msg.ToUpper() = "DONE"

                Console.WriteLine("The server has been disconnected.")
            Catch ex As Exception
                ' Display any errors to the screen.
                Console.WriteLine(ex.ToString)
            Finally
                ' Close up the streams and make sure the pipe is shut down.
                If w IsNot Nothing Then w.Close()
                If r IsNot Nothing Then r.Close()

                If namedPipeServer.IsConnected = True Then ➡
namedPipeServer.Disconnect()
                namedPipeServer.Close()
            End Try

            ' Wait to continue.
            Console.WriteLine(Environment.NewLine)
            Console.WriteLine("Main method complete.  Press Enter.")
            Console.ReadLine()
```

```
        End Sub

    End Class
End Namespace
```

The following code is a basic example of creating a named pipe client. It connects to the TestPipeServer, created with the previous code example, running on the local system. Once the connection has been successfully established, the client sends some information to and receives some information from the server before it terminates the server by passing DONE.

```
Imports System
Imports System.IO
Imports System.Net
Imports System.Net.Sockets
Imports System.IO.Pipes

Namespace Apress.VisualBasicRecipes.Chapter11

    Public Class Recipe11_13Client

        Public Shared Sub Main()

            Dim pipeClient As NamedPipeClientStream = Nothing
            Dim w As StreamWriter = Nothing
            Dim r As StreamReader = Nothing

            Try

                ' Create the named client pipe and configure it to support both
                ' input and output.
                pipeClient = New NamedPipeClientStream(".", "TestPipeServer", ➥
PipeDirection.InOut)

                Console.WriteLine("Connecting to TestPipeServer server...")

                ' Attempt to connect to the named server pipe.
                pipeClient.Connect()
                Console.WriteLine("Connection established with server.")

                ' Create a StreamWriter for writing to the stream.
                w = New StreamWriter(pipeClient)
                w.AutoFlush = True

                ' Create a StreamReader for reading from the stream.
                r = New StreamReader(pipeClient)

                ' Send some text to the server pipe.
                w.WriteLine("Hello Server.  I have some information to send.")

                ' Display text sent from the server pipe.
                Console.WriteLine("From Server:  {0}", r.ReadLine())
                Console.WriteLine("From Server:  {0}", r.ReadLine())
```

```
              ' Generate and send some sample information to the server pipe.
              Console.WriteLine("Sending some information to the server.")
              For i = 1 To 10
                  w.WriteLine(Guid.NewGuid().ToString())
              Next

              ' Send the text to trigger the server pipe to close.
              Console.WriteLine("Sending 'DONE' to the server.")
              w.WriteLine("DONE)

          Catch ex As Exception
              ' Display any errors to the screen.
              Console.WriteLine(ex.ToString)
          Finally
              ' Close up the streams and make sure the pipe is shutdown.
              If w IsNot Nothing Then w.Close()
              If r IsNot Nothing Then r.Close()
              pipeClient.Close()
          End Try

          ' Wait to continue.
          Console.WriteLine(Environment.NewLine)
          Console.WriteLine("Main method complete.  Press Enter.")
          Console.ReadLine()
      End Sub

  End Class
End Namespace
```

Usage

To run this example, you must first launch the Recipe11-13Server.exe application to create the named pipe server. Once you've done that, you can run the Recipe11-13Client.exe application, which will establish a connection with the server and produce these results on the server:

```
Waiting for client connection...
Connection established with client.
From Client:  Hello Server.  I have some information to send.
From Client:  7c4abfce-19c5-499c-8f39-4d02e9d1cac6
From Client:  ca559189-af63-4290-ab43-8894ce7f70e6
From Client:  3cf12f00-f5e9-4809-86e1-84c7bd325e42
From Client:  394ba658-cf1f-49c9-beb5-dee2b1d99e38
From Client:  e7e94e22-09a1-4d67-9056-2511d1953280
From Client:  e12d6b2f-9b67-4df1-8d9a-e28b3a38985b
From Client:  be319951-51d7-4da6-b84c-fd674aca75f5
From Client:  921bd692-5ae7-4cdd-9129-5ca5acd818c3
From Client:  b06c42d0-500b-4c55-ae94-eac9dd79f0a9
From Client:  03730f41-ff3c-4a28-a8ab-023ab3e10023
From Client:  DONE
The server has been disconnected.

Main method complete.  Press Enter.
```

And here's a sample connection transcript on the client side:

```
Connecting to TestPipeServer server...
Connection established with server.
From Server:  Welcome to the server.  Please send me some information.
From Server:  Send the string 'DONE' when you are done.
Sending some information to the server.
Sending 'DONE' to the server.

Main method complete.  Press Enter.
```

11-14. Make an Object Remotable

Problem

You need to create a class that can be accessed from another application or another computer on the network. However, you don't need cross-platform compatibility, and you want optimum performance.

Solution

Make the class remotable by deriving from System.MarshalByRefObject, and create a component host that registers the class with the .NET remoting infrastructure.

How It Works

Remoting allows you to make an object accessible across process and machine boundaries. Although web services are ideal when you need to share functionality across platforms or trust boundaries, remoting is one of the best-performing choices for a closed system in which all components are built on .NET and the Windows operating system. Since serialization is used to perform this behavior, the object in question must be serializable. To use .NET remoting, you need the following ingredients, each of which must reside in a separate assembly:

- *A component host*: This application registers the remotable type with the .NET remoting infrastructure using the RemotingConfiguration class from the System.Runtime.Remoting namespace. You can use any type of long-running .NET Framework application for a component host (including Windows Forms–based applications, Windows services, console applications, and even IIS). As long as the component host is running, remote clients can create or connect to existing instances of the remotable object. The component host never interacts with the remotable objects directly. All it does is register the appropriate types with the .NET remoting infrastructure. After this point, clients can create object instances, and the server application can continue with other tasks. However, when the component host is closed, any remotable objects will be destroyed, and no more hosted objects can be created.

- *A client application*: This application can create or connect to instances of the remotable class in the component host process and interact with them. The client uses the RemotingConfiguration class to register the types it wants to access remotely. The client application uses the RemotingConfiguration.Configure method to register the remote objects it wants to call. Once this step is taken, the client can create the object exactly as it would create a local object. However, the object will actually be created in the component host.

Figure 11-2 shows how these three parts interact. This example has only one client. However, it's also possible for multiple clients to create instances of the remotable class at the same time. In this case, you can configure the remoting host, whether each client has its own remotable object instance or all clients share a single instance.

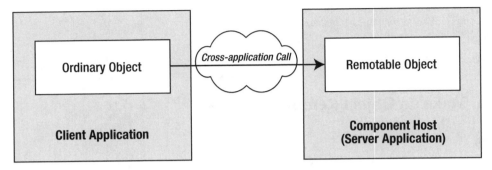

Figure 11-2. *Using a remotable class*

■**Note** Ideally, the remote object won't retain any state. This characteristic allows you to use single-call activation, in which object instances are created at the beginning of each method call and released at the end, much like a web service. This ensures your objects consume the fewest possible server resources and saves you from the added complexity of implementing a lease policy to configure object lifetime.

The Code

The following example demonstrates the declaration of a remotable class that reads data from the Person.Contact table of the AdventureWorks database and returns a System.Data.DataTable. Notice that the only remoting-specific code is the derivation of the class from the System.MarshalByRef class.

```
Imports System
Imports System.Data
Imports System.Data.SqlClient

Namespace Apress.VisualBasicRecipes.Chapter11

    ' Define a class that extends MarshalByRefObject, making it remotable.
    Public Class Recipe11_14
        Inherits MarshalByRefObject

        Private Shared connectionString As String = "Data Source=.\sqlexpress;" & ➥
"Initial Catalog=AdventureWorks;Integrated Security=SSPI;"

        ' The DataTable returned by this method is serializable, meaning that the
        ' data will be physically passed back to the caller across the network.
        Public Function GetContacts() As DataTable

            Dim SQL As String = "SELECT * FROM Person.Contact;"
```

```vbnet
        ' Create ADO.NET objects to execute the DB query.
        Using con As New SqlConnection(connectionString)
            Using com As New SqlCommand(SQL, con)
                Dim adapter As New SqlDataAdapter(com)
                Dim ds As New DataSet

                ' Execute the command.
                Try
                    con.Open()
                    adapter.Fill(ds, "Contacts")
                Catch ex As Exception
                    Console.WriteLine(ex.ToString)
                Finally
                    con.Close()
                End Try

                ' Return the first DataTable in the DataSet to the caller.
                Return ds.Tables(0)

            End Using
        End Using

    End Function

    ' This method allows you to verify that the object is running remotely.
    Public Function GetHostLocation() As String
        Return AppDomain.CurrentDomain.FriendlyName
    End Function

    End Class
End Namespace
```

Usage

To use the Recipe11_14 class remotely, you must host it and then create a client that uses the remote object. Here is the code for a simple console component host:

```vbnet
Imports System
Imports System.Runtime.Remoting

Namespace Apress.VisualBasicRecipes.Chapter11
    Public Class Recipe11_14Host

        Public Shared Sub Main()

            ' Register the remotable classes defined in the specified
            ' configuration file.
            RemotingConfiguration.Configure("Recipe11-14Host.exe.config", False)
```

```
' As long as this application is running, the registered remote
' objects will be accessible.
Console.Clear()
Console.WriteLine("Press Enter to shut down the host.")
Console.ReadLine()

    End Sub

End Class
End Namespace
```

The component host uses a new section in the standard configuration file (in this case Recipe11-14 Host.exe.config) to configure the classes it will support, the ports it will support for network communication, and the URI that the client will use to access the object. The host application must have a reference to the assembly, the Recipe11-14 assembly in this case, containing the implementation of the remote object class. The configuration file also configures the remote object to use single-call activation, meaning that a new object is created for each client call.

```
<?xml version="1.0" encoding="utf-8" ?>
<configuration>
  <system.runtime.remoting>
    <application>

      <!-- Define the remotable types. -->
      <service>
        <wellknown
            mode = "SingleCall"
            type = "Apress.VisualBasicRecipes.Chapter11.Recipe11_14, Recipe11-14"
            objectUri = "Recipe11-14.rem" />
      </service>

      <!-- Define the protocol used for network access.
           You can use tcp or http channels. -->
      <channels>
        <channel ref="tcp" port="19080" />
      </channels>


    </application>
  </system.runtime.remoting>
</configuration>
```

The following sample code shows a simple client that uses the remote object created earlier. Notice that in this example, the configuration of the remoting infrastructure is performed programmatically instead of using the configuration file. You should avoid such an approach when using shared configuration values because using configuration files provides more flexibility. If you did use a configuration file for the client, it would look similar to this:

```
<?xml version="1.0" encoding="utf-8" ?>
<configuration>
  <system.runtime.remoting>
    <application>
```

```
    <client>
      <wellknown
          type="Apress.VisualBasicRecipes.Chapter11.Recipe11_14,Recipe11_14"
          url="tcp://localhost:19080/Recipe11-14.rem" />
    </client>

  </application>
 </system.runtime.remoting>
</configuration>
```

However, if you want to dynamically configure the remoting infrastructure, you will need to be familiar with the approach demonstrated here. For detailed information, see *Advanced .NET Remoting, Second Edition* by Ingo Rammer and Mario Szpuszta (Apress, 2005). Note that as with the host, the assembly containing the declaration of the class that will be accessed remotely must still be explicitly referenced by the application.

```
Imports System
Imports System.Runtime.Remoting
Imports System.Runtime.Remoting.Channels
Imports System.Runtime.Remoting.Channels.Tcp
Imports System.Data

Namespace Apress.VisualBasicRecipes.Chapter11
    Public Class Recipe11_14Client

        Public Shared Sub Main()

            ' Register a new TCP Remoting channel to communicate with the
            ' remote object.
            ChannelServices.RegisterChannel(New TcpChannel, False)

            ' Register the classes that will be accessed remotely.
            RemotingConfiguration.RegisterWellKnownClientType( ➡
GetType(Recipe11_14), "tcp://localhost:19080/Recipe11-14.rem")

            ' Now any attempts to instantiate the Recipe11_14 class
            ' will actually create a proxy to a remote instance.

            ' Interact with the remote object through a proxy.
            Dim proxy As New Recipe11_14

            Try
                ' Display the name of the component host application domain
                ' where the object executes.
                Console.WriteLine("Object executing in: " & proxy.GetHostLocation)
            Catch ex As Exception
                Console.WriteLine(ex.ToString)
            End Try

            ' Get the DataTable from the remote object and display its contents.
            Dim dt As DataTable = proxy.GetContacts

            For Each row As DataRow In dt.Rows
                Console.WriteLine("{0}, {1}", row("LastName"), row("FirstName"))
            Next
```

```
            '  Wait to continue.
            Console.WriteLine(Environment.NewLine)
            Console.WriteLine("Main method complete.  Press Enter.")
            Console.ReadLine()

        End Sub

    End Class
End Namespace
```

11-15. Register All the Remotable Classes in an Assembly

Problem

You want to register all the remotable classes that are defined in an assembly without having to specify them in a configuration file.

Solution

Load the assembly with the remotable classes using reflection. Loop through all its Public types, and use the RemotingConfiguration.RegisterWellKnownServiceType method to register every remotable class.

How It Works

.NET makes it equally easy to register remotable classes through a configuration file or programmatically with code. The type being registered must extend MarshalByRefObject, and then you call RemotingConfiguration.RegisterWellKnownServiceType, passing on the type, the URI on which remote clients can connect to the type, and a value of the System.Runtime.Remoting.WellKnownObjectMode enumeration, which describes how the remoting infrastructure should map client calls to object instances. The possible values are SingleCall, in which every incoming call is serviced by a new object, and Singleton, in which every incoming call is serviced by the same object. When using singleton objects, accurate state management and thread synchronization become critical.

The Code

The following server code searches for remotable classes in an assembly that is specified as a command-line argument. Each class derived from MarshalByRefObject is registered, and then the example displays the channel where the remotable object is available.

```
Imports System
Imports System.Reflection
Imports System.Runtime.Remoting
Imports System.Runtime.Remoting.Channels
Imports System.Runtime.Remoting.Channels.Tcp

Namespace Apress.VisualBasicRecipes.Chapter11
    Public Class Recipe11_15

        Public Shared Sub Main(ByVal args As String())

            '  Ensure there is an argument. We assume it is a valid
            '  filename.
```

```
            If Not args.Length = 1 Then Exit Sub

            ' Register a new TCP remoting channel to communicate with
            ' the remote object.
            ChannelServices.RegisterChannel(New TcpChannel(19080), False)

            ' Get the registered remoting channel.
            Dim channel As TcpChannel = ➡
DirectCast(ChannelServices.RegisteredChannels(0), TcpChannel)

            ' Create an Assembly object representing the assembly
            ' where remotable classes are defined.
            Dim remoteAssembly As Assembly = Assembly.LoadFrom(args(0))

            ' Process all the public types in the specified assembly.
            For Each remType As Type In remoteAssembly.GetExportedTypes()

                ' Check if type is remotable.
                If remType.IsSubclassOf(GetType(MarshalByRefObject)) Then
                    ' Register each type using the type name as the URI.
                    Console.WriteLine("Registering {0}", remType.Name)
                    RemotingConfiguration.RegisterWellKnownServiceType(remType, ➡
remType.Name, WellKnownObjectMode.SingleCall)

                    ' Determine the URL where this type is published.
                    Dim urls As String() = channel.GetUrlsForUri(remType.Name)
                    Console.WriteLine("Url:  {0}", urls(0))
                End If

            Next

            ' As long as this application is running, the registered remote
            ' objects will be accessible.
            Console.WriteLine(Environment.NewLine)
            Console.WriteLine("Press Enter to shut down the host.")
            Console.ReadLine()

        End Sub

    End Class
End Namespace
```

Usage

Place the Recipe11-14.dll assembly in the directory where this recipe is and run the following command line:

```
recipe11-15 recipe11-14.dll
```

This will produce results similar to the following output:

```
Registering Recipe11_14
Url:  tcp://192.168.239.80:19080/Recipe11_14
```

Notes

The preceding code determines if a class is remotable by examining whether it derives from `MarshalByRefObject`. This approach always works, but it could lead you to expose some types that you don't want to make remotable. For example, the `System.Windows.Forms.Form` object derives indirectly from `MarshalByRefObject`. This means that if your remote object library contains any forms, they will be exposed remotely. To avoid this problem, don't include remotable types in your assembly unless you want to make them publicly available. Alternatively, identify the types you want to register with a custom attribute. You could then check for this attribute before registering a type.

11-16. Host a Remote Object in IIS

Problem

You want to create a remotable object in IIS (perhaps so that you can use SSL or IIS authentication) instead of a dedicated component host.

Solution

Place the configuration file and assembly in a directory (configured as an application within IIS), and modify the object URI so that it ends in .rem or .soap.

How It Works

Instead of creating a dedicated component host, you can host a remotable class in IIS. This allows you to ensure that the remotable classes will always be available, and it allows you to use IIS features such as SSL encryption and Integrated Windows authentication.

To host a remotable class in IIS, you must first have a directory configured as an application. The directory will contain two things: a configuration file named Web.config that registers the remotable classes and a Bin directory where you must place the corresponding class library assembly (or install the assembly in the GAC).

The configuration file for hosting in IIS is quite similar to the configuration file you use with a custom component host. However, you must follow several additional rules:

- You must use the HTTP channel (although you can use the binary formatter for smaller message sizes).

- You cannot specify a specific port number for listening. IIS listens on all the ports you have configured in IIS Manager. Typically, this will be ports 80 and 443 (for secure SSL communication).

- The object URI must end with .rem or .soap.

- When using IIS, you are stepping into ASP.NET territory. The configuration file you use here for remoting must be named Web.config, which is the configuration file used by ASP.NET applications.

The Code

Here's an example Web.config file that registers the remote class shown in recipe 11-14:

```
<?xml version="1.0"?>
<configuration>
  <system.runtime.remoting>
    <application>
      <!-- Define the remotable types. -->
      <service>
        <wellknown mode="SingleCall" ➥
type="Apress.VisualBasicRecipes.Chapter11.Recipe11_14,Recipe11-14" ➥
objectUri="Recipe11-14.rem" />
      </service>

      <!-- Define the protocol used for network access.
      You can use only the http channel. -->
      <channels>
        <channel ref="http" />
      </channels>

      <!-- Uncomment the following section if you want to use the
      binary formatter rather than the default SOAP formatter.-->
      <!--
      <serverProviders>
        <formatter ref="binary" />
      </serverProviders>
      -->
    </application>
  </system.runtime.remoting>
</configuration>
```

Usage

A client can use an object hosted in IIS in the same way as an object hosted in a custom component host. However, if a directory name is present, it will become part of the object URI. For example, if the Web.config file shown in the preceding code is hosted in the directory `http://localhost/RemoteObjects`, the full URL will be `http://localhost/RemoteObjects/Recipe11-14.rem`.

■**Note** When hosting an object with IIS, the account used to execute the object is the ASP.NET account defined in the Machine.config file. If this account doesn't have the rights to access the database (which is the default situation), you will receive an error when you try this example. Look at the .NET Framework for documentation on the `<processModel>` element.

11-17. Control the Lifetime of a Remote Object

Problem

You want to configure how long a singleton or client-activated object lives while not in use.

Solution

Configure a lease policy by using configuration file settings, override the `MarshalByRefObject.InitializeLifetimeService` method, or implement a custom lease provider.

How It Works

If a remotable object uses single-call activation, it will be destroyed automatically at the end of each method call. This behavior changes with client-activated and singleton objects, which are given a longer lifetime dictated by a *lifetime lease*. With the default settings, a remote object will be automatically destroyed if it's inactive for 2 minutes, provided it has been in existence for at least 5 minutes.

The component host, remote object, and client each have the opportunity to change lifetime settings, as described here:

- The component host can specify different lease lifetime defaults in the configuration file using the `<lifetime>` element, which is a child of the `<system.runtime.remoting>` element. The `leaseTime` attribute of the element specifies the default lifetime for all hosted objects. The `renewOnCallTime` attribute specifies the amount of time by which the lease is extended when a call is made against a hosted object. You can specify the values for both attributes as positive integers with a time unit suffix for days (D), hours (H), minutes (M), or seconds (S). For example, 10 hours is 10H, and 30 seconds is 30S.

- The remote class can override its `InitializeLifetimeService` method (inherited from `MarshalByRefObject`) to modify its initial lease settings by configuring and returning an object that implements the `System.Runtime.Remoting.Lifetime.ILease` interface. You obtain an `ILease` instance by calling the base class method `InitializeLifetimeService`. Then configure the returned `ILease` by setting the `InitialLeaseTime` and `RenewOnCallTime` properties to the desired values using `System.TimeSpan` objects. If you want the object to have an unlimited lifetime, simply return a `Nothing` reference instead of an `ILease` object. This is most commonly the case if you are creating a singleton object that needs to run independently (and permanently), even if clients aren't currently using it.

- The client can call the `MarshalByRefObject.GetLifetimeService` method on a specific remote object to retrieve an `ILease` instance. The client can then call the `ILease.Renew` method to specify a minimum amount of time the object should be kept alive.

The Code

The following example demonstrates how to use a component host's configuration file to control lifetime leases. The configuration gives each hosted object an initial lifetime of 10 minutes, and each time a member of the object is invoked, the lifetime is set to be at least 3 minutes.

```
<?xml version="1.0" encoding="utf-8" ?>
<configuration>
  <system.runtime.remoting>
    <application>

      <!-- Define the remotable types. -->
      <service>
        <wellknown
            mode = "SingleCall"
            type = "Apress.VisualBasicRecipes.Chapter11.Recipe11_17, Recipe11-17"
            objectUri = "Recipe11-17" />
      </service>

      <!-- Define the protocol used for network access.
           You can use tcp or http channels. -->
      <channels>
        <channel ref="tcp" port="19080" />
      </channels>
```

```
    <lifetime leaseTime="10M" renewOnCallTime="3M" />

  </application>
 </system.runtime.remoting>
</configuration>
```

The following example demonstrates how to use the second approach outlined where the remotable object overrides the `InitializeLifetimeService` method and takes control of its own lifetime. The example shows a remotable object that gives itself a default 10-minute lifetime and 3-minute renewal time.

```vbnet
Imports System
Imports System.Runtime.Remoting.Lifetime

Namespace Apress.VisualBasicRecipes.Chapter11

    ' Define a class that extends MarshalByRefObject, making it remotable.
    Public Class Recipe11_17
        Inherits MarshalByRefObject

        Public Overrides Function InitializeLifetimeService() As Object

            Dim lease As ILease = DirectCast(MyBase.InitializeLifetimeService(), ➥
ILease)

            ' Lease can only be configured if it is in an initial state.
            If lease.CurrentState = LeaseState.Initial Then
                lease.InitialLeaseTime = TimeSpan.FromMinutes(10)
                lease.RenewOnCallTime = TimeSpan.FromMinutes(3)
            End If

            Return lease

        End Function

        ...

    End Class
End Namespace
```

11-18. Control Versioning for Remote Objects

Problem

You want to create a component host that can host more than one version of the same object.

Solution

Install all versions of the remotable object into the global assembly cache (GAC), and explicitly register each version at a different URI endpoint. See recipe 1-17 for details on how to manage the assemblies in the GAC.

How It Works

.NET remoting doesn't include any intrinsic support for versioning. When a client creates a remote object, the component host automatically uses the version in the local directory or, in the case of a shared assembly, the latest version from the GAC. To support multiple versions, you have three choices:

- *Create separate component host applications*: Each component host will host a different version of the remote object assembly and will register its version with a different URI. This approach forces you to run multiple component host applications at once and is most practical if you are using IIS hosting (as described in recipe 11-16).

- *Create an entirely new remote object assembly (instead of simply changing the version)*: You can then register the classes from both assemblies at different URIs by using the same component host.

- *Install all versions of the remote object assembly in the GAC*: You can now create a component host that maps different URIs to specific versions of the remote object assembly.

The Code

Installing all versions of the remote object assembly in the GAC is the most flexible approach in cases where you need to support multiple versions. The following configuration file registers two versions of the RemoteObjects assembly at two different endpoints. Notice that you need to include the exact version number and public key token when using assemblies from the GAC. You can find this information by viewing the assembly in the Windows Explorer GAC plug-in (browse to C:\ [*WindowsDir*]\Assembly). The client configuration file won't change at all (aside from possibly updating the URI and ensuring that the correct version is referenced). The client "chooses" the version it wants to use by using the corresponding URI.

```
<configuration>
  <system.runtime.remoting>
    <application>

      <service>

        <!-- The type information is split over two lines to accommodate the
             bounds of the page. In the configuration file, this information
             must all be placed on a single line. -->
        <wellknown mode="SingleCall"
          type="RemoteObjects.RemoteObject, RemoteObjects, Version 1.0.0.1,
              Culture=neutral, PublicKeyToken=8b5ed84fd25209e1"
          objectUri="RemoteObj_1.0" />

        <wellknown mode="SingleCall"
          type="RemoteObjects.RemoteObject, RemoteObjects, Version 2.0.0.1,
              Culture=neutral, PublicKeyToken=8b5ed84fd25209e1"
          objectUri="RemoteObj_2.0" />
      </service>

      <channels>
        <channel ref="tcp" port="19080" />
      </channels>

    </application>
  </system.runtime.remoting>
</configuration>
```

11-19. Consume an RSS Feed

Problem

You need to consume (or retrieve data from) a Real Simple Syndication (RSS) feed.

Solution

Use the shared Load method of the SyndicationFeed class, which is located in the System.ServiceModel.Syndication namespace.

How It Works

In previous versions of the .NET Framework, consuming an RSS feed required downloading the file, using a method similar to the one covered by recipe 11-4, and parsing the returned XML information. To accurately parse the information, you needed to have fairly extensive knowledge of the RSS specifications in which the feed was written.

The SyndicationFeed class, which is part of the Windows Communication Foundation (WCF) piece released with .NET 3.0 and represents the feed itself, greatly simplifies this process. The shared Load method, which can accept the source as an Uri or an XmlReader, downloads the specified feed, parses the information, and returns a SyndicationFeed instance that contains the data from the feed.

The Code

The following example retrieves and displays some of the data contained in the specified RSS feed:

```
Imports System
Imports System.ServiceModel.Syndication

Namespace Apress.VisualBasicRecipes.Chapter11
    Public Class Recipe11_19

        Public Shared Sub main(ByVal args As String())

            ' Attempt to establish a connection to the feed represented by the URL
            ' passed into this method.
            Dim rssFeed As SyndicationFeed
            Try
                rssFeed = SyndicationFeed.Load(New Uri(args(0)))

                ' Display a few of the RSS feeds properties to the screen.
                Console.WriteLine("Title: {0}", rssFeed.Title.Text)
                Console.WriteLine("Description: {0}", rssFeed.Description.Text)
                Console.WriteLine("Copyright: {0}", rssFeed.Copyright.Text)
                Console.WriteLine("ImageUrl: {0}", rssFeed.ImageUrl.ToString)
                Console.WriteLine("LastUpdated: {0}", ➥
rssFeed.LastUpdatedTime.ToString())
                Console.WriteLine("Language: {0}", rssFeed.Language)

                ' Just show the first link (if there is more than one)
                Console.WriteLine("Link: {0}", rssFeed.Links(0).Uri.ToString())
```

```
        ' Now, show information for each item contained in the feed.
        Console.WriteLine("Items:")
        For Each item As SyndicationItem In rssFeed.Items
            Console.WriteLine("Title: {0}", item.Title.Text)
            Console.WriteLine("Description: {0}", item.Summary.Text)
            ' Just show the first link (if there is more than one)
            Console.WriteLine("Link: {0}", item.Links(0).Uri.ToString())
        Next
        Console.WriteLine(Environment.NewLine)

    Catch ex As Exception
        Console.WriteLine("Unable to retrieve the feed because of " & ➥
"the following error:  {0}", ex.ToString)
    End Try

    ' Wait to continue.
    Console.WriteLine(Environment.NewLine)
    Console.WriteLine("Main method complete.  Press Enter.")
    Console.ReadLine()

    End Sub
End Class

End Namespace
```

Usage

Running the example with the following command line:

recipe11-19 http://www.apress.com/resource/feed/newbook

will produce results similar to the following:

```
Title: Apress Newest Title List
Description: Apress's recent publish
Copyright: &#169; Copyright 2007, Apress. All Rights Reserved.
ImageUrl: http://www.apress.com/img/apress_RSS_logo.gif
LastUpdated: 1/1/0001 12:00:00 AM
Language: en-us
Link: http://www.apress.com/book?newest=1
Items:
Title: The Definitive Guide to Django: Web Development Done Right
Description: <p>In <i>The Definitive Guide to Django: Web Development Done Right
</i>, one of Django&rsquo;s creators and a Django lead developer show you how th
ey use this framework to create award&ndash;winning web sites. Over the course o
f three sections plus multiple appendixes, you&rsquo;ll learn about Django funda
mentals, complex features, and configuration options.</p>
Link: http://www.apress.com/book/view/1590597257
...
```

CHAPTER 12

■■■

Security and Cryptography

A principal goal of the Microsoft .NET Framework is to make computing more secure, especially with respect to the use of mobile code and distributed systems. Most modern operating systems (including Microsoft Windows) support user-based security, allowing you to control the actions and resources to which a user has access. However, in the highly connected world resulting from the proliferation of computer networks, particularly the Internet, it's insufficient to base security solely on the identity of a system's user. In the interest of security, code should not automatically receive the same level of trust that you assign to the person running the code.

The .NET Framework incorporates two complementary security models that address many of the issues associated with user and code security: code access security (CAS) and role-based security (RBS). CAS and RBS do not replace or duplicate the security facilities provided by the underlying operating system. They are platform-independent mechanisms that provide additional security capabilities to augment and enhance the overall security of your managed solutions. CAS uses information about the source and origin of an assembly (*evidence*) gathered at runtime to determine which actions and resources code from the assembly can access (*permissions*). The .NET Framework *security policy*—a hierarchical set of configurable rules—defines the mapping between evidence and permissions. The building blocks of security policy are *code groups*, which allow you to configure the mapping between evidence and permissions. The set of permissions granted to an assembly as a result of the security policy is known as the assembly's *grant set*.

The .NET Framework class library uses permission *demands* to protect its most important functionality from unauthorized access. A demand forces the common language runtime (CLR) to ensure that the whole stack of code calling a protected method has a specific permission. CAS ensures that the runtime capabilities of code depend on the level of trust you place in the creator and source of the code, not the level of trust you place in the user running the code.

Following a more traditional security model, RBS allows you to make runtime decisions based on the identity and roles of the user on whose behalf an application is running. On the Windows operating system, this equates to making decisions based on the Windows username and the Windows groups to which that user belongs. However, RBS provides a generic security mechanism that is independent of the underlying operating system, allowing you (with some development) to integrate with any user account system.

Another important aspect of the security features provided by the .NET Framework is *cryptography*. Cryptography is one of the most complex aspects of software development that any developer will use. The theory of modern cryptographic techniques is extremely difficult to understand and requires a level of mathematical knowledge that relatively few people have or need. Fortunately, the .NET Framework class library provides easy-to-use implementations of the most commonly used cryptographic techniques and support for the most popular and well-understood algorithms.

This chapter provides a wide variety of recipes that cover some of the more commonly used security capabilities provided by the .NET Framework. As you read the recipes in this chapter and think about how to apply the techniques to your own code, keep in mind that individual security features are rarely effective when implemented in isolation. In particular, cryptography does not equal security; the use of cryptography is merely one small element of creating a secure solution.

The recipes in this chapter cover the following:

- Developing strong-named assemblies that can still be called by partially trusted code (recipe 12-1)

- Configuring the .NET Framework security policy to turn off CAS execution permission checks (recipes 12-2)

- Requesting specific code access permissions for your assemblies, determining at runtime what permissions the current assembly has, and inspecting third-party assemblies to determine what permissions they need in order to run correctly (recipes 12-3, 12-4, 12-5, and 12-6)

- Controlling inheritance and member overrides using CAS (recipe 12-7)

- Inspecting the evidence presented by an assembly to the runtime when the assembly is loaded (recipe 12-8)

- Integrating with Windows security to determine whether a user is a member of a specific Windows group, restricting which users can execute your code, and impersonating other Windows users (recipes 12-9, 12-10, and 12-11)

- Generating random numbers that are nondeterministic and are suitable for use in security-sensitive applications (recipe 12-12)

- Using hash codes and keyed hash codes to store user passwords and determine whether files have changed (recipes 12-13, 12-14, 12-15, and 12-16)

- Using encryption to protect sensitive data both in memory and when it is stored to disk (recipes 12-17 and 12-18)

■**Note** For a broader explanation of secure programming and where cryptography fits in the overall security landscape, read *Writing Secure Code, Second Edition* by Michael Howard and David LeBlanc (Microsoft Press, 2003), a modern classic of computer literature that contains a wealth of practical field-tested information. For more comprehensive coverage of the .NET security classes, see *Programming .NET Security* by Adam Freeman and Allen Jones (O'Reilly and Associates, 2003). Although not yet updated for .NET Framework 3.5, *Programming .NET Security* provides easily understood descriptions of security fundamentals, covers most of the .NET security classes in detail, and demonstrates how to extend most aspects of the security framework.

12-1. Allow Partially Trusted Code to Use Your Strong-Named Assembly

Problem

You need to write a shared assembly that is accessible to code that is not fully trusted. By default, the runtime does not allow partially trusted code to access the types and members contained in a strong-named assembly.

Solution

Apply the assembly-level attribute System.Security.AllowPartiallyTrustedCallersAttribute to your shared assembly.

How It Works

To minimize the security risks posed by malicious code, the runtime does not allow assemblies granted only partial trust to access strong-named assemblies. This restriction dramatically reduces the opportunity for malicious code to attack your system, but the reasoning behind such a heavy-handed approach requires some explanation.

Assemblies that contain important functionality that is shared between multiple applications are usually strong-named and often installed in the global assembly cache (GAC). This is particularly true of the assemblies that constitute the .NET Framework class library. Other strong-named assemblies from well-known and widely distributed products will also be in the GAC and accessible to managed applications. The high chance that certain assemblies will be present in the GAC, their easy accessibility, and their importance to many different applications makes strong-named assemblies the most likely target for any type of subversive activity by malicious managed code.

Generally, the code most likely to be malicious is that which is loaded from remote locations, such as the Internet, over which you have little or no control. Under the default security policy in version 3.5 of the .NET Framework, all code run from the local machine has full trust, whereas code loaded from remote locations has only partial trust. Stopping partially trusted code from accessing strong-named assemblies means that partially trusted code has no opportunity to use the features of the assembly for malicious purposes, and cannot probe and explore the assembly to find exploitable holes. Of course, this theory hinges on the assumption that you correctly administer your security policy. If you simply assign all code full trust, not only will any assembly be able to access your strong-named assembly, but the code will also be able to access all of the functionality of the .NET Framework and even Win32 or any COM object through P/Invoke and COM Interop. That would be a security disaster!

■Note If you design, implement, and test your shared assembly correctly using CAS to restrict access to important members, you do not need to impose a blanket restriction to prevent partially trusted code from using your assembly. However, for an assembly of any significance, it's impossible to prove there are no security holes that malicious code can exploit. Therefore, you should carefully consider the need to allow partially trusted code to access your strong-named assembly before applying the AllowPartiallyTrustedCallers attribute. However, you might have no choice. If you are exposing public classes that provide events, you must apply this attribute. If you do not, an assembly that is not strong-named will be allowed to register a handler for one of your events, but when it is called, a security exception will be thrown. Code in an assembly that is not strong-named is not allowed to call code in a strong-named assembly.

The runtime stops partially trusted code from accessing strong-named assemblies by placing an implicit LinkDemand for the FullTrust permission set on every Public and Protected member of every publicly accessible type defined in the assembly. A LinkDemand verifies that the caller has the specified permissions, during just-in-time (JIT) compilation. This means that only assemblies granted the permissions equivalent to the FullTrust permission set are able to access the types and members from the strong-named assembly. Applying AllowPartiallyTrustedCallersAttribute to your strong-named assembly signals the runtime not to enforce the LinkDemand on the contained types and members.

■Note The runtime is responsible for enforcing the implicit LinkDemand security actions required to protect strong-named assemblies. The VB .NET assembler does not generate declarative LinkDemand statements at compile time.

The Code

The following code fragment shows the application of the attribute
`AllowPartiallyTrustedCallersAttribute`. Notice that you must prefix the attribute with `Assembly:`
to signal to the compiler that the target of the attribute is the assembly (also called a *global attribute*).
Because you target the assembly, the attribute must be positioned after any top-level `Imports` statements, but before any namespace or type declarations.

```
Imports System.Security

<Assembly: AllowPartiallyTrustedCallers()>

Namespace Apress.VisualBasicRecipes.Chapter12

    Public Class Recipe12_01
        '  Implementation code...
    End Class

End Namespace
```

■**Tip** It's common practice to contain all global attributes in a file separate from the rest of your application code.
Microsoft Visual Studio uses this approach, creating a file named AssemblyInfo.vb (located in the My Projects folder,
which is hidden by default) to contain all global attributes.

Notes

If, after applying `AllowPartiallyTrustedCallersAttribute` to your assembly, you want to restrict
partially trusted code from calling only specific members, you should implement a `LinkDemand` for
the `FullTrust` permission set on the necessary members, as shown in the following code fragment:

```
<System.Security.Permissions.PermissionSet(SecurityAction.LinkDemand, ➡
Name:="FullTrust")> _
Public Sub SomeMethod()
    '  Method code...
End Sub
```

12-2. Disable Execution Permission Checks

Problem

You need to load assemblies at runtime without the runtime checking them for execution permission.

Solution

In code, set the property `CheckExecutionRights` of the class `System.Security.SecurityManager` to `False`
and persist the change by calling `SecurityManager.SavePolicy`. Alternatively, use the Code Access Security Policy tool (Caspol.exe), and execute the command `caspol -e off` from the command line.

How It Works

Code Access Security (CAS) is a key element of the .NET runtime's security model and one that sets
it apart from many other computing platforms. As the runtime loads each assembly, it ensures that

the assembly's grant set (the permissions assigned to the assembly based on the security policy) includes the Execution element of SecurityPermission. The runtime implements a lazy policy resolution process, meaning that the grant set of an assembly is not calculated until the first time a security demand is made against the assembly. Not only does execution permission checking force the runtime to check that every assembly has the execution permission, but it also indirectly causes policy resolution for every assembly loaded, effectively negating the benefits of lazy policy resolution. These factors can introduce a noticeable delay as assemblies are loaded, especially when the runtime loads a number of assemblies together, as it does at application startup.

In many situations, simply allowing code to load and run is not a significant risk, as long as all other important operations and resources are correctly secured using CAS and operating system security. The SecurityManager class contains a set of Shared methods and properties that provide access to critical security functionality and data. For example, the CheckExecutionRights property turns on and off execution permission checks.

To modify the value of CheckExecutionRights, your code must have the ControlPolicy element of SecurityPermission. The change will affect the current process immediately, allowing you to load assemblies at runtime without the runtime checking them for execution permission. However, the change will not affect other existing processes. You must call the SavePolicy method to persist the change to the Windows registry for it to affect new processes.

The Code

The following example contains two methods (ExecutionCheckOn and ExecutionCheckOff) that demonstrate the code required to turn on and off execution permission checks and persist the configuration change:

```vb
Imports System.Security

Namespace Apress.VisualBasicRecipes.Chapter12
    Public Class Recipe12_02

        ' A method to turn on execution permission checking
        ' and persist the change.
        Public Sub ExecutionCheckOn()
            ' Turn on CAS checks.
            SecurityManager.CheckExecutionRights = True

            ' Persist the configuration change.
            SecurityManager.SavePolicy()

        End Sub

        ' A method to turn off execution permission checking
        ' and persist the change.
        Public Sub ExecutionCheckOff()
            ' Turn on CAS checks.
            SecurityManager.CheckExecutionRights = False

            ' Persist the configuration change.
            SecurityManager.SavePolicy()

        End Sub

    End Class
End Namespace
```

Notes

The .NET runtime allows you to turn off the automatic checks for execution permissions from within code or by using Caspol.exe. When you enter the command `caspol -e off` or its counterpart `caspol -e on` from the command line, the Caspol.exe utility actually sets the `CheckExecutionRights` property of the `SecurityManager` class before calling `SecurityManager.SavePolicy`.

12-3. Ensure the Runtime Grants Specific Permissions to Your Assembly

Problem

You need to ensure that the runtime grants your assembly those code access permissions that are critical to the successful operation of your application.

Solution

In your assembly, use permission requests to specify the code access permissions that your assembly must have. You declare permission requests using assembly-level code access permission attributes.

How It Works

The name *permission request* is a little misleading given that the runtime will never grant permissions to an assembly unless security policy dictates that the assembly should have those permissions. However, naming aside, permission requests serve an essential purpose, and although the way the runtime handles permission requests might initially seem strange, the nature of CAS does not allow for any obvious alternative.

Permission requests identify permissions that your code *must* have to function. For example, if you wrote a movie player that your customers could use to download and view movies from your web server, it would be disastrous if the user's security policy did not allow your player to open a network connection to your media server. Your player would load and run, but as soon as the user tried to connect to your server to play a movie, the application would crash with the exception `System.Security.SecurityException`. The solution is to include in your assembly a permission request for the code access permission required to open a network connection to your server (`System.Net.WebPermission` or `System.Net.SocketPermission`, depending on the type of connection you need to open).

The runtime honors permission requests using the premise that it's better that your code never load than to load and fail sometime later when it tries to perform an action that it does not have permission to perform. Therefore, if after security policy resolution the runtime determines that the user does not have the appropriate permissions to satisfy the assembly's permission requests, the runtime will fail to load the assembly and will instead throw the exception `System.Security.Policy.PolicyException`. Since your own code failed to load, the runtime will handle this security exception during the assembly loading and transform it into a `System.IO.FileLoadException` exception that will terminate your program.

When you try to load an assembly from within code (either automatically or manually), and the loaded assembly contains permission requests that the security policy does not satisfy, the method you use to load the assembly will throw a `PolicyException` exception, which you must handle appropriately.

To declare a permission request, you must use the attribute counterpart of the code access permission that you need to request. All code access permissions have an attribute counterpart that you use to construct declarative security statements, including permission requests. For example, the attribute counterpart of `SocketPermission` is `SocketPermissionAttribute`, and the attribute counterpart of WebPermission is WebPermissionAttribute. All permissions and their attribute counterparts follow the same naming convention and are members of the same namespace.

When making a permission request, it's important to remember the following:

- You must declare the permission request after any top-level Imports statements but before any namespace or type declarations.

- The attribute must target the assembly, so you must prefix the attribute name with Assembly.

- You do not need to include the Attribute portion of an attribute's name, although you can.

- You must specify SecurityAction.RequestMinimum as the first positional argument of the attribute. This value identifies the statement as a permission request.

- You must configure the attribute to represent the code access permission you want to request using the attribute's properties. Refer to the .NET Framework SDK documentation for details of the properties implemented by each code access security attribute.

- To make more than one permission request, simply include multiple permission request statements.

The Code

The following example is a console application that includes two permission requests: one for SocketPermission and the other for SecurityPermission. If you try to execute the PermissionRequestExample application and your security policy does not grant the assembly the requested permissions, you will get a FileLoadException exception, and the application will not execute. Using the default security policy, this will happen if you run the assembly from a network share, because assemblies loaded from the intranet zone are not granted SocketPermission.

```
Imports System
Imports System.Net
Imports System.Security.Permissions

'  Permission request for SocketPermission that allows the code to
'  open a TCP connection to the specified host and port.
<Assembly: SocketPermission(SecurityAction.RequestMinimum, Access:="Connect", ➥
Host:="www.fabrikam.com", Port:="3538", Transport:="Tcp")>

'  Permission request for the UnmanagedCode element of SecurityPermission,
'  which controls the code's ability to execute unmanaged code.
<Assembly: SecurityPermission(SecurityAction.RequestMinimum, UnmanagedCode:=True)>

Namespace Apress.VisualBasicRecipes.Chapter12
    Public Class Recipe12_03

        Public Shared Sub Main()

            '  Do something

            '  Wait to continue.
            Console.Write("Main method complete.  Press Enter.")
            Console.ReadLine()

        End Sub

    End Class
End Namespace
```

12-4. Limit the Permissions Granted to Your Assembly

Problem

You need to restrict the code access permissions granted to your assembly, ensuring that people and other software can never use your code as a mechanism through which to perform undesirable or malicious actions.

Solution

Use declarative security statements to specify optional permission requests and permission refusal requests in your assembly. Optional permission requests define the maximum set of permissions that the runtime will grant to your assembly. Refused permission requests specify particular permissions that the runtime should not grant to your assembly.

How It Works

In the interest of security, it's ideal if your code has only those code access permissions required to perform its function. This minimizes the opportunities for people and other code to use your code to carry out malicious or undesirable actions. The problem is that the runtime resolves an assembly's permissions using security policy, which a user or an administrator configures. Security policy could be different in every location where your application is run, and you have no control over what permissions the security policy assigns to your code.

Although you cannot control security policy in all locations where your code runs, the .NET Framework provides two mechanisms through which you can reject permissions granted to your assembly:

- *Optional permission request*: This defines the maximum set of permissions that the runtime can grant to your assembly. If the final grant set of an assembly contains any permissions other than those specified in the optional permission request, the runtime removes those permissions. Unlike as with a minimum permission request (discussed in recipe 12-3), the runtime will not refuse to load your assembly if it cannot grant all of the permissions specified in the optional request.

- *Refused permission request*: This defines the set of permissions that the runtime should never grant to your assembly. Even if the assembly would normally be granted a permission, it will be refused if it is part of the refused permission set.

The approach you use depends on how many permissions you want to reject. If you want to reject only a handful of permissions, a refuse request is easier to code. You just specify the permissions that you do not want to grant to your assembly. However, if you want to reject a large number of permissions, it's easier to code an optional request for the few permissions that you do want; all others not specified will be refused by the assembly.

You include optional and refuse requests in your code using declarative security statements with the same syntax as the minimum permission requests discussed in recipe 12-3. The only difference is the value of the System.Security.Permissions.SecurityAction that you pass to the permission attribute's constructor. Use SecurityAction.RequestOptional to declare an optional permission request and SecurityAction.RequestRefuse to declare a refuse request. As with minimal permission requests, you must declare optional and refuse requests as global attributes by beginning the permission attribute name with the prefix Assembly. In addition, all requests must appear after any top-level Imports statements but before any namespace or type declarations.

The Code

The code shown here demonstrates an optional permission request for the Internet permission set. The Internet permission set is a named permission set defined by the default security policy. When the runtime loads the example, it will not grant the assembly any permission that is not included within the Internet permission set. (Consult the .NET Framework SDK documentation for details of the permissions contained in the Internet permission set.)

```
Imports System.Security.Permissions

<Assembly: PermissionSet(SecurityAction.RequestOptional, Name:="Internet")>

Namespace Apress.VisualBasicRecipes.Chapter12

    Public Class Recipe12_04_OptionalRequest
        ' Class implementation...
    End Class

End Namespace
```

In contrast to the preceding example, the following example uses a refuse request to single out the permission System.Security.Permissions.FileIOPermission—representing write access to the C: drive—for refusal:

```
Imports System.Security.Permissions

<Assembly: FileIOPermission(SecurityAction.RequestRefuse, Write:="C:\")>

Namespace Apress.VisualBasicRecipes.Chapter12

    Public Class Recipe12_04_RefuseRequest
        ' Class implementation...
    End Class

End Namespace
```

12-5. View the Permissions Required by an Assembly

Problem

You need to view the permissions that an assembly must be granted in order to run correctly.

Solution

Use the Permissions Calculator (Permcalc.exe) supplied with the .NET Framework SDK.

How It Works

To configure security policy correctly, you need to know the code access permission requirements of the assemblies you intend to run. This is true of both executable assemblies and libraries that you access from your own applications. With libraries, it's also important to know which permissions the assembly refuses so that you do not try to use the library to perform a restricted action, which would result in a System.Security.SecurityException exception.

The Permissions Calculator (Permcalc.exe) supplied with the .NET Framework SDK walks through an assembly and provides an estimate of the permissions the assembly requires to run, regardless of whether they are declarative or imperative. Declarative permissions are those that are defined directly on a class or method, while imperative permissions are demanded by code.

The Code

The following example shows a class that declares a minimum, optional, and refusal request, as well as a number of imperative security demands:

```
Imports System
Imports System.Net
Imports System.Security.Permissions

'  Minimum permission request for SocketPermission.
<Assembly: SocketPermission(SecurityAction.RequestMinimum, Unrestricted:=True)>

'  Optional permission request for IsolatedStorageFilePermission.
<Assembly: IsolatedStorageFilePermission(SecurityAction.RequestOptional, ➥
Unrestricted:=True)>

'  Refuse request for ReflectionPermission.
<Assembly: ReflectionPermission(SecurityAction.RequestRefuse, Unrestricted:=True)>

Namespace Apress.VisualBasicRecipes.Chapter12
    Public Class Receipe12_05

        Public Shared Sub Main()

            '  Create and configure a FileIOPermission object that represents
            '  write access to the C:\Data folder.
            Dim fileIOPerm As New FileIOPermission(FileIOPermissionAccess.Write, ➥
"C:\Data")

            '  Make the demand.
            fileIOPerm.Demand()

            '  Do something...

            '  Wait to continue.
            Console.Write("Main method complete.  Press Enter.")
            Console.ReadLine()

        End Sub

    End Class
End Namespace
```

Usage

Executing the command permcalc -sandbox Recipe12-05.exe will generate a file named sandbox. PermCalc.xml that contains XML representations of the permissions required by the assembly. The sandbox parameter creates a private area (or *sandbox*) for an application, with the minimum permissions in which the application requires to run. Where the exact requirements of a permission cannot be determined (because it is based on runtime data), Permcalc.exe reports that unrestricted permissions of that type are required. You can instead default to the Internet zone permissions using the -Internet flag. Here are the contents of sandbox.PermCalc.xml when run against the sample code:

```
<?xml version="1.0"?>
<Sandbox>
  <PermissionSet version="1" class="System.Security.PermissionSet">
    <IPermission Write="C:\Data" version="1"
        class="System.Security.Permissions.FileIOPermission, mscorlib,
        Version=2.0.0.0, Culture=neutral,
        PublicKeyToken=b77a5c561934e089" />
    <IPermission version="1"
        class="System.Security.Permissions.SecurityPermission,
        mscorlib, Version=2.0.0.0, Culture=neutral,
        PublicKeyToken=b77a5c561934e089" Flags="Execution" />
    <IPermission version="1" class="System.Security.Permissions.UIPermission,
        mscorlib, Version=2.0.0.0, Culture=neutral,
        PublicKeyToken=b77a5c561934e089" Unrestricted="true" />
    <IPermission version="1" class="System.Net.SocketPermission, System,
        Version=2.0.0.0, Culture=neutral, PublicKeyToken=b77a5c561934e089"
        Unrestricted="true" />
  </PermissionSet>
</Sandbox>
```

12-6. Determine at Runtime Whether Your Code Has a Specific Permission

Problem

You need to determine at runtime whether your assembly has a specific permission, such as write access to files.

Solution

Instantiate and configure the permission you want to test for, and then pass it as an argument to the Shared method IsGranted of the class System.Security.SecurityManager.

How It Works

Using minimum permission requests, you can ensure that the runtime grants your assembly a specified set of permissions. As a result, when your code is running, you can safely assume that it has the requested minimum permissions. However, you might want to implement opportunistic functionality that your application offers only if the runtime grants your assembly appropriate permissions. This approach is partially formalized using optional permission requests, which allow you to define a set of permissions that your code could use if the security policy granted them, but are not essential for the successful operation of your code. (Recipe 12-4 provides more details on using optional permission requests.)

The problem with optional permission requests is that the runtime has no ability to communicate to your assembly which of the requested optional permissions it has granted. You can try to use a protected operation and fail gracefully if the call results in the exception System.Security. SecurityException. However, it's more efficient to determine in advance if you have the necessary permissions. You can then build logic into your code to avoid invoking secured members that will cause stack walks and raise security exceptions.

The Code

The following example demonstrates how to use the IsGranted method to determine if the assembly has write permission to the directory C:\Data. You could make such a call each time you needed to test for the permission, but it's more efficient to use the returned Boolean value to set a configuration flag indicating whether to allow users to save files.

```
Imports System.Security
Imports System.Security.Permissions

Namespace Apress.VisualBasicRecipes.Chapter12
    Public Class Recipe12_06
        ' Define a variable to indicate whether the assembly has write
        ' access to the C:\Data folder.
        Private canWrite As Boolean = False

        Public Sub New()
            ' Create and configure a FileIOPermission object that
            ' represents write access the C:\Data folder.
            Dim fileIOPerm As New FileIOPermission(FileIOPermissionAccess.Write, ➥
"C:\Data")

            ' Test if the current assembly has the specified permission.
            canWrite = SecurityManager.IsGranted(fileIOPerm)

        End Sub

    End Class
End Namespace
```

12-7. Restrict Who Can Extend Your Classes and Override Class Members

Problem

You need to control what code can extend your classes through inheritance and which class members a derived class can override.

Solution

Use declarative security statements to apply the SecurityAction.InheritanceDemand to the declarations of the classes and members that you need to protect.

How It Works

Language modifiers such as NotOverridable, NotInheritable, Public, Private, and Overridable give you a level of control over the ability of classes to inherit from your class and override its members. However, these modifiers are inflexible, providing no selectivity in restricting which code can extend a class or override its members. For example, you might want to allow only code written by your company or department to extend business-critical classes. By applying an InheritanceDemand to your class or member declaration, you can specify runtime permissions that a class must have to extend your class or override particular members. Remember that the permissions of a class are the permissions of the assembly in which the class is declared.

Although you can demand any permission or permission set in your InheritanceDemand, it's more common to demand identity permissions. Identity permissions represent evidence presented to the runtime by an assembly. If an assembly presents certain types of evidence at load time, the runtime will automatically assign the assembly the appropriate identity permission. Identity permissions allow you to use regular imperative and declarative security statements to base security decisions directly on code identity, without the need to evaluate evidence objects directly. Table 12-1 lists the type of identity permission generated for each type of evidence. (Evidence types are members of the System.Security.Policy namespace, and identity permission types are members of the System. Security.Permissions namespace.)

Table 12-1. *Evidence Type Classes That Generate Identity Permissions*

Evidence Class	Identity Permission
Publisher	PublisherIdentityPermission
Site	SiteIdentityPermission
StrongName	StrongNameIdentityPermission
Url	UrlIdentityPermission
Zone	ZoneIdentityPermission

Note   The runtime assigns identity permissions to an assembly based on the evidence presented by the assembly. You cannot assign additional identity permissions to an assembly through the configuration of security policy.

You must use declarative security syntax to implement an InheritanceDemand, and so you must use the attribute counterpart of the permission class that you want to demand. All permission classes, including InheritanceDemand, have an attribute counterpart that you use to construct declarative security statements. For example, the attribute counterpart of PublisherIdentityPermission is PublisherIdentityPermissionAttribute, and the attribute counterpart of StrongNameIdentityPermission is StrongNameIdentityPermissionAttribute. All permissions and their attribute counterparts follow the same naming convention and are members of the same namespace.

To control which code can extend your class, apply the InheritanceDemand to the class declaration using one of the permissions listed in Table 12-1. To control which code can override specific members of a class, apply the InheritanceDemand to the member declaration.

The Code

The following example demonstrates the use of an InheritanceDemand on both a class and a method. Applying a PublisherIdentityPermissionAttribute to the Recipe12_07 class means only classes in assemblies signed by the publisher certificate contained in the pubcert.cer file (or assemblies granted FullTrust) can extend the class. The contents of the pubcert.cer file are read at compile time, and the necessary certificate information is built into the assembly metadata. To demonstrate that other permissions can also be used with an InheritanceDemand, the PermissionSetAttribute is used to allow only classes granted the FullTrust permission set to override the method SomeProtectedMethod.

```
Imports System.Security.Permissions
Namespace Apress.VisualBasicRecipes.Chapter12

    <PublisherIdentityPermission(SecurityAction.InheritanceDemand, ➡
CertFile:="pubcert.cer")> _
    Public Class Recipe12_07

        <PermissionSet(SecurityAction.InheritanceDemand, Name:="FullTrust")> _
        Public Sub SomeProtectedMethod()
            ' Method implementation...
        End Sub

    End Class
End Namespace
```

12-8. Inspect an Assembly's Evidence

Problem

You need to inspect the evidence that the runtime assigned to an assembly.

Solution

Obtain a System.Reflection.Assembly object that represents the assembly in which you are interested. Get the System.Security.Policy.Evidence class from the Evidence property of the Assembly object, and access the contained evidence objects using the GetEnumerator, GetHostEnumerator, or GetAssemblyEnumerator method of the Evidence class.

How It Works

The Evidence class represents a collection of evidence objects. The read-only Evidence property of the Assembly class returns an Evidence collection object that contains all of the evidence objects that the runtime assigned to the assembly as the assembly was loaded.

The Evidence class actually contains two collections, representing different types of evidence:

- *Host evidence* includes those evidence objects assigned to the assembly by the runtime or the trusted code that loaded the assembly.

- *Assembly evidence* represents custom evidence objects embedded into the assembly at build time.

The Evidence class implements three methods for enumerating the evidence objects it contains: GetEnumerator, GetHostEnumerator, and GetAssemblyEnumerator. The GetHostEnumerator and GetAssemblyEnumerator methods return a System.Collections.IEnumerator instance that enumerates only those evidence objects from the appropriate collection. The GetEnumerator method, which is used when you perform a For Each on the Evidence class, returns an IEnumerator instance that enumerates *all* of the evidence objects contained in the Evidence collection.

> **■Note** Evidence classes do not extend a standard base class or implement a standard interface. Therefore, when working with evidence programmatically, you need to test the type of each object and know what particular types you are seeking. (See recipe 3-11 for details on how to test the type of an object at runtime.)

The Code

The following example demonstrates how to display the host and assembly evidence of an assembly on the console. The example relies on the fact that all standard evidence classes override the Object. ToString method to display a useful representation of the evidence object's state. Although interesting, this example does not always show the evidence that an assembly would have when loaded from within your program. The runtime host (such as the Microsoft ASP.NET or Internet Explorer runtime host) is free to assign additional host evidence as it loads an assembly.

```vbnet
Imports System
Imports System.Reflection
Imports System.Collections
Imports System.Security.Policy

Namespace Apress.VisualBasicRecipes.Chapter12
    Public Class Recipe12_08

        Public Shared Sub Main(ByVal args As String())

            ' Load the specified assembly.
            Dim a As Assembly = Assembly.LoadFrom(args(0))

            ' Get the evidence collection from the
            ' loaded assembly.
            Dim e As Evidence = a.Evidence

            ' Display the host evidence.
            Dim x As IEnumerator = e.GetHostEnumerator

            Console.WriteLine("HOST EVIDENCE COLLECTION:")

            While x.MoveNext
                Console.Write(x.Current.ToString)
                Console.Write("Press Enter to see next evidence.")
                Console.Write(Environment.NewLine)
                Console.ReadLine()
            End While

            ' Display the assembly evidence.
            x = e.GetAssemblyEnumerator()

            Console.WriteLine("ASSEMBLY EVIDENCE COLLECTION:")
```

```
        While x.MoveNext
            Console.Write(x.Current.ToString)
            Console.Write("Press Enter to see next evidence.")
            Console.Write(Environment.NewLine)
            Console.ReadLine()
        End While

        ' Wait to continue.
        Console.Write("Main method complete.  Press Enter.")
        Console.ReadLine()

    End Sub

  End Class
End Namespace
```

Note All of the standard evidence classes provided by the .NET Framework are immutable, ensuring that you cannot change their values after the runtime has created them and assigned them to the assembly. In addition, you cannot add or remove items while you are enumerating across the contents of a collection using an IEnumerator; otherwise, the MoveNext method throws a System.InvalidOperationException exception.

Usage

You would execute the example using Recipe12-08.exe Recipe12-08.exe. This will produce output similar to the following:

```
HOST EVIDENCE COLLECTION:
<System.Security.Policy.Zone version="1">
<Zone>MyComputer</Zone>
</System.Security.Policy.Zone>
Press Enter to see next evidence.

<System.Security.Policy.Url version="1">
<Url>file:///F:/Programming/Visual Studio 2008/Visual Basic 2008 Recipes/Chapter
12/Recipe12-08/bin/Debug/Recipe12-08.EXE</Url>
</System.Security.Policy.Url>
Press Enter to see next evidence.

<System.Security.Policy.Hash version="1">
<RawData>4D5A900003000000040000000FFFF0000B80000000000000040000000000000000000000
000000000000000000000000000000000000000000000800000000E1FBA0E00B409CD21B8014

...

0000000000000000000000000</RawData>
</System.Security.Policy.Hash>
Press Enter to see next evidence.

ASSEMBLY EVIDENCE COLLECTION:
Main method complete.  Press Enter.
```

12-9. Determine Whether the Current User Is a Member of a Specific Windows Group

Problem

You need to determine if the current user of your application is a member of a specific Windows user group.

Solution

Obtain a `System.Security.Principal.WindowsIdentity` object representing the current Windows user by calling the `Shared` method `WindowsIdentity.GetCurrent`. Create a `System.Security.Principal.WindowsPrincipal` class using the `WindowsIdentity` class, and then call the method `IsInRole` of the `WindowsPrincipal` object.

How It Works

The role-based security (RBS) mechanism of the .NET Framework abstracts the user-based security features of the underlying operating system through the following two key interfaces:

- The `System.Security.Principal.IIdentity` interface, which represents the entity on whose behalf code is running; for example, a user or service account.

- The `System.Security.Principal.IPrincipal` interface, which represents the entity's `IIdentity` and the set of roles to which the entity belongs. A *role* is simply a categorization used to group entities with similar security capabilities, such as a Windows user group.

To integrate RBS with Windows user security, the .NET Framework provides the following two Windows-specific classes that implement the `IIdentity` and `IPrincipal` interfaces:

- `System.Security.Principal.WindowsIdentity`, which implements the `IIdentity` interface and represents a Windows user.

- `System.Security.Principal.WindowsPrincipal`, which implements `IPrincipal` and represents the set of Windows groups to which the user belongs.

Because .NET RBS is a generic solution designed to be platform-independent, you have no access to the features and capabilities of the Windows user account through the `IIdentity` and `IPrincipal` interfaces, and you must frequently use the `WindowsIdentity` and `WindowsPrincipal` objects directly.

To determine if the current user is a member of a specific Windows group, you must first call the `Shared` method `WindowsIdentity.GetCurrent`. The `GetCurrent` method returns a `WindowsIdentity` object that represents the Windows user on whose behalf the current thread is running. An overload of the `GetCurrent` method takes a `Boolean` argument and allows you to control what is returned by `GetCurrent` if the current thread is impersonating a user different from the one associated with the process. If the argument is `True`, `GetCurrent` returns a `WindowsIdentity` representing the imperson-ated user, or it returns `Nothing` if the thread is not impersonating a user. If the argument is `False`, `GetCurrent` returns the `WindowsIdentity` of the thread if it is impersonating a user, or it returns the `WindowsIdentity` of the process if the thread is not currently impersonating a user. Calling `GetCurrent` and passing `False` is the same as calling `GetCurrent` with no parameter.

■**Note** The `WindowsIdentity` class provides overloaded constructors that, when running on Microsoft Windows Server 2003, Windows Vista, or Windows Server 2008, allow you to obtain a `WindowsIdentity` object representing a named user. You can use this `WindowsIdentity` object and the process described in this recipe to determine if that user is a member of a specific Windows group. If you try to use one of these constructors when running on an earlier version of Windows, the `WindowsIdentity` constructor will throw an exception. On Windows platforms preceding Windows Server 2003, you must use native code to obtain a Windows access token representing the desired user. You can then use this access token to instantiate a `WindowsIdentity` object. Recipe 12-11 explains how to obtain Windows access tokens for specific users.

Once you have a `WindowsIdentity`, instantiate a new `WindowsPrincipal` object, passing the `WindowsIdentity` object as an argument to the constructor. Finally, call the `IsInRole` method of the `WindowsPrincipal` object to test if the user is in a specific group (role). `IsInRole` returns `True` if the user is a member of the specified group; otherwise, it returns `False`. The `IsInRole` method provides three additional overloads:

- The second `IsInRole` overload accepts an `Integer`, which specifies a Windows role identifier (RID). RIDs provide a mechanism to identify groups that is independent of language and localization.

- The third `IsInRole` overload accepts a member of the `System.Security.Principal.WindowsBuiltInRole` enumeration. The `WindowsBuiltInRole` enumeration defines a set of members that represent each of the built-in Windows groups. As with RIDs, these groups are independent of language and localization.

- The fourth `IsInRole` overload accepts a `System.Security.Principal.SecurityIdentifier` object that represents the security identifier (SID) of the group for which you want to test.

Table 12-2 lists the name, RID, and `WindowsBuiltInRole` value for each of the standard Windows groups.

Table 12-2. *Windows Built-In Account Names and Identifiers*

Account Name	RID (Hex)	WindowsBuiltInRole Value
BUILTIN\Account Operators	0x224	AccountOperator
BUILTIN\Administrators	0x220	Administrator
BUILTIN\Backup Operators	0x227	BackupOperator
BUILTIN\Guests	0x222	Guest
BUILTIN\Power Users	0x223	PowerUser
BUILTIN\Print Operators	0x226	PrintOperator
BUILTIN\Replicators	0x228	Replicator
BUILTIN\Server Operators	0x225	SystemOperator
BUILTIN\Users	0x221	Use

The Code

The following example demonstrates how to test whether the current user is a member of a set of named Windows groups. You specify the groups that you want to test for as command-line arguments. Remember to prefix the group name with the machine or domain name, or BUILTIN for standard Windows groups.

```vb
Imports System
Imports System.Security.Principal

Namespace Apress.VisualBasicRecipes.Chapter12
    Public Class Recipe12_09

        Public Shared Sub Main(ByVal args As String())

            ' Obtain a WindowsIdentity object representing the currently
            ' logged on Windows user.
            Dim identity As WindowsIdentity = WindowsIdentity.GetCurrent

            ' Create a Windows Principal object that represents the security
            ' capabilities of the specified WindowsIdentity; in this case,
            ' the Windows groups to which the current user belongs.
            Dim principal As New WindowsPrincipal(identity)

            ' Iterate through the group names specified as command-line
            ' arguments and test to see if the current user is a member of
            ' each one.
            For Each role As String In args
                Console.WriteLine("Is {0} a member of {1}? = {2}", identity.Name, ➥
role, principal.IsInRole(role))
            Next

            ' Wait to continue.
            Console.WriteLine(Environment.NewLine)
            Console.Write("Main method complete.  Press Enter.")
            Console.ReadLine()

        End Sub

    End Class
End Namespace
```

Usage

If you run this example while logged in as a user named Guy on a computer named MACHINE using this command:

```
Recipe12-09 BUILTIN\Administrators BUILTIN\Users MACHINE\Accountants
```

you will see console output similar to the following:

```
Is MACHINE\Guy a member of BUILTIN\Administrators? = False
Is MACHINE\Guy a member of BUILTIN\Users? = True
Is MACHINE\Guy a member of MACHINE\Accountants? = True
```

12-10. Restrict Which Users Can Execute Your Code

Problem

You need to restrict which users can execute elements of your code based on the user's name or the roles of which the user is a member.

Solution

Use the permission class System.Security.Permissions.PrincipalPermission and its attribute counterpart System.Security.Permissions.PrincipalPermissionAttribute to protect your program elements with RBS demands.

How It Works

The .NET Framework supports both imperative and declarative RBS (refer to recipe 12-9) demands. The class PrincipalPermission provides support for imperative security statements, and its attribute counterpart PrincipalPermissionAttribute provides support for declarative security statements. RBS demands use the same syntax as CAS demands, but RBS demands specify the name the current user must have, or more commonly, the roles of which the user must be a member. An RBS demand instructs the runtime to look at the name and roles of the current user, and if that user does not meet the requirements of the demand, the runtime throws a System.Security.SecurityException exception.

To make an imperative security demand, you must first create a PrincipalPermission object specifying the username or role name you want to demand, and then you must call its Demand method. You can specify only a single username and role name per demand. If either the username or the role name is Nothing, any value will satisfy the demand. Unlike with code access permissions, an RBS demand does not result in a stack walk; the runtime evaluates only the username and roles of the current user.

To make a declarative security demand, you must annotate the class or member you want to protect with a correctly configured PrincipalPermissionAttribute attribute. Class-level demands apply to all members of the class, unless a member-specific demand overrides the class demand.

Generally, you are free to choose whether to implement imperative or declarative demands. However, imperative security demands allow you to integrate RBS demands with code logic to achieve more sophisticated demand behavior. In addition, if you do not know the role or usernames to demand at compile time, you must use imperative demands. Declarative demands have the advantage that they are separate from code logic and easier to identify. In addition, you can view declarative demands, but not imperative ones, using the Permview.exe tool (discussed in recipe 12-5). Whether you implement imperative or declarative demands, you must ensure that the runtime has access to the name and roles for the current user to evaluate the demand correctly.

The System.Threading.Thread class represents an operating system thread running managed code. The Shared property CurrentPrincipal of the Thread class contains an IPrincipal instance representing the roles on whose behalf the managed thread is running.

At the operating system level, each thread also has an associated Windows access token (represented by the WindowsIdentity class), which represents the Windows account on whose behalf the thread is running. The IPrincipal instance and the Windows access token are two separate entities. Windows uses its access token to enforce operating system security, whereas the .NET runtime uses its IPrincipal instance to evaluate application-level RBS demands. The identity and principal are separate entities, and they may represent different user accounts, as noted in recipe 12-11.

The benefit of this approach is that you can implement a user and an RBS model within your application using a proprietary user accounts database, without the need for all users to have Windows user accounts. This is a particularly useful approach in large-scale, publicly accessible Internet applications.

By default, the `Thread.CurrentPrincipal` property is undefined. Because obtaining user-related information can be time-consuming, and only a minority of applications use this information, the .NET designers opted for lazy initialization of the `CurrentPrincipal` property. The first time code gets the `Thread.CurrentPrincipal` property, the runtime assigns an `IPrincipal` instance to the property using the following logic:

- If the application domain in which the current thread is executing has a default principal, the runtime assigns this principal to the `Thread.CurrentPrincipal` property. By default, application domains do not have default principals. You can set the default principal of an application domain by calling the method `SetThreadPrincipal` on a `System.AppDomain` object that represents the application domain you want to configure. Code must have the `ControlPrincipal` element of `SecurityPermission` to call `SetThreadPrincipal`. You can set the default principal only once for each application domain; a second call to `SetThreadPrincipal` results in the exception `System.Security.Policy.PolicyException`.

- If the application domain does not have a default principal, the application domain's principal policy determines which `IPrincipal` implementation to create and assign to `Thread.CurrentPrincipal`. To configure principal policy for an application domain, obtain an `AppDomain` object that represents the application domain and call the object's `SetPrincipalPolicy` method. The `SetPrincipalPolicy` method accepts a member of the enumeration `System.Security.Principal.PrincipalPolicy`, which specifies the type of `IPrincipal` object to assign to `Thread.CurrentPrincipal`. Code must have the `ControlPrincipal` element of `SecurityPermission` to call `SetPrincipalPolicy`. Table 12-3 lists the available `PrincipalPolicy` values; the default value is `UnauthenticatedPrincipal`.

- If your code has the `ControlPrincipal` element of `SecurityPermission`, you can instantiate your own `IPrincipal` object and assign it to the `Thread.CurrentPrincipal` property directly. This will prevent the runtime from assigning default `IPrincipal` objects or creating new ones based on principal policy.

Table 12-3. *Members of the PrincipalPolicy Enumeration*

Member Name	Description
NoPrincipal	No `IPrincipal` object is created. `Thread.CurrentPrincipal` returns `Nothing`.
UnauthenticatedPrincipal	An empty `System.Security.Principal.GenericPrincipal` object is created and assigned to `Thread.CurrentPrincipal`.
WindowsPrincipal	A `WindowsPrincipal` object representing the currently logged-on Windows user is created and assigned to `Thread.CurrentPrincipal`.

Whatever method you use to establish the `IPrincipal` for the current thread, you must do so before you use RBS demands, or the correct user (`IPrincipal`) information will not be available for the runtime to process the demand. Normally, when running on the Windows platform, you would set the principal policy of an application domain to `PrincipalPolicy.WindowsPrincipal` (as shown here) to obtain Windows user information.

```
' Obtain a reference to the current application domain.
Dim currentAppDomain As AppDomain = System.AppDomain.CurrentDomain

' Configure the current application domain to use Windows-based principals.
currentAppDomain.SetPrincipalPolicy( ➥
Security.Principal.PrincipalPolicy.WindowsPrincipal)
```

The Code

The following example demonstrates the use of imperative and declarative RBS demands. The example shows three methods protected using imperative RBS demands (Method1, Method2, and Method3), and then three other methods protected using the equivalent declarative RBS demands (Method4, Method5, and Method6).

```
Imports System
Imports System.Security.Permissions

Namespace Apress.VisualBasicRecipes.Chapter12
    Public Class Recipe12_10

        Public Shared Sub Method1()

            ' An imperative role-based security demand for the current
            ' principal to represent an identity with the name Jeremy. The
            ' roles of the principal are irrelevant.
            Dim perm As New PrincipalPermission("MACHINE\Jeremy", Nothing)

            ' Make the demand.
            perm.Demand()

        End Sub

        Public Shared Sub Method2()

            ' An imperative role-based security demand for the current
            ' principal to be a member of the roles Managers or Developers.
            ' If the principal is a member of either role, access is granted.
            ' Using the PrincipalPermission, you can express only an OR type
            ' relationship. This is because the PrincipalPolicy.Intersect method
            ' always returns an empty permission unless the two inputs are the
            ' same. However, you can use code logic to implement more complex
            ' conditions. In this case, the name of the identity is irrelevant.
            Dim perm1 As New PrincipalPermission(Nothing, "MACHINE\Managers")
            Dim perm2 As New PrincipalPermission(Nothing, "MACHINE\Developers")

            ' Make the demand.
            perm1.Union(perm2).Demand()

        End Sub

        Public Shared Sub Method3()

            ' An imperative role-based security demand for the current principal
            ' to represent an identity with the name Jeremy AND be a member of the
            ' Managers role.
            Dim perm As New PrincipalPermission("MACHINE\Jeremy", ➥
    "MACHINE\Managers")

            ' Make the demand.
            perm.Demand()

        End Sub
```

```vb
' A declarative role-based security demand for the current principal
' to represent an identity with the name Jeremy.
<PrincipalPermission(SecurityAction.Demand, Name:="MACHINE\Jeremy")> _
Public Shared Sub Method4()

    ' Method implementation...

End Sub

' A declarative role-based security demand for the current principal
' to be a member of the roles Managers OR Developers. If the principal
' is a member of either role, access is granted. You can express only
' an OR type relationship, not an AND relationship.
<PrincipalPermission(SecurityAction.Demand, Role:="MACHINE\Managers"), ➥
PrincipalPermission(SecurityAction.Demand, Role:="MACHINE\Developers")> _
    Public Shared Sub Method5()

        ' Method implementation...

    End Sub

' A declarative role-based security demand for the current principal
' to represent an identity with the name Jeremy and be a member of the
' Managers role.
<PrincipalPermission(SecurityAction.Demand, Name:="MACHINE\Jeremy", ➥
Role:="MACHINE\Managers")> _
    Public Shared Sub Method6()

        ' Method implementation...

    End Sub

End Class
End Namespace
```

12-11. Impersonate a Windows User

Problem

You need your code to run in the context of a Windows user other than the currently active user account.

Solution

Obtain a System.Security.Principal.WindowsIdentity object representing the Windows user you need to impersonate, and then call the Impersonate method of the WindowsIdentity object.

How It Works

Every Windows thread has an associated *access token*, which represents the Windows account on whose behalf the thread is running. The Windows operating system uses the access token to determine whether a thread has the appropriate permissions to perform protected operations on behalf of the account, such as read and write files, reboot the system, and change the system time.

By default, a managed application runs in the context of the Windows account that executed the application. This is normally desirable behavior, but sometimes you will want to run an application in the context of a different Windows account. This is particularly true in the case of server-side applications that process transactions on behalf of the users remotely connected to the server.

It's common for a server application to run in the context of a Windows account created specifically for the application—a service account. This service account will have minimal permissions to access system resources. Enabling the application to operate as though it were the connected user permits the application to access the operations and resources appropriate to that user's security clearance. When an application assumes the identity of another user, it's known as *impersonation*. Correctly implemented, impersonation simplifies security administration and application design, while maintaining user accountability.

▮**Note** As discussed in recipe 12-10, a thread's Windows access token and its .NET principal are separate entities and can represent different users. The impersonation technique described in this recipe changes only the Windows access token of the current thread; it does not change the thread's principal. To change the thread's principal, code must have the ControlPrincipal element of SecurityPermission and assign a new System. Security.Principal.IPrincipal object to the CurrentPrincipal property of the current System. Threading.Thread.

The System.Security.Principal.WindowsIdentity class provides the functionality through which you invoke impersonation. However, the exact process depends on which version of Windows your application is running. For example, the WindowsIdentity class supports constructor overloads that create WindowsIdentity objects based on the account name of the user you want to impersonate. These overloads work only when used on a Windows Server 2003 or 2008 domain.

On all previous versions of Windows, you must first obtain a System.IntPtr containing a reference to a Windows access token that represents the user to impersonate. To obtain the access token reference, you must use a native method such as the LogonUser function from the Win32 API.

▮**Caution** A major issue with performing impersonation on Microsoft Windows 2000 and Windows NT is that an account must have the Windows privilege SE_TCB_NAME to execute LogonUser. This requires you to configure Windows security policy and grant the account the right to "act as part of operating system." This grants the account a very high level of trust. You should never grant the privilege SE_TCB_NAME directly to user accounts. The requirement for an account to have the SE_TCB_NAME privilege no longer exists for Windows 2003, Windows XP, and Windows Vista.

Once you have a WindowsIdentity object representing the user you want to impersonate, call its Impersonate method. From that point on, all actions your code performs occur in the context of the impersonated Windows account. The Impersonate method returns a System.Security.Principal. WindowsSecurityContext object, which represents the active account prior to impersonation. To revert to the original account, call the Undo method of this WindowsSecurityContext object.

The Code

The following example demonstrates impersonation of a Windows user. The example uses the LogonUser function of the Win32 API to obtain a Windows access token for the specified user, impersonates the user, and then reverts to the original user context.

```vb
Imports System
Imports System.IO
Imports System.Security.Principal
Imports System.Security.Permissions
Imports System.Runtime.InteropServices

' Ensure the assembly has permission to execute unmanaged code
' and control the thread principal.
<Assembly: SecurityPermission(SecurityAction.RequestMinimum, UnmanagedCode:=True, ➥
ControlPrincipal:=True)>
Namespace Apress.VisualBasicRecipes.Chapter12
    Public Class Recipe12_11

        ' Define some constants for use with the LogonUser function.
        Const LOGON32_PROVIDER_DEFAULT As Integer = 0
        Const LOGON32_LOGON_INTERACTIVE As Integer = 2

        ' Import the Win32 LogonUser function from advapi32.dll. Specify
        ' "SetLastError = True" to correctly support access to Win32 error
        ' codes.
        <DllImport("advapi32.dll", SetLastError:=True, CharSet:=CharSet.Unicode)> _
        Private Shared Function LogonUser(ByVal userName As String, ➥
ByVal domain As String, ByVal password As String, ByVal logonType As Integer, ➥
ByVal logonProvider As Integer, ByRef accessToken As IntPtr) As Boolean
        End Function

        Public Shared Sub Main(ByVal args As String())

            ' Create a new IntPtr to hold the access token returned by the
            ' LogonUser function.
            Dim accessToken As IntPtr = IntPtr.Zero

            ' Call the LogonUser function to obtain an access token for the
            ' specified user. The accessToken variable is passed to LogonUser
            ' by reference and will contain a reference to the Windows access
            ' token if LogonUser is successful.
            Dim success As Boolean = LogonUser(args(0), ".", args(1), ➥
LOGON32_LOGON_INTERACTIVE, LOGON32_PROVIDER_DEFAULT, accessToken)

            ' If LogonUser returns false, an error has occurred.
            ' Display the error and exit.
            If Not success Then
                Console.WriteLine("LogonUser returned error {0}", ➥
Marshal.GetLastWin32Error())
            Else
                ' Display the active identity.
                Console.WriteLine("Identity before impersonation = {0}", ➥
WindowsIdentity.GetCurrent.Name)
                ' Create a new WindowsIdentity from the Windows access token.
                Dim identity As New WindowsIdentity(accessToken)
```

```
                            '  Impersonate the specified user, saving a reference to the
                            '  returned WindowsImpersonationContext, which contains the
                            '  information necessary to revert to the original user context.
                            Dim impContext As WindowsImpersonationContext = ➥
identity.Impersonate

                            '  Display the active identity.
                            Console.WriteLine("Identity during impersonation = {0}", ➥
WindowsIdentity.GetCurrent.Name)

                            '  Perform actions as the impersonated user...

                            '  Revert to the original Windows user using the
                            '  WindowsImpersonationContext object.
                            impContext.Undo()

                            '  Display the active identity.
                            Console.WriteLine("Identity after impersonation = {0}", ➥
WindowsIdentity.GetCurrent.Name)

                            '  Wait to continue.
                            Console.WriteLine(Environment.NewLine)
                            Console.WriteLine("Main method complete.  Press Enter.")
                            Console.ReadLine()

                    End If

                End Sub

        End Class
End Namespace
```

Usage

The example expects two command-line arguments: the account name of the user on the local machine to impersonate and the account's password. For example, the command `Recipe12-11 Administrator password` impersonates the user Administrator, as long as that user exists in the local accounts database and has the password "password."

If you used the previous command while logged on as user TestUser, you would receive results similar to the following:

```
Identity before impersonation = TestDomain\TestUser
Identity during impersonation = TestDomain\Administrator
Identity after impersonation = TestDomain\TestUser

Main method complete.  Press Enter.
```

12-12. Create a Cryptographically Random Number

Problem

You need to create a random number that is suitable for use in cryptographic and security applications.

Solution

Use a cryptographic random number generator, derived from `System.Security.Cryptography.RandomNumberGenerator` such as the `System.Security.Cryptography.RNGCryptoServiceProvider` class.

How It Works

The `System.Random` class is a pseudo-random number generator that uses a mathematical algorithm to simulate the generation of random numbers. In fact, the algorithm it uses is deterministic, meaning that you can always calculate what the next number will be based on the previously generated number. This means that numbers generated by the `Random` class are unsuitable for use in situations in which security is a priority, such as generating encryption keys and passwords.

When you need a nondeterministic random number for use in cryptographic or security-related applications, you must use a random number generator derived from the class `RandomNumberGenerator`. The `RandomNumberGenerator` class is an abstract (`MustInherit`) class from which all concrete .NET random number generator classes should inherit. Currently, the `RNGCryptoServiceProvider` class is the only concrete implementation provided. The `RNGCryptoServiceProvider` class provides a managed wrapper around the `CryptGenRandom` function of the Win32 CryptoAPI, and you can use it to fill `Byte` arrays with cryptographically random `Byte` values.

■Note The numbers produced by the `RNGCryptoServiceProvider` class are not truly random. However, they are sufficiently random to meet the requirements of cryptography and security applications in most commercial and government environments.

As is the case with many of the .NET cryptography classes, the `RandomNumberGenerator` base class is a factory for the concrete implementation classes that derive from it. Calling `RandomNumberGenerator.Create("System.Security.Cryptography.RNGCryptoServiceProvider")` will return an instance of `RNGCryptoServiceProvider` that you can use to generate random numbers. In addition, because `RNGCryptoServiceProvider` is the only concrete implementation provided, it's the default class created if you call the `Create` method without arguments, as in `RandomNumberGenerator.Create()`.

Once you have a `RandomNumberGenerator` instance, the method `GetBytes` fills a `Byte` array with random `Byte` values. As an alternative, you can use the `GetNonZeroBytes` method if you need random data that contains no zero values.

The Code

The following example instantiates an `RNGCryptoServiceProvider` object and uses it to generate random values:

```
Imports System
Imports System.Security.Cryptography

Namespace Apress.VisualBasicRecipes.Chapter12
    Public Class Recipe12_12

        Public Shared Sub Main()

            ' Create a byte array to hold the random data.
            Dim number As Byte() = New Byte(32) {}

            ' Instantiate the default random number generator.
            Dim rng As RandomNumberGenerator = RandomNumberGenerator.Create

            ' Generate 32 bytes of random data.
            rng.GetBytes(number)

            ' Display the random number.
            Console.WriteLine(BitConverter.ToString(number))

            ' Wait to continue.
            Console.WriteLine(Environment.NewLine)
            Console.WriteLine("Main method complete.  Press Enter.")
            Console.ReadLine()

        End Sub

    End Class
End Namespace
```

■**Note** The computational effort required to generate a random number with RNGCryptoServiceProvider is significantly greater than that required by Random. For everyday purposes, the use of RNGCryptoServiceProvider is overkill. You should consider the quantity of random numbers you need to generate and the purpose of the numbers before deciding to use RNGCryptoServiceProvider. Excessive and unnecessary use of the RNGCryptoServiceProvider class could have a noticeable effect on application performance if many random numbers are generated.

12-13. Calculate the Hash Code of a Password

Problem

You need to store a user's password securely so that you can use it to authenticate the user in the future.

Solution

Create and store a cryptographic hash code of the password using a hashing algorithm class derived from the System.Security.Cryptography.HashAlgorithm class. On future authentication attempts, generate the hash of the password entered by the user and compare it to the stored hash code.

How It Works

Hashing algorithms are one-way cryptographic functions that take plaintext of variable length and generate a fixed-size numeric value. They are *one-way* because it's nearly impossible to derive the original plaintext from the hash code. Hashing algorithms are deterministic; applying the same hashing algorithm to a specific piece of plaintext always generates the same hash code. This makes hash codes useful for determining if two blocks of plaintext (passwords in this case) are the same. The design of hashing algorithms ensures that the chance of two different pieces of plaintext generating the same hash code is extremely small (although not impossible). In addition, there is no correlation between the similarity of two pieces of plaintext and their hash codes; minor differences in the plaintext cause significant differences in the resulting hash codes.

When using passwords to authenticate a user, you are not concerned with the content of the password that the user enters. You need to know only that the entered password maches the password that you have recorded for that user in your accounts database.

The nature of hashing algorithms makes them ideal for storing passwords securely. When the user provides a new password, you must create the hash code of the password and store it, and then discard the plaintext password. Each time the user tries to authenticate with your application, calculate the hash code of the password that user provides and compare it with the hash code you have stored.

■**Note** People regularly ask how to obtain a password from a hash code. The simple answer is that you cannot. The whole purpose of a hash code is to act as a token that you can freely store without creating security holes. If a user forgets a password, you cannot derive it from the stored hash code. Rather, you must either reset the account to some default value or generate a new password for the user.

Generating hash codes is simple in the .NET Framework. The MustInherit class HashAlgorithm provides a base from which all concrete hashing algorithm implementations derive. The .NET Framework class library includes the hashing algorithm implementations listed in Table 12-4. The classes are members of the System.Security.Cryptography namespace and come in three flavors (noted by the class names suffix): CryptoServiceProvider, Cng, and Managed.

The CryptoServiceProvider classes wrap functionality provided by the native Win32 CryptoAPI (CAPI), whereas the Managed classes are fully implemented in managed code. The Cng classes are new to .NET 3.0 and 3.5 and wrap functionality provided by the native Win32 Cryptographic Next Generation (CNG) API. CNG is the replacement for CAPI and is currently available only on Windows Vista and Windows Server 2008.

As the table shows, most of the algorithms have multiple implementations. The algorithms themselves are the same but differ only in how they are implemented. For example, in the case of sha1, SHA1CryptoServiceProvider, SHA1Managed, and SHA1Cng, each implements the same algorithm, but the SHA1Managed class uses the *managed* library, while the SHA1CryptoServiceProvider and SHA1Cng classes wrap CryptoAPI and CNG, respectively.

Table 12-4. *Hashing Algorithm Implementations*

Class Name	Algorithm Name	Hash Code Size (in Bits)
MD5CryptoServiceProvider	MD5	128
*MD5Cng	MD5	128
RIPEMD160Managed	RIPEMD160 or RIPEMD-160	160
SHA1CryptoServiceProvider	SHA or SHA1	160

Table 12-4. *Hashing Algorithm Implementations (Continued)*

Class Name	Algorithm Name	Hash Code Size (in Bits)
SHA1Managed	N/A	160
*SHA1Cng	SHA1	160
*SHA256CryptoServiceProvider	N/A	256
SHA256Managed	SHA256 or SHA-256	256
*SHA256Cng	SHA256	256
*SHA384CryptoServiceProvider	N/A	384
SHA384Managed	SHA384 or SHA-384	384
*SHA384Cng	SHA384	384
*SHA512CryptoServiceProvider	N/A	512
SHA512Managed	SHA512 or SHA-512	512
*SHA512Cng	SHA512	512

* *These classes are new to the .NET Framework 3.5.*

Although you can create instances of the hashing algorithm classes directly, the HashAlgorithm base class is a factory for some of the concrete implementation classes that derive from it. Calling the Shared method HashAlgorithm.Create will return an object of the specified type. The following list contains the names of the classes that the Create method currently supports:

- MD5CryptoServiceProvider
- RIPEMD160Managed
- SHA1CryptoServiceProvider
- SHA256Managed
- SHA384Managed
- SHA512Managed

Using the factory approach allows you to write generic code that can work with any hashing algorithm implementation. Note that unlike in recipe 12-12, you are not required to provide the complete class name; instead, you pass the algorithm name (as shown in Table 12-4). If you do not specify an algorithm name, the default, SHA1Managed, is used. Any classes that are not supported by the Create factory method must be instantiated directly.

Once you have a HashAlgorithm object, its ComputeHash method accepts a Byte array argument containing plaintext and returns a new Byte array containing the generated hash code. Table 12-4 also shows the size of hash code (in bits) generated by each hashing algorithm class.

The Code

The example shown here demonstrates the creation of a hash code from a string, such as a password. The application expects two command-line arguments: the name of the hashing algorithm to use and the string from which to generate the hash. Because the HashAlgorithm.ComputeHash method requires a Byte array, you must first byte-encode the input string using the class System.Text.Encoding, which provides mechanisms for converting strings to and from various character-encoding formats.

Since not everyone has Vista or Windows Server 2008, this example does not use any of the algorithm classes that rely on the Cryptographic Next Generation (CNG) API.

```vb
Imports System
imports System.Text
imports System.Security.Cryptography

Namespace Apress.VisualBasicRecipes.Chapter12
    Public Class Recipe12_13

        Public Shared Sub Main(ByVal args As String())

            ' Create a HashAlgorithm of the type specified by the first
            ' command-line argument.
            Dim hashAlg As HashAlgorithm = Nothing

            ' Some of the classes cannot be instantiated using the
            ' factory method so they most be directly created.
            Select Case args(0).ToUpper()
                Case "SHA1MANAGED"
                    hashAlg = New SHA1Managed
                Case "SHA256CRYPTOSERVICEPROVIDER"
                    hashAlg = New SHA256CryptoServiceProvider
                Case "SHA384CRYPTOSERVICEPROVIDER"
                    hashAlg = New SHA384CryptoServiceProvider
                Case "SHA512CRYPTOSERVICEPROVIDER"
                    hashAlg = New SHA512CryptoServiceProvider
                Case Else
                    hashAlg = HashAlgorithm.Create(args(0))
            End Select

            Using hashAlg

                ' Convert the password string, provided as the second
                ' command-line argument, to an array of bytes.
                Dim pwordData As Byte() = Encoding.Default.GetBytes(args(1))

                ' Generate the hash code of the password.
                Dim hash As Byte() = hashAlg.ComputeHash(pwordData)

                ' Display the hash code of the password to the console.
                Console.WriteLine(BitConverter.ToString(hash))

                ' Wait to continue.
                Console.WriteLine(Environment.NewLine)
                Console.WriteLine("Main method complete.  Press Enter.")
                Console.ReadLine()

            End Using

        End Sub

    End Class
End Namespace
```

Usage

Running the following command:

`Recipe12-13 SHA1 ThisIsMyPassword`

will display the following hash code to the console:

`30-B8-BD-58-29-88-89-00-D1-5D-2B-BE-62-70-D9-BC-65-B0-70-2F`

In contrast, executing this command:

`Recipe12-13 RIPEMD-160 ThisIsMyPassword2`

will display the following hash code:

`97-78-D5-0C-33-7E-FB-44-AC-DC-0A-71-20-53-29-9A-14-79-97-8D`

12-14. Calculate the Hash Code of a File

Problem

You need to determine if the contents of a file have changed over time.

Solution

Create a cryptographic hash code of the file's contents using the `ComputeHash` method of the `System.Security.Cryptography.HashAlgorithm` class. Store the hash code for future comparison against newly generated hash codes.

How It Works

As well as allowing you to store passwords securely (discussed in recipe 12-13), hash codes provide an excellent means of determining if a file has changed. By calculating and storing the cryptographic hash of a file, you can later recalculate the hash of the file to determine if the file has changed in the interim. A hashing algorithm will produce a very different hash code even if the file has been changed only slightly, and the chances of two different files resulting in the same hash code are extremely small.

■**Caution** Standard hash codes are not suitable for sending with a file to ensure the integrity of the file's contents. If someone intercepts the file in transit, that person can easily change the file and recalculate the hash code, leaving the recipient none the wiser. Recipe 12-16 discusses a variant of the hash code—a keyed hash code—that is suitable for ensuring the integrity of a file in transit.

The `HashAlgorithm` class makes it easy to generate the hash code of a file. First, instantiate one of the concrete hashing algorithm implementations derived from the `HashAlgorithm` class. To instantiate the desired hashing algorithm class, pass the name of the hashing algorithm to the `HashAlgorithm.Create` method, as described in recipe 12-13. See Table 12-4 for a list of valid hashing algorithm names. Then, instead of passing a `Byte` array to the `ComputeHash` method, you pass a `System.IO.Stream` object representing the file from which you want to generate the hash code. The `HashAlgorithm` object handles the process of reading data from the Stream and returns a Byte array containing the hash code for the file.

Note The SHA1Managed algorithm cannot be implemented using the factory approach. It must be instantiated directly.

The Code

The example shown here demonstrates the generation of a hash code from a file. The application expects two command-line arguments: the name of the hashing algorithm to use and the name of the file from which the hash is calculated.

```
Imports System
Imports System.IO
Imports System.Security.Cryptography

Namespace Apress.VisualBasicRecipes.Chapter12
    Public Class Recipe12_14

        Public Shared Sub Main(ByVal args As String())

            ' Create a HashAlgorithm of the type specified by the first
            ' command-line argument.
            Dim hashAlg As HashAlgorithm = Nothing

            ' The SHA1Managed algorithm cannot be implemented using the
            ' factory approach. It must be instantiated directly.
            If args(0).CompareTo("SHA1Managed") = 0 Then
                hashAlg = New SHA1Managed
            Else
                hashAlg = HashAlgorithm.Create(args(0))
            End If

            ' Open a FileStream to the file specified by the second
            ' command-line argument.
            Using fileArg As New FileStream(args(1), FileMode.Open, FileAccess.Read)

                ' Generate the hash code of the password.
                Dim hash As Byte() = hashAlg.ComputeHash(fileArg)

                ' Display the hash code of the password to the console.
                Console.WriteLine(BitConverter.ToString(hash))

                ' Wait to continue.
                Console.WriteLine(Environment.NewLine)
                Console.WriteLine("Main method complete.  Press Enter.")
                Console.ReadLine()

            End Using

        End Sub

    End Class
End Namespace
```

Usage

Running this command:

```
Recipe12-14 SHA1 Recipe12-14.exe
```

will display the following hash code to the console:

```
F9-0E-31-C7-57-82-12-A3-9B-9F-0C-A3-CB-54-4C-34-68-30-19-58
```

In contrast, executing this command:

```
Recipe12-14 RIPEMD-160 Recipe12-14.exe
```

will display the following hash code:

```
FB-21-82-E7-0F-BA-71-C4-0B-A0-9A-EB-BC-9D-D3-44-6E-D7-5A-CA
```

12-15. Verify a Hash Code

Problem

You need to verify a password or confirm that a file remains unchanged by comparing two hash codes.

Solution

Convert both the old and the new hash codes to hexadecimal code strings, Base64 strings, or `Byte` arrays and compare them.

How It Works

You can use hash codes to determine if two pieces of data (such as passwords or files) are the same, without the need to store, or even maintain access to, the original data. To determine if data changes over time, you must generate and store the original data's hash code. Later, you can generate another hash code for the data and compare the old and new hash codes, which will show if any change has occurred. The format in which you store the original hash code will determine the most appropriate way to verify a newly generated hash code against the stored one.

Note The recipes in this chapter use the `ToString` method of the class `System.BitConverter` to convert `Byte` arrays to hexadecimal string values for display. Although easy to use and appropriate for display purposes, this approach may be inappropriate for use when storing hash codes, because it places a hyphen (-) between each byte value (for example, 4D-79-3A-C9-. . .). In addition, the `BitConverter` class does not provide a method to parse such a string representation back into a `Byte` array.

Hash codes are often stored in text files, either as hexadecimal strings (for example, *89D22213170A9CFF09A392F00E2C6C4EDC1B0EF9*), or as Base64-encoded strings (for example, *idIiExcKnP8Jo5LwDixsTtwbDvk=*). Alternatively, hash codes may be stored in databases as raw byte values. Regardless of how you store your hash code, the first step in comparing old and new hash codes is to get them both into a common form.

The Code

This following example contains three methods that use different approaches to compare hash codes:

- VerifyHexHash: This method converts a new hash code (a Byte array) to a hexadecimal string for comparison to an old hash code. Other than the BitConverter.ToString method, the .NET Framework class library does not provide an easy method to convert a Byte array to a hexadecimal string. You must program a loop to step through the elements of the byte array, convert each individual byte to a string, and append the string to the hexadecimal string representation of the hash code. The use of a System.Text.StringBuilder avoids the unnecessary creation of new strings each time the loop appends the next byte value to the result string. (See recipe 2-1 for more details.)

- VerifyB64Hash: This method takes a new hash code as a Byte array and the old hash code as a Base64-encoded string. The method encodes the new hash code as a Base64 string and performs a straightforward string comparison of the two values.

- VerifyByteHash: This method compares two hash codes represented as Byte arrays. The .NET Framework class library does not include a method that performs this type of comparison, and so you must program a loop to compare the elements of the two arrays. This code uses a few timesaving techniques, namely ensuring that the Byte arrays are the same length before starting to compare them and returning False on the first difference found.

```vbnet
Imports System
Imports System.Text
Imports System.Security.Cryptography

Namespace Apress.VisualBasicRecipes.Chapter12
    Public Class Recipe12_15

        ' A method to compare a newly generated hash code with an
        ' existing hash code that's represented by a hex code string.
        Private Shared Function VerifyHexHash(ByVal hash As Byte(), ➥
ByVal oldHashString As String)

            ' Create a string representation of the hash code bytes.
            Dim newHashString As New StringBuilder(hash.Length)

            ' Append each byte as a two-character uppercase hex string.
            For Each b As Byte In hash
                newHashString.AppendFormat("{0:X2}", b)
            Next

            ' Compare the string representation of the old and new hash
            ' codes and return the result.
            Return oldHashString.Replace("-", "") = newHashString.ToString

        End Function

        ' A method to compare a newly generated hash code with an
        ' existing hash code that's represented by a Base64-encoded
        ' string.
        Private Shared Function VerifyB64Hash(ByVal hash As Byte(), ➥
ByVal oldHashString As String) As Boolean
```

```
            ' Create a Base64 representation of the hash code bytes.
            Dim newHashString As String = Convert.ToBase64String(hash)

            ' Compare the string representations of the old and new hash
            ' codes and return the result.
            Return oldHashString = newHashString

        End Function

        ' A method to compare a newly generated hash code with an
        ' existing hash code represented by a byte array.
        Private Shared Function VerifyByteHash(ByVal hash As Byte(), ➥
    ByVal oldHash As Byte()) As Boolean

            ' If either array is nothing or the arrays are different lengths,
            ' then they are not equal.
            If hash Is Nothing Or oldHash Is Nothing Or Not (hash.Length = ➥
    oldHash.Length) Then
                Return False
            End If

            ' Step through the byte arrays and compare each byte value.
            For count As Integer = 0 To hash.Length - 1
                If Not hash(count) = oldHash(count) Then Return False
            Next

            ' Hash codes are equal.
            Return True

        End Function

    End Class
End Namespace
```

12-16. Ensure Data Integrity Using a Keyed Hash Code

Problem

You need to transmit a file to someone and provide the recipient with a means to verify the integrity of the file and its source.

Solution

Share a secret key with the intended recipient. This key would ideally be a randomly generated number, but it could also be a phrase that you and the recipient agree to use. Use the key with one of the keyed hashing algorithm classes derived from the System.Security.Cryptography.KeyedHashAlgorithm class to create a keyed hash code. Send the hash code with the file. On receipt of the file, the recipient will generate the keyed hash code of the file using the shared secret key. If the hash codes are equal, the recipient knows that the file is from you and that it has not changed in transit.

How It Works

Hash codes are useful for comparing two pieces of data to determine if they are the same, even if you no longer have access to the original data. However, you cannot use a hash code to reassure the recipient of data as to the data's integrity. If someone could intercept the data, that person could replace the data and generate a new hash code. When the recipient verifies the hash code, it will seem correct, even though the data is actually nothing like what you sent originally.

A simple and efficient solution to the problem of data integrity is a *keyed hash code*. A keyed hash code is similar to a normal hash code (discussed in recipes 12-13 and 12-14); however, the keyed hash code incorporates an element of secret data—a *key*—known only to the sender and the receiver. Without the key, a person cannot generate the correct hash code from a given set of data. When you successfully verify a keyed hash code, you can be certain that only someone who knows the secret key could generate the hash code.

The keyed hash algorithms supplied by the .NET Framework are provided by the HMAC and MACTripleDes classes. Generating these keyed hash codes is similar to generating normal hash codes. All HMAC algorithm classes derive themselves from the HMAC base class, which inherits the KeyedHashAlgorithm class, which inherits the HashAlgorithm class. MACTripleDES inherits the KeyedHashAlgorithm base class directly. The .NET Framework class library includes the seven keyed hashing algorithm implementations listed in Table 12-5. Each implementation is a member of the namespace System.Security.Cryptography.

Table 12-5. *Keyed Hashing Algorithm Implementations*

Algorithm/Class Name	Key Size (in Bits)	Hash Code Size (in Bits)
HMACMD5	Any	128
HMACRIPEMD160	Any	160
HMACSHA1	Any	160
HMACSHA256	Any	256
HMACSHA384	Any	384
HMACSHA512	Any	512
MACTripleDES	128, 192	6

As with the standard hashing algorithms, you can either create keyed hashing algorithm objects directly or use the Shared factory method KeyedHashAlgorithm.Create and pass the algorithm name as an argument. Using the factory approach allows you to write generic code that can work with any keyed hashing algorithm implementation, but as shown in Table 12-5, MACTripleDES supports fixed key lengths that you must accommodate in generic code.

If you use constructors to instantiate a keyed hashing object, you can pass the secret key to the constructor. Using the factory approach, you must set the key using the Key property inherited from the KeyedHashAlgorithm class. Then call the ComputeHash method and pass either a Byte array or a System.IO.Stream object. The keyed hashing algorithm will process the input data and return a Byte array containing the keyed hash code. Table 12-5 shows the size of hash code generated by each keyed hashing algorithm.

The Code

The following example demonstrates the generation of a keyed hash code from a file. The example uses the given class to generate the keyed hash code, and then displays it to the console. The example requires three command-line arguments: the name of the file from which the hash is calculated, the name of the algorithm to instantiate, and the key to use when calculating the hash.

```vb
Imports System
Imports System.IO
Imports System.Text
Imports System.Security.Cryptography

Namespace Apress.VisualBasicRecipes.Chapter12
    Public Class Recipe12_16

        Public Shared Sub Main(ByVal args As String())

            ' Create a byte array from the key string, which is the
            ' third command-line argument.
            Dim key As Byte() = Encoding.Default.GetBytes(args(2))

            ' Create a KeyedHashAlgorithm derived object to generate the keyed
            ' hash code for the input file. Pass the byte array representing
            ' the key to the constructor.
            Using hashAlg As KeyedHashAlgorithm = KeyedHashAlgorithm.Create(args(1))

                ' Assign the key.
                hashAlg.Key = key

                ' Open a FileStream to read the input file. The file name is
                ' specified by the first command-line argument.
                Using argFile As New FileStream(args(0), FileMode.Open, ➥
FileAccess.Read)

                    ' Generate the keyed hash code of the file's contents.
                    Dim hash As Byte() = hashAlg.ComputeHash(argFile)

                    ' Display the keyed hash code to the console.
                    Console.WriteLine(BitConverter.ToString(hash))

                End Using
            End Using

            ' Wait to continue.
            Console.WriteLine(Environment.NewLine)
            Console.WriteLine("Main method complete.  Press Enter.")
            Console.ReadLine()

        End Sub

    End Class
End Namespace
```

Usage

Executing the following command:

```
Recipe12-16 Recipe12-16.exe HMACSHA1 secretKey
```

will display the following hash code to the console:

```
53-E6-03-59-C8-BB-F6-74-51-BF-B6-C3-75-B2-78-0B-43-01-3A-E0
```

In contrast, executing this command:

```
Recipe12-16 Recipe12-16.exe HMACSHA1 anotherKey
```

will display the following hash code to the console:

```
73-09-27-07-08-4C-48-13-F9-6A-A6-BA-D4-0E-87-57-CC-7F-05-D7
```

12-17. Work with Security-Sensitive Strings in Memory

Problem

You need to work with sensitive string data, such as passwords or credit card numbers, in memory and need to minimize the risk of other people or processes accessing that data.

Solution

Use the class System.Security.SecureString to hold the sensitive data values in memory.

How It Works

Storing sensitive data such as passwords, personal details, and banking information in memory as String objects is insecure for many reasons, including the following:

- String objects are not encrypted.

- The immutability of String objects means that whenever you change the String, the old String value is left in memory until it is dereferenced by the garbage collector and eventually overwritten.

- Because the garbage collector is free to reorganize the contents of the managed heap, multiple copies of your sensitive data may be present on the heap.

- If part of your process address space is swapped to disk or a memory dump is written to disk, a copy of your data may be stored on the disk.

Each of these factors increases the opportunities for others to access your sensitive data. The SecureString class, first introduced in .NET Framework 2.0, is used to simplify the task of working with sensitive String data in memory.

You create a SecureString as either initially empty or from a pointer to a character (Char) array. Then you manipulate the contents of the SecureString one character at a time using the methods AppendChar, InsertAt, RemoveAt, and SetAt. As you add characters to the SecureString, they are encrypted using the capabilities of the Data Protection API (DPAPI).

The SecureString class also provides a method named MakeReadOnly. As the name suggests, calling MakeReadOnly configures the SecureString to no longer allow its value to be changed. Attempting to modify a SecureString marked as read-only results in the exception System.InvalidOperationException being thrown. Once you have set the SecureString to read-only, it cannot be undone.

The SecureString class has a ToString method, but rather than retrieving a string representation of the contained data, it returns only a representation of the type (System.Security.SecureString). Instead, the class System.Runtime.InteropServices.Marshal implements a number of Shared methods that take a SecureString object; decrypts it; converts it to a binary string, a block of ANSI, or a block of Unicode data; and returns a System.IntPtr object that points to the converted data. The Marshal class also offers Shared methods for displaying the contents referenced by an IntPtr. Here is a code snippet to demonstrate this:

```
' Retrieve a pointer to the data contained in a
' SecureString.
Dim secureStringPtr As IntPtr = ➡
Marshal.SecureStringToGlobalAllocUnicode(mySecureString)

' Retrieve a string representation of the data
' referenced by a pointer.
Dim clearText As String = Marshal.PtrToStringAuto(secureStringPtr)

' Display the secure string contents in clear text.
Console.WriteLine(clearText))
```

At any time, you can call the SecureString.Clear method to clear the sensitive data, and when you have finished with the SecureString object, call its Dispose method to clear the data and free the memory. SecureString implements System.IDisposable.

■**Note** Although it might seem that the benefits of the SecureString class are limited, because there is no way in Windows Forms applications to get such a secured string from the GUI without first retrieving a nonsecured String through a TextBox or another control, it is likely that third parties and future additions to the .NET Framework will use the SecureString class to handle sensitive data. This is already the case in System.Diagnostics. ProcessStartInfo, where using a SecureString, you can set the Password property to the password of the user context in which the new process should be run.

The Code

The following example reads a username and password from the console and starts Notepad.exe as the specified user. The password is masked on input and stored in a SecureString in memory, maximizing the chances of the password remaining secret.

```
Imports System
Imports System.Security
Imports System.Diagnostics

Namespace Apress.VisualBasicRecipes.Chapter12
    Public Class Recipe12_17

        Public Shared Function ReadString() As SecureString

            ' Create a new empty SecureString.
            Dim str As New SecureString
```

```vb
    ' Read the string from the console one
    ' character at a time without displaying it.
    Dim nextChar As ConsoleKeyInfo = Console.ReadKey(True)

    ' Read characters until Enter is pressed.
    While Not nextChar.Key = ConsoleKey.Enter

        If nextChar.Key = ConsoleKey.Backspace Then
            If str.Length > 0 Then
                ' Backspace pressed. Remove the last character.
                str.RemoveAt(str.Length - 1)

                Console.Write(nextChar.KeyChar)
                Console.Write(" ")
                Console.Write(nextChar.KeyChar)
            Else
                Console.Beep()
            End If
        Else
            ' Append the character to the SecureString and
            ' display a masked character.
            str.AppendChar(nextChar.KeyChar)
            Console.Write("*")
        End If

        ' Read the next character.
        nextChar = Console.ReadKey(True)

    End While

    ' String entry finished.  Make it read-only.
    str.MakeReadOnly()

    Return str

End Function

Public Shared Sub Main()

    Dim user As String = ""

    ' Get the username under which Notepad.exe will be run.
    Console.Write("Enter the user name: ")
    user = Console.ReadLine

    ' Get the user's password as a SecureString.
    Console.Write("Enter the user's password: ")
    Using pword As SecureString = ReadString()

        ' Start Notepad as the specified user.
        Dim startInfo As New ProcessStartInfo
```

```
                    startInfo.FileName = "Notepad.exe"
                    startInfo.UserName = user
                    startInfo.Password = pword
                    startInfo.UseShellExecute = False

                    ' Create a new Process object.
                    Using proc As New Process

                        ' Assign the ProcessStartInfo to the Process object.
                        proc.StartInfo = startInfo

                        Try
                            ' Start the new process.
                            proc.Start()
                        Catch ex As Exception
                            Console.WriteLine(Environment.NewLine)
                            Console.WriteLine(Environment.NewLine)
                            Console.WriteLine("Could not start Notepad process.")
                            Console.WriteLine(ex.ToString)
                        End Try

                    End Using

                End Using

                ' Wait to continue.
                Console.WriteLine(Environment.NewLine)
                Console.WriteLine("Main method complete.  Press Enter")
                Console.ReadLine()

            End Sub

        End Class
    End Namespace
```

12-18. Encrypt and Decrypt Data Using the Data Protection API

Problem

You need a convenient way to securely encrypt data without the headache associated with key management.

Solution

Use the ProtectedData and ProtectedMemory classes of the System.Security.Cryptography namespace to access the encryption and key management capabilities provided by the DPAPI.

How It Works

Given that the .NET Framework provides you with well-tested implementations of the most widely used and trusted encryption algorithms, the biggest challenge you face when using cryptography is key management—namely the effective generation, storage, and sharing of keys to facilitate the use of cryptography. In fact, key management is the biggest problem facing most people when they want to securely store or transmit data using cryptographic techniques. If implemented incorrectly, key management can easily render useless all of your efforts to encrypt your data.

DPAPI provides encryption and decryption services without the need for you to worry about key management. DPAPI automatically generates keys based on Windows user credentials, stores keys securely as part of your profile, and even provides automated key expiry without losing access to previously encrypted data.

Note DPAPI is suitable for many common uses of cryptography in Windows applications, but will not help you in situations that require you to distribute or share secret or public keys with other users.

The `System.Security` namespace includes two classes that provide easy access to the encryption and decryption capabilities of DPAPI: `ProtectedData` and `ProtectedMemory`. Both classes allow you to encrypt a `Byte` array by passing it to the `Shared` method `Protect`, and decrypt a `Byte` array of encrypted data by passing it the `Shared` method `Unprotect`. The difference in the classes is in the scope that they allow you to specify when you encrypt and decrypt data.

Caution You must use `ProtectedData` if you intend to store encrypted data and reboot your machine before decrypting it. `ProtectedMemory` will be unable to decrypt data that was encrypted before a reboot.

When you call `ProtectedData.Protect`, you specify a value from the enumeration `System.Security.Cryptography.DataProtectionScope`. The following are the possible values:

- `CurrentUser`, which means that only code running in the context of the current user can decrypt the data

- `LocalMachine`, which means that any code running on the same computer can decrypt the data

When you call `ProtectedMemory.Protect`, you specify a value from the enumeration `System.Security.Cryptography.MemoryProtectionScope`. The possible values are as follows:

- `CrossProcess`, which means that any code in any process can decrypt the encrypted data

- `SameLogon`, which means that only code running in the same user context can decrypt the data

- `SameProcess`, which means that only code running in the same process can decrypt the data

Both classes allow you to specify additional data (*entropy*) when you encrypt your data. This entropy, in the form of byte arrays, is used to further encrypt the data, making certain types of cryptographic attacks less likely to succeed. If you choose to use entropy when you protect data, you must use the same entropy value when you unprotect the data. It is not essential that you keep the entropy data secret, so it can be stored freely without encryption.

The Code

The following example demonstrates the use of the `ProtectedData` class to encrypt a string entered at the console by the user. Note that you need to reference the `System.Security` assembly.

```
Imports System
Imports System.Text
Imports System.Security.Cryptography
```

```vb
Namespace Apress.VisualBasicRecipes.Chapter12
    Public Class Recipe12_18

        Public Shared Sub Main()

            ' Read the string from the console.
            Console.Write("Enter the string to encrypt: ")
            Dim str As String = Console.ReadLine

            ' Create a byte array of entropy to use in the encryption process.
            Dim entropy As Byte() = {0, 1, 2, 3, 4, 5, 6, 7, 8}

            ' Encrypt the entered string after converting it to a
            ' byte array. Use CurrentUser scope so that only the
            ' current user can decrypt the data.
            Dim enc As Byte() = ProtectedData.Protect( ➥
Encoding.Default.GetBytes(str), entropy, DataProtectionScope.CurrentUser)

            ' Display the encrypted data to the console.
            Console.WriteLine(Environment.NewLine)
            Console.WriteLine("Encrypted string = {0}", BitConverter.ToString(enc))

            ' Attempt to decrypt the data using CurrentUser scope.
            Dim dec As Byte() = ProtectedData.Unprotect(enc, entropy, ➥
DataProtectionScope.CurrentUser)

            ' Display the data decrypted using CurrentUser scope.
            Console.WriteLine(Environment.NewLine)
            Console.WriteLine("Decrypted data using CurrentUser scope = {0}", ➥
Encoding.Default.GetString(dec))

            ' Wait to continue.
            Console.WriteLine(Environment.NewLine)
            Console.WriteLine("Main method complete.  Press Enter.")
            Console.ReadLine()

        End Sub

    End Class
End Namespace
```

CHAPTER 13

■■■

Code Interoperability

The Microsoft .NET Framework is an extremely ambitious platform, combining a managed runtime (the common language runtime, or CLR), a platform for hosting web applications (Microsoft ASP. NET), and an extensive class library for building all types of applications. However, as expansive as the .NET Framework is, it does not duplicate all the features that are available in unmanaged code. Currently, the .NET Framework does not include every function that is available in the Win32 API, and many businesses are using complex proprietary solutions that they have built with COM-based languages such as Microsoft Visual Basic 6 (VB 6) and Visual C++ 6.

Fortunately, Microsoft does not intend for businesses to abandon the code base they have built up when they move to the .NET platform. Instead, the .NET Framework is equipped with interoperability features that allow you to use legacy code from .NET Framework applications and even access .NET assemblies as though they were COM components.

The recipes in this chapter cover the following:

- Calling functions defined in an unmanaged DLL, getting the handles for a control or window, invoking an unmanaged function that uses a structure, invoking unmanaged callback functions, and retrieving unmanaged error information (recipes 13-1 through 13-5)

- Using COM components from .NET Framework applications, releasing COM components, and using optional parameters (recipes 13-6 through 13-8)

- Using ActiveX controls from .NET Framework applications (recipe 13-9)

- Exposing the functionality of a .NET assembly as a COM component (recipe 13-10)

- Using a Windows Presentation Foundation (WPF) component within a Windows Form application (recipe 13-11)

Although most of the recipes in this chapter deal with working with and exchanging information between managed and unmanaged components, situations may arise where you need to perform the same functionality between managed components. This chapter includes a recipe on using Windows Presentation Foundation (WPF) components within a Windows Forms application (both of which are managed components).

■**Note** *Managed* code refers to code developed in a .NET language (such as VB .NET and C#). This code is compiled to Microsoft Intermediary Language (MSIL) and runs within the CLR. When the code is executed, it is compiled to machine language using the just-in-time (JIT) compiler. *Unmanaged* code refers to code developed in a non-.NET language (such as C++ or VB 6). This code is compiled directly to machine language. If you use Visual C++ .NET, you can create managed or unmanaged code, depending on the project type you select.

13-1. Call a Function in an Unmanaged DLL

Problem

You need to call a function in a DLL. This function might be part of the Win32 API or your own legacy code.

Solution

Declare a method in your VB .NET code that you will use to access the unmanaged function. Declare this method as Shared, and apply the attribute System.Runtime.InteropServices.DllImportAttribute to specify the DLL file and the name of the unmanaged function.

How It Works

To use a function from an external library (such as one written in C or C++), all you need to do is declare it appropriately. The CLR automatically handles the rest, including loading the DLL into memory when the function is called and marshaling the parameters from .NET data types to C data types (or the data types appropriate for the external library's language). The .NET service that supports this cross-platform execution is named Platform Invoke (PInvoke), and the process is usually seamless. Occasionally, you will need to do a little more work, such as when you need to support in-memory structures, callbacks, or mutable strings.

PInvoke is often used to access functionality in the Win32 API, particularly Win32 features that are not present in the set of managed classes that make up the .NET Framework. Three core libraries make up the Win32 API:

- Kernel32.dll includes operating system–specific functionality such as process loading, context switching, and file and memory I/O.

- User32.dll includes functionality for manipulating windows, menus, dialog boxes, icons, and so on.

- GDI32.dll includes graphical capabilities for drawing directly on windows, menus, and control surfaces, as well as for printing.

As an example, consider the Win32 API functions used for writing and reading INI files, such as GetPrivateProfileString and WritePrivateProfileString in Kernel32.dll. The .NET Framework does not include any classes that wrap this functionality. However, you can import these functions using the attribute DllImportAttribute, like this:

```
<DllImport("kernel32.dll", EntryPoint:="WritePrivateProfileString")> _
Private Shared Function WritePrivateProfileString(ByVal lpAppName As String, ➥
    ByVal lpKeyName As String, ByVal lpString As String, ➥
    ByVal lpFileName As String) As Boolean
End Function
```

The arguments specified in the signature of the WritePrivateProfileString method must match the DLL method, or a runtime error will occur when you attempt to invoke it. Remember that you do not define any method body, because the declaration refers to a method in the DLL. The EntryPoint portion of the attribute DllImportAttribute is optional in this example. You do not need to specify the EntryPoint when the declared function name matches the function name in the external library.

The Code

The following is an example of using some Win32 API functions to get INI file information. It declares the unmanaged functions used and exposes Public methods to call them. The code first displays the current value of a key in the INI file, modifies it, retrieves the new value, and then writes the default value.

```
Imports System
Imports System.Runtime.InteropServices
Imports System.Text


Namespace Apress.VisualBasicRecipes.Chapter13
    Public Class Recipe13_01

        ' Declare the unmanaged functions
        <DllImport("kernel32.dll", EntryPoint:="GetPrivateProfileString")> _
        Private Shared Function GetPrivateProfileString(ByVal lpAppName As ➡
String, ByVal lpKeyName As String, ByVal lpDefault As String, ByVal ➡
lpReturnedString As StringBuilder, ByVal nSize As Integer, ByVal lpFileName As ➡
String) As Integer
        End Function

        <DllImport("kernel32.dll", EntryPoint:="WritePrivateProfileString")> _
        Private Shared Function WritePrivateProfileString(ByVal lpAppName As ➡
String, ByVal lpKeyName As String, ByVal lpString As String, ByVal lpFileName As ➡
String) As Boolean
        End Function

        Public Shared Sub Main(ByVal args As String())

            Dim val As String

            ' Obtain current value.
            val = GetIniValue("SampleSection", "Key1", args(0))
            Console.WriteLine("Value of Key1 in [SampleSection] is: {0}", val)

            ' Write a new value.
            WriteIniValue("SampleSection", "Key1", "New Value", args(0))

            ' Obtain the new value.
            val = GetIniValue("SampleSection", "Key1", args(0))
            Console.WriteLine("Value of Key1 in [SampleSection] is now: {0}", val)

            ' Write original value.
            WriteIniValue("SampleSection", "Key1", "Value1", args(0))

            ' Wait to continue.
            Console.WriteLine(Environment.NewLine)
            Console.WriteLine("Main method complete.  Press Enter.")
            Console.ReadLine()

        End Sub
```

```
        Public Shared Function GetIniValue(ByVal section As String, ➥
ByVal key As String, ByVal fileName As String) As String

            Dim chars As Integer = 256
            Dim buffer As New StringBuilder(chars)

            If Not GetPrivateProfileString(section, key, "", buffer, chars, ➥
fileName) = 0 Then
                Return buffer.ToString
            Else
                Return Nothing
            End If

        End Function

        Public Shared Function WriteIniValue(ByVal section As String, ➥
ByVal key As String, ByVal value As String, ByVal fileName As String) As String
            Return WritePrivateProfileString(section, key, value, fileName)
        End Function

    End Class
End Namespace
```

■**Note** The `GetPrivateProfileString` method is declared with one `StringBuilder` parameter (`lpReturnedString`). This is because this string must be mutable; when the call completes, it will contain the returned INI file information. Whenever you need a mutable string, you must substitute `StringBuilder` in place of the `String` class. Often, you will need to create the `StringBuilder` object with a character buffer of a set size and then pass the size of the buffer to the function as another parameter. You can specify the number of characters in the `StringBuilder` constructor. See recipe 2-1 for more information about using the `StringBuilder` class.

Usage

To test this example, first create a test file such as the inittest.ini file shown here:

```
[SampleSection]
Key1=Value1
```

Now, execute the command `Recipe13-01.exe initest.ini`. You will get an output such as this:

```
Value of Key1 in [SampleSection] is: Value1
Value of Key1 in [SampleSection] is now: New Value
```

```
Main method complete. Press Enter.
```

13-2. Get the Handle for a Control, Window, or File

Problem

You need to call an unmanaged function, such as GetWindowText, that requires the handle for a control, a window, or a file.

Solution

Many classes, including all Control-derived classes and the FileStream class, return the handle of the unmanaged Windows object they are wrapping as an IntPtr through a property named Handle. Other classes also provide similar information; for example, the System.Diagnostics.Process class provides a Process.MainWindowHandle property in addition to the Handle property.

How It Works

The .NET Framework does not hide underlying details such as the operating system handles used for controls and windows. Although you usually will not use this information, you can retrieve it if you need to call an unmanaged function that requires it. Many Microsoft Win32 API functions, for example, require control or window handles.

The Code

As an example, consider the Windows-based application shown in Figure 13-1. It consists of a single window that always stays on top of all other windows regardless of focus. (This behavior is enforced by setting the Form.TopMost property to True.) The form also includes a timer that periodically calls the unmanaged GetForegroundWindow and GetWindowText Win32 API functions to determine which window is currently active and its caption, respectively.

Figure 13-1. *Retrieving information about the active window*

One additional detail in this example is that the code also uses the Form.Handle property to get the handle of the main application form. It then compares it with the handle of the active form to test whether the current application has focus. The following is the complete code for this form:

```vb
Imports System
Imports System.Windows.Forms
Imports System.Runtime.InteropServices
Imports System.Text

'  All designed code is stored in the autogenerated partial
'  class called ActiveWindowInfo.Designer.vb. You can see this
'  file by selecting Show All Files in Solution Explorer.
Partial Public Class ActiveWindowInfo

    '  Declare external functions.
    <DllImport("user32.dll")> _
    Private Shared Function GetForegroundWindow() As IntPtr
    End Function

    <DllImport("user32.dll")> _
    Private Shared Function GetWindowText(ByVal hWnd As IntPtr, ➥
ByVal text As StringBuilder, ByVal count As Integer) As Integer
    End Function

    Private Sub tmrRefresh_Tick(ByVal sender As System.Object, ➥
ByVal e As System.EventArgs) Handles tmrRefresh.Tick

        Dim chars As Integer = 256
        Dim buff As New StringBuilder(chars)

        '  Obtain the handle of the active window.
        Dim handle As IntPtr = GetForeGroundWindow()

        '  Update the controls.
        If GetWindowText(handle, buff, chars) > 0 Then
            lblCaption.Text = buff.ToString
            lblHandle.Text = handle.ToString

            If handle = Me.Handle Then
                lblCurrent.Text = "True"
            Else
                lblCurrent.Text = "False"
            End If

        End If

    End Sub
End Class
```

■**Caution** The Windows Forms infrastructure manages window handles for forms and controls transparently. Changing some of their properties can force the CLR to create a new native window behind the scenes, and a new handle gets wrapped with a different handle. For that reason, you should always retrieve the handle before you use it (rather than storing it in a member variable for a long period of time).

13-3. Call an Unmanaged Function That Uses a Structure

Problem

You need to call an unmanaged function, such as GetVersionEx, that accepts a structure as a parameter.

Solution

Define the structure in your VB .NET code. Use the attribute System.Runtime.InteropServices. StructLayoutAttribute to configure how the structure fields are laid out in memory. Use the Shared SizeOf method of the System.Runtime.InteropServices.Marshal class if you need to determine the size of the unmanaged structure in bytes.

How It Works

In VB .NET code, you are not able to directly control how type fields are laid out once the memory is allocated. Instead, the CLR is free to arrange fields to optimize performance, especially in the context of moving memory around during garbage collection. This can cause problems when interacting with legacy functions, such as those written in C, that expect structures to be laid out sequentially in memory to follow their definition in include files. Fortunately, the .NET Framework allows you to solve this problem by using the attribute StructLayoutAttribute, which lets you specify how the members of a given class or structure should be arranged in memory.

The Code

As an example, consider the unmanaged GetVersionEx function provided in the Kernel32.dll file. This function accepts a pointer to an OSVERSIONINFO structure and uses it to return information about the current operating system version. To use the OSVERSIONINFO structure in VB .NET code, you must define it with the attribute StructLayoutAttribute, as shown here:

```
<StructLayout(LayoutKind.Sequential)> _
Public Structure OSVersionInfo

    Public dwOSVersionInfoSize As Integer
    Public dwMajorVersion As Integer
    Public dwMinorVersion As Integer
    Public dwBuildNumber As Integer
    Public dwPlatformId As Integer
    <MarshalAs(UnmanagedType.ByValTStr, SizeConst:=128)> _
    Public szCSDVersion As String

End Structure
```

Note that this structure also uses the attribute System.Runtime.InteropServices. MarshalAsAttribute, which is required for fixed-length strings. In this example, MarshalAsAttribute specifies the string will be passed by value and will contain a buffer of exactly 128 characters, as specified in the OSVERSIONINFO structure. This example uses sequential layout, which means the data types in the structure are laid out in the order they are listed in the class or structure.

Instead of using sequential layout, you could use LayoutKind.Explicit; in that case, you must define the byte offset of each field using FieldOffsetAttribute. This layout is useful when dealing with an irregularly packed structure or one where you want to omit some of the fields that you do not want to use. Here is an example that defines the OSVersionInfo class with an explicit layout:

```
<StructLayout(LayoutKind.Explicit)> _
Public Structure OSVersionInfo2

    <FieldOffset(0)> Public dwOSVersionInfoSize As Integer
    <FieldOffset(4)> Public dwMajorVersion As Integer
    <FieldOffset(8)> Public dwMinorVersion As Integer
    <FieldOffset(12)> Public dwBuildNumber As Integer
    <FieldOffset(16)> Public dwPlatformId As Integer
    <MarshalAs(UnmanagedType.ByValTStr, SizeConst:=128)> _
    <FieldOffset(20)> Public szCSDVersion As String

End Structure
```

Now that you've defined the structure used by the GetVersionEx function, you can declare the function and then use it. The following console application shows all the code you will need. A parameter marked with InAttribute (<[In]()>) is marshaled from the calling assembly to the unmanaged function, while one marked with OutAttribute (<Out()>) is marshaled in the opposite direction. If neither of these attributes is used, then marshaling is decided based on how the parameter is passed (ByRef equals *In* and *Out*, while ByVal equals *In*). In this example, you need to make sure that OSVersionInfo is marshaled in both directions, so both attributes are applied. In addition, the code uses the Marshal. SizeOf method to calculate the size the marshaled structure will occupy in memory.

```
Imports System
Imports System.Runtime.InteropServices

Namespace Apress.VisualBasicRecipes.Chapter13

    <StructLayout(LayoutKind.Sequential)> _
    Public Structure OSVersionInfo

        Public dwOSVersionInfoSize As Integer
        Public dwMajorVersion As Integer
        Public dwMinorVersion As Integer
        Public dwBuildNumber As Integer
        Public dwPlatformId As Integer
        <MarshalAs(UnmanagedType.ByValTStr, SizeConst:=128)> _
        Public szCSDVersion As String

    End Structure

    Public Class Recipe13_03

        ' Declare the external function.
        <DllImport("kernel32.dll")> _
```

```
        Public Shared Function GetVersionEx(<[In](), Out()> ByRef osvi As ➡
OSVersionInfo) As Boolean
        End Function

        Public Shared Sub Main()

            Dim osvi As New OSVersionInfo

            osvi.dwOSVersionInfoSize = Marshal.SizeOf(osvi)

            ' Obtain the OS version information.
            GetVersionEx(osvi)

            ' Display the version information from the OSVersionInfo structure.
            Console.WriteLine("Class Size: " & osvi.dwOSVersionInfoSize.ToString)
            Console.WriteLine("Major Version: " & osvi.dwMajorVersion.ToString)
            Console.WriteLine("Minor Version: " & osvi.dwMinorVersion.ToString)
            Console.WriteLine("Build Number: " & osvi.dwBuildNumber.ToString)
            Console.WriteLine("Platform Id: " & osvi.dwPlatformId.ToString)
            Console.WriteLine("CSD Version: " & osvi.szCSDVersion.ToString)

            ' Display some information from the Environment class.
            Console.WriteLine("Platform: " & ➡
Environment.OSVersion.Platform.ToString)
            Console.WriteLine("Version: " & Environment.OSVersion.Version.ToString)

            ' Wait to continue.
            Console.WriteLine(Environment.NewLine)
            Console.WriteLine("Main method complete.  Press Enter.")
            Console.ReadLine()


        End Sub

    End Class
End Namespace
```

Usage

If you run this application on a Windows Vista system, you will see information such as this:

```
Class Size: 148
Major Version: 6
Minor Version: 0
Build Number: 6000
Platform Id: 2
CSD Version:
Platform: Win32NT
Version: 6.0.6000.0

Main method complete.  Press Enter.
```

13-4. Call an Unmanaged Function That Uses a Callback

Problem

You need to call an asynchronous unmanaged function, such as EnumWindows, and allow it to call a method, or make a *callback*, in your code.

Solution

Create a delegate that has the required signature for the callback. Use this delegate when defining and using the unmanaged function.

How It Works

Many of the Win32 API functions use callbacks. For example, if you want to retrieve the name of all the top-level windows that are currently open, you can call the unmanaged EnumWindows function in the User32.dll file. When calling EnumWindows, you need to supply a pointer to a function in your code. The Windows operating system will then call this function repeatedly, once for each top-level window that it finds, and pass the window handle to your code.

The .NET Framework allows you to handle callback scenarios like this without resorting to pointers and unsafe code blocks. Instead, you can define and use a delegate that points to your callback function. When you pass the delegate to the EnumWindows function, for example, the CLR will automatically marshal the delegate to the expected unmanaged function pointer.

The Code

The following is a console application that uses EnumWindows with a callback to display the name of every open window:

```
Imports System
Imports System.Text
Imports System.Runtime.InteropServices

Namespace Apress.VisualBasicRecipes.Chapter13
    Public Class Recipe13_04

        ' The signature for the callback method.
        Public Delegate Function CallBack(ByVal hwnd As IntPtr, ➥
ByVal lParam As Integer) As Boolean

        ' The unmanaged function that will trigger the callback
        ' as it enumerates the open windows.
        <DllImport("user32.dll")> _
        Public Shared Function EnumWindows(ByVal windowCallback As CallBack, ➥
ByVal param As Integer) As Integer
        End Function

        <DllImport("user32.dll")> _
        Public Shared Function GetWindowText(ByVal hWnd As IntPtr, ➥
ByVal text As StringBuilder, ByVal count As Integer) As Integer
        End Function
```

```
Public Shared Sub Main()

    ' Request that the operating system enumerate all windows,
    ' and trigger your callback with the handle of each one.
    EnumWindows(AddressOf DisplayWindowInfo, 0)

    ' Wait to continue.
    Console.WriteLine(Environment.NewLine)
    Console.WriteLine("Main method complete.  Press Enter.")
    Console.ReadLine()

End Sub

' The method that will receive the callback. The second
' parameter is not used, but is needed to match the
' callback's signature.
Public Shared Function DisplayWindowInfo(ByVal hWnd As IntPtr, ➥
ByVal lParam As Integer) As Boolean

    Dim chars As Integer = 100
    Dim buf As New StringBuilder(chars)

    If Not GetWindowText(hWnd, buf, chars) = 0 Then
        Console.WriteLine(buf)
    End If
    Return True

End Function

    End Class
End Namespace
```

13-5. Retrieve Unmanaged Error Information

Problem

You need to retrieve error information (either an error code or a text message) explaining why a Win32 API call failed.

Solution

On the declaration of the unmanaged method, set the SetLastError field of DllImportAttribute to True. If an error occurs when you execute the method, call the Shared Marshal.GetLastWin32Error method to retrieve the error code. To get a text description for a specific error code, use the unmanaged FormatMessage function.

How It Works

You cannot retrieve error information directly using the unmanaged GetLastError function. The problem is that the error code returned by GetLastError might not reflect the error caused by the unmanaged function you are using. Instead, it might be set by other .NET Framework classes or the CLR. You can retrieve the error information safely using the Shared Marshal.GetLastWin32Error method. This method should be called immediately after the unmanaged call, and it will return the error information only once. (Subsequent calls to GetLastWin32Error will simply return the error code 127.) In addition, you must specifically set the SetLastError field of the DllImportAttribute to True to indicate that errors from this function should be cached.

```
<DllImport("user32.dll", SetLastError:=True)>
```

You can extract additional information from the Win32 error code using the unmanaged FormatMessage function from the Kernel32.dll file.

The Code

The following console application attempts to show a message box but submits an invalid window handle. The error information is retrieved with Marshal.GetLastWin32Error, and the corresponding text information is retrieved using FormatMessage.

```
Imports System
Imports System.Runtime.InteropServices

Namespace Apress.VisualBasicRecipes.Chapter13
    Public Class Recipe13_05

        ' Declare the unmanaged functions.
        <DllImport("kernel32.dll")> _
        Private Shared Function FormatMessage(ByVal dwFlags As Integer, ➥
ByVal lpSource As Integer, ByVal dwMessage As Integer, ➥
ByVal dwLanguageId As Integer, ByRef lpBuffer As String, ByVal nSize As Integer, ➥
ByVal Arguments As Integer) As Integer
        End Function

        <DllImport("user32.dll", SetLastError:=True)> _
        Public Shared Function MessageBox(ByVal hWnd As IntPtr, ➥
ByVal pText As String, ByVal pCaption As String, ByVal uType As Integer) As Integer
        End Function

        Public Shared Sub Main()

            ' Invoke the MessageBox function passing an invalid
            ' window handle and thus forcing an error.
            Dim badWindowHandle As IntPtr = New IntPtr(-1)

            MessageBox(badWindowHandle, "Message", "Caption", 0)

            ' Obtain the error information.
            Dim errorCode As Integer = Marshal.GetLastWin32Error

            If Not errorCode = 0 Then
                Console.WriteLine(errorCode)
                Console.WriteLine(GetErrorMessage(errorCode))
            End If
```

```
        ' Wait to continue.
        Console.WriteLine(Environment.NewLine)
        Console.WriteLine("Main method complete.  Press Enter.")
        Console.ReadLine()

    End Sub

    ' GetErrorMessage formats and returns an error message
    ' corresponding to the input error code.
    Public Shared Function GetErrorMessage(ByVal errorCode As Integer) As String

        Dim FORMAT_MESSAGE_ALLOCATE_BUFFER As Integer = &H100
        Dim FORMAT_MESSAGE_IGNORE_INSERTS As Integer = &H200
        Dim FORMAT_MESSAGE_FROM_SYSTEM As Integer = &H1000

        Dim messageSize As Integer = 255
        Dim lpMsgBuf As String = ""
        Dim dwFlags As Integer = FORMAT_MESSAGE_ALLOCATE_BUFFER Or ➥
FORMAT_MESSAGE_FROM_SYSTEM Or FORMAT_MESSAGE_IGNORE_INSERTS

        Dim retVal As Integer = FormatMessage(dwFlags, 0, errorCode, 0, ➥
lpMsgBuf, messageSize, 0)
        If retVal = 0 Then
            Return Nothing
        Else
            Return lpMsgBuf
        End If

    End Function

    End Class
End Namespace
```

13-6. Use a COM Component in a .NET Client

Problem

You need to use a COM component, such as the older ADODB components, in a .NET client.

Solution

Use a primary interop assembly (PIA), if one is available. Otherwise, generate a runtime callable wrapper (RCW) using the Type Library Importer (Tlbimp.exe) or the Add Reference feature in Visual Studio 2008.

How It Works

The .NET Framework includes extensive support for COM interoperability. To allow .NET clients to interact with a COM component, .NET uses an RCW—a special .NET proxy class that sits between your .NET code and the COM component. The RCW handles all the details, including marshaling data types, using the traditional COM interfaces, and handling COM events.

You have the following three options for using an RCW:

- Obtain an RCW from the author of the original COM component. In this case, the RCW is created from a PIA provided by the publisher, as Microsoft does for Microsoft Office and ADODB.

- Generate an RCW using the Tlbimp.exe command-line utility or Visual Studio 2008.

- Create your own RCW using the types in the `System.Runtime.InteropServices` namespace. (This can be an extremely tedious and complicated process.)

If you want to use Visual Studio 2008 to generate an RCW, you simply need to select Add Reference from the Project menu and then select the appropriate component from the COM tab. When you click OK, the RCW will be generated and added to your project references. After that, you can use the Object Browser to inspect the namespaces and classes that are available.

If possible, you should always use a PIA instead of generating your own RCW. PIAs are more likely to work as expected, because they are created and digitally signed by the original component publisher. They might also include additional .NET refinements or enhancements. If a PIA is registered on your system for a COM component, Visual Studio 2008 will automatically use that PIA when you add a reference to the COM component. For example, the .NET Framework includes an adodb. dll assembly that allows you to use the ADO classic COM objects. If you add a reference to the Microsoft ActiveX Data Objects component, this PIA will be used automatically; no new RCW will be generated. Similarly, Microsoft Office 2007 provides a PIA that improves .NET support for Office Automation. However, you must download this assembly from the MSDN web site (at http://www.microsoft.com/ downloads/details.aspx?familyid=59DAEBAA-BED4-4282-A28C-B864D8BFA513&displaylang=en).

If you are not using Visual Studio 2008, you can create a wrapper assembly using the Tlbimp.exe command-line utility that is included with the .NET Framework. The only mandatory piece of information is the file name that contains the COM component. For example, the following statement creates an RCW with the default file name and namespace, assuming that the MyCOMComponent. dll file is in the current directory:

```
tlbimp MyCOMComponent.dll
```

Assuming that MyCOMComponent.dll has a type named `MyClasses`, the generated RCW file will have the name MyClasses.dll and will expose its classes through a namespace named `MyClasses`. You can also configure these options with command-line parameters, as described in the MSDN reference. For example, you can use `/out:[Filename]` to specify a different assembly file name and `/namespace:[Namespace]` to set a different namespace for the generated classes. You can also specify a key file using `/keyfile[keyfilename]` so that the component will be signed and given a strong name, allowing it to be placed in the global assembly cache (GAC). Use the `/primary` parameter to create a PIA.

The Code

The following example shows how you can use COM Interop to access the classic ADO objects from a .NET Framework application:

```
Imports System

Namespace Apress.VisualBasicRecipes.Chapter13
    Public Class Recipe13_06

        ' Be sure to add a reference to ADODB (runtime version 1.1.4322)
        ' to the project.
        Public Shared Sub Main()
```

```
        ' This example assumes that you have the AdventureWorks
        ' sample database installed. If you don't, you will need
        ' to change the connectionString accordingly.

        ' Create a new ADODB connection.
        Dim con As New ADODB.Connection
        Dim connectionString As String = "Provider=SQLOLEDB.1;Data " & ➥
Source=.\sqlexpress;Initial Catalog=AdventureWorks;Integrated Security=SSPI;"

        con.Open(connectionString, Nothing, Nothing, 0)

        ' Execute a SELECT query.
        Dim recordsAffected As Object = Nothing
        Dim rs As ADODB.Recordset = con.Execute("SELECT * FROM " & ➥
HumanResources.Employee;", recordsAffected, 0)

        ' Print out the results.
        While Not rs.EOF = True

            Console.WriteLine(rs.Fields("EmployeeID").Value)
            rs.MoveNext()

        End While

        ' Wait to continue.
        Console.WriteLine(Environment.NewLine)
        Console.WriteLine("Main method complete.  Press Enter.")
        Console.ReadLine()

    End Sub

End Class
End Namespace
```

13-7. Release a COM Component Quickly

Problem

You need to ensure that a COM component is removed from memory immediately, without waiting for garbage collection to take place, or you need to make sure that COM objects are released in a specific order.

Solution

Release the reference to the underlying COM object using the `Shared Marshal.` `FinalReleaseComObject` method and passing the appropriate RCW reference.

How It Works

COM uses reference counting to determine when objects should be released. When you use an RCW, the reference will be held to the underlying COM object, even when the object variable goes out of scope. The reference will be released only when the garbage collector disposes of the RCW object. As a result, you cannot control when or in what order COM objects will be released from memory.

To get around this limitation, you usually use the `Marshal.ReleaseComObject` method. However, if the COM object's pointer is marshaled several times, you need to repeatedly call this method to decrease the count to zero. However, the `FinalReleaseComObject` method allows you to release all references in one go by setting the reference count of the supplied RCW to zero. This means you do not need to loop and invoke `ReleaseComObject` to completely release an RCW. Once an object is released in this manner, it can no longer be used unless it's re-created.

For example, in the ADO example in recipe 13-6, you could release the underlying ADO `Recordset` and `Connection` objects by adding these two lines to the end of your code:

```
System.Runtime.InteropServices.Marshal.FinalReleaseComObject(rs)
System.Runtime.InteropServices.Marshal.FinalReleaseComObject(con)
```

■**Note** The `ReleaseComObject` method does not actually release the COM object; it just decrements the reference count. If the reference count reaches zero, the COM object will be released. `FinalReleaseComObject` works by setting the reference count of an RCW to zero. It thus bypasses the internal count logic and releases all references.

13-8. Use Optional Parameters

Problem

You need to call a method in a COM component without supplying all the required parameters.

Solution

Use the `Type.Missing` field.

How It Works

The .NET Framework is designed with a heavy use of method overloading. Most methods are overloaded several times so that you can call the version that requires only the parameters you choose to supply. COM, on the other hand, does not support method overloading. Instead, COM components usually use methods with a long list of optional parameters. You do not need to specify values for the optional parameters. For example, if a method includes three optional parameters, you can assign a value to the first and third one, skipping the second one. Passing `Nothing` to the second optional parameter would have the same effect. However, COM parameters are often passed by reference, which means your code cannot simply pass a `Nothing` reference. Instead, it must declare an object variable and then pass that variable.

You can mitigate the problem to some extent by supplying the `Type.Missing` field whenever you want to omit an optional parameter. If you need to pass a parameter by reference, you can simply declare a single object variable, set it equal to `Type.Missing`, and use it in all cases, like this:

```
Private Shared n As Object = Type.Missing
```

The Code

The following example uses the Microsoft Word COM objects to programmatically create and show a document. Many of the methods the example uses require optional parameters passed by reference. You will notice that the use of the Type.Missing field simplifies this code greatly. Each use is emphasized in bold in the code listing.

```vbnet
Imports System
Imports Microsoft.Office.Interop

Namespace Apress.VisualBasicRecipes.Chapter13

    ' This recipe requires a reference to Word and
    ' Microsoft.Office.Core or Microsoft.Office.Interop.Word.
    Public Class Recipe13_08

        Private Shared n As Object = Type.Missing

        Public Shared Sub Main()

            ' Start Word in the background.
            Dim app As New Word.Application
            app.DisplayAlerts = Word.WdAlertLevel.wdAlertsNone

            ' Create a new document (this is not visible to the user).
            Dim doc As Word.Document = app.Documents.Add(n, n, n, n)

            Console.WriteLine()
            Console.WriteLine("Creating new document.")
            Console.WriteLine()

            ' Add a heading and two lines of text.
            Dim range As Word.Range = doc.Paragraphs.Add(n).Range

            range.InsertBefore("Test Document")
            range.Style = "Heading 1"

            range = doc.Paragraphs.Add(n).Range
            range.InsertBefore("Line one." & ControlChars.CrLf & "Line two.")
            range.Font.Bold = 1

            ' Show a print preview, and make Word visible.
            doc.PrintPreview()
            app.Visible = True

            ' Wait to continue.
            Console.WriteLine(Environment.NewLine)
            Console.WriteLine("Main method complete.  Press Enter.")
            Console.ReadLine()

        End Sub

    End Class
End Namespace
```

13-9. Use an ActiveX Control in a .NET Client

Problem

You need to place an ActiveX control on a form or a user control in a .NET Framework application.

Solution

Use an RCW exactly as you would with an ordinary COM component (see recipe 13-6). To work with the ActiveX control at design time, add it to the Visual Studio 2008 Toolbox.

How It Works

As with COM components, the .NET Framework fully supports the use of ActiveX controls. When working with COM (detailed in recipe 13-6), an RCW is required to allow communication between your code and the COM object. An ActiveX control differs in that it requires two RCWs. The first RCW provides communication between the COM object and the second RCW. The second RCW is required to communicate between the first COM object and your Windows Form.

This extra wrapper is required because any control you use on your form *must* derive from System.Windows.Forms.Control. The second wrapper derives from the System.Windows.Forms.AxHost class, which derives from System.Windows.Forms.Control. This provides the standard .NET control properties, methods, and events (such as Location, Size, Anchor, and so on).

Several methods are available for creating the necessary RCWs. One method is to use the Aximp. exe command-line utility. This tool is the equivalent to Tlbimp.exe, which is used to generate an RCW for COM components. You just run aximp and supply the path to the ActiveX component. The following is an example of using this tool on the Microsoft Masked Edit control:

```
aximp c:\windows\system32\msmask32.ocx
```

This will generate MSMask.dll, the *first* wrapper, and AxMSMask.dll, the *second* wrapper. The MSMask.dll file is identical to the RCW that Tlbimp.exe would have produced for a COM component. The main component of the AxMSMask.dll file is the AxMaskEdBox class, which is part of the AxMSMask namespace. The Ax prefix represents the word *ActiveX* and indicates which wrapper derives from the AxHost class. To use the control in your project, you just need to add a reference to both these assemblies and then create an instance of the control. The following code snippet demonstrates creating an instance of the control and adding it to a form:

```
' Create a new instance of the ActiveX control.
Dim AxMaskEdBox1 As New AxMSMask.AxMaskEdBox

' Set some properties.
AxMaskEdBox1.Location = New Point(0, 0)
AxMaskEdBox1.Size = New Size(200, 50)

' Add the control to the form.
Me.Controls.Add(AxMaskEdBox1)
```

The .NET Framework also offers the AxImporter class, found in the System.Windows.Forms. Design namespace. This class lets you generate the appropriate wrapper assemblies by using the GenerateFromFile or GenerateFromTypeLibrary method. Both methods return the assembly-qualified name for the ActiveX control defined by the newly created assemblies. The AxImporter constructor takes an AxImporter.Option class instance. This class contains several properties that represent options the importer will use, but only the OutputDirectory property is required. You then use one of the methods, such as GenerateFromFile, to create the necessary wrappers. Once the assemblies have been generated, you can reference them at design time, as you would any other component, or you can reference them at runtime using reflection (described in Chapter 3). The following sample code demonstrates using AxImporter to create and use an instance of the Masked Edit control at runtime:

```
' Create the AxImporter options and set the output
' directory.
Dim axOptions As New AxImporter.Options
axOptions.outputDirectory = "C:\"

' Create the AxImporter object and generate the wrappers
' for the c:\windows\system32\msmask32.ocx file.
Dim aximp As New AxImporter(axOptions)
Dim fi As New FileInfo("C:\windows\system32\msmask32.ocx")
Dim assemblyName As String = aximp.GenerateFromFile(fi)

' Load the ActiveX RCW and create an instance of the control
' type named in assemblyName (which is "AxMSMask.AxMaskEdBox,AxMSMask").
Dim MSMaskAssembly As Assembly = Assembly.LoadFrom("C:\AxMSMask.dll")
Dim AxMaskEdBox1 As Object = ➠
MSMaskAssembly.CreateInstance(assemblyName.Substring(0, ➠
assemblyName.IndexOf(",")))

' Set some properties.
AxMaskEdBox1.Location = New Point(0, 0)
AxMaskEdBox1.Size = New Size(200, 50)

' Add the control to the form.
Me.Controls.Add(AxMaskEdBox1)
```

The simplest method, if you are using Visual Studio, is to add the ActiveX control to the Toolbox. You do this by selecting Choose Toolbox Items from the Tools menu. This will add an icon representing the ActiveX control to the Toolbox. Once you place the control on your form, the required RCWs will be created, and the appropriate references will be added to your project. The only difference between these generated files and those created by the two previous methods are the names. This method will name the files AxInterop.MSMask.dll and Interop.MSMask.dll.

Adding the control in this manner will automatically generate code in the hidden designer region of your form. That code will look similar to this:

```
Me.AxMaskEdBox1 = New AxMSMask.AxMaskEdBox
CType(Me.AxMaskEdBox1, System.ComponentModel.ISupportInitialize).BeginInit()
'
'AxMaskEdBox1
'
Me.AxMaskEdBox1.Location = New System.Drawing.Point(10, 15)
Me.AxMaskEdBox1.Name = "AxMaskEdBox1"
Me.AxMaskEdBox1.OcxState = CType(resources.GetObject("AxMaskEdBox1.OcxState"), ➠
System.Windows.Forms.AxHost.State)
Me.AxMaskEdBox1.Size = New System.Drawing.Size(247, 43)
Me.AxMaskEdBox1.TabIndex = 0
Me.Controls.Add(Me.AxMaskEdBox1)
```

13-10. Expose a .NET Component to COM

Problem

You need to create a .NET component that can be called by a COM client.

Solution

Create an assembly that follows certain restrictions identified in this recipe. Export a type library for this assembly using the Type Library Exporter (Tlbexp.exe) command-line utility.

How It Works

The .NET Framework includes support for COM clients to use .NET components. When a COM client needs to create a .NET object, the CLR creates the managed object and a COM-callable wrapper (CCW) that wraps the object. The COM client interacts with the managed object through the CCW. No matter how many COM clients are attempting to access a managed object, only one CCW is created for it.

Types that need to be accessed by COM clients must meet certain requirements:

- The managed type (class, interface, struct, or enum) must be `Public`.

- If the COM client needs to create the object, it must have a `Public` default constructor. COM does not support parameterized constructors.

- The members of the type that are being accessed must be `Public` instance members. `Private`, `Protected`, `Friend`, and `Shared` members are not accessible to COM clients.

In addition, you should consider the following recommendations:

- You should not create inheritance relationships between classes, because these relationships will not be visible to COM clients (although .NET will attempt to simulate this by declaring a shared base class interface).

- The classes you are exposing should implement an interface. If they don't implement an interface, one will be generated automatically. Changing the class in the future may cause versioning issues, so implementing your own interface is highly suggested. You use the `ClassInterfaceAttribute` to turn off the automatic generation of the interface and specify your own. For added versioning control, you can use the attribute `System.Runtime.InteropServices.GuidAttribute` to specify the GUID that should be assigned to an interface.

- Ideally, you should give the managed assembly a strong name so that it can be installed into the GAC and shared among multiple clients.

For a COM client to create the .NET object, it requires a type library (a .tlb file). The type library can be generated from an assembly using the Tlbexp.exe command-line utility. Here is an example of the syntax you use:

```
tlbexp ManagedLibrary.dll
```

Tlbexp.exe includes several options that affect how the tool runs and the output is produced. For example, you can use `/out` to specify the path and/or name produced by the utility. If you don't use this option, the file is created in the current directory with a name based on the assembly name and ending with .tlb. For automation purposes, you could use the `/silent` option to suppress all messages.

Once you generate the type library, you can reference it from the unmanaged development tool. With Visual Basic 6, you reference the .tlb file from the dialog box that opens when you select Project ➤ References. In Visual C++ 6, you can use the `#import` statement to import the type definitions from the type library.

13-11. Use a Windows Presentation Foundation Control from a Windows Form

Problem

You need to use a Windows Presentation Foundation (WPF) control or controls from a Windows Forms application rather than from a WPF application.

Solution

Use the `ElementHost` control to host the desired WPF control.

How It Works

Windows Presentation Foundation (WPF), discussed in some detail in Chapter 10, is a new application framework, introduced in .NET Framework 3.0. WPF includes enhanced controls and functionality for building Windows applications with a more advanced user interface. They are constructed in a similar manner as ASP.NET applications in that the interface is designed using a markup language (XAML, in this case) and events are handled with managed code.

WPF includes many of the same controls (such as `Button`, `TextBox`, `ListBox`, and so on) that can be found in a Windows Forms application, but many of them include more events (`MouseEnter`, `MouseLeave`, and so on) and more functionality. Windows Forms and WPF applications are two completely different .NET entities and cannot interact with one another without some sort of intermediary.

To allow the interoperability between WPF and Windows Forms, the .NET Framework provides the `ElementHost` control, which is part of the `System.Windows.Forms.Integration` namespace. You can easily add this control to your form by dragging it from the Toolbox. This will add the following required references to your project: `PresentationCore`, `PresenatationFramework`, `UIAutomationProvider`, `WindowsBase`, and `WindowsFormsIntegration`.

The `ElementHost` control works as a container for a single component that derives from `UIElement`, which is the base class for all WPF components. If you need to host more than one WPF element (or component), then you must create a composite user control in WPF and add a reference to it in your Windows Forms project. Once you have done this, you can then add it to an `ElementHost` control as you would normally by assigning an instance of the desired WPF control to the `ElementHost.Child` property.

The Code

This example displays a WPF button on a Windows Forms application using the `ElementHost` control. The `Click` event is handled to display a message when the button is clicked.

```
Imports System
Imports System.Windows.Controls

'  All designed code is stored in the autogenerated partial
'  class called Recipe13-11.Designer.vb.  You can see this
'  file by selecting Show All Files in Solution Explorer.
```

```vb
Public Class Recipe13_11

    Dim WithEvents wpfButton As System.Windows.Controls.Button

    Private Sub Recipe13_11_Load(ByVal sender As System.Object, ➥
ByVal e As System.EventArgs) Handles MyBase.Load

        ' Create a new button instance.
        wpfButton = New System.Windows.Controls.Button

        ' Set a few properties.
        wpfButton.Name = "WPF_Button"
        wpfButton.Content = "WPF BUTTON"

        ' Add the button to the ElementHost control.
        ElementHost1.Child = wpfButton

    End Sub

    Private Sub wpfButton_Click(ByVal sender As Object, ➥
ByVal e As System.Windows.RoutedEventArgs) Handles wpfButton.Click

        MessageBox.Show("You just clicked the WPF Button.", ➥
"WPF Button clicked", MessageBoxButtons.OK)

    End Sub

End Class
```

When you run the application, you will see a window similar to the one shown in Figure 13-2.

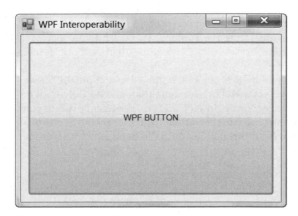

Figure 13-2. *WPF InteroperabilityWindow*

CHAPTER 14

■ ■ ■

Commonly Used Interfaces and Patterns

The recipes in this chapter show you how to implement patterns you will use frequently during the development of Microsoft .NET Framework applications. Some of these patterns are formalized using interfaces defined in the .NET Framework class library. Others are less rigid but still require you to take specific approaches to their design and implementation of your types. The recipes in this chapter cover the following:

- Creating serializable types that you can easily store to disk, sending across the network, or passing by value across application domain boundaries (recipe 14-1)

- Providing a mechanism that creates accurate and complete copies (clones) of objects (recipe 14-2)

- Implementing types that are easy to compare and sort (recipe 14-3)

- Supporting the enumeration of the elements contained in custom collections by creating a custom iterator (recipe 14-4)

- Ensuring that a type that uses unmanaged resources correctly releases those resources when they are no longer needed (recipe 14-5)

- Displaying string representations of objects that vary based on format specifiers (recipe 14-6)

- Correctly implementing custom exception and event argument types, which you will use frequently in the development of your applications (recipes 14-7 and 14-8)

- Implementing the commonly used Singleton and Observer design patterns using the built-in features of VB .NET and the .NET Framework class library (recipes 14-9 and 14-10)

14-1. Implement a Serializable Type

Problem

You need to implement a custom type that is serializable, allowing you to do the following:

- Store instances of the type to persistent storage (for example, a file or a database).

- Transmit instances of the type across a network.

- Pass instances of the type "by value" across application domain boundaries.

Solution

For serialization of simple types, apply the attribute `System.SerializableAttribute` to the type declaration. For types that are more complex, or to control the content and structure of the serialized data, implement the interface `System.Runtime.Serialization.ISerializable`.

How It Works

Recipe 2-13 showed how to serialize and deserialize an object using the formatter classes provided with the .NET Framework class library. However, types are not serializable by default. To implement a custom type that is serializable, you must apply the attribute `SerializableAttribute` to your type declaration. As long as all the data fields in your type are serializable types, applying `SerializableAttribute` is all you need to do to make your custom type serializable. If you are implementing a custom class that derives from a base class, the base class must also be serializable.

■**Caution** Classes that derive from a serializable type don't inherit the attribute `SerializableAttribute`. To make derived types serializable, you must explicitly declare them as serializable by applying the `SerializableAttribute` attribute.

Each formatter class contains the logic necessary to serialize types decorated with `SerializableAttribute` and will correctly serialize all `Public`, `Protected`, and `Private` fields. You can exclude specific fields from serialization by applying the attribute `System.NonSerializedAttribute` to those fields. As a rule, you should exclude the following fields from serialization:

- Fields that contain nonserializable data types

- Fields that contain values that might be invalid when the object is deserialized, such as memory addresses, thread IDs, and unmanaged resource handles

- Fields that contain sensitive or secret information, such as passwords, encryption keys, and the personal details of people and organizations

- Fields that contain data that is easily re-creatable or retrievable from other sources, especially if the data is large

If you exclude fields from serialization, you must implement your type to compensate for the fact that some data will not be present when an object is deserialized. Unfortunately, you cannot create or retrieve the missing data fields in an instance constructor, because formatters do not call constructors during the process of deserializing objects. The best approach for achieving fine-grained control of the serialization of your custom types is to use the attributes from the `System.Runtime.Serialization` namespace described in Table 14-1. These attributes allow you to identify methods of the serializable type that the serialization process should execute before and after serialization and deserialization. Any method annotated with one of these attributes must take a single `System.Runtime.Serialization.StreamingContext` argument, which contains details about the source or intended destination of the serialized object so that you can determine what to serialize. For example, you might be happy to serialize secret data if it's destined for another application domain in the same process, but not if the data will be written to a file.

As types evolve, you often add new member variables to support new features. This new state causes a problem when deserializing old objects because the new member variables are not part of the serialized object. .NET Framework 2.0 introduced the attribute `System.Runtime.Serialization.OptionalFieldAttribute`. When you create a new version of a type and add data members, annotate them with `OptionalFieldAttribute` so that the deserialization process will not fail if they are not present.

Table 14-1. *Attributes to Customize the Serialization and Deserialization Processes*

Attribute	Description
OnSerializingAttribute	Apply this attribute to a method to have it executed before the object is serialized. This is useful if you need to modify object state before it is serialized. For example, you may need to convert a DateTime field to UTC time for storage.
OnSerializedAttribute	Apply this attribute to a method to have it executed after the object is serialized. This is useful in case you need to revert the object state to what it was before the method annotated with OnSerializingAttribute was run.
OnDeserializingAttribute	Apply this attribute to a method to have it executed before the object is deserialized. This is useful if you need to modify the object state prior to deserialization.
OnDeserializedAttribute	Apply this attribute to a method to have it executed after the object is deserialized. This is useful if you need to re-create additional object state that depends on the data that was deserialized with the object or modify the deserialized state before the object is used.

You can then annotate new methods with OnDeserializedAttribute (see Table 14-1) to configure the new member variables appropriately.

For the majority of custom types, the mechanisms described will be sufficient to meet your serialization needs. If you require more control over the serialization process, you can implement the interface ISerializable. The formatter classes use different logic when serializing and deserializing instances of types that implement ISerializable. To implement ISerializable correctly, you must do the following:

- Declare that your type implements ISerializable.

- Apply the attribute SerializableAttribute to your type declaration as just described. What gets serialized is determined by the GetObjectData method, rather than relying on automatic serialization. For this reason, you shouldn't use NonSerializedAttribute because it will have no effect.

- Implement the ISerializable.GetObjectData method (used during serialization), which takes the argument types System.Runtime.Serialization.SerializationInfo and System.Runtime.Serialization.StreamingContext.

- Implement a nonpublic constructor (used during deserialization) that accepts the same arguments as the GetObjectData method. Remember that if you plan to derive classes from your serializable class, you should make the constructor Protected.

- If you are creating a serializable class from a base class that also implements ISerializable, your type's GetObjectData method and deserialization constructor must call the equivalent method and constructor in the base class.

During serialization, the formatter calls the GetObjectData method and passes it SerializationInfo and StreamingContext references as arguments. Your type must populate the SerializationInfo object with the data you want to serialize. The SerializationInfo class acts as a list of field/value pairs and provides the AddValue method to let you store a field with its value. In each call to AddValue, you must specify a name for the field/value pair; you use this name during deserialization to retrieve the value of each field. The AddValue method has 16 overloads that allow you to add values of different data types to the SerializationInfo object.

When a formatter deserializes an instance of your type, it calls the deserialization constructor, again passing a SerializationInfo and a StreamingContext reference as arguments. Your type must extract the serialized data from the SerializationInfo object using one of the SerializationInfo. Get* methods; for example, using GetString, GetInt32, or GetBoolean. The StreamingContext object provides information about the purpose and destination of the serialized data, allowing you to choose which data to serialize. During deserialization, the StreamingContext object provides information about the source of the serialized data, allowing you to mirror the logic you implemented for serialization.

Note During standard serialization operations, the formatters do not use the capabilities of the StreamingContext object to provide specifics about the source, destination, and purpose of serialized data. However, if you want to perform customized serialization, your code can configure the formatter's StreamingContext object prior to initiating serialization and deserialization. Consult the .NET Framework SDK documentation for details of the StreamingContext class.

The Code

The following example demonstrates a serializable Employee class that implements the ISerializable interface. In this example, the Employee class does not serialize the Address property if the provided StreamingContext object specifies that the destination of the serialized data is a file. The Main method demonstrates the serialization and deserialization of an Employee object.

```
Imports System
Imports System.IO
Imports System.Text
Imports System.Runtime.Serialization
Imports System.Runtime.Serialization.Formatters.Binary

Namespace Apress.VisualBasicRecipes.Chapter14

    <Serializable()> _
    Public Class Employee
        Implements ISerializable

        Private m_Name As String
        Private m_Age As Integer
        Private m_Address As String

        ' Simple Employee constructor.
        Public Sub New(ByVal name As String, ByVal age As Integer, ➥
ByVal address As String)

            m_Name = name
            m_Age = age
            m_Address = address

        End Sub

        ' Constructor required to enable a formatter to deserialize an
        ' Employee object. You should declare the constructor nonpublic
        ' to help ensure it is not called unnecessarily.
```

```vb
    Private Sub New(ByVal info As SerializationInfo, ➥
ByVal context As StreamingContext)

        ' Extract the name and age of the employee, which will always be
        ' present in the serialized data regardless of the value of the
        ' StreamingContext.
        m_Name = info.GetString("Name")
        m_Age = info.GetInt32("Age")

        ' Attempt to extract the employee's address and fail gracefully
        ' if it is not available.
        Try
            m_Address = info.GetString("Address")
        Catch ex As SerializationException
            m_Address = Nothing
        End Try

    End Sub

    ' Public property to provide access to the employee's name.
    Public Property Name() As String
        Get
            Return m_Name
        End Get
        Set(ByVal Value As String)
            m_Name = Value
        End Set
    End Property

    ' Public property to provide access to the employee's age.
    Public Property Age() As Integer
        Get
            Return m_Age
        End Get
        Set(ByVal value As Integer)
            m_Age = value
        End Set
    End Property

    ' Public property to provide access to the employee's address.
    ' Uses lazy initialization to establish address because a
    ' deserialized object may not have an address value.

    Public Property Address() As String
        Get
            If m_Address Is Nothing Then
                ' Load the address from persistent storage.
                ' In this case, set it to an empty string.
                m_Address = String.Empty
            End If

            Return m_Address
        End Get
```

```vbnet
            Set(ByVal value As String)
                m_Address = value
            End Set
        End Property

        ' Declared by the ISerializable interface, the GetObjectData method
        ' provides the mechanism with which a formatter obtains the object
        ' data that it should serialize.
        Public Sub GetObjectData(ByVal info As SerializationInfo, ➥
ByVal context As StreamingContext) Implements.ISerializable.GetObjectData

            ' Always serialize the employee's name and age.
            info.AddValue("Name", Name)
            info.AddValue("Age", Age)

            ' Don't serialize the employee's address if the StreamingContext
            ' indicates that the serialized data is to be written to a file.
            If (context.State And StreamingContextStates.File) = 0 Then
                info.AddValue("Address", Address)
            End If

        End Sub

        ' Override Object.ToString to return a string representation of the
        ' Employee state.
        Public Overrides Function ToString() As String

            Dim str As New StringBuilder

            str.AppendFormat("Name: {0}{1}", Name, ControlChars.CrLf)
            str.AppendFormat("Age: {0}{1}", Age, ControlChars.CrLf)
            str.AppendFormat("Address: {0}{1}", Address, ControlChars.CrLf)

            Return str.ToString

        End Function

    End Class

    ' A class to demonstrate the use of Employee.
    Public Class Recipe14_01

        Public Shared Sub Main()

            ' Create an Employee object representing an employee named Alex.
            Dim emp As New Employee("Aidan", 35, "Retroville")

            ' Display Employee object.
            Console.WriteLine(emp.ToString())

            ' Serialize the Employee object specifying another application domain
            ' as the destination of the serialized data. All data including the
            ' employee's address is serialized.
            Dim str As Stream = File.Create("Aidan.bin")
            Dim bf As New BinaryFormatter
```

```
bf.Context = New StreamingContext(StreamingContextStates.CrossAppDomain)
bf.Serialize(str, emp)
str.Close()

' Deserialize and display the Employee object.
str = File.OpenRead("Aidan.bin")
bf = New BinaryFormatter
emp = DirectCast(bf.Deserialize(str), Employee)
str.Close()
Console.WriteLine(emp.ToString())

' Serialize the Employee object specifying a file as the destination
' of the serialized data. In this case, the employee's address is not
' included in the serialized data.
str = File.Create("Aidan.bin")
bf = New BinaryFormatter
bf.Context = New StreamingContext(StreamingContextStates.File)
bf.Serialize(str, emp)
str.Close()

' Deserialize and display the Employee.
str = File.OpenRead("Aidan.bin")
bf = New BinaryFormatter
emp = DirectCast(bf.Deserialize(str), Employee)
str.Close()
Console.WriteLine(emp.ToString())

' Wait to continue.
Console.WriteLine(Environment.NewLine)
Console.WriteLine("Main method complete.  Press Enter.")
Console.ReadLine()

    End Sub

End Class
End Namespace
```

14-2. Implement a Cloneable Type

Problem

You need to create a custom type that provides a simple mechanism for programmers to create copies of type instances.

Solution

Implement the System.ICloneable interface.

How It Works

When you assign one value type to another, you create a copy of the value. No link exists between the two values—a change to one will not affect the other. However, when you assign one reference type to another (excluding strings, which receive special treatment by the runtime), you do not create a new copy of the reference type. Instead, both reference types refer to the same object, and changes to the value of the object are reflected in both references. To create a true copy of a reference type, you must *clone* the object to which it refers.

The ICloneable interface identifies a type as cloneable and declares the Clone method as the mechanism through which you obtain a clone of an object. The Clone method takes no arguments and returns a System.Object, regardless of the implementing type. This means that once you clone an object, you must explicitly cast the clone to the correct type.

The approach you take to implementing the Clone method for a custom type depends on the data members declared within the type. If the custom type contains only value-type (Integer, Byte, and so on) and System.String data members, you can implement the Clone method by instantiating a new object and setting its data members to the same values as the current object. The Object class (from which all types derive) includes the Protected method MemberwiseClone, which automates this process.

If your custom type contains reference-type data members, you must decide whether your Clone method will perform a *shallow copy* or a *deep copy*. A shallow copy means that any reference-type data members in the clone will refer to the same objects as the equivalent reference-type data members in the original object. A deep copy means that you must create clones of the entire object graph so that the reference-type data members of the clone refer to physically independent copies (clones) of the objects referenced by the original object.

A shallow copy is easy to implement by calling the MemberwiseClone method from within your Clone method. However, a deep copy is often what programmers expect when they first clone an object, but it's rarely what they get. This is especially true of the collection classes in the System. Collections namespace, which all implement shallow copies in their Clone methods. Although it would often be useful if these collections implemented a deep copy, there are two key reasons why types (especially generic collection classes) do not implement deep copies:

- Creating a clone of a large object graph is processor-intensive and memory-intensive.

- General-purpose collections can contain wide and deep object graphs consisting of any type of object. Creating a deep-copy implementation to cater to such variety is not feasible because some objects in the collection might not be cloneable, and others might contain circular references, which would send the cloning process into an infinite loop.

For strongly typed collections in which the nature of the contained elements are understood and controlled, a deep copy can be a very useful feature; for example, the System.Xml.XmlNode implements a deep copy in its Clone method. This allows you to create true copies of entire XML object hierarchies with a single statement.

■**Tip** If you need to clone an object that does not implement ICloneable but is serializable, you can often serialize and then deserialize the object to achieve the same result as cloning. However, be aware that the serialization process might not serialize all data members (as discussed in recipe 14-1). Likewise, if you create a custom serializable type, you can potentially use the serialization process just described to perform a deep copy within your ICloneable.Clone method implementation. To clone a serializable object, use the class System.Runtime. Serialization.Formatters.Binary.BinaryFormatter to serialize the object to, and then deserialize the object from a System.IO.MemoryStream object.

The Code

The following example demonstrates various approaches to cloning. The simple class named Employee contains only String and Integer members and so relies on the inherited MemberwiseClone method to create a clone. The Team class contains an implementation of the Clone method that performs a deep copy. The Team class contains a collection of Employee objects, representing a team of people. When you call the Clone method of a Team object, the method creates a clone of every contained Employee object and adds it to the cloned Team object. The Team class provides a Private constructor to simplify the code in the Clone method. The use of constructors is a common approach to simplify the cloning process.

```
Imports System
Imports System.Text
Imports System.Collections.Generic

Namespace Apress.VisualBasicRecipes.Chapter14

    Public Class Employee
        Implements ICloneable

        Public Name As String
        Public Title As String
        Public Age As Integer

        ' Simple Employee constructor.
        Public Sub New(ByVal _name As String, ByVal _title As String, ➥
ByVal _age As Integer)

            Name = _name
            Title = _title
            Age = _age

        End Sub

        ' Create a clone using the Object.MemberwiseClone method because
        ' the Employee class contains only string and value types.
        Public Function Clone() As Object Implements System.ICloneable.Clone
            Return Me.MemberwiseClone
        End Function

        ' Returns a string representation of the Employee object.
        Public Overrides Function ToString() As String
            Return String.Format("{0} ({1}) - Age {2}", Name, Title, Age)
        End Function

    End Class

    Public Class Team
        Implements ICloneable

        ' A List to hold the Employee team members.
        Public TeamMembers As New List(Of Employee)

        Public Sub New()
        End Sub

        ' Override Object.ToString to return a string representation
        ' of the entire team.
```

```vb
        Public Overrides Function ToString() As String

            Dim str As New StringBuilder

            For Each e As Employee In TeamMembers
                str.AppendFormat("  {0}{1}", e, ControlChars.CrLf)
            Next

            Return str.ToString

        End Function

        ' Implementation of ICloneable.Clone.
        Public Function Clone() As Object Implements System.ICloneable.Clone

            ' Create a deep copy of the team.
            Dim newTeam As New Team

            For Each e As Employee In Me.TeamMembers
                ' Clone the individual Employee objects and
                ' add them to the List.
                newTeam.TeamMembers.Add(DirectCast(e.Clone, Employee))
            Next

            Return newTeam

        End Function

    End Class


    ' A class to demonstrate the use of Employee.
    Public Class Recipe14_02

        Public Shared Sub Main()

            ' Create the original team.
            Dim originalTeam As New Team
            originalTeam.TeamMembers.Add(New Employee("Kai", "Genius", 34))
            originalTeam.TeamMembers.Add(New Employee("Jeremy", ➡
"Jack-Of-All-Trades", 35))
            originalTeam.TeamMembers.Add(New Employee("Guy", "Developer", 25))

            ' Clone the original team.
            Dim clonedTeam As Team = DirectCast(newTeam.Clone, Team)

            ' Display the original team.
            Console.WriteLine("Original Team:")
            Console.WriteLine(originalTeam)

            ' Display the cloned team.
            Console.WriteLine("Cloned Team:")
            Console.WriteLine(clonedTeam)
```

```
            '  Make change.
            Console.WriteLine("*** Make a change to original team ***")
            Console.WriteLine(Environment.NewLine)

            originalTeam.TeamMembers(0).Name = "Joed"
            originalTeam.TeamMembers(0).Title = "Manager"
            originalTeam.TeamMembers(0).Age = 30

            '  Display the original team.
            Console.WriteLine("Original Team:")
            Console.WriteLine(originalTeam)

            '  Display the cloned team.
            Console.WriteLine("Cloned Team:")
            Console.WriteLine(clonedTeam)

            '  Wait to continue.
            Console.WriteLine(Environment.NewLine)
            Console.WriteLine("Main method complete.  Press Enter.")
            Console.Read()

        End Sub

    End Class
End Namespace
```

14-3. Implement a Comparable Type

Problem

You need to provide a mechanism that allows you to compare custom types, enabling you to easily sort collections containing instances of those types.

Solution

To provide a standard comparison mechanism for a type, implement the generic System.IComparable(Of T) interface. To support the comparison of a type based on more than one characteristic, create separate types that implement the generic System.Collections.Generic.IComparer(Of T) interface.

■**Note** The nongeneric System.IComparable and System.Collections.IComparer interfaces, available prior to .NET Framework 2.0, still exist but do not use generics to ensure type safety. If you use these interface, you must take extra precautions to ensure the objects passed to the methods of these interfaces are of the appropriate type.

How It Works

To sort a collection, such as a List(Of T), you would call its Sort method. This method sorts the objects based on their implementation of the IComparable(Of T) interface. IComparable(Of T) defines a single method named CompareTo, shown here:

```
Public Function CompareTo(ByVal other As T) As Integer
End Function
```

The value returned by CompareTo should be calculated as follows:

- If the current object is less than other, return less than zero (for example, –1).
- If the current object has the same value as other, return zero.
- If the current object is greater than other, return greater than zero (for example, 1).

What these comparisons mean depends on the type implementing the IComparable interface. For example, if you were sorting people based on their surname, you would do a String comparison on this field. However, if you wanted to sort by birthday, you would need to perform a comparison of the corresponding System.DateTime fields.

To support a variety of sort orders for a particular type, you must implement separate helper types that implement the IComparer(Of T) interface, which defines the Compare method shown here:

```
Public Function Compare(ByVal x As T, ByVal y As T) As Integer
End Function
```

These helper types must encapsulate the necessary logic to compare two objects and return a value based on the following logic:

- If x has the same value as y, return zero.
- If x is greater than y, return greater than zero (for example, 1).

To use any of these helper types, you would pass them into an overloaded version of the collections Sort method that accepts an IComparer(Of T) .

The Code

The Newspaper class listed here demonstrates the implementation of both the IComparable and IComparer interfaces. The Newspaper.CompareTo method performs a case-insensitive comparison of two Newspaper objects based on their Name properties. A Private nested class named AscendingCirculationComparer implements IComparer and compares two Newspaper objects based on their Circulation properties. An AscendingCirculationComparer object is obtained using the Shared Newspaper.CirculationSorter property.

The Main method shown here demonstrates the comparison and sorting capabilities provided by implementing the IComparable and IComparer interfaces. The method creates a System.Collections. Generic.List(Of T) collection containing five Newspaper objects. Main then sorts the List(Of T) twice using the .Sort method. The first Sort operation uses the default Newspaper comparison mechanism provided by the IComparable.CompareTo method. The second Sort operation uses an AscendingCirculationComparer object to perform comparisons through its implementation of the IComparer.Compare method.

```
Imports System
Imports System.Collections.Generic

Namespace Apress.VisualBasicRecipes.Chapter14
    Public Class Newspaper
        Implements IComparable(Of Newspaper)

        Private _name As String
        Private _circulation As Integer

        ' Simple Newspaper constructor.
        Public Sub New(ByVal name As String, ByVal circulation As Integer)
```

```vb
            _name = name
            _circulation = circulation

        End Sub


        ' Declare a read-only property to access _name field.
        Public ReadOnly Property Name() As String
            Get
                Return _name
            End Get
        End Property


        ' Declare a read-only property to access _circulation field.
        Public ReadOnly Property Circulation() As String
            Get
                Return _circulation
            End Get
        End Property


        ' Declare a read-only property that returns an instance of the
        ' AscendingCirculationComparer.
        Public Shared ReadOnly Property CirculationSorter() As ➡
IComparer(Of Newspaper)
            Get
                Return New AscendingCirculationComparer
            End Get
        End Property


        ' Override Object.ToString.
        Public Overrides Function ToString() As String
            Return String.Format("{0}: Circulation = {1}", _name, _circulation)
        End Function


        ' Implementation of IComparable.CompareTo. The generic definition
        ' of IComparable allows us to ensure that the argument provided
        ' must be a Newspaper object. Comparison is based on a case-
        ' insensitive comparison of the Newspaper names.
        Public Function CompareTo(ByVal other As Newspaper) As Integer ➡
Implements System.IComparable(Of Newspaper).CompareTo

            ' IComparable dictates that an object is always considered
            ' greater than nothing.
            If other Is Nothing Then Return 1

            ' Short-circuit the case where the other Newspaper object is a
            ' reference to this one.
            If other Is Me Then Return 0

            ' Calculate return value by performing a case-insensitive
            ' comparison of the Newspaper names.
```

```vb
                    ' Because the Newspaper name is a string, the easiest approach
                    ' is to reply on the comparison capabilities of the string
                    ' class, which perform culture-sensitive string comparisons.
                    Return String.Compare(Me.Name, other.Name, True)

            End Function

            Private Class AscendingCirculationComparer
                Implements IComparer(Of Newspaper)

                    ' Implementation of IComparer.Compare. The generic definition of
                    ' IComparer allows us to ensure both arguments are Newspaper
                    ' objects.
                    Public Function Compare(ByVal x As Newspaper, ➡
ByVal y As Newspaper) As Integer Implements ➡
System.Collections.Generic.IComparer(Of Newspaper).Compare

                        ' Handle logic for nothing reference as dictated by the
                        ' IComparer interface. Nothing is considered less than
                        ' any other value.
                        If x Is Nothing And y Is Nothing Then
                            Return 0
                        ElseIf x Is Nothing Then
                            Return -1
                        ElseIf y Is Nothing Then
                            Return 1
                        End If

                        ' Short-circuit condition where x and y are references.
                        ' to the same object.
                        If x Is y Then
                            Return 0
                        End If

                        ' Compare the circulation figures. IComparer dictates that:
                        '       return less than zero if x < y
                        '       return zero if x = y
                        '       return greater than zero if x > y
                        ' This logic is easily implemented using integer arithmetic.
                        Return x.Circulation - y.Circulation

                    End Function

            End Class
    End Class

    ' A class to demonstrate the use of Newspaper.
    Public Class Recipe14_03

        Public Shared Sub Main()

            Dim newspapers As New List(Of Newspaper)
```

```
newspapers.Add(New Newspaper("The Washington Post", 125780))
newspapers.Add(New Newspaper("The Times", 55230))
newspapers.Add(New Newspaper("The Sun", 88760))
newspapers.Add(New Newspaper("The Herald", 5670))
newspapers.Add(New Newspaper("The Gazette", 235950))

Console.Clear()
Console.WriteLine("Unsorted newspaper list:")

For Each n As Newspaper In newspapers
    Console.WriteLine("  {0}", n)
Next

'  Sort the newspaper list using the object's implementation
'  of IComparable.CompareTo.
Console.WriteLine(Environment.NewLine)
Console.WriteLine("Newspaper list sorted by name (default order):")
newspapers.Sort()

For Each n As Newspaper In newspapers
    Console.WriteLine("  {0}", n)
Next

'  Sort the newspaper list using the supplied IComparer object.
Console.WriteLine(Environment.NewLine)
Console.WriteLine("Newspaper list sorted by circulation:")
newspapers.Sort(Newspaper.CirculationSorter)

For Each n As Newspaper In newspapers
    Console.WriteLine("  {0}", n)
Next

'  Wait to continue.
Console.WriteLine(Environment.NewLine)
Console.WriteLine("Main method complete.  Press Enter.")
Console.ReadLine()

        End Sub

    End Class
End Namespace
```

14-4. Implement an Enumerable Type Using a Custom Iterator

Problem

You need to create a collection type whose contents you can enumerate using a For Each statement.

Solution

Implement the interface System.Collections.IEnumerable or System.Collections.Generic.
IEnumerable(Of T) on your collection type. The GetEnumerator method of the IEnumerable and
IEnumerable(Of T) interfaces returns an *enumerator*, which is an object that implements either

the System.Collections.IEnumerator or System.Collections.Generic.IEnumerator(Of T) interface, respectively. The IEnumerator and IEnumerator(Of T) interfaces define the methods used by the For Each statement to enumerate the collection.

Implement a private iterator class within the enumerable type that implements either the IEnumerator or IEnumerator(Of T) interface and can iterate over the enumerable type while maintaining appropriate state information. In the GetEnumerator method of the enumerable type, create and return an instance of the iterator class.

How It Works

A numeric indexer allows you to iterate through the elements of most standard collections using a For loop. However, this technique does not always provide an appropriate abstraction for nonlinear data structures, such as trees and multidimensional collections. The For Each statement provides an easy-to-use and syntactically elegant mechanism for iterating through a collection of objects, regardless of their internal structures. This recipe will focus on the standard (nongeneric) implementation of an enumerable type.

To support For Each semantics, the type containing the collection of objects should implement the IEnumerable interface. The IEnumerable interface declares a single method named GetEnumerator, which does not take any arguments and returns an object that implements IEnumerator.

The next step is to implement a separate class that implements the IEnumerator interface. The IEnumerator interface provides a read-only, forward-only cursor for accessing the members of the underlying collection. Table 14-2 describes the members of the IEnumerator interface. The IEnumerator instance returned by GetEnumerator is your custom iterator—the object that actually supports enumeration of the collection's data elements.

Table 14-2. *Members of the IEnumerator Interface*

Member	Description
Current	Property that returns the current data element. When the enumerator is created, Current refers to a position preceding the first data element. This means you must call MoveNext before using Current. If Current is called and the enumerator is positioned before the first element or after the last element in the data collection, Current must throw a System.InvalidOperationException.
MoveNext	Method that moves the enumerator to the next data element in the collection. Returns True if there are more elements; otherwise, it returns False. If the underlying source of data changes during the life of the enumerator, MoveNext must throw an InvalidOperationException.
Reset	Method that moves the enumerator to a position preceding the first element in the data collection. If the underlying source of data changes during the life of the enumerator, Reset must throw an InvalidOperationException.

If your collection class contains different types of data that you want to enumerate separately, implementing the IEnumerable interface on the collection class requires some extra work. One option, since each item is returned as an Object, is to add checks to handle each different type within the For Each loop.

Another possible option would be to implement a number of properties that return different IEnumerator instances that handle each specific data type. For example, you might have a class that includes a collection of employees and a collection of tasks. You would create the Employees property, which would return an IEnumerator for the employee collection and the Tasks property, which would return an IEnumerator for the task collection.

The Code

The TeamMember, Team, and TeamMemberEnumerator classes in the following example demonstrate the implementation of a custom iterator using the IEnumerable and IEnumerator interfaces. The TeamMember class represents a member of a team. The Team class, which represents a team of people, is a collection of TeamMember objects. Team implements the IEnumerable interface and declares a separate class, named TeamMemberEnumerator, to provide enumeration functionality. Team implements the *Observer pattern* using delegate and event members to notify all TeamMemberEnumerator objects if their underlying Team changes. (See recipe 14-10 for a detailed description of the Observer pattern.) The TeamMemberEnumerator class is a Private nested class, so you cannot create instances of it other than through the Team.GetEnumerator method.

This example also demonstrates what happens when you attempt to change the collection you are enumerating through. In this case, an InvalidOperationException is thrown.

```vb
Imports System
Imports System.Collections.Generic
Imports System.Text.RegularExpressions

Namespace Apress.VisualBasicRecipes.Chapter14

    ' The TeamMember class represents an individual team member.
    Public Class TeamMember

        Public Name As String
        Public Title As String

        ' Simple TeamMember constructor.
        Public Sub New(ByVal _name As String, ByVal _title As String)

            Me.Name = _name
            Me.Title = _title

        End Sub


        ' Returns a string representation of the TeamMember.
        Public Overrides Function ToString() As String
            Return String.Format("{0} ({1})", Name, Title)
        End Function

    End Class

    ' Team class represents a collection of TeamMember objects.
    ' It implements the IEnumerable interface to support enumerating
    ' TeamMember objects.
    Public Class Team
        Implements IEnumerable
```

```vb
        ' A delegate that specifies the signature that all team change
        ' event handler methods must implement.
        Public Delegate Sub TeamChangedEventHandler(ByVal source As Team, ➡
ByVal e As EventArgs)

        ' A List to contain the TeamMember objects.
        Private teamMembers As List(Of TeamMember)

        ' The event used to notify that the Team  has changed.
        Public Event TeamChange As TeamChangedEventHandler

        ' Team constructor.
        Public Sub New()
            teamMembers = New List(Of TeamMember)
        End Sub

        ' Implement the IEnumerable.GetEnumerator method.
        Public Function GetEnumerator() As IEnumerator ➡
Implements System.Collections.IEnumerable.GetEnumerator
            Return New TeamMemberEnumerator(Me)
        End Function

        ' Adds a TeamMember object to the Team.
        Public Sub AddMember(ByVal member As TeamMember)

            teamMembers.Add(member)

            ' Notify listeners that the list has changed.
            RaiseEvent TeamChange(Me, EventArgs.Empty)

        End Sub

        ' TeamMemberEnumerator is a private nested class that provides
        ' the functionality to enumerate the TeamMembers contained in
        ' a Team collection. As a nested class, TeamMemberEnumerator
        ' has access to the private members of the Team class.
        Private Class TeamMemberEnumerator
            Implements IEnumerator

            ' The Team that this object is enumerating.
            Private sourceTeam As Team

            ' Boolean to indicate whether underlying Team has changed
            ' and so is invalid for further enumeration.
            Private teamInvalid As Boolean = False

            ' Integer to identify the current TeamMember. Provides
            ' the index of the TeamMember in the underlying List
            ' used by the Team collection. Initialize to -1, which is
            ' the index prior to the first element.
            Private currentMember As Integer = -1
```

```vbnet
        ' The constructor takes a reference to the Team that is
        ' the source of the enumerated data.
        Friend Sub New(ByVal _team As Team)

            Me.sourceTeam = _team

            ' Register with sourceTeam for change notifications.
            AddHandler Me.sourceTeam.TeamChange, AddressOf Me.TeamChange

        End Sub


        ' Implement the IEnumerator.Current property.
        Public ReadOnly Property Current() As Object Implements ➥
System.Collections.IEnumerator.Current
            Get
                ' If the TeamMemberEnumerator is positioned before
                ' the first element or after the last element, then
                ' throw an exception.
                If currentMember = -1 Or currentMember > ➥
(sourceTeam.teamMembers.Count - 1) Then
                    Throw New InvalidOperationException
                End If

                ' Otherwise, return the current TeamMember.
                Return sourceTeam.teamMembers(currentMember)

            End Get
        End Property


        ' Implement the IEnumerator.MoveNext method.
        Public Function MoveNext() As Boolean Implements ➥
System.Collections.IEnumerator.MoveNext

            ' If underlying Team is invalid, throw exception.
            If teamInvalid Then
                Throw New InvalidOperationException("Team modified")
            End If

            ' Otherwise, progress to the next TeamMember.
            currentMember += 1

            ' Return false if we have moved past the last TeamMember.
            If currentMember > (sourceTeam.teamMembers.Count - 1) Then
                Return False
            Else
                Return True
            End If

        End Function


        ' Implement the IEnumerator.Reset method. This method
        ' resets the position of the TeamMemberEnumerator to
        ' the top of the TeamMembers collection.
```

```vbnet
            Public Sub Reset() Implements System.Collections.IEnumerator.Reset

                ' If underlying Team is invalid, throw exception.
                If teamInvalid Then
                    Throw New InvalidOperationException("Team modified")
                End If

                ' Move the currentMember pointer back to the index
                ' preceding the first element.
                currentMember = -1

            End Sub

            ' An event handler to handle notification that the underlying
            ' Team collection has changed.
            Friend Sub TeamChange(ByVal source As Team, ByVal e As EventArgs)

                ' Signal that the underlying Team is now invalid.
                teamInvalid = True

            End Sub

        End Class
End Class

' A class to demonstrate the use of Team.
Public Class Recipe14_04

    Public Shared Sub Main()

        ' Create a new Team.
        Dim newTeam As New Team

        newTeam.AddMember(New TeamMember("Leah", "Biologist"))
        newTeam.AddMember(New TeamMember("Romi", "Actress"))
        newTeam.AddMember(New TeamMember("Gavin", "Quantum Physicist"))

        ' Enumerate the Team.
        Console.Clear()
        Console.WriteLine("Enumerate with a for each loop:")


        For Each member As TeamMember In newTeam
            Console.WriteLine(member.ToString)
        Next

        ' Enumerate using a while loop.
        Console.WriteLine(Environment.NewLine)
        Console.WriteLine("Enumerate with while loop:")

        Dim e As IEnumerator = newTeam.GetEnumerator

        While e.MoveNext
            Console.WriteLine(e.Current)
        End While
```

```
'  Enumerate the Team and try to add a Team Member.
'  Since adding a member will invalidate the collection,
'  the MoveNext method, of the TeamMemberEnumerator class,
'  will throw an exception.
Console.WriteLine(Environment.NewLine)
Console.WriteLine("Modify while enumerating:")

For Each member As TeamMember In newTeam
    Console.WriteLine(member.ToString)
    newTeam.AddMember(New TeamMember("Joed", "Linguist"))
Next

'  Wait to continue.
Console.WriteLine(Environment.NewLine)
Console.WriteLine("Main method complete.  Press Enter.")
Console.ReadLine()

        End Sub

    End Class
End Namespace
```

Notes

The preceding example demonstrates creating your own iterator for a custom collection. You could have simply created a new collection that inherits from one of the base generic classes, such as List(Of T). Since the base class is already enumerable, your class would automatically have this ability. You would not need to create your own enumerator class as required in the previous example. If you wanted to try this, you would replace the entire Team class with this version:

```
'  Team class represents a generic collection of TeamMember objects.
'  It inherits the List(Of TeamMember) class so it automatically
'  supports enumerating TeamMember objects.
Public Class Team
    Inherits List(Of TeamMember)

    '  A delegate that specifies the signature that all Team change
    '  event handler methods must implement.
    Public Delegate Sub TeamChangedEventHandler(ByVal source As Team, ➥
ByVal e As EventArgs)

    '  The event used to notify that the Team has changed.
    Public Event TeamChange As TeamChangedEventHandler

    '  Team constructor.
    Public Sub New()
    End Sub

    '  Adds a TeamMember object to the Team.
    Public Overloads Sub Add(ByVal member As TeamMember)

        MyBase.Add(member)
```

```
        ' Notify listeners that the list has changed.
        RaiseEvent TeamChange(Me, EventArgs.Empty)

    End Sub

End Class
```

Here, to mimic the main example, you override the base Add method so you can raise the TeamChange event. This means you need to replace calls to the AddMember method with calls to the Add method.

14-5. Implement a Disposable Class

Problem

You need to create a class that references unmanaged resources and provide a mechanism for users of the class to free those unmanaged resources deterministically.

Solution

Implement the System.IDisposable interface, and release the unmanaged resources when client code calls the IDisposable.Dispose method.

How It Works

An unreferenced object continues to exist on the managed heap and consume resources until the garbage collector releases the object and reclaims the resources. The garbage collector will automatically free managed resources (such as memory), but it will not free unmanaged resources (such as file handles and database connections) referenced by managed objects. If an object contains data members that reference unmanaged resources, the object must free those resources explicitly, or they will remain in memory for an unknown length of time.

One solution is to declare a destructor—or finalizer—for the class (*destructor* is a C++ term equivalent to the more general .NET term *finalizer*). Prior to reclaiming the memory consumed by an instance of the class, the garbage collector calls the object's finalizer. The finalizer can take the necessary steps to release any unmanaged resources. Unfortunately, because the garbage collector uses a single thread to execute all finalizers, use of finalizers can have a detrimental effect on the efficiency of the garbage collection process, which will affect the performance of your application. In addition, you cannot control when the runtime frees unmanaged resources because you cannot call an object's finalizer directly, and you have only limited control over the activities of the garbage collector using the System.GC class.

As a complementary mechanism to using finalizers, the .NET Framework defines the *Dispose pattern* as a means to provide deterministic control over when to free unmanaged resources. To implement the Dispose pattern, a class must implement the IDisposable interface, which declares a single method named Dispose. In the Dispose method, you must implement the code necessary to release any unmanaged resources and remove the object from the list of objects eligible for finalization if a finalizer has been defined.

Instances of classes that implement the Dispose pattern are called *disposable objects*. When code has finished with a disposable object, it calls the object's Dispose method to free all resources and make it unusable, but it still relies on the garbage collector to eventually release the object memory. It's important to understand that the runtime does not enforce disposal of objects; it's the responsibility of the client to call the Dispose method. However, because the .NET Framework class library uses the Dispose pattern extensively, VB .NET provides the Using statement to simplify the correct use of disposable objects. The following code shows the structure of a Using statement:

```
Using fs As New FileStream("SomeFile.txt", FileMode.Open)
    ' do some work
End Using
```

When the code reaches the end of the block in which the disposable object was declared, the object's Dispose method is automatically called, even if an exception is raised. Furthermore, once you leave the Using block, the object is out of scope and can no longer be accessed, so you cannot use a disposed object accidentally.

Here are some points to consider when implementing the Dispose pattern:

- Client code should be able to call the Dispose method repeatedly with no adverse effects.

- In multithreaded applications, it's important that only one thread execute the Dispose method concurrently. It's normally the responsibility of the client code to ensure thread synchronization, although you could decide to implement synchronization within the Dispose method.

- The Dispose method should not throw exceptions.

- Because the Dispose method does all necessary cleaning up of both managed and unmanaged objects, you do not need to call the object's finalizer. Your Dispose method should call the GC.SuppressFinalize method to ensure the finalizer is not called during garbage collection.

- Implement a finalizer that calls the unmanaged cleanup part of your Dispose method as a safety mechanism in case client code does not call Dispose correctly. However, avoid referencing managed objects in finalizers, because you cannot be certain of the object's state.

- If a disposable class extends another disposable class, the Dispose method of the child must call the Dispose method of its base class. Wrap the child's code in a Try block and call the base class' Dispose method in a Finally clause to ensure execution.

- Other instance methods and properties of the class should throw a System.ObjectDisposedException exception if client code attempts to execute a method on an already disposed object.

The Code

The following example demonstrates a common implementation of the Dispose pattern where a new Dispose method, which accepts a Boolean parameter, overrides the base Dispose method. If this parameter is True, managed and unmanaged objects will be properly disposed. If it is False, only the unmanaged objects will be properly disposed. The base Dispose method calls the new method passing True into the disposing parameter, while the Finalize method, which overrides the base Finalize method, passes False.

```
Imports System

Namespace Apress.VisualBasicRecipes.Chapter14

    ' Implement the IDisposable interface in an
    ' example class.
    Public Class DisposeExample
        Implements IDisposable

        ' Private data member to signal if the object has already
        ' been disposed.
        Private isDisposed As Boolean = False
```

```vbnet
' Private data member that holds the handle to an unmanaged
' resource.
Private resourceHandle As IntPtr

' Constructor.
Public Sub New()

    ' Constructor code obtains reference to an unmanaged
    ' resource.
    resourceHandle = IntPtr.Zero

End Sub

' Protected overload of the Dispose method. The disposing argument
' signals whether the method is called by consumer code (true), or by
' the garbage collector (false). Note that this method is not part
' of the IDisposable interface because it has a different signature to
' the parameterless Dispose method.
Protected Overridable Sub Dispose(ByVal disposing As Boolean)

    ' Don't try to dispose of the object twice.
    If Not Me.isDisposed Then

        ' Determine if consumer code or the garbage collector is
        ' calling. Avoid referencing other managed objects during
        ' finalization.
        If disposing Then
            ' Method called by consumer code. Call the Dispose method
            ' of any managed data members that implement the IDisposable
            ' interface.
            ' ...
        End If

        ' Whether called by consumer code or the garbage collector,
        ' free all unmanaged resources and set the value of managed
        ' data members to nothing. In the case of an inherited type,
        ' call base.Dispose(disposing).
    End If

    ' Signal that this object has been disposed.
    Me.isDisposed = True
End Sub

' Public implementation of the IDisposable.Dispose method, called
' by the consumer of the object in order to free unmanaged resources.
Public Sub Dispose() Implements IDisposable.Dispose

    ' Call the protected Dispose overload and pass a value of "True"
    ' to indicate that Dispose is being called by consumer code, not
    ' by the garbage collector.
    Dispose(True)

    ' Because the Dispose method performs all necessary cleanup,
    ' ensure the garbage collector does not call the class destructor.
    GC.SuppressFinalize(Me)
```

```vb
    End Sub

    ' Destructor / Finalizer. Because Dispose calls GC.SuppressFinalize,
    ' this method is called by the garbage collection process only if
    ' the consumer of the object does not call Dispose as it should.
    Protected Overrides Sub Finalize()

        ' Call the Dispose method as opposed to duplicating the code to
        ' clean up any unmanaged resources. Use the protected Dispose
        ' overload and pass a value of "False" to indicate that Dispose is
        ' being called during the garbage collection process, not by the
        ' consumer code.
        Dispose(False)

    End Sub

    ' Before executing any functionality, ensure that Dispose had not
    ' already been executed on the object.
    Public Sub SomeMethod()

        ' Throw an exception if the object has already been disposed.
        If isDisposed Then
            Throw New ObjectDisposedException("DisposeExample")
        End If

        ' Execute method functionality.
        ' ...

    End Sub

End Class

' A class to demonstrate the use of DisposeExample.
Public Class Recipe14_05

    Public Shared Sub Main()

        ' The Using statement ensures the Dispose method is called
        ' even if an exception occurs.
        Using d As New DisposeExample
            ' Do something with d.
        End Using

        ' Wait to continue.
        Console.WriteLine(Environment.NewLine)
        Console.WriteLine("Main method complete.  Press Enter.")
        Console.ReadLine()

    End Sub

End Class
End Namespace
```

14-6. Implement a Type That Can Be Formatted

Problem

You need to implement a type that can create different string representations of its content based on the use of format specifiers for use in formatted strings.

Solution

Implement the System.IFormattable interface.

How It Works

The following code fragment demonstrates the use of format specifiers in the WriteLine method of the System.Console class. The codes in the braces (emphasized in the example) are the format specifiers.

```
Dim a As Double = 345678.5678
Dim b As UInteger = 12000
Dim c As Byte = 254

Console.WriteLine("a = {0}, b = {1}, and c = {2}", a, b, c)
Console.WriteLine("a = {0:c0}, b = {1:n4}, and c = {2,10:x5}", a, b, c)
```

When run on a machine configured with English (United States) regional settings, this code will result in the output shown here:

```
a = 345678.5678, b = 12000, and c = 254
a = $345,679, b = 12,000.0000, and c =      000fe
```

As you can see, changing the contents of the format specifiers changes the format of the output significantly, even though the data has not changed. To enable support for format specifiers in your own types, you must implement the IFormattable interface. IFormattable declares a single method named ToString with the following signature:

```
Public Function ToString(ByVal format As String, ByVal formatProvider As ➥
IFormatProvider) As String
End Function
```

The format argument is a System.String containing a *format string*. The format string is the portion of the format specifier that follows the colon. For example, in the format specifier {2,10:x5} used in the previous example, x5 is the format string. The format string contains the instructions the IFormattable instance should use when it's generating the string representation of its content. The .NET Framework documentation for IFormattable states that types that implement IFormattable must support the G (general) format string, but that the other supported format strings depend on the implementation. The format argument will be Nothing if the format specifier does not include a format string component, for example, {0} or {1,20}.

The formatProvider argument is a reference to an instance of a type that implements System. IFormatProvider, and that provides access to information about the cultural and regional preferences to use when generating the string representation of the IFormattable object. This information includes data such as the appropriate currency symbol or number of decimal places to use. By default, formatProvider is Nothing, which means you should use the current thread's regional and cultural settings, available through the Shared method CurrentCulture of the System.Globalization. CultureInfo class. Some methods that generate formatted strings, such as String.Format, allow you to specify an alternative IFormatProvider to use, such as CultureInfo, DateTimeFormatInfo, or NumberFormatInfo.

The .NET Framework uses IFormattable primarily to support the formatting of value types, but it can be used to good effect with any type.

The Code

The following example contains a class named Person that implements the IFormattable interface. The Person class contains the title and names of a person and will render the person's name in different formats depending on the format strings provided. The Person class does not make use of regional and cultural settings provided by the formatProvider argument. The Main method demonstrates how to use the formatting capabilities of the Person class.

```vb
Imports System

Namespace Apress.VisualBasicRecipes.Chapter14
    Public Class Person
        Implements IFormattable

        ' Private members to hold the person's title and name details.
        Private title As String
        Private names As String()

        ' Constructor used to set the person's title and names.
        Public Sub New(ByVal _title As String, ByVal ParamArray _names As String())

            Me.title = _title
            Me.names = _names

        End Sub

        ' Override the Object.ToString method to return the person's
        ' name using the general format.
        Public Overrides Function ToString() As String
            Return ToString("G", Nothing)
        End Function

        ' Implementation of the IFormattable.ToString method to return the
        ' person's name in different forms based on the format string
        ' provided.
        Public Overloads Function ToString(ByVal format As String, ➡
ByVal formatProvider As System.IFormatProvider) As String ➡
Implements System.IFormattable.ToString

            Dim result As String = Nothing

            ' Use the general format if none is specified.
            If format Is Nothing Then format = "G"

            ' The contents of the format string determine the format of the
            ' name returned.
```

```vb
        Select Case format.ToUpper()(0)
            Case "S"
                ' Use short form - first initial and surname if a surname
                ' was supplied.
                If names.Length > 1 Then
                    result = names(0)(0) & ". " & names(names.Length - 1)
                Else
                    result = names(0)
                End If
            Case "P"
                ' Use polite form - title, initials, and surname.
                ' Add the person's title to the result.
                If title IsNot Nothing And Not title.Length = 0 Then
                    result = title & ". "
                End If

                ' Add the person's initials and surname.
                For count As Integer = 0 To names.Length - 1

                    If Not count = (names.Length - 1) Then
                        result += names(count)(0) & ". "
                    Else
                        result += names(count)
                    End If

                Next
            Case "I"
                ' Use informal form - first name only.
                result = names(0)

            Case Else
                ' Use general.default form - first name and surname (if
                ' a surname is supplied).
                If names.Length > 1 Then
                    result = names(0) & " " & names(names.Length - 1)
                Else
                    result = names(0)
                End If
        End Select

    Return result

End Function

' A class to demonstrate the use of Person.
Public Class Recipe14_06

    Public Shared Sub Main()

        ' Create a Person object representing a man with the name
        ' Dr. Gaius Baltar.
        Dim newPerson As New Person("Dr", "Gaius", "Baltar")
```

```
' Display the person's name using a variety of format strings.
Console.WriteLine("Dear {0:G}", newPerson)
Console.WriteLine("Dear {0:P}", newPerson)
Console.WriteLine("Dear {0:I},", newPerson)
Console.WriteLine("Dear {0}", newPerson)
Console.WriteLine("Dear {0:S},", newPerson)

' Wait to continue.
Console.WriteLine(Environment.NewLine)
Console.WriteLine("Main method complete.  Press Enter.")
Console.ReadLine()

        End Sub

    End Class

    End Class
End Namespace
```

14-7. Implement a Custom Exception Class

Problem

You need to create a custom exception class so that you can use the runtime's exception-handling mechanism to handle application-specific exceptions.

Solution

Create a serializable class that inherits the System.Exception class. Add support for any custom data members required by the exception, including constructors and properties required to manipulate the data members.

■Tip If you need to define a number of custom exceptions for use in a single application or library, you should define a single custom exception that extends System.Exception and use this as a common base class for all your other custom exceptions. There is very little point in extending System.ApplicationException, as is often recommended. Doing so simply introduces another level in your exception hierarchy and provides little if any benefit when handling your exception classes—after all, catching a nonspecific exception like ApplicationException is just as bad a practice as catching Exception.

How It Works

Exception classes are unique in that you do not declare new classes solely to implement new or extended functionality. The runtime's exception-handling mechanism—exposed by the VB .NET statements Try, Catch, and Finally—works based on the *type* of exception thrown, not the functional or data members implemented by the thrown exception.

If you need to throw an exception, you should use an existing exception class from the .NET Framework class library, if a suitable one exists. For example, some useful exceptions include the following:

- System.ArgumentNullException, thrown when code passes a Nothing argument value to your method that does not support Nothing arguments

- System.ArgumentOutOfRangeException, thrown when code passes an inappropriately large or small argument value to your method

- System.FormatException, thrown when code attempts to pass your method a String argument containing incorrectly formatted data

If none of the existing exception classes meets your needs or you feel your application would benefit from using application-specific exceptions, it's a simple matter to create your own exception class. To integrate your custom exception with the runtime's exception-handling mechanism and remain consistent with the pattern implemented by .NET Framework–defined exception classes, you should do the following:

- Give your exception class a meaningful name ending in the word Exception, such as TypeMismatchException or RecordNotFoundException.

- Mark your exception class as NotInheritable if you do not intend other exception classes to extend it.

- Implement at least one of the Public constructors with the signatures shown here and ensure they call the base class constructor. Best practices dictate that you should implement the first three constructors. The last constructor is used if your type is serializable.

```
Public Sub New
    MyBase.New
End Sub

Public Sub New(ByVal msg As String)
    MyBase.New(msg)
End Sub

Public Sub New(ByVal msg As String, ByVal inner As Exception)
    MyBase.New(msg, inner)
End Sub

Public Sub New(ByVal info As SerializationInfo, ➡
ByVal context As StreamingContext)
    MyBase.New(info, context)
End Sub
```

- Make your exception class serializable so that the runtime can marshal instances of your exception across application domain and machine boundaries. Applying the attribute System.SerializableAttribute is sufficient for exception classes that do not implement custom data members. However, because Exception implements the interface System.Runtime.Serialization.ISerializable, if your exception declares custom data members, you must override the ISerializable.GetObjectData method of the Exception class as well as implement a deserialization constructor with this signature. If your exception class is NotInheritable, mark the deserialization constructor as Private; otherwise, mark it as Protected. The GetObjectData method and deserialization constructor must call the equivalent base class method to allow the base class to serialize and deserialize its data correctly. (See recipe 14-1 for details on making classes serializable.)

■**Tip** In large applications, you will usually implement quite a few custom exception classes. It pays to put significant thought into how you organize your custom exceptions and how code will use them. Generally, avoid creating new exception classes unless code will make specific efforts to catch that exception; use data members, not additional exception classes, to achieve informational granularity.

The Code

The following example is a custom exception named CustomException that extends Exception and declares two custom data members, a String named stringInfo and a Boolean named booleanInfo:

```vbnet
Imports System
Imports System.Runtime.Serialization

Namespace Apress.VisualBasicRecipes.Chapter14

    ' Mark CustomException as Serializable.

    <Serializable()> _
    Public NotInheritable Class CustomException
        Inherits Exception

        ' Custom data members for CustomException.
        Private m_StringInfo As String
        Private m_BooleanInfo As Boolean

        ' Three standard constructors that simply call the base
        ' class constructor of System.Exception.
        Public Sub New()
            MyBase.New()
        End Sub

        Public Sub New(ByVal message As String)
            MyBase.New(message)
        End Sub

        Public Sub New(ByVal message As String, ByVal inner As Exception)
            MyBase.New(message, inner)
        End Sub

        ' The deserialization constructor required by the ISerialization
        ' interface. Because CustomException is NotInheritable, this constructor
        ' is private. If CustomException were not NotInheritable, this constructor
        ' should be declared as protected so that derived classes can call
        ' it during deserialization.
        Private Sub New(ByVal info As SerializationInfo, ➥
ByVal context As StreamingContext)
            MyBase.New(info, context)

            ' Deserialize each custom data member.
            m_StringInfo = info.GetString("StringInfo")
            m_BooleanInfo = info.GetBoolean("BooleanInfo")

        End Sub
```

```vb
        ' Additional constructors to allow code to set the custom data
        ' members.
        Public Sub New(ByVal _message As String, ByVal _StringInfo As String, ➡
ByVal _BooleanInfo As Boolean)
            MyBase.New(_message)

            m_StringInfo = _StringInfo
            m_BooleanInfo = _BooleanInfo

        End Sub

        Public Sub New(ByVal _message As String, ByVal inner As Exception, ➡
ByVal _stringinfo As String, ByVal _booleanInfo As Boolean)
            MyBase.New(_message, inner)


            m_StringInfo = _stringinfo
            m_BooleanInfo = _booleanInfo

        End Sub

        ' Read-only properties that provide access to the custom data members.
        Public ReadOnly Property StringInfo() As String
            Get
                Return m_StringInfo
            End Get
        End Property

        Public ReadOnly Property BooleanInfo() As Boolean
            Get
                Return m_BooleanInfo
            End Get
        End Property

        ' The GetObjectData method (declared in the ISerializable interface)
        ' is used during serialization of CustomException. Because
        ' CustomException declares custom data members, it must override
        ' the base class implementation of GetObjectData.
        Public Overrides Sub GetObjectData(ByVal info As SerializationInfo, ➡
ByVal context As StreamingContext)

            ' Serialize the custom data members.
            info.AddValue("StringInfo", m_StringInfo)
            info.AddValue("BooleanInfo", m_BooleanInfo)

            ' Call the base class to serialize its members.
            MyBase.GetObjectData(info, context)

        End Sub

        ' Override the base class Message property to include the custom data
        ' members.
```

```vb
        Public Overrides ReadOnly Property Message() As String
            Get
                Dim msg As String = MyBase.Message

                If StringInfo IsNot Nothing Then
                    msg += Environment.NewLine & StringInfo & " = " & BooleanInfo
                End If

                Return msg
            End Get
        End Property

    End Class

    '  A class to demonstrate the use of CustomException.
    Public Class Recipe14_07

        Public Shared Sub Main()

            Try
                '  Create and throw a CustomException object.
                Throw New CustomException("Some error", "SomeCustomMessage", True)
            Catch ex As CustomException
                Console.WriteLine(ex.Message)
            End Try

            '  Wait to continue.
            Console.WriteLine(Environment.NewLine)
            Console.WriteLine("Main method complete.  Press Enter.")
            Console.ReadLine()

        End Sub

    End Class
End Namespace
```

14-8. Implement a Custom Event Argument

Problem

When you raise an event, you need to pass an object that contains data related to the event that would be useful when handling it. For example, the MouseEventArgs class (used by the MouseDown event) includes the Button property, which indicates which mouse button was pressed.

Solution

Create a custom event argument class derived from the System.EventArgs class. When you raise the event, create an instance of your event argument class and pass it to the event handlers.

How It Works

When you declare your own event types, you will often want to pass event-specific state to any listening event handlers. To create a custom event argument class that complies with the *Event pattern* defined by the .NET Framework, you should do the following:

- Derive your custom event argument class from the EventArgs class. The EventArgs class contains no data and is used with events that do not need to pass event state.

- Give your event argument class a meaningful name ending in EventArgs, such as DiskFullEventArgs or MailReceivedEventArgs.

- Mark your argument class as NotInheritable if you do not intend other event argument classes to extend it.

- Implement additional data members and properties to support event state that you need to pass to event handlers. It's best to make event state immutable, so you should use Private ReadOnly data members and use Public properties to provide read-only access to the data members.

- Make your event argument class serializable so that the runtime can marshal instances of it across application domain and machine boundaries. Applying the attribute System. SerializableAttribute is usually sufficient for event argument classes. However, if your class has special serialization requirements, you must also implement the interface System.Runtime. Serialization.ISerializable. (See recipe 14-1 for details on making classes serializable.)

The Code

The following example demonstrates the implementation of an event argument class named MailReceivedEventArgs. Theoretically, an e-mail server passes instances of the MailReceivedEventArgs class to event handlers in response to the receipt of an e-mail message. The MailReceivedEventArgs class contains information about the sender and subject of the received e-mail message.

```
Imports System

Namespace Apress.VisualBasicRecipes.Chapter14

    <Serializable()> _
    Public NotInheritable Class MailReceivedEventArgs
        Inherits EventArgs

        ' Private read-only members that hold the event state that is to be
        ' distributed to all event handlers. The MailReceivedEventArgs class
        ' will specify who sent the received mail and what the subject is.
        Private ReadOnly m_From As String
        Private ReadOnly m_Subject As String

        ' Constuctor, initializes event state.
        Public Sub New(ByVal _from As String, ByVal _subject As String)

            Me.m_From = _from
            Me.m_Subject = _subject

        End Sub
```

```vbnet
        ' Read-only properties to provide access to event state.
        Public ReadOnly Property From() As String
            Get
                Return m_From
            End Get
        End Property

        Public ReadOnly Property Subject() As String
            Get
                Return m_Subject
            End Get
        End Property

    End Class

    ' A class to demonstrate the use of MailReceivedEventArgs.
    Public Class Recipe14_08

        Public Shared Sub Main()

            Dim args As New MailReceivedEventArgs("Amy", "Work Plan")

            Console.WriteLine("From: {0}, Subject: {1}", args.From, args.Subject)

            ' Wait to continue.
            Console.WriteLine(Environment.NewLine)
            Console.WriteLine("Main method complete.  Press Enter.")
            Console.ReadLine()

        End Sub

    End Class
End Namespace
```

Notes

The preceding example mainly deals with creating a custom `EventArgs` class. If the example were part of a full application, you would most likely have an event (such as `MailReceived`) that would accept an instance of `MailReceivedEventArgs` as the second parameter. Your `Mail` class would appropriately raise this event, passing an instance of `MailReceivedEventArgs`. Recipe 14-10 goes into more detail on handling custom events and event arguments this way.

14-9. Implement the Singleton Pattern

Problem

You need to ensure that only a single instance of a type exists at any given time and that the single instance is accessible to all elements of your application.

Solution

Implement the type using the *Singleton pattern.*

How It Works

Of all the identified patterns, the Singleton pattern is perhaps the most widely known and commonly used. The purpose of the Singleton pattern is to ensure that only one instance of a type exists at a given time and to provide global access to the functionality of that single instance. You can implement the type using the Singleton pattern by doing the following:

- Implement a Private Shared member within the type to hold a reference to the single instance of the type.

- Implement a publicly accessible Shared property in the type to provide read-only access to the singleton instance.

- Implement only a Private constructor so that code cannot create additional instances of the type.

The Code

The following example demonstrates an implementation of the Singleton pattern for a class named SingletonExample:

```
Imports System

Namespace Apress.VisualBasicRecipes.Chapter14
    Public Class SingletonExample

        ' A shared member to hold a reference to the singleton instance.
        Private Shared m_Instance As SingletonExample

        ' A shared constructor to create the singleton instance. Another
        ' alternative is to use lazy initialization in the Instance property.
        Shared Sub New()
            m_Instance = New SingletonExample
        End Sub

        ' A private constructor to stop code from creating additional
        ' instances of the singleton type.
        Private Sub New()
        End Sub

        ' A public property to provide access to the singleton instance.
        Public Shared ReadOnly Property Instance() As SingletonExample
            Get
                Return m_Instance
            End Get
        End Property

        ' Public methods that provide singleton functionality.
        Public Sub TestMethod1()
            Console.WriteLine("Test Method 1 ran.")
        End Sub

        Public Sub TestMethod2()
            Console.WriteLine("Test Method 2 ran.")
        End Sub
```

```
        End Class
End Namespace
```

Usage

To invoke the functionality of the SingletonExample class, you can obtain a reference to the singleton using the Instance property and then call its methods. Alternatively, you can execute members of the singleton directly through the Instance property. The following code shows both approaches:

```
Public Class Recipe14_09
    Public Shared Sub Main()

        ' Obtain reference to a singleton and invoke methods.
        Dim s As SingletonExample = SingletonExample.Instance
        s.TestMethod1()

        ' Execute singleton functionality without a reference.
        SingletonExample.Instance.TestMethod2()

        ' Wait to continue.
        Console.WriteLine(Environment.NewLine)
        Console.WriteLine("Main method complete.  Press Enter.")
        Console.ReadLine()

    End Sub
End Class
```

14-10. Implement the Observer Pattern

Problem

You need to implement an efficient mechanism for an object (the *subject*) to notify other objects (the *observers*) about changes to its state.

Solution

Implement the *Observer pattern* using delegate types as type-safe function pointers and event types to manage and notify the set of observers.

How It Works

The traditional approach to implementing the Observer pattern is to implement two interfaces: one to represent an observer (IObserver) and the other to represent the subject (ISubject). Objects that implement IObserver register with the subject, indicating that they want to be notified of important events (such as state changes) affecting the subject. The subject is responsible for managing the list of registered observers and notifying them in response to events affecting the subject. The subject usually notifies observers by calling a Notify method declared in the IObserver interface. The subject might pass data to the observer as part of the Notify method, or the observer might need to call a method declared in the ISubject interface to obtain additional details about the event.

Although you are free to implement the Observer pattern in VB .NET using the approach just described, the Observer pattern is so pervasive in modern software solutions that VB .NET and the .NET Framework include event and delegate types to simplify its implementation. The use of events and delegates means that you do not need to declare IObserver and ISubject interfaces. In addition, you do not need to implement the logic necessary to manage and notify the set of registered observers—the area where most coding errors occur.

The .NET Framework uses one particular implementation of the event-based and delegate-based Observer pattern so frequently that it has been given its own name: the *Event pattern*. (Pattern purists might prefer the name *Event idiom*, but Event pattern is the name most commonly used in Microsoft documentation.)

The Code

The example for this recipe contains a complete implementation of the Event pattern, which includes the following types:

- Thermostat class (the subject of the example), which keeps track of the current temperature and notifies observers when a temperature change occurs

- TemperatureChangedEventArgs class, which is a custom implementation of the System.EventArgs class used to encapsulate temperature change data for distribution during the notification of observers

- TemperatureChangedEventHandler delegate, which defines the signature of the method that all observers of a Thermostat object should implement if they want to be notified in the event of temperature changes

- TemperatureChangeObserver and TemperatureAverageObserver classes, which are observers of the Thermostat class

The TemperatureChangedEventArgs class (in the following listing) derives from the class System.EventArgs. The custom event argument class should contain all of the data that the subject needs to pass to its observers when it notifies them of an event. If you do not need to pass data with your event notifications, you do not need to define a new argument class; simply pass EventArgs.Empty or Nothing as the argument when you raise the event. (See recipe 14-8 for details on implementing custom event argument classes.)

```vb
Namespace Apress.VisualBasicRecipes.Chapter14

    ' An event argument class that contains information about a temperature
    ' change event. An instance of this class is passed with every event.
    <Serializable()> _
    Public Class TemperatureChangedEventArgs
        Inherits EventArgs

        ' Private data members contain the old and new temperature readings.
        Private ReadOnly m_OldTemperature As Integer
        Private ReadOnly m_NewTemperature As Integer

        ' Constructor that takes the old and new temperature values.
        Public Sub New(ByVal oldTemp As Integer, ByVal newTemp As Integer)

            m_OldTemperature = oldTemp
            m_NewTemperature = newTemp

        End Sub

        ' Read-only properties provide access to the temperature values.
        Public ReadOnly Property OldTemperature()
```

```
            Get
                Return m_OldTemperature
            End Get
        End Property

        Public ReadOnly Property NewTemperature()
            Get
                Return m_NewTemperature
            End Get
        End Property

    End Class
End NameSpace
```

The following code shows the declaration of the TemperatureChangedEventHandler delegate. Based on this declaration, all observers must implement a subroutine (the name is unimportant), which takes two arguments: an Object instance as the first argument and a TemperatureChangedEventArgs object as the second. During notification, the Object argument is a reference to the Thermostat object that raises the event, and the TemperatureChangedEventArgs argument contains data about the old and new temperature values.

Namespace Apress.VisualBasicRecipes.Chapter14

```
    '  A delegate that specifies the signature that all temperature event
    '  handler methods must implement.
    Public Delegate Sub TemperatureChangedEventHandler(ByVal sender As Object, ➥
ByVal args As TemperatureChangedEventArgs)
```

End NameSpace

For the purpose of demonstrating the Observer pattern, the example contains two different observer types: TemperatureAverageObserver and TemperatureChangeObserver. Both classes have the same basic implementation. TemperatureAverageObserver keeps a count of the number of temperature change events and the sum of the temperature values, and displays an average temperature when each event occurs. TemperatureChangeObserver displays information about the change in temperature each time a temperature change event occurs.

The following listing shows the TemperatureChangeObserver and TemperatureAverageObserver classes. Notice that the constructors take references to the Thermostat object that the TemperatureChangeObserver or TemperatureAverageObserver object should observe. When you instantiate an observer, pass it a reference to the subject. The observer's constructor must handle the observer's event by using AddHandler and specifying the delegate method preceded by the AddressOf keyword.

Once the TemperatureChangeObserver or TemperatureAverageObserver object has registered its delegate instance with the Thermostat object, you need to maintain a reference to this Thermostat object only if you want to stop observing it later. In addition, you do not need to maintain a reference to the subject, because a reference to the event source is included as the first argument each time the Thermostat object raises an event through the TemperatureChange method.

Namespace Apress.VisualBasicRecipes.Chapter14

```
    '  A thermostat observer that displays information about the change in
    '  temperature when a temperature change event occurs.
    Public Class TemperatureChangeObserver
```

```vb
        '  A constructor that takes a reference to the Thermostat object that
        '  the TemperatureChangeObserver object should observe.
        Public Sub New(ByVal t As Thermostat)

            '  Add a handler for the TemperatureChanged event.
            AddHandler t.TemperatureChanged, AddressOf Me.TemperatureChange

        End Sub

        '  The method to handle temperature change events.
        Public Sub TemperatureChange(ByVal sender As Object, ➥
ByVal args As TemperatureChangedEventArgs)

            Console.WriteLine("ChangeObserver: Old={0}, New={1}, Change={2}", ➥

args.OldTemperature, args.NewTemperature, args.NewTemperature - args.OldTemperature)
        End Sub

    End Class

    '  A Thermostat observer that displays information about the average
    '  temperature when a temperature change event occurs.
    Public Class TemperatureAverageObserver

        '  Sum contains the running total of temperature readings.
        '  Count contains the number of temperature events received.
        Private sum As Integer = 0
        Private count As Integer = 0

        '  A constructor that takes a reference to the Thermostat object that
        '  the TemperatureAverageObserver object should observe.
        Public Sub New(ByVal T As Thermostat)

            '  Add a handler for the TemperatureChanged event.
            AddHandler T.TemperatureChanged, AddressOf Me.TemperatureChange

        End Sub

        '  The method to handle temperature change events.
        Public Sub TemperatureChange(ByVal sender As Object, ➥
ByVal args As TemperatureChangedEventArgs)

            count += 1
            sum += args.NewTemperature

            Console.WriteLine("AverageObserver: Average={0:F}", ➥
CDbl(sum) / CDbl(count))

        End Sub

    End Class
End NameSpace
```

Finally, the Thermostat class is the observed object in this Observer (Event) pattern. In theory, a monitoring device sets the current temperature by calling the Temperature property on a Thermostat object. This causes the Thermostat object to raise its TemperatureChange event and send a TemperatureChangedEventArgs object to each observer.

The example contains a Recipe14_10 class that defines a Main method to drive the example. After creating a Thermostat object and two different observer objects, the Main method repeatedly prompts you to enter a temperature. Each time you enter a new temperature, the Thermostat object notifies the listeners, which display information to the console. The following is the code for the Thermostat class:

```vbnet
Namespace Apress.VisualBasicRecipes.Chapter14

    ' A class that represents a Thermostat, which is the source of temperature
    ' change events. In the Observer pattern, a Thermostat object is the
    ' subject that observers listen to for change notifications.
    Public Class Thermostat

        ' Private field to hold current temperature.
        Private m_Temperature As Integer = 0

        ' The event used to maintain a list of observer delegates and raise
        ' a temperature change event when a temperature change occurs.
        Public Event TemperatureChanged As TemperatureChangedEventHandler

        ' A protected method used to raise the TemperatureChanged event.
        ' Because events can be triggered only from within the containing
        ' type, using a protected method to raise the event allows derived
        ' classes to provide customized behavior and still be able to raise
        ' the base class event.
        Protected Overridable Sub OnTemperatureChanged(ByVal args As➡
TemperatureChangedEventArgs)

            ' Notify all observers.
            RaiseEvent TemperatureChanged(Me, args)

        End Sub

        ' Public property to get and set the current temperature. The "set"
        ' side of the property is responsible for raising the temperature
        ' change event to notify all observers of a change in temperature.
        Public Property Temperature() As Integer
            Get
                Return m_Temperature
            End Get
            Set(ByVal value As Integer)
                ' Create a new event argument object containing the old and
                ' new temperatures.
                Dim args As New TemperatureChangedEventArgs(m_Temperature, value)

                ' Update the current temperature.
                m_Temperature = value
```

```vbnet
                    '  Raise the temperature change event.
                    OnTemperatureChanged(args)

            End Set
        End Property

    End Class

    '  A class to demonstrate the use of the Observer pattern.
    Public Class Recipe14_10

        Public Shared Sub Main()

            '  Create a Thermostat instance.
            Dim myThemoStat As New Thermostat

            '  Create the Thermostat observers.
            Dim changeObserver As New TemperatureChangeObserver(myThemoStat)
            Dim averageObserver As New TemperatureAverageObserver(myThemoStat)

            '  Loop, getting temperature readings from the user.
            '  Any non-integer value will terminate the loop.
            Do
                Console.WriteLine(Environment.NewLine)
                Console.Write("Enter current temperature: ")

                Try
                    '  Convert the user's input to an integer and use it to set
                    '  the current temperature of the Thermostat.
                    myThemoStat.Temperature = Int32.Parse(Console.ReadLine)
                Catch ex As Exception
                    '  Use the exception condition to trigger termination.
                    Console.WriteLine("Terminating Observer Pattern Example.")

                    '  Wait to continue.
                    Console.WriteLine(Environment.NewLine)
                    Console.WriteLine("Main method complete.  Press Enter.")
                    Console.ReadLine()
                    Return

                End Try
            Loop While True

        End Sub

    End Class
End Namespace
```

Usage

The following listing shows the kind of output you should expect if you build and run the previous example. The bold values show your input:

```
Enter current temperature: 35
ChangeObserver: Old=0, New=35, Change=35
AverageObserver: Average=35.00

Enter current temperature: 37
ChangeObserver: Old=35, New=37, Change=2
AverageObserver: Average=36.00

Enter current temperature: 40
ChangeObserver: Old=37, New=40, Change=3
AverageObserver: Average=37.33
```

CHAPTER 15

■ ■ ■

Windows Integration

The intention of the Microsoft .NET Framework is to run on a wide variety of operating systems to improve code mobility and simplify cross-platform integration. At the time this book was written, versions of the .NET Framework were available for various operating systems, including Microsoft Windows, FreeBSD, Linux, and Mac OS X. However, many of these implementations are yet to be widely adopted. Microsoft Windows is currently the operating system on which the .NET Framework is most commonly installed.

The .NET Framework includes functionality for working with several components (such as the registry and event log) that are integrated with the Windows operating system. Although other platforms may provide equivalent functionality, the recipes in this chapter focus specifically on the Windows implementations. The recipes in this book cover the following topics:

- Retrieving runtime environment information (recipes 15-1 and 15-2)
- Writing to the Windows event log (recipe 15-3)
- Reading, writing, and searching the Windows registry (recipes 15-4 and 15-5)
- Creating and installing Windows services (recipes 15-6 and 15-7)
- Creating a shortcut on the Windows Start menu or desktop (recipe 15-8)

■Note The majority of functionality discussed in this chapter is protected by code access security permissions enforced by the common language runtime (CLR). See the .NET Framework software development kit (SDK) documentation for the specific permissions required to execute each member.

15-1. Access Runtime Environment Information

Problem

You need to access information about the runtime environment and platform in which your application is running.

Solution

Use the members of the System.Environment class.

How It Works

The Environment class provides a set of Shared members that you can use to obtain (and in some cases modify) information about the environment in which an application is running. Table 15-1 describes some of the most commonly used Environment members.

Table 15-1. *Commonly Used Members of the Environment Class*

Member	Description
Properties	
CommandLine	Gets a String containing the command line used to execute the current application, including the application name. (See recipe 1-7 for details.)
CurrentDirectory	Gets and sets a String containing the current application directory. Initially, this property will contain the name of the directory in which the application was started.
HasShutdownStarted	Gets a Boolean that indicates whether the CLR has started to shut down or the current application domain has started unloading.
MachineName	Gets a String containing the name of the machine.
OSVersion	Gets a System.OperatingSystem object that contains information about the platform and version of the underlying operating system. See the paragraph following this table for more details.
ProcessorCount	Gets the number of processors on the machine.
SystemDirectory	Gets a String containing the fully qualified path of the system directory, that is, the system32 subdirectory of the Windows installation folder.
TickCount	Gets an Integer representing the number of milliseconds that have elapsed since the system was started.
UserDomainName	Gets a String containing the Windows domain name to which the current user belongs. This will be the same as MachineName if the user has logged in on a machine account instead of a domain account.
UserInteractive	Gets a Boolean indicating whether the application is running in user interactive mode; in other words, its forms and message boxes will be visible to the logged-on user. UserInteractive will return False when the application is running as a service or is a web application.
UserName	Gets a String containing the name of the user that started the current thread, which can be different from the logged-on user in case of impersonation.
Version	Gets a System.Version object that contains information about the version of the CLR.
Methods	
ExpandEnvironmentVariables	Replaces the names of environment variables in a String with the value of the variable. (See recipe 15-2 for details.)

Table 15-1. *Commonly Used Members of the Environment Class*

Member	Description
GetCommandLineArgs	Returns a String array containing all elements of the command line used to execute the current application, including the application name. (See recipe 1-5 for details.)
GetEnvironmentVariable	Returns a String containing the value of a specified environment variable. (See recipe 15-2 for details.)
GetEnvironmentVariables	Returns an object implementing System.Collections.IDictionary, which contains all environment variables and their values. (See recipe 15-2 for details.)
GetFolderPath	Returns a String containing the path to a special system folder specified using the System.Environment.SpecialFolder enumeration. This includes folders for the Internet cache, cookies, history, desktop, and favorites. (See the .NET Framework SDK documentation for a complete list of values.)
GetLogicalDrives	Returns a String array containing the names of all logical drives, including network mapped drives. Note that each drive has the following syntax: <drive letter>:\.

The System.OperatingSystem object returned by OSVersion contains four properties:

- The Platform property returns a value of the System.PlatformID enumeration identifying the current operating system; valid values are Unix, Win32NT, Win32S, Win32Windows, and WinCE.

- The ServicePack property returns a String identifying the service pack level installed on the computer. If no service packs are installed or service packs are not supported, an empty String is returned.

- The Version property returns a System.Version object that identifies the specific operating system version. This class includes the Build, Major, MajorRevision, Minor, MinorRevision, and Revision properties, which allow you to get each specific part of the complete version number.

- The VersionString property returns a concatenated string summary of the Platform, ServicePack, and Version properties.

To determine the operating system on which you are running, you must use both the platform and the version information, as detailed in Table 15-2.

Table 15-2. *Determining the Current Operating System*

PlatformID	Major Version	Minor Version	Operating System
Win32Windows	4	10	Windows 98
Win32Windows	4	90	Windows ME
Win32NT	4	0	Windows NT 4
Win32NT	5	0	Windows 2000
Win32NT	5	1	Windows XP
Win32NT	5	2	Windows Server 2003
Win32NT	6	0	Windows Vista

The Code

The following example uses the `Environment` class to display information about the current environment to the console:

```vb
Imports System

Namespace Apress.VisualBasicRecipes.Chapter15
    Public Class Recipe15_01

        Public Shared Sub Main()

            ' Command line.
            Console.WriteLine("Command line : " & Environment.CommandLine)

            ' OS and CLR version information.
            Console.WriteLine(Environment.NewLine)
            Console.WriteLine("OS PlatformID : " & Environment.OSVersion.Platform)
            Console.WriteLine("OS Major Version : " & ➡
Environment.OSVersion.Version.Major)
            Console.WriteLine("OS Minor Version : " & ➡
Environment.OSVersion.Version.Minor)
            Console.WriteLine("CLR Version : " & Environment.Version.ToString)

            ' User, machine, and domain name information.
            Console.WriteLine(Environment.NewLine)
            Console.WriteLine("User Name : " & Environment.UserName)
            Console.WriteLine("Domain Name : " & Environment.UserDomainName)
            Console.WriteLine("Machine Name : " & Environment.MachineName)

            ' Other environment information.
            Console.WriteLine(Environment.NewLine)
            Console.WriteLine("Is interactive? : " & Environment.UserInteractive)
            Console.WriteLine("Shutting down? : " & Environment.HasShutdownStarted)
            Console.WriteLine("Ticks since startup : " & Environment.TickCount)

            ' Display the names of all logical drives.
            Console.WriteLine(Environment.NewLine)
            For Each s As String In Environment.GetLogicalDrives
                Console.WriteLine("Logical drive : " & s)
            Next

            ' Standard folder information.
            Console.WriteLine(Environment.NewLine)
            Console.WriteLine("Current folder : " & Environment.CurrentDirectory)
            Console.WriteLine("System folder : " & Environment.SystemDirectory)

            ' Enumerate all special folders and display them.
            Console.WriteLine(Environment.NewLine)
            For Each s As Environment.SpecialFolder In ➡
[Enum].GetValues(GetType(Environment.SpecialFolder))
                Console.WriteLine("{0} folder : {1}", s, ➡
Environment.GetFolderPath(s))
            Next
```

```
        '  Wait to continue.
        Console.WriteLine(Environment.NewLine)
        Console.WriteLine("Main method complete.  Press Enter.")
        Console.ReadLine()

    End Sub

  End Class
End Namespace
```

15-2. Retrieve the Value of an Environment Variable

Problem

You need to retrieve the value of an environment variable for use in your application.

Solution

Use the GetEnvironmentVariable, GetEnvironmentVariables, and ExpandEnvironmentVariables methods of the Environment class.

How It Works

The GetEnvironmentVariable method allows you to retrieve a string containing the value of a single named environment variable, whereas the GetEnvironmentVariables method returns an object implementing IDictionary that contains the names and values of all environment variables as strings. .NET Framework 2.0 introduced additional overloads of the GetEnvironmentVariable and GetEnvironmentVariables methods, which take a System.EnvironmentVariableTarget argument, allowing you to specify a subset of environment variables to return based on the target of the variable: Machine, Process, or User.

The ExpandEnvironmentVariables method provides a simple mechanism for substituting the value of an environment variable into a string by including the variable name enclosed in percent signs (%) within the string.

The Code

Here is an example that demonstrates how to use all three methods:

```
Imports System
Imports System.Collections

Namespace Apress.VisualBasicRecipes.Chapter15
    Public Class Recipe15_02

        Public Shared Sub Main()

            '  Retrieve a named environment variable.
            Console.WriteLine("Path = " & GetEnvironmentVariable("Path"))
            Console.WriteLine(Environment.NewLine)

            '  Substitute the value of named environment variables.
            Console.WriteLine(ExpandEnvironmentVariables("The Path on " & ➥
"%computername% is %path%"))
```

```
          ' Retrieve all environment variables targeted at the process and
          ' display the values of all that begin with the letter U.
          Dim vars As IDictionary = ➡
GetEnvironmentVariables(EnvironmentVariableTarget.Process)

          For Each s As String In vars.Keys
              If s.ToUpper.StartsWith("U") Then
                  Console.WriteLine(s & " = " & vars(s))
              End If
          Next

          ' Wait to continue.
          Console.WriteLine(Environment.NewLine)
          Console.WriteLine("Main method complete.  Press Enter.")
          Console.ReadLine()

      End Sub

    End Class
End Namespace
```

15-3. Write an Event to the Windows Event Log

Problem

You need to write an event to the Windows event log.

Solution

Use the members of the System.Diagnostics.EventLog class to create a log (if required), register an event source, and write events.

How It Works

You can write to the Windows event log using the Shared methods of the EventLog class, or you can create an EventLog object and use its members. Whichever approach you choose, before writing to the event log, you must decide which log you will use and register an event source against that log. The event source is simply a string that uniquely identifies your application. An event source may be registered against only one log at a time.

By default, the event log contains three separate logs: Application, System, and Security. Usually, you will write to the Application log, but you might decide your application warrants a custom log in which to write events. You do not need to explicitly create a custom log; when you register an event source against a log, if the specified log doesn't exist, it's created automatically.

Once you have decided on the destination log and registered an event source, you can start to write event log entries using the WriteEntry method. WriteEntry provides a variety of overloads that allow you to specify some or all of the following values:

- A String containing the event source for the log entry (Shared versions of WriteEntry only).

- A String containing the message for the log entry.

- A value from the System.Diagnostics.EventLogEntryType enumeration, which identifies the type of log entry. Valid values are Error, FailureAudit, Information, SuccessAudit, and Warning.

- An Integer that specifies an application-specific event ID for the log entry.

- A Short that specifies an application-specific subcategory for the log entry.

- A Byte array containing any raw data to associate with the log entry.

Note The methods of the EventLog class also provide overloads that support the writing of events to the event log of remote machines. See the .NET Framework SDK documentation for more information.

The Code

The following example demonstrates how to use the Shared members of EventLog class to write an entry to the event log of the local machine:

```
Imports System
Imports System.Diagnostics

Namespace Apress.VisualBasicRecipes.Chapter15
    Public Class Recipe15_03

        Public Shared Sub Main()

            ' If it does not exist, register an event source for this
            ' application against the Application log of the local machine.
            ' Trying to register an event source that already exists on the
            ' specified machine will throw a System.ArgumentException.
            If Not EventLog.SourceExists("Visual Basic 2008 Recipes") Then
                EventLog.CreateEventSource("Visual Basic 2008 Recipes", ➥
"Application")
            End If

            ' Write an event to the event log.
            EventLog.WriteEntry("Visual Basic 2008 Recipes", ➥
"A simple test event.", EventLogEntryType.Information, 1, 0, ➥
New Byte() {10, 55, 200})

            ' Wait to continue.
            Console.WriteLine(Environment.NewLine)
            Console.WriteLine("Main method complete.  Press Enter.")
            Console.ReadLine()

            ' Remove the event source.
            EventLog.DeleteEventSource("Visual Basic 2008 Recipes")

        End Sub

    End Class
End Namespace
```

Usage

After you run the sample code, launch the Event Viewer (EventVwr.exe), and find the last entry with a source of "Visual Basic 2008 Recipes." Figure 15-1 shows how the log entry will look.

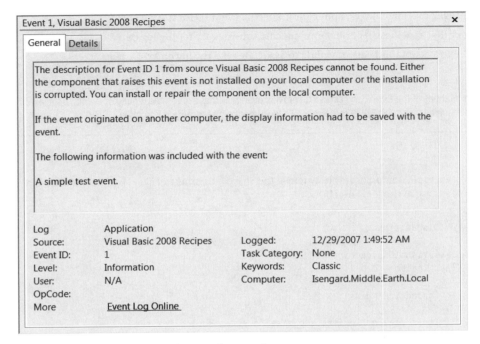

Figure 15-1. *Custom message written to the event log*

15-4. Read and Write to the Windows Registry

Problem

You need to read information from, or write information to, the Windows registry.

Solution

Use the methods GetValue and SetValue of the Microsoft.Win32.Registry class.

■**Tip** The GetValue and SetValue methods open a registry key, get or set its value, and close the key each time they are called. This means they are inefficient when used to perform many read or write operations. The GetValue and SetValue methods of the Microsoft.Win32.RegistryKey class, discussed in recipe 15-5, will provide better performance if you need to perform many read or write operations on the registry.

How It Works

The GetValue and SetValue methods allow you to read and write named values in named registry keys. GetValue takes three arguments:

- A String containing the fully qualified name of the key you want to read. The key name must start with one of the following root key names:

  - HKEY_CLASSES_ROOT
  - HKEY_CURRENT_CONFIG
  - HKEY_CURRENT_USER
  - HKEY_DYN_DATA
  - HKEY_LOCAL_MACHINE
  - HKEY_PERFORMANCE_DATA
  - HKEY_USERS

- A String containing the name of the value in the key you want to read.
- An Object containing the default value to return if the named value is not present in the key.

GetValue returns an Object containing either the data read from the registry or the default value specified as the third argument if the named value is not found. If the specified key does not exist, GetValue returns Nothing.

SetValue offers two overloads. The most functional expects the following arguments:

- A String containing the fully qualified name of the key you want to write. The key must start with one of the root key names specified previously. If the registry key does not exist, it is created automatically.
- A String containing the name of the value in the key you want to write.
- An Object containing the value to write.
- An element of the Microsoft.Win32.RegistryValueKind enumeration that specifies the registry data type that should be used to hold the data.

The second overload allows you to call the SetValue method without specifying the RegistryValueKind argument. In this case, SetValue attempts to automatically determine what the data type should be, based on the data type of the Object argument. A 32-bit integer type will be inferred as a Dword value, and any other numeric type will be inferred as a String. Environment variables, such as %PATH%, will be ignored by this overload and inferred as a normal String. Use the previously mentioned overload if you need to ensure the correct data type is used.

The My object offers the My.Computer.Registry class as an alternative. This class includes only two methods, SetValue and GetValue, which are identical to the SetValue and GetValue methods from the Microsoft.Win32.Registry class. (Refer to Chapter 5 for more information about the My object.)

The Code

The following example demonstrates how to use GetValue and SetValue to read from and write to the registry. Every time the example is run, it reads usage information from the registry and displays it to the screen. The example also updates the stored usage information, which you can see the next time you run the example.

```
Imports System
Imports Microsoft.Win32

Namespace Apress.VisualBasicRecipes.Chapter15
    Public Class Recipe15_04
```

```vbnet
Public Shared Sub Main()

    ' Variables to hold usage information read from registry.
    Dim lastUser As String
    Dim lastRun As String
    Dim runCount As Integer

    ' Read the name of the last user to run the application from the
    ' registry. This is stored as the default value of the key and is
    ' accessed by not specifying a value name. Cast the returned object
    ' to a string.
    lastUser = DirectCast(Registry.GetValue("HKEY_CURRENT_USER\" & ➥
"Software\Apress\Visual Basic 2008 Recipes", "", "Nobody"), String)

    ' If lastUser is Nothing, it means that the specified registry key
    ' does not exist.
    If lastUser Is Nothing Then
        lastUser = "Nobody"
        lastRun = "Never"
        runCount = 0
    Else
        ' Read the last run date and specify a default value of
        ' Never. Cast the returned Object to a String.
        lastRun = DirectCast(Registry.GetValue("HKEY_CURRENT_USER\" & ➥
"Software\Apress\Visual Basic 2008 Recipes", "LastRun", "Never"), String)

        ' Read the run count value and specify a default value of
        ' 0 (zero). Cast the returned Object to an Integer.
        runCount = DirectCast(Registry.GetValue("HKEY_CURRENT_USER\" & ➥
"Software\Apress\Visual Basic 2008 Recipes", "RunCount", 0), Integer)
    End If

    ' Display the usage information.
    Console.WriteLine("Last user name: " & lastUser)
    Console.WriteLine("Last run date/time: " & lastRun)
    Console.WriteLine("Previous executions: " & runCount)

    ' Update the usage information. It doesn't matter if the registry
    ' key exists or not; SetValue will automatically create it.

    ' Update the last user information with the current username.
    ' Specify that this should be stored as the default value
    ' for the key by using an empty string as the value name.
    Registry.SetValue("HKEY_CURRENT_USER\Software\Apress\Visual Basic " & ➥
"2008 Recipes", "", Environment.UserName, RegistryValueKind.String)

    ' Update the last run information with the current date and time.
    ' Specify that this should be stored as a String value in the
    ' registry.
    Registry.SetValue("HKEY_CURRENT_USER\Software\Apress\" & ➥
"Visual Basic 2008 Recipes", "LastRun", DateTime.Now.ToString, ➥
RegistryValueKind.String)
```

```
              ' Update the usage count information. Specify that this should
              ' be stored as an Integer value in the registry.
              runCount += 1
              Registry.SetValue("HKEY_CURRENT_USER\Software\Apress\" & ➥
"Visual Basic 2008 Recipes", "RunCount", runCount, RegistryValueKind.DWord)

              ' Wait to continue.
              Console.WriteLine(Environment.NewLine)
              Console.WriteLine("Main method complete.  Press Enter.")
              Console.ReadLine()

        End Sub

    End Class
End Namespace
```

15-5. Search the Windows Registry

Problem

You need to search the Windows registry for a key that contains a specific value or content.

Solution

Use the `Microsoft.Win32.Registry` class to obtain a `Microsoft.Win32.RegistryKey` object that repre-sents the root key of a registry hive you want to search. Use the members of this `RegistryKey` object to navigate through and enumerate the registry key hierarchy, as well as to read the names and content of values held in the keys.

How It Works

You must first obtain a `RegistryKey` object that represents a base-level key and navigate through the hierarchy of `RegistryKey` objects as required. The `Registry` class implements a set of seven `Shared` properties that return `RegistryKey` objects representing base-level registry keys; Table 15-3 describes the registry location to where each of these fields maps. The `My` object offers the `My.Computer.Registry` class, which includes an identical set of properties that provide the same functionality as their `Microsoft.Win32.Registry` counterparts. (Refer to Chapter 5 for more information about the `My` object.)

Table 15-3. *Shared Fields of the Registry Class*

Field	Registry Mapping
ClassesRoot	HKEY_CLASSES_ROOT
CurrentConfig	HKEY_CURRENT_CONFIG
CurrentUser	HKEY_CURRENT_USER
DynData	HKEY_DYN_DATA
LocalMachine	HKEY_LOCAL_MACHINE
PerformanceData	HKEY_PERFORMANCE_DATA
Users	HKEY_USERS

■**Tip** The Shared method RegistryKey.OpenRemoteBaseKey allows you to open a registry base key on a remote machine. See the .NET Framework SDK documentation for details of its use.

Once you have the base-level RegistryKey object, you must navigate through its child subkeys recursively. To support navigation, the RegistryKey class allows you to do the following:

- Get a String array containing the names of all subkeys using the GetSubKeyNames method.
- Get a RegistryKey reference to a subkey using the OpenSubKey method. The OpenSubKey method provides two overloads: the first opens the named key as read-only, and the second accepts a Boolean argument that, if true, will open a writable RegistryKey object.

Once you obtain a RegistryKey, you can create, read, update, and delete subkeys and values using the methods listed in Table 15-4. Methods that modify the contents of the key require you to have a writable RegistryKey object.

Table 15-4. *RegistryKey Methods to Create, Read, Update, and Delete Registry Keys and Values*

Method	Description
CreateSubKey	Creates a new subkey with the specified name and returns a writable RegistryKey object. If the specified subkey already exists, CreateSubKey returns a writable reference to the existing subkey.
DeleteSubKey	Deletes the subkey with the specified name, which must be empty of subkeys (but not values); otherwise, a System.InvalidOperationException is thrown.
DeleteSubKeyTree	Deletes the subkey with the specified name along with all of its subkeys.
DeleteValue	Deletes the value with the specified name from the current key.
GetValue	Returns the value with the specified name from the current key. The value is returned as an Object, which you must cast to the appropriate type. The simplest form of GetValue returns Nothing if the specified value doesn't exist. An overload allows you to specify a default value to return (instead of Nothing) if the named value doesn't exist.
GetValueKind	Returns the registry data type of the value with the specified name in the current key. The value is returned as a member of the Microsoft.Win32. RegistryValueKind enumeration.
GetValueNames	Returns a String array containing the names of all values in the current registry key. If the key includes a default value, represented by an empty string, the empty string will be included in the array of names returned by this method.
SetValue	Creates (or updates) the value with the specified name. You can specify the data type used to store the value with the overload that takes a RegistryValueKind as the last parameter. If you don't provide such a value, one will be calculated automatically, based on the managed type of the object you pass as the value to set.

The RegistryKey class implements IDisposable. You should call the IDisposable.Dispose method to free operating system resources when you have finished with the RegistryKey object.

The Code

The following example takes a single command-line argument and recursively searches the CurrentUser hive of the registry looking for keys with names matching the supplied argument. When the example finds a match, it displays all String type values contained in the key to the console.

```
Imports System
Imports Microsoft.Win32

Namespace Apress.VisualBasicRecipes.Chapter15
    Public Class Recipe15_05

        Public Shared Sub SearchSubKeys(ByVal root As RegistryKey, ➥
ByVal searchKey As String)

            ' Loop through all subkeys contained in the current key.
            For Each keyName As String In root.GetSubKeyNames

                Try
                    Using key As RegistryKey = root.OpenSubKey(keyName)
                        If keyName = searchKey Then PrintKeyValues(key)
                        SearchSubKeys(key, searchKey)
                    End Using
                Catch ex As Security.SecurityException
                    ' Ignore SecurityException for the purpose of this example.
                    ' Some subkeys of HKEY_CURRENT_USER are secured and will
                    ' throw a SecurityException when opened.
                End Try
            Next

        End Sub

        Public Shared Sub PrintKeyValues(ByVal key As RegistryKey)

            ' Display the name of the matching subkey and the number of
            ' values it contains.
            Console.WriteLine("Registry key found : {0} contains {1} values", ➥
key.Name, key.ValueCount)

            ' Loop through the values and display.
            For Each valueName As String In key.GetValueNames

                If TypeOf key.GetValue(valueName) Is String Then
                    Console.WriteLine("  Value : {0} = {1}", valueName, ➥
key.GetValue(valueName))
                End If

            Next

        End Sub

        Public Shared Sub Main(ByVal args As String())

            If args.Length > 0 Then
                ' Open the CurrentUser base key.
```

```
            Using root As RegistryKey = Registry.CurrentUser
                '  Search recursively through the registry for any keys
                '  with the specified name.
                SearchSubKeys(root, args(0))
            End Using
        End If

        '  Wait to continue.
        Console.WriteLine(Environment.NewLine)
        Console.WriteLine("Main method complete.  Press Enter.")
        Console.ReadLine()

    End Sub

  End Class
End Namespace
```

Usage

Running the example using the command `Recipe15-05 Environment` will display output similar to the following when executed using the command on a machine running Windows Vista:

```
Registry key found : HKEY_CURRENT_USER\Environment contains 3 values
  Value : TEMP = C:\Users\ Todd \AppData\Local\Temp
  Value : TMP = C:\Users\Todd\AppData\Local\Temp
...

Main method complete.  Press Enter.
```

15-6. Create a Windows Service

Problem

You need to create an application that will run as a Windows service.

Solution

Create a class that extends `System.ServiceProcess.ServiceBase`. Use the inherited properties to control the behavior of your service, and override inherited methods to implement the functionality required. Implement a `Main` method that creates an instance of your service class and passes it to the `Shared ServiceBase.Run` method.

■**Note** The ServiceBase class is defined in the System.ServiceProcess assembly, so you must include a reference to this assembly when you build your service class.

How It Works

To create a Windows service manually, you must implement a class derived from the `ServiceBase` class. The `ServiceBase` class provides the base functionality that allows the Windows Service Control

Manager (SCM) to configure the service, operate the service as a background task, and control the life cycle of the service. The SCM also controls how other applications can manage the service programmatically.

■**Tip** If you are using Microsoft Visual Studio, you can use the Windows Service project template to create a Windows service. The template provides the basic code infrastructure required by a Windows service class, which you can extend with your custom functionality.

To control your service, the SCM uses the eight Protected methods inherited from ServiceBase class described in Table 15-5. You should override these virtual methods to implement the functionality and behavior required by your service. Not all services must support all control messages. The CanXXX properties inherited from the ServiceBase class declare to the SCM which control messages your service supports. Table 15-5 specifies the property that controls each operation.

Table 15-5. *Methods That Control the Operation of a Service*

Method	Description
OnStart	All services must support the OnStart method, which the SCM calls to start the service. The SCM passes a String array containing arguments specified for the service. These arguments can be specified when the ServiceController. Start method is called and are usually configured in the service's property window in Windows Control Panel. However, they are rarely used because it is better for the service to retrieve its configuration information directly from a configuration file or the Windows registry. The OnStart method must normally return within 30 seconds, or the SCM will abort the service. Your service must call the RequestAdditionalTime method of the ServiceBase class if it requires more time; specify the additional milliseconds required as an Integer.
OnStop	Called by the SCM to stop a service. The SCM will call OnStop only if the CanStop property is set to True, which it is by default.
OnPause	Called by the SCM to pause a service. The SCM will call OnPause only if the CanPauseAndContinue property, which is False by default, is set to True.
OnContinue	Called by the SCM to continue a paused service. The SCM will call OnContinue only if the CanPauseAndContinue property, which is False by default, is set to True.
OnShutdown	Called by the SCM when the system is shutting down. The SCM will call OnShutdown only if the CanShutdown property, which is False by default, is set to True.
OnPowerEvent	Called by the SCM when a system-level power status change occurs, such as a laptop going into suspend mode. The SCM will call OnPowerEvent only if the CanHandlePowerEvent property, which is False by default, is set to True.
OnCustomCommand	Allows you to extend the service control mechanism with custom control messages. See the .NET Framework SDK documentation for more details.
OnSessionChange	Called by the SCM when a change event is received from the Terminal Services session or when users log on and off the local machine. A System. ServiceProcess.SessionChangeDescription object passed as an argument by the SCM contains details of what type of session change occurred. The SCM will call OnSessionChange only if the CanHandleSessionChangeEvent property, which is False by default, is set to True.

As mentioned in Table 15-5, the OnStart method is expected to return within 30 seconds, so you should not use OnStart to perform lengthy initialization tasks when you can avoid it. A service class should implement a constructor that performs initialization, including configuring the inherited properties of the ServiceBase class. In addition to the properties that declare the control messages supported by a service, the ServiceBase class implements three other important properties:

- ServiceName is the name used internally by the SCM to identify the service and must be set before the service is run.

- AutoLog controls whether the service automatically writes entries to the event log when it receives any of the OnStart, OnStop, OnPause, and OnContinue control messages (see Table 15-5).

- EventLog provides access to an EventLog object that's preconfigured with an event source name that's the same as the ServiceName property registered against the Application log. (See recipe 15-3 for more information about the EventLog class.)

The final step in creating a service is to implement a Shared Main method. The Main method must create an instance of your service class and pass it as an argument to the Shared method ServiceBase.Run.

The Code

The following Windows service example uses a configurable System.Timers.Timer to write an entry to the Windows event log periodically. You can start, pause, and stop the service using the Services application in the Control Panel.

```
Imports System
Imports System.Timers
Imports System.ServiceProcess

Namespace Apress.VisualBasicRecipes.Chapter15

    Class Recipe15_06
        Inherits ServiceBase

        ' A timer that controls how frequently the example writes to the

        ' event log.
        Private serviceTimer As Timer

        Public Sub New()

            ' Set the ServiceBase.ServiceName property.
            ServiceName = "Recipe 15_06 Service"

            ' Configure the level of control available on the service.
            CanStop = True
            CanPauseAndContinue = True
            CanHandleSessionChangeEvent = True

            ' Configure the service to log important events to the
            ' Application event log automatically.
            AutoLog = True

        End Sub
```

```vb
          ' The method executed when the timer expires and writes an
          ' entry to the Application event log.
          Private Sub WriteLogEntry(ByVal sender As Object, ➥
ByVal e As ElapsedEventArgs)

              ' In case this is a long-running process, stop the timer
              ' so it won't attempt to execute multiple times.
              serviceTimer.Stop()

              ' Use the EventLog object automatically configured by the
              ' ServiceBase class to write to the event log.
              EventLog.WriteEntry("Recipe15_06 Service active : " & e.SignalTime)

              ' Restart the timer.
              serviceTimer.Start()

          End Sub

          Protected Overrides Sub OnStart(ByVal args() As String)

              ' Obtain the interval between log entry writes from the first
              ' argument. Use 5000 milliseconds by default and enforce a 1000
              ' millisecond minimum.
              Dim interval As Double

              Try
                  interval = Double.Parse(args(0))
                  interval = Math.Max(1000, interval)
              Catch ex As Exception
                  interval = 5000
              End Try

              EventLog.WriteEntry(String.Format("Recipe15_06 Service starting." & ➥
"Writing log entries every {0} milliseconds...", interval))

              ' Create, configure and start a System.Timers.Timer to
              ' periodically call the WriteLogEntry method. The Start
              ' and Stop methods of the System.Timers.Timer class
              ' make starting, pausing, resuming, and stopping the
              ' service straightforward.
              serviceTimer = New Timer
              serviceTimer.Interval = interval
              serviceTimer.AutoReset = True
              AddHandler serviceTimer.Elapsed, AddressOf WriteLogEntry
              serviceTimer.Start()

          End Sub

          Protected Overrides Sub OnStop()

              EventLog.WriteEntry("Recipe15_06 Service stopping...")
              serviceTimer.Stop()
```

```
        ' Free system resources used by the Timer object.
        serviceTimer.Dispose()
        serviceTimer = Nothing

    End Sub

    Protected Overrides Sub OnPause()

        If serviceTimer IsNot Nothing Then
            EventLog.WriteEntry("Recipe15_06 Service pausing...")
            serviceTimer.Stop()
        End If

    End Sub

    Protected Overrides Sub OnContinue()

        If serviceTimer IsNot Nothing Then
            EventLog.WriteEntry("Recipe15_06 Service resuming...")
            serviceTimer.Start()
        End If

    End Sub

    Protected Overrides Sub OnSessionChange(ByVal changeDescription As ➥
System.ServiceProcess.SessionChangeDescription)

        EventLog.WriteEntry("Recipe15_06 Session change..." & ➥
changeDescription.Reason)

    End Sub

    Public Shared Sub Main()

        ' Create an instance of the Recipe15_06 class that will write
        ' an entry to the Application event log. Pass the object to the
        ' shared ServiceBase.Run method.
        ServiceBase.Run(New Recipe15_06)

    End Sub

    End Class
End Namespace
```

Usage

If you want to run multiple services in a single process, you must create an array of ServiceBase objects and pass it to the ServiceBase.Run method. Although service classes have a Main method, you can't execute service code directly. Attempting to run a service class directly results in Windows displaying the Windows Service Start Failure message box, as shown in Figure 15-2. Recipe 15-7 describes what you must do to install your service before it will execute.

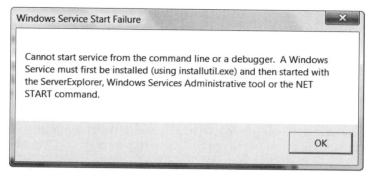

Figure 15-2. *The Windows Service Start Failure message box*

15-7. Create a Windows Service Installer

Problem

You have created a Windows service application and need to install it.

Solution

Add a new class to your Windows service project that extends the `System.Configuration.Install.` `Installer` class to create an installer class containing the information necessary to install and configure your service class. Use the Installer tool (Installutil.exe) to perform the installation, which is installed as part of the .NET Framework.

■**Note** You must create the installer class in the same assembly as the service class for the service to install and function correctly.

How It Works

As stated in recipe 15-6, you cannot run service classes directly. The high level of integration with the Windows operating system and the information stored about the service in the Windows registry means services require explicit installation.

   If you have Microsoft Visual Studio, you can create an installation component for your service automatically by right-clicking in the design view of your service class and selecting Add Installer from the context menu. This will generate a class called `ProjectInstaller`. `ServiceProcessInstaller` and `ServiceInstaller` components will be added to the class and configured for your service automatically. You can call this installation class by using deployment projects or by using the Installer tool to install your service.

   You can also create installer components for Windows services manually by following these steps:

   1. In your project, create a class derived from the `Installer` class.

   2. Apply the attribute `System.ComponentModel.RunInstallerAttribute(True)` to the installer class.

3. In the constructor of the installer class, create a single instance of the System.ServiceProcess. ServiceProcessInstaller class. Set the Account, Username, and Password properties of ServiceProcessInstaller to configure the account under which your service will run. The Account property is set to one of the values of the ServiceAccount enumerator that represents the type of account the service will run under: LocalService, LocalSystem, NetworkService, or User. The default is User and means that you must specify an account to be used via the Username and Password properties.

4. In the constructor of the installer class, create one instance of the System.ServiceProcess. ServiceInstaller class for each individual service you want to install. Use the properties of the ServiceInstaller objects to configure information about each service, including the following:

   - ServiceName, which specifies the name that Windows uses internally to identify the service. This must be the same as the value assigned to the ServiceBase.ServiceName property.

   - DisplayName, which provides a user-friendly name for the service. This property will use the value of ServiceName by default.

   - StartType, which uses values of the System.ServiceProcess.ServiceStartMode enumeration to control whether the service is started automatically or manually or is disabled.

   - ServiceDependsUpon, which allows you to provide a string array containing a set of service names that must be started before this service can start.

5. Add the ServiceProcessInstaller object and all ServiceInstaller objects to the System. Configuration.Install.InstallerCollection object accessed through the Installers property, which is inherited by your installer class from the Installer base class.

The Code

The following example is an installer for the Recipe15_06 Windows service created in recipe 15-6. The sample project contains the code from recipe 15-6 and for the installer class. This is necessary for the service installation to function correctly. To compile the example, you must reference two additional assemblies: System.Configuration.Install.dll and System.ServiceProcess.dll.

```
Imports System.Configuration.Install
Imports System.ServiceProcess
Imports System.ComponentModel

Namespace Apress.VisualBasicRecipes.Chapter15

    <RunInstaller(True)> _
    Public Class Recipe15_07
        Inherits Installer

        Public Sub New()

            ' Instantiate and configure a ServiceProcessInstaller.
            Dim ServiceExampleProcess As New ServiceProcessInstaller
            ServiceExampleProcess.Account = ServiceAccount.LocalSystem

            ' Instantiate and configure a ServiceInstaller.
            Dim ServiceExampleInstaller As New ServiceInstaller
            ServiceExampleInstaller.DisplayName = "Visual Basic 2008 " & ➥
"Recipes Service Example"
```

```
        ServiceExampleInstaller.ServiceName = "Recipe 15_06 Service"
        ServiceExampleInstaller.StartType = ServiceStartMode.Automatic

        ' Add both the ServiceProcessInstaller and ServiceInstaller to
        ' the installers collection, which is inherited from the
        ' Installer base class.
        Installers.Add(ServiceExampleInstaller)
        Installers.Add(ServiceExampleProcess)

    End Sub

  End Class
End Namespace
```

Usage

To install the Recipe15_06 service, build the project, navigate to the directory where Recipe15-07.exe is located (bin\Debug by default), and execute the command Installutil Recipe15-07.exe. You will see output similar to the following:

```
Microsoft (R) .NET Framework Installation utility Version 2.0.50727.42
Copyright (c) Microsoft Corporation.  All rights reserved.

Running a transacted installation.

Beginning the Install phase of the installation.
See the contents of the log file for the C:\Recipe15-07\Recipe15-07.exe assembly's
progress.
The file is located at C:\Recipe15-07\Recipe15-07.InstallLog.
Installing assembly 'C:\Recipe15-07\Recipe15-07.exe'.
Affected parameters are:
   logtoconsole =
   assemblypath = C:\Recipe15-07\Recipe15-07.exe
   logfile = C:\Recipe15-07\Recipe15-07.InstallLog
Installing service Recipe 15_06 Service...
Service Recipe 15_06 Service has been successfully installed.
Creating EventLog source Recipe 15_06 Service in log Application...

The Install phase completed successfully, and the Commit phase is beginning.
See the contents of the log file for the C:\Recipe15-07\Recipe15-07.exe assembly's
progress.
The file is located at C:\Recipe15-07\Recipe15-07.InstallLog.
Committing assembly 'C:\Recipe15-07\Recipe15-07.exe'.
Affected parameters are:
   logtoconsole =
   assemblypath = C:\Recipe15-07\Recipe15-07.exe
   logfile = C:\Recipe15-07\Recipe15-07.InstallLog

The Commit phase completed successfully.

The transacted install has completed.
```

■**Note** You can use your ServiceInstaller instance automatically with a Visual Studio Setup project. You can find details on how to do this at http://support.microsoft.com/kb/317421.

You can then see and control the Recipe15_06 service using the Windows Computer Management console. However, despite specifying a StartType of Automatic, the service is initially installed unstarted. You must start the service manually (or restart your computer) before the service will write entries to the event log. Once the service is running, you can view the entries it writes to the Application event log using the Event Viewer application. To uninstall the Recipe15_06 service, add the /u switch to the Installutil command as follows: Installutil /u Recipe15-07.exe. You will get output similar to the following:

```
Microsoft (R) .NET Framework Installation utility Version 2.0.50727.42
Copyright (c) Microsoft Corporation.  All rights reserved.

The uninstall is beginning.
See the contents of the log file for the C:\Recipe15-07\Recipe15-07.exe assembly's
progress.
The file is located at C:\Recipe15-07\Recipe15-07.InstallLog.
Uninstalling assembly 'C:\Recipe15-07\Recipe15-07.exe'.
Affected parameters are:
   logtoconsole =
   assemblypath = C:\Recipe15-07\Recipe15-07.exe
   logfile = C:\Recipe15-07\Recipe15-07.InstallLog
Removing EventLog source Recipe 15_06 Service.
Service Recipe 15_06 Service is being removed from the system...
Service Recipe 15_06 Service was successfully removed from the system.

The uninstall has completed.
```

■**Note** If you have the Service application from the Control Panel open when you uninstall the service, the service will not uninstall completely until you close the Service application. Once you close the Service application, you can reinstall the service; otherwise, you will get an error telling you that the installation failed because the service is scheduled for deletion.

15-8. Create a Shortcut on the Desktop or Start Menu

Problem

You need to create a shortcut on the user's Windows desktop or Start menu.

Solution

Use COM Interop to access the functionality of the Windows Script Host. Create and configure an IWshShortcut instance that represents the shortcut. The folder in which you save the shortcut determines whether it appears on the desktop or in the Start menu.

How It Works

The .NET Framework class library does not include the functionality to create desktop or Start menu shortcuts; however, this is relatively easy to do using the Windows Script Host component accessed through COM Interop. Chapter 13 describes how to create an interop assembly that provides access to a COM component. If you are using Visual Studio, add a reference to the Windows Script Host Object Model listed in the COM tab of the Add Reference dialog box. If you don't have Visual Studio, use the Type Library Importer (Tlbimp.exe) to create an interop assembly for the wshom.ocx file, which is usually located in the Windows\System32 folder. (You can obtain the latest version of the Windows Script Host from `http://www.microsoft.com/downloads/details.` `aspx?FamilyID=47809025-D896-482E-A0D6-524E7E844D81&displaylang=en`. At the time of this writing, the latest version is 5.7)

Once you have generated and imported the interop assembly into your project, follow these steps to create a desktop or Start menu shortcut:

1. Instantiate a `WshShell` object, which provides access to the Windows shell.

2. Use the `SpecialFolders` property of the `WshShell` object to determine the correct path of the folder where you want to put the shortcut. You must specify the name of the folder you want as an index to the `SpecialFolders` property. To create a desktop shortcut, specify the value `Desktop`; to create a Start menu shortcut, specify `StartMenu`. Using the `SpecialFolders` property, you can obtain the path to any of the special system folders. If the specified folder does not exist on the platform you are running on, `SpecialFolders` returns an empty `String`. Other commonly used values include `AllUsersDesktop` and `AllUsersStartMenu`. You can find the full list of special folder names in the section on the `SpecialFolders` property in the Windows Script Host documentation.

3. Call the `CreateShortcut` method of the `WshShell` object, and provide the fully qualified filename of the shortcut file you want to create. The file should have the extension .lnk. `CreateShortcut` will return an `IWshShortcut` instance.

4. Use the properties of the `IWshShortcut` instance to configure the shortcut. You can configure properties such as the executable that the shortcut references, a description for the shortcut, a hotkey sequence, and the icon displayed for the shortcut.

5. Call the `Save` method of the `IWshShortcut` instance to write the shortcut to disk. The shortcut will appear either on the desktop or in the Start menu (or elsewhere), depending on the path specified when the `IWshShortcut` instance was created.

The Code

The following example class creates a shortcut to Notepad.exe on both the desktop and Start menu of the current user. The example creates both shortcuts by calling the `CreateShortcut` method and specifying a different destination folder for each shortcut file. This approach makes it possible to create the shortcut file in any of the special folders returned by the `WshShell.SpecialFolders` property.

```
Imports System
Imports System.IO
Imports IWshRuntimeLibrary

Namespace Apress.VisualBasicRecipes.Chapter15
    Public Class Recipe15_08

        Public Shared Sub CreateShortcut(ByVal destination As String)
```

```vbnet
        ' Create a WshShell instance through which to access the
        ' functionality of the Windows shell.
        Dim hostShell As New WshShell

        ' Assemble a fully qualified name that places the Notepad.lnk
        ' file in the specified destination folder. You could use the
        ' System.Environment.GetFolderPath method to obtain a path, but
        ' the WshShell.SpecialFolders method provides access to a wider
        ' range of folders. You need to create a temporary object
        ' reference to the destination string to satisfy the requirements of
        ' the item method signature.
        Dim destFolder As Object = DirectCast(destination, Object)
        Dim fileName As String = ➥
Path.Combine(DirectCast(hostShell.SpecialFolders.Item(destFolder), String), ➥
"Notepad.lnk")

        ' Create the shortcut object. Nothing is created in the
        ' destination folder until the shortcut is saved.
        Dim shortcut As IWshShortcut = ➥
DirectCast(hostShell.CreateShortcut(fileName), IWshShortcut)

        ' Configure the fully qualified name to the executable.
        ' Use the Environment class for simplicity.
        shortcut.TargetPath = ➥
Path.Combine(Environment.GetFolderPath(Environment.SpecialFolder.System), ➥
"notepad.exe")

        ' Set the working directory to the Personal (My Documents) folder.
        shortcut.WorkingDirectory = ➥
Environment.GetFolderPath(Environment.SpecialFolder.Personal)

        ' Provide a description for the shortcut.
        shortcut.Description = "Notepad Text Editor"

        ' Assign a hotkey to the shortcut.
        shortcut.Hotkey = "CTRL+ALT+N"

        ' Configure Notepad to always start maximized.
        shortcut.WindowStyle = 3

        ' Configure the shortcut to display the first icon in Notepad.exe.
        shortcut.IconLocation = "notepad.exe,0"

        ' Save the configured shortcut file.
        shortcut.Save()

    End Sub

    Public Shared Sub Main()

        ' Create the Notepad shortcut on the desktop.
        CreateShortcut("Desktop")
```

```vbnet
        ' Create the Notepad shortcut on the Windows Start menu of
        ' the current user.
        CreateShortcut("StartMenu")

        ' Wait to continue.
        Console.WriteLine(Environment.NewLine)
        Console.WriteLine("Main method complete.  Press Enter.")
        Console.ReadLine()

    End Sub

    End Class
End Namespace
```

Index

You Need the Companion eBook

Your purchase of this book entitles you to buy the companion PDF-version eBook for only $10. Take the weightless companion with you anywhere.

We believe this Apress title will prove so indispensable that you'll want to carry it with you everywhere, which is why we are offering the companion eBook (in PDF format) for $10 to customers who purchase this book now. Convenient and fully searchable, the PDF version of any content-rich, page-heavy Apress book makes a valuable addition to your programming library. You can easily find and copy code—or perform examples by quickly toggling between instructions and the application. Even simultaneously tackling a donut, diet soda, and complex code becomes simplified with hands-free eBooks!

Once you purchase your book, getting the $10 companion eBook is simple:

❶ Visit **www.apress.com/promo/tendollars/**.

❷ Complete a basic registration form to receive a randomly generated question about this title.

❸ Answer the question correctly in 60 seconds, and you will receive a promotional code to redeem for the $10.00 eBook.

THE EXPERT'S VOICE™

2855 TELEGRAPH AVENUE | SUITE 600 | BERKELEY, CA 94705

Offer valid through 10/28/08.